D1488476

SEXUAL FUNCTION
IN PEOPLE WITH DISABILITY AND CHRONIC ILLNESS

A HEALTH PROFESSIONAL'S GUIDE

MARCA L. SIPSKI, MD
Director of Medical Systems Development
Kessler Rehabilitation Corporation
West Orange, New Jersey
Associate Professor of Physical Medicine and Rehabilitation
UMDNJ–New Jersey Medical School
Newark, New Jersey

CRAIG J. ALEXANDER, PhD
Director of Psychology and Neuropsychology
Kessler Institute for Rehabilitation
West Orange, New Jersey
Associate Professor of Physical Medicine and Rehabilitation
UMDNJ–New Jersey Medical School
Newark, New Jersey

AN ASPEN PUBLICATION®
Aspen Publishers, Inc.
Gaithersburg, Maryland
1997

The authors have made every effort to ensure the accuracy of the information herein. However, appropriate information sources should be consulted, especially for new or unfamiliar procedures. It is the responsibility of every practitioner to evaluate the appropriateness of a particular opinion in the context of actual clinical situations and with due considerations to new developments. Authors, editors, and the publisher cannot be held responsible for any typographical or other errors found in this book.

Library of Congress Cataloging-in-Publication Data

Sexual function in people with disability and chronic illness:
a health professional's guide/
[edited by] Marca L. Sipski, Craig J. Alexander.
p. cm.
Includes bibliographical references and index.
ISBN 0-8342-0886-5
1. Handicapped—Sexual behavior.
2. Chronically ill—Sexual behavior.
3. Sexual disorders. I. Sipski, Marca L.
II. Alexander, Craig J.
[DNLM: 1. Sex Disorders—etiology.
2. Sex Disorders—therapy. 3. Chronic Disease.
4. Disabled. 5. Sexuality.
WJ 709 S5185 1997]
HQ30.5.S2 1997
306.7'087—dc21
DNLM/DLC
for Library of Congress
97-14397
CIP

Aspen Publishers, Inc., grants permission for photocopying for limited personal or internal use. This consent does not extend to other kinds of copying, such as copying for general distribution, for advertising or promotional purposes, for creating new collective works, or for resale. For information, address Aspen Publishers, Inc., Permissions Department, 200 Orchard Ridge Drive, Suite 200, Gaithersburg, Maryland 20878.

Orders: (800) 638-8437
Customer Service: (800) 234-1660

About Aspen Publishers • For more than 35 years, Aspen has been a leading professional publisher in a variety of disciplines. Aspen's vast information resources are available in both print and electronic formats. We are committed to providing the highest quality information available in the most appropriate format for our customers. Visit Aspen's Internet site for more information resources, directories, articles, and a searchable version of Aspen's full catalog, including the most recent publications: **http://www.aspenpub.com**
Aspen Publishers, Inc. • The hallmark of quality in publishing
Member of the worldwide Wolters Kluwer group

Editorial Resources: Jane Colilla
Library of Congress Catalog Card Number: 97-14397
ISBN: 0-8342-0886-5

Printed in the United States of America

1 2 3 4 5

To my mother, Sophia Marcewicz Sipski, and my father, Joseph Sipski, whose love, hard work, and dedication to me set me on my path in life.

Marca L. Sipski, MD

To my late parents, Bernard Irving Alexander and Margaret Ann Barber Alexander, whose living example of love, respect, compassion, and sensitivity along with their commitment to humanistic values helped to shape my understanding of sexuality.

Craig J. Alexander, PhD

Table of Contents

Contributors

Craig J. Alexander, PhD
Director of Psychology and
  Neuropsychology
Kessler Institute for Rehabilitation
West Orange, New Jersey
Associate Professor of Physical
  Medicine and Rehabilitation
UMDNJ—New Jersey Medical
  School
Newark, New Jersey

John R. Bach, MD
Professor of Physical Medicine and
  Rehabilitation
Vice Chairman
Department of Physical Medicine
  and Rehabilitation
UMDNJ—New Jersey Medical
  School
Newark, New Jersey

Joan L. Bardach, PhD
Clinical Professor of Rehabilitation
  Medicine (Psychology)
Department of Rehabilitation
  Medicine
New York University Medicine
  Center
New York, New York

Barbara T. Benevento, MD
Staff Physiatrist
Kessler Institute for
  Rehabilitation
West Orange, New Jersey
Department of Physical Medicine
  and Rehabilitation
UMDNJ—New Jersey Medical
  School
Newark, New Jersey

Michael B. Chancellor, MD
Associate Professor of Urologic
  Surgery
Director of Neurourology and
  Urinary Incontinence
  Programs
University of Pittsburgh School of
  Medicine
Pittsburgh, Pennsylvania

José M. Colón, MD
Associate Professor of Clinical
  Obstetrics and Gynecology
UMDNJ—New Jersey Medical
  School
Newark, New Jersey

Stanley H. Ducharme, PhD
Professor of Rehabilitation Medicine
Assistant Professor of Urology
Boston University School of
    Medicine
Clinical/Health Psychologist
Boston Medical Center
Boston, Massachusetts

Kathleen L. Dunn, MS, RN, CRRN
Clinical Nurse Specialist, Spinal
    Cord Injury Center
San Diego Veterans Affairs
    Healthcare System
San Diego, California

Barbara Eliasof, MS, RN, CS, OCN
Clinical Nurse Specialist
Pascack Valley Hospital
Westwood, New Jersey
Private Practice
Ramsey, New Jersey

Lisa Engel, MSW
Clinical Social Worker
Social Work Department
University of Michigan Medical
    Center
Ann Arbor, Michigan

Carolyn A. Gerdes, PhD Candidate
Assistant Professor
Department of Physical Education,
    Recreation, and Health
Kean College of New Jersey
Union, New Jersey
Part-Time Lecturer, Department of
    Psychology
Rutgers, The State University of
    New Jersey
Newark, New Jersey

Kathleen M. Gill, PhD
Private Practice
Wellesley, Massachusetts
Consultant, Sexual Function Clinic
Lahey-Hitchcock Medical Center
Burlington and Peabody,
    Massachusetts
Lecturer in Psychiatry
Harvard Medical School
Boston, Massachusetts

Carol Howland
Assistant Professor
Department of Physical Medicine
    and Rehabilitation
Baylor College of Medicine
Houston, Texas

Karen Hwang, MEd
Research Assistant
Kessler Institute for Rehabilitation
West Orange, New Jersey

C. Leith Kelley, RN, PhD
Clinical Coordinator, Multiple
    Sclerosis Center
Department of Neurology
Allegheny University of the Health
    Sciences
Philadelphia, Pennsylvania

Anthony J. Kerrigan, PhD
Clinical Assistant Professor
Department of Psychiatry and
    Behavioral Sciences
Baylor College of Medicine
Staff Psychologist, Psychology
    Service
Houston Veterans Affairs Medical
    Center
Houston, Texas

Donald Kewman, PhD
Clinical Associate Professor
Department of Physical Medicine
and Rehabilitation
University of Michigan Medical
School
Ann Arbor, Michigan

Kenneth A. Lefebvre, PhD
Senior Psychologist
Orthopedic, Amputee, and Spinal
Cord Injury Programs
Rehabilitation Institute of Chicago
Assistant Professor of Physical
Medicine and Rehabilitation
Chicago, Illinois

Todd A. Linsenmeyer, MD
Director of Urology
Kessler Institute for Rehabilitation
West Orange, New Jersey
Associate Professor of Physical
Medicine and Rehabilitation
UMDNJ—New Jersey Medical
School
Newark, New Jersey

Karen Brash McGreer, RN, MEd
Nurse Psychotherapist/Sex Counselor
Brash McGreer Counseling Associates
Cherry Hill, New Jersey

Elizabeth A. McNeff, MPA:HA
Portland, Oregon

**Trilok N. Monga, MD, PRCP(C),
MRCP(I)**
Professor of Physical Medicine and
Rehabilitation
Baylor College of Medicine

Chief of Physical Medicine and
Rehabilitation Service
Houston Veterans Affairs Medical
Center
Houston, Texas

Scott Nadler, DO
Instructor
Department of Physical Medicine
and Rehabilitation
Attending Physiatrist
UMDNJ—New Jersey Medical
School
Newark, New Jersey

Margaret A. Nosek, PhD
Associate Professor
Department of Physical Medicine
and Rehabilitation
Baylor College of Medicine
Houston, Texas

David A. Rivas, MD
Assistant Professor of Urology
Jefferson Medical College
Thomas Jefferson University
Philadelphia, Pennsylvania

Raymond C. Rosen, PhD
Professor of Psychiatry and
Medicine
Co-Director, Center for Sexual and
Marital Health
UMDNJ—Robert Wood Johnson
Medical School
Piscataway, New Jersey

S. Chris Saad, PhD
School of Education
University of Pennsylvania
Philadelphia, Pennsylvania

M. Elizabeth Sandel, MD
Director of the Division of
  Neurorehabilitation
Associate Professor
Department of Rehabilitation
  Medicine
Hospital of the University of
  Pennsylvania
Philadelphia, Pennsylvania

Marca L. Sipski, MD
Director of Medical Systems
  Development
Kessler Rehabilitation Corporation
West Orange, New Jersey
Associate Professor of Physical
  Medicine and Rehabilitation
UMDNJ—New Jersey Medical School
Newark, New Jersey

**Suzane C. Smeltzer, RN, EdD,
  FAAN**
Associate Professor
Villanova University College of
  Nursing
Villanova, Pennsylvania

Todd P. Stitik, MD
Assistant Professor
Department of Physical Medicine and
  Rehabilitation
UMDNJ—New Jersey Medical School
Newark, New Jersey

**Mitchell S. Tepper, MPH,
  PhD Candidate**
President
The Sexual Health Network, LLC
Huntington, Connecticut

Margaret C. Tilton, MS, MD
Private Practice
Seacoast Area Physiatry
Portsmouth, New Hampshire

Tracey L. Waldman, PhD
Clinical Psychologist
Kessler Institute of Rehabilitation
West Orange, New Jersey
Intervention Strategies International,
  Inc.
Teaneck, New Jersey

Seth Warschausky, PhD
Assistant Professor
Department of Physical Medicine
  and Rehabilitation
University of Michigan Medical
  School
Ann Arbor, Michigan

William J. Warzak, PhD
Associate Professor
Department of Pediatrics
University of Nebraska Medical
  Center/Meyer Rehabilitation
  Center
Omaha, Nebraska

Daniel N. Weiner, PhD
Postdoctoral Fellow
Center for Sexual and Marital
  Health
UMDNJ—Robert Wood Johnson
  Medical School
Piscataway, New Jersey

Sandra L. Welner, MD
Primary Care Gynecology
Gynecologic Care for Women with
  Disabilities
Silver Spring, Maryland

Beverly Whipple, PhD, RN, FAAN
Associate Professor
College of Nursing
Rutgers, The State University of
  New Jersey
Newark, New Jersey

Preface

This book is designed to allow the reader to peruse through the volume as a whole and gain an overall understanding about sexuality and disability. Conversely, it is designed to allow the reader to research a particular topic of interest. Part I provides an overview of specific issues related to the evaluation of sexuality and sexual function. In Part II, specific disabilities and illnesses are addressed in individual chapters. The goal of these chapters is to provide an overview of each particular disability and illness and what is known about male and female sexual response as well as sexuality and fertility issues with that particular disability. Part III is dedicated to treatment of specific aspects of sexual dysfunction that may occur in individuals with any of the various disabilities or in able-bodied individuals.

Any interested health care professional may use this book to learn about the varying types of disabilities, their effects on human sexuality, and available treatment methods. Because this area is often addressed by members of the interdisciplinary rehabilitation team, the target audience includes not only those professionals who may be doing the primary counseling and education of patients, but also those individuals who may be asked questions by their patients in the course of treatment. Sex counselors and therapists will also benefit from the use of this book, because part of their practice undoubtedly includes treatment of individuals with chronic disability and illness. In addition, this volume will provide them with a perspective of issues facing patients with disabilities.

We hope you enjoy reading this volume and learning about sexuality and disability. Because of space and information constraints, we are unable to cover every possible diagnosis; rather, we have chosen to provide information about certain major diagnostic categories. However, we cannot emphasize enough how important we believe it is to effectively address this issue with all people regardless of the degree of their disability or illness. The chapters comprising this text have been contributed by a range of interesting and highly qualified people. Professional discipline, gender, race, able-bodied or disabled, sexual orientation, and personal values and beliefs are widely represented here. Each author's unique sense of sexuality is expressed throughout these pages. We hope the knowledge disseminated through this approach will foster further interaction through the disciplines and promote increased research aimed at improving the sexuality and quality of life for people with disabilities and chronic illnesses.

Acknowledgments

In writing this book, I would like to acknowledge the invaluable assistance of my assistant and right-hand woman Ruth Sullivan. I thank my mentor, Dr. John Ditunno, Jr., for his invaluable support and confidence in me throughout my professional development in the rehabilitation field, and for his continuing friendship. Thanks also to Dr. Ray Rosen, who has provided support in my studies of female sexuality. Finally, I acknowledge the support of my co-author and husband, Craig Alexander, who makes my life, personally and professionally, whole, exciting, and worth living.

Marca L. Sipski, MD

I owe thanks and appreciation, both personally and professionally, to my wife, best friend, and colleague, Marcalee Sipski. This book was her idea, and I owe her thanks for her support and patience with me throughout its development—the most difficult period of my life.

Craig J. Alexander, PhD

Introduction

WHERE WE ARE AND HOW WE GOT THERE

Over the past 40 years, there has been a virtual revolution in American and international societies pertaining to sexuality and the "proper" roles of males and females. In the first half of the 20th century, much of society functioned with a typical family core—the male went to work outside the home and the female stayed home with the children. As we move into the 21st century, having families in which both the male and the female work is more the rule than the exception. Furthermore, it is becoming increasingly common to have single-parent families or to have same-sex relationships be sanctioned in marriage or to have same-sex parents raise children.

During this same period we have seen a shift in the type of sexual behaviors undertaken by men and women. Whereas in the 1940s and 1950s premarital sex was considered improper and many marriages occurred because they "had to," in the 1960s and 1970s, free love became the rule and societies moved more toward "love the one you're with." At least partially because of the acquired immune deficiency syndrome epidemic, which was recognized in the early 1980s, there appears to be a trend in society to participate less frequently in multiple sexual encounters and to develop more stable, longer-lasting sexual relationships, or what has been referred to as "serial monogamy." Furthermore, these relationships may be of a homosexual, heterosexual, or bisexual nature.

Not only have able-bodied people experienced changes in sexuality and roles over the past five decades, but patients with disabilities have also witnessed changes in their roles in society. These changes have affected an understanding of sexuality issues within the population with disabilities and illnesses. An analysis of the following enhances an understanding of these changes: the demographics of disability and illness, what is known about sexuality and various disabilities, what is known about fertility in people with various disabilities, and how funding for research and health care has varied.

Over the past 50 years, there has been an increase in the number of people with disabilities. Better preventive measures performed at the scene of accidents have allowed more people with disabilities to survive. Likewise, better medical care has allowed individuals with medical illnesses to live longer, even with a disability. In addition, the development of systems of care and the maturing of specialties such as physical medicine and rehabilitation have enabled people with disabilities such as spinal cord injuries to live longer, thereby increasing the prevalence of this particular disability.

The increase in the number of people with disabilities and the improvements in life expectancy and their overall health have led to a change in focus on particular issues. For example, now, rather than being worried about whether someone will survive pneumonia, it is meaningful to worry about whether appropriate assistive devices are provided for parenting by people with disabilities or what can be done to improve the sexual satisfaction of a woman with a disability.

Sexuality issues related to people with disabilities and illness have been inadequately addressed, probably, in part, because of a societal belief that it is unacceptable for the person with a disability to be a sexual being. Moreover, most of the research that has pertained to issues of sexuality and disability has been performed in a retrospective fashion on small numbers of patients with varying degrees of disabilities. Control groups have been relatively nonexistent and the major area addressed has been male erectile function; female sexual function has been ignored.

There have been major inroads in therapies available for the treatment of sexual dysfunctions in the able-bodied population and those populations with particular disabilities such as spinal cord injuries. Unfortunately, most of these therapies have not been studied for the treatment of sexual dysfunctions in people with other disabilities. In addition, there is often little collaboration between the fields of clinical psychology, sex therapy, physical medicine and rehabilitation, urology, and obstetrics and gynecology. A person with a neurologic disability, for instance, may have a combined psychological and mechanical problem associated with his or her disability that results in sexual dysfunction. One professional may believe the problem is a psychological one, hence referring the patient to another professional who may think the problem is neurological; yet another professional may believe the problem is entirely mechanical. As a result, the patient receives no care. Furthermore, new treatments in the field of sex therapy may never make it to the disability population at all.

Many inroads also have been made in the treatment of infertility for able-bodied men and women. Likewise, there have been many advances made in the treatment of infertility for individuals with certain types of disabilities. Specifically, the use of electroejaculation, which was borrowed from the field of animal husbandry, has allowed some men with spinal cord injuries to father children. In addition, electrovibration is a viable alternative for producing ejaculation. Other new techniques continue to be developed.

As these positive changes have allowed people with disabilities to have more fulfilling sexual and family lives, there have been shifts in funding for research pertaining to disability and sexuality as well as the clinical treatment of people with disabilities. Recent funding for new research programs under the auspices of the National Center for Medical Rehabilitation Research has enabled issues pertaining to the disabled population to be addressed. For example, this funding has supported the study of sexuality in women with spinal cord injuries and other disabilities—an area largely overlooked in the literature. In addition, funding has supported the study of methods for improving the fertility potential in men who are unable to ejaculate because of spinal cord injuries or other neurologic deficits.

As an offshoot of the increased funding for research pertaining to sexuality and disability, there has been an increase in the level of communication between clinicians in the field of rehabilitation and the field of sex therapy. Until recently, professionals in these areas have infrequently shared their knowledge and ideas with the major disciplines involved: psychology and medicine. It is hoped that this improved communication will lead to further increases in research ideas and productivity regarding the subject of sexuality and disability. Moreover, such discussion and information should positively affect the sexuality and overall quality of life for the disabled as well as the nondisabled populations.

WHAT IS SEXUALITY?

Any discussion regarding sexuality must consider the broad picture. Chipouras, Cornelius, Daniels, and Makas (1979) indicated that sexuality is the major way in which people define and present themselves to others as people, and as men and women. Although people commonly think of issues pertaining to sexuality as those physical behaviors that occur in bed—that is, the sex act—a range of other issues also encompasses the term *sexuality*. Trieschmann (1988) has emphasized the need to differentiate the sex act from the sex drive from the broader issue of sexuality. The sensuality of sex is expressed through the full scope of our senses. Expression of a person's sexuality involves the way one dresses, the way one carries oneself, the way one looks at others and oneself, the way one speaks to other people, the way one touches other people and oneself, the way one smells, or the way one tastes.

People may also express their sexuality by the way they think and feel about themselves or another person, regardless of whether those thoughts and feelings are communicated through external behaviors. Rotberg (1987) indicated that sexuality includes many facets of an individual's personality including, but not limited to, affection, companionship, intimacy, and love. Ducharme, Gill, Biener-Bergman, and Fertitta (1993) defined *sexuality* as "the integration of physical, emotional, intellectual and social aspects of an individual's personality that expresses maleness or femaleness" (p. 763). These authors also asserted that sexuality might just be the most important part of rehabilitation because of its relationship to self-esteem and body image, among other factors. They pointed out the importance that Sigmund Freud and others have placed on the role of love and work as the hallmarks of good mental health. To the extent that one subscribes to this notion, the role of sexuality cannot be overemphasized in the process of rehabilitation.

REFERENCES

Chipouras, S., Cornelius, D., Daniels, S.M., & Makas, E. (1979). *Who cares: A handbook on sex education and counseling services for disabled people.* Austin, TX: PRO:ED.

Ducharme, S., Gill, K.M., Biener-Bergman, S., & Fertitta, L.C. (1993). Sexual functioning: Medical and psychological aspects. In J.A. DeLisa (Ed.), *Rehabilitation medicine: Principles and practice* (2nd ed., pp. 763–782). Philadelphia: J.B. Lippincott.

Rotberg, A. (1987). An introduction to the study of women, aging, and sexuality. *Physical and Occupational Therapy in Geriatrics, 5*(3), 3–12.

Trieschmann, R.B. (1988). *Spinal cord injuries: Psychological, social, and vocational rehabilitation* (2nd ed.). New York: Demos.

General Sexual Function

CHAPTER 1

Impact of Disability or Chronic Illness on Sexual Function

Marca L. Sipski and Craig J. Alexander

GENERAL PHYSIOLOGIC CONCERNS REGARDING DISABILITY OR CHRONIC ILLNESS

The terms *disability* and *chronic illness* represent an array of possible disorders; consequently, it is almost impossible to group them as a whole. Yet, such grouping is often done in communications pertaining to the disabled population, as compared with the able-bodied population. Although such grouping may be appropriate for political purposes or to express the demographics of society, it is inappropriate when discussing or researching the impact of sexuality on disability.

To fully examine the physiologic effects of disability or chronic illness on a person's sexuality, two factors must be considered: (1) the type of disability or chronic illness by which the person is affected and (2) the individual strengths and weaknesses of the person affected by the disability or chronic illness. Issues pertaining to the type of disability or chronic illness include the overall consequences of the disability or specific illness, whether there is an effect on genital function, secondary complications, whether the disorder is static or progressive, iatrogenic concerns, and concomitant medical problems associated with the disability or illness.

Overall Effects of the Disability or Chronic Illness

Some disabilities have a major impact on the nervous system, such as complete spinal cord injuries or cerebrovascular accidents. As a result of the original neurologic deficit, there may be concomitant organ system dysfunctions, including changes in genital sexual function. Illnesses such as leukemia may not directly affect the genitals, but the profound impact on overall bodily function may

3

leave individuals without energy for sexual activity. Furthermore, sexual activity may be prohibited in people with marked leukopenia. In contrast, people may also suffer from a disability if they have significant osteoarthritis in one knee. It is apparent that the sexual function would be affected differently in people with arthritis as compared with people with leukemia or spinal cord injury.

Impact on Genital Function

Some disabilities or chronic illnesses may directly affect genital function. For instance, a person with a penile carcinoma who requires subsequent surgery will undoubtedly have a different degree of sexual dysfunction than a person with a partial foot amputation. Likewise, a person with multiple sclerosis with resultant neurogenic bladder and bowel will have a different degree of sexual dysfunction than a person with multiple sclerosis whose symptomatology is limited to optic neuritis.

Secondary Complications

Some of the more profound disabilities such as traumatic brain injury or some of the muscular dystrophies can be associated with secondary complications such as pressure sores, respiratory failure, spasticity, or contractures that may also affect a person's ability to engage in sexual activity. Secondary complications can be significant and should not be taken lightly because they may have just as great an impact on a person's sexual function as the primary disability itself. For instance, people with a mild traumatic brain injury and severe adductor spasticity can have problems with positioning for intercourse. Moreover, the development of a severe pressure sore in the sacrum will prohibit a person from lying on his or her back, thereby temporarily ruling out this position for sexual activity.

Contrast these complications with the effects of a disability such as peripheral nerve injury that results in a foot drop in one leg. People with such a disability will not have concomitant problems in other organ systems, nor will they have associated genital dysfunction. Obviously, the physiological impact on the sexual function of a person with a foot drop is less than that on a person with a complete spinal cord injury.

Static versus Progressive Disorder

The physiologic effects of disability or chronic illness will also vary depending on whether the condition is static or progressive. Individuals with paraplegia secondary to multiple sclerosis will have the potential for further progressive disability because of the nature of their disease. In contrast, individuals with paraplegia with spinal cord injury will know that their disability is static and will not worsen. The physical impact of multiple sclerosis on individuals therefore will require adaptation to the current level of function; however, they will realize that there is always the risk that their medical condition will worsen. Alternatively, people with paraplegia resulting from spinal cord injury will be able to adapt to the current level of function with the security that their condition will not decline further.

The static or progressive nature of a condition will have both a psychological and physical effect on sexual functioning. Psychologically it follows that people with a progressive disability will have the added stress of worrying how and when their condition will worsen. From a physical standpoint, progressive disorders can carry with them fatigue as the condition worsens. People need to functionally adapt to the physical progression of their illness. For instance, a person with multiple sclerosis may first have little physical disability associated with the multiple sclerosis, with no impact on sexual function. As the disease progresses, he or she may suffer from paralysis, cognitive dysfunction, development of neurogenic bladder, bowel and sexual dysfunction, and difficulties with speech and swallowing. Clearly, this person will need to adjust to these changes both physically and functionally. Furthermore, the person will also need to adjust to the effect of these changes on his or her sexual function and sexuality.

Associated Iatrogenic Effects

Treatments may or may not be available, depending on the nature of a person's disability or illness. In some cases, the treatments may not affect a person's sexuality or sexual function. Alternatively, prescribed treatments can sometimes lead to more problems in sexual function than the disorders themselves. For instance, the use of pelvic irradiation for carcinoma in women can cause ovarian failure with resultant symptoms of premature menopause. Furthermore, damage to the vaginal epithelium can lead to vaginal dryness and fibrosis. Certain prescribed medications are also known to cause various effects on sexual function, for example, tricyclic antidepressants that are used for neurogenic pain that frequently occurs after spinal cord injury. Although alterations in sexual function occur after spinal cord injuries, the increase or decline in libido, impotence, and painful ejaculation that can occur with the administration of some tricyclic antidepressants can be more powerful than the impact of the spinal cord injury itself.

Similarities Between the Disability, Other Disabilities, and Chronic Illness

For many disabilities, there is inadequate information available regarding the effects on sexual function. In those cases, the similarities between different disabilities and chronic illnesses may provide a framework for understanding the impact of the uncommon disability on sexuality. Where in the body is the pathology located and is there a similar disorder that exists? The answers to this question can help in understanding disorders such as multiple sclerosis in which the pathologic lesions can occur in the brain, similar to those with stroke, or in the spinal cord, similar to a person with a spinal cord injury. With this information, one then may be able to partially extrapolate from the knowledge about the impacts of a specific type of stroke or spinal cord injury to understand the effects of the multiple sclerosis.

Disability and illness can be acquired or congenital. When a disability is acquired, it can occur at any time in a person's life. The effect of a disability will vary greatly depending on the specific point in the life cycle when the disability occurs. For instance, the impact of a below-knee amputation in a 15-year-old male who is planning to be an athlete will certainly differ from the impact in a 42-year-old male construction worker or a 72-year-old male retiree. Similarly, the impact of a particular disability on a person's sexual function will vary depending on his or her age. A 15-year-old with an amputation will most likely be less sexually experienced than the 42-year-old and therefore may be more adaptable to necessary changes in sexual position. Concomitantly, the 15-year-old will be at a different point in life, and issues regarding attracting a mate may be more important than in the 42-year-old. An even more dramatic contrast is between the needs of the 15-year-old, who is on the upswing in his sexuality and desires and the 72-year-old, who most likely has the majority of his sexual experiences behind him.

Impact of Preexisting Medical Status

The physical impact of disability on people also depends on their preexisting medical problems. A person with diabetes and hypertension who must have a below-knee amputation because of a skin condition will have a different experience than a person who has an amputation because of a traumatic injury. The person with diabetes and hypertension will have more difficulty progressing in his or her rehabilitation and in regaining the ability to ambulate than the person who is otherwise healthy. Moreover, the impact on the sexuality of the person with diabetes, hypertension, and amputation may be different than that of the otherwise healthy amputee because diabetes, hypertension, and amputation may all independently cause sexual dysfunction, compounding the resultant problems.

Disability or Illness and Concomitant Medical Problems

Another concern when evaluating the impact of disability or chronic illness on people's sexual function is their ongoing, unrelated concomitant medical problems. Two people with right-sided cerebrovascular accidents whose functional deficits are similar and are limited to an inability to ambulate for long distances will have significantly different situations if one develops a malignant melanoma requiring surgery and radiation subsequent to his or her stroke. Likewise, two people with similar levels of complete paraplegia will have different outcomes if one suffers from daily severe migraine headaches and the other is otherwise healthy.

Therefore, a discussion of the issues of sexuality and disability or chronic illness must consider the nature and degree of the disability or chronic illness, whether there are genital and other organ system effects, and the impact of any ongoing treatments. Other issues to consider are who the person is, where he or she is in the life cycle, and any preexisting and forthcoming medical problems. Consideration of these issues will lead to an understanding of how a particular disability affects a person's physiologic sexual function and sexuality; however, it will not give the whole picture. When dealing with issues of sexual function and sexuality, one must consider not only an individual's physical concerns but also his or her psychological concerns, as well as the partner's psychological concerns.

GENERAL PSYCHOLOGICAL CONCERNS

The majority of sexual dysfunctions originate in reaction to psychologic processes or are compounded by psychologic reaction to organic pathology (Masters & Johnson, 1970). Thus, a discussion of sexuality must examine the emotional and physical elements involved. The following discussion artificially separates these two components. However, in actuality, sexuality involves an interplay between the psychological and the physical, and their effects are not always discernable or attributable to one factor or another.

A myriad of issues, including psychological, situational, cultural, and couples, must be examined when assessing sexuality. Disability and chronic illness can have a profound psychological effect on people, greatly influencing their sexual adjustment. Perhaps the most important factor in people's psychological well-being is that of self-esteem. Disability affects the way in which people feel about themselves. If their self-esteem is damaged, their sense of sexuality will certainly be similarly affected. Other related concepts include *self-image,* or the way in which people perceive themselves, and *self-efficacy,* or people's perceived ability to successfully complete a thought or action. Disability, which frequently interferes in these areas, can often lead to mood disorder—the most common being depression and anxiety—which certainly will interfere with a person's sexuality.

An often overlooked issue is that involving the age of onset of a disability and its effect on an individual's overall emotional and sexual adjustment. Many developmental psychologists have theorized various critical stages of both psychological and sexual development. When traumatic events occur that interfere with the smooth progression through these developmental stages, emotional problems can ensue. Take, for example, a catastrophic injury leading to a disability. The impact of a spinal cord injury on a 17-year-old male will be different from that on a 50-year-old man. A high incidence of spinal cord injuries occurs in young, active males who are usually in their late teens or early adulthood. Examining this scenario from the perspective of the psychologist Erik Erikson, late adolescence and early adulthood is the critical time for a person to resolve the developmental conflicts of identity versus role confusion as well as intimacy versus isolation (Erikson, 1968). It is during this critical period of life that a person answers the question, Who am I?, becomes comfortable with his or her physical and sexual development, achieves a sense of independence from family, and develops the skills necessary for sexual intimacy. Most people can think back and relate to that time in our lives when we, as teenagers, looked forward with enthusiasm and excitement in search of our freedom and independence, the very aspects interfered with by the paralyzing effects of a spinal cord injury. The young victim of a spinal cord injury will struggle maybe more than his or her able-bodied counterpart at developing a sense of self and identity and, along with it, a sense of self-esteem, self-image, and intimacy gained through productive relationships with peers of the same and opposite sex. Presumably, in the previous example, the 50-year-old will have already experienced and resolved these psychosocial developmental crises. Thus, the age of onset of a disability or chronic illness will affect the kinds of issues a person must address. Clearly, these psychological issues are closely linked to a person's sense of sexuality.

Disability and illness affect both the person and his or her partner. Thus, when evaluating a person's sexuality, clinicians must closely examine the factors affecting the couple. Many of the issues will have existed before the onset of disability and illness and will have become exacerbated; however, in some cases, an illness might introduce a new issue. The clinician must determine the degree of conflict that presently exists between the partners and to what extent it is related to the illness. Disability and illness certainly lead to stress, which can lead to increased conflict. Similarly, the amount of hostility in both the patient and partner must be assessed. Following illness or disability, there is the inevitable question, Why did this happen to me? Because there usually is no good answer to this question, the patient often becomes frustrated and angry. The partner, too, has similar questions and can be left feeling cheated and hostile about his or her life situation. The usual balance of power that exists within any relationship is disrupted by disability, leading to struggles to regain a homeostasis with which both partners are comfortable. The disabled person may feel particularly vulnerable and replete with fears that may be rational or irrational. The disabled partner might harbor feelings of inadequacy, both as a person as well as a sexual partner. Those feelings can lead to an intense fear of disappointing his or her partner sexually or even a more broader fear of abandonment—that the partner will leave for a more "adequate," "healthy," and "worthy" person. Disability and illness may have changed the couple's lives significantly to the point that life goals that were once compatible may no longer be compatible.

Situational and cultural factors can also interfere with a couple's sexual relationship. Disability and illness may highlight issues that existed previously but posed little problems. Differing attitudes and values regarding intimacy, religion, and roles within the family system can lead to conflict both within an individual and between the partners. A common scenario is when the traditional role played by the male (i.e., masculine, wage earner) is disrupted by disability, forcing a reversal of roles with his wife. In those cultures that place a premium on maintaining the traditional masculine role, any deviation can be a blow to a man's self-esteem, leading to a variety of insecurities and conflicts.

These issues underscore the need for healthy communication, mutual trust, openness, and a strong sense of commitment on the part of each partner. These issues are not unique to the disabled; however, given the magnitude of the potential problems, these qualities of communication, trust, and commitment are even more important for the satisfaction of the couple's relationship and sexual lives. It has been said that there is no greater test of love than disability. With the problems and obstacles resulting from a disability, though, comes the opportunity through resolution for an even greater degree of intimacy and satisfaction for a couple.

SEXUALITY COUNSELING

Sexuality continues to be a sensitive topic that many clinicians feel uncomfortable addressing with patients. The reasons are at least twofold. First, few clinicians have received professional training in the area of sexuality. Second, the subject of sexuality is replete with the clinician's own personal values and biases based on his or her own upbringing, values, and life experiences. For many clinicians, it is difficult to separate their own values and attitudes on sexuality to address the issue objectively. It is not surprising therefore that the subject is either not approached with patients, is raised inappropriately, or is simply dismissed when the patient raises the topic. Annon (1976) has proposed a multilayered framework for sexual counseling that incorporates all health care personnel who are working with the patient. The so-called PLISSIT model is an acronym for *per*mission, *l*imited *i*nformation, *s*pecific *s*uggestions, and *i*ntensive *t*herapy. According to this model, all personnel working with the patient should feel comfortable enough with their own sexuality and be knowledgeable enough to engage in the first two levels of the model. Professionals should feel comfortable raising the issue with the patient to "permit" discussion of the topic. In addition, professionals should possess enough information about sexuality and the specific disability or illness to impart limited information. Moreover, they should possess enough information to know their limits or to "know what they do not know." In that case, they would move up to the next level of the model, that is, referring the patient to a more knowledgeable professional for specific suggestions or intensive therapy. Successful implementation of the model would require an ongoing institutional commitment to train all staff who have contact with patients on basic sexuality issues. The model also argues for the existence of a standing multidisciplinary hospitalwide committee that would address sexuality issues, including education of patients and staff, and ongoing ethical issues.

The need for sexual counseling has been reported differently, depending on the population. In the past, Pauly and Goldstein (1970) reported that 10% of the general population needed sexual counseling. Burnap and Golden (1967) reported that 15% of their general medical practice needed sexual therapy, whereas Stuntz (1988) stated that 50% of his gynecological patients needed sexual counseling. More recently, Alexander, Sipski, and Findley (1993) and Sipski and Alexander (1993) reported that 27% of their male and 20% of their female spinal cord–injured subjects acknowledged poor sexual adjustment. Moreover, those researchers reported that 74% of their male and 44% of their female spinal cord–injured subjects claimed that their disability significantly and negatively affected the quality of their sexual relationships.

Schover (1989) described a model for brief, problem-focused sexual counseling following chronic illness. According to her model, there are at least five criteria for counseling:

1. a sexual dysfunction that predates the illness or disability
2. a relationship that is conflicted by the illness
3. sexual dysfunction resulting from poor coping
4. difficulty coping with severe changes in sexual self-image
5. adjustment to medical or surgical procedures

The model calls for practical, realistic, and humane interventions with clear goals. When referring patients for sexual counseling, the clinician must be sensitive to their emotional concerns. When a patient is referred for sexual counseling, he or she may react with disapproval for fear that the problem may be interpreted as emotional. However, a patient referred to the urologist with erectile dysfunction following illness or disability will probably be quite receptive to help. This situation, viewed as clearly medical, is less threatening and therefore more acceptable to the individual. Thus, sensitivity is essential in educating patients about the role of both the emotional and physical aspects involved in their sexual problems.

Schover (1989) also has delineated five aspects to her model of brief sexual counseling:

1. providing sexual education
2. changing maladaptive sexual attitudes
3. helping couples resume sex
4. overcoming the physical handicaps
5. decreasing any marital conflict

Couples must be educated about the normal sexual response cycle and the impact of their physiologic condition on the sexual response cycle. Couples also must be knowledgeable about the impact of medications, lifestyle, and the aging process on their sexuality. Chronic illness and disability often results in maladaptive attitudes (e.g., sex is unhealthy, sex must be spontaneous, intercourse is the only worthwhile form of sexual expression) that must be challenged and corrected (Schover, 1989). Not infrequently, couples will need assistance resuming their sexual activity, which can be accomplished by improving communication and self-esteem and by educating couples on alternative methods of sexual expression and caring. Such education will help decrease any performance anxiety. Disability will usually present physical barriers that must be hurdled successfully. Issues such as diminished movement and sensation, bowel and bladder programs, and pain must be addressed. When marital conflict exists because of a change in roles, changes in the homeostasis of power in the relationship, or fear that the able-bodied partner will leave, it must be confronted and corrected. An all too common conflict arises when the spouse ends up serving in the dual role as caregiver, a situation that should be actively avoided whenever possible.

Sexuality involves an interplay between physiologic and psychological components, and disability and illness affect each of these areas. As Trieschmann (1982) has noted, the physiologic and psychological contributions to the sexual act, the desire for sex, and the broader concept of sexuality must be assessed. When discussing sexuality, clinicians all too often only focus on the aspect of the sexual act and forget the more important aspect of sexuality. The late and noted social worker Mary Romano (1973) eloquently described female sexuality as the following:

> Sexuality is more than the act of sexual intercourse. It involves for most women the whole business of relating to another person; the tenderness, the desire to give as well as take, the compliments, casual caresses, reciprocal concerns, tolerance, the forms of communication that both include and go beyond words. For women, sexuality includes a range of behaviors from smiling through orgasm; it is not just what happens between two people in bed. (p. 28)

The goal in our work with couples in sexual counseling is to help them increase their personal definition of sexuality. To the extent that their personal definition is narrow they will have more difficulties adjusting to disability. On the other hand, when their definition of sexuality is broad and encompassing, they will likely adjust more smoothly to the physical challenges in their lives.

REFERENCES

Alexander, C.J., Sipski, M.L., & Findley, T.W. (1993). Sexual activities, desire, and satisfaction in males pre- and post-spinal cord injury. *Archives of Sexual Behavior, 22*(3), 217–228.

Annon, J. (1976). *The behavioral treatment of sexual problems: Brief therapy.* New York: Harper & Row.

Burnap, D.W., & Golden, J.S. (1967). Sexual problems in medical practice. *Journal of Medical Education, 42,* 673–680.

Erikson, E.H. (1968). *Identity: Youth and crisis.* New York: Norton.

Masters, W.H., & Johnson, V.E. (1970). *Human sexual inadequacy.* Boston: Little, Brown.

Pauly, I.H., & Goldstein, S.G. (1970). Prevalence of sexual dysfunction. *Medical Aspects of Human Sexuality, 4,* 48–52.

Romano, M. (1973). Sexuality and the disabled female. *Accent on Living* (Winter), 27–34.

Schover, L.R. (1989). Sexual problems in chronic illness. In S.R. Leiblum & R.C. Rosen (Eds.), *Principles and practice of sex therapy: Update for the 1990s* (2nd ed., pp. 319–351). New York: Guilford Press.

Sipski, M.L., & Alexander, C.J. (1993). Sexual activities, response and satisfaction in women pre- and post-spinal cord injury. *Archives of Physical Medicine and Rehabilitation, 74,* 1025–1029.

Stuntz, R.C. (1988). Assessment of organic factors in sexual dysfunctions. In R.A. Brown & J.R. Field (Eds.), *Treatment of sexual problems in individual and couples therapy* (pp. 187–207). Columbia, MD: PMA.

Trieschmann, R.B. (1982). *Spinal cord injuries: Psychological, social and vocational adjustment.* New York: Pergamon Press.

CHAPTER 2

Performing the Medical Sexual History and Physical

Marca L. Sipski

Before performing the sexual history and physical examination on someone with a disability or chronic illness, the practitioner must determine whether the condition is acquired or congenital. If the condition is acquired, the practitioner must then consider those issues the individual faced before his or her disability or chronic illness. Next, the practitioner must take into account the individual's current medical and psychological status. The practitioner must analyze these issues to develop an etiology for the individual's sexual condition and to determine an appropriate treatment program.

SEXUAL HISTORY

The sexual history, like all other histories, should start with a query of the person's chief complaint. If someone is being seen as part of a specific sexuality program, it is appropriate for the practitioner to begin by introducing himself or herself and then ask the person what brings him or her there and whether the individual has any specific concerns. Alternatively, if an assessment of sexual function is being performed as part of a routine history and physical, it is probably most natural to ask about a person's sexual function after the routine history is performed and the person is queried about bladder and bowel function.

Once the practitioner has obtained the chief complaint, it is necessary to inquire about the history of the person's current illness: How long has the person been ill or injured? What is known about the diagnosis? What treatments have been rendered? Elicit specific symptoms of the person's condition and review all systems to avoid any omissions. Record any surgical procedures performed, as well as any history of radiation or hormonal therapy. Furthermore, obtain a list of the person's current medications and allergies. In women, assess the presence and quality of their menstrual cycles; moreover, in those subjects who are menopausal, address the timing and conditions associated with the cessation of their periods.

Ask males about the quality of their erections, whether they are able to achieve them by psychogenic and reflex mechanisms, how long they last, whether they are adequate for penetration, and whether they are satisfied with them. Assess any difficulties in the time it takes to achieve ejaculation and the quality of ejaculate. Moreover, address whether there is a difference in any of these functions with intercourse, oral sex, or masturbation, and whether they are related to the sexual partner. Assess the ability to achieve orgasm and the quality of the orgasms. Document whether there has been a significant change in sexual function since an injury, illness, or other treatment, and explore the nature of this change.

Ask females about their ability to be sexually aroused and whether they are able to achieve reflex or psychogenic lubrication. Address whether their lubrication is sufficient to permit acceptance of the penis during intercourse and whether the ability to achieve lubrication is related to a specific sexual activity. Furthermore, assess whether the woman is able to achieve orgasm, the time it takes to achieve orgasm, and the activities that will allow her to achieve orgasm. Address the ability to achieve multiple orgasms and whether the ability to achieve any of these functions is related to the sexual partner. Document whether there has been a change in sexual function since an injury, illness, or other treatment, and explore the nature of this change.

Past medical history should address all previous medical illnesses, hospitalizations, surgeries, and significant therapeutics such as the use of hormones, radiation, or medications that can result in sexual dysfunction. Also, document the use of cigarettes, drugs, and alcohol.

Explore the person's psychosocial history by determining his or her sexual orientation, relationship, and family status and making an attempt to elicit specific interpersonal conflicts or concerns. Determine the person's current and former occupations and ascertain functional status and any implications it has on the person's relationships. In addition, elicit any information about transportation difficulties that might decrease the individual's ability to contact others.

PHYSICAL EXAMINATION

A physical examination of a person with disability or chronic illness is the same as a basic medical physical examination. However, pay attention to those areas that may affect sexual function.

Assess the head, eyes, ears, nose, and throat; note any problems with hearing and vision; and verify appropriate treatment. Determine if there are any difficulties with production of saliva, lingual mobility, and swallowing problems. Examine the neck to determine any limitations resulting from pain or range of motion that could contribute to mobility problems.

Auscultate the heart and lungs and assess cardiac rate, rhythm, and any adventitious sounds. Note breathing rate and pattern, breath sounds, and any long-standing changes such as a barrel chest or kyphoscoliosis. Abdominal examination should include attention to any scarring from previous surgery or radiation, the presence of bowel sounds, and any abnormal masses.

Examine genitalia externally for their presence, shape, and size. Note hair pattern distribution. Furthermore, note the use of any external or internal collection mechanisms for urine. In males, the practitioner should note whether the penis is circumcised and whether there is any evidence of scarring or Peyronie's disease. Note also the presence and size of the testicles. Rectal examination in the male should include palpation of the prostate for size and consistency. In females, note the clitoral size and the condition of the labia. Furthermore, in both sexes, look for any discharge, skin lesions, swelling, or areas of tenderness or hypersensitivity. In females, an internal pelvic examination may be appropriate, but is not discussed in this text because this type of specialized examination should remain under the purview of a gynecologist.

Examine extremities to determine the presence and strength of peripheral pulses and whether any edema is present. Assess joints for range of motion and the presence of any pain, swelling, or warmth. Address any evidence of skin lesions and the presence of any limb abnormalities.

The neurologic examination should include verification of orientation to person, place, and time. For those people with any evidence of cerebral or cognitive dysfunction, a complete mental status examination is appropriate. Assess cranial nerves to determine the presence of any dysfunction, with particular attention given to those nerves that relate to visual, auditory, and swallowing functions. Test sensation throughout. In individuals with spinal cord damage or neuropathy, pay particular attention to the T-11 to L-2 and S-2 to S-4 dermatomes to determine the presence of any loss of the ability to perceive pinprick sensation in those areas. Furthermore, seek the presence of peripheral sensory deficits to light touch, position, or vibration and any areas of hypersensitivity. Test motor strength throughout to determine any segmental losses, side-to-side discrepancies, or distal weakness. Test cerebellar function as appropriate to determine any difficulties with balance and test deep tendon reflexes. Rectal examination should include special attention to the presence or absence of the ability to perceive light touch and pinprick sensation in addition to the ability to voluntarily squeeze the examiner's finger. Elicit the quality of the bulbocavernosus and the anal wink reflexes.

Exhibit 2–1 Sexual Dysfunctions

Sexual Desire Disorders

302.71   Hypoactive Sexual Desire Disorder
302.79   Sexual Aversion Disorder

Sexual Arousal Disorders

302.72   Female Sexual Arousal Disorder
302.72   Male Erectile Disorder

Orgasmic Disorders

302.73   Female Orgasmic Disorder
302.74   Male Orgasmic Disorder
302.75   Premature Ejaculation

Sexual Pain Disorders

302.76   Dyspareunia (not due to a general medical condition)
306.51   Vaginismus (not due to a general medical condition)

Sexual Dysfunction Due to a General Medical Condition

625.8   Female Hypoactive Sexual Desire Disorder Due to [INDICATE GEN-
          ERAL MEDICAL CONDITION]
608.89   Male Hypoactive Sexual Desire Disorder Due to [INDICATE GEN-
          ERAL MEDICAL CONDITION]
607.84   Male Erectile Disorder Due to [INDICATE GENERAL MEDICAL
          CONDITION]
625.0   Female Dyspareunia Due to [INDICATE GENERAL MEDICAL
          CONDITION]
608.89   Male Dyspareunia Due to [INDICATE GENERAL MEDICAL
          CONDITION]
625.8   Other Female Sexual Dysfunction Due to [INDICATE GENERAL
          MEDICAL CONDITION]
608.89   Other Male Sexual Dysfunction Due to [INDICATE GENERAL
          MEDICAL CONDITION]
——.—   Substance-Induced Sexual Dysfunction (refer to Substance-Related
          Disorders for substance-specific codes)
          Specify if: With Impaired Desire/With Impaired Arousal/With Impaired
          Orgasm/With Sexual Pain
          Specify if: With Onset During Intoxication
302.70   Sexual Dysfunction Not Otherwise Specified

Note: The following specifiers apply to all primary sexual dysfunctions: Lifelong Type/
Acquired Type; Generalized Type/Situational Type; Due to Psychological Factors/Due to
Combined Factors.

Source: Reprinted with permission from the *Diagnostic and Statistical Manual of Mental Disorders*, Fourth Edition. Copyright 1994 American Psychiatric Association.

Skin examination should cover the entire body. Note the presence of any scarring, rashes, or lesions. Furthermore, note any signs of inflammation or hypersensitivity.

ASSESSMENT AND TREATMENT

Based on the preliminary history and physical examination, develop a differential diagnosis of the patient's sexual difficulties. If the person's sexual concerns are long-standing and predating any acquired illness or disability, then his or her disorder is of a primary sexual nature and the person happens to have a disability or illness that has confounded the problem. Alternatively, the person's sexual problem may simply be secondary to the impact of his or her particular disability or illness. Moreover, other confounding factors may be involved, and further testing may be necessary to obtain a diagnosis.

The *Diagnostic and Statistical Manual of Mental Disorders-IV* (*DSM-IV*; American Psychiatric Association, 1994) provides a nomenclature for the classification of sexual dysfunctions (Exhibit 2–1). If the sexual problem predates the disability or chronic illness, code it based on *DSM-IV* criteria. If the diagnosis is secondary to the illness or disability, or if there is an additional diagnosis due to the illness or disability, it should be coded under "Sexual Dysfunction Due to a Medical Condition." For this diagnostic category to be clinically useful, however, more detailed information should be provided about the medical condition, the sexual dysfunction, and the relationship between both. A complete discussion of the *DSM-IV* diagnostic system is beyond the scope of this chapter; refer to the source for more information.

REFERENCE

American Psychiatric Association. (1994). *Diagnostic and statistical manual of mental disorders-IV*. Washington, DC: Author.

CHAPTER 3

Performing a Sexual Evaluation on the Person with Disability or Illness

Kenneth A. Lefebvre

The discussion of sexuality cannot begin without a proper understanding of its place within the person and within the society that the person calls home. Those characteristics affect both practitioners and consumers of care. Both professionals and people interested in the area of sexuality must have a comprehensive and precise understanding of the complexity of sexual behaviors.

TALKING ABOUT SEXUALITY—THE BASICS: SEXUALITY, SEXUALITY DISCUSSIONS, AND COMFORT LEVEL

Why is the discussion of sexuality important and how should such issues be addressed in the health care system? Sexuality is important because it is integral to self-image, influenced by many health care decisions, and too frequently ignored or overlooked. Sexuality is difficult to discuss because there are many components of the concept and many different and sometimes incomplete or conflicting definitions. For some people, sexuality is how they feel about themselves and how they think others perceive them in terms of attractiveness or desirability. Sexuality can be a basic component of self-identity that can define sexual orientation and lifestyle. It can reflect political positions and human rights policies. It can encompass issues of power and control, affiliation, or hate. Sexuality can mean so many different things and include so many different constructs that misunderstanding and poor communication are almost inevitable unless an operational definition can be agreed on.

The definition proposed by Thorn-Gray and Kern (1983) seems to be most helpful and inclusive for most cases and problems: "Sexuality is the verbal, visual, tactual, and olfactory communication which expresses love and intimacy between two people" (p. 138). This definition is a great heuristic tool because it is broad and is not as functionally based or performance oriented as others. However, it has both requirements and limitations. The requirements are that the participants have the ability to communicate and the ability and skills to carry on an intimate emotional relationship. The limitations entail excluding those people who are isolated or so schizoid they shun others, or who are unable to communicate because of medical, psychiatric, or other reasons.

The need to use a definition gives clinicians an opportunity to examine their personal biases and values and perhaps an opportunity to evaluate how these biases affect their ability to work with certain kinds of clients or problems. It is important to examine how often clinicians think of sexuality as exclusively genital or always better if genital sex is included. The practitioner should have a clear understanding of how he or she conceptualizes sexuality in groups that are older or younger than the practitioner. Practitioners should examine their attitudes or prejudices about sexuality issues for people who have significant disabilities and chronic medical problems. They should try to re-think their biases about sexuality for those they consider "unattractive" or disfigured. Furthermore, practitioners have to consider the roles of sexual orientation, countertransference to certain sexual states, cultural factors, and practices accepted by certain religious, socioeconomic, and ethnic groups that might be different, considered offensive, or even seen as destructive.

SIGNIFICANT ROLES OF AFFILIATION AND POWER

The Thorn-Gray and Kern definition has affiliation as a major component. *Affiliation* can be operationally defined as a person's desire to either associate with others or be separate from others. This is clearly something many societies favor and a bias that seems to make cultural sense. Psychological theories support the idea that much of human behavior is directed toward achieving goals that can be understood as being fueled by these needs. Interpersonal theories have been less used than others because it has been difficult to quantify and test those kinds of theories using traditional testing techniques.

Behavior is also complimentary in nature. Each bit of behavior is both a stimulus to the other person and a response to what the other person has "done." The causality rules of this kind of system are circular, not linear. In this kind of system, no one is the cause and no one has the blame for behavior, whether good or bad. Instead, the behavior is the result of the interactions in the system. In this system it makes no sense to blame. When there is a "problem," the person has to ask, What am I doing to allow this interaction to continue this way? What could I do to change my behavior? Power and affiliation are key factors in communication theory (Watzlawick, Heimich, & Johnson, 1967) and communication is central to sexuality as defined.

Certain rules of communication and communication theory are important to remember:

- It is impossible not to communicate.
- All communications have two parts, the process and the content.
- Process is concerned with issues of power and status—"who is right" issues.
- Communications are often based on "quid pro quos," essentially an exchange between participants for items or behaviors having perceived equal values.
- Communication is both verbal and nonverbal.
- If there is a conflict between verbal and nonverbal components, the subjects will more often rely on the nonverbal component.
- The more time and effort that is spent on process in relation to content, the more pathological the communication.
- Communication options include accepting, rejecting, and disqualifying statements.
- Accepting and rejecting responses are equal and have no positive or negative values.
- Disqualifying statements are destructive and are to be avoided. A *disqualifying statement* is one that invalidates another person's rights, competencies, or opinions and that attempts to establish the unassailable authority of the speaker (e.g., "You just don't know what you are talking about!").

It is crucial for providers to be especially concerned about "process" issues because health care is often perceived as an area in which power and control issues are more important than people want to realize. *Process* often refers to issues concerning who is "right" or who has the authority to issue directives to others. Many health care teams that comprise well-educated and trained people have difficulty solving process problems. In working with patients, providers must remember that they should have the most flexibility and options in their interactions. They have the choice of how aware they can become of their communication style and their relationship with power in themselves and others. They have a choice in how they react to others. They can learn new and different communication styles that will result in new and more positive emotional feelings in themselves and others.

Providers have the choice of perceiving themselves as either vendors or stewards. As vendors, they must focus on providing the best value. There must be a concern for the bottom line, and obligations are based on "quid pro quos." A steward relationship is based on the distribution of resources. It is not concerned with finances, and obligations are based on personal values and not quid pro quos.

DISABILITY, TRANSFERENCE, AND COUNTERTRANSFERENCE

When working with patients with disability or chronic illness, it is likely that practitioners will encounter issues of transference and countertransference. To better appreciate the context that encourages such interactions, it is important to understand the major emotional and status changes patients may have experienced. From the patient's point of view, many changes may have occurred. Some of the more significant changes might involve sensory experiences. Patients may have had different bodily and cognitive experiences since illness onset. Their body may feel and perceive differently than before disease or disability onset. There may be inattention, neglect, lack of sensation, pain, and concerns about bowel and bladder function that did not exist before. They may view their body as a source of inconvenience and distress rather than as a vehicle for giving and receiving pleasure. Their view of the world may have changed. Instead of a place that provides opportunities for recreation and work along with a sense of community, they may see the world as a dangerous place, not as accessible as before, and inhospitable to people with medical conditions. People may develop a distrust of themselves and others.

At some level, they may feel that their actions or the actions of others (medical providers, family members, or accident participants) are or have been dangerous, and a protective sense of isolation and distrust develops. For these reasons, and especially if there has been a shift to a more negative self-image, patients can develop an internal prejudice toward themselves. Before the disability or illness, there existed a set of attitudes and beliefs toward people with disabilities or illness. These attitudes may have been built on fear, ignorance, or primal prejudice. As their bodies become more disabled, their attitudes may reflect these pre-onset attitudes and impair their ability to incorporate the illness or medical condition into a more positive post-onset self-image. In effect, these constructs result in considerable self-prejudice. Until that self-prejudice is resolved, self-acceptance and the ability to feel that they deserve a healthy sexual relationship is limited. Some patients will routinely disenfranchise themselves from a variety of activities because they are "too much trouble" or because they cannot participate or enjoy them like they used to.

Another important factor is the power of countertransference. Countertransference is a problem for both patients and providers. Gunther (1994) has pointed out that countertransference is not a singular concept, but rather a combination of feelings, attitudes, ideas, and behaviors that usually arise unexpectedly around a specific problem or issues within a working relationship. Countertransference is important because it leads to some form of response believed to be appropriately useful (by the therapist or provider), but ultimately not so. Countertransference characteristics are behavior that contains some degree of anxiety, special intensity of feeling, or nonspecific upset that goes unrecognized by the caregiver. The caregiver may feel that the patient is behaving in a provocative or disappointing way and may, in response, act more rigid or insistent. The caregiver is seldom troubled by doubt or curiosity regarding his or her own reactions or understanding. The patient may experience the caregiver's response as mean or uncaring. The sources of countertransference may be the vulnerabilities of professional self-esteem or professional expectations, which are provoked when patients do not give signs that they respect or appreciate the professional's skills or training. Countertransference is provoked by patients who are severely regressed either psychologically or physically. In addition, patient behaviors such as swearing, physical aggression, exhibitionism, homelessness, drug use, narcissistic display, or entitlement requests are possible precipitants. Countertransference also can rise from the therapists' own narcissistic vulnerability and the unconscious reaction to their own fear of becoming disabled or ill when they see the burden that results in the patients with whom they work. Countertransference is often seen in the team when a particular patient is characterized as a "baby," "disturbed," or as being more responsible for his or her particular disability than other patients.

COMMUNICATION AND RULES

Communication within the health care system should have six goals:

1. to establish rapport
2. to determine a basic medical and interpersonal history
3. to assess the role and nature of relationships in the patient's life
4. to identify what changes have occurred since the onset of the disability or illness
5. to determine how those changes have been explained to the patient and how the changes have affected quality of life
6. to communicate in such a way so that questions are encouraged

These tasks are a lot to remember, and therapists often feel so rushed during their day that giving them another task is counterproductive. However, therapists may be helped at times by referring to these following seven "rules":

1. It is okay to be stupid—just do not work at it. (Working at it means the therapist thinks he or she already knows all the answers and has the "right intervention" for every problem.)
2. No one ever tells the therapist the truth the first time.
3. Not everyone is a nice person.

4. It is not up to the therapist to "fix" everything.
5. Except in unusual circumstances, sex occurs within a social environment.
6. Most sexual problems are less concerned with sex and more concerned with something else (e.g., social skills, lack of a partner, finances, privacy issues, and depression).
7. Although everyone may have the "right" to be sexual, sexuality within a relationship implies a certain set of responsibilities.

INTERVIEW AND TREATMENT PLANNING

An interview to discuss sexuality issues should never be done in isolation. A general interview should always be conducted first. This interview should include general questions on lifestyle and personality issues, health status, experience in the health care system, etiology of the illness or disability, the reactions of the patient and significant others, reactions to the hospital or treatment environment, and abuse issues.

It is crucial that the therapist sets the stage for the interview, especially if the patient has not requested the evaluation, by describing his or her position, title, and how he or she is involved with the patient's care. The therapist must explain his or her job carefully—not everyone knows what a psychologist or an occupational therapist does. The therapist should also carefully explain the purpose of the interview and ask if the patient has ever talked to someone like the therapist and, if so, how the patient evaluated that interview or service. The provider should not use language or jargon that the patient might not understand. Setting the stage for the interview might go as follows, for example:

> I am Dr. Lefebvre. I am the psychologist who works with the spinal cord service. It is routine for me to talk to new patients. Have you ever talked to a psychologist before? The reason I am seeing you is because you have had a significant injury that resulted in your coming to this hospital. I am going to ask about your injury; your treatment at other hospitals; how the injury has affected you, your friends, and your relatives; and some other questions about lifestyle and health. I am not here to see if you are "crazy." Is it okay for me to proceed? Do you have any questions?

At the start of the general interview, the provider must review with the patient the information that may be contained in transfer notes or chart reviews. He or she should look for errors and areas that need to be clarified. It is not unusual to find errors. The clinician must let the patient know he or she trusts the patient and values the patient's perspective more than what others may have written about the patient. For example, a patient may be described as having a history of depression because she has been taking antidepressant medication. On inquiry, however, the provider determines that the person has been prescribed antidepressants for treatment of dysesthetic pain.

The general interview needs to cover the following topics:

- *Who:* Obtain information on basic demographics, age, sex, education, work history, marital status, children, and marital history. Discuss the patient's relationship with his or her children, especially if the children are adults.
- *What:* Discuss the nature of the disease, disability, or circumstances that brings the patient into the health care system. Assess to what the patient attributes this change.
- *Where/when:* Ask, Did the problem arise in a certain context or place? Is it acute or chronic?
- *Problem:* Ask, How does the patient perceive the "problem"? What are the patient's goals?
- *Previous history:* Determine what previous history is important for the provider.
- *General history:* Assess important historical issues, previous experience with the health care system, and history of significant stressors involving interpersonal issues, health, finances, and losses. Significant losses include experiences with death, change in personal status, and significant change in financial status. Specific questions can be asked about abortions, interrupted pregnancies, and deaths of children.
- *Essential issues:* Assess significant developmental issues such as abuse history including physical, psychological, sexual, and substance. If possible, determine if the patient ever abused others. Ask about substance use and abuse history. Remember that some patients may not consider use of certain "recreational" drugs as abuse.
- *Sex-specific issues:* Explore sexual abuse; sexually transmitted disease; abortion or unplanned pregnancies (explore this issue with both men and women); body image; sexual concerns; and sexual consequences of life changes (change in sexual orientation, sexual reassignment, intersex status, sexual addictions, and so on). Determine the level of sexual knowledge and priority of sexual concerns in context of other problems, if possible.
- *Family and friends:* Assess the reactions of relations, children, work colleagues, and employer. Ask for perceived effect on work relationships and romantic relationships. In some settings, the provider will find that patients have both spouses and significant others both known and unknown to the spouse. Patients may also have two spouses.
- *Expectations:* Assess the patient's chief concerns and complaints. Determine the place and importance of sexuality concerns.

Three basic assumptions underlie Cole's (1991) approach to sexuality: (1) sexuality is a health issue that, in many settings, is not acknowledged and therefore may not be readily accepted as such; (2) the person working with sexuality must have a good understanding of his or her own sexuality, and it is incorrect for the practitioner to impose on the client the provider's personal view of sexuality; and (3) sexuality should be addressed in the same way as other important issues in the health care setting. Cole has indicated a preference for an interview format because the fundamental issue is to determine whether the "problem" is primarily or only secondarily related to a disability. He has correctly pointed out that the presence of a physical disability does not mean that the sexual dysfunction and the disability are causally linked. He has emphasized that taking a sexual history involves both receiving information while simultaneously providing education. Patient education is mandatory during the history taking and, if it is not provided, the patient may become frightened. A sexual history must include a social history. Cultural diversity makes it imperative to touch on religious, moral, and cultural influences that may influence sexuality. If privacy and personal comfort are compromised by living arrangements, then they may be major factors in sexual dysfunction.

Cole (1991) has identified important ground rules for the interview. The patient has to know that there is no obligation to answer any question. The examiner, however, needs to watch for unconscious disruptive body language or other negative communications from either himself or herself or the patient. It is necessary to acknowledge "The elephant in the room," which refers to an obvious and significant fact or experience that occurs in the interview. Examples are abuse histories, chemical dependency, or overt hostility. Ignoring the obvious is dysfunctional; rather, the interview has to be forthright and supportive. Training, supervision, and retraining are necessary to impart and maintain high-level interview skills.

Donohue and Gebhard (1995) mentioned similar issues and concerns when they reported on the long delayed but recently published Kinsey Institute/Indiana University report on sexuality and spinal cord injury. In that study, which was conducted in the 1970s, the protocol was designed for interviews rather than a self-administered questionnaire. It was believed that the interviewer sets the tone of the interview. If the interviewer is an interested and sympathetic listener, it is possible to establish rapport quickly and earn the trust of the subject. If the subject gives a vague response or if the question appears to have been misunderstood, the interviewer is able to clarify the question and seek additional information if necessary. Also, this method is the only way to catch discrepancies in responses that have appeared in different parts of the interview. Discrepancies are quite common and usually indicate a poor understanding of the question or an interpretation of the question that reflects personal or idiosyncratic views. The authors have indicated that the interview format allows both the subject and the investigator to ask questions immediately that help to clarify and better define the information being discussed and gathered. This type of personal interaction helps the respondent feel more at ease with those questions that might otherwise cause discomfort and ensures the completeness and detail from each case. Donohue and Gebhard (1995) also observed that some of the interviewers in the study were better trained than others and they emphasized that training is necessary because this type of interviewing is complicated. "Taking a thorough and good sexual case history requires special skills, persistence, adequate time, and an acute sensitivity for contradiction, internal inconsistencies and ambiguity" (p. 10).

Bridge Statements: Definition, Function, and Utility

Not all questions are easy to ask and some questions must be asked more than once. Some patients will give different answers to different therapists and will have engaged the rule of electing not to tell the truth the first time. This is understandable, because they may have had no chance to develop any trust with the provider before being asked intimate and potentially embarrassing questions. However, other sets of questions are not asked because of the therapist's reluctance or because the provider thought the patient did not seem "ready" for them. *Bridge statements* (including questions) facilitate the transition from easy, comfortable topics to those that are difficult or awkward. They require a proper conceptualization of "the problem." Every aspect of a person's life interacts with and affects other aspects. Bridge statements proceed from the general to the more specific and acknowledge prerequisite events implicitly or explicitly. They emphasize the professional relationship between patient and therapist, help to clarify the content component of communications, and focus on permission giving and permission seeking. Bridge statements provide support for the therapist for those questions that are easy to "forget" to ask, or that are not asked because the patient is not "ready" for them. In especially difficult cases, patient readiness is often assessed unilaterally and telepathically (to spare the therapist discomfort). Bridge statements are a way to overcome this difficulty. Their utility is to incorporate difficult topics into an assessment, reduce discomfort, gain valuable information, and legitimatize personal inquiry. Their goal is to facilitate interactions that minimize awkwardness and maximize permission seeking.

The following are examples of bridge statements:

- Has anyone talked to you about how your injury [illness] can affect your ability to have sex [or a sexual relationship]?
- Since your injury [illness], has your relationship with your [spouse, partner, lover, significant other] changed? Has there been any change in your physical relationship?

- How has your [arthritis, multiple sclerosis, amputation] changed the kinds of things you and your [spouse, partner, lover] do together? Does he or she treat you any differently now? How has your sexual relationship been affected? What was it like before [onset or first diagnosis]?
- How has your libido [your desire for sex, your interest in sex] changed? How has it affected the way you feel sexually about your partner?
- Were you romantically involved with anyone when you were injured? [A "yes" gets this probe:] Were you sexually involved?
- [If a spouse has died, ask for the cause of death:] Was your husband's or wife's death a surprise? How did it affect you? Have you been involved in any romantic relationships since? Have those relationships included a sexual relationship?
- [For the topic of abuse:] Has there ever been any kind of abuse in your life? Any kind of physical, mental, or psychological abuse? Any kind of sexual abuse?

Although bridge satements are designed to solicit information and increase communication, there is another type of statement that hinders information seeking and creates anxiety in patients, family members, and staff. These are called Barnum statements, named after P.T. Barnum, and are statements that are so general and contain so many truisms that they are empty in content, although fashioned to sound either encouraging, optimistic, or both. Examples of Barnum statements are as follows: [To an anxious patient:] "You're in the best hospital for your condition. The doctors will do everything they can. You don't need to worry. Just take one day at a time. There's someone for everybody in this world [not even mathematically true]. Come on, smile—it's a wonderful day." Even if it is a wonderful day for most people, it may not be one for your patient. Barnum statements minimize and depersonalize the patient's problem. They prohibit the practitioner from understanding the problem from the patient's perspective. Barnum statements should, therefore, be avoided.

Treatment Planning

Treatment planning is determined by a number of factors. Not all teams have a member who is comfortable asking about sexuality. On other teams, two or three different team members will have inquired without prior knowledge of the other member's activities and without coordination of effort. Basic sexuality training for all staff is an important way for institutions to address this need as a common problem. It is also good to have an ad hoc or standing sexuality committee that can help address the issues of training, coordination of services, use of explicit sexual materials, sexuality programs for children and other special need populations, and coordination of sexuality training and research.

Although sexuality is not the same for all people it is generally subsumed under the concept of self-image. Different hospital and clinic settings will have clients with different presentations of self-image. Different cultures and subcultures will be represented. Some facilities may have a larger number of patients involved with drug- or alcohol-related incidents. Others will have a greater proportion of gunshot victims as a result of either gang or street violence. Practitioners need to remember not to make value judgments or criticize their patients, but, rather, to work with them. Practitioners may encounter many patients whom they would not choose as neighbors or friends. But all patients deserve at least an inquiry into sexuality concerns that they may be experiencing and an opportunity to be educated. Not all facilities will be able to offer treatment in the usual sense, but all should be able to impart the message that sexuality is an integral aspect of self-image and is affected by other health conditions.

Common Sexual Concerns

In almost any facility that treats patients with chronic disease or disability, it is reasonable to think that a majority of patients will be affected by at least two or three sexual concerns. *Sexual infantilization* is the process of treating someone as if he or she had no sexual concerns or interests. People born with developmental disabilities or congenital medical problems are at risk for being treated this way. Also at risk are individuals with progressive neurologic disorders. As their condition deteriorates, they increasingly may be treated in a childlike manner to spare family members from dealing with the area of sexuality in their impaired family members. Family members may fear that the patient may begin to express sexual urges that can only cause "trouble." Sometimes, parents infantilize their children while simultaneously taking the Barnum approach for the future by implying directly and indirectly that their children will "find someone" and get married. Significant others of the progressive neurologically impaired may find their deteriorating physical presentation and impaired cognitive skills repulsive and unsettling. Confused by guilt over their unacceptable negative feelings and ashamed of being unable to "stand by" their loved one, it is easy to see how redefining a person as nonsexual is an easy and comforting position. The same kind of thinking may be operative for patients who have had a traumatic significant injury or illness and whose impaired status and capabilities make sex the last thing that family members want to think about. Sometimes patients are infantilized because it is too difficult to think of "crippled" people as sexual.

Many other patients' conditions fall into the category of sex deprivation. Sometimes providers take sexual behavior in themselves for granted. They may be used to having some kind of (genital) sexual event twice weekly and may daily appreciate in themselves and others good looks, good grooming, self-affirming statements, and the ability to use their bodies to give themselves or others pleasure in a variety of ways (e.g., sports, body language, or exercise). Chronically ill or disabled people may not have the same opportunities or the same ease in satisfying those needs. Sex deprivation can be a major loss for those individuals.

Role changes, sex role changes, and role reversal affect a great proportion of individuals with chronic disease or disability. Individuals who have been caregivers most of their lives find themselves too ill to help others. Spouses who once provided support for their family may now be unable to control their bowels or bladder. Independent successful businesspeople may not remember their medical history or if they are in a hospital or a restaurant. New parents who have had their fingers amputated may wonder what kind of a parent they will be to their 8-month-old baby. Every history has a different story that can tug at one's heart.

Sexual Behavior and Competency

Another aspect of treatment planning concerns how competency in sexuality is determined. There are no guidelines for this kind of determination. Assuredly, some individuals who have entered the health care system will have been abused and will have abused others. Individuals who are parents of children may be neglectful or incapable of caring for them and seemingly unconcerned about what others perceive as an irresponsible attitude. Except for the most infamous cases, those individuals and their problems are usually ignored. Hospitals know that getting involved can be expensive in terms of time and effort and that there is little chance of actually changing these situations. Furthermore, such areas are politically and culturally sensitive. The courts have been unwilling to abridge the rights of individuals to engage in sexual behavior, procreate, and parent. Individuals have a constitutional right to be sexual. What educational programs can emphasize is that sexual activity per se does not equal sexual competency. Programs can redefine *sexuality* from a right to an activity that can be improved by skill enhancement techniques and that can be enjoyed more in a responsible way. Although everyone may have the right to be sexual, sexual behavior with another person implies responsibilities as well.

Acquired and Developmental Conditions

Providers should address sexuality differently for those people with acquired and developmental disabilities. It is easy to overlook how much important developmental sexual behavior is absent in the lives of some children with developmental disabilities. For example, how does a young girl in a wheelchair visit her friends in a nonaccessible apartment? How does she learn how adults are sexual if her parents are afraid to be that way in front of her? How does she explore her parents' drawers when they are out and find books, movies, condoms, sponges, lingerie, and so forth—as many youths do—if she cannot get into their bedroom? How can she find her brother's copies of sexually explicit publications if she cannot get under his bed where they are stashed? Patients with developmental disabilities may come to a provider as an adult and not have had sufficient experience or information to know their sexual orientation and sexual interests. Providers need to offer support and education for parents of children with chronic conditions and disabilities and focus on the areas of sexuality and socialization.

In the development of treatment planning, all of these factors are important. The person the clinician sees is not the person the clinician might have seen pre-injury. Someone who has had a condition for a long time may have a different view of the world than the provider might guess. The importance of a pre-injury personality cannot be overemphasized. Research on posttraumatic stress disorder has found that disaster is not an equal opportunity event. Individuals affected by such trauma often have psychological or behavioral histories that put them at higher risk for emotional and sexual problems than others in the population (North & Smith, 1990).

Practitioner Roles and Obligations

Practitioners have an obligation to be aware of their limits and deficiencies in the area of sexuality. They and their facility should have the capability to train in-house staff as necessary or refer, if appropriate. Practitioners must realize that they have both an implied and explicit obligation to establish a therapeutic contract with patients that is understandable and acceptable to patients. If a patient does not identify something as a problem, a practitioner either has to get better at getting the patient to identify problems or move on. Practitioners must maintain balance and respect in what they do. Emotional reactions are often the sign of countertransference. Practitioners should try to maintain a cognitive, problem-solving position. Patients come into a provider's life for only a short time—even if they are long-term patients.

In treatment, three constructs interact: hope, complexity, and the unknown. Much of what is really known of most patients is insignificant when compared with the unknown. Practitioners are responsible for remembering how little they may really know about what the patient has experienced and the patient's personal history. Providers must hesitate from making quick judgments and decisions for patients they hardly know in an area that is so complex.

Patient Questions

Sometimes questions that seem straightforward are really disguised requests or covers for questions that the patient is uncomfortable asking. For example, the question, Will I be able to have children? may be a question about fertility, erection capability, mobility, attractiveness, or desirability. It also may be a way of asking the therapist if he or she finds the patient attractive. It also may be a way of expressing a romantic or sexual interest in the therapist. Therapists do develop both negative and positive feelings toward patients that are motivated by different needs. Each facility has to determine its own policy about staff–patient interactions.

Some staff see nothing wrong in socializing with patients. Some socialize with those they treat, others with those they do not treat. Socializing can develop into sexual relationships, marriage, breakups, acceptance, and rejection. Some facilities have taken the stand that any interaction between staff and therapists is prohibited unless that activity is part of a treatment plan and authorized by the patient's physician. Other facilities have not yet addressed this issue. Close professional relationships can turn into emotional and sexual relationships. The most dangerous position for an institution to take is to assume that emotional and sexual relationships between patients and their therapists do not exist, or if they do, they are no one's business. People with disability or chronic disease may be especially vulnerable for exploitation or abuse; abuse may often come from family members or acquaintances. The consequences of staff–patient interactions have never been rigorously studied and they probably need to be examined. But such interactions often put patients in a more vulnerable psychological position than the potential benefits justify.

Sexuality Program Goals

One method of providing a basic level of sexuality information and education is with sexuality programs that are designed either for a general medical population or especially directed toward the needs of individuals with specific diagnoses. Information and education is the major focus of such programs (Schuler, 1982). The major objective is to increase understanding and encourage new expectations. Sexuality programs are best when they offer information and skill training in the following seven areas:

1. information and education about the sexual response cycle and how disease and disability might impair or change the cycle
2. techniques to increase mutual responsibility for relationships and sexuality goals
3. information, exercises, and techniques to facilitate attitude change and to help the participants adopt different criteria to evaluate relationships
4. techniques and exercises designed to minimize performance anxiety
5. skills to increase communication
6. exercises that prescribe behavior change
7. examination of lifestyle and organized efforts to change destructive lifestyle or sex roles

SEXUAL ASSESSMENT PROFILE: HOW PRACTITIONERS WILL KNOW WHEN THEY KNOW ENOUGH

Many patients can be helped by sexuality education and nearly all will benefit from some basic education. Not all patients will have partners who can or will want to participate. Other patients could benefit from a more individualized program but may require a more extensive evaluation. Sometimes it is difficult for therapists to know if they have obtained enough information. The very idea of sexuality may cause some anxiety, and that coupled with a person's complicated life history can make it difficult for therapists to proceed. Sometimes, therapists will offer information and suggestions that are incongruent with a patient's acceptance level. Other times, there is a "rush to intervention," and education is focused either in the wrong area or at the wrong level. There is always the reluctance to address destructive lifestyles.

Lefebvre (1990) has reported on a technique called Sexual Assessment Planning (SAP), which is designed to help clinicians in several ways. Its goal is to prevent clinicians from rushing into interventions with patients about whom they need more information. SAP relies on history provided by patients. It can help assess the potential of a patient to benefit from specific interventions. It assesses a patient's needs. It guides and limits interventions, often defining and restricting them to better address patient limitations. SAP can be modified to suit the preferences of individual therapists and the special needs of different client populations.

Essentially a therapist identifies specific categories of assessment or constructs that may be most important based on a preliminary patient history. For example, one set of categories might be cognitive status, relationship history, personal responsibility, grief and loss issues, patient personal prejudices, finances, and the patient's view of the world. The therapist then structures the evaluation to focus on these areas. When done, the therapist rates each area. Categories with more positive content are rated +1; with more negative content, -1; and with uncertain content, 0. Zero content scores require more evaluation. Positive categories are viewed as strengths and may be used to help balance deficiencies in other areas. Categories with -1 should be considered as areas that will impair sexuality skills and need to be specifically addressed as liabilities, not just normal variance. This approach can help therapists to more thoughtfully address the area of sexuality and identify areas that require more intensive or comprehensive rehabilitation.

Sexuality, an integral part of self-identity and self-image, is a complicated concept involving power, communication, affiliation, and reproduction. It is heavily influenced by cultural and societal values and rules. It certainly is influenced by many health care practices and interventions. In the current changing health care climate, often only the most pressing issues get addressed. Facilities that work with people with chronic illness or disability should include sexuality as one of their concerns. Institutional rules and policies will affect how therapists work with this issue and, consequently, with patients. Sexuality is a complicated process that must be assessed carefully. Although it is difficult to identify and address destructive lifestyles and behaviors, such actions are necessary to offer healthier options. Not every therapist can work with disabled or chronically ill people, though. Nearly every provider who does work with this population can learn the basic skills to ask fundamental questions that identify sexuality as a concern integral to health care and of interest to the medical team. Letting patients know that their sexuality concerns are something the medical team is interested in will open the door for further education and intervention.

Self-Report Questionnaires Assessing Sexual Behavior

Many questionnaires have been developed for a variety of different specialized clinical and research populations. Each instrument has questions of reliability, generalizability, and application with a disabled population. However, only a few instruments have been developed specifically to assess sexuality in people with physical disabilities generally because the researchers were required to develop their own instruments—either none was available or none was suited and standardized on the population being studied. Of those instruments specially developed most have been adapted for a single physical impairment, such as spinal cord injury, traumatic brain injury, multiple sclerosis, or stroke. Furthermore, most questions on those questionnaires have been geared to the concerns of men or have investigated the reactions of wives to their husband's disability. A complete review of sexuality questionnaires is beyond the scope of this chapter. The reader is referred to other sources for reviews of this information (e.g., Conte, 1983; Derogatis, Lopez, & Zinzeletta, 1988; LoPiccolo & Steger, 1974; Nosek et al., 1994, 1996).

Although questionnaires have a valuable role to play in clinical and research settings, each questionnaire is so individual and different from others that the particular utility of any one instrument is impossible to assess. Clearly the most comprehensive models are the most time consuming. Questionnaires used with the disabled population must be presented in multiple formats to facilitate response by subjects with more disabling conditions. Questionnaires can, by design, limit the responses that an individual will give and, thus, may allow respondents to select answers that mask other more serious problems. Questionnaires are relatively cheap, can be mailed or transmitted all over the country to provide statistically representative samples, and are anonymous. They also can be developed to study specific, narrowly focused topics.

Furthermore, questionnaires have the advantages of ensuring that each subject will be exposed to the same question. However, they do not offer the potential for education and emotional support that a well-trained and experienced interviewer can provide. Several authors (Cole, 1991; Donohue & Gebhard, 1995; Sbrocco, Weisberg, & Barlow, 1995) have noted that education is especially important in the area of sexuality and have pointed out how an interview format allows the researcher to elaborate on questions if necessary, inquire into answers that seem to be contradictory, and provide comfort when necessary to subjects who might be confused or distressed. Questionnaires, however, are not an appropriate instrument for individuals who are illiterate or who are too disabled to respond. Adaptive techniques are available for use under such circumstances.

The Open Ended Sexuality Limited Organizing Worksheet (OPEN SLOW)

The OPEN SLOW is a semistructured questionnaire that has many open-ended questions and can be used for clinical or training purposes (see Appendix 3–A). This method provides the strengths of both the questionnaire and interview methods. In addition, it is designed for disabled or medically ill populations and is free of gender bias. It is good for gathering a basic history. Other questionnaires designed for specific problems or clinical interest can be used to augment the information that the OPEN SLOW can provide.

CONCLUSION

Sexuality is a pervasive issue that is often unexplored. Practitioners may fear that they are undertrained or underequipped to address sexual concerns. However, it is crucial for both the practitioner and the patient to understand that sexuality is much more than the functional status of the genitals. Many patients need education about sexuality and may have a distorted idea about sexual ideals. By using some of the techniques outlined in this chapter, the practitioner can develop confidence and a better appreciation for the complex interactions between self-image, health care, and sexuality. Ultimately, practitioners will be able to incorporate the psychosocial and psychosexual features of the patient into the overall treatment plan.

REFERENCES

Cole, T.M. (1991). Gathering a sex history for a physically disabled adult. *Sexuality and Disability, 9,* 29–37.

Conte, H.R. (1983). Development and use of self report techniques for assessing sexual functioning: A review and critique. *Archives of Sexual Behavior, 12,* 555–567.

Derogatis, L.R., Lopez, M.C., & Zinzeletta, E.M. (1988). Clinical applications of the DSFI in the assessment of sexual dysfunctions. In R.A. Brown & J.R. Field (Eds.), *Treatment of sexual problems in individual and couples therapy.* Columbia, MD: PMA Publishing.

Donohue, J., & Gebhard, P. (1995). The Kinsey Institute/Indiana University report on sexuality and spinal cord injury. *Sexuality and Disability, 13,* 7–85.

Gunther, M.S. (1994). Countertransference: Issues in staff caregivers who work to rehabilitate catastrophic-injury survivors. *American Journal of Psychotherapy, 48,* 208–220.

Lefebvre, K.A. (1990). Sexual assessment planning. *Journal of Head Trauma Rehabilitation, 5,* 25–30.

LoPiccolo, J., & Steger, J.C. (1974). The sexual interaction inventory: A new instrument for assessment of sexual dysfunction. *Archives of Sexual Behavior, 3,* 585–595.

North C.S., & Smith, E.M. (1990). Post traumatic stress disorder in disaster survivors. *Comprehensive Therapy, 16*(12), 3–9.

Nosek, M.A., Howland, C.A., Young, M.E., Georgiou, D., Rintala, D.H., Foley, C.C., Bennett, J.A., & Smith, Q. (1994). Wellness models and sexuality among women with physical disabilities. *Journal of Applied Rehabilitation Counseling, 25,* 50–58.

Nosek, M.A., Rintala, D.H., Young, M.E., Howland, C.A., Foley, C.C., Rossi, D., & Champong, G. (1996). Sexual functioning among women with physical disabilities. *Archives of Physical Medicine and Rehabilitation, 77,* 107–115.

Sbrocco, T., Weisberg, B.A., & Barlow, D. (1995). Sexual dysfunction in the older adult: Assessment of psychosocial factors. *Sexuality and Disability, 13,* 201–216.

Schuler, M. (1982). Sexual counseling for the spinal cord injured: A review of five programs. *Journal of Sex and Marital Therapy, 8*(3), 241–251.

Thorn-Gray, B., & Kern, L. (1983). Sexual dysfunction associated with physical disability: A treatment guide for the rehabilitation practitioner. *Rehabilitation Literature, 44*(5–6), 138–144.

Watzlawick, P., Heimich, J., & Johnson, D.D. (1967). *Pragmatics of human communication: A study of interactional patterns, pathologies, and paradoxes.* New York: Norton.

SUGGESTED READINGS

Annon, J.S. (1975). *The behavioral treatment of sexual problems, brief therapy.* New York: Harper & Row.

Benjamin, L.S. (1974). Structural analysis of social behavior. *Psychological Review, 81,* 392–425.

The Committee on Medical Education. (1974). *Assessment of sexual function: A guide to interviewing.* New York: Jason Aronson.

Gans, J. (1983). Hate in the rehabilitation setting. *Archives of Physical Medicine and Rehabilitation, 64,* 176–179.

McLemore, C.W., & Benjamin, L.S. (1979). Whatever happened to interpersonal diagnosis? A psychosocial alternative to DSM-III. *American Psychologist, 34,* 17–34.

Mooney, T.O., Cole, T.M., & Chilgren, R.A. (1975). *Sexual options for paraplegics and quadriplegics.* Boston: Little, Brown.

Novak, P.P., & Mitchell, M.M. (1988). Professional involvement in sexuality counseling for patients with spinal cord injuries. *American Journal of Occupational Therapy, 42*(2), 105–112.

Romano, M.D. (1978). Sexuality and the disabled female. *Sexuality and Disability, 1,* 27–33.

Sipski, M.L., & Alexander, C.J. (1993). Sexual activities, response and satisfaction in women pre- and post-spinal cord injury. *Archives of Physical Medicine and Rehabilitation, 74,* 1025–1029.

Sipski, M.L., Alexander, C.J., & Rosen, R.C. (1995a). Orgasm in women with spinal cord injuries: A laboratory-based assessment. *Archives of Physical Medicine and Rehabilitation, 76,* 1097–1102.

Sipski, M.L., Alexander, C.J., & Rosen, R.C. (1995b). Physiological parameters associated with psychogenic sexual arousal in women with complete spinal cord injuries. *Archives of Physical Medicine and Rehabilitation, 76,* 811–818.

Sipski, M.L., Rosen, R.C., & Alexander, C.J. (1996). Physiological parameters associated with the performance of a distracting task and genital self-stimulation in women with complete spinal cord injuries. *Archives of Physical Medicine and Rehabilitation, 77,* 419–424.

Tepper, M.S. (1992). Sexual education in spinal cord injury rehabilitation: Current trends and recommendations. *Sexuality and Disability, 10*(1), 15–31.

The OPEN SLOW

Instructions: This is to be used with individuals who have expressed a desire to either work on or discuss the area of sexuality. The language can and should be modified to ensure patient understanding and comfort, if necessary. The focus of the interview should be to gather basic information that may be helpful to better understand the patient's problem.

1. What is the most serious problem you have right now?

2. How does this problem affect your sexuality?

3. *Sexuality* means different things to different people. What does it mean for you?

4. What are the most important parts (or aspects) of sexuality for you?

5. Describe the problem that you are having with your sexual life.

6. How long have you had this problem?

7. Have you ever gone to anyone for help with this problem?

   If yes, when?

   What happened?

8. In your opinion, is this problem connected to your medical condition (or disability)?

9. Has your physician ever talked to you about how your medical condition might affect your ability to have a sexual relationship?

10. What is the hardest part about talking about sexual things?

11. Have you ever asked anyone on your medical team sex questions?

12. How did they react?

13. What is different about sexuality since you developed _____ (medical condition) or became disabled?

14. Do you think that getting more information would help?

15. Here is a list of topics that people often have questions about. Circle those topics you would like to have more information about:

Sexual positions   Sexual diseases   Finding someone to be with

Having children   How my body works   Having more pleasure

How to keep people away   Other (please describe)

16. Are any of these topics involved with your problem?

17. Are you involved in a romantic or sexual relationship(s) at this time?

    If so, how would you describe it?

18. How satisfied are you with this relationship?

19. How satisfied do you think your partner(s) is (are)?

20. How could things be better?

    Have they been better in the past?

21. How could things be worse?

    Have they been worse in the past?

22. How often do you and your partner(s) engage in some kind of sexual behavior?

23. Please list the sexual behavior you and your partner(s) engage in.

24. Are there things you would like to do that you do not do?

25. Are there things your partner(s) would like to do that your partner(s) does (do) not do?

26. Do you ever feel forced to engage in some behavior you would rather avoid?

    If yes, please describe:

27. Do you ever want to engage in some behavior that you do not try?

    If yes, please describe:

28. Are concerns about sexual behavior a big part of your problem?

29. Have you ever been forced to engage in sexual behavior when you didn't want to?

30. How old were you when you first began to engage in sexual behavior?

31. When you were younger, how did you learn about sexuality and sexual behavior?

32. What messages did you get about how to behave as a sexual person?

33. How comfortable was your family with sexuality topics?

34. Have you ever had any problems with nervous or mental conditions?

Please describe the following:

Circumstances:

Treatment:

Outcome:

35. Are nervous or mental conditions a part of your problem now?

36. Have you ever been involved in or affected by the following (circle all those that apply):

Forced sex

An unplanned pregnancy

Rape or sexual assault

Sexual abuse

A miscarriage

The death of a child

The death of a sex or romantic partner

An abortion

37. Do you use tobacco?

    Do you have any health problems associated with tobacco?

    Is tobacco use a part of your sexual problem?

38. Do you use alcohol?

    Do you have any health problems associated with alcohol?

    Is alcohol a part of your sexual problem?

39. Do you think that you have ever been dependent on prescription drugs?

    Has anyone ever told you that they thought you were dependent on prescription drugs?

    Are prescription drugs a part of your sexual problem?

    What type of nonprescription drugs (like aspirin, laxatives, or special herbs) do you use?

What type of "recreational drugs" do you use—like marijuana, cocaine, crack, or other drugs that you might buy on the street?

Are these drugs a part of your sexual problem?

40. Have you heard (or are you familiar with) the term "safe sex"?

41. What does that term mean to you? Please describe what safe sex means.

42. Tell me the things that you do to practice safe sex.

43. Tell me what you could do to make your sexual activity even "safer."

44. Have you ever had a disease from having sex? How was it treated?

45. Please describe where you live.

    Would you prefer to live somewhere else?

46. Is where you live a part of your problem?

47. Describe your health.

    Is your health a part of your problem?

48. Are there things that you know you should be doing to make things better but that you just can't do?

49. What are the sources of your income?

    Is your income adequate?

50. Do you currently have any big financial problems?

51. Are these financial problems a part of your sexual problem?

52. What is the biggest sexual problem you have?

53. Do you think it can be helped?

54. Why did you come in at this time?

55. Do you have any questions for me?

CHAPTER 4

Psychophysiologic and Laboratory Testing

Carolyn A. Gerdes

The study of human sexual function has changed dramatically over the past 100 years. It was not until the late 19th century that a scientific approach was applied to the study of human sexuality, and not until the 1950s were the first laboratory studies concerning human sexual function conducted. There continue to be many unresolved questions regarding the exact neural and vascular events that are involved in controlling sexual responses. Many of these questions remain as a result of the challenges associated with conducting research on human sexual function. One major obstacle that has prohibited additional research regarding human sexual function is that funding for such research has been virtually nonexistent. In addition, many sex researchers have found there is a general lack of support from many of their peers. It is not unusual for sex researchers to have to defend the scientific importance of their research.

Over the past 100 years, the methods applied to the study of human sexual function have changed significantly. Many of the early writings relating to human sexual function were mostly based on case studies of individuals with sexual deviations. One of the earliest publications that examined human sexual behaviors from a medical perspective was *Psychopathia Sexualis*, written in 1886 by German psychiatrist Richard von Krafft-Ebing. *Psychopathia Sexualis* contained more than 200 hundred detailed case histories of various types of sexual deviations. However, Krafft-Ebing wrote the sections that contained explicit details of sexual variations in Latin to protect the lay reader from graphic sexual details (Rosen & Beck, 1988). Other early influential writings that were also highly criticized included the *Studies in the Psychology of Sex*, which were written and periodically updated by Havelock Ellis between 1896 and 1928. Despite that Ellis based all his writings on material that had been previously published and never conducted any original research, he still had to face much social disapproval (Katchadourian, 1989). Even though the Victorian era had supposedly come to an

47

end by this point, it is clearly evident that many of the sex-negative attitudes of that era had carried over well into the 20th century.

Then, in the mid-20th century, large-scale sex surveys became the popular way of examining issues related to human sexual function. Between 1938 and 1956, Alfred Kinsey and his colleagues collected detailed sexual histories by way of personal interviews from nearly 12,000 people. The information collected from many of these interviews was incorporated into two published works, *Sexual Behavior in the Human Male* (1948), and *Sexual Behavior in the Human Female* (1953). However, even just interviewing people about their sexuality resulted in ridicule of Kinsey and his colleagues. In their first publication, *Sexual Behavior in the Human Male*, Kinsey, Pomeroy, and Martin (1948) gave a detailed report of the difficulties they encountered while trying to conduct their interviews. Over the years, they had to face opposition from various sources that included medical associations and law enforcement agencies.

It was not until the 1950s that the laboratory studies of human sexual responses by William Masters and Virginia Johnson truly revolutionized the study of human sexual function. Today, Masters and Johnson are recognized as pioneers in the field of human sexual physiology. However, with all the opposition they had to face over the years, it is quite amazing they persisted with their research efforts. When Masters, a medical doctor, first approached his superiors at Washington University Medical School in St. Louis, Missouri, about conducting research on human sexual function, he did not immediately receive their approval. In 1954, when Masters finally received the official word that he could begin his investigations into human sexual function, he was basically starting from scratch, because there were no reference materials available that he could consult for information regarding the physiology of the sexual systems. When Masters tried to obtain a text entitled *Atlas of Human Sexual Anatomy* from his university library, he found that his borrowing privileges denied him access to this text. Apparently, the library had restricted the access of this text to only full professors, and Masters at that time only held the rank of associate professor (Allgeier, 1984). Through the assistance of his department chairperson, Masters finally did obtain the text; however, he found it to be of little help in designing his studies.

The participants in Masters's earliest studies were all prostitutes—a group of people who by no means were considered representative of the general population. However, in 1957, when Masters hired Virginia Johnson as his research assistant, they began a broader investigation of the physiologic basis of human sexual response using a total of 694 male and female volunteers. Using both standard physiologic recording devices, such as electrocardiographs and electromyographs, and specially developed equipment that included a so-called "artificial coital device," Masters and Johnson observed and collected physiologic measurements of more than 10,000 episodes of sexual arousal that were experienced by the 694 volunteers while in the laboratory (Masters & Johnson, 1966). With the aid of the clear penis-shaped artificial coital device, Masters and Johnson were even able to observe and film changes inside the vagina during periods of sexual stimulation that simulated intercourse. It was these classic studies that provided the first insight into the physiologic mechanisms that are involved in controlling human sexual responses.

However, in 1966, when Masters and Johnson published their physiologic findings in their first book, *Human Sexual Response*, they received many angry letters from medical professionals who claimed that their work was "an unacceptable departure from traditional medicine and was therefore not respectable" (Masters, Johnson, & Kolodny, 1995). Others have criticized the work of Masters and Johnson, claiming they used biased samples, that there were biases in the methods, and that they themselves were biased (Tiefer, 1991). However, the criticisms that Masters and Johnson had to face were not unique to just their studies. Still to this day, all studies concerning human sexual function are highly scrutinized by many for the same reasons Masters and Johnson were criticized.

Over the past few decades, the incorporation of psychophysiologic methods into studies of human sexual function have aided in the elucidation of many of the neural and vascular mechanisms that are involved in controlling sexual responses. However, there still exist many uncertainties concerning the underlying mechanisms that regulate events such as erection, orgasm, and lubrication.

To date, the majority of the research studies that have been conducted on sexual function have focused primarily on the male. Much of what practitioners assume to be true regarding female sexual function is actually based on studies that were conducted on males. Understanding the physiologic mechanisms that underlie normal sexual responses is of significant importance if a provider wants to be able to accurately diagnose and treat dysfunctional states. Because sexual dysfunctions, such as erectile failure in the male and lack of vaginal lubrication or anorgasmia in the female, often cause a person to seek medical attention, researchers within the medical community have recently shown increased interest in the physiologic mechanisms that control sexual responses. Many medical professionals seeking to learn if a dysfunctional state is of an organic or psychogenic nature have begun to incorporate psychophysiologic techniques of testing sexual function into their practices. However, much of the new psychophysiologic research being conducted on dysfunctional states still ignores the female. Bancroft (1992) stated "that we can therefore, with some confidence, conclude that the 'medicalization' of sexuality that we have been observing in recent years is in the male and not the female domain" (pp. vii–xv).

Not only is there a lack of basic knowledge concerning female sexual function, but there is also little known about the effects that many common chronic illnesses and physical disabilities have on the sexual systems. Although many common ailments such as cardiovascular diseases, neurologic disorders, diabetes, renal disorders, and spinal cord injuries can have devastating effects on sexual function, little is known about the underlying mechanisms that are responsible for altering sexual function in patients with these illnesses and disabilities. This lack of knowledge is not at all surprising. All too often chronically ill or disabled people are viewed as being nonsexual people by their family, friends, and even many medical professionals. Therefore, they are not routinely included in studies of sexual function. Medical professionals often even do not inquire about a chronically ill or physically disabled patient's sexual relations. For this reason, patients with chronic illnesses and physical disabilities often do not receive sufficient information regarding sexual function from their health care providers.

It is unfortunate but true that sexual function is a topic that few health care providers routinely discuss with their patients, both disabled or nondisabled. In a recent survey of 171 cardiac nurses, it was found that, during the past year, 75% of the nurses had offered to discuss sexual concerns with fewer than 2% of their patients (Steinke & Patterson, 1995). In a recent survey of women with spinal cord injuries, Sipski and Alexander (1993) found that, after their injuries, few of the women received any information concerning sexual function. In addition, a study of 27 women who had undergone surgical and radiological treatments for endometrial and cervical cancer found that 59% of the women received no form of sexual counseling (Jenkins, 1988). However, many patients do desire information regarding sexual function. Studies of men and women with various chronic illnesses have shown that they would prefer to receive information regarding sexual function from their primary caregivers, rather than from sexuality specialists (Schover & Jensen, 1988). However, before practitioners can better educate a person with a chronic illness or disability about sexual function, there need to be more research studies that focus on the chronically ill or disabled populations.

DESIGN OF A PSYCHOPHYSIOLOGIC LABORATORY STUDY

When designing a laboratory study concerning sexual function, researchers must consider numerous factors. Selection and recruitment of study participants is always challenging. Researchers are concerned that the findings obtained from a laboratory study are not going to be representative of the general population. A truly representative sample of the general population is difficult to achieve when conducting any type of research study. Volunteer bias has been documented in all areas of psychological research. People who volunteer to participate in research studies tend to have higher educational levels, higher occupational status, higher need for approval, and lower authoritarianism scores than nonvolunteers (Rosenthal & Rosnow, 1969).

Volunteers who take part in sex research studies also tend to be more sexually liberal and more curious about sex than nonvolunteers (Wolchik, Braver, & Jensen, 1985). Additionally, volunteers tend to be more sexually experienced (Farkas, Sine, & Evans, 1978), masturbate more frequently (Wolchik, Spencer, & Lisi,

1983), and have had more sexual partners (Wolchik et al., 1985) than nonvolunteers. Riley (1990) conducted a study that compared the responses to sexual questionnaires and demographic data on women who had taken part in laboratory studies of sexual response with those of women who had been unwilling to participate in the laboratory sexual response study. Findings indicated that women who had been unwilling to participate in sexual response studies showed differences in their questionnaire responses to questions on masturbation and sexual arousal when compared with the group that had taken part in a sexual response study. Practitioners must, therefore, exercise caution when extrapolating findings from laboratory studies to people of the general population.

Any proposed research project that involves human subjects needs to have the approval of an appointed review board before the study can begin. The members of a review board typically include representatives from the scientific community, medical and legal professions, and religious organizations. The purpose of the review board is to ensure that the proposed research is scientifically warranted, that it will not purposely cause harm to the participants, and that appropriate informed consent will be provided to subjects.

All study participants need be informed of all research procedures and oriented to the research facility and equipment before they agree to participate in the research project. Once a person has volunteered to participate in the research project, he or she should sign and date an informed consent form. The construction of an informed consent form needs to be done carefully, with close attention given to the description of the research protocol and to the assurance of confidentiality. The informed consent form should also clearly state any risks or benefits that may result from participation in the study. Additionally, any provisions for medical or psychological services that may be available to the participant either during or after his or her participation in the research study should also be clearly stated.

Each participant should always be in control of the experimental proceedings at all times and should be free to terminate participation in the study at any time without any penalties. If the research protocol includes invasive procedures or drug administration, the informed consent form should also include the signature of a witness. At the conclusion of the study, each participant should be debriefed to ensure that he or she has not experienced any unforeseen effects and should also be made aware of any use of deception that might have occurred during the experimental proceedings.

Maintaining confidentiality is also a critical responsibility of the researcher. Researchers should keep all data and other information collected on all study participants in locked files. In addition, they should assign to all participants a code number that is used in all publications; a participant's identity should never be revealed in publications. The key to the subject codes should be kept in a separate locked file and known by only those directly involved in the research project.

Researchers also must consider technical matters when designing a psychophysiologic laboratory study. The location selected for the laboratory should be quiet and free of possible sources of distraction. The laboratory needs to have adequate ventilation and researchers should be able to access temperature controls. Temperature control is of special importance in laboratories that contain temperature-sensitive pieces of equipment such as thermistors, because they are reactive to ambient temperature changes. The type of light source also needs to be considered when designing a psychophysiology laboratory, because fluorescent lights generate a 60 Hz electric noise that can interfere with physiologic signals. Therefore, incandescent lights are recommended.

If the study is going to include participants with physical disabilities or chronic illnesses, the researcher may need to make slight modifications in the research protocol. Because many research facilities are located outside of a hospital setting, this location may restrict the number of chronically ill or disabled people who can travel to the research laboratory. The entire research facility also needs to be wheelchair accessible. For patients who have limited travel capabilities, some of the preliminary screenings or assessments may need to be conducted in another location, such as in a hospital room. If this is the case, it is important that these proceedings be conducted in private to maintain confidentiality. In addition, some medications or medical treatments may cause a person with a disability or chronic illness to tire easily. Therefore, the research proceedings may need to be conducted over time, rather than in just one session. Participants who have limited use of their extremities may require special assistance in performing certain tasks.

The remainder of this chapter provides readers with a detailed description of the most common psychophysiologic techniques used to assess sexual function in research settings. Although many studies also include nongenital measures of sexual arousal such as heart rate, blood pressure, skin temperature changes, and pupillary responses, there are many uncertainties about the reliability of those measures in indicating genital sexual arousal. Those measures are at best only weakly associated with sexual stimuli or subjective ratings of sexual arousal (Geer, O'Donohue, & Schorman, 1986). Therefore, this chapter focuses on the advantages and disadvantages of the most commonly used methods in the assessment of male and female genital responses.

SEXUAL FUNCTION IN THE MALE

The majority of studies that have examined male sexual function have focused on the male's ability to achieve and maintain an erection. One of the main concerns that has often arisen with studies of erectile capabilities is whether the physiologic measures of erection correspond to the subjects' self-reports of arousal.

Presently, most sexuality researchers accept that the most valid and reliable measure of sexual arousal in the male is penile erection (Masters & Johnson, 1966; Zuckerman, 1971). Nevertheless, it should not be overlooked that there are other important measurable changes that occur in other external and internal sexual structures during sexual arousal. However, a male's familiarity with his own penis and its easy accessibility make erectile responses easy to study.

Over the past 20 years, major advances have been made in elucidating the complex neural and vascular mechanisms that control erection. However, still to this date, the exact mechanisms that control erection have not been fully established. It was once commonly believed that erection was exclusively controlled by the parasympathetic nervous system. Today, however, it is known that the sympathetic nervous system as well as numerous neurotransmitters and complex hemodynamic processes are also involved in mediating erectile function. Erection of the penis results when the smooth muscle of the penile corpora relaxes and the penile arteries dilate. Penile erection can normally be elicited by either reflexogenic or psychogenic stimuli; often in the healthy male it is a combination of these two stimuli. However, there are numerous physiologic and psychological factors that can impair erectile function.

The inability to achieve or maintain an erection sufficient enough to allow for sexual intercourse is a problem that will affect between 10% and 20% of all males at least once during their life (Shvartzman, 1994). Erectile failure has also been reported to be the most common complaint of men seeking treatment at sex therapy clinics (Spector & Carey, 1990). Age, chronic illnesses, alcohol consumption, psychological factors, pharmacologic therapies, and medical treatments can all contribute to erectile difficulties. Until about 30 years ago, it was commonly believed that the majority of cases of erectile difficulties were purely psychogenic in nature. However, better diagnostic techniques in recent years have increased the understanding of the factors that contribute to erectile dysfunctions. Currently, it is generally accepted that physical factors contribute to more than 50% of all cases of erectile dysfunctions (Morley, 1986). These new diagnostic techniques have also been instrumental in the development of new treatments for erectile dysfunctions.

Although erectile function has been extensively studied in the laboratory, orgasm has not. Numerous problems are associated with studying orgasm in the laboratory. First and foremost, there is not even a standard universally accepted definition of orgasm. There are also social and professional limits on the types of sexual behaviors that can be monitored and measured in the laboratory. In addition, to prevent measurement artifacts, movement of the subject needs to be limited. To date, most publications that examine orgasmic responses are based on interviews or survey findings, and not on laboratory studies. In one laboratory study that examined anal contractions during orgasm, Bohlen, Held, and Sanderson

(1980) found that anal contractions did not correlate with the participants' subjective reports of the intensity of the orgasm or of their arousal levels. In addition, they found that the periods of anal contractions did not always correspond to when the participants reported experiencing orgasm. However, the number of males and females seeking treatment for orgasm disorders has been on the rise in recent years (Leiblum & Pervin, 1980). This increase in the number of people seeking treatments for orgasm disorders is likely to bring about the development of additional ways of assessing orgasm in the laboratory; most laboratory studies of sexual function currently focus on assessing vasocongestion and not orgasm.

LABORATORY ASSESSMENT OF ERECTILE FUNCTION

Nocturnal Penile Tumescence

In 1944, Ohlmeyer, Brilmayer, and Hullstrung first described the use of kymograph penile recordings for monitoring nocturnal penile erections. Since then, studies of nocturnal penile tumescence (NPT) have become the most widely used laboratory method of assessing male sexual function. NPT monitoring has long been considered the ideal way to distinguish between organic and psychogenic causes of erectile dysfunction. It was long assumed that if erectile difficulties were the result of an organic cause, such as vascular blockage or a neurologic disorder, periods of NPT should either be absent or greatly diminished. In contrast, if erectile difficulties were the result of a psychogenic cause, it was commonly believed that measurable periods of NPT would still occur. Over the years, though, there has been mounting evidence that factors such as aging, pharmacologic therapies, sleep disorders, and mental illnesses can disrupt NPT periods. In addition, many cases of erectile difficulties result from a combination of factors; hence, the presence or absence of NPT periods should not be used as the sole diagnostic criteria when evaluating patients with erectile dysfunction. Considering all these factors reinforces the importance of collecting and including a detailed medical and psychosexual history as part of all studies that concern sexual function.

The earliest devices that were developed to measure penile tumescence were actually used to detect and prevent masturbation (Mountjoy, 1974). Today, numerous different devices have been developed to assess erectile function. The first devices used in laboratory settings that provided useful objective measures of erections were circular rings that could be fitted around the penis (Ohlmeyer et al., 1944). Mounted within the circular ring was a simple electromechanical transducer that produced a simple binary signal in either the presence or absence of an erection.

Volumetric Devices

Volumetric measurement of penile tumescence has been one of the most common laboratory techniques used in the study of male sexual function. The principle behind volumetric plethysmography is that when a body part such as the penis is placed within a sealed container that is filled with a known volume of fluid, any changes in the size of the body part will result in a displacement of the fluid into an attached reservoir. Fisher, Gross, and Zuch (1965) developed a volumetric plethysmograph filled with water. They used that device in laboratory studies of NPT, although, like many of the other earlier volumetric devices, it was bulky and difficult to work with.

To date, the most commonly used volumetric device in laboratory studies has been the penile plethysmograph, which originally was developed in Czechoslovakia by Freund and his colleagues (Freund, 1963; Freund, Sedlacek, & Knob, 1965). The penile plethysmograph consists of multiple parts, including an inflatable air cuff that fits around the penis. Changes in penile blood volume are determined by measuring the amount of air that has been displaced into a volumetric strain gauge during episodes of penile engorgement. This device has been most commonly used in studies conducted to determine sexual preference in heterosexual and homosexual subjects and in the evaluation of deviant arousal patterns (Freund, 1963, 1967).

Although volumetric plethysmography is a highly sensitive way of measuring penile tumescence, it does have drawbacks. The operation of volumetric devices requires the use of additional complex and costly pieces of equipment. In addition, unexpected movements or changes in position of the participant can easily produce measurement artifacts. The types of studies into which volumetric devices can be incorporated are also limited; the devices are useless in masturbation studies or in NPT studies.

Strain Gauges

Current studies of erectile functioning have commonly involved measures of penile circumference, which have been found to be reliable and highly adaptable (Rosen & Keefe, 1978). Over the years, the various devices developed to measure penile circumference have had the advantage of being small, simple to use, and generally reliable.

The most commonly used devices in laboratory evaluations of penile circumference are the mercury-in-rubber and electromechanical strain gauges. The mercury-in-rubber strain gauge was first used in NPT studies in 1965; those early studies were successful in demonstrating the association of rapid eye movement (REM) sleep with periods of NPT in healthy males (Fisher et al., 1965). The mercury-in-rubber strain gauge consists of a narrow-diameter rubber tube filled with mercury and sealed at the ends with platinum electrodes. The electrodes are then attached to a device that balances the resistances; the device, in turn, is connected to a polygraph. Before each recording, the strain gauge should be calibrated against an object with known diameters. This calibration process allows for the polygraph recordings to later be converted to an absolute scale of circumference change. As engorgement of the penis occurs, the rubber tube placed around the penis becomes stretched, which causes a narrowing of the mercury column contained within the rubber tube. As the mercury column narrows, there is an increase in resistance, which is recorded by the polygraph. All changes in resistance are directly proportional to changes in penile circumference (Geer, 1976). In general, the mercury-in-rubber strain gauge is ideal for overnight studies because it is relatively unaffected by temperature changes (Earls & Jackson, 1981) and movement artifacts are easily detected (Laws & Holmen, 1978).

Bancroft, Gwynne Jones, and Pullan (1966) developed a variation of the mercury-in-rubber strain gauge that they used in laboratory studies of normal and deviant arousal patterns. Their device was mounted onto a moveable platform, which permitted individual fitting before use. The modifications allowed for the accommodation of a wider range of penis sizes. Today, a variety of mercury strain gauges in a range of sizes is commercially available. These gauges are easily adaptable to almost any laboratory study and have been found to be generally reliable in different laboratory studies (Rosen & Keefe, 1978).

The other widely used device that measures penile circumference is the electromechanical strain gauge, which was developed by Barlow, Becker, Leitenberg, and Agras (1970). The electromechanical strain gauge consists of a pair of arcs made from surgical spring material and connected to a pair of mechanical strain gauges. The mechanical strain gauges are then connected to a polygraph. The penis is placed within the arcs and, during arousal states, an increase in penile circumference causes a flexing of the mechanical gauges. The flexing of the mechanical stain gauges causes a change in resistance, which is recorded by the polygraph. Just as with the mercury-in-rubber strain gauge, the electromechanical device should be calibrated before each use. Although the construction of the electromechanical gauge makes it more durable and longer lasting than the mercury-in-rubber gauges, apparently the electromechanical device is more susceptible to movement and positioning artifacts (Geer, 1980).

These devices are relatively easy to use; however, they are not problem free. The use of both devices requires a laboratory that is equipped with a polygraph. Laboratory assessment of NPT can be quite costly—a few thousand dollars—and therefore may not be an option for patients. The use of the devices also does not guarantee an accurate measure of NPT. Patients' unfamiliarity with the sleep laboratory may cause anxiety, which can interfere with sleep patterns and periods of NPT. Therefore, it is strongly recommended that patients be evaluated for at least

2 nights, with the first night considered an adjustment night. In addition, use of the NPT monitoring devices fails to provide any information regarding the firmness or rigidity of the penis. Just because periods of NPT may be detected does not mean that penile rigidity is sufficient to allow for penetration during periods of sexual activity. To aid in the assessment of penile rigidity during NPT monitoring, a technician can make visual ratings. However, visual ratings are highly subjective and their reliability has not been firmly established. Karacan (1978) has developed a device that, when used with the strain gauges, measures the axial force required to bend the penis, known as the *buckling pressure*. A buckling pressure of less than 100 mmHg is considered to be insufficient for penetration to occur (Wabrek, 1986). It has been suggested that penile buckling measurements may be useful when assessing younger patients, but not for older patients (Schiavi, 1992). In the older patient, rapid detumescence at the time of testing may not allow for an accurate measurement.

Interpreting the results of studies that have used strain gauge measurements can be complicated by several factors. Strain gauges are sensitive to movement, which makes artifacts in the recordings relatively common. In addition, at the onset of penile erection, there is a dramatic increase in penile length that is associated with a simultaneous decrease in penile circumference (Earls & Marshall, 1982). Therefore, measurements taken during the early arousal states will most likely be inaccurate. Moreover, several researchers have noted that circumference gauges may be unreliable at the upper end of the tumescence curve (Rosen & Beck, 1988).

Home Monitoring Devices

Over the years, researchers have tried to develop effective ways of evaluating NPT that do not require the use of a sleep laboratory. Barry, Blank, and Boileau (1980) developed an inexpensive and simple method that a patient can use at home to detect NPT. Using their method, the patient attaches a ring of connected stamps around the penis at bedtime. On waking, the patient examines the ring for rips or breaks. A rip or break in the ring is associated with at least one period of NPT. This test, though, neither provides information regarding the number of episodes of NPT that occurred during the night nor information on their firmness. The stamps also may break as the patient moves while sleeping. Additional questions regarding the validity of this procedure have been raised in studies of erotically induced erections (Marshall, Earls, Morales, & Surridge, 1982) and of sleep erections (Marshall, Morales, Phillips, & Fenemore, 1983).

The snap gauge developed by Ek, Bradley, and Krane (1983) has been widely used to assess NPT outside of the laboratory. This device, which fits around the penis, consists of small bands that contain plastic strips that are sequentially forced open as penile circumference increases. In a study that compared the opening of the strips with visual estimates of penile rigidity, Ellis, Doghramji, and Bagley (1988) showed that the snap gauge correctly predicted 77.5% of the patients with rigid or nonrigid erections. Disadvantages associated with the snap gauge include its inability to determine the frequency or duration of NPT episodes and the possibility that the strips of the snap gauge may accidentally open if the patient moves a great deal during sleep.

The newest devices developed to monitor NPT episodes are portable monitors that have the advantage of being able to record information concerning the frequency, degree, and duration of erectile activity. One of the most widely used home monitoring devices is the Rigi-Scan monitor manufactured by the Dacomed Corporation of Minneapolis, Minnesota. The Rigi-Scan device consists of an ambulatory data recording unit and a microcomputer system. Two loops that are placed around the base and tip of the penis are attached to a sensor in the body of the ambulatory unit, which can provide approximately 10 hours of continuous monitoring and recording of penile circumference and rigidity. While the patient sleeps, the body of the ambulatory unit is attached to either the patient's leg or abdomen by a large self-adhesive band (Kaneko & Bradley, 1986). To help ensure reliable measures of NPT, subjects are typically requested to use the device for at least 2 consecutive nights. Data are stored by microchips in the body of the ambulatory unit and then transferred to a disk. Data on the disk are then analyzed using commercially available software (Levine & Carroll, 1994). One advantage of home monitoring devices is that they can be used in patients' natural surroundings, which is less likely to create stress than having patients spend 2 or 3 nights in a sleep laboratory. However, on the downside, movement artifacts are also common with the use of the Rigi-Scan. In addition, without a sleep laboratory it is impossible to tell in what stages of sleep NPT periods occurred.

Waking Erectile Assessment

Recently, psychophysiologic methods have also been incorporated into studies of waking erectile assessment (WEA). It is often assumed that the findings of NPT studies can be used to predict daytime erectile function (Everaerd, 1993). However, it has been shown that many healthy older males and diabetic males who have decreased episodes of NPT are still able to achieve daytime erections that allow them to remain sexually functional (Schiavi, 1988). Janssen, Everaerd, Van Lunsen, and Oerlemans (1994) have investigated the potential value of using WEA in the diagnosis of erectile disorders. Using a mechanical penile strain gauge, they evaluated the erectile responses of 50 sexually functional and 100 dysfunctional men during periods of visual erotic stimuli and vibratory tactile stimulation of the penis. Patients whose erectile difficulties were purely psychogenic in nature showed a greater increase in penile circumference than did patients who had an organic factor that contributed to their dysfunctional state. This finding suggests that WEA may be a relatively inexpensive useful initial screening procedure in the evaluation of patients with erectile difficulties. One consideration when incorporating the use of visual erotic stimuli into studies of sexual functioning is that the visual material may not be sexually arousing to all participants, especially if a patient does not find pornographic material arousing or objects to such material because of moral or religious reasons.

Gordon and Carey (1995) have also examined the possibility of assessing erectile functioning during morning naps. Monitoring penile tumescence in 30 modestly sleep-deprived sexually functional males during two early morning naps, Gordon and Carey found that 80% of the males experienced periods of REM sleep and that 73% also experienced tumescence episodes consistent with previous studies of NPT. These findings suggest that assessing erectile function during morning naps may be another inexpensive and less time-consuming alternative to the conventional NPT sleep laboratory studies. However, additional research is needed to establish the validity and reliability of WEA studies.

Thermistor Devices

Variations in the skin temperature of the penile surface have also been used to detect increases in penile tumescence. The first attempts in recording changes in penile skin temperature involved using a small thermistor attached to the dorsal surface of the penis. However, one of the major drawbacks of using temperature changes as an indicator of vasocongestion is that the thermistor often will not remain attached to the skin surface for an extended period. This problem was extremely prevalent in the early studies of changes in penile skin temperature, which is why so many of the early studies that used thermistor devices were highly unsuccessful (Fisher et al., 1965).

By using a mercury-in-rubber strain gauge and a thermistor probe attached to the dorsal surface of the penis by two rubber bands, Solnick and Birren (1977) were able to obtain both temperature and circumference measures during periods of penile tumescence. Their findings suggested that there is a good correlation ($r = .75$) between penile circumference and changes in temperature. Their data also suggested that age is a factor that must be considered when examining arousal responses, because younger subjects showed a greater temperature change and larger increase in penile circumference than did older subjects.

VASCULAR ASSESSMENT OF ERECTILE FUNCTION

In recent years, researchers have developed highly technical methods of measuring erectile function. Although many of these new methods have important diagnostic capabilities, they are often costly and more invasive than many of the routinely used older methods of assessing erectile function. The majority of erectile dysfunctional states that are the result of an organic nature are believed to involve a vascular component (Krane, Goldstein, & Saenz de Tejada, 1989). Recent years have brought about the development of more accurate ways of assessing vascular problems such as arterial insufficiency and venous leakage. Techniques researchers have used to assess penile blood flow include Doppler ultrasound, intracorporal pharmacologic testing, duplex ultrasonography, cavernosography, cavernosometry, and radioisotope techniques.

One of the most routinely used procedures to assess penile vasculature is the measurement of blood pressure. Measurement of penile blood pressure is a noninvasive procedure that involves the use of a Doppler ultrasound flow detector and a pneumatic cuff that is placed around the base of the penis. The flow detector measures the occlusion pressures in the six penile arteries. Penile blood pressure is then compared with the brachial systolic pressure, which provides a measure known as the penile–brachial index (PBI). It is generally accepted that PBI values below 0.6 strongly suggest that erectile difficulties are of a vascular etiology and that PBI values between 0.6 and 0.75 suggest that arterial insufficiency is the cause of the erectile difficulties (Queral et al., 1979). Although obtaining the PBI entails a fairly straightforward noninvasive procedure, it does have one major drawback. Obtaining an accurate PBI is a challenging task because it is difficult to obtain reliable recordings from the cavernosal arteries, which are the main arteries responsible for penile vasocongestion.

Duplex ultrasonography, which also has been used in the vascular assessment of erectile function, provides visualization of the corpora cavernosa and the cavernosal arteries. This visualization allows for a detailed evaluation of the vascular components of penile vasocongestion. Duplex ultrasonography can also be used to measure blood flow through the penile vessels in either the flaccid or erect state. Changes in the diameter of the cavernosal arteries are measured by an ultrasound transducer, and changes in blood flow in the other penile arteries can be monitored using a pulsed Doppler transducer. The use of duplex ultrasonography has also been incorporated into studies that have assessed erectile capabilities through pharmacologic testing with vasodilators such as papaverine (Chen, Chou, Chang, & Chen, 1992; Nelson & Lue, 1989). During erection, blood flow to the erectile tissue as well as to nonerectile tissues (e.g., corpus spongiosum, penile skin, and subcutaneous tissue) increases. Standard penile circumference measures can be misleading because they measure blood flow to both erectile and nonerectile tissues. However, with the use of duplex ultrasonography, a direct measure of only the erectile volume of corpora cavernosa is obtained, therefore yielding a more accurate measure of penile erectile volume. To help ensure accurate measurements, only specially trained technicians should perform these highly specialized techniques.

Techniques such as cavernosometry and cavernosography specifically assess cavernosal venous outflow resistance. Cavernosometry tests for venous insufficiency by monitoring the perfusion rate of a saline solution that is infused into the corpora cavernosa to create an artificial erection. Venous insufficiency is indicated by an elevated infusion flow rate and low intracavernosal pressure (Buvat, Lemaire, Dehaene, Buvat-Herbaut, & Guien, 1986). Cavernosography involves the infusion of a contrast media into the corpora cavernosa. On visualization of the contrast media, any sites of venous leakage can be easily located. Both techniques have been incorporated into studies of pharmacologically induced erections (Lue, Hricak, Schmidt, & Tanagho, 1986). These two invasive techniques of vascular assessment are highly complex and therefore are not routinely incorporated into research studies.

The use of radioisotopes has also recently been incorporated into studies of penile blood flow. In a study of both sexually functional and dysfunctional men, Miraldi, Nelson, Jones, Thompson, and Kursh (1992) demonstrated that both arterial and venous vasculature could be assessed during a pharmacologically induced erection by a dual-radioisotope technique that used xenon 133 and technetium. This recently developed dual-radioisotope technique warrants further study because it has the potential for becoming a valuable tool in the diagnosis of vascular dysfunctions and in the study of the physiology of erection. However, there are numerous limitations to radioisotope studies. Even though the exposure to radioactive materials is small, such exposure may deter some men from having this procedure performed. In addition, the need to be near a nuclear medicine facility restricts the use of this technique to only select locations.

NEUROLOGIC ASSESSMENT OF ERECTILE FUNCTION

Numerous methods have been developed to assess the role that the nervous system plays in controlling erectile function. However, many of the currently used neurologic assessments of erectile function are limited in scope because they are designed to only assess the pudendally mediated afferent component of the erectile reflex.

Measuring the latency of the bulbocavernosus reflex was one of the earliest tests used to determine if cases of erectile difficulties involved a neurogenic component. This test consists of applying an electric stimulus to the dorsal nerve of the penis, which is a terminal branch of the pudendal, and recording the latency of the electromyograph response of the bulbocavernosus muscles (Rushworth, 1967). Prolonged or absent reflex latency is an indication of damage to the pundendal nerve or to the S-2 to S-4 region of the spinal cord. Although this test is frequently used when assessing cases of erectile dysfunction that are suspected to be neurogenic in nature, there has been controversy regarding the value of this test in discriminating between neurogenic and other causes of erectile dysfunction (Lavoisier, Proulx, Courtois, & deCarufel, 1989).

Penile biothesiometry is of great value in evaluating the integrity of penile afferent sensory pathways. Penile biothesiometry involves the use of a fixed frequency electromagnetic vibratory device whose vibration amplitude can be varied by adjusting the voltage required to produce the electromagnetic energy. The vibration amplitude is linearly related to the voltage. Patients are asked to verbally report when they first perceive the vibratory stimulus, at which time the amplitude of the vibratory perception threshold is recorded off of the voltage scale. However, researchers need to exercise caution when interpreting the results because a decrease in penile sensitivity may be the result of damage to the nerves that innervate the penis. In addition, a decrease in penile sensitivity is known to occur with aging (Newman, 1970). Therefore, researchers should always compare all results with age-appropriate controls.

In recent years, smaller and more lightweight minivibrators have been used in the measurement of penile sensitivity. These smaller devices have been shown to produce similar results regarding penile vibratory thresholds in both sexually functional and dysfunctional patients when compared with the older, larger devices (Rowland, Geilman, Brouwer, & Slob, 1992). Furthermore, these smaller devices do not lose contact with the penis during erection because they are able to be directly attached to the patient's penis. Although, penile biothesiometry is an inexpensive, noninvasive test that is easy to conduct, when used alone it is an inadequate measure of penile innervation (Bemelmans et al., 1995). However, when penile biothesiometry is used in combination with other neurophysiologic tests, neurologic lesions in either the peripheral or central somatic pathways can be identified (Anten, van Waalwijk van Doorn, & Debruyne, 1987).

Electrophysiologic evaluation of the conduction velocity of the dorsal nerve of the penis has also been used as a means of diagnosing and evaluating neurogenic dysfunctional states. When first developed (Bradley, Lin, & Johnson, 1984), this technique lacked validation. Recently, Clawson and Cardenas (1991) introduced a new technique of evaluating orthodromic dorsal nerve conduction velocity by using a simple traction device that elongates the penis. Recent findings of a study of patients with neurogenic erectile disorders suggested that diagnostic sensitivity of the newer peripheral nerve conduction tests are comparable with the results of bulbocavernosus reflex latency tests (Espino, 1994).

In a sexually functional male, electrical stimulation of the dorsal nerve of the penis should evoke a measurable electroencephalograph (EEG) response in the cerebral cortex. Through the use of the test known as the somatosensory evoked potential, an EEG recording is made of the cerebral cortex immediately following electric stimulation of the dorsal nerve of the penis. The total conduction time is believed to be an accurate measure of the peripheral and central pudendal afferent pathways (Oposomer, Guerit, & Wese, 1986). However, this is a relatively complicated procedure to perform and its capability of identifying lesions of the pudendal nerve is debatable.

SUMMARY OF MALE SEXUAL FUNCTION

Even though the past decade has brought about major advances in the diagnosis and treatment of erectile dysfunctions, the reliability and validity of many of these new techniques and devices have yet to be fully established. Furthermore, additional research is still needed to fully elucidate the underlying physiologic mechanisms that control erectile function. However, as these underlying mechanisms become clarified, practitioners will certainly see the development of more aggressive and effective treatments of erectile disorders. Nevertheless, before these changes can occur, additional basic physiologic studies must be conducted.

To help improve the effectiveness of treatments for dysfunctional states, there needs to be a more comprehensive understanding of the neural mechanisms that control erection and ejaculation. Furthermore, the interactions of the various neurotransmitters and neuromodulators that are found in the nerve terminals of the male sexual structures need to be examined in more detail. With an increased understanding of the roles of these neurotransmitters and neuromodulators, it is likely that practitioners will see the development of new pharmacologic treatments for erectile disorders.

SEXUAL FUNCTION IN THE FEMALE

The study of female sexual function is still in its infancy. The number of methods for assessing female sexual function in the laboratory are fewer when compared with laboratory methods available for assessing male sexual function. In the female, examination of changes in blood flow to the capillaries of the vagina is the main psychophysiologic measure used to assess sexual function. However, it was not even until the late 1960s that the first psychophysiologic techniques were developed to measure genital blood flow in the female (Palti & Bercovici, 1967). Also, most of the early genital blood flow studies were not concerned with sexual function as they were almost exclusively with predicting ovulation or other related reproductive concerns.

Just as in males, females with chronic illnesses, such as diabetes and hypertension, or physical impairments caused by injuries to the spinal cord or neurologic disorders, such as myelopathies and polyneuropathies, often report changes in sexual function. Sexual problems experienced by women with neurologic impairments included decreased sexual desire, anorgasmia, lack of vaginal lubrication, pelvic muscle weakness, and decreased genital sensations (Lundberg, 1992). However, these same problems are also experienced by other chronically ill or disabled women as well as by "healthy" women. Response to a sexual function questionnaire distributed to 329 healthy women who visited a women's wellness center indicated that they commonly reported vaginal dryness, lack of sexual pleasure, and difficulty in achieving orgasm (Rosen, Taylor, & Leiblum, 1993). However, few studies have focused exclusively on the physiology of the female sexual system.

A knowledge of the anatomy and physiology of the female sexual system is important if the researcher is to understand the principles on which these devices that measure changes in vaginal blood flow work. In the sexually unaroused adult female, the vagina is a collapsed tube that is approximately 8 to 10 cm in length. The entire length of the vagina is lined with squamous epithelia cells and its inner surface consists of folds of tissue known as *rugae*. It is these folds that allow the vagina to expand so it can accommodate a penis during intercourse or serve as a passageway for an infant during parturition.

During sexual arousal, there is an increase in blood flow to the vaginal capillaries. It is the vasocongestion of these vaginal capillaries that is responsible for producing vaginal lubrication, because there are no secretory cells located within the walls of the vagina. As these vaginal capillaries become engorged with blood, it is believed that the hydrostatic pressure within the capillaries causes them to "sweat." It is this "sweat" that is believed to be the source of vaginal lubrication. Evidence to support this theory comes from chemical analysis studies of vaginal fluid, which suggest that the fluid that lubricates the vagina during periods of sexual arousal is a modified form of plasma (Levin, 1981).

In the female, vasocongestion brings about notable changes in a variety of internal and external structures. Hence, numerous devices used to measure genital blood flow in the female have been developed. These devices are divided into three general classes:

1. devices that use mechanical means to measure changes in genital vasocongestion
2. devices that indirectly measure blood flow by techniques of heat dissipation and photometry
3. devices that monitor other changes in the sexual structures that relate to vasocongestion

All of the devices currently used in psychophysiologic studies provide an indirect measure of vasocongestion; other methods of directly measuring genital blood flow that have been developed to date have been too invasive to incorporate into human studies.

Vaginal Photoplethysmography

Many of the earliest devices developed to assess genital blood flow in the female proved to be excessively bulky and difficult to use. However, it was the development of vaginal photoplethysmograph that revolutionized the measurement of genital blood flow in the female. The first reliable vaginal photoplethysmograph was developed by Sintchak and Geer in 1975. Their device comprised an incandescent light source and a photodetector contained within a 2 cm × 5 cm tampon-shaped acrylic probe. Over the years, minor modifications such as switching the light source to a light-emitting diode (LED) and using a phototransistor instead of a photocell have helped to reduce the likelihood of measurement artifacts. Today, the vaginal photoplethysmograph is the most commonly used device for measuring genital blood flow in the female.

When the LED illuminates the vaginal walls, an indirect measure of vasocongestion is produced by the backscattering of light off of the vaginal walls. The amount of light that is backscattered is measured by the photodetector and then coupled to a signal. Two different measurements can be obtained through the use of the vaginal photoplethysmograph. When the signal is coupled to an alternating current (AC), a measure of vaginal pulse amplitude (VPA) is obtained. Coupling the signal to a direct current (DC) measures the total pooled vaginal blood volume (VBV). Because of its ability to better discriminate between response to erotic and nonerotic presentations, VPA is the more widely used signal (Rosen & Beck, 1988). However, some investigators use both AC- and DC-coupled measures in their studies because there exists some debate on the reliability of using the measure of the total VBV as an indicator of sexual arousal (Rosen & Beck, 1988).

Before every use, the researcher should calibrate each vaginal probe to help ensure intersession and interlaboratory consistency. Calibration allows for the determination of a relative response of a probe to a known change in reflectance (for a review, see Hoon, Murphy, Laughter, & Abel, 1984). During experimental proceedings, it is important to try and minimize all sources of measurement artifact. Factors such as the position of the probe within the vagina, contractions of the vagina, movement of the subject, and the subject's respiratory pattern can all cause artifacts to be introduced into the recordings. On conclusion of the experimental proceedings, the researcher should sterilize all equipment that has been in contact with the study participant, using a standard solution of Cidex or other similar germicidal agent.

One question faces all researchers using measures of vasocongestion: What is the correlation between genital blood flow and a female's subjective report of sexual arousal? Unfortunately, there is no easy answer to this question—the literature on this topic is divided. Generally, studies that have compared VPA and VBV with subjective reports of sexual arousal have found little correlation between the two (Geer, Morokoff, & Greenwood, 1974; Heiman, 1977; Henson, Rubin, & Henson, 1979).

Rogers, Van de Castle, Evans, and Critelli (1985) used vaginal photoplethys- mography to measure VPA during waking erotic conditions and during sleep in both sexually functional and dysfunctional women. All potential participants were given the Sexual Arousability Inventory questionnaire (Hoon, Hoon, & Wincze, 1976) to complete, and only the females whose responses placed them at the bottom one-third or at the top one-third of the scale were chosen to participate in the study. When the two groups were compared, they did not show any differ- ences in VPA during either periods of erotic visual stimuli or during sleep. How- ever, in both groups, nocturnal VPA varied throughout the sleep cycle, with the highest levels occurring during REM sleep. It was also found that the two groups did not vary significantly in their subjective ratings of their sexual arousal during the erotic visual stimuli. An examination of the research population raises the question of whether it was a representative sample of the general population. All participants were recruited from either human sexuality or nursing classes, in which students with sex-positive attitudes are more likely to be found. Neverthe- less, the findings do suggest that self-reports of low arousal levels do not corre- spond to poor physiologic responses. Increases in vaginal blood flow during REM sleep in healthy volunteers have also been reported by others (Hayashi, Hoon, Amberson, & Murphy, 1986). The findings of changes in vaginal blood flow during different stages of sleep suggest that nocturnal evaluation of vaginal blood flow, similar to NPT monitoring in the male, may be useful in the differential diagnosis of organic versus psychogenic dysfunctional states.

Studies of VPA have also been of great value in elucidating the factors that contribute to the dysfunctional states that females with diabetes often experience. Sexual dysfunctional states in males with diabetes are most often organic in na- ture, whereas in females with diabetes, sexual dysfunctional states are more likely to be of a psychogenic nature (Thomas & LoPiccolo, 1994). A critical review of the literature concerning diabetes and female sexual function by Spector, Leiblum, Carey, and Rosen (1993) revealed that pyschosocial factors such as disease ac- ceptance, relationship adjustment, and depressive states were better predictors of sexual dysfunctions than were vascular involvement, age of onset, duration of disease, or glucose control. However, there are female diabetic patients who do suffer from sexual dysfunctions that have an organic etiology. Using vaginal photoplethysmography, Wincze, Albert, and Bansal (1993) measured VPA during exposure to erotic visual stimuli in women with diabetes and in a matched control group without diabetes. They found that the group of women with diabetes expe- rienced significantly less vasocongestion in response to erotic stimuli than did the control group of women without diabetes. In contrast, in a study that exam- ined changes in labial temperature in response to erotic visual stimuli, Slob, Koster,

Radder, and Van der Werff ten Bosch (1990) found that there were no significant differences in the elevation of labial temperature in response to erotic stimuli between women with diabetes and a control group of women without diabetes.

Clitoral Blood Flow Measures

The clitoris of a female is a richly innervated, highly sensitive structure that develops from the same embryonic tissue from which the male penis develops. Therefore, these two structures are considered to be homologous. Just like the shaft of the penis, the clitoral shaft comprises two corpora cavernosa and a corpus spongiosum. During sexual arousal in the female, engorgement of the corpora causes erection of the clitoral shaft. Animal studies have even suggested that the sensory innervation of the clitoris is more important for female sexual function than is the sensory innervation of the penis for male sexual function (Campbell, 1976). Despite the important role of the clitoris in female sexual arousal, few physiologic studies have focused on the clitoris.

Using Doppler ultrasonography, Lavoisier, Aloui, Schmidt, and Watrelot (1995) examined the vascular changes of the clitoral arteries in response to pressure applied to the vagina by a water-filled pressure probe device. Doppler signals revealed that, as vaginal pressure stimuli increased, the blood flow and blood velocity into the clitoral arteries in 9 out of 10 healthy, nondysfunctional women also increased. The response seen in those women is similar to what is observed in the cavernous arteries of males when pressure is applied to the glans penis. These findings warrant further investigation into the use of Doppler ultrasonography as a possible means of assessing genital blood flow in the female.

Measures of Heat Dissipation

The first attempts at measuring changes in temperature of the external genitalia in relation to states of sexual arousal were made by Jovanovic in 1971. Jovanovic used a thermistor device to measure changes in the temperature of the clitoris during states of sexual arousal. More recent studies have focused on measuring changes in labial temperature as a means of assessing genital blood flow. By using a three-conductor wire clip to attach a thermistor to the labia minora, Henson, Rubin, Henson, and Williams (1977) monitored changes in labial temperature while participants viewed erotic films. They reported significant correlations between changes in labial temperature and the participants' subjective reports of arousal levels. Positive correlations have also been found when changes in labial temperature have been compared with measures of VPA and VBV (Henson, Rubin, & Henson, 1982). However, one drawback of assessing genital blood flow by measuring changes in labial temperature in laboratory studies is that, after exposure to an erotic stimulus, it takes considerable time for the labial temperature to return to the prestimulus resting state.

Changes in vaginal temperature are also known to occur during states of sexual arousal in the female. By using a vaginal thermistor probe, Fisher and colleagues (1983) examined changes in vaginal temperature in 10 volunteers during exposure to visual erotic stimuli and during sleep. Elevation in vaginal temperature was noted to occur during periods of erotic stimuli and during masturbatory activities. In addition, cyclic changes in vaginal temperature were noted during periods of sleep. However, the reliability and validity of using vaginal temperature changes as a measure of sexual response or sexual arousal still needs to be established. Nevertheless, future psychophysiologic studies are likely to incorporate the use of the vaginal thermistor into their protocols because movement artifacts are rare. Moreover, the vaginal thermistor can be used in either daytime or nighttime assessment studies of genital blood flow.

Measures of Oxygenation and Temperature

Changes in vaginal blood flow have also been assessed through the use of isothermally maintained, heated, oxygen electrodes. This method of assessing vaginal blood flow measures transcutaneous oxygen pressure (pO_2) along with heat dissipation (Levin & Wagner, 1977). Using this method involves placing an oxygen electrode inside a suction cup that is then placed against the vaginal wall. The electrode is capable of providing measures of surface oxygenation and heat dissipation. Levels of vaginal pO_2 have been found to be lower in the sexually unaroused state when compared with measurements taken during periods of genital stimulation (Wagner & Levin, 1978). The increased levels of pO_2 during genital stimulation suggest a greater inflow of oxygenated blood into the vaginal capillaries. To date, the use of this device has been limited because it is rather expensive and its use is restricted to 1- to 1½- hour sessions. However, further research is necessary to determine if the oxygen probe is a reliable method of measuring genital blood flow in the female.

Changes in vaginal blood flow during orgasm have also been examined using a similar method. Levin and Wagner (1985) examined vaginal blood flow during orgasm by monitoring changes in heat clearance from a small silver disc that was placed against the vaginal wall and heated by an electric current to 43°C. Changes in vaginal blood flow would result in changes in the amount of electric power needed to maintain the preset temperature. The changes in electric power consumption, measured in milliwatts, are used as an index of change in blood flow (Levin, 1981). When study participants reported experiencing an orgasm, blood flow to the vagina was found to have increased. However, there was no significant correlation found to exist between the duration of orgasm and the increase in vaginal blood flow. In addition, there was also no significant correlation found to exist between power consumption and the participants' subjective grading of the strength of their orgasms (Levin & Wagner, 1985).

Other Measurements of Female Genital Responses

The vaginal perineometer is a small dumbbell-shaped pressure-sensitive device that was first used by Kegel (1948, 1952) in his studies of the role of the pubococcygeus muscle in urinary stress incontinence and sexual function in the female. Since its development, numerous researchers have used the perineometer or modifications of it, such as the vaginal myograph (Perry, 1980), to examine the role of the pubococcygeus muscle in female sexual responses. Graber and Kline-Graber (1979) used the vaginal perineometer to determine resting pubococcygeus muscle tone as well as sustained contractile strength. Perry and Whipple (1982), through the use of the vaginal perineometer, found that women who reported more intense orgasms had greater pubococcygeus muscle strength. However, researchers must consider the following when analyzing perineometer readings. Levitt, Konovsky, Freese, and Thompson (1979) have demonstrated that readings can be highly influenced by the position of the subject's legs and torso. The perineometer also does not provide a direct measure of muscle activity. Furthermore, the exact role that the pubococcygeus muscle has in sexual responses has never been firmly established.

CONCLUSION

Even with the medical advances that have been made within the past few decades, there still exists a gross lack of knowledge concerning the physiologic mechanisms that regulate female sexual function. Because of the invasiveness of the devices used to measure changes in vaginal vasocongestion, many researchers and research subjects find them unappealing and are uncomfortable using them. There are also relatively few research facilities that have the equipment and trained personnel to conduct research studies that focus on female sexual function.

In addition, only recently has the pharmaceutical industry begun to examine the effects that commonly prescribed medications such as antidepressants and antihypertensives may have on female sexual function. As the American population grows older, more women are bound to seek treatment for numerous medical conditions that may also interfere with normal sexual function. Future studies need to focus on elucidating the underlying physiologic mechanisms of the female sexual system. Before researchers and practitioners can develop reliable means of diagnosing and treating female sexual disorders, they must first understand how the female sexual system normally functions.

REFERENCES

Allgeier, E.R. (1984). The personal perils of sex researchers: Vern Bullough and William Masters. *SIECUS Reports, 12*(4), 16–19.

Anten, H.W.M., van Waalwijk van Doorn, E.S.C., & Debruyne, F.M.J. (1987). Evoked responses for differentiating neurogenic lesions in the urogenital system in patients with diabetes mellitus. In G.H. Jacobi (Ed.), *Investigative urology 2* (pp. 117–123). New York: Springer-Verlag.

Bancroft, J. (1992). Erectile disorders. In R. Rosen & S. Lieblum (Eds.), *Erectile disorders* (pp. vii–xv). New York: Guilford Press.

Bancroft, J.H., Gwynne Jones, H.E., & Pullan, B.P. (1966). A simple transducer for measuring penile erection with comments on its use in the treatment of sexual disorders. *Behaviour Research and Therapy, 4*, 239–241.

Barlow, D.H., Becker, R., Leitenberg, H., & Agras, W.S. (1970). A mechanical strain gauge for recording penile circumference change. *Journal of Applied Behavior Analysis, 3*, 73–76.

Barry, J.M., Blank, B., & Boileau, M. (1980). Nocturnal penile tumescent monitoring with stamps. *Urology, 15*, 171–173.

Bemelmans, B., Hendrikx, L.B., Koldewijn, E., Lemmens, W., Debruyne, F., & Meuleman, E. (1995). Comparison of biothesiometry and neuro-urophysiological investigations for the clinical evaluation of patients with erectile dsyfunction. *Journal of Urology, 153*, 1483–1486.

Bohlen, J.G., Held, J.P., & Sanderson, M.D. (1980). The male orgasm: Pelvic contractions measured by anal probe. *Archives of Sexual Behavior, 9*, 503–521.

Bradley, W.E., Lin, J.T.Y., & Johnson, B. (1984). Measurement of the conduction velocity of the dorsal nerve of the penis. *Journal of Urology, 131*, 1127–1129.

Buvat, J.J., Lemaire, A., Dehaene, J.L., Buvat-Herbaut, M., & Guien, J.D. (1986). Venous incompetence: Critical study of the organic basis of high maintenance flow rates during artificial erection test. *Journal of Urology, 135*, 926–928.

Campbell, B. (1976). Neurophysiology of the clitoris. In T.P. Lowry & T.S Lowry (Eds.), *The clitoris* (pp. 35–74). St. Louis, MO: Green.

Chen, K., Chou, Y., Chang, L.S., & Chen, M. (1992). Sonographic measurement of penile erectile volume. *Journal of Clinical Ultrasound, 20*, 247–253.

Clawson, D.R., & Cardenas, D.D. (1991). Dorsal nerve of the penis nerve conduction velocity: A new technique. *Muscle & Nerve, 14*(9), 845–849.

Earls, C.M., & Jackson, D.R. (1981). The effects of temperature on the mercury-in-rubber strain gauge. *Behavior Assessment, 3*, 145–149.

Earls, C.M., & Marshall, W.L. (1982). The simultanous and independent measurement of penile circumference and length. *Behavior Research Methods and Instrumentation, 14*, 447–450.

Ek, A., Bradley, W.E., & Krane, R.J. (1983). Snap-gauge band: New concept in measuring penile rigidity. *Urology, 21*, 63–67.

Ellis, D.J., Doghramji, K., & Bagley, D.H. (1988). Snap-gauge band versus penile rigidity in impotence assessment. *Journal of Urology, 140*, 61–63.

Espino, P. (1994). Neurogenic impotence: Diagnostic value of nerve conduction studies, bulbocavernosus reflex, and heart rate variability. *Electromyography & Clinical Neurophysiology, 34*(6), 373–376.

Everaerd, W. (1993). Male erectile disorder. In W. O'Donohue, & J.H. Geer (Eds.), *Handbook of sexual dysfunctions: Assessment and treatment* (pp. 201–224). Needham Heights, MA: Allyn & Bacon.

Farkas, G.M., Sine, L.F., & Evans, I.M. (1978). Personality, sexuality, and demographic differences between volunteers and nonvolunteers for a laboratory study of male sexual behavior. *Archives of Sexual Behavior, 7*, 513–520.

Fisher, C., Cohen, H.D., Schiavi, R.C., Davis, D., Furman, B., Ward, K., Edwards, A., & Cunningham, J. (1983). Patterns of female sexual arousal during sleep and waking: Vaginal thermo-conductance studies. *Archives of Sexual Behavior, 12*, 97–122.

Fisher, C., Gross, J., & Zuch, J. (1965). Cycle of penile erection synchronous with dreaming (REM) sleep: Preliminary report. *Archives of General Psychiatry, 12*, 29–45.

Freund, K. (1963). A laboratory method for diagnosing predominance of homo- or hetero-erotic interest in the male. *Behaviour Research and Therapy, 1*, 85–93.

Freund, K. (1967). Diagnosing homo- or heterosexuality and erotic age-preference by means of a psychophysiological test. *Behaviour Research and Therapy, 5*, 339–348.

Freund, K., Sedlacek, F., & Knob, K. (1965). A simple transducer for mechanical plethysmography of the male genital. *Journal of the Experimental Analysis of Behavior, 8*, 169–170.

Geer, J.H. (1976). Genital measures: Comments on their role in understanding human sexuality. *Journal of Sex and Marital Therapy, 2*, 165–172.

Geer, J.H. (1980). Measurement of genital arousal in human males and females. In I. Martin & P.H. Venables (Eds.), *Techniques in psychophysiology* (pp. 431–459). New York: Wiley.

Geer, J.H., Morokoff, P., & Greenwood, P. (1974). Sexual arousal in women: The development of a measurement device for vaginal blood volume. *Archives of Sexual Behavior, 3*, 559–564.

Geer, J.H., O'Donohue, W.T., & Schorman, R.H. (1986). Sexuality. In M.G.H. Coles, E. Donchin, & S.W. Porges (Eds.), *Psychophysiology* (pp. 407–427). New York: Guilford Press.

Gordon, C.M., & Carey, M.P. (1995). Penile tumescence monitoring during morning naps to assess male erectile functioning: An initial study of healthy men of varied ages. *Archives of Sexual Behavior, 24*(3), 291–307.

Graber, B., & Kline-Graber, G. (1979). Female orgasm: Role of pubococcygeus muscle. *Journal of Clinical Psychiatry, 40*, 33–39.

Hayashi, J., Hoon, P., Amberson, J., & Murphy, W.D. (1986). The reliability of nocturnal vaginal blood flow. *Journal of Psychopathology & Behavioral Assessment, 8*(4), 281–288.

Heiman, J. (1977). A psychophysiological exploration of sexual arousal patterns in females and males. *Psychophysiology, 14*(3), 266–274.

Henson, C., Rubin, H.B., & Henson, D.E. (1979). Women's sexual arousal concurrently assessed by three genital measures. *Archives of Sexual Behavior, 8*, 459–469.

Henson, D.E., Rubin, H.B., & Henson, C. (1982). Labial and vaginal blood volume responses to visual and tactile stimuli. *Archives of Sexual Behavior, 11*, 23–31.

Henson, D.E., Rubin, H.B., Henson, C., & Williams, J. (1977). Temperature changes of the labia minora as an objective measure of human female eroticism. *Journal of Behavior Therapy and Experimental Psychiatry, 8*, 401–410.

Hoon, E., Hoon, P., & Wincze, J. (1976). An inventory for the measurement of female sexual arousability: The SAI. *Archives of Sexual Behavior, 5*(4), 291–300.

Hoon, P.W., Murphy, W.D., Laughter, J.S., & Abel, G.G. (1984). Infrared vaginal photoplethysmography: Construction, calibration, and sources of artifact. *Behavioral Assessment, 6*, 141–152.

Janssen, E., Everaerd, W., Van Lunsen, R.H.W., & Oerlemans, S. (1994). Validation of a psychophysiological waking erectile assessment (WEA) for the diagnosis of male erectile disorder. *Urology, 43*(5), 686–695.

Jenkins, B. (1988). Patients' reports of sexual changes after treatment for gynecological cancer. *Oncology Nursing Forum, 15*(3), 349–354.

Jovanovic, U.J. (1971). The recording of physiological evidence of genital arousal in human males and females. *Archives of Sexual Behavior, 1*, 309–320.

Kaneko, S., & Bradley, W.E. (1986). Evaluation of erectile dysfunction with continuous monitoring of penile rigidity. *Journal of Urology, 136*, 1026–1029.

Karacan, I. (1978). Advances in the psychophysiological evaluation of male erectile impotence. In J. LoPiccolo & L. LoPiccolo (Eds.), *Handbook of sex therapy* (pp. 137–146). New York: Plenum.

Katchadourian, H.A. (1989). *Fundamentals of human sexuality.* New York: Holt, Rinehart & Winston.

Kegel, A. (1948). The non-surgical treatment of genital relaxation. *Annals of Western Medical Surgery, 2*, 213–216.

Kegel, A. (1952). Sexual functions of the pubococcygeus muscle. *Western Journal of Surgery, Obstetrics, and Gynecology, 60*, 521–524.

Kinsey, A.C., Pomeroy, W.B., & Martin, C.E. (1948). *Sexual behavior in the human male.* Philadelphia: W.B. Saunders.

Kinsey, A.C., Pomeroy, W.B., Martin, C.E., & Gebhard, P.H. (1953). *Sexual behavior in the human female.* Philadelphia: W.B. Saunders.

Krane, R.J., Goldstein, I., & Saenz de Tejada, I. (1989). Impotence. *New England Journal of Medicine, 321*, 1648–1659.

Lavoisier, P., Aloui, R., Schmidt, M.H., & Watrelot, A. (1995). Clitoral blood flow increases following vaginal pressure stimulation. *Archives of Sexual Behavior, 24*(1), 37–45.

Lavoisier, P., Proulx, J., Courtois, F., & deCarufel, F. (1989). Bulbocavernosus reflex: Its validity as a diagnostic test for neurogenic impotence. *Journal of Urology, 141*, 311–314.

Laws, D.R., & Holmen, M.L., (1978). Sexual response faking by pedophiles. *Criminal Justice and Behavior, 5*, 343–356.

Leiblum, S.R., & Pervin, L.A. (Eds.). (1980). *Principles and practices of sex therapy.* New York: Guilford Press.

Levin, R.J. (1981). The female orgasm—current appraisal. *Journal of Psychosomatic Research, 25*, 119–133.

Levin, R.J., & Wagner, G. (1977). Haemodynamic changes of the human vagina during sexual arousal assessed by a heated oxygen electrode. *Journal of Physiology, 275*, 23–24.

Levin, R.J., & Wagner, G. (1985). Orgasm in women in the laboratory—quantitative studies on duration, intensity, latency, and vaginal blood flow. *Archives of Sexual Behavior, 14*(5), 439–449.

Levine, L.A., & Carroll, R.A. (1994). Nocturnal penile tumescence and rigidity in men without complaints of erectile dysfunction using a new quantitative analysis software. *Journal of Urology, 152*, 1103–1107.

Levitt, E.E., Konovsky, M., Freese, M.P., & Thompson, J.F. (1979). Intravaginal pressure assessed by the Kegel perineometer. *Archives of Sexual Behavior, 8*, 425–430.

Lue, T.F., Hricak, H., Schmidt, R.A., & Tanagho, E.A. (1986). Functional evaluation of penile veins by cavernosography in papaverine-induced erection. *Journal of Urology, 135*, 479–482.

Lundberg, P.O. (1992). Sexual dysfunction in patients with neurological disorders. *Annual Review of Sex Research, 3*, 121–150.

Marshall, P., Earls, C., Morales, A., & Surridge, D. (1982). Nocturnal penile tumescence recording with stamps: A validity study. *Journal of Urology, 128*, 946–947.

Marshall, P., Morales, A., Phillips, P., & Fenemore, J. (1983). Nocturnal penile tumescence with stamps: A comparative study under sleep laboratory conditions. *Journal of Urology, 130*, 88–89.

Masters, W.H., & Johnson, V.E. (1966). *Human sexual response*. Boston: Little, Brown.

Masters, W.H., Johnson, V.E., & Kolodny R.C. (1995). *Human sexuality*. New York: HarperCollins.

Miraldi, F., Nelson, A.D., Jones, W.T., Thompson, S., & Kursh, E.D. (1992). A dual-radioisotope technique for the evaluation of penile blood flow during tumescence. *The Journal of Nuclear Medicine, 33*(1), 41–46.

Morley, J.E. (1986). Impotence. *American Journal of Medicine, 80*, 897–905.

Mountjoy, P.T. (1974). Some early attempts to modify penile erection in horse and human. *Psychological Record, 24*, 291–308.

Nelson, R.P., & Lue, T.F. (1989). Determination of penile erectile volume by ultrasonography. *Journal of Urology, 141*, 1123–1126.

Newman, A.F. (1970). Vibratory sensitivity of the penis. *Fertility and Sterility, 21*, 791–795.

Ohlmeyer, P., Brilmayer, H., & Hullstrung, H. (1944). Periodische Vorgange im Schlaf. *Pfluegers Archiv fuer Die Gesamte Physiologie, 251*, 110–114.

Oposomer, R.J., Guerit, J.M., & Wese, T.X. (1986). Pudendal cortical somatosensory evoked potentials. *Journal of Urology, 135*, 1216–1218.

Palti, Y., & Bercovici, B. (1967). Photoplethysmographic study of the vaginal blood pulse. *American Journal of Obstetrics and Gynecology, 97*, 143–153.

Perry, J.D. (1980, April). *Two devices for the physiological measurement of sexual activity*. Paper presented at the meeting of the Society for the Scientific Study of Sex, Philadelphia.

Perry, J.D., & Whipple, B. (1982). Vaginal myography. In B. Graber (Ed.), *Circumvaginal musculature and sexual function* (pp. 61–73). Basel, Switzerland: Karger.

Queral, L.A., Whitehouse, W.M, Flinn, W.R., Zarins, C.K, Bergan, J.J., & Yao, J.S.T. (1979). Pelvic hemodynamics after aortoiliac reconstruction. *Surgery, 86*, 799–804.

Riley, A. (1990). Are women who volunteer for sexual response studies representative of women in general? *Sexual & Marital Therapy, 5*(2), 131–140.

Rogers, G.S., Van de Castle, R.L., Evans, W.S., & Critelli, J.W. (1985). Vaginal pulse amplitude response patterns during erotic conditions and sleep. *Archives of Sexual Behavior, 14*(4), 327–342.

Rosen, R.C., & Beck, J.G. (1988). *Patterns of sexual arousal*. New York: Guilford Press.

Rosen, R.C., & Keefe, F.J. (1978). The measurement of human penile tumescence. *Psychophysiology, 15*, 366–376.

Rosen, R.C., Taylor, J.F., & Leiblum, S.R. (1993). Prevalence of sexual dysfunction in women: Results of a survey study of 329 women in an outpatient gynecological clinic. *Journal of Sex and Marital Therapy, 13*(3), 171–188.

Rosenthal, R., & Rosnow, R.L. (1969). The volunteer subject. In R. Rosenthal & R.L. Rosnow (Eds.), *Artifact in behavioral research* (pp. 59–118). New York: Academic Press.

Rowland, D.L., Geilman, C., Brouwer, A.A., & Slob, A.K. (1992). New device for penile vibrotactile stimulation: Description and preliminary results. *Urological Research, 20*(5), 365–368.

Rushworth, G. (1967). Diagnostic value of the electromyographic study of reflex activity in man. *Electroencephalography and Clinical Neurophysiology, 25*(Suppl.), 65–73.

Schiavi, R.C. (1988). Nocturnal penile tumescence in the evaluation of erectile disorders: A critical review. *Journal of Sex and Marital Therapy, 14*, 83–97.

Schiavi, R.C. (1992). Laboratory methods for evaluating erectile dysfunction. In R.C. Rosen & S.R. Leiblum (Eds.), *Erectile disorders* (pp. 141–170). New York: Guilford Press.

Schover, L.R., & Jensen, S.B. (1988). *Sexuality and chronic illness: A comprehensive approach*. New York: Guilford Press.

Shvartzman, P. (1994). The role of nocturnal penile tumescence and rigidity monitoring in the evaluation of impotence. *Journal of Family Practice, 39*(3), 279–282.

Sintchak, G., & Geer, J.H. (1975). A vaginal plethysmograph system. *Psychophysiology, 12,* 113–115.

Sipski, M., & Alexander, C. (1993). Sexual activities, response and satisfaction in women pre- and post-spinal cord injury. *Archives of Physical Medicine and Rehabilitation, 74*(10), 1025–1029.

Slob, A.K., Koster, J., Radder, J.K., & Van der Werff ten Bosch, J.J. (1990). Sexuality and psycho-physiological functioning in women with diabetes mellitus. *Journal of Sex and Marital Therapy, 16*(2), 59–69.

Solnick, R.L., & Birren, J.E. (1977). Age and male erectile responsiveness. *Archives of Sexual Behavior, 6,* 1–9.

Spector, I.P., & Carey, M.P. (1990). Incidence and prevalence of the sexual dysfunctions: A critical review of the empirical literature. *Archives of Sexual Behavior, 19,* 389–408.

Spector, I.P., Leiblum, S.R., Carey, M.P., & Rosen, R.C. (1993). Diabetes and female sexual function: A critical review. *Annals of Behavioral Medicine, 15*(4), 257–264.

Steinke, E.E., & Patterson, P. (1995). Sexual counseling of MI patients by cardiac nurses. *Journal of Cardiovascular Nursing, 10*(1), 81–87.

Thomas, A., & LoPiccolo, J. (1994). Sexual functioning in persons with diabetes: Issues in research, treatment, and education. *Clinical Psychology Review, 14*(1), 61–86.

Tiefer, L. (1991). Historical, scientific, clinical and feminist criticisms of the "human sexual response cycle" model. *Annual Review of Sex Research, 2,* 1–23.

Wabrek, A.J. (1986). In-hospital nocturnal penile tumescence (NPT) monitoring and penile-rigidity determination in the differential diagnosis of erectile dysfunction. *Journal of Psychosomatic Obstetrics and Gynecology, 5,* 137–145.

Wagner, G., & Levin, R.J. (1978). Oxygen tension of the vaginal surface during sexual stimulation in the human. *Fertility and Sterility, 30,* 50–53.

Wincze, J.P., Albert, A., & Bansal, S. (1993). Sexual arousal in diabetic females: Physiological and self-report measures. *Archives of Sexual Behavior, 22*(6), 587–601.

Wolchik, S.A., Braver, S.L, & Jensen, K. (1985). Volunteer bias in erotic research: Effects of intrusiveness of measure and sexual background. *Archives of Sexual Behavior, 14,* 93–107.

Wolchik, S.A., Spencer, S.L., & Lisi, I.S. (1983). Volunteer bias in research employing vaginal measures of sexual arousal. Demographic, sexual, and personality characteristics. *Archives of Sexual Behavior, 12,* 399–408.

Zuckerman, M. (1971). Physiological measures of sexual arousal in the human. *Physiological Bulletin, 75,* 297–329.

CHAPTER 5

Basic Sexual Function over Time

Marca L. Sipski and Craig J. Alexander

As people age, there are predictable physiologic alterations in their sexual responses. Before the 1980s, these changes were thought to be accompanied by a large decrease in a person's participation in sexual activity (Kleitsch & O'Donnell, 1990). However, more recently, Starr and Weiner (1981) noted that, for many elderly subjects (ages 60 to 91) surveyed, there was not a significant change in their sexual activity when compared with their frequency during their forties and fifties. Masters and Johnson (1966) also noted that the greatest predictor of sexual activity in aging is the level of previous activity in the early and middle adult years. In contrast, Labby (1985) reported that the sooner someone began to be sexually active the more likely he or she was to continue to be sexually active in old age. The maintenance of a high frequency of sexual activity has been associated with a high level of health and fitness. Whitten and Whiteside (1989) noted that in 160 master's-level competition male and female swimmers, the frequency of intercourse in those swimmers aged 60 years and older was nearly as great as those in their forties. Furthermore, for those individuals in their forties, the frequency of intercourse was about seven times a month, similar to the frequency reported by many people in their twenties and thirties.

NORMAL SEXUAL RESPONSE CYCLE

Multiple models of sexual response are available. Probably the most well-known model is the one developed by Masters and Johnson (1966), which includes four phases: excitement, plateau, orgasm, and resolution. Depending on the sex of the individual, there are specific physiologic changes that occur during each phase. Furthermore, in the female, the capacity to achieve multiple orgasms may exist before moving on to the resolution phase (Figure 5–1; Sipski, 1991).

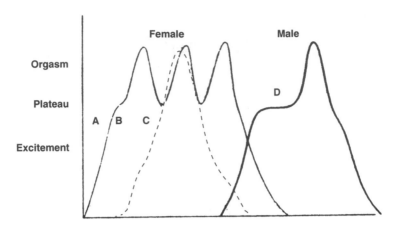

Figure 5–1 Sexual Response Cycle. (**A**) multiple orgasms (**B**) no orgasm, individual fails to go past plateau (**C**) single orgasm (**D**) single orgasm. *Source:* Reprinted with permission from M.L. Sipski, Spinal Cord Injury: What Is the Effect on Sexual Response? *Journal of the American Paraplegia Society,* Vol. 14, pp. 40–43, © 1991, American Paraplegia Society.

Male Sexual Response Cycle

Changes in the excitement phase in the male include engorgement of the corpora cavernosa of the penis with resultant erection, flattening of the scrotal skin, and the beginning elevation of the testicles. Furthermore, two-thirds of patients demonstrate nipple erection.

Changes in the plateau phase include the results of further vasocongestion. Both the diameter and color of the glans penis increase. Furthermore, a drop of secretion can occur from the Cowper's gland at the urethral meatus. There is also an increase in heart rate, blood pressure, respiratory rate, and general muscle tone. The testicles increase in size by 50% to 100% and the sex flush—a measles-like rash—can appear over the face, neck, and chest.

During orgasm, heart rate, blood pressure, and respiratory rate increase further. There is also contraction of the prostate, seminal vesicles, and vas deferens, which bring the seminal fluid into the urethra; further contractions of the urethra lead to ejaculation. Concomitantly, the bladder neck closes to prevent retrograde ejaculation. Five to seven rhythmic contractions of the perineal musculature occur, each lasting from 0.7 to 1.0 seconds (see Figure 5–1, pathway D).

The resolution phase brings gradual reversal of the anatomical and physical changes. Furthermore, there is generalized perspiration. A refractory period will occur for repeated ejaculation.

Female Sexual Response Cycle

Changes in the female during the excitement phase include clitoral enlargement in diameter, beginning dilation of the upper two-thirds and constriction of the lower one-third of the vagina, beginning uterine elevation out of the deep pelvis, and vaginal lubrication. Furthermore, nipple erection occurs in two-thirds of women.

During the plateau phase, the upper two-thirds of the vagina balloons, with the associated formation of the orgasmic platform. The clitoral glans and shaft retract against the pubic symphysis. Heart rate, respiratory rate, muscle tone, and blood pressure increase, and breast size can increase up to 50%. Additionally, the sex flush may appear over the face, neck, and chest. For those females who suffer from primary or secondary anorgasmia, the individual may reach this phase of sexual excitement, staying at the plateau level for a prolonged period, and slowly returning back to baseline levels (see Figure 5–1, pathway B).

Orgasm results in further increases in generalized muscle tone, heart rate, blood pressure, and respiratory rate in addition to rhythmic contractions in the perineal musculature, similar to the male. Contraction also occurs in the fallopian tubes and uterus. This phase is different in females than in males because females may experience one orgasm or multiple orgasms (see Figure 5–1, pathways A and C).

The resolution phase in the female is similar to that in males. Heart rate, respiratory rate, and breathing rate gradually return to baseline levels, and generalized perspiration appears. Although some women may report the presence of a refractory period for further sexual activity postorgasm, Masters and Johnson (1966) have reported that the refractory period only occurs in the male.

Kaplan (1977, 1979) also developed a model for sexual response. The main difference from the Masters and Johnson model is that libido or desire for sexual activity is considered. In the Kaplan model, desire is the first phase of sexual response, the second stage is excitement, and the last phase is orgasm. Desire consists of sensations that motivate the person to initiate or respond to sexual stimulation. Excitement is equated with reflex genital vasocongestion, and orgasm involves reflex pelvic muscle contractions (Rosen & Beck, 1988). Because of the attention to desire, Kaplan's model of sexual response has been found useful for classification of sexual dysfunction.

CHANGES IN SEXUAL RESPONSE THAT OCCUR WITH AGING

Just as there are changes in most organ systems with aging, there are also changes in sex organs and sexual function. Unfortunately, most people are not apprised of these normal changes and therefore may misconstrue them as occurring because of psychological and not physiologic reasons. This belief can lead to a vicious cycle, with secondary psychological concerns compounding the physiologic effects. For instance, the elderly man who takes more time to achieve an erection but is unaware that this is a normal byproduct of aging may become worried about his delay in performance. This worry may then result in further, psychologically induced, erectile dysfunction that could be prevented through basic education.

Changes in Aging Females

Most genital changes that occur in aging females are attributed to menopause and the accompanying decline in estrogen levels. Genital appearance is altered with loss of fullness in the labia and thinning of pubic hair. Skin changes also occur in the vaginal mucosa including dryness, thinning, and increased friability. Furthermore, in those women who are sexually abstinent, narrowing and stenosis of the introitus and vaginal vault can occur (Leiblum & Segraves, 1989).

Masters and Johnson (1966) studied the sexual responses of 61 females, ranging in age from 41 to 78 years. During the excitement phase, there was a smaller increase in breast size. Flattening, separation, and elevation of the major labia was lost and vaginal lubrication took longer and was decreased in amount. Vasocongestive thickening of the genital organs during advanced excitement also decreased.

According to Masters and Johnson (1966), the plateau phase was remarkable for a decrease in the intensity of areolar engorgement. Fewer women developed the sex flush. Loss of the preorgasmic color change of the minor labia occurred, and the vasocongestion of the outer one-third of the vagina was reduced.

During orgasm, Masters and Johnson (1966) noted an overall decrease in myotonia, with less muscular tension during both voluntary and involuntary contractions. Rectal contractions occurred less frequently and contractions of the orgasmic platform were limited to 3 to 5, as compared with 5 to 10 in younger women. Minimal involuntary distension of the external meatus was noted with intense orgasm. Uterine contractility was thought to be the same; however, cramping was thought to occur with uterine contractions. Those women who were noted to be more sexually active, however, were not found to have changes in muscular contractions.

Changes in Aging Males

Masters and Johnson (1966) also studied the sexual responses of 39 men between the ages of 51 and 90 years. During the excitement phase, penile erection took at least two to three times longer to develop. Moreover, the older the male was, the longer it took to achieve an erection. Once a full erection was achieved and lost without ejaculation, it was more difficult to regain. The scrotal vasocongestive response was also markedly reduced in males older than age 60 years. The folding pattern would persist without tensing or flattening, and thickening of the skin and dartos might not occur. At the same time, a decrease in testicular elevation was found.

During the plateau phase, nipple turgidity was reduced and the sex flush was lost in the aging male. Overall myotonia was diminished, except in the more sexually active men, with little incidence of involuntary spasm occurring in men older than age 50 years. Testicular elevation occurred later in the plateau phase and was decreased, with full excursion not always occurring before orgasm. There was an absence of the color change in the glans penis that occurred with young males. Erection might be maintained for a long time without ejaculation and full erection might not occur at all.

The orgasm phase was remarkable for the overall decrease in myotonia along with less frequent contractions of the rectal sphincter and fewer penile contractions. The decrease in myotonia might also have contributed to the distance semen may travel: 6 to 12 inches, as compared with 12 to 24 inches in young males. There was also a decrease in the amount of ejaculatory fluid.

The resolution phase in elderly males was remarkable for an extended refractory period, which may last for days. Furthermore, once orgasm occurred, penile detumescence and testicular descent were much more rapid.

RELATIONSHIP BETWEEN AGE AND SEXUALITY

At least five major research endeavors have been reported in the literature that have examined sexual behavior beyond age 60 years. The first to study the effects of aging on sexuality was probably Alfred Kinsey and colleagues (Kinsey, Pomeroy, & Martin, 1948; Kinsey, Pomeroy, Martin, & Gebhard, 1953). Kinsey reported that, although sexual activity persisted later in life, a gradual decline in sexual activity for both males and females occurred with aging. Kinsey's sample, however, was quite small and therefore limited the generalizability of his findings.

Masters and Johnson (1966, 1970) conducted laboratory-based studies of the physiology of sexual response in approximately 150 women and 200 men aged 50 to 90 years. They reported that all age groups were sexually active, although there was a slower, less intense sexual response as a result of the aging process. The frequency of sexual activity in earlier years was most predictive of level of sexual activity in older years. For women, the quality of their relationship was related to sexual activity. Men reported that numerous factors interfered with aging and a satisfying sexual relationship, including fatigue, boredom, illness, overeating, and performance anxiety.

A series of studies conducted at the Duke University Center for the Study of Aging and Human Development (Pfeiffer, 1974) have been reported in the literature. Between 1953 and 1965, the center sampled more than 250 men and women between the ages of 60 and 90 years. In addition, since 1968, more than 500 men and women between the ages of 45 and 69 years have been assessed. The center's researchers concluded that more than 70% of healthy couples were sexually active at age 68 years. However, sexual interest and activity tended to decline with time. Men tended to be more sexually active than women.

Starr and Weiner (1981) conducted a questionnaire study with 280 males and 520 females aged 60 to 91 years. Their results were somewhat surprising. Starr and Weiner reported that more than 80% of their sample was sexually active. Of the sample, 50% engaged in regular sexual activity. Of those individuals, 50% engaged in intercourse at least once per week.

Brecher (1984) conducted a Consumers Union survey of more than 4,000 men and women aged 50 to 93 years. Results were published in his book *Love, Sex and Aging*. Of the men, 79% and 65% of the women aged 50 to 91 years reported that they were sexually active. Of the respondents, 58% of men and 50% of women reported weekly sex.

More recently, Michael, Gagnon, Laumann, and Kolata (1994), working through the National Opinion Research Center at the University of Chicago, spent 7 months using 220 interviewers to question 3,432 randomly selected Americans between the ages of 18 and 59 years on their sexual attitudes and behaviors. They attempted to improve on the methodological shortcomings inherent in most of the previously published reports on sexuality attitudes and behaviors. As George and Weiler (1981) have noted, research in this area suffers from a lack of representativeness in sampling, confounding cohort effects inherent in cross-sectional designs, and inadequate statistical control of relevant variables such as marital status. The Michael et al. (1994) study, though, is a comprehensive and methodologically sound survey of America's sexual practices and beliefs. Only one-third of Americans surveyed had sex as often as twice a week. Moreover, only three factors contributed to the frequency of sex: (1) age, (2) whether people were married or cohabitating, and (3) how long the couple had been together. The youngest and oldest people surveyed had the least sex. People in their twenties had the most sex. For people aged 50 to 59 years, one-third of the men and more than half of the women had no sex at all or sex only a few times during the past year. Married and cohabitating people reported having the most sex. The authors concluded that the critical factor in sexual activity is not age but rather the availability of a sexual partner.

PSYCHOSOCIAL ISSUES, AGING, AND SEXUALITY

Taken as a whole, the studies concluded that the loss of sexuality is not an inevitable aspect of aging (Kaplan, 1990). Sexuality is multifaceted, including affection, companionship, intimacy, and love (Rotberg, 1987). The need for love and belonging is timeless and ageless (Burnside, Ebersole, & Monea, 1979). Research has shown that sexual enjoyment is a significant predictor of happiness in aging males (Palmore & Kivett, 1977). Other research has shown that the quality of the sexual relationship is closely related to overall happiness in the marital relationship (Libman, Takefman, & Brender, 1980).

It is the emotional and psychological difficulties that are most likely to interfere with sexual performance in old age (Charatan, 1978). The American Medical Association Human Sexuality Committee in 1972 concluded that anxiety and internalization of societal pressures are responsible for most of the problems of impotence (Kay & Neelley, 1982). Psychological issues, couples' concerns related to the quality of the relationship, and cultural factors all contribute to sexual difficulties with aging. Depression, a common problem among elderly people, contributes to sexual dysfunction. Depression can be associated with any of the large number of potential losses inherent with aging. The loss of job or career, good health, attractive physical appearance, or close friends or family, including children who have left home, can result in depression. Anxiety about inadequate sexual performance or fear of disappointing a partner will most likely lead to sexual dysfunction. A person's basic attitudes toward sexuality are important throughout the aging process. If a person associates guilt and shame with sexual expression, especially as he or she ages, sexual performance and satisfaction will obviously be hampered. The issue of body image and self-esteem continues to be important even into the later years when a person's physical appearance changes.

The quality of the relationship, quality of communication, degree of mutual intimacy, and level of commitment are vital to sexual satisfaction. The partner's expectations, flexibility, and willingness to experiment are important. Couples must be sensitive to each other's needs and fears and have the ability to communicate without being perceived as criticizing. When any of these problems exist, they might be acted out in the bedroom.

The impact of societal and cultural factors on the partners throughout the aging process cannot be overemphasized. Western culture tends to value productivity and activity and, not infrequently, equate old age with dependency, slowness, and reduced output. Some people subscribe to the myth that lovemaking is only for the beautiful. Thus, elderly people may be viewed as asexual. Westerners tend to identify older people with their parents, and the thought of parents as sexual beings can tend to create more than just a little discomfort. As Rubin (1965) indicated, what is "virility" at age 25 years becomes "lechery" at age 65 years.

Starr and Weiner (1981) have pointed out that sexual expression remains important throughout the lifespan: "Despite what society has conditioned us to believe, our data clearly show that the need to be touched, stroked, cuddled, and caressed is a lifelong one. Physical contact is a basic human need and that need is as powerful in the 60's, 70's and 80's as it is in infancy, childhood and early adulthood" (p. 9). Brown (1989) has offered a question and an answer that have become paradoxical in our society: "What is it that everyone wants to become but no one wants to be?" The answer, obviously, is, "We want to become old" (p. 75).

REFERENCES

Brecher, E. (1984). *Love, sex and aging*. Boston: Little, Brown.

Brown, L. (1989). Is there sexual freedom for our aging population in long-term care institutions? *Journal of Gerontological Social Work, 13*(3/4), 75–93.

Burnside, M., Ebersole, P., & Monea, H.E. (1979). *Psychosocial caring throughout the life span*. New York: McGraw-Hill.

Charatan, F.B. (1978). Sexual function in old age. *Medical Aspects in Human Sexuality, 12*, 151–160.

George, L.K., & Weiler, S.J. (1981). Sexuality in middle and late life. *Archives of General Psychiatry, 38*, 919–923.

Kaplan, H.S. (1977). Hypoactive sexual desire. *Journal of Sex and Marital Therapy, 3*, 3–9.

Kaplan, H.S. (1979). *Disorders of sexual desire*. New York: Brunner/Mazel.

Kaplan, H.S. (1990). Sex, intimacy, and the aging process. *Journal of the American Academy of Psychoanalysis, 18*(2), 185–205.

Kay, B., & Neelley, J.N. (1982). Sexuality and the aging: A review of current literature. *Sexuality and Disability, 5*(1), 38–46.

Kinsey, A.C., Pomeroy, W.B., & Martin, C.E. (1948). *Sexual behavior in the human male*. Philadelphia: W.B. Saunders.

Kinsey, A.C., Pomeroy, W.B., Martin, C.E., & Gebhard, P.H. (1953). *Sexual behavior in the human female*. Philadelphia: W.B. Saunders.

Kleitsch, E.C., & O'Donnell P.D. (1990). Sex and aging. *Physical medicine and rehabilitation: State of the art reviews, 4*(1), 121–134.

Labby, D.H. (1985). Aging's effects on sexual function. *Postgraduate Medicine, 78*, 32–43.

Leiblum, S.R., & Segraves, R.T. (1989). Sex therapy with aging adults. In S.R. Leiblum & R.C. Rosen (Eds.), *Principles and practice of sex therapy: Update for the 1990s.* (2nd ed., pp. 352–381). New York: Guilford Press.

Libman, E., Takefman, J., & Brender, W. (1980). A comparison of sexually dysfunctional, maritally disturbed and well-adjusted couples. *Personality and Individual Differences, 1*, 219–227.

Masters, W.H., & Johnson, V.E. (1966). *Human sexual response*. Boston: Little, Brown.

Masters, W.H., & Johnson, V.E. (1970). *Human sexual inadequacy*. Boston: Little, Brown.

Michael, R.T., Gagnon, J.H., Laumann, E.O., & Kolata, G. (1994). *Sex in America: A definitive survey*. New York: Little, Brown.

Palmore, E., & Kivett, V. (1977). Change in life satisfaction: A longitudinal study of persons aged 46–70. *Journal of Gerontology, 32*, 311–316.

Pfeiffer, E. (1974). *Successful aging*. Durham, NC: Duke University Center for the Study of Aging and Human Development.

Rosen, R.C., & Beck, J.G. (1988). Patterns of sexual response. In R.C. Rosen & J.G. Beck (Eds.), *Patterns of sexual arousal: Psychophysiological processes and clinical applications* (pp. 23–52). New York: Guilford Press.

Rotberg, A. (1987). An introduction to the study of women, aging, and sexuality. *Physical and Occupational Therapy in Geriatrics, 5*(3), 3–12.

Rubin, I. (1965). *Sexual life after sixty*. New York: Basic Books.

Sipski, M.L. (1991). Spinal cord injury: What is the effect on sexual response? *Journal of the American Paraplegia Society, 14*, 40–43.

Starr, B.D., & Weiner, M.B. (1981). *The Starr-Weiner report on sex and sexuality in the mature years*. New York: McGraw-Hill.

Whitten, P., & Whiteside, E.J. (1989, April). Can exercise make you sexier? *Psychology Today*, pp. 42–44.

CHAPTER 6

Medications and Their Impact

Daniel N. Weiner and Raymond C. Rosen

For many patients suffering from disability or chronic illness, medication use is a necessary and integral component of health maintenance. In recent years, clinicians and researchers have focused increasingly on quality of life issues related to chronic medication use and sexual sequelae, in particular (Crenshaw & Goldberg, 1996; Rosen, 1991). Recent clinical trials of drug efficacy in chronic illness have highlighted quality of life assessments, in addition to more traditional health outcome measures (e.g., Croog et al., 1986; Kostis et al., 1992). Among the major components of quality of life are social and physical function, mood state, cognitive performance, and sexual satisfaction. In addition to the potential effect on quality of life, a major reason for the present concern with sexual side effects of medical therapy is the potential threat to treatment compliance in many individuals (Watts, 1981).

Sexual performance may be affected directly or indirectly by a variety of pharmacologic agents. Normal sexual function depends on multiple physiologic mechanisms, including vascular, hormonal, neurologic, and psychological processes (Rosen & Beck, 1988). Drugs used in the treatment of various medical or psychiatric conditions (e.g., hypertension, hypercholesterolemia, or depression) may adversely affect one or more of the physiologic mechanisms that underly normal sexual function. Alternatively, drug therapy may affect sexual function indirectly through concomitant effects on mood state, mental alertness, or social interactions. Thus, pharmacologic treatments may have direct or indirect effects on sexual function by way of multiple physiological and psychologic pathways.

Many prescription drugs are viewed as *anaphrodisiacs*, or substances that are likely to diminish or impair sexual performance. However, some agents are currently being investigated for their potential prosexual, or positive, effects on sexual function (Rosen & Ashton, 1993). Although much of the literature discussed in this chapter concerns adverse sexual side effects of prescription drugs, this chapter also addresses the use of pharmacologic antidotes for treating sexual dysfunction associated with certain drugs, as well as prosexual drugs for the management of a variety of sexual disorders. Specific drugs used for the treatment of male erectile disorder are discussed in another chapter (see Chapter 22).

Before reviewing the effects of particular drugs on sexual function, several characteristics of the overall literature on the topic should be addressed. Drug effects on sexual response are strongly influenced by a number of demographic or clinical variables, including the dosage and duration of medication use; past history and characteristics of the individual (e.g., age, sex, or overall health); and the context in which the drug is taken. Much of the literature is based on studies of individuals with preexisting medical or psychological disorders. Sexual difficulties in these individuals may stem either from the underlying disorder or from the direct effects of the treatment (Buffum, 1982). The effects of labeling an individual as ill may also play a role in a patient's subsequent sexual interactions (Bansal, 1988). Nonspecific effects of various drugs on mood state, energy level, and overall well-being may also influence sexual desire and performance in some individuals (Bancroft, 1989; Schover & Jensen, 1988). Furthermore, many of the drugs to be considered have complex pharmacologic actions, affecting multiple neurotransmitter and hormonal mechanisms (Segraves, 1989).

Unfortunately, a gender bias is evident in much of the research on this topic. Relatively few studies to date have evaluated drug effects on female sexual response, and clinical guidelines are most often addressed to male disorders (e.g., erectile dysfunction or delayed ejaculation). In some instances, it is unclear whether women are at greater or lesser risk for adverse sexual side effects in comparison with men. Generalization of the findings on male patients to female sexual function is certainly questionable. Similarly, relatively few studies have addressed the effects of drugs on sexual function in older patients, despite the widespread use of prescription drugs among elderly people.

To maximize clinical relevance, this chapter is limited to studies of drug effects on sexual function in humans (see Appendix 6–A). Uncontrolled case studies and clinical reports have been generally excluded, except when they include medications not studied in a controlled fashion, or when the findings are relevant to a broader understanding of drug effects on sexual response. Except for the use of pharmacologic antidotes in cases of drug-induced sexual dysfunction, pharmacotherapy for male erectile disorder is not addressed in this chapter. The presentation of material is organized by drug class.

CARDIOVASCULAR DRUGS

Antihypertensive Agents

Antihypertensive drugs are currently among the most commonly prescribed medications in most industrialized societies. Concerns about potential sexual side effects of these drugs have increased markedly over the past decade (e.g., Bansal, 1988; Duncan & Bateman, 1993; Smith & Talbert, 1986; Wicklund, 1994). In a large-scale study of the effects of antihypertensive medications on quality of life, Breckenridge (1991) reported that sexual side effects were among the most common reasons for noncompliance with medical treatment of this problem. Estimates of the incidence of sexual dysfunction in patients with hypertension have varied widely, ranging from fewer than 10% for patients on vasodilators and angiotensin-converting enzyme (ACE) inhibitors (Heel, Brogden, Speight, & Avery, 1979) to more than 30% of patients on alpha-agonist drugs (Croog, Levine, Sudilovsky, Baume, & Clive, 1988). Different drug mechanisms, patient characteristics, and study procedures likely contribute to the widely varying reported prevalence. In addition to the effects of drug treatment, prevalence statistics may also reflect the association between sexual dysfunction and hypertension per se (Bauer, Hunyor, Baker, & Marshall, 1981; Bulpitt, Dollery, & Carne, 1976). The mechanisms underlying this association are currently unclear.

Two major classes of antihypertensive drugs have been strongly associated with adverse effects on sexual function: (1) sympatholytic, or adrenergic-inhibiting, drugs (e.g., reserpine, central alpha-agonists, or beta-blockers); and (2) diuretics (e.g., thiazides or spironolactone). An early study (Hogan, Wallin, & Baer, 1980) investigated the sexual side effects of these and other drugs. Questionnaires were administered to evaluate sexual dysfunction in 861 hypertensive men. Results indicated that sexual dysfunction was most common in patients treated with a combination of propranolol and diuretics (23%), followed by clonidine (15%), and methyldopa (13%). In contrast, the authors found a low rate of dysfunction in untreated controls (4%).

In a multicenter, prospective study of 620 male hypertensive patients receiving methyldopa, propranolol, or captopril (an ACE inhibitor), Croog et al. (1988) found a greater incidence of erectile dysfunction and other sexual difficulties in patients on propranolol compared with patients on captopril or methyldopa. When a diuretic was added to the treatment regimens, both the propranolol and methyldopa groups showed greater impairment in sexual function compared with the captopril group. Generalizability of these findings is limited by the lack of placebo control and concomitant use of diuretics in all treatment groups.

Thiazide diuretics are one of the most commonly prescribed treatments for hypertension. In a randomized placebo-controlled study of 176 men, Chang et al. (1991) found that thiazide treatment adversely affected sex drive, erectile functioning, and ejaculatory ability. No differences were found on other quality of life variables such as mood and alertness. Importantly, the study found that sexual difficulties were reported by subjects on self-report questionnaires more often than in response to direct clinician questioning. This finding highlights the utility of well-constructed self-report measures in the clinical setting for detecting sexual side effects in men on antihypertensive medication.

Over the past 10 years, several new antihypertensive agents have been accepted in clinical practice. The effects on sexual function of several of these drugs have been evaluated in recent studies. For example, Weir et al. (1991) compared the effects of nicardipine and propranolol on quality of life variables. Although both drugs effectively reduced blood pressure, only patients treated with nicardipine experienced improvement on questionnaire measures of several quality of life variables, including sexual function. Novel methods of administration for antihypertensive drugs have also been tested. In some cases, the nontraditional methods of administration have been associated with fewer negative sexual side effects. For example, clonidine has recently been tested in a transdermal patch preparation (Burris, 1993). Clinical trials documented the effectiveness of the patch in reducing blood pressure. In comparison with oral administration of clonidine, the transdermal patch was associated with a reduced incidence and severity of sexual side effects, as well as other side effects such as dry mouth and drowsiness. Not surprisingly, the study also found that patients commonly preferred the patch over the oral medication preparation.

A major drawback of many studies is the exclusive reliance on subjective measures, such as clinician ratings or retrospective reports of sexual dysfunction by patients, both of which may be susceptible to bias. To circumvent these problems, investigators have used laboratory measures of nocturnal penile tumescence (NPT) to objectively assess the effects of antihypertensive medications on sexual function. In the first study of this type, Rosen, Kostis, and Jekelis (1988) demonstrated that pindolol increased latency to NPT in normal volunteer subjects. Atenolol, metoprolol, and propranolol did not significantly diminish NPT in that study, although all medications significantly decreased testosterone levels. In a subsequent study with hypertensive male patients, Kostis et al. (1990) found that both propranolol and clonidine resulted in diminished NPT in men with mild hypertension.

To evaluate the hypothesis that decrements in sexual function on antihypertensives are directly related to the blood pressure–lowering effects of the drugs, Kostis et al. (1992) compared propranolol treatment with both double-blind placebo and a nondrug treatment program consisting of diet, exercise, and stress management training in mildly hypertensive men. Although both treatment conditions resulted in lowered blood pressure, only the propranolol condition was associated with impaired NPT and self-reported sexual dysfunction. In contrast, NPT was unaffected, and self-report indices of sexual function were improved in the nondrug treatment. In sum, propranolol was found to negatively affect both subjective and physiologic measures of sexual function, whereas nondrug intervention improved subjective measures of sexual function without significantly altering NPT.

Two relatively new antihypertensive medications, nifedipine and atenolol, were tested for effects on morning erection (a crude measure of NPT) in a double-blind placebo crossover study by Morrissette, Skinner, Hoffman, Levine, and Davidson (1993). In the study, men with mild-to-moderate hypertension completed daily logs assessing morning erection and erectile capacity during intercourse and other sexual activities. Based on these measures, neither drug significantly affected morning erection. Decrease in erection firmness during masturbation in the nifedipine condition was the only significant change found. It was concluded that these two newer medications are unlikely to be associated with sexual side effects in men with mild-to-moderate hypertension.

Clinically, it is important to identify risk factors, such as age or a previous history of sexual dysfunction, that may increase susceptibility to the sexual side effects of antihypertensives. In one study, Rosen, Kostis, Jekelis, and Taska (1994) evaluated the susceptibility to sexual side effects of antihypertensive therapy in a sample of men with a prior history of sexual dysfunction. Despite the small sample size of the study ($n = 13$), all patients showed a decline in sexual function over the course of the study. Adverse effects on both physiologic and self-reported measures of sexual function were observed.

Taken together, the studies have suggested that patients with treated or untreated hypertension showed diminished NPT compared with nonhypertensive controls. Antihypertensive drugs, particularly the centrally active or sympatholytic agents, have been associated with decreased NPT and waking sexual function in several studies. Clinical recommendations include the use of nondrug therapy, wherever possible, for the control of mild-to-moderate hypertension, or the use of newer calcium channel blockers or ACE inhibitor drugs.

Fewer studies have evaluated sexual side effects of pharmacologic therapy in women. In their review of the literature, Duncan and Bateman (1993) noted that, of the few published studies addressing sexual side effects of antihypertensives in women, most are anecdotal or lack control groups. In general, those studies reported that clonidine, methyldopa, guanethidine, reserpine, propranolol, and spironolactone have all been associated with decreased sexual desire or orgasmic difficulties. No negative sexual side effects have been reported in women for nadolol, atenolol, labetalol, and hydralazine. Thiazide diuretics have been associated with loss of sexual desire and decreased vaginal lubrication in some studies (Moss & Procci, 1982; Semmens & Semmens, 1978; Stevenson & Umstead, 1984; Wartman, 1983). However, Wassertheil-Smoller et al. (1991) found that a weight-reduction diet decreased the incidence of female sexual problems while on chlorthalidone, although the mechanism by which this effect occurred remains unclear. Schoenberger, Testa, Ross, Brennan, and Bannon (1990) found that sexual function in hypertensive women tended to improve when patients were switched from beta-blockers to captopril. However, no improvements were found when women switched from calcium antagonists to captopril.

In a meta-analysis that included three studies that assessed sexual function in men and women, Beto and Bansal (1992) found trends toward diminished sexual function for beta-blockers and centrally acting alpha-2 antagonists. Smaller trends for increased sexual function were found for ACE inhibitors and calcium channel blockers. None of the pre–postmedication effect sizes reached statistical significance, however. Comparisons of effect sizes by gender were also generally nonsignificant. However, the power of these analyses was limited by the small representation (20%) of women in the studies included for analysis.

Recently, a handful of prospective studies on the sexual side effects of antihypertensives drugs were conducted in women. For example, Hodge, Harward, West, Krongaard-DeMong, and Kowal-Neeley (1991) used questionnaire measures to investigate the sexual function of 18 hypertensive women taking clonidine, prazosin, or placebo in a crossover design study. Although no significant differences were found between the drug conditions, trends were found for women to be less receptive to sexual approach by their partners while on antihypertensive medications. In contrast, orgasmic strength was reportedly increased during clonidine treatment. This study was limited by its small sample size and reliance on self-report measures.

More recently, Fernandez-Lopez, Siegrist, Hernandez-Mejia, Brorer, and Cueto-Espinar (1994) compared 115 hypertensive men and women with 115 normotensive controls on questionnaire measures of sexual function. Medication status was not assessed in the study. Results indicated that, although male hypertensives were more likely than male controls to report sexual impairment, female hypertensives reported similar levels of sexual impairment compared with normotensive controls. Because medication use was not reported in the study, conclusions regarding effects of specific treatments on sexual function cannot be drawn. However, other studies have also noted that women treated with antihypertensives have reported levels of sexual impairment similar to controls (Prisant, Carr, Bottini, Solursh, & Solursh, 1994).

In summary, studies that have assessed the effects of antihypertensive agents on women's sexual function have had mixed results. Taken together, the studies have suggested that certain drugs had a negative impact, but the effect appeared to be weaker than that on men, although data were clearly equivocal. Overall, there have been far fewer studies conducted on women, and fewer still using objective or reliable assessment methods. Notably, no physiologic assessment studies of the effects of antihypertensive medications on women's sexual arousal have been conducted to date.

Anticholesterolemic Agents

Hypercholesterolemia is highly prevalent in this society and is associated with a variety of health risks. In particular, elevated cholesterol levels have been associated with heightened risk for erectile dysfunction in male patients, even after adjustment for potential confounding factors such as age, cigarette smoking, and hypertension (Wei et al., 1994). Clofibrate, a relatively older anticholesterolemic agent, has been associated with erectile dysfunction and low sexual desire in several studies (Blane, 1987; Coronary Drug Project Research Group, 1975; Schneider & Kaffarnik, 1975). In contrast, newer agents such as pravastatin and lovastatin have been associated with slight improvements in erectile function (Kostis, Rosen, & Wilson, 1994). In the Kostis et al. study, pravastatin and lovastatin significantly increased NPT in middle-aged, hyperlipidemic men after 2 weeks of treatment. Although trends for increased NPT were maintained, differences were not significant after 6 weeks of treatment. The finding of improved NPT should be interpreted cautiously, however, given the small sample size ($n = 22$) and brief duration of treatment (6 weeks) in this study.

In summary, although older hypolipidemic agents (e.g., clofibrate) were associated with significant adverse effects on sexual function, there may be an advantage for males with elevated cholesterol and erectile dysfunction in the use of one of the newer agents, such as pravastatin or lovastatin. No studies to date have evaluated the effects of these drugs on sexual function in women.

Digoxin

Digoxin is used in the treatment of various cardiac conditions. The drug has been associated with increased estrogen and decreased testosterone and luteinizing hormone levels in male patients (Stoffer, Hynes, Jiang, & Ryan, 1973). Neri, Aygen, Zukerman, and Bahary (1980) found diminished sexual desire, arousal, and erectile functioning in men treated with digoxin for at least 2 years in comparison with other treatments. Sexual dysfunction in the digoxin-treated group was associated with decreased plasma testosterone and luteinizing hormone levels. Thus, it appears that digoxin adversely affects male sexual function through hormonal mechanisms.

Antiarrhythmic Drugs

Despite the widespread use of antiarrhythmic drugs for the control of cardiac arrythmias, few studies have examined the sexual side effects of these drugs. Two case reports have documented a dose–response relationship between disopyramide and erectile dysfunction (Ahmad, 1980; McHaffie, Guz, & Johnston, 1977). There are no reports in the literature of sexual side effects of antiarrythmics in women. Clearly, further research is needed to elucidate the effects of these drugs on sexual function in both sexes.

PSYCHOTROPIC DRUGS

A variety of drugs are included in the category of psychotropic agents, including tricyclic antidepressants (e.g., imipramine or amitriptyline); monoamine oxidase inhibitors (MAOIs; e.g., phenelzine or isocarboxid); selective serotonin reuptake inhibitors (SSRIs; e.g., fluoxetine or sertraline); lithium carbonate; antianxiety agents (benzodiazepines; e.g., diazepam or alprazolam); and neuroleptics (e.g., chlorpromazine, thioridazine, or haloperidol). Despite widespread use of these drugs, there are little systematic data available concerning their effects on sexual function.

Generalizations about the sexual side effects of psychotropic drugs in psychiatric patients are limited by several factors. In addition to the previously mentioned confounds, there are major difficulties in separating the effects of the illness itself from possible side effects of the drugs used in treatment. Severely depressed or psychotic individuals, in particular, have poor interpersonal relationships (Verhulst & Schneidman, 1981) and a chronic history of sexual inadequacy (Nestoros, Lehman, & Ban, 1981; Schover & Jensen, 1988). Obtaining reliable self-reports from such individuals may present a challenge, given their communication difficulties and possible distortions in self-perception. Pharmacologic effects of most psychotropic drugs on central and peripheral neurotransmitters are also highly complex and not fully understood at present (Segraves, 1989).

Antidepressants

Antidepressants have been shown to adversely affect sexual performance in both sexes. Among the major drugs in this category are the tricyclics (e.g., imipramine, amitriptyline, or clomipramine) and MAOIs. In evaluating the effects of antidepressants on sexual function, consider that depressed individuals frequently show markedly decreased sexual desire or arousal associated with the disorder (Mathew & Weinman, 1982; Merikangas, Prusoff, Kupfer, & Frank, 1985). Depressed affect itself has been demonstrated to attenuate sexual arousal in normal controls (Mitchell et al., 1992). In addition to the clinical manifestations of decreased sexual desire, impaired NPT response has also been shown in depressed individuals (Thase et al., 1987). Several of the men with depression-related sexual dysfunction and impaired NPT in the Thase et al. study showed marked improvement in both sexual desire and NPT on recovery from their depression.

Sexual side effects of antidepressants were first reported by Simpson, Blair, and Amuso (1965), who evaluated both clinical patients and normal volunteers. The tricyclic antidepressant imipramine was associated with either erectile or ejaculatory problems in about one-third of subjects. Couper-Smartt and Rodham (1973) found similarly high rates of sexual dysfunction in male patients treated with imipramine. Subsequently, a double-blind, placebo-controlled study comparing imipramine and phenelzine was conducted in 79 male and female depressed patients (Harrison et al., 1985). Both drugs were found to adversely affect sexual function in men and women. More than half of male patients reported problems with arousal and orgasm with both drugs, whereas more females experienced sexual problems with phenelzine (57%) compared with imipramine (27%).

In a subsequent double-blind study of the tricyclic antidepressant clomipramine in patients with obsessive–compulsive disorder, Monteiro, Noshirvani, Marks, and Lelliott (1987) reported high rates of anorgasmia in both men and women. In one case, yohimbine administration resolved clomipramine-related anorgasmia (Price & Grunhaus, 1990). Interestingly, other reports have documented spontaneous orgasms and ejaculation related to clomipramine administration (McLean, Forsythe, & Kapkin, 1983). To date, there is no satisfactory explanation of those discrepant results.

Several case reports have described orgasmic problems in both men and women who were taking other antidepressants, including imipramine (Balon, Yeragani, Pohl, & Ramesh, 1993; Riley & Riley, 1986a; Sovner, 1983), amoxapine (Kulik & Wilbur, 1982; Shen, 1982), and MAOIs (Lesko, Stotland, & Segraves, 1982; Nurnberg & Levine, 1987). Balon et al. (1993) surveyed 22 men and 38 women with anxiety and mood disorders who were taking antidepressant medication. Overall incidence of sexual dysfunction was 43%, with dysfunction occurring across diagnostic groups and medications. Notably, 18% of males in their study reported painful orgasm while on antidepressant medication.

The effect of antidepressant medications on NPT has been investigated in normal males (Kowalski, Stanley, Dennerstein, Burrows, & Maguire, 1985). In that study, amitriptyline and mianserin were administered to six subjects in a double-blind fashion for 2 weeks. Results of NPT testing following the 2-week treatment period revealed significantly reduced NPT response in subjects taking either medication, compared with the placebo. Lack of control for the sleep-altering effects of the drugs may have confounded the results of the study.

SSRIs

Recently, SSRIs have revolutionized treatment of depression and anxiety disorders (Ashton, Hamer, & Rosen, 1996). This group of drugs includes fluoxetine, sertraline, paroxetine, and venlafaxine. Treatment refractory conditions such as dysthymia (Rosenthal et al., 1992; Hellerstein, Yanowitch, & Rosenthal, 1993) and obsessive–compulsive disorder (Fontaine & Chouinard, 1986) have been responsive to these agents. These medications have also been associated with a much lower incidence of adverse side effects, such as anticholinergic reactions, sedation, and orthostatic hypotension. SSRIs also have a larger therapeutic window and are safer in cases of overdose (Haider, Miller, & Staton, 1993).

Unfortunately, relatively high levels of sexual dysfunction have been associated with most SSRIs. Gitlin (1994) noted that SSRIs have been associated with more sexual side effects than expected from prerelease studies of those drugs. For example, Patterson (1993) found the incidence of fluoxetine-related sexual dysfunction to be 75%. Several case studies have documented the adverse effects of fluoxetine on sexual function (Meston & Gorzalka, 1992). Orgasmic difficulty secondary to fluoxetine use has been reported in both depressed women (Zajecka, Fawcett, Schaff, Jeffriess, & Guy, 1991) and men (Kline, 1989).

Interestingly, other case studies have shown fluoxetine to have an excitatory effect on sexual behavior. Modell (1989) reported a case of a depressed woman with no history of sexual problems who indicated having spontaneous orgasms and increased sexual excitement while on fluoxetine. Smith and Levitt (1993) found that fluoxetine improved sexual function in three elderly men with histories of erectile dysfunction in conjunction with depression or obsessive–compulsive disorder. In their report, improvement in sexual function was apparently unrelated to abatement of the other psychiatric conditions. Other SSRIs have also been associated with sexual dysfunction. For example, Dorevitch and Davis (1994) reported two cases of ejaculatory difficulties subsequent to fluvoxamine treatment for depression.

In a recent large-scale study of the incidence of adverse side effects during SSRI administration, Fisher, Kent, and Bryant (1995) found a higher incidence of sexual side effects in patients on sertraline compared with patients on fluoxetine. In contrast, Hsu and Shen (1995) found an equal incidence of sexual dysfunction across fluoxetine, sertraline, and paroxetine. Similar results were obtained in a recent large-scale study (Ashton et al., 1996) in which retrospective chart review was conducted on 596 men and women taking SSRIs. Patients were prescribed either fluoxetine, sertraline, paroxetine, or venlafaxine. Sexual dysfunction was associated with SSRI administration in 97 (16.3%) cases. Dysfunction was usually reported within 1 to 2 months of beginning SSRI treatment or increasing dosage. Anorgasmia and decreased sexual desire were the most commonly reported symptoms. Sexual difficulties were more common among males (23.4%) than females (13.8%). These estimates are likely conservative, because patients were not specifically evaluated for sexual dysfunction. As in the study by Hsu and Shen (1995), diagnosis and type of SSRI were unrelated to occurrence of sexual dysfunction. A clinically important finding was that dysfunction associated with one SSRI did not necessarily predict dysfunction with another drug. Thus, it may be useful to switch from one SSRI to another in some cases of SSRI-related sexual dysfunction.

Orgasmic difficulties were the most common sexual problems reported with all four SSRIs. In contrast to reports of dysfunction in patients on MAOIs and tricyclic antidepressants, inhibited arousal or erection problems were reported less frequently. Several patients reported a combination of problems in sexual desire, arousal, and orgasm. No association was found between gender and type of dysfunction. Of the patients with sexual dysfunction, 14 of 97 (14%) withdrew from SSRI treatment because of ongoing sexual difficulties, underscoring the importance of addressing these side effects clinically.

With the documentation of a relatively high incidence of sexual side effects associated with SSRI treatment, researchers have begun to investigate methods to diminish these side effects. For example, Rothschild (1995) examined the effectiveness of "drug holidays" in 30 patients reporting diminished sexual function during SSRI treatment. Subjects were instructed to discontinue their SSRIs during the weekend, for four consecutive weekends. Results indicated no significant increase in depression during drug discontinuation. In contrast, subjects prescribed sertraline and paroxetine reported improvement in sexual function during periodic drug discontinuation. Subjects taking fluoxetine, which has a much longer half-life, reported no change in sexual function during discontinuation. The authors concluded that, in some patients taking sertraline or paroxetine, drug holidays may serve as a useful means to temporarily improve sexual function without affecting mood.

Another approach to minimizing sexual side effects is the administration of pharmacologic antidotes in conjunction with SSRI treatment. Cyproheptadine and yohimbine are two medications that have proven effective for this purpose in several case studies (Gitlin, 1994). In the study by Ashton et al. (1996), the charts of 65 patients who were prescibed either yohimbine (average dose, 16.2 mg/day), amantadine (200 mg/day), or cyproheptadine (8.6 mg/day) as antidotes for SSRI-related sexual dysfunction were analyzed. Mean duration of antidote treatment was between 1.4 and 2.4 months. Results indicated that 81% of patients responded positively to yohimbine, 42% responded positively to amantadine, and 48% responded positively to cyproheptadine. Analyses revealed that patients on yohimbine were significantly more likely than patients on the other two agents to show improvement in sexual function. Failure of one antidote did not predict failure of the other antidotes in individual cases. Thus, selecting an alternative antidote may be an effective strategy when one antidote fails to improve sexual function or is not well tolerated by the patient.

Antidepressants with Minimal Sexual Side Effects

In recent years, several antidepressant agents have been found to exhibit fewer sexual side effects than the traditional medications previously reviewed. Some of these drugs—bupropion, trazodone, and nefazodone (a new-generation SSRI)—may actually improve sexual function in certain patients.

Bupropion is an antidepressant agent associated with fewer anticholinergic and antiadrenergic effects than other traditional antidepressants. Gardner and Johnston

(1985) administered bupropion (300 to 600 mg/day) to 40 male patients with depression, 28 of whom complained of sexual side effects with other antidepressants. Almost all patients experienced resolution of their drug-related sexual difficulties. The authors concluded that this drug may be particularly appropriate for use in patients with a previous history of sexual dysfunction.

Mildly positive effects of bupropion were found in one study of sexually dysfunctional men and women (Crenshaw, Goldberg, & Stern, 1987). Patients in that study were assigned to a 12-week, double-blind trial of bupropion or placebo, following which detailed assessments of sexual function were obtained by way of interview. Results indicated slight improvement in global ratings of sexual function in the bupropion group, although those changes did not appear to be clinically significant.

Trazodone, an atypical antidepressant with serotonergic properties, has been associated with increased sexual desire in both male and female patients (Gartrell, 1986; Sullivan, 1988). In both studies, improved sexual desire was not directly related to the mood-altering effects of the drug, because some patients experienced resolution of depression without increased desire. In one study (Sullivan, 1988), when patients were taken off trazodone, sexual desire diminished, suggesting that the observed effects were specific to the drug. Albo and Steers (1993) found that trazodone (50 to 150 mg/day) improved sexual function in 64% of their sample of 33 men with erectile dysfunction of mixed organic and psychologic etiology. Trazodone has also been associated with increased NPT in normal male subjects (Ware, Pittard, Nadig, Morrison, and Quinn, 1987), providing further evidence of the potential prosexual effects of this drug.

In a few instances, priapism has been reported as an adverse sexual side effect of trazodone (Scher, Krieger, & Jergens, 1983; Warner, Peabody, & Whiteford, 1987). One case study documented trazodone-induced priapism that required surgical treatment (Patt, 1985). Another study reported nocturnal erections approaching 6 hours in duration during trazodone treatment (Saenz de Tejada et al., 1991), suggesting potentially damaging erectile activity during sleep. Analogous to penile priapism, clitoral priapism and enlargement have been reported in a small number of women taking trazodone alone (Thompson, Ware, & Blashfield, 1990) and in combination with testosterone (Crenshaw & Goldberg, 1996). According to some authors (Warner et al., 1987), the incidence of priapism is relatively rare (1 in 10,000). However, patients should be informed about this potentially dangerous side effect and its treatment.

Nefazodone is a new SSRI designed to act specifically on 5-HT2A receptors, which are thought to be criticially involved in the pathophysiology of depression (Preskorn, 1995). The specificity of action of nefazodone has been hypothesized to decrease the side effect profile of this drug in comparison with other SSRIs that affect 5-HT receptors more generally. In a recent review, Preskorn concluded that, compared with traditional SSRIs, nefazodone has a much lower rate of associated sexual side effects. Similarly, Crenshaw and Goldberg (1996) reported that, in their clinical experience with the drug, sexual desire difficulties reported during use of another SSRI tended to resolve when patients were changed to nefazodone. Replication of these results in controlled, prospective studies is warranted.

In summary, there is strong evidence of an association between antidepressant drug use and sexual dysfunction. In particular, several SSRIs that are widely used at present have been associated with orgasmic difficulties and loss of sexual desire. However, preliminary data have suggested that SSRI-related sexual dysfunctions are responsive to a variety of interventions. For the clinician, several options are available for management of SSRI-related sexual dysfunction. For some patients, drug holidays may be sufficient to improve sexual function for selected intervals. Other patients may benefit from a change to another SSRI agent. Antidote medications, most notably yohimbine, can restore sexual function in some patients undergoing SSRI therapy. Several alternative drugs, including bupropion, trazodone, and nefazodone, have been associated with fewer adverse effects on sexual desire, arousal, and orgasmic capacity than other antidepressants, and may improve sexual performance in some patients with a history of sexual dysfunction.

Lithium Carbonate

Despite its common use in the treatment of bipolar disorder, few studies have assessed the sexual side effects of lithium carbonate. An early study by Vinarova, Uhlir, Stika, and Vinar (1972) found increased erectile dysfunction in a double-blind placebo-controlled trial of lithium in male patients with affective disorders. In their study, 20% of patients treated with active drug reported erectile dysfunction. Similar findings were reported by Blay, Ferraz, and Galil (1982), who described erectile impairment in two patients treated for bipolar disorder using chronic lithium therapy. Decreased sexual desire and erectile difficulties associated with lithium have also been reported by Raboch, Smolik, and Soucek (1983). A more recent retrospective interview study found few differences in sexual function between patients taking lithium and controls (Kristensen & Jorgensen, 1987). Other studies have documented sexual difficulties in patients on lithium in conjunction with other medications such as antidepressants, neuroleptics, and bezodiazepines, but few adverse effects with lithium alone (Ghadirian, Annable, & Belanger, 1992; Page, Benamin, & Lappin, 1987). None of the studies to date have evaluated the effects of lithium on sexual function in women.

In summary, few studies have examined the effects of lithium on sexual function. Results to date are equivocal regarding whether this widely used drug adversely affects sexual function. However, lithium use in conjunction with other medications has been consistently associated with sexual impairment.

Anxiolytics/Sedative–Hypnotics

Benzodiazepines are often used as antianxiety agents and sedative–hypnotics. These drugs, which include diazepam and alprazolam, have been associated with negative effects on sexual function in some studies. The most common problems reported are anorgasmia in women (Nutt, Hackman, & Hawton, 1986; Riley & Riley, 1986b; Sangal, 1985; Uhde, Tancer, & Shea, 1988) and delayed ejaculation in men (Hughs, 1964; Segraves, 1987). In a placebo-controlled study of normal women, diazepam was found to delay orgasm during masturbation (Riley & Riley, 1986b). Decreased sexual desire and arousal have also been reported in some studies (Balon, Ramesh, & Pohl, 1989; Nutt et al., 1986). In a retrospective questionnaire study of 9 men and 32 women, Lydiard, Howell, Laraia, and Balenger (1987) found mixed effects of benzodiazepines on sexual function. After starting benzodiazepine treatment, almost half (47%) of the patients reported decreased sexual desire, whereas 25% of the remaining patients reported increased sexual drive. Of the patients, 50% reported inhibition of orgasm following onset of treatment, whereas 9% indicated enhancement of orgasm. Of the men in the study, 5 (55%) reported diminished or absent erection. Thus, it appears that diazepam has the potential to either inhibit or facilitate sexual response in different individuals.

In select circumstances, benzodiazepines may exert a positive effect on sexual function as a result of their anxiolytic properties. Patients suffering from sexual dysfunction secondary to anxiety may benefit from low-dose benzodiazepine treatment. Typically, doses lower than those used for treatment of anxiety disorders are most effective (Crenshaw & Goldberg, 1996). This effect may be the result of a release of sexual inhibitions at low doses that are obscured by the depressant effects on physiologic processes underlying sexual response at higher doses. For instance, low-dose alprazolam has been associated with enhanced sexual desire, receptivity, and orgasm in some cases (Ghadirian et al., 1992; Post, 1994).

Buspirone is a relatively recent nonsedating antianxiety agent that has not been associated with negative sexual side effects to date. In selected case reports of patients who had experienced sexual side effects while on benzodiazepines, Crenshaw and Goldberg (1996) noted improvement in sexual desire and response after tapering patients off benzodiazepines, while gradually replacing the benzodiazepines with buspirone. In one open trial, buspirone was associated with improved sexual function in sexually dysfunctional patients with severe anxiety disorders (Othmer & Othmer, 1987). However, double-blind placebo-controlled studies have yet to be conducted with this medication, and it is impossible to draw firm conclusions about the effects of buspirone on sexual function.

In summary, benzodiazepines appear to have generally mixed effects on sexual response. Although several case studies have documented impaired sexual function while on benzodiazepines, others have found enhanced sexual response, especially at low doses. Buspirone, an atypical anxiolytic, shows promise as a treatment for anxiety that is not associated with adverse sexual side effects, and may improve sexual function in some cases. Large-scale, placebo-controlled studies of the sexual side effects of these agents are clearly needed.

Neuroleptics

Commonly used neuroleptics include the phenothiazines (e.g., chlorpromazine or thioridazine) and the butyrophenones (e.g., haloperidol). Many of these medications have been associated with diminished sexual performance and arousal. Thioridazine, in particular, has been associated with delayed ejaculation, absent ejaculation, and erectile dysfunction in several studies (Blair & Simpson, 1966; Segraves, Madsen, Carter, & Davis, 1985; Shader, 1964). For example, Blair and Simpson (1966) found that approximately 30% of patients receiving thioridazine complained of difficulty reaching orgasm. To test the severity of ejaculatory inhibition, vibratory stimulation was applied, which, in most patients, failed to elicit ejaculation.

In a study of 87 sexually active male psychiatric patients without concomitant medical conditions, Kotin, Wilbert, Verburg, and Soldinger (1976) found a markedly higher incidence of both ejaculatory and erectile problems with thioridazine treatment in comparison with other antipsychotic medications. Of the patients receiving thioridazine, 60% complained of sexual dysfunction, including orgasm without ejaculation, and painful ejaculation, compared with only 25% of patients on other neuroleptics. Almost half of the patients on thioridazine reported delayed ejaculation, whereas no patients on other medications reported this problem. Gold and Justino (1988) reported that the delay in ejaculation in patients on thioridazine can result in firm and sustained, but nonpainful, erections. Ejaculatory difficulties in those patients are likely due to alpha-adrenergic blockade caused by thioridazine.

Other neuroleptics have been associated with sexual dysfunction in some psychiatric patients. For instance, Ghadirian, Chouinard, and Annable (1982) found that male and female schizophrenic patients reported increased sexual dysfunction, and women reported menstrual irregularities while on fluphenazine. Consistent with the preceding reports, more than half of the men in the study reported difficulties with ejaculation or orgasm, and 38% had erectile difficulties while on the drug. Desire and arousal problems were reported by 44% of the female patients in the study, and almost 80% complained of menstrual irregularities. Sexual dysfunction was associated with elevations in prolactin in male, but not female, patients.

Certain commonly prescribed neuroleptics, including haloperidol, have been associated with changes in prolactin and occasional erectile failure in men (Kolodny, Masters, & Johnson, 1979). Several studies by Rubin and his colleagues (Rubin, Poland, O'Connor, Gouin, & Tower, 1976; Rubin, Poland, & Tower, 1976) have indicated that single doses of haloperidol given to normal male subjects result in increases in plasma prolactin levels, which can persist for up to 4 hours following drug administration. At present, it is unclear whether changes in prolactin following haloperidol administration are related to sexual dysfunction in male patients. As noted by Segraves (1989), the effect of increased prolactin release associated with most neuroleptic drugs appears to be related to the dopamine-inhibiting effects of the drugs. Thus, the mechanism of therapeutic action of these drugs may directly result in inhibited sexual function in many patients.

Reports of priapism have been associated with a variety of neuroleptics, including thrioridazine, chlorpromazine, fluphenazine, mesoridazine, haloperidol, molindone, trifluoperizine, perphenazine, and chlorprothixene (Griffith & Zil, 1984; Winter & McDonell, 1988). Therefore, male patients taking these drugs should be warned of this potentially dangerous side effect and given specific instructions to seek immediate treatment should priapism occur.

Most studies of sexual side effects of neuroleptics reviewed thus far have included only small-to-moderate sample sizes. In a large-scale study of 2,391 men and women with various psychiatric disorders, Lingjaerde, Ahlfors, Bech, Dencker, and Elgen (1987) found reduction in sexual desire to be the most common sexual dysfunction associated with neuroleptic use, occurring in approximately one-third of all patients. Difficulties with orgasm, sexual arousal, and ejaculation occurred in about one-quarter of subjects. Sexual dysfunction occurred in subjects of all ages, with older subjects tending to be more susceptible to sexual side effects. Overall, negative effects on sexual function continued to increase in severity up to approximately 6 months of treatment, after which time the symptoms persisted at a relatively stable level for as long as treatment was continued. In general, high-potency, low-dose neuroleptics such as fluphenazine and flupenthixol were associated with fewer sexual side effects than the low-potency, high-dose neuroleptics, including chlorpromazine and chlorprothixene.

Recently, atypical antipsychotic medications have been introduced in the United States. This class of medications includes clozapine and risperidone. For many years, clozapine use was not permitted in the United States following the discovery of the rare but potentially lethal side effect of agranulocytosis (Krupp & Barnes, 1992). However, with improved methods of monitoring white blood cell count and research that has indicated the usefulness of the drug in treating otherwise treatment-refractory psychotic patients, the drug is now being used increasingly in this country. Although there are no data assessing the sexual side effects of the drug, its side effects profile—including extensive weight gain, sedation, dizziness, and constipation—has been noted to be unlikely to enhance sexual function (Crenshaw & Goldberg, 1996). Limited data exist on sexual side effects of risperidone, and include dose-related erectile dysfunction, diminished sexual desire, orgasm or ejaculation disturbance, and priapism (Lindenmeyer, 1994; Marder & Meibach, 1994; Meltzer, Lee, & Ranjan, 1994). These difficulties were associated with decreased compliance in one study (Lindenmeyer, 1994).

Taken together, the studies reviewed have suggested that sexual side effects of neuroleptic agents are relatively common—sometimes severe. Some clinicians, however, may assume that the side effects are outweighed by the beneficial antipsychotic effects of the medications. Clinicians may assume that psychotic symptoms are considered more troubling by most patients than the potential sexual side effects of the drugs. To test these assumptions, Finn, Bailey, Schultz, and Faber (1990) asked 41 patients on neuroleptic medications to rate the level of distress associated with both psychotic symptoms and sexual side effects of medications. Results indicated that sexual side effects were generally rated by patients as more distressing than psychotic symptoms. Erectile dysfunction, in particular, was rated as more bothersome than any of the psychotic symptoms. Those results have suggested that sexual side effects should not be taken lightly by clinicians, even when the drug is being used to treat severe psychopathology involving psychotic symptoms. Proper management of sexual side effects will likely increase compliance to treatment regimens and decrease patient distress. Unfortunately, there is little information to date about how to successfully manage sexual side effects of these medications. Clearly, this is an area worthy of investigation.

Stimulants/Anorectics

These medications are used primarily for weight control and treatment of attention deficit disorder. Most of these drugs increase adrenergic and dopaminergic tone. Little data exist on sexual side effects of these drugs. Mazindol, a sympathomimetic agent, has been associated with pain in the testes and spontaneous orgasmless ejaculation in some men (McEwen & Meyboom, 1983), and, in one published case, increased sexual desire in a woman (Friesen, 1976). The sexual side effects of fenfluramine, an anorectic drug affecting mainly serotonergic systems, have not been studied systematically, although disturbing increases in sexual desire and arousal have been reported in several cases of women taking the drug for bulimia (Stevenson & Solyom, 1990). Methylphenidate, used primarily in treatment of attention deficit and hyperactivity disorder, also has not been systematically evaluated for sexual side effects, although one report indicated that the drug was associated with increased orgasmic potential in two women (Wood, Reimherr, Wender, & Johnson, 1976). The limited data available to date have suggested that stimulant/anorectic medications may increase sexual desire (sometimes to disturbingly high levels) and may cause painful genital symptoms in some men.

OTHER MEDICATIONS

Anticonvulsants

Epileptic patients have been noted to have symptoms of hyposexuality in several studies (e.g., Christianson, Silfvenius, Saisa, & Nilsson, 1995; Pritchard, 1980; Toone, 1985; Toone, Wheeler, & Fenwick, 1980). Moreover, the severity of epileptic symptoms appears to correlate with the degree of sexual dysfunction (Christianson et al., 1995). In the only laboratory study of waking physiologic sexual response in epileptic patients, Morrell, Sperling, Stecker, and Dichter (1994) found that men and women with epilepsy responded less to erotic stimulation than normal controls.

Anticonvulsants used to control epilepsy have also been found to contribute to sexual dysfunction. For example, phenobarbital and primidone were associated with erectile dysfunction and diminished sexual desire in one study (Mattson et al., 1985). Primidone and phenobarbital were associated with sexual dysfunction more frequently than other anticonvulsants in another study (Mattson & Cramer, 1985). Consistent with the preceding findings, Kolodny et al. (1979) reported decreased orgasmic ability in patients treated with barbiturates. Recently, Bergen, Daugherty, and Eckenfels (1992) found that a subgroup of women taking antiepileptic drugs experienced sexual dysfunction including diminished sexual desire.

Some anticonvulsants have been associated with marked increases in plasma sex hormone–binding globulin and decreased free testosterone levels in male epileptic patients (Barragry, Makin, Trafford, & Scott, 1978; Brunet et al., 1995; Isojarvi, Repo, Pakarinen, Lukkarinen, & Myllyla, 1995; Murialdo et al., 1995). Fenwick et al. (1986) documented diminished NPT in medicated male epileptics with low testosterone, suggesting hormonal involvement in medication-related changes in sexual function. Based on findings of diminished testosterone in epileptic patients, Fenwick et al. suggested testosterone replacement therapy for treatment of sexual dysfunction in male epileptic patients, although this treatment has yet to be evaluated clinically. Recent evidence has suggested that changes in free testosterone and sex hormone–binding globulin per se may not correlate with erectile dysfunction in epileptic men but that increases in estradiol predict erectile dysfunction in those patients (Murialdo et al., 1995).

It has been argued that past studies of sexual dysfunction in epileptic patients may have been confounded by factors such as selection of the most severe patients, use of multiple medications, and lack of control groups (Jensen et al., 1990). These factors may have led to inflated estimates of sexual dysfunction in epileptic patients. In a study of 86 well-controlled epileptic patients receiving monotherapy with either carbamazepine, valprolate, or phenytoin, Jensen et al. (1990) found that the prevalence of sexual dysfunction in men on those medications was no greater than that of controls, and significantly less than that of diabetic patients. In women, no differences were found between the three diagnostic groups. However, approximately 20% of patients in the study reported past sexual problems while taking anticonvulsant drugs, particularly phenobarbital, clonazepam, and phenytoin.

In summary, there are conflicting data regarding the negative effects of antiepileptic medications on sexual function. Although several studies have documented such effects, one methodologically rigorous study failed to detect differences in occurrence of sexual dysfunction between subjects who were taking antiepileptic medications and controls. Increased baseline prevalence of sexual dysfunction in epileptic patients may complicate interpretation of case studies.

Antiulcer Drugs

Cimetidine, a histamine antagonist widely used in the treatment of peptic ulcer disease, has been shown to have disruptive effects on sexual function in a number of studies. In particular, several case reports have described low libido and erectile dysfunction in association with cimetidine treatment (e.g., Niv, 1986; Wolfe, 1979). In most cases, sexual function returns to normal within a few months after cessation of cimetidine (e.g., Galeone et al., 1978). However, cases have been reported in which sexual dysfunction does not improve after cessation of cimetidine (Peden, Cargill, Browning, Saunders, & Wormsley, 1979).

In addition to sexual dysfunction, cimetidine has been linked to other sex-related changes. Van Thiel, Gavaler, Smith, and Paul (1979) reported decreased sperm count in patients who were taking 1,200 mg/day cimetidine. Several studies have found an association between cimetidine treatment and gynecomastia, which usually takes several months to become evident and resolves after discontinuation of the drug (Jensen et al., 1983; Spence & Celestin, 1979). These changes in sexual function and breast size may be the result of the potential of cimetidine for increasing prolactin (Knigge, Thuesen, & Christiansen, 1986) and estradiol (Galbraith & Michnovicz, 1989) levels.

Ranitidine, another commonly used antiulcer drug, appears to have fewer sexual side effects than cimetidine. Moreover, negative sexual symptoms resulting from cimetidine use can often be reversed by switching to ranitidine. For example, Peden and Wormsley (1982) reported a case of a man who developed erectile dysfunction and gynecomastia while taking cimetidine. After being switched to ranitidine, both sexual symptoms resolved. Similar results were obtained in a double-blind study of cimetidine and ranitidine (Jensen et al., 1984). In the study, 60% of men taking cimetidine developed erectile dysfunction or gynecomastia. NPT testing confirmed the presence of drug-related organic erectile dysfunction in three patients who reported complete lack of erection while on cimetidine. In all cases, sexual side effects were resolved after switching to ranitidine.

Anticancer Drugs

Pharmacologic treatment of cancer has understandably focused on preservation of life and prevention of pain, with minimal attention to sexual side effects (Crenshaw & Goldberg, 1996). Drugs used for this purpose have generally been limited to toxic agents that cause suppression of malignant cell growth, which are likely to adversely affect sexual function. Sexual dysfunction may sometimes persist past the point of discontinuation of chemotherapy (Chapman, Sutcliffe, & Malpas, 1981), although it is difficult to ascertain whether this is the result of the impact of the disease itself or permanent side effects of medication. Some anticancer drugs, such as procarbazine, busulfan, chlorambucil, and cyclophosphamide, have been shown to have lasting negative effects on sperm production in men, and to cause amenorrhea in women (Averette, Boike, & Jarrell, 1990; Chapman, 1984). Chapman, Sutcliffe, and Malpas (1979) reported that, after starting cancer treatment, women had a decreased frequency of sexual behavior, despite frequent self-reports of no change in sexual desire. As Crenshaw and Goldberg (1996) noted, during cancer treatment, sexual desire may shift to a desire for intimate closeness, independent of actual sexual behavior. Consistent with this notion, Chapman (1984) reported that, within 3 years of chemotherapy, 70% of women acknowledged decreased or totally absent sexual desire. In the future, locally applied chemotherapies may decrease the incidence of side effects from anticancer medications (Crenshaw & Goldberg, 1996).

Recently, tamoxifen has received attention for its ability to reduce relapse in women treated for breast cancer and to reduce the incidence of breast cancer when used prophylactically (Plowman, 1993). This medication has been associated with both vaginal dryness and excessive vaginal lubrication, as well as occasional decrease in sexual desire and orgasmic ability in some cases (Kaplan, 1992).

Treatment of prostate cancer often involves suppression of androgens, which frequently results in negative effects on all aspects of sexual function (Schover, 1993). A recent study (Goldenberg, Bruchovsky, Gleave, Sullivan, & Akakura, 1995) has shown that intermittent androgen suppression can control prostate cancer in some cases and that, during off-treatment periods, sexual function and other quality of life measures improve significantly. These preliminary data have suggested that a drug holiday approach may decrease the impact of prostate cancer treatment on sexual function.

In summary, cancer and its medical treatments are associated with diminished sexual function in many patients. New treatment techniques are currently being investigated that may result in fewer decrements in all areas of quality of life, including sexual function.

Medications for Other Prostate Conditions

Treatment for benign prostatic hyperplasia has traditionally involved endocrinologically active drugs, which can adversely affect sexual function. For instance, Eri and Tveter (1994) noted that erectile function and sexual activity were markedly diminished in all patients receiving treatment with leuprolide, a luteinizing hormone–releasing hormone agonist. In contrast, doxazosin has recently been shown to be effective in treatment of benign prostatic hyperplasia, with no clinically significant changes in sexual function (Chapple et al., 1995). Clearly, this is preferable from the perspective of preserving adequate sexual function in the large number of men receiving treatment for this highly prevalent condition.

CONCLUSION

Overall, sexual response in both genders is mediated by multiple physiologic and psychological mechanisms, each of which can be interrupted by the effects of specific drugs. Much attention has been focused on the sexual side effects of antihypertensive and other cardiovascular drugs, although major inconsistencies have been noted in the pattern of effects observed from one drug to another. Psychotropic medications also have been frequently associated with sexual side effects. In particular, the neuroleptic and antidepressant drugs have frequently been associated with adverse sexual side effects. However, in many instances, it is difficult to differentiate sexual side effects of drug therapy from the effects of the underlying disease process. This is particularly evident in conditions such as epilepsy or cancer, which may independently affect sexual function. The review of the literature in this chapter revealed a major gender bias. Relatively few studies have specifically investigated the sexual side effects of drugs in female patients. Results of the studies have also been inconsistent, and it is unclear whether women are at greater or lesser risk of sexual side effects of chronic drug therapy. Given the strong association between sexual function and overall quality of life, it is essential for clinicians and researchers to pay greater attention to this critical aspect of patient care.

REFERENCES

Ahmad, S. (1980). Disopyrimide and impotence [Letter to the editor]. *Southern Medical Journal, 73*, 958.

Albo, M., & Steers, W.D. (1993). Oral trazodone as initial therapy for management of impotence. *Journal of Urology, 149*(Suppl.), 344A.

Ashton, A.K., Hamer, R., & Rosen, R.C. (1996). *SSRI-induced sexual dysfunction and its treatment: A large-scale retrospective study of 596 psychiatric outpatients*. Manuscript submitted for publication.

Averette, H.E., Boike, G.M., & Jarrell, M.A. (1990). Effects of cancer chemotherapy on gonadal function and reproduction. *CA-A Cancer Journal for Clinicians, 40*, 199–209.

Balon, R., Ramesh, C., & Pohl, R. (1989). Sexual dysfunction associated with diazepam but not clonazepam. *Canadian Journal of Psychiatry, 34*, 947–948.

Balon, R., Yeragani, V.K., Pohl, R., & Ramesh, C. (1993). Sexual dysfunction during antidepressant treatment. *Journal of Clinical Psychiatry, 54*, 209–212.

Bancroft, J. (1989). *Human sexuality and its problems*. New York: Churchill Livingstone.

Bansal, S. (1988). Sexual dysfunction in hypertensive men: A critical review of the literature. *Hypertension, 12*, 1–10.

Barragry, J.M., Makin, H.L.J., Trafford, D.J., & Scott, D.F. (1978). Effect of anticonvulsants on plasma testosterone and sex hormone binding globulin levels. *Journal of Neurology, Neurosurgery, and Psychiatry, 41*, 913–914.

Bauer, G.E., Hunyor, S.N., Baker, J., & Marshall, P. (1981). Clinical side effects during antihypertensive therapy: A placebo-controlled double-blind study. *Postgraduate Medical Communications, 1*, 49–54.

Bergen, D., Daugherty, S., & Eckenfels, E. (1992). Reduction of sexual activities in females taking antiepileptic drugs. *Psychopathology, 25*, 1–4.

Beto, J.A., & Bansal, V.K. (1992). Quality of life in treatment of hypertension: A metaanalysis of clinical trials. *American Journal of Hypertension, 5*, 125–133.

Blair, J.H., & Simpson, G.M. (1966). Effects of antipsychotic drugs on reproductive functions. *Diseases of the Nervous System, 27*, 645–647.

Blane, G.F. (1987). Comparative toxicity and safety profile of fenofibrate and other fibric acid derivatives. *American Journal of Medicine, 83*, 26–36.

Blay, S.L., Ferraz, M.P., & Galil, H.M. (1982). Lithium-induced male sexual impairment: Two case reports. *Journal of Clinical Psychiatry, 43*, 497–498.

Breckenridge, A. (1991). Angiotensin converting enzyme inhibitors and quality of life. *American Journal of Hypertension, 4*, 79S–82S.

Brunet, M., Rodamilans, M., Martinez-Osaba, M.J., Santamaria, J., To-Figueras, J., Torra, M., Corbella, J., & Rivera, F. (1995). Effects of long-term antiepileptic therapy on the catabolism of testosterone. *Pharmacology and Toxicology, 76*, 371–375.

Buffum, J. (1982). Pharmacosexology: The effects of drugs on sexual function. *Journal of Psychoactive Drugs, 14*, 5–44.

Bulpitt, C.J., Dollery, C.T., & Carne, S. (1976). Change in symptoms of hypertensive patients after referral to hospital clinic. *British Heart Journal, 38*, 121–128.

Burris, J.F. (1993). The USA experience with the clonidine transdermal therapaeutic system. *Clinical Autonomic Research, 3*, 391–396.

Chang, S.W., Fine, R., Siegel, D., Chesney, M., Black, D., & Hulley, S.B. (1991). The impact of diuretic therapy on reported sexual function. *Archives of Internal Medicine, 151*, 2402–2408.

Chapman, R.M. (1984). Effect of cytotoxic therapy on sexuality and gonadal function. In M.C. Perry & J.W. Yarbro (Eds.), *Toxicity in chemotherapy* (pp. 343–363). New York: Grune & Stratton.

Chapman, R.M., Sutcliffe, S.B., & Malpas, J.S. (1979). Cytotoxic-induced ovarian failure in women with Hodgkin's disease: Hormone function. *Journal of the American Medical Association, 24*, 1877–1881.

Chapman, R.M., Sutcliffe, S.B., & Malpas, J.S. (1981). Male gonadal dysfunction in Hodgkin's disease. *Journal of the American Medical Association, 245*, 1323–1328.

Chapple, C.R., Carter, P., Christmas, T.J., Kirby, R.S., Bryan, J., Milroy, E.J., & Abrams, P. (1995). A three month double-blind study of doxazosin as treatment for benign prostatic bladder obstruction. *British Journal of Urology, 75*, 809–810.

Christianson, S.A., Silfvenius, H., Saisa, J., & Nilsson, M. (1995). Life satisfaction and sexuality in patients operated for epilepsy. *Acta Neurologica Scandinavica, 92*, 1–6.

Coronary Drug Project Research Group. (1975). Clofibrate and niacin in coronary heart disease. *Journal of the American Medical Association, 231*, 360–388.

Couper-Smartt, J.D., & Rodham, R. (1973). A technique for surveying side effects of tricyclic drugs with reference to reported side effects. *Journal of Internal Medicine and Research, 1*, 473–476.

Crenshaw, T.L., & Goldberg, J.P (1996). *Sexual pharmacology: Drugs that affect sexual functioning*. New York: Norton.

Crenshaw, T.L., Goldberg, J.P., & Stern, W.C. (1987). Pharmacologic modification of psychosexual dysfunction. *Journal of Sex and Marital Therapy, 13*, 239–253.

Croog, S.H., Levine, S., Sudilovsky, A., Baume, R.M., & Clive, J. (1988). Sexual symptoms in hypertensive patients: A clinical trial of antihypertensive medications. *Archives of Internal Medicine, 148*, 788–794.

Croog, S.H., Levine, S., Testa, M.A., Brown, B., Bulpitt, C.J., Jenkins, C.D., Klerman, G.L., & Williams, G.H. (1986). The effects of antihypertensive therapy on the quality of life. *New England Journal of Medicine, 314*, 1657–1664.

Dorevitch, A., & Davis, H. (1994). Fluvoxamine-associated sexual dysfunction. *Annals of Pharmacotherapy, 28*, 872–874.

Duncan, L.D., & Bateman, N.B. (1993). Sexual function in women: Do antihypertensive drugs have an impact? *Drug Safety, 8*, 225–234.

Eri, L.M., & Tveter, K.J. (1994). Safety, side effects, and patient acceptance of the luteinizing hormone releasing hormone agonist leuprolide in treatment of benign prostatic hyperplasia. *Journal of Urology, 152*, 448–452.

Fenwick, P.B.C., Mercer, S., Grant, R., Wheeler, M., Nanjee, N., Toone, B., & Brown, D. (1986). Nocturnal penile tumescence and serum testosterone levels. *Archives of Sexual Behavior, 15*, 247–257.

Fernandez-Lopez, J.A., Siegrist, J., Hernandez-Mejia, R., Brorer, M., & Cueto-Espinar, A. (1994). Study of quality of life on rural hypertensive patients: Comparison with the general population of the same environment. *Journal of General Internal Medicine, 6*, 290–294.

Finn, S.E., Bailey, J.M., Schultz, R.T., & Faber, R. (1990). Subjective utility ratings of neuroleptics in treating schizophrenia. *Psychological Medicine, 20*, 843–848.

Fisher, S., Kent, T.A., & Bryant, S.G. (1995). Postmarketing surveillance by patient self-monitoring: Preliminary data for sertraline versus fluoxetine. *Journal of Clinical Psychiatry, 56*, 288–296.

Fontaine, F., & Chouinard, G. (1986). An open trial of fluoxetine in the treatment of obsessive–compulsive disorder. *Journal of Clinical Psychopharmacology, 6,* 98–101.

Friesen, L.V.C. (1976). Aphrodisia with mazindol. *Lancet, 2,* 974.

Galbraith, R.A., & Michnovicz, J.J. (1989). The effects of cimetidine on the oxidative metabolism of estradiol. *New England Journal of Medicine, 321,* 269–274.

Galeone, M., Moise, G., Ferrante, F., Cacioli, D., Casula, P.L., & Bignamini, A.A. (1978). Double-blind clinical comparison between a gastric-receptor agonist, proglumide, and a histamine-H$_2$ blocker, cimetidine. *Current Medical Research and Opinion, 5,* 376–382.

Gardner, E.A., & Johnston, J.A. (1985). Bupropion—An antidepressant without sexual pathophysiological action. *Journal of Clinical Psychopharmacology, 5,* 24–29.

Gartrell, N. (1986). Increased libido in women receiving trazodone. *American Journal of Psychiatry, 143,* 781–782.

Ghadirian, A.M., Annable, L., & Belanger, M.C. (1992). Lithium, benzodiazepines, and sexual function in bipolar patients. *American Journal of Psychiatry, 149,* 801–805.

Ghadirian, A.M., Chouinard, G., & Annable, L. (1982). Sexual dysfunction and plasma prolactin levels in neuroleptic-treated schizophrenic outpatients. *Journal of Nervous and Mental Disease, 170,* 643–647.

Gitlin, M.J. (1994). Psychotropic medications and their effects on sexual function: Diagnosis, biology, and treatment approaches. *Journal of Clinical Psychiatry, 55,* 406–413.

Gold, D.D., & Justino, J.D. (1988). "Bicycle kickstand" phenomenon: Prolonged erections associated with antipsychotic agents. *Southern Medical Journal, 81,* 792–794.

Goldenberg, S.L., Bruchovsky, N., Gleave, M.E., Sullivan, L.D., & Akakura, K. (1995). Intermittent androgen suppression in the treatment of prostate cancer: A preliminary report. *Urology, 45,* 839–844.

Griffith, S.R., & Zil, J.S. (1984). Priapism in a patient receiving antipsychotic therapy. *Psychosomatics, 25,* 629–631.

Haider, A., Miller, D.R., & Staton, R.D. (1993). Use of serotonergic drugs for treating depression in older patients. *Geriatrics, 48,* 48–51.

Harrison, W.M., Stewart, J., Ehrhardt, A.A., Rabkin, J., McGrath, P., Liebowitz, M., & Quitkin, F.M. (1985). Effects of antidepressants on sexual function: A controlled study. *Journal of Clinical Psychopharmacology, 6,* 144–149.

Heel, R.C., Brogden, R.N., Speight, T.M., & Avery, G.S. (1979). Atenolol: A review of its pharmacological properties and therapeutic efficacy in angina pectoris and hypertension. *Drugs, 17,* 425–460.

Hellerstein, D., Yanowitch, P., & Rosenthal, J. (1993). A randomized double-blind study of fluoxetine versus placebo in treatment of dysthymia. *American Journal of Psychiatry, 150,* 1169–1175.

Hodge, R.H., Harward, M.P., West, M.S., Krongaard-DeMong, L., & Kowal-Neeley, M.B. (1991). Sexual function of women taking antihypertension agents: A comparative study. *Journal of General Internal Medicine, 6,* 290–294.

Hogan, M.J., Wallin, J.D., & Baer, R.M. (1980). Antihypertensive therapy and male sexual dysfunction. *Psychosomatics, 21,* 235–237.

Hsu, J.H., & Shen, W.W. (1995). Male sexual side effects associated with antidepressants: A descriptive clinical study of 32 patients. *International Journal of Psychiatry in Medicine, 25,* 191–201.

Hughs, J.M. (1964). Failure to ejaculate with chlordiazepoxide. *American Journal of Psychiatry, 121,* 610–611.

Isojarvi, J.I., Repo, M., Pakarinen, A.J., Lukkarinen, O., & Myllyla, V.V. (1995). Carbamazepine, phenytoin, sex hormones, and sexual function in men with epilepsy. *Epilepsia, 36,* 366–370.

Jensen, R.T., Collen, M.J., McAuthur, K.E., Howard, J.M., Maton, P.N., Cherner, G., & Gordner, J.D. (1984). Comparison of the effectiveness of ranitidine and cimetidine in inhibiting acid secretions in patients with gastric hypersecretory states. *American Journal of Medicine, 77,* 90–105.

Jensen, R.T., Collen, M.J., Pandol, S.J., Allende, H.D., Raufman, J.P., Bissonnette, B.M., Duncan, R.C., Durgin, P.L., Gillin, J.C., & Gardner, J.D. (1983). Cimetidine-induced impotence and breast changes in patients with gastric hypersecretory states. *New England Journal of Medicine, 308,* 883–887.

Jensen, P., Jensen, S.B., Sorensen, P.S., Bjerre, B.D., Klysner, R., Brinch, K., Jespersen, B., & Nielsen, H. (1990). Sexual dysfunction in male and female patients with epilepsy: A study of 86 outpatients. *Archives of Sexual Behavior, 19,* 1–14.

Kaplan, H.S. (1992). A neglected issue: The sexual side effects of current treatments for breast cancer. *Journal of Sex and Marital Therapy, 18,* 3–19.

Kline, M.D. (1989). Fluoxetine and anorgasmia. *American Journal of Psychiatry, 146,* 804–805.

Knigge, U., Thuesen, B., & Christiansen, P.M. (1986). Histaminergic regulation of prolactin secretion: Dose–response relationship and possible involvement of the dopaminergic system. *Journal of Clinical Endocrinology and Metabolism, 62,* 491–496.

Kolodny, R.C., Masters, W.H., & Johnson, V.E. (1979). *Textbook of sexual medicine.* Boston: Little, Brown.

Kostis, J.B., Rosen, R.C., Brondolo, E., Taska, L., Smith, D.E., & Wilson, A.C. (1992). Superiority of nonpharmacological therapy compared to propranolol and placebo in men with mild hypertension: A randomized, prospective trial. *American Heart Journal, 123,* 466–467.

Kostis, J.B., Rosen, R.C., Holzer, B.C., Randolph, C., Taska, L.S., & Miller, M.II. (1990). CNS effects side effects of centrally-active antihypertensive agents: A prospective, placebo-controlled study of sleep, mood state, and cognitive and sexual function in hypertensive males. *Psychopharmacology, 102,* 163–170.

Kostis, J.B., Rosen, R.C., & Wilson, A.C. (1994). Central nervous system effects of HMG CoA reductase inhibitors: Lovastatin and pravastatin on sleep and cognitive performance in patients with hypercholesterolemia. *Journal of Clinical Pharmacology, 34,* 989–996.

Kotin, J., Wilbert, D.E., Verburg, D., & Soldinger, S.M. (1976). Thioridazine and sexual dysfunction. *American Journal of Psychiatry, 133,* 82–85.

Kowalski, A., Stanley, R., Dennerstein, L., Burrows, G., & Maguire, K.P. (1985). The sexual side effects of antidepressant medication: A double-blind comparison of two antidepressants in a non-psychiatric population. *British Journal of Psychiatry, 147,* 413–418.

Kristensen, E., & Jorgensen, P. (1987). Sexual function in lithium-treated manic–depressive patients. *Pharmacopsychiatry, 20,* 165–167.

Krupp, P., & Barnes, P. (1992). Clozapine-associated agranulocytosis: Risk and etiology. *British Journal of Psychiatry, 160*(Suppl. 17), 38–40.

Kulik, F.A., & Wilbur, R. (1982). Case report of painful ejaculation as a side effect of amoxapine. *American Journal of Psychiatry, 139,* 234–235.

Lesko, L.M., Stotland, N.L., & Segraves, R.T. (1982). Three cases of female anorgasmia associated with MAOIs. *American Journal of Psychiatry, 139,* 1353–1354.

Lindenmeyer, J.P. (1994). Risperidone: Efficacy and side effects. *Journal of Clinical Psychiatry Monograph, 12,* 53–60.

Lingjaerde, O., Ahlfors, U.G., Bech, P., Dencker, S.J., & Elgen, K. (1987). The UKU side effect rating scale: A new comprehensive rating scale for psychotropic drugs and cross-sectional study of side effects in neuroleptic-treated patients. *Acta Psychiatrica Scandinavica, 76*(Suppl. 334), 1–99.

Lydiard, R.B., Howell, E.F., Laraia, M.T., & Balenger, J.C. (1987). Sexual side effects of alprazolam [Letter to the editor]. *American Journal of Psychiatry, 144*, 254–255.

Marder, S.R., & Meibach, R.C. (1994). Risperidone in the treatment of schizophrenia. *American Journal of Psychiatry, 151*, 825–835.

Mathew, R.J., & Weinman, M.L. (1982). Sexual dysfunctions in depression. *Archives of Sexual Behavior, 11*, 323–328.

Mattson, R.H., & Cramer, J.A. (1985). Epilepsy, sex hormones, and antiepileptic drugs. *Epilepsia, 26*, 540–541.

Mattson, R.H., Cramer, J.A., Collins, J.F., Smith, D.B., Delgado-Escucta, A.V., Browne, T.R., Williamson, P.D., Treiman, D.M., McNamara, J.D., & McCutcheon, C.B. (1985). Comparison of carbamazepine, phenobarbital, phenytoin, and primidone in partial and secondary generalized tonic–clonic seizures. *New England Journal of Medicine, 313*, 145–151.

McEwen, J., & Meyboom, R.H.B. (1983). Testicular pain caused by mazindol. *British Medical Journal, 287*, 1763–1764.

McHaffie, D.J., Guz, A., & Johnston, A. (1977). Impotence in a patient on disopyramide. *Lancet, 1*, 859.

McLean, J.D., Forsythe, R.G., & Kapkin, I.A. (1983). Unusual side effects of clomipramine associated with yawning. *Canadian Journal of Psychiatry, 28*, 569–570.

Meltzer, H.Y., Lee, M.A., & Ranjan, R. (1994). Recent advances in the pharmacotherapy of schizophrenia. *Acta Psychiatrica Scandinavica, 90*(Suppl. 384), 95–101.

Merikangas, J., Prusoff, B.A., Kupfer, D.J., & Frank, E. (1985). Marital adjustment in major depression. *Journal of Affective Disorders, 9*, 5–11.

Meston, C.M., & Gorzalka, B.B. (1992). Psychoactive drugs and human sexual behavior: The role of serotonergic activity. *Journal of Psychoactive Drugs, 24*, 1–40.

Mitchell, W., Barlow, D.H., Wackett, A., Rozalewycz, J., Sbrocco, T., & Weiner, D.N. (1992, November). *Sexual responsiveness under affect induction.* Paper presented at the annual meeting of the Association for Advancement of Behavior Therapy, Boston.

Modell, J.G. (1989). Repeated observations of yawning, clitoral engorgement, and orgasm associated with fluoxetine administration. *Journal of Clinical Psychopharmacology, 9*, 63–65.

Monteiro, W.O., Noshirvani, H.F., Marks, I.M., & Lelliott, P.T. (1987). Anorgasmia from clomipramine in obsessive–compulsive disorder: A controlled trial. *British Journal of Psychiatry, 151*, 107–112.

Morrell, M.J., Sperling, M.R., Stecker, M., & Dichter, M.A. (1994). Sexual dysfunction in partial epilepsy: A deficit in physiologic sexual arousal. *Neurology, 44*, 243–247.

Morrissette, D.L., Skinner, M.H., Hoffman, B.B., Levine, R.E., & Davidson, J.M. (1993). Effects of antihypertensive drugs atenolol and nifedipine on sexual function in older men: A placebo-controlled, crossover study. *Archives of Sexual Behavior, 22*, 99–109.

Moss, H.B., & Procci, W.R. (1982). Sexual dysfunction associated with oral antihypertensive medication: A critical survey of the literature. *General Hospital Psychiatry, 4*, 121–129.

Murialdo, G., Galimbert, C.A., Fonzi, S., Manni, R., Costelli, P., Parodi, C., Solinas, G.P., Amoretti, G., & Tartara, A. (1995). Sex hormones and pituitary function in male epileptic patients with altered or normal sexuality. *Epilepsia, 36*, 360–365.

Neri, A., Aygen, M., Zukerman, Z., & Bahary, C. (1980). Subjective asssessment of sexual dysfunction of patients on long-term administration of digoxin. *Archives of Sexual Behavior, 9,* 343–347.

Nestoros, J.N., Lehman, H.E., & Ban, T.A. (1981). Sexual behavior of the male schizophrenic: The impact of illness and medications. *Archives of Sexual Behavior, 10,* 421–442.

Niv, Y. (1986). Male sexual dysfunction due to cimetidine. *Irish Medical Journal, 79,* 352.

Nurnberg, H.G., & Levine, P.E. (1987). Spontaneous remission of MAOI-induced anorgasmia. *American Journal of Psychiatry, 144,* 805–807.

Nutt, D., Hackman, A., & Hawton, K. (1986). Increased sexual function in benzodiazepine withdrawal. *Lancet, 2,* 1101–1102.

Othmer, E., & Othmer, S.C. (1987). Effect of buspirone on sexual dysfunction in patients with generalized anxiety disorder. *Journal of Clinical Psychiatry, 48,* 201–203.

Page, C., Benamin, S., & Lappin, F. (1987). A long-term retrospective follow-up study of patients treated with prophylactic lithium carbonate. *British Journal of Psychiatry, 150,* 175–179.

Patt, N. (1985). More on trazodone and priapism [Letter to the editor]. *American Journal of Psychiatry, 142,* 783–784.

Patterson, W.M. (1993). Fluoxetine induced sexual dysfunction [Letter to the editor]. *Journal of Clinical Psychiatry, 54,* 71.

Peden, N.R., Cargill, N.R., Browning, M.C., Saunders, J.H., & Wormsley, K.G. (1979). Male sexual dysfunction during treatment with cimetidine. *British Medical Journal, 1,* 659.

Peden, N.R., & Wormsley, K.G. (1982). Effect of cimetidine on gonadal function in man [Letter to the editor]. *British Journal of Clinical Pharmacology, 14,* 565.

Plowman, P.N. (1993). Tamoxifen as adjuvant therapy in breast cancer: Current status. *Drugs, 46,* 819–833.

Post, L.L. (1994). Sexual side effects of psychiatric medications in women. *American Journal of Psychiatry, 151,* 1246–1247.

Preskorn, S.H. (1995). Comparison of the tolerability of bupropion, fluoxetine, imipramine, nefazodone, paroxetine, sertraline, and venlafaxine. *Journal of Clinical Psychiatry, 56*(Suppl.), 12–21.

Price, J., & Grunhaus, L.J. (1990). Treatment of clomipramine-induced anorgasmia: A case report. *Journal of Clinical Psychiatry, 51,* 32–33.

Prisant, L.M., Carr, A.A., Bottini, P.B., Solursh, D.S., & Solursh, L.P. (1994). Sexual dysfunction with antihypertensive drugs. *Archives of Internal Medicine, 154,* 730–736.

Pritchard, P.B. (1980). Hyposexuality: A complication of partial-complex epilepsy. *Transactions of the American Neurological Association, 105,* 32–33.

Raboch, J., Smolik, P., & Soucek, V. (1983). Lithium and male sexuality. *Ceskoslovaska Psychiatrie, 79,* 19–21.

Riley, A.J., & Riley, E.J. (1986a). Cyproheptadine and antidepressant-induced anorgasmia. *British Journal of Psychiatry, 148,* 217–218.

Riley, A.J., & Riley, E.J. (1986b). The effect of a single dose of diazepam on female sexual response induced by masturbation. *Sexual and Marital Therapy, 1,* 49–53.

Rosen, R.C. (1991). Alcohol and drug effects on sexual response: Human experimental and clinical studies. *Annual Review of Sex Research, 2,* 119–180.

Rosen, R.C., & Ashton, A.K. (1993). Prosexual drugs: Empirical status of the "new aphrodisiacs." *Archives of Sexual Behavior, 22,* 521–543.

Rosen, R.C., & Beck, J.G. (1988). *Patterns of sexual arousal: Psychophysiological processes and clinical applications*. New York: Guilford Press.

Rosen, R.C., Kostis, J.B., & Jekelis, A.W. (1988). Beta-blocker effects on sexual function in normal males. *Archives of Sexual Behavior, 17*, 241–255.

Rosen, R.C., Kostis, J.B., Jekelis, A.W., & Taska, L.S. (1994). Sexual sequelae of antihypertensive drugs: Treatment effects on self-report and physiological measures in middle-aged male hypertensives. *Archives of Sexual Behavior, 23*, 135–152.

Rosenthal, J., Hemlock, C., Hellerstein, D.J., Yanowitch, P., Kasch, K., Schupak, C., Samstag, L., & Winston, A. (1992). A preliminary study of serotonergic antidepressants in treatment of dysthymia. *Progress in Neuro-Psychopharmacology and Biological Psychiatry, 16*, 933–941.

Rothschild, A.J. (1995). Selective serotonin reuptake inhibitor-induced sexual dysfunction: Efficacy of a drug holiday. *American Journal of Psychiatry, 152*, 1514–1516.

Rubin, R.T., Poland, R.E., O'Connor, D., Gouin, P.R., & Tower, B.B. (1976). Selective neuroendocrine effects of low-dose haloperidol in normal adult men. *Psychopharmacology, 47*, 135–140.

Rubin, R.T., Poland, R.E., & Tower, B.B. (1976). Prolactin-related testosterone secretion in normal adult men. *Journal of Clinical Endocrinology and Metabolism, 42*, 112–116.

Saenz de Tejada, I., Ware, J.C., Blanco, R., Pittard, J.T., Nadig, P.W., Azadzoi, K.M., Krane, R.J., & Goldstein, I. (1991). Pathophysiology of prolonged penile erection associated with trazodone use. *Journal of Urology, 145*, 60–64.

Sangal, R. (1985). Inhibited female orgasm as a side effect of alprazolam. *American Journal of Psychiatry, 142*, 1223–1224.

Scher, M., Krieger, J., & Jergens, S. (1983). Trazodone and priapism. *American Journal of Psychiatry, 140*, 1362–1363.

Schneider, J., & Kaffarnik, H. (1975). Impotence in patients treated with clofibrate. *Atherosclerosis, 21*, 455–475.

Schoenberger, J.A., Testa, M., Ross, A.D., Brennan, W.K., & Bannon, J.A. (1990). Efficacy, safety, and quality-of-life assessment of captopril antihypertensive therapy in clinical practice. *Archives of Internal Medicine, 150*, 301–306.

Schover, L.R. (1993). Sexual rehabilitation after treatment for prostate cancer. *Cancer, 71*, 1024–1030.

Schover, L.R., & Jensen, S.B. (1988). *Sexuality and chronic illness: A comprehensive approach*. New York: Guilford Press.

Segraves, R.T. (1987). Treatment of premature ejaculation with lorazepam. *American Journal of Psychiatry, 144*, 1240.

Segraves, R.T. (1989). Effects of psychotropic drugs on human erection and ejaculation. *Archives of General Psychiatry, 46*, 275–284.

Segraves, R.T., Madsen, R., Carter, C.S., & Davis, J.M. (1985). Erectile dysfunction associated with pharmacological agents. In R.T. Segraves & H.W. Schoenberg (Eds.), *Diagnosis and treatment of erectile disturbances* (pp. 23–63). New York: Plenum Press.

Semmens, J.P., & Semmens, F.J. (1978). Inadequate vaginal lubrication. *Medical Aspects of Human Sexuality, 12*, 58–71.

Shader, R.I. (1964). Sexual dysfunction associated with thioridazine hydrochloride. *Journal of the American Medical Association, 188*, 1007–1009.

Shen, W.W. (1982). Female orgasmic inhibition by amoxapine. *American Journal of Psychiatry, 139*, 1220–1221.

Simpson, G.M., Blair, J.H., & Amuso, D. (1965). Effects of antidepressants on genitourinary function. *Diseases of the Nervous System, 26*, 787–789.

Smith, D.M., & Levitt, S.S. (1993). Association of fluoxetine and return of sexual potency in three elderly men. *Journal of Clinical Psychiatry, 54*, 317–319.

Smith, P.J., & Talbert, R.L. (1986). Sexual dysfunction with antihypertensive and antipsychotic agents. *Clinical Pharmacology, 5*, 373–384.

Sovner, R. (1983). Anorgasmia associated with imipramine but not desipramine: Case report. *Journal of Clinical Psychiatry, 44*, 345–346.

Spence, R.W., & Celestin, L.R. (1979). Gynaecomastia associated with cimetidine. *Gut, 20*, 154–157.

Stevenson, J.G., & Umstead, G.S. (1984). Sexual dysfunction due to antihypertensive agents. *Drug Intelligence and Clinical Pharmacology, 18*, 113–121.

Stevenson, R.W.D., & Solyom, L. (1990). The aphrodisiac effect of fenfluramine: Two case reports of a possible side effect to the use of fenfluramine in the treatment of bulimia. *Journal of Clinical Psychopharmacology, 10*, 69–71.

Stoffer, S.S., Hynes, K.M., Jiang, N.S., & Ryan, R.J. (1973). Digoxin and abnormal serum hormone levels. *Journal of the American Medical Association, 225*, 1643–1644.

Sullivan, G. (1988). Increased libido in three men treated with trazodone. *Journal of Clinical Psychiatry, 49*, 202–203.

Thase, M.E., Reynolds, C.F., Glanz, C.M., Jennings, J.R., Sewitch, D.E., Kupfer, D.J., & Frank, E. (1987). Nocturnal penile tumescence in depressed men. *American Journal of Psychiatry, 144*, 89–92.

Thompson, J.W., Ware, M.R., & Blashfield, R.K. (1990). Psychotropic medication and priapism: A comprehensive review. *Journal of Clinical Psychiatry, 51*, 430–433.

Toone, B.K. (1985). Sexual disorders in epilepsy. In T.A. Redley & B.S. Meldrum (Eds.), *Recent advances in epilepsy* (pp. 233–260). Edinburgh, Scotland: Churchill Livingstone.

Toone, B.K., Wheeler, M., & Fenwick, P.B.C. (1980). Sex hormone changes in male epileptics. *Clinical Endocrinology, 12*, 391–395.

Uhde, T.W., Tancer, M.E., & Shea, C.A. (1988). Sexual dysfunction related to alprazolam treatment of social phobia [Letter to the editor]. *American Journal of Psychiatry, 145*, 531–532.

Van Thiel, P.H., Gavaler, B.S., Smith, W.I., & Paul, G. (1979). Hypothalamic-pituitary-gonadal dysfunction in men using cimetidine. *New England Journal of Medicine, 300*, 1012–1015.

Verhulst, J., & Schneidman, B. (1981). Schizophrenia and sexual functioning. *Hospital & Community Psychiatry, 32*, 259–262.

Vinarova, E., Uhlir, O., Stika, L., & Vinar, O. (1972). Side effects of lithium administration. *Activitas Nervosa Sperior (Praha), 14*, 105–107.

Ware, J.C., Pittard, J.T., Nadig, P.W., Morrison, J.L., & Quinn, J.B. (1987). Trazodone: Its effects on nocturnal penile tumescence. *Sleep Research, 16*, 157.

Warner, M.D., Peabody, C.A., & Whiteford, H.A. (1987). Trazodone and priapism. *Journal of Clinical Psychiatry, 48*, 244–245.

Wartman, S.A. (1983). Sexual side effects of antihypertensive drugs: Treatment strategies and strictures. *Postgraduate Medicine, 73*, 133–138.

Wassertheil-Smoller, S., Blaufox, M.D., Oberman, A., Davis, B.R., Swencionis, C., Knerr, M.O., Hawkins, C.M., & Langford, H.G. (1991). Effects of antihypertensives on sexual function and quality of life: The TAIM Study. *Annals of Internal Medicine, 114*, 613–620.

Watts, R.J. (1981). Sexual functioning, health beliefs, and compliance with high blood pressure medications. *Nursing Research, 31*, 278–283.

Wei, M., Macera, C.A., Davis, D.R., Hornung, C.A., Nankin, H.R., & Blair, S.N. (1994). Total cholesterol and high density lipoprotein cholesterol as important predictors of erectile dysfunction. *American Journal of Epidemiology, 140*, 930–937.

Weir, M.R., Josselson, J., Ekelund, L.G., Korc, M., Pool, J.L., Stein, G.H. Wolbach, R.A., & Champion, D. (1991). Nicardipine as antihypertensive monotherapy: Positive effects on quality of life. *Journal of Human Hypertension, 5*, 205–213.

Wicklund, I. (1994). Quality of life and cost-effectiveness in the treatment of hypertension. *Journal of Clinical Pharmacology and Therpaeutics, 19*, 81–87.

Winter, C.C., & McDonell, G. (1988). Experience with 105 patients with priapism: Update review of all aspects. *Journal of Urology, 140*, 980–983.

Wolfe, M.M. (1979). Impotence on cimetidine therapy. *New England Journal of Medicine, 300*, 94.

Wood, D.R., Reimherr, F.W., Wender, P.H., & Johnson, G.E. (1976). Diagnosis and treatment of minimal brain dysfunction in adults. *Archives of General Psychiatry, 33*, 1453–1460.

Zajecka, J., Fawcett, J., Schaff, M., Jeffriess, H., & Guy, C. (1991). The role of serotonin in sexual dysfunction: Fluoxetine-associated orgasm dysfunction. *Journal of Clinical Psychiatry, 52*, 66–68.

Summary of Prescription Drug Effects on Sexual Function

Drug	Desire	Arousal	Orgasm	Other
Antihypertensives				
amlodipine				0 (general sexual function)
atenolol	0	0	0	Decreased testosterone
betaxolol				0 (general sexual function)
captopril				0 (general sexual function)
clonidine	M-, F-	M-, F-	F+	Decreased testosterone
enalapril				0 (general sexual function)
guanethidine	F-		F-	Limited data
hydralazine				0 (female general sexual function); limited data
labetalol				0 (female general sexual function); limited data

Note: M+, data indicate excitatory effect on this aspect of sexual function in men; M-, data indicate inhibitory effect on this aspect of sexual function in men; F+, data indicate excitatory effect on this aspect of sexual function in women; F-, data indicate inhibitory effect on this aspect of sexual function in women; 0, data indicate no effect on this aspect of sexual function.

Drug	Desire	Arousal	Orgasm	Other
methyldopa	M-	M-		Decreased testosterone
nadolol				0 (female general sexual function); limited data
nicardipine				Improved general sexual function
nifedipine	0	0	0	
pindolol		M-		
prazosin	F-			
propranolol	M-, F-	M-, F-	F-	Decreased testosterone
reserpine	F-		F-	Limited data
spironolactone	F-		F-	Limited data
thiazide (oral)	M-, F-	M-, F-	M-	Decreased testosterone
thiazide (transdermal patch)				Fewer sexual problems than oral administration
Anticholesterolemics				
clofibrate	M-	M-		
lovastatin		M+		
pravastatin		M+		
Digoxin	M-	M-	M-	Increased luteinizing hormone; decreased testosterone
Antiarrhythmics				
disopyramide		M-		
Antidepressants				
amitriptyline		M-		
amoxapine		M-, F-		
bupropion	M+, F+		F+	Increased global ratings on sexuality
clomipramine			M-, F-	Spontaneous ejaculation
fluoxetine			M-, F-	In some cases, spontaneous orgasm
fluvoxamine			M-	
imipramine		M-, F-	M-, F-	
lithium carbonate	M-	M-		
mianserin		M-		
monoamine oxidase inhibitors (in general)			M-, F-	
nefazodone	0	0	0	

Drug	Desire	Arousal	Orgasm	Other
paroxetine			M-, F-	
phenelzine		M-, F-	M-, F-	
sertraline			M-, F-	
trazodone	M+, F+	M+		Penile and clitoral priapism
venlafaxine			M-, F-	
Anxiolytics				Positive effects may be more likely in anxious patients
alprazolam	M-, F- M+, F-	M-, F-	M-, F- M+, F+	
buspirone	0	0	0	
diazepam	M-, F- M+, F+	M-	M-, F- M+, F+	
Neuroleptics	M-, F-	M-, F-	M-, F-	Priapism
chlorpromazine				Priapism; high levels of general sexual dysfunction
chlorprothixene				Priapism; high levels of general sexual dysfunction
flupenthixol				Low levels of general sexual dysfunction
fluphenazine	F-	M-, F-	M-	Menstrual irregularities; priapism; low levels of general sexual dysfunction
haloperidol		M-		Priapsim
mesoridazine				Priapism
molindone				Priapism
perphenazine				Priapism
risperidone	M-, F-	M-, F-	M-, F-	Priapism
thioridazine		M-	M-	Painful ejaculation; sustained nonpainful erection
trifluoperizine				Priapism
Stimulants				
fenfluramine	F+			Disturbing increase of desire reported
mazindol	F+		M-	

Drug	Desire	Arousal	Orgasm	Other
methylphenidate			F+	
Anticonvulsants				
carbamazepine				Equivocal data; general sexual problems reported
clonazepam				General sexual problems; limited data
phenobarbital	M-	M-	M-, F-	
phenytoin				General sexual problems reported
primidone	M-	M-		
valprolate				Equivocal data; general sexual problems reported
Antiulcer				
cimetidine	M-, F-	M-		Gynecomastia; decreased sperm count; hormonal disturbances
ranitidine	0	0	0	
Anticancer				
antiandrogens	M-	M-	M-	
busulfan				Decreased sperm count; amenorrhea
chlorambucil				Decreased sperm count; amenorrhea
cyclophosphamide				Decreased sperm count; amenorrhea
procarbazine				Decreased sperm count; amenorrhea
tamoxifen	F-	F+, F-		
Prostate				
doxazosin	0	0	0	
leuprolide	M-	M-	M-	

CHAPTER 7

Living with a Disability:
A Woman's Perspective

Karen Hwang

Maintaining a sexual identity as a woman with a disability is no easy task. For years, sexuality and disability have been considered mutually exclusive terms. People with disabilities have traditionally been viewed by society as incomplete humans, often pitied, avoided, and treated as second class, even by health care professionals. Even today, there is still a prevailing social attitude that individuals with disabilities are incapable of, or simply not inclined toward, engaging in the same kind of sexual relationships that nondisabled individuals are. Women in particular are affected by this stereotype. In a society that still often judges a woman's attractiveness and desirability largely on standards of physical perfection, women with disabilities are by definition excluded.

This social attitude is manifested in a number of ways. Girls who are either born disabled or incur a disability in childhood tend to be treated differently from nondisabled girls (Brecker, 1993; Carolan, 1984). They are frequently overprotected by their parents and especially sheltered from men. Parents of girls with disabilities often have trouble acknowledging their daughters as potentially sexual beings who are capable of making and rearing their own families. Such sheltering can lead to general social inhibition and emotional problems, although one researcher (Brecker, 1993) has suggested that girls with disabilities who leave home and reside at college have a better self-concept compared with those who remain at home. Few ever receive sex education in schools, partially because many sex education classes are offered during gym classes, from which they are likely to be excused. Mostly, though, they do not receive sex education because of a general attitude that sex education is unnecessary—as the girls so often hear, "No one is going to marry them anyway." As a result of this lack of preparation, as well as the devastating blows to self-esteem that such repeated messages can deliver, girls with disabilities also tend to be at greater risk physically and psychologically to abuse, a topic that is discussed in this chapter.

Women who acquire a disability after adulthood face a different set of issues, mostly centered around the attitudes toward disability they had previously held. Predisability stereotypes and change in roles may also affect self-esteem. For instance, women whose cultural roles have revolved primarily around the bearing and rearing of children may suddenly find themselves valueless with the perceived loss of that role. On the dating scene, there is evidence suggesting that the romantic interests of single women with disabilities sometimes are not reciprocated (Brecker, 1993). The same study found that married women's relationships are less affected, although other findings have indicated that many established marriages break down when one partner becomes totally dependent (Greengross, 1976), especially when wives become disabled, likely because of the loss of the wife's traditional role as caregiver. However, the more solid the marriage is on other levels, the better able it is to withstand the emotional crises brought on by an adult-onset disability (Brecker, 1993; Greengross, 1976).

Institutional policies are also built around the stereotype of people with disabilities as sexless beings. Until recently, most of the residential care facilities and independent living centers that house a large number of disabled residents simply paid no attention to residents' sexual needs. Living arrangements today still tend to be sex-segregated for convenience, and staff are often puritanical in outlook, viewing issues of sex and sexual feelings as "inconvenient" rather than natural (Carolan, 1984). In addition, facilities tend to be understaffed, and little provision is made for privacy for couples. Even couples living in the community face social and economic handicaps as well. Many personal care attendant programs are set up to accommodate only one person. In addition, if one or both parties involved depends on Medicaid or Supplemental Security Income (SSI), there are severe financial consequences for marriage (Brecker, 1993).

Another concern for women in the community is the lack of access to reproductive health care, particularly the lack of accessible gynecology offices (Brecker, 1993). Gynecologists' examination tables are obviously designed primarily for the convenience of the doctor, not the patient. The height and the short length of the table makes transferring from a wheelchair extremely difficult with assistance and just about impossible without. In addition, many women complain that physicians who are inadequately informed about the specific conditions of their disability may ignore their input, overtreat them, or be unaware of the complications and side effects that may be associated with the use of certain contraceptives and other medications (Charlifue, Gerhart, Menter, Whiteneck, & Manley, 1992).

In addition, the portrayal of characters with disabilities—especially women—in films and television programs is overwhelmingly asexual (Medgyesi, 1994). Although representation is increasing, the characters portrayed are nevertheless generally expected to look attractive and practice "appropriate" gender-specific behaviors. Husbands tragically unable to pursue new loves because they are burdened by disabled, insane, or chronically ill wives have been a staple of romantic fiction since Charlotte Bronte wrote *Jane Eyre*. Women with disabilities in soap operas generally tend to languish pathetically at home clad in robes until they have the decency to die poignantly. Or, they remove themselves from the plot so their husbands can find "real" women; that is, unless they become miraculously "cured" and then go on to resume normal lives. Although a few exceptions do exist, the vast majority of Hollywood productions still tend to portray disabled individuals of both sexes as heroic, tragic, or angry—in short, as anything but real people attempting to lead normal lives.

Members of the disabled community have been trying to change this view. In 1987, a woman with quadriplegia posed for *Playboy* magazine, a move that drew much public attention but received mixed reactions from feminists and disability activists alike. In addition, advertisements aimed at members of the disabled community have begun to expand the scope of images of women. A recent wheelchair company advertisement, for example, showed a beautiful model draped sensually over her wheelchair; another depicted a pregnant woman in a wheelchair, also suggestively posed. Some viewers may have found those images offensive and sexist, exploiting women with disabilities to sell a commercial product the way nondisabled women have traditionally been exploited. Others may have applauded the advertisers for taking a bold stance in breaking down attitudinal barriers.

I know that before I became disabled (from a spinal cord injury in 1988), the most thought I had ever given to any of these issues was when I wrote a brief chapter on disability during an undergraduate women's studies class. I must admit I never thought those issues would apply to me. At the time I wrote this chapter on living with a disability, I was a 29-year-old spinal cord–injury survivor of almost 8 years, single, with a master's degree, and reasonably free from economic worries. Therefore, keep in mind that certain experiences or insights may not necessarily resonate with women of different ages, disabilities, or other life circumstances. Where possible, I have drawn on outside sources to supplement my own experiences.

I have a spinal cord injury at the C-3 to C-4 level, which means I have no functional sensation or mobility below the top of my shoulders. Yet I suppose in many ways I could have been much worse off. Women who were injured at any level 20 to 30 years ago were told point-blank to expect no picture of future sexuality at all. I was lucky, too, to have a partner who was extremely accepting of my disability, and who was actually more convinced than I that I was still desirable and worth keeping as a romantic partner. To this day, I have no doubt that having someone who loved me and believed in me was invaluable in helping me bolster my self-image and keep up the self-confidence to face the world with a newly acquired spinal cord injury.

There is no hiding the wheelchair—it's impossible. The best thing a person can do is simply treat the wheelchair as just another aspect of one's physical appearance, the way a person might treat his or her height or weight—and be natural and comfortable with it. A large component of attractiveness depends not on what a woman looks like, but how she presents herself. I have heard many women in wheelchairs admit that they frequently have to become more assertive and forward when pursuing a romantic partner. The truth is, if a person does not see himself or herself as attractive and desirable, then likely nobody else will either. It is a little surprising to admit this, but since I have become disabled, I am much less anxious about my physical appearance. It is almost as if knowing I have much less chance at being considered attractive in the conventional sense has freed me from the temptation to conform to the standards of conventional attractiveness and has allowed me instead to concentrate on developing and projecting the inner qualities that are uniquely mine.

SURVEY SAYS...

Just out of curiosity, I did a little research to find out just where my own experience fell within the experience of spinal cord–injured women in general. Searching through the MEDLINE database, I was able to find broad-based surveys aimed at assessing the sexual activities and concerns of spinal cord–injured women following rehabilitation.

The first study compared the pre- and postinjury attitudes toward sexuality of spinal cord–injured women who had done their initial rehabilitation at Craig Hospital in Colorado (Charlifue et al., 1992). As I expected, this survey found a general decrease in sexual activity following injury and rehabilitation. In addition, nearly half the respondents described sex to be "less important" to them than before. That priority shift made me wonder: Is it an indication that everyday activities—such as dressing, transferring, and engaging in general personal care—simply need greater attention than previously? Or, more disturbingly, did it indicate that messages received during rehabilitation somehow lead women to internalize the expectation that women with disabilities learn to subjugate and devalue their sexual selves? Respondents also reported they felt less sexually desirable and skillful following injury; women with higher-level injuries rated themselves the lowest in these categories. Clearly, pre-injury attitudes about disability—and the nondisabled ideal—have a great impact on self-confidence and self-image.

The second study (White, Rintala, Hart, & Fuhrer, 1993), conducted in Texas, focused on current attitudes and behaviors of spinal cord–injured women living in the community. As one might expect, given the results of the Craig Hospital study, the researchers found that sex life received a low priority rating and a low satisfaction rating among women. These two findings are related in that lack of satisfaction with a certain feature of a person's life may lead him or her to downplay the importance of that feature. Interestingly, the category of "family relationships" received much higher ratings in both indexes. For many women, the categories of sexuality and family relationships may be so tightly linked—particularly for those women who identify strongly with roles as wives or mothers—that the format of the survey may impose an artificial distinction.

Despite these apparently discouraging attitudes, women with spinal cord injuries are living sexually active lives. In the Texas sample of women surveyed (White et al., 1993), 83% had engaged in physical relationships postinjury and 65% within the preceding 12 months (physical relationships not necessarily involving intercourse). This strong evidence negates the stereotypical image of women with disabilities as nonsexual. The most relevant factor regarding sexual activity was not the level of injury or functional impairment but the length of time postinjury, which should be encouraging information to pass on to all newly injured women, especially those with higher-level injuries. The Texas sample also showed that concerns with personal unattractiveness were less prevalent among women who had more years postinjury. Clearly, even though women with spinal cord injuries need a certain amount of time to cope and make adjustments, their self-esteem and sexual activity do eventually rebound following reintegration into the community.

A third study by Sipski and Alexander (1993) that compared pre- and postinjury patterns of sexual behavior in women also found a general decrease in sexual activity overall postinjury. Although there was a change in the preference of sexual activities enjoyed by subjects, most of the respondents reported they were adjusting "well" after injury. In addition, this particular study found that individual differences in pre-injury sexual behavior (rather than any factor related to the disability itself) appeared to be the best predictor of behavior postinjury. These findings should come as an encouragement to any woman who may believe that sexual life stops with a spinal cord injury.

DATING AND OTHER SOCIAL HAZARDS

For the woman with a disability looking to enter or reenter the world of romance, the process can be frustrating and sometimes dangerous. As a result of a variety of social attitudes about women and disability, these women often are to rejected as romantic and sexual partners. To make matters worse, some men in wheelchairs will reject out of hand the idea of dating or marrying a woman with a disability (Medgyesi, 1994). Because women in wheelchairs fail to live up to society's expectation of how a "real" woman looks, disabled men—particularly men disabled late in life—may look for nondisabled women to make them feel equal and whole in the eyes of society. In addition, men who expect women to assume the traditional caregiving role in a relationship often unfairly assume that a disability renders a woman incapable of nurturing.

Disability advocate Barbara Waxman (as cited in Medgyesi, 1994) has suggested that disabled men who reject disabled women do so out of their own self-hatred and because they have the mistaken notion that being coupled with a nondisabled partner reduces the social stigma of their own disability. According to this argument, a man with a disability who wishes to deny or avoid that aspect of himself purposely seeks a nondisabled woman as a "trophy" to validate his manhood. Ironically, this attitude may have been inadvertently encouraged during early attempts at sexual counseling by rehabilitation therapists, who would show male inpatients films of quadriplegic and paraplegic men in various sexual positions with nondisabled women (Medgyesi, 1994).

On the other hand, some men and women are *attracted* to disability (Storrs, 1996). If that sounds too good to be true, it is. Psychologists generally believe that these "devotees" need the kind of attention and love that they feel can be met by having a disability, and that their attraction is thus actually a form of projection. Relationships with devotees seldom work out in the long term. For the person fixated on a body part, projection becomes impossible when the wheelchair (or cast, or stump) becomes a real person.

I like to think that the great majority of men are neither unduly repelled by disability nor unduly fascinated by it. Perhaps it has simply never occurred to them that a woman with a disability can be considered a candidate for romance or marriage. At the same time, it is unreasonable to blame every rejection on the wheelchair. It is up to a woman to present herself as a full package, to make herself interesting enough so that potential romantic partners will see beyond the stereotypes. Sometimes a woman with a disability has to function in society as an educator and "consciousness-raiser," especially if the people around her are unfamiliar or uncomfortable with disability. This responsibility can seem burdensome, but the results may be well worth the effort.

CARE AND MAINTENANCE OF INTIMATE RELATIONSHIPS

For women already involved in relationships or embarking on new relationships, disability presents a unique constellation of problems and challenges. Wheelchairs, especially the large-power variety, can present physical barriers to touching, hugging, and closeness. In addition, pain and spasticity can also limit physical or psychological closeness. Decreased mobility and the need for physical assistance can result in a significant loss of spontaneity, and physical dependency often forces a couple to completely reinvent the dynamics of their relationship in terms of roles, power, and communication.

An important lesson to keep in mind in terms of sustaining a relationship is that it is impossible to expect a spouse or partner to be both a lover and a caregiver all the time. Spouses who help care for disabled partners are more at risk for emotional stress, burnout, and depression than those who do not (Alexander, 1991; Smith, 1989). It is important for both the disabled and nondisabled partners in the relationship to find peers who are going through similar experiences to share, support, and validate each other's feelings. Also, couples should not expect to spend all their time together. Partners should be allowed to take an occasional break and pursue separate interests without feeling guilty.

Relationships in which both partners are disabled present their own problems. A disabled partner might be more understanding about the headaches and frustrations that come from living with a disability, but one cannot always make that assumption. Being physically unable to take care of one another means that a couple's range of activities can be quite limited. In addition, having to rely on an aide makes privacy difficult. Couples in this situation need to come up with ways to preserve privacy, by setting up boundaries in the home with live-in aides or by making time to be by themselves. Above all, they should not be afraid to speak out and be honest. Being physically dependent does not imply becoming passive. By contrast, the less people are able to do for themselves, the more clear and direct they must be when making their wishes known.

At times, it is hard not to feel like a burden on one's partner. Partial or total physical dependency can put a unique strain on a relationship, although having a partner with a positive attitude is certainly helpful. Because women have traditionally been socialized to assume the role of caregiver, some men, particularly more conservative ones, may feel uncomfortable taking on this role. In addition, a woman may be unused to assuming a directive role during intimacy and sex. There are no easy solutions; each couple needs to find their own comfort level in this situation. It helps if they can view it as a challenge and are willing to be creative.

Interestingly, there is evidence of a difference between women and men in terms of the main impact of a disability on a relationship (White et al., 1993). Women after a spinal cord injury appear to place a higher priority on seeking emotional coping techniques for themselves and their partners than about methods and techniques for achieving sexual satisfaction. In contrast, spinal cord–injured men have more concerns with achieving sexual satisfaction, perhaps because a spinal cord injury has a greater direct effect on the physical aspect of male sexual function, or perhaps because sexuality discussions during rehabilitation focus overwhelmingly on men's issues. Alternatively, perhaps men and women are socialized to view sexual relationships in different ways and, thus, assign primary importance to different elements. This is, of course, not to say that men are only out for their own satisfaction, but merely to suggest that a disability may affect different partners in different ways.

More than ever, communication is vital, especially during intimacy and sex. If mobility and sensation are impaired, then a couple may have to rely on verbal and auditory cues to maintain arousal. Often, a disability forces a couple to redefine sex. Although many nondisabled people view sex as simply a means to an orgasm, I think the experience for people with disabilities becomes broadened to encompass any form of sharing of mental or physical pleasure with a partner. To love your partner means to enjoy whatever pleasures can be shared by both. For many people, actual intercourse becomes less essential; as long as love exists between partners, satisfaction will be the culmination of whatever type of sex that couple is able (or simply chooses) to have.

Pregnancy and motherhood constitute a vital part of the sexual identity for many women. In the past, pregnancy was almost always contraindicated for women with disabilities. One reason was the so-called eugenics argument (Brecker, 1993), the idea that congenitally disabled women be discouraged from having children and passing on their "defective" genes. Another reason was the traditional view held by society that women with disabilities are frail and would simply be physically and psychologically overwhelmed by the demands of pregnancy, childbirth, and child rearing. This lack of information and understanding, unfortunately, has led to a high number of coerced sterilizations and hysterectomies (Brecker, 1993). However, with a little extra monitoring, pregnancy and natural childbirth are becoming acceptable—even routine—for women with disabilities. Furthermore, contrary to popular belief, there is no evidence to indicate that disabled mothers are any less effective at parenting than their nondisabled peers (Smith, 1989).

A very real hazard for women with disabilities in relationships is abuse. The proportion of women with disabilities who have experienced domestic violence has been estimated as high as 60%, compared with 33% of women in general (Russell, 1995). In addition, the incidence of sexual abuse among girls with disabilities is twice as high as among nondisabled girls. Much of the reason for this abuse is that women with disabilities are perceived as particularly easy targets by people—particularly men—who feel a need to dominate and control. Violence can take the form of verbal humiliation, physical battering, intimidation, forced isolation, or a combination of factors. A batterer may also take advantage of his or her victim's disability, for example, by withholding medications or by disconnecting the wheelchair.

The reasons why women with disabilities stay in abusive relationships are similar to those cited by nondisabled women: shame, financial dependency, or perceptions of aloneness (Russell, 1995). Many have also internalized the societal myths that keeping a man is worth any price and that domestic violence is the woman's fault. These women in particular suffer from a double stigma: Their disability already makes them outcasts; compounded with the abuse, they retreat further from society rather than come out. Physical barriers also present a problem, because shelters are frequently inaccessible.

Women need to stay alert to the signs of violence and learn to recognize the characteristics of a typical batterer. Simultaneously, they must realistically evaluate their options for escape. Getting out is important, but it also carries an element of risk, because batterers tend to become even more violent when women try to leave (Russell, 1995). Women with disabilities, though, are seriously underserved by helping agencies. If the batterer is also disabled, the police may underestimate or completely discount the batterer's capability for abuse. In addition, disabled women fleeing abusive relationships also need to deal with obstacles in obtaining SSI, Medicaid, accessible housing, or attendant care.

A greater availability of resources will enable more women with disabilities to break the cycle of domestic violence. Advocates for the disabled are using the Americans with Disabilities Act compliance rules to increase funding for accessible shelters. But the existence of shelters will not be sufficient without open channels of communication among medical, social, and legislative agencies. Physicians and therapists need to be able to identify the physical and psychological indicators of abuse in women. They must also be willing to listen and discuss the issue without judgment. They also should be aware of the availability and location of accessible shelters, hotlines, and counselors, and be able to make the appropriate referrals.

IMPLICATIONS FOR PRACTITIONERS

The degree and quality of sexual counseling during rehabilitation can help women maintain their sexual identity following disability. Although research has shown a significant correlation between a healthy sexuality and improved self-esteem (Sidman, 1977), sexual readjustment following disability has been an area too often underexplored or ignored entirely by health care professionals because of the social stereotypes internalized by patients and practitioners alike. In a study involving the experiences of spinal cord–injury survivors, Yoshida (1994) documented how institutionalization, even within the rehabilitation setting, can curtail an individual's self-concept because of the constant and persistent focus on the disability and the "disabled" self at the cost of those aspects that constitute the "nondisabled" self, including sexual concerns. Health professionals may be reluctant to speak or answer questions about sexuality either because they have inadequate knowledge or are uncomfortable discussing the topic, especially with women.

Until recently, there has also been a considerable dearth of available medical research on sexuality in women with disabilities. Reasons range from the devaluation of women's sexual concerns because of women's traditionally "passive" role in the sex act (Sidman, 1977); to the lack of sufficient numbers of women with specific disabilities such as spinal cord injury, for statistical sampling (White et al., 1993); to the technological difficulties of measuring sexual response in internal genitalia (Sipski, 1995). In addition, research on female sexuality has traditionally focused mainly on fertility, pregnancy, and childbearing. In disabilities such as spinal cord injury or multiple sclerosis in which fertility is basically unaffected, the assumption has been that sexuality itself is generally unaffected. Nothing could be farther from the truth.

Obviously, sexuality encompasses far more than childbearing. A disability impacts not just the physical aspects of sexuality, but also the emotional, psychological, and social elements of a woman's self-image as a sexual being. Actual research into this area, though, is especially rare. This is a particularly unfortunate omission, because complete and accurate information, in my experience, does lead to fewer problems in adjustment. In addition, too many medical practitioners have a tendency to address all bodily functions in strictly clinical terms (with the unfortunate result that sometimes your physician may ask about your bowel function in the middle of an occupational therapy room or, worse, your lunch period). As a result, women who have been through the rehabilitation process often complain that what limited sexuality counseling they do receive is approached on an overly medical level that focuses primarily on the physical act of intercourse and is often removed from the context of the entire relationship (Yoshida, 1994). Sexual instruction frequently comes loaded with admonitions about cleanliness, catheterizations, insufficient lubrication, and the possibility of bowel and bladder accidents. Given this approach, is it any wonder that the picture of future sexuality most women receive is ambiguous at best?

Evidence suggests that messages received during rehabilitation are being internalized. Women's greatest concerns regarding sexual activity include both the physical (fear of bladder and bowel accidents) and the psychosocial (not satisfying a partner or feeling unattractive) areas (White et al., 1993). However, although the feelings of unattractiveness seem to diminish over time, the physical concerns do not. Aside from the background literature, many spinal cord–injured women with whom I have spoken to have reported that what they remember the most from rehabilitation was being told to expect bowel and bladder accidents, muscle spasms, and many other negative possibilities. Instead of preparing women for sex after disability, these admonitions—coming as they do when self-confidence is at its most uncertain—may be inadvertently scaring women away from it. Disabled women are constantly told if an involuntary bowel movement happens to treat it as no big deal. However, although helpful messages might be received on an intellectual level, this does not necessarily mean that they are any easier to swallow on an emotional "gut" level.

In addition, because the overwhelming majority of spinal cord injuries occur in men (about 85%), doctors and therapists may unwittingly focus all their attention on primarily male matters, and, as a result, women may feel their concerns are being devalued. Separate discussion and education sessions exclusively for and about women should be implemented so that women have full access to a wide range of information and can talk freely without fear or embarrassment. Indeed, women who have had access to such groups often feel better informed and more comfortable with themselves than those who have not (Charlifue et al., 1992). If videotapes are used, they too should address both men's and women's concerns.

Given the research results cited, my experiences, and the experiences of those women I have interviewed, I suggest that the main objective of sexual counseling in rehabilitation should be to reassure the newly disabled women that they will be able to have a satisfying sex life. Thus, it is important that the entire rehabilitation staff be supportive and work together toward that end. Physicians and nurses can help by treating patients with dignity and respect for their integrity as individuals, rather than as collections of medical symptoms. Warnings about possible problems should be realistic—but not overwhelming—and, whenever possible, the focus should be on solutions, not problems. Physical and occupational therapists can help to address the effects of disability by discussing issues in a nonjudgmental way and by helping patients to minimize physical pain and dysfunction as much as possible. In addition, peer counselors can be extremely helpful, not just in adding credibility, but also in presenting positive role models of people with disabilities who are active, successful, and comfortable with themselves. Self-confidence enhances a person's acceptability to potential mates; self-acceptance affects a person's ability to relate to others.

Because the concept of sexuality may involve not just the individual but also her partner and family, therapists should encourage families to attend patient education sessions and to provide both individual and couple counseling with an emphasis on communication exercises to help partners to express emotion verbally. Counselors should not underrate the pressures of a disability on the patient's spouse or partner, especially when the spouse is also pulled into the role of caregiver. Working together, *all* participants in the rehabilitation process can help a woman to deal more effectively with the physical, psychological, and social challenges of maintaining her sexuality while living with a disability.

REFERENCES

Alexander, C.J. (1991). Psychological assessment and treatment of sexual dysfunctions following spinal cord injury. *Journal of the American Paraplegia Society, 14*, 127–131.

Brecker, L.R. (1993, October 18). Women with disabilities struggle for a healthy view of their sexuality. *ADVANCE for Physical Therapists*, pp. 11–12, 23.

Carolan, C. (1984). Sex and disability: "Handicap—Less important than loving." *Nursing Times, 80*(39), 28–30.

Charlifue, S.W., Gerhart, K.A., Menter, R.R., Whiteneck, G.G., & Manley, M.S. (1992). Sexual issues of women with spinal cord injuries. *Paraplegia 30*(3), 192–199.

Greengross, W. (1976). *Entitled to love.* London: Malaby Press.

Medgyesi, V. (1994). I don't do crips. *New Mobility, 5*(15), 39–41.

Russell, M. (1995). Piercing the veil of silence: Domestic violence and disability. *New Mobility, 6*(26), 44–49, 53.

Sidman, J.M. (1977). Sexual functioning and the physically disabled adult. *American Journal of Occupational Therapy, 31*(2), 81–85.

Sipski, M.L. (1995). The sexuality of women with disability and chronic illness. *New Jersey Rehab, 8*(9), 12–17.

Sipski, M.L., & Alexander, C.J. (1993). Sexual activities, response and satisfaction in women pre- and post-spinal cord injury. *Archives of Physical Medicine and Rehabilitation, 74,* 1025–1029.

Smith, I. (1989). Shattering the myths: Sexuality in rehabilitation for spinal cord injury. *Rehab Management, 2,* 28–34.

Storrs, B. (1996). Caveat dater: Devotees of disability. *New Mobility, 7*(28), 50–53.

White, M.J., Rintala, D.H., Hart, K.A., & Fuhrer, M.J. (1993). Sexual activities, concerns and interests of women with spinal cord injury living in the community. *American Journal of Physical Medicine and Rehabilitation 72*(6), 372–378.

Yoshida, K.K. (1994). Institutional impact on self-concept among persons with spinal cord injury. *International Journal of Rehabilitation Research, 17*(2), 95–107.

CHAPTER 8

Living with a Disability: A Man's Perspective

Mitchell S. Tepper

In this chapter, I share my personal story and professional perspectives on the impact of disability on male sexuality. Because disability is experienced in the context of gender, I have integrated literature on concepts of male socialization and learning about sex. I explore how acquiring a disability may affect sexuality and create treatment concerns. Finally, I make treatment suggestions for working with men with disability or chronic illness.

PERSONAL PERSPECTIVES

I was baptized into disability on July 27, 1982. I was a lifeguard at the time, approaching the end of my shift. In the moments before I broke my neck, I was heading out to fix some buoys. I had sun-bleached hair, a golden tan, and a lean, muscular body. I was 20 years old and at my prime. Everything was perfect except for the ileostomy bag I hid under my shorts.

I had to wear the bag because I had a large section of my intestines removed earlier in 1982. I had been diagnosed with Crohn's disease at age 12 years, when it was apparent I was not growing at nearly the same rate as other pubescent boys. I was hospitalized once at age 17, and by age 20, the disease was no longer manageable with diet and drug therapy. I left school in the middle of the spring semester of my junior year for an emergency hemicolectomy. Before being discharged, I had a bout with peritonitis that resulted in a second surgery and the temporary ileostomy.

It was 3 months after this surgery when I headed out to fix the buoys. I ran into the lake with a wrench in my left hand. As I dove over the line that separated the depths, I placed my right hand over my bag to prevent it from coming off. The combination of diving over the line and grabbing my bag resulted in angling too deep. My left arm alone was not enough to protect my head from planting firmly in the bottom of the lake. I heard a noise from within my head. It sounded like air rushing quickly out of a tire. I floated to the surface of the water and then struggled unsuccessfully to lift my head up to take a breath. A fellow lifeguard came to my rescue. He asked if I was ok. I said no. I knew I was in trouble. It was at that point my life as a person with a disability began.

Growing up with a chronic illness such as Crohn's disease, I had already developed what I thought were exceptional coping skills. I dealt with managing pain, cramps, diarrhea, special diets, side effects of medications, name-calling by peers, and despair about my body. I also had to cope with the emotional stress and discomfort of having my private parts exposed in teaching hospitals, the embarrassment of unwelcomed erections during medical procedures, the mortification of waking up from surgery to discover a tube in my penis, and the invasion of being catheterized after the tube was removed. I was just learning to deal with wearing an ileostomy bag and the significant scarring on my abdomen.

I guess it is my love for life and fighting spirit that helped me cope overall. But what helped me deal with the ileostomy bag was the relief from the pain, cramping, and diarrhea it provided. The absence of pain was pleasure. Feeling good again motivated me to get back into life. Pleasure helped me to compensate for the blow to my body image and ask for my summer job back as a lifeguard. I had just started working and dating again when I broke my neck and became disabled.

As a young man with a C-6 to C-7 spinal cord injury, I would have to deal with much more. I had to face changes in sexual function and response, career options, independence, relating to others, and how others related to me. I would have to deal with bowel routines, wearing an external-dwelling catheter and a leg bag, and depending on a wheelchair to get around. I would have to deal with a quad belly, atrophied muscles, paralysis, and spasticity. And, I would have to deal with how all this affected my sexuality.

I was deeply concerned about my sexual capabilities from the moment the breathing apparatus was removed and I was able to speak again. My first sexual question was whether I could still have children. I was single at the time and had hardly thought about marriage, let alone having children. I did not understand the complexity of that question at the time, nor did my physician. I was told my chances of having children were less than 5%. That was it.

There was no acknowledgment of my sexual concerns from the doctor, no follow-up questions, no discussion about other changes in sexual response I might experience, no referral to someone who might help me with my other sexual questions and concerns, and no offer of hope for a sexual future. In retrospect, this is not surprising based on the general level of ignorance about sexuality and disability and the limited amount of sexuality education doctors received in their formal education and training.

My mother seemed to be the only one at the time who recognized my continuing need for love and affection. She added the statements "I need a hug" and "I need a kiss" to the list of basic needs on my communication board. These two statements gave me a vehicle for sexual overtures even before I could speak.

My recovery and rehabilitation were riddled with sexual experiences and exploration of my sexuality. The sexual experiences started with the reflex erection I became aware of when I first awoke in intensive care, which nobody talked about, and the limited, pessimistic response from my doctor to my question regarding children. With the limited information available to me and the many questions and concerns I had regarding my sexuality and my manhood, I had to work out these issues on my own.

It has been 14 years since I was baptized in Lake Mohegan in Fairfield, Connecticut, and I have recently celebrated my 10th wedding anniversary. Cheryl and I are expecting our first child, and I have moved from a career in finance to a calling in sexuality education and research focusing on disability and chronic illness. My life since sustaining a spinal cord injury has been a slow and steady process of change and growth. It took a while for me to reflect on what had value for me. It also took time to fully accept my disabilities and to come out to others as a person with a disability. I first connected with others who had a spinal cord injury and eventually connected with others who had different disabilities. I am eternally grateful to my disabled peers who served as role models, mentors, and guides.

Along the way I did a lot of experimentation, at times hurting others' feelings and getting my own feelings hurt, too. I sought out every opportunity to express my sexuality and have it affirmed. I was a consummate flirt, always testing my abilities. With each date I would experiment sexually as much as the particular relationship would allow.

My male energy drove me to deal with my disability. Competitive swimming, diving, and especially the discipline and focus I learned in karate prepared me well for the rehabilitation process. I was stoic, strong, independent, and hard working. I forged ahead, always looking to protect the ones I loved from my misfortunes. But at the same time, masculinity had its detrimental affects. I pushed away my girlfriend whom I started seeing after my ileostomy and was still dating at the time I broke my neck. I also pushed away my mother, or at least rebelled strongly against her when she tried to take care of me. I reacted most strongly when she was trying to feed me.

As I regained more functional ability, I fought my mother's suggestions to finish school nearby so I could live at home with her. After finishing my outpatient rehabilitation, I returned to Bryant College in Rhode Island where I had been enrolled as an undergraduate finance major before leaving school for surgery. The college assigned a suite mate who was on work study to help me with my personal care. My roommate and closest friends had already graduated and I did not feel much like making a whole new set of friends. I was primarily focused on finishing my degree as quickly as possible but I was still interested in finding a girlfriend.

In the first year following my injury, I took solace in knowing that I could still please a woman. I was not too concerned about my own sexual pleasure or what else I needed from a relationship. Just being able to attract a sexual partner was a boost to my self- and sexual-esteem. Once that was established, I began looking for a more "serious" relationship. Finding that relationship as a quadriplegic, outside the comfortable walls of the rehabilitation hospital and outside the comfortable relationships of ex-girlfriends and strangers who pursued me, was a more risky and painful experience.

I had no problem making female friends. In college, my roommates were jealous of the amount of female attention I attracted and said it was only because of my wheelchair. What they did not understand is that these women were looking for male friendship that was free of sexual pressure. The women assumed I was safe. I was not perceived as a potential sexual partner, but the perennial friend. It seemed impossible to make the transition from friend to sexual partner in relationships in which I had established an intimate connection. I even brought this up as a primary concern with my physiatrist. His meager consolation was that some people are lucky to find love only once in their lives.

I felt like I was never going to connect sexually with someone on the level that I was interested in again until I met Cheryl more than 12 years ago in a computer class at Bryant College (Tepper & Tepper, 1996). It turned out that we lived diagonally across the hall from each other. My father-in-law always asks us who made the first move. I think she did; she thinks I did. The truth is that there was a real mutual attraction.

I knew Cheryl was right for me because I felt totally accepted when I was with her; I did not feel my disability was an issue at all. I had made myself a promise even before I broke my neck that I would marry the first person I dated for 6 months. I was so overwhelmed with this requited love that by 5 months I proposed. I was afraid if I lost Cheryl I might never find a love like her's again. We were married 18 months later.

There were concerns from both families because of my disability and our differences in religion. My mother expressed concern about the religion of our children. This prompted me to reveal to her the doubts of my being able to father children. I also told my mother about my discussions with Cheryl about adopting a child if it turned out that I could not impregnate her. Both my mother and Cheryl's parents were concerned for Cheryl and the burden I would be on her over the long run. Fortunately, neither Cheryl nor I saw me as a burden.

We have a wonderful marriage. We have adopted a lifestyle that is less traditional than other heterosexual marriages and it works well for us. I do the dishes and the laundry and clean the bathrooms; my wife is the primary breadwinner. I enjoy decorating, shopping, and picking out clothes. Cheryl puts up the shelves, fixes the dryer when it breaks, washes the car, paints, and hangs wallpaper. The formula that works for our relationship is based on equality, respect, mutual acceptance, trust, realistic expectations, open and honest communication, and flexibility in roles. Although none of these qualities is unique to a relationship in which one or both partners have a chronic illness or disability, we believe they are critical for long-term success and happiness.

I was not born into disability secure in my manhood or comfortable breaking out of stereotypical male roles. What it meant to be a "real" man was deeply ingrained in me by the time I was 20. Fortunately, after many years of work, I am relatively free of socially imposed concepts of male sexuality and masculinity. Even at this juncture in my life, however, I sometimes wrestle with internalized notions of male roles as I prepare to stay home with our baby when my wife goes back to work.

What I have learned since formally studying human sexuality is that male sexuality goes way beyond the apparent issues of erectile function, who should do the dishes, and who should make more money. There are lasting and lingering effects of the indirect education and training to be a man in the United States. Although each man's experience may be different, men still live in a society that is androcentric, gender polarized, and works to socially construct our gender (Bem, 1993). *Androcentrism* refers to male-centeredness, "a definition of males and male experience as a neutral standard or norm, and females and female experience as a sex-specific deviation from that norm" (p. 2). *Gender polarization* refers to the perceived differences between women and men that are used as an organizing principle for the social life of the culture. According to Bem, gender polarization operates by defining mutually exclusive scripts for being male and female and by defining any person or behavior that deviates from these scripts as problematic; androcentrism and gender polarization work to limit options and, hence, human potential.

> The gender-polarizing concepts of a real man and a real woman give both men and women the feeling that their maleness or femaleness is something they must continually construct and reconstruct, rather than something they can simply take for granted. In the context of an androcentric culture it is the males in particular who are made to feel the most insecure about the adequacy of their gender. Androcentrism exacerbates the male's insecurity about his status as a real man in at least two different ways. It so thoroughly devalues whatever thoughts, feelings, and behaviors that are culturally defined as feminine that the

gender boundary has a more negative cultural meaning for men that it has for women—which means, in turn, that male gender-boundary-crossers are much more culturally stigmatized than female gender-boundary-crossers. At the same time, androcentrism provides such an unreachable definition of what a real man is supposed to be that only a few men can ever begin to meet it. (Bem, 1993, p. 150)

How men are socialized into gender will affect their reactions to events that threaten their identity and will also affect how they deal with changes in their ability to perform expected gender roles.

MALE SOCIALIZATION AND MASCULINITY

The social construction of masculinity begins as soon as males are born and continues for the rest of their lives (Bem, 1993; Money & Tucker, 1975; Zilbergeld, 1992). Money and Tucker (1975) have asserted that people learn gender identities and expected gender roles much the same way they attain speech. Humans are born hardwired for speech, but not programmed. Programming for speech occurs as people are exposed to the language spoken to them by their parents and those around them in society. From the moment the physician pronounces, "It's a boy," males begin to establish a sense of gender identity. By the time people can speak, they can already identify their gender (Thompson, 1975). As people learn the language of their society, they also learn what the expected gender roles are for them. According to Bem (1993), "Male-female difference is superimposed on so many aspects of the social world that a cultural connection is thereby forged between sex and virtually every other aspect of human experience, including modes of dress and social roles and even ways of expressing emotion and experiencing sexual desire" (p. 2).

According to Zilbergeld (1992), by the age of 6 or 7 years, most of the important lessons in male socialization have been learned. One of these messages is "don't be like a girl" (p. 23). As Zilbergeld has explained, "Since females of all ages are the softer ones—the people who express feelings, who cry, who are people oriented—not being like them is an effective way to suppress the softer side of males" (p. 23). Negative reinforcers such as name-calling—"sissy," "girl," or "faggot"—keep boys from straying too far from what is expected. They also send the message that to be masculine, you must be heterosexual (Herek, 1986).

Homophobic name-calling is used to keep boys in line (Linn, Stein, & Young, 1992). Name-calling creates or reinforces hostility toward the gay and lesbian population, and it forces all children to follow strict sex-role behaviors to avoid ridicule (Gordon, 1983). Homophobia, in this sense, a fear of being perceived as gay, is said to be perhaps the greatest pressure boys face while growing up (Friedman, 1989) and is considered the ultimate weapon in reinforcing rigid sex-role conformity ("Homophobia and Education," 1983). According to Friedman (1989), homophobia sparks male hatred of women and fear of closeness to other people. Rigid sex-role stereotypes prevent heterosexual males from establishing meaningful and intimate relationships with other men and women and set up male–female relationships based on male superiority that preclude the possibility of true intimacy (Neisen, 1990).

Boys also learn the primary thing in life is performing (Farrell, 1986; Zilbergeld, 1992) or "getting the job done" (Bem, 1974, p. 156). In general, masculinity and masculine behavior seems to reflect a "competency cluster" of character traits (Broverman, Broverman, Clarkson, Rosenkrantz, & Vogel, 1970). The end result of male socialization is a set of defaults that are programmed by society, culture, media, family, and religion. The typical male attributes are supposed to be strength and self-reliance; success; no "sissy" stuff (do not be like women); sexual interest and prowess; active; independent; tough; aggressive; dominant; stoic; and never cries (Bem, 1974; Broverman et al., 1970; Herek, 1986; Zilbergeld, 1992). These defaults define a fanciful standard of masculinity. Males who internalize these standards are prone to experience anxiety that they will fail to measure up to their role. According to Herek (1986), "The source of this anxiety is fear of losing one's sense of self, or identity, as a heterosexual man (which is equivalent to a male's identity as a person)" (p. 567). The socialization of males provides very little that is of value in the formation and maintenance of intimate relationships. Male socialization also carries over into what boys learn about sex.

What Boys Learn about Sex and Manhood

What boys learn about sex and manhood becomes a critical treatment concern when they reach adulthood and are faced with sexual dysfunction resulting from a disability or illness. According to Zilbergeld (1992), boys learn that their manhood is tied to their penis, and having and using erections has something to do with masculinity. "Before having sex with partners or even themselves, boys know that sexual interest and prowess are crucial to being a man. . . . Since sexuality is such a crucial component of masculinity, males feel pressured to act interested in sex whether or not they really are. . . . This is a great setup for faking, lying, and feeling inadequate" (p. 32). Zilbergeld has asserted that what adolescent boys learn about penis-centered sexuality creates an incredible confusion between personhood or identity and one's sexual organ. When their penis does not operate according to certain specifications, men equate this with loss of manhood. This is no different for a man who acquires a disability.

According to Zilbergeld (1992), boys learn a fantasy model of sex: "It's two feet long, hard as steel, always ready, and will knock your socks off" (p. 37). Furthermore,

> Sexual education goes on all the time . . . [via sexual jokes, sexually
> implicit or explicit movies, novels or television that involves sex or adult
> relationships]. . . . Because all the media portray essentially the same
> sexual message, it's virtually assured that all men and women will learn
> the same model of sex. . . . The sexual messages conveyed in our culture
> are the stuff of fantasy. . . . Because we don't have any realistic models
> or standards in sex, we tend to measure ourselves against these fanta-
> sies. . . . We usually aren't even aware that we're comparing ourselves to
> anything. We just know that we feel bad because our equipment and
> performances aren't what we wish they were. . . . [We] end up feeling
> inadequate about our bodies and our partners'. . . . We compare our-
> selves to what we have learned, and almost everyone feels that they've
> come out on the short end. (pp. 37–42)

Add an Acquired Disability

What happens if a man loses his ability to attain or maintain an erection or to
ejaculate as a result of an acquired disability? What happens if a man loses sensation in his genitals, if he uses a catheter, or if he has physical limitations? Whether
resulting from Crohn's disease, spinal cord injury, or any other acquired disability
or chronic illness, a medical impairment inevitably impacts male sexuality. Issues
such as dependency, diminished body image, impaired sexual function, and loss
of earning potential may threaten a man's gender identity or core sense of himself
as a man and his ability to carry out established gender roles.

Men arrive at rehabilitation with all the baggage society, culture, the media,
parents, friends, and religion packed for them. Men were socialized to be strong
and self-reliant, successful, manly, and sexual performers. They learned the same
myths and fantasy model of sex as their peers. What happens when men are faced
with the loss of strength and self-reliance, loss of sexual prowess, and loss of
success? What happens when men do not have their penis to fall back on?

For some men with an acquired disability, loss of strength and self-reliance,
loss of sexual prowess, and loss of success can equate to loss of manhood. To men
who are faced with sexual problems and physical impairments, the perceived loss
of their manhood or sexuality could be devastating. Zilbergeld (1992) has discussed this link between gender roles and gender identity as follows:

> Because we learn from an early age that manhood is conditional rather
> than absolute, males are in constant danger of losing their manhood
> and their identities. Not making the team, not being willing to fight, not
> performing in bed, losing a job—that's all it takes and our man no longer
> believes that he's a man. . . . [Furthermore,] their behavior must con-

form to what is considered manly. Any slight deviation, small sign of weakness, and they might lose their place among other men and be labeled "lady," "woman," or "pussy"—all signifying a non-man or less than a man. But if a man isn't a man, then what is he? The answer most seem to believe is: Nothing at all. For their identities are inextricably linked to their gender-roles. If the results of changing one's behavior can be so dire as a loss of identity, one doesn't take change lightly. (p. 20)

If it is impossible for an able-bodied man to meet the fantasy model of sex, a man with a disability faces an even more devastating task to live up to the ideal male model. As long as a nondisabled man continues to function and perform sexually, as long as he still attains an erection and ejaculates, he can continue to strive for the fantasy and operate under the myths described earlier. The able-bodied, sexually functioning man may never have reason to question the quality of his sexual encounters. For the man with a disability with impaired sexual function, the realization that he does not match up may be painfully clear.

If these fantasies and myths are not dispelled in sexual health care, the man with erectile dysfunction, inhibited ejaculation, loss of sensation, or physical limitations might conclude that his sex life is over. Attempts at sex may lead to frustration or anger and to relationship conflict. The recall of predisability performance is highly subjective and still clouded by the fantasy model. When sexual function is lost or impaired, men will need help in redefining their concept of good sex and of manhood to be capable of finding enjoyment in their sexuality.

But society teaches men many destructive myths about sexuality that must be surmounted first. Some of these myths are described by Zilbergeld (1992) as follows:

- "We're liberated folks who are all comfortable with sex" (p. 42). This myth is inconsistent with messages people receive growing up that sexual pleasure is bad and that sex is private. It also leads to arrogance and narrow-mindedness about sex, thus making communication and learning more difficult.
- "A real man isn't into sissy stuff like feelings and communicating" (p. 44). Sex is used for expression of emotions instead of verbal communication. Therefore, men never have the opportunity to develop comfort or skill in talking about sex. However, communication around sexual issues is crucial to adapting to sexual changes and maintaining intimacy with a partner after acquiring a disability.
- "All touching is sexual or should lead to sex" (p. 45). As a result, most men are closed to touch as an option for getting needs for signs of love and support met and for bonding. Men also may distance themselves physically in the presence of a disability that impairs sexual function.

- "A man is always interested in and always ready for sex" (p. 47). This belief leads to pressure to be sexual before men are ready. There is pressure for men to become sexually active to prove to themselves and others that they are still "normal" (Blumenfeld, 1994).
- "A real man performs in sex" (Zilbergeld, 1992, p. 48). Therefore, performance proves a person to be a man. Conversely, if men cannot perform, then they are not real men anymore.
- "Sex is centered on a hard penis and what's done with it" (p. 49). This myth creates pressure to have and to keep an erection because "the desired penis functions automatically and predictably, just like a well-oiled machine" and "the penis should function regardless of any other considerations" (p. 51).
- "Sex equals intercourse" (p. 51). The absolute need to have intercourse as a necessary part of sex can create a number of problems. "When the penis doesn't operate as we want it to, many of us get upset and refuse to have sex at all. If we can't do it the right way, 'why do it at all'?" (p. 52). This thinking leaves men to deprive themselves of pleasure because they cannot perform sexually like they did before disability or illness.
- "A man should be able to make the earth move for his partner, or at the very least knock her socks off" (p. 53). This myth keeps the performance pressure on and the focus more on the pleasure of the partner. "It can [also] make it difficult for a man to feel good about a sexual encounter that consists primarily of being pleasured by his partner" (p. 54).
- "Good sex requires orgasm" (p. 55). Orgasm and, more specifically, ejaculation in men is interpreted as a clear sign of enjoyment. Because, according to Zilbergeld, many men do not get much out of sex besides ejaculatory release, they do not see the point in sex without it. It is easy for men who have not experienced orgasm or ejaculation after disability or illness to adopt this attitude.
- "Good sex is spontaneous, with no planning and no talking" (p. 59). Men hold on to the idea of fantasy sex in which "people instinctively know what the other wants and willingly provide it, where there are no serious problems, where we can have whatever we want and all we want of it" (p. 59). It is more comfortable to hold onto the fantasy because planning requires talking and explicit approval. The perceived loss of spontaneity after disability or illness gives men another reason to believe good sex is no longer possible.
- "Real men don't have sex problems" (p. 60). Therefore, men are not readily willing to admit or acknowledge sexual problems because sexual problems are equated with diminished manhood. The health practitioner will need to take responsibility for gently initiating the discussion of sexual problems.

Zilbergeld (1992) and Farrell (1986) have argued that men get a raw deal in their socialization because men live fewer years than women, and men are more likely to commit suicide, become dependent on drugs or alcohol, become psychotic, suffer from stress-related illnesses like ulcers and heart disease, and be involved in serious accidents. Potential violence is a fact of life for boys from the first day they encounter other boys. It is easy to see how these facts contribute to the overrepresentation of men in rehabilitation units and hospitals who are left with permanent disabilities.

TREATMENT CONCERNS

The subtle and not-so-subtle messages accumulated over the years can leave men with an acquired disability feeling the loss of manhood. Medical impairment leads to disability, and disability to dependency. Often after a disability, a man moves from a position of independence to a situation in which he is forced to depend on his mother or spouse or partner. Dependency makes a man feel child-like, like a non-man. Complicating the matter is that the majority of rehabilitation nurses on whom the man in the rehabilitation unit or hospital depends for his basic care are women.

When faced with loss of strength and self-reliance, men are unable to express the fear and despair they are feeling with their new disability because they are trained to mistrust and dislike the more vulnerable and expressive side of themselves (Zilbergeld, 1992). Men's inability to express fear and despair limits their ability to get comforted and to find release in tears, and may manifest itself in denial or anger. Denial and anger may, in turn, impede the rehabilitation process. "Because anger is one of the few feelings men believe they can have, it's often a mask for other feelings, especially such as feeling hurt or fear, that suggest weakness. It's much easier for men to deal with anger than these other emotions" (Zilbergeld, 1992, p. 239). Accordingly, men have a tendency to display excessive masculinity when they are afraid and, conversely, to act out of a sense of imperfect masculinity (Pittman, 1991).

Because of emphasis on strength and self-reliance, men may deny they need help adjusting (Zilbergeld, 1992). They try to go through the rehabilitation process on their own. They often have trouble admitting they need help and do not want to burden their loved ones with complaints. Therefore, men do not acknowledge worries or fears to providers or partners. This hinders intimacy with their partners, which adds distance in a relationship when closeness is needed.

"Men drown feelings in drugs, alcohol, or sex to satisfy need for body contact/ touch and distraction from feelings" (Zilbergeld, 1992, p. 30). Therefore, unexpressed feelings over losses may lead to substance abuse. Rehabilitation providers and loved ones may overlook the substance abuse because they feel that the abuse is justified because of the dreaded physical condition of the man.

Because "parents stop touching their boys early on . . . men lose sight of their need for touching except as a part of roughhousing or sex" (Zilbergeld, 1992, p. 27). Therefore, many men are closed to touch. If the disability results in diminished or lost ability to sense genital stimulation, men are usually unaware of the sensual potential of other parts of their body. Sexual satisfaction becomes impossible.

Many men still have sports as an outlet. "In sports many of the prohibitions on males are lifted. A man can be as emotional and expressive about his favorite team and players as he wants. . . . Playfulness and creativity are allowed. . . . There's even a lot of physical contact . . . one could express anger without much risk. . . . Sports is one of the few places where men can safely become boys again . . . [displaying] expressiveness and playfulness" (Zilbergeld, 1992, p. 31). Sports provides men an opportunity to prove themselves and can be a vehicle to help men reestablish their masculine identity.

Treatment Suggestions for Sexual Health Care

Attention to comprehensive sexual health care is desperately needed to help restore a man's sense of manhood and help him enjoy his sexuality once again. Several possible concerns to address during treatment are:

- childlike feelings of dependency
- physiologic changes in sexual function
- inability to express fear and disapproval
- denial, repression, anger, and misinformation regarding sexual issues
- the wish not to burden loved ones
- the potential for substance abuse to soften the sexual trauma

I believe restoring a sense of manhood and enjoyment of sexuality is possible based on my personal experiences and my theoretical understanding of the social construction of gender and of sexuality. The theory operates under the assumption that what is socially constructed can be deconstructed and reconstructed (Herek, 1986).

Health practitioners can assist in the process of deconstruction and reconstruction by

- helping men unlearn sexual myths by facilitating the critical examination of what men learn about sex and manhood
- helping men learn or relearn facts about human sexuality to help compensate for the general lack of accurate sexual information people have before their disability or illness
- helping men to understand the physiologic effects of disability on their sexual function
- providing information on solutions to impaired sexual function and options for sexual expression

- helping men to improve their communication skills as they relate to sexual issues
- reacting constructively to anger by deflecting the words or behavior whenever possible and guiding men to explore the underlying causes of their emotions
- anticipating sexual questions and concerns and looking for teachable moments during times of intimate care to broach the subject
- encouraging men to take control and direct their own rehabilitation process as much as possible
- providing competitive, recreational activities
- spelling out the benefits of adapting a more flexible gender role
- teaching men to focus on pleasure and intimacy instead of performance and orgasm
- addressing substance abuse when it is involved

In theory, if men were taught as children that being a man is not conditional and that manhood cannot be lost through loss of genital function or the inability to perform other traditionally male-coded sex roles (Bem, 1993; Money & Tucker, 1975), then men would not suffer the same major blow to their masculine identities when confronted with the changes associated with disabilities. But reconstructing concepts of gender identity as men age, like learning a new language, is not easy. Learning the basics of a language in the classroom is only a start, as is the limited amount of sexuality education health practitioners are able to provide, considering shorter lengths of stay in rehabilitation hospitals today. To really learn a language, it is helpful to be submersed in the culture in which the language is spoken. Likewise, to really accept a new image of male sexuality, men must have an opportunity to learn from others with spinal cord injury who have maintained a positive sense of their sexuality with disability (Tepper, 1992).

The reeducation process will entail assessing the man's sexual knowledge, attitudes, and behaviors acquired before and after his disability. The sexual assessment should be followed by the provision of appropriate information, suggestions, and referrals, if necessary. Ideally, there should be health practitioners on staff who have received specialized training in providing comprehensive sexual health care. Like comprehensive rehabilitation, comprehensive sexual health care addresses sexuality from a biopsychosocial perspective using an interdisciplinary team approach (Tepper, in press). Hospitals, professional organizations, and universities that wish to provide continuing education and training in comprehensive sexual health care to health practitioners can now obtain an extensive curriculum that was developed with the support of a grant from the Paralyzed Veterans of America, Spinal Cord Injury Education and Training Foundation (Tepper, 1994).

Sexual Healing

Sexual health care must deal directly with issues of sexual pleasure if there is going to be total sexual healing. Men need new messages to replace the old ones learned over a lifetime. Suggested messages include the following:

- ejaculation and orgasm are not the same thing
- it is not necessary to ejaculate every time you have sex
- orgasm is possible without ejaculation
- sexual activity without orgasm or ejaculation is still sex and is a viable alternative to having no sexual contact at all
- there are many ways to receive and to give sexual satisfaction without penile–vaginal intercourse
- sexual pleasure and even orgasm is possible through touching, kissing, hugging, masturbation, and oral and anal sexual activities
- good sex does not have to be spontaneous—talking about sex and planning sex can lead to good sex

Simply sending messages will not be enough, though. Assuming a man desires to be sexually active again, assuming excitement problems of attaining and maintaining an erection are organically based and managed with one of the options for erectile dysfunction, or assuming he decides to have sex without an erection, he will need guidance in finding out his optimal conditions for arousal. Common conditions men have reported as necessary to enjoy good sex and that lead to increased arousal include being more open to the experience, more confident, more rested, and more relaxed (Zilbergeld, 1992). Achieving those conditions subsequent to acquiring a disability is not a quick and easy path and will require implementation of the aforementioned treatment suggestions.

A man will also need guidance in relearning about his body and what types of stimulation bring him pleasure. Commonly used techniques can help increase awareness to areas of the body where sensation is still intact and where a person may be open to sexual stimulation. Sensate focus exercises described by Masters and Johnson (1970), pleasure mapping described by Stubbs (1988), and charting of a person's personal extragenital matrix described by Whipple and Ogden (1989) are three options for increasing sexual communication and sexual pleasure. Men may perform some of these sexual exercises by themselves, whereas others will require the help of a partner or sexual surrogate. It takes many painful steps to recover sexual pleasure after a disability. But it can be done. I have done it.

REFERENCES

Bem, S.L. (1974). The measurement of psychological androgyny. *Journal of Consulting and Clinical Psychology, 42*(2), 155–162.

Bem, S.L. (1993). *The lenses of gender: Transforming the debate on sexual inequality.* New Haven, CT: Yale University Press.

Blumenfeld, W.J. (1994). Gay, lesbian, bisexual and questioning youth. In J.C. Drolet & K. Clark (Eds.), *The sexuality education challenge: promoting healthy sexuality in young people* (pp. 321–341). Santa Cruz, NM: ETR Associates.

Broverman, I.K., Broverman, D.M., Clarkson, F.E., Rosenkrantz, P.S., & Vogel, S.R. (1970). Sex-role stereotypes and clinical judgments of mental health. *Journal of Consulting and Clinical Psychology, 34*(1), 1–7.

Farrell, W. (1986). *Why men are the way they are.* New York: Berkley Books.

Friedman, J. (1989, May–June). The impact of homophobia on male sexual development. *SIECUS Report,* pp. 8–9.

Gordon, L. (1983). What do we do when we fear "faggot"? *Interracial Books for Children, 14,* 25–27.

Herek, G.M. (1986). On heterosexual masculinity. *American Behavioral Scientist, 29*(5), 563–577.

Homophobia and education: How to deal with name-calling. (1983). *Interracial Books for Children, 14,* 3.

Linn, E., Stein, N.D., & Young, J. (1992). Bitter lessons for all: Sexual harassment in schools. In J.T. Sears (Ed.), *Sexuality and the curriculum: The politics and practices of sexuality education* (pp. 106–123). New York: Teachers College Press.

Masters, W.H., & Johnson, V.E. (1970). *Human sexual inadequacy.* Boston: Little, Brown.

Money, J., & Tucker, P. (1975). *Sexual signatures: On being a man or a woman.* Boston: Little, Brown.

Neisen, J.H. (1990, Fall). Heterosexism or homophobia? The power of the language we use. *Out/Look,* pp. 36–37.

Pittman, F.S. (1991). The secret passions of men. *Journal of Marital and Family Therapy, 17*(1), 17–23.

Stubbs, K.R. (1988). *Romantic interludes: A sensuous lovers guide.* Larkspur, CA: Secret Garden.

Tepper, M.S. (1992). Sexual education in spinal cord injury rehabilitation: Current trends and recommendations. *Sexuality and Disability, 10,* 15–31.

Tepper, M. S. (1994). *Providing comprehensive sexual health care in spinal cord injury rehabilitation: Continuing education and training for health professionals.* Huntington, CT: Author.

Tepper, M.S. (in press). Providing comprehensive sexual health care in spinal cord injury rehabilitation: Implementation and evaluation of a new curriculum for health professionals. *Sexuality and Disability.*

Tepper, M.S., & Tepper, C.A. (1996). Finding the right mate. *The Conn-Cord Newsletter, 2,* pp. 1–4.

Thompson, S.K. (1975). Gender labels and early sex role development. *Child Development, 46,* 339–347.

Whipple, B., & Ogden, G. (1989). *Safe encounters: How women can say yes to pleasure and no to unsafe sex*. New York: Pocket Books.

Zilbergeld, B. (1992). *The new male sexuality*. New York: Bantam Books.

Specific Disabilities
and Illnesses

CHAPTER 9

Spinal Cord Injury and Sexual Function: An Educational Model

Marca L. Sipski

Spinal cord injuries (SCIs) are thought to affect some 200,000 Americans (Go, DeVivo, & Richards, 1995), whereas spinal cord disease is thought to affect an additional 300,000. SCIs and diseases affect not only the spinal cord itself, but multiple organ systems through the spinal cord itself. Therefore, the impact on sexual function must be taken in context with the effects on other organ systems.

The nuances of sexuality are only moderately understood after SCI. Nevertheless, there are two reasons that SCI is an important model to study to understand other disabilities. Health practitioners probably know more about sexual function and sexuality after SCI than about any other disability. Moreover, the nature of SCI is such that practitioners are often able to determine the exact level of neuropathology. Therefore, knowledge about the effects of specific types of SCIs on sexual function will assist in an understanding of other neurologic disorders and their effects on sexual functioning.

LEVEL OF INJURY

When discussing the impact of an SCI, the level and degree of injury must be known. The level and degree of injury are most properly defined using the *International Standards for Neurological and Functional Classification of Spinal Cord Injury* (American Spinal Injury Association [ASIA], 1992). Spinal cord injuries can result in *tetraplegia,* which is paralysis and loss of sensation in all four limbs, or *paraplegia*, which indicates paralysis and loss of sensation in the lower extremities and not the upper extremities. Injuries are also classified as complete or incomplete, depending on whether there is preservation of voluntary contraction of the external anal sphincter on digital rectal examination and whether there is preservation of anal sensation.

149

The level of SCI is determined by measurement of motor strength and sensory function at specific points (Figure 9–1). The level of injury is then defined as the last normal neurologic level, including both motor and sensory functions. Classification of an SCI also includes determination of a motor score that indicates the degree of preservation of motor strength in 20 specific muscle groups based on a maximum score of 100. Furthermore, sensation to pinprick and light touch is quantified for each of 64 dermatomes, and a score based on a maximum score of 112 for each modality is provided. When considering the impact of an SCI on a person's sexual function, it is important to understand the level and degree of SCI injury the person sustained. This information will then allow the clinician to more accurately estimate the anticipated physiologic changes in the patient's sexual function, which should occur as a result of the particular SCI. This knowledge is particularly important after SCI because psychologic and physiologic issues can easily be confused.

A complete discussion of the effects of SCI on various organ systems is beyond the scope of this text. However, in general, changes can include bladder and bowel incontinence with the need for external bladder management and bowel program; spasticity with resultant involuntary movements of the legs, trunk, and arms; and chronic neurogenic pain. As with all other disorders, the impact of the primary condition on other organ systems must be considered when treating the person's sexual concerns. However, one disorder, *autonomic dysreflexia,* deserves mention because it is unique to patients with SCIs and is a common occurrence among those patients. Noxious stimuli—most commonly bladder or bowel distension (however, sexual activity and labor can also be inciting stimuli)—causes sympathetic vasoconstriction, sweating, and piloerection below the level of injury. What follows is the sudden onset of headache and hypertension, and sometimes anxiety and bradycardia or tachycardia. Because of the involvement of the splanchnic bed, the syndrome is most common in injuries at the level of T-6 and above. Treatment involves monitoring blood pressure, elevating the person's head, and removing the offending stimulus. For prolonged and dangerous hypertension, immediate treatment of blood pressure is appropriate (Staas et al., 1993). Left untreated, autonomic dysreflexia can cause intracerebral hemorrhage and death (Erickson, 1980).

Although there is more information on sexuality and SCI than on sexuality and any other neurologic disorder, a review of the literature reveals large gaps. Male sexual response, impotence, and treatment of infertility are mentioned often; however, only recently has there been any in-depth look at female sexual response or satisfaction. In contrast, a number of studies have discussed the impact of an SCI on pregnancy. This chapter systematically discusses the impact of SCI on various aspects of sexual response, sexuality, and infertility.

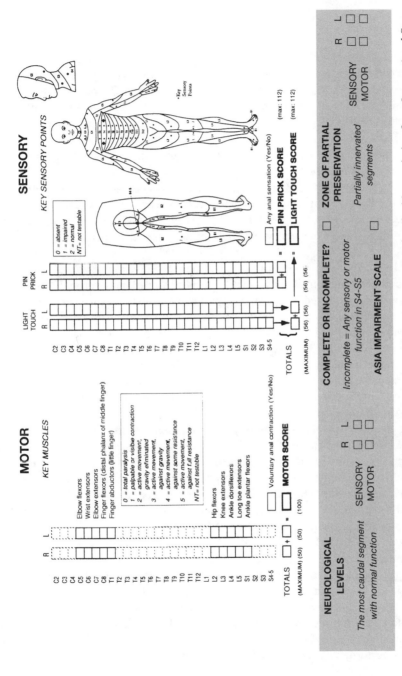

Figure 9–1 Standard neurologic classification of spinal cord injury. *Source:* Reprinted with permission from *International Standards for Neurological and Functional Classification of Spinal Cord Injury,* Revised 1996, © 1996 American Spinal Injury Association.

MALE SEXUAL RESPONSE

An understanding of the sexual response cycle of the able-bodied individual will enable clinicians to better understand the impact of SCIs on sexual response. Information on the sexual response cycle can be found in Chapter 5. Once a spinal cord injury occurs, sexual response will be altered in a predictable fashion based on the level and degree of injury and what physiologic processes have been interrupted.

To understand how a specific SCI affects sexual response, clinicians must first consider the level and degree of the SCI. Then, they must determine whether the injury at the sacral roots is upper motor neuron (UMN) or lower motor neuron (LMN) through the performance of a bulbocavernosus or anal wink reflex (these reflexes test the integrity of the sacral reflex arc) (Comarr & Vigue, 1978a, 1978b). Next, clinicians must consider on which aspect of sexual response they must focus.

Probably the first component of sexual response that clinicians should consider is erectile function. Reflex erectile response originates through sacral stimulation and is mediated by the parasympathetic nervous system, whereas psychogenic erectile function is controlled by the hypogastric plexus, which originates at the T-11 to L-2 levels in addition to the sacral plexus (Bennett, Seager, Vasher, & McGuire, 1988; Linsenmeyer, 1991). Based on the knowledge available on neurophysiology, males with complete UMN injury should retain the ability to achieve reflex but not psychogenic erections. However, based on self-reports, only 70% (Talbot, 1955) to 93% (Bors & Comarr, 1960) of men noted this ability.

With incomplete UMN injuries, it follows that reflex erection should be maintained and a certain percentage of men should have psychogenic erections. Comarr and Vigue (1978a) further reported that the potential to achieve psychogenic erections should remain if men with SCIs retained penile, scrotal, and perianal pinprick sensation. Based on the ASIA criteria, those areas reflect the L-1 and L-2 and S-4 and S-5 dermatomes, which, with respect to level of injury, roughly correspond to the areas described for control of psychogenic erectile function. Furthermore, at T-11 to L-2, the proximity of the intermediolateral cell columns, where sympathetic neurons originate, and the spinothalamic tracts, which control the perception of pain, should lead to a correlation between the ability to appreciate pinprick sensation in these dermatomes and the presence of psychogenic erection. Yet, questionnaire studies have indicated only that 80% of males with incomplete UMN injuries have reflex erections and 19% have some type of combination erection (Bors & Comarr, 1960). To resolve these discrepancies, researchers should perform prospective laboratory-based evaluations of specific male sexual responses.

In males with incomplete and complete LMN injuries affecting the sacral roots, preservation of the ability to discriminate pinprick sensation in the T-11 to L-2 dermatomes should predict the ability to achieve psychogenic lubrication. Furthermore, preservation of this sensation in the S-4 to S-5 dermatomes may also be predictive. Reflex erections should not be present in men with complete injuries and should be partially present with incomplete injuries. Self-report studies have revealed 26% of men with complete injuries reported they could achieve psychogenic erection but none could achieve reflex erection (Bors & Comarr, 1960). With incomplete LMN injuries, 67% (Comarr & Vigue, 1978a) to 95% (Geiger, 1979) of men reportedly maintained some type of erectile function.

Ejaculation is a more complex process requiring coordination of the sympathetic, parasympathetic, and somatic nervous systems to propel semen out of the body. After an SCI, it is not uncommon to suffer from *retrograde ejaculation* in which semen is ejected into the bladder instead of out of the urethral meatus because of a lack of closure of the bladder neck. There apparently have not been any hypotheses stating the natural history of ejaculation post-SCI. Furthermore, the ability to achieve an ejaculate recently has been greatly augmented through the use of vibratory stimulation and electroejaculation. Findings of questionnaire studies have revealed that 4% of men with complete UMN SCIs reported the ability to ejaculate, whereas 32% of the men with incomplete UMN SCIs reported they could ejaculate (Bors & Comarr, 1960). Of the population with complete LMN SCIs, 18% ejaculated; those individuals who retained the ability to achieve psychogenic erection had a greater likelihood of ejaculation (Bors & Comarr, 1960). Of those men with incomplete LMN SCIs, 70% reported the ability to ejaculate (Bors & Comarr, 1960).

According to self-report studies (Alexander, Sipski, & Findley, 1993; Phelps et al., 1983), orgasm occurs in men with a history of SCI. Of the subjects in the Phelps et al. (1983) report, 42% achieved orgasm, whereas 47% of those in the Alexander et al. (1983) report were orgasmic. Men described their orgasms as similar, weaker, or different after their SCI. Furthermore, 38% of men with complete SCIs reported the ability to achieve orgasm (Alexander et al., 1993). According to Bors and Comarr (1960), "Orgasm in one form or another may be retained as long as either the autonomic innervation of the adnexa or the somatic innervation of the pelvic floor musculature remains intact" (p. 215). Clinicians should perform further laboratory-based studies of orgasm in men with SCIs to determine whether there is a significant difference in the ability of men with different degrees of SCI to achieve orgasm and what physiologic responses accompany their orgasms.

FEMALE SEXUAL RESPONSE

Until recently, most information about female sexual response after SCI was anecdotal. Hypotheses about female sexual response after an SCI were derived primarily from self-report studies of males with SCIs. It is generally accepted that vaginal lubrication is the parallel to male erectile function. Those women with SCIs and resultant complete UMN injuries affecting the sacral segments should retain the ability for reflex lubrication but not the ability for psychogenic lubrication (Berard, 1989; Geiger, 1979). With incomplete UMN injuries, women should all have the capacity for reflex lubrication and may be able to achieve psychogenic lubrication (Berard, 1989). For those women with complete LMN injuries, 25% should achieve psychogenic lubrication, whereas none should have the capacity for reflex lubrication (Sipski, 1991). Furthermore, with incomplete LMN injuries, 95% of women should have some type of combined psychogenic/reflex lubrication (Sipski, 1991). Recently, attempts were made to query women with specific types of injuries about their abilities to lubricate (Sipski & Alexander, 1993); however, a significant percentage of women reported they did not have any knowledge of their ability to lubricate.

Griffith and Trieschmann (1975) have discussed another parallel to ejaculation consisting of smooth muscle contractions of the fallopian tubes, uterus, and paraurethral Skene's glands, followed by contraction of the striated musculature located in the pelvic floor, perineum, and anal sphincter. Sipski (1991) noted that if male sexual function and female sexual function are similar, then 4% of women with complete UMN injuries affecting the sacral segments should experience the ejaculatory equivalent, whereas 32% of women with incomplete UMN injuries should do the same. Sipski (1991) further hypothesized that 25% of women with complete LMN injuries would experience this ejaculatory equivalent and that 70% of the women with incomplete LMN injuries would achieve the ejaculatory equivalent.

The topic of female orgasm has been discussed both anecdotally and through self-report studies. Although early reports described orgasms as "phantom" (Money, 1960) or revealed that orgasm was nonexistent or rare in women with SCIs (Guttmann, 1969; Jackson, 1972), more recent reports have revealed that approximately 50% of women with all degrees of SCI reported the ability to achieve orgasms (Charlifue, Gerhart, Menter, Whiteneck, & Manley, 1992; Sipski & Alexander, 1993). Unfortunately, the topic of female orgasm, similar to the issues of lubrication and ejaculation, cannot adequately be addressed through self-report data because of the inherent biases in those data and the inability of women to assess their own genital and nongenital responses.

To fill the gaps in the knowledge about female sexual response after an SCI, Sipski and colleagues (Sipski, Alexander, & Rosen, 1995a, 1995b; Sipski, Rosen, & Alexander, 1996) conducted a controlled laboratory-based study designed to examine the impact of different degrees and types of SCIs on sexual response to varying combinations of psychogenic and manual erotic stimulation. Specifically, the effect of SCIs on vaginal pulse amplitude (a correlate of lubrication), heart rate, blood pressure, respiratory rate, and subjective level of arousal was recorded in response to different experimental conditions.

A comparison of the responses of able-bodied subjects and subjects with complete SCIs to audiovisual stimulation alone revealed that those subjects with complete SCIs did not demonstrate a significant increase in vaginal pulse amplitude, whereas able-bodied subjects did. Concomitantly, both groups of subjects had similar significant increases in their levels of subjective sexual arousal. With the addition of manual clitoral stimulation to the audiovisual stimulation, both groups of subjects developed similar increases in vaginal pulse amplitude; however, only the able-bodied subjects showed a further significant increase in their level of subjective sexual arousal. Nongenital parameters of sexual arousal were generally similar. In all, the results support the hypothesis that women with complete SCIs with UMN lesions affecting the sacral spinal segments will have reflex lubrication but not psychogenic lubrication (Sipski et al., 1995b).

Subjects with incomplete SCIs were also studied to observe their responses to audiovisual stimulation and audiovisual combined with manual stimulation (Sipski, Alexander, & Rosen, 1997). Subjects were grouped based on their ability to discriminate pinprick from light touch sensation in the T-11 to L-2 dermatomes. Those subjects with preservation of pinprick sensation in the T-11 to L-2 dermatomes demonstrated a significant increase in vaginal pulse amplitude in response to audiovisual stimulation alone, whereas those subjects with preservation of only light touch sensation in the T-11 to L-2 dermatomes did not. Concomitantly, both groups of subjects showed similar significant increases in their levels of subjective sexual arousal. When manual clitoral stimulation was added to the audiovisual stimulation, both groups of subjects demonstrated similar significant increases in vaginal pulse amplitude. During this experimental condition, however, only those subjects with preservation of T-11 to L-2 pinprick sensation demonstrated a further significant increase in their level of subjective sexual arousal. Both groups of subjects had similar nongenital responses. Furthermore, both groups of subjects had increased blood pressure in response to the addition of manual clitoral stimulation; however, at no time were there any recorded blood pressures that were considered dangerously high. Overall, the results support the hypotheses that the ability to achieve psychogenic lubrication in women with incomplete UMN SCIs can be predicted based on the preservation of the ability to perceive pinprick sensation in the T-11 to L-2 dermatomes and that women with incomplete SCIs with UMN injuries affecting the sacral spinal segments will retain the capacity for reflex lubrication.

To definitively prove that women with SCIs with UMN injuries affecting the sacral spinal segments have the capacity for reflex lubrication, subjects underwent an additional experimental protocol designed to determine their responses to genital stimulation during the performance of a distracting task (Sipski et al., 1996). Based on similar testing of able-bodied males and males with complete SCIs, performance of the Stroop test (Stroop, 1935) was used as a means to distract the subjects during masturbation, thus allowing the visualization of the effects of reflex genital stimulation. Whereas males with complete SCIs achieved erections under conditions of the Stroop test plus manual genital stimulation, able-bodied men did not (Sipski, 1992). In contrast, able-bodied women and women with preservation of T-11 to L-2 pinprick sensation developed significant increases in vaginal pulse amplitude during the performance of the Stroop test in conjunction with genital stimulation, and women with complete SCIs and women with preservation of only light touch sensation in the genital regions did not. These experimental conditions were thought to isolate reflex vaginal lubrication because subjective arousal increased only slightly during the conditions and continued to increase when the Stroop test was removed and women just masturbated. However, as the results stand, they do not support the hypothesis that women with SCIs with UMN injuries affecting the sacral spinal segments will achieve reflex lubrication. Review of the conditions of the experimental protocol led the authors to conclude that the preceding hypothesis is probably true and that it was too taxing for women with SCIs with deficits in hand function to perform the Stroop test in conjunction with manual genital stimulation. Therefore, the authors indicated they did not get a true reading of the women's ability to achieve reflex lubrication; they plan to study women with SCIs and normal hand function to confirm this postulation. Furthermore, results obtained in the able-bodied females in the study underscored the dangers of equating the sexual responses of males with females. In that instance, the responses of males and females may have been different because it was more difficult to achieve an erection than it was to have a significant increase in vaginal pulse amplitude; however, further physiologic testing will be required to resolve this issue.

As part of the same study, subjects were brought in the laboratory and asked to stimulate themselves to orgasm in any way they chose (Sipski et al., 1995a). All able-bodied subjects were able to achieve orgasm, whereas only 52% of the women with SCIs achieved orgasm. The ability of women with SCIs to achieve orgasm was unrelated to the type or degree of incompleteness of their injury. However, the able-bodied women achieved orgasm more quickly, followed by women with partial lower-extremity paralysis. Women with complete lower-extremity paralysis took the longest time. Heart rates and respiratory rates were significantly higher at orgasm compared with the baseline in both subjects with SCIs and able-bodied subjects. Systolic blood pressure responses were significantly higher at orgasm only in subjects with SCIs; however, at no time during the experimental protocol did any women with SCIs develop dangerously elevated blood pressure responses. Subjective descriptions of orgasm were generally similar between able-bodied subjects and women with SCIs (Table 9–1). The only two variables that were significantly different in women who could and could not achieve orgasm were the presence of greater sexual knowledge and higher sex drive in women who achieved orgasms.

Whipple, Gerdes, and Komisaruk (1996) have also recently reported that women with complete SCIs are capable of experiencing orgasm in response to both geni-

Table 9–1 Percentage of Females Indicating Desire, Arousal, and Satisfaction Pre-SCI and Post-SCI

	All Subjects (n = 25)		Quadriplegics Complete (n = 5)		Quadriplegics Incomplete (n = 9)		Paraplegics Complete (n = 4)		Paraplegics Incomplete (n = 7)	
	Pre-SCI	Post-SCI	Pre-SCI	Post-SCI	Pre-SCI	Post-SCI	Pre-SCI	Post-SCI	Pre-SCI	Post-SCI
Desire pre- and post-SCI										
None to low	20	44	0	20	22	33	50	75	14	57
Appropriate	44	32	40	20	33	44	50	0	57	43
High	36	24	60	60	44	22	0	25	29	0
Satisfaction pre- and post-SCI										
Very dissatisfied	4	8	0	0	0	0	0	0	0	14
Dissatisfied	4	16	0	0	0	0	0	0	0	14
Indifferent	20	28	20	20	22	11	20	75	14	29
Satisfied	28	28	60	20	11	22	60	25	14	43
Very satisfied	44	20	20	60	55	22	20	0	57	0
Arousability post-SCI										
None to low		32		20		22		50		29
Appropriate		40		20		56		25		57
High		28		60		22		25		14

Source: Reprinted with permission from M.L. Sipski, C.J. Alexander, Sexual Activities, Response and Satisfaction in Women Pre- and Post-Spinal Cord Injury, *Archives of Physical Medical Rehabilitation*, Vol. 74, pp. 1025–1029, W.B. Saunders Company.

tal and nongenital forms of stimulation. They monitored changes in heart rate, blood pressure, and arousal levels in 16 women with complete SCIs and 5 able-bodied women in response to periods of vaginal self-stimulation, cervical self-stimulation, and hypersensitive area stimulation. Three women with complete SCIs and one able-bodied woman self-reported experiencing orgasms while in the laboratory. Self-reports of orgasms in the women with complete SCIs included one woman who reported experiencing multiple orgasms from vaginal and cervical self-stimulation, a second woman who reported experiencing one orgasm from cervical self-stimulation and multiple orgasms from vaginal self-stimulation and hypersensitive area stimulation, and a third woman who reported one orgasm in response to cervical self-stimulation. During self-reported orgasm, heart rate and blood pressure significantly increased over resting baseline levels in the able-bodied female, and a significant increase in blood pressure over baseline resting levels was observed in the women with SCIs. Whipple and colleagues (1996) have proposed that blood pressure and heart rate in women with complete SCIs are possibly mediated by different mechanisms, which can account for why they did not observe an increase in heart rate during self-reported orgasms in the women with SCIs.*

In summary, recent research aimed at studying the sexual responses of women with SCIs has begun to confirm previous hypotheses about what responses should and should not occur in women with different levels and degrees of SCIs. Thus far, data support the hypothesis that women with complete UMN SCIs affecting their sacral spinal segments will retain the ability for reflex but not psychogenic lubrication. Supporting data have also been found for the hypothesis that the ability to achieve psychogenic lubrication in women with incomplete SCIs will be predictable based on the preservation of the ability to discriminate pinprick from light touch sensation in the T-11 to L-2 dermatomes. Furthermore, data have supported the hypothesis that women with incomplete SCIs with UMN injuries affecting their sacral spinal segments will retain the capacity for reflex lubrication. Moreover, observation of women with SCIs has confirmed that, despite the presence of complete SCIs, women retain the capacity to achieve orgasm, and orgasm is accompanied by physiologic and subjective changes similar to those of able-bodied women. It is important that similar physiologic studies of women with other levels and patterns of SCIs continue to develop an overall picture of how SCIs affect sexual response. Furthermore, information obtained about the impact of various lesions can be used to begin to understand the impact of various neurologic disorders on sexual response.

MALE SEXUALITY

This section examines what is known about sexual desire, arousal, activities, and satisfaction after an SCI. These topics are subjective and generally without standardized definitions, and measures are generally unavailable pertaining to people with SCIs (Willmuth, 1987). Perhaps this is why information in the literature is inconsistent.

Sexual desire has been shown to decrease after an SCI (Alexander et al., 1993); however, the majority of males with SCIs still demonstrate interest in sexual activity (Alexander et al., 1993; Berkman, Weissman, & Frielich, 1978; Phelps et al., 1983). Berkman et al. (1978) found that 95% of 145 males with SCIs continued to have an interest in sex. Alexander et al. (1993) further found that 78% of 38 males with SCIs still rated their sexual desire as appropriate or high. Similarly, Phelps et al. (1983) found that only 20% of 50 males with SCIs reported their

---

*The author gratefully acknowledges Carolyn Gerdes for the preceding summary of the research she and her colleagues have performed.

sexual desire was weak or very weak. Whereas early reports (Hohmann, 1972; Janos & Hakmiller, 1975) indicated the more severe the level of injury the greater the decrease in sexual desire, more recent reports have noted preservation of sensation is unnecessary for sexual excitement (Alexander et al., 1993).

The ability to become sexually aroused in specific body parts and overall has been examined and is known to be altered by SCIs. Phelps et al. (1983) found that 75% of paraplegics versus 40% of quadriplegics enjoyed nipple stimulation, and concluded these subjects were able to do so because the area around the level of injury was hypersensitive and an erogenous zone. Thus, stimulation above the level of injury is often recommended in sexuality education programs. Concomitantly, 72% of males in the Phelps et al. (1983) study indicated genital stimulation was arousing. Likewise, Alexander et al. (1993) found that 59% of subjects reported their penis as arousable and 41% reported their testicles were arousable after SCIs, even though the majority of the subjects had complete SCIs. Whereas 81% of the Alexander et al. (1993) study subjects reported their overall ability to become sexually aroused as appropriate to high, arousability did not correlate with age or level of injury. This finding is not surprising given the ability of body parts both above and below the level of injury to be aroused.

The majority of patients with SCIs resume sexual activity within 1 year of injury (Alexander et al., 1993). However, despite resumption of activity, the frequency of sexual activity has consistently been shown to diminish after SCIs. Sjogren and Egberg (1983) demonstrated a decrease in coital frequency by half from three to four times per week pre-SCI to one to two times per week post-SCI. Similarly, Alexander et al. (1993) indicated that 52% of their subjects had sex two to three times per week and 48% had sex once a week or less before their injury; however, postinjury, only 30% had sex two to three times per week and 70% had sex once a week or less. The reason for the decline in sexual activity following SCIs has been studied: Phelps et al. (1983) noted fewer opportunities for sex, whereas Alexander et al. (1993) found that the partner's desire for sex correlated with the frequency of sexual activity. This finding was in contrast with pre-injury, when both the patient's and their partner's desire for sex correlated with frequency of sexual activity. Level and degree of SCI were not found to correlate with frequency of sexual activity post-SCI. Overall, Alexander et al. (1993) concluded that frequency of sexual activity postinjury was contingent on the ability to meet, or the availability of, potential interested sexual partners.

The types of sexual activities men engage in after an SCI have also been studied. Phelps et al. (1983) commented on the sexual techniques used by their subjects post-SCI. Of the subjects, 78% reported engaging in oral–vaginal stimulation, 76% reported stroking the penis, and only 54% reported engaging in penile–vaginal intercourse. No information was provided on the frequency of activities before injury. Alexander et al. (1993) also queried their subjects on the sexual activities they participated in before their SCIs, and found that, before their injuries, 97% of men engaged in sexual intercourse; 97%, in kissing; 89%, in hugging; and 87%, in touching. However, postinjury, 84% of men engaged in kissing; 79%, in hugging; 76%, in touching; and only 61%, in penile–vaginal intercourse. This change in activities parallels the subject's change in preference for activities. Before injury, 99% of men reported penile–vaginal intercourse was their favorite activity, whereas postinjury, only 16% of men preferred the same. Instead, most men postinjury preferred oral sex, kissing, and hugging. Those same subjects reported they engaged in the same range of activities for their partner's pleasure both before and after their SCIs.

Sexual satisfaction has consistently been shown to decrease after an SCI; however, agreement has not been reached on why. Berkman et al. (1978) found that 77% of men with SCIs reported decreased sexual satisfaction after injury. Subsequently, Phelps et al. (1983) reported that 42% of their male subjects with SCIs were sexually dissatisfied. Sjogren and Egberg (1983) further reported that 61% of 21 males with SCIs had decreased sexual satisfaction primarily because of decreased ability to achieve orgasm and problems with immobility. Halstead, Halstead, Salhoot, Stock, and Sparks (1978) agreed that there were high levels of dissatisfaction among men with SCIs; however, they reported the men were dissatisfied because they did not have a sexual partner. Alexander et al. (1993) also found that 41% of the subjects were sexually dissatisfied. Furthermore, they observed two major factors related to sexual satisfaction post-SCI: the patient's feelings and their partner's feelings about intercourse.

FEMALE SEXUALITY

The study of female sexuality after an SCI, similar to that of sexual response, has recently begun to receive more attention. In addition, a more optimistic picture of women's abilities has been painted. Much of the early works focused merely on the documentation of the persistent sexual feeling in women with SCIs. Money (1960) was one of the first researchers to comment on the sexuality of women with SCIs. He reported on seven women, three of whom had traumatic SCIs and four who had nontraumatic SCIs. Those women were markedly limited in their desire for sexual activity and their ability to be aroused; however, review of the women's pre-injury status revealed that three of these women's problems predated their SCIs.

Bregman and Hadley (1976) studied the sexuality of women with SCIs. They performed semistructured interviews with 31 women and used interview results to develop overall sexual adjustment scores for the women. The result were then correlated with the length of time postinjury and the level of sexual education the women received. The scores were found to be independent of both variables; rather, those women who accepted and understood their disabilities were more likely to achieve satisfactory sexual adjustment. This study is notable because it was the first to look at the sexuality of women with SCIs in greater depth; however, similar to most other reports, it suffered from the lack of a control group and provided inadequate data about the subjects queried.

Fitting, Salisbury, Davies, and Mayclin (1978) also performed semistructured interviews of 24 women with SCIs. Of those women, 13 reported that sexual relations were highly enjoyable before their injuries. In general, the authors concluded that the sexual interest of the women appeared to be similar both pre-SCI and post-SCI. A detailed review of the subjects' makeup, however, revealed the women to be an older, highly educated sample, and without an able-bodied control group, it is uncertain whether the results were biased because of the women's status in life.

More than 10 years passed before the study of sexuality in women with SCIs was resumed. Kettl et al. (1991) performed a mail survey of 74 women with SCIs and received responses from 27. The authors found a 23% decrease in sexual satisfaction postinjury along with a 15% decrease in the women's satisfaction with the frequency of their sexual activities. Women with complete quadriplegia reported sex was less satisfying and less important than those women with incomplete paraplegia. However, the level and degree of the women's injuries was only known in 17 women through self-report, so its reliability is uncertain. Another finding was that the women perceived their bodies only about half as attractive postinjury as they were pre-injury.

Charlifue et al. (1992) interviewed a total of 231 women with SCIs, of which approximately equal numbers were paraplegic and quadriplegic. Of the subjects, 46% indicated that sex was less important postinjury and 43% of the women reported they were less desirable postinjury. Those women who were quadriplegic generally reported themselves to have fewer sexual skills postinjury, whereas those women with paraplegia did not report this change. Although that study provided an excellent sample size, the reliance of self-report information for the women's neurologic status still limits researchers' abilities to draw conclusions from the data.

Sipski and Alexander (1993) eliminated this problem in their examination of the sexuality of women with SCIs by confirming the patients' neurologic status through physical examination. Of 25 subjects with SCIs, there were 5 women with complete quadriplegia, 4 with complete paraplegia, 7 with incomplete paraplegia, and 9 with incomplete quadriplegia. Although 76% of the women reported they had made a satisfactory sexual adjustment after their SCIs, 44% indicated that their disability negatively affected their sexual relationships. Detailed information provided about the women's sexual desire, satisfaction, and arousability post-SCI revealed that, like the males' sexual satisfaction, satisfaction in those areas significantly decreased post-SCI (Table 9–2). Attempts were made to find associations that could predict the reason for decreased sexual satisfaction after an SCI; however, no positive associations were found. In contrast, degree of desire and ability to be aroused were shown to significantly correlate postinjury.

Early information about sexual activities women with SCIs engaged in merely mentioned coitus and upper-body stimulation (Money, 1960). According to the women studied, sex was a "waste of time." Bregman and Hadley (1976) reported that women and their partners enjoyed "body massages with creams or oils; rubbing each other's backs with tongue and hands; rubbing each other's genitals; oral–genital intercourse and sucking the women's breasts" (p. 449). Comarr and Vigue (1978b) provided case histories of the activities in which women with SCIs engaged, including kissing, mild petting, fellatio, cunnilingus, and the use of a vaginal vibrator. More recently, reports have revealed that there is generally little change in the types of activities in which women with SCIs engage, compared with the able-bodied population (Charlifue et al., 1992; Kettl et al., 1991; Sipski & Alexander, 1993). One area of significant difference, however, is that fewer women masturbate post-SCI. Although types of activities engaged in do not change, women's preference for activities post-SCI have been found to change. Although intercourse was the preferred activity pre-injury, Sipski and Alexander (1993) reported that their subjects preferred kissing, hugging, and touching postinjury. Furthermore, most of the subjects reported arousability of the mouth and lips, whereas only 32% reported arousability of their clitoris.

Frequency of sexual activity has generally been shown to decrease post-SCI. Zwerner (1982) reported that 45% of the respondents studied had a decrease in sexual activity post-SCI, 37% had no change, and 15% had an increase in activity. Those women who were sexually active on a daily or monthly basis pre-injury had less change in their level of activity postinjury than those who were active two to three times per week. Furthermore, Charlifue et al. (1992) reported that those subjects who were sexually active at least once per week decreased from 76% to 52% post-SCI.

In summary, studies of sexuality in males and females with SCIs have revealed similar results. An SCI results in a significant decrease in sexual satisfaction and frequency of sexual activity. The reasons for this decrease in satisfaction and frequency have not been well studied but are probably related to a decrease in the availability and interest of a partner. The sexual activities in which a person engages after an SCI generally remain unchanged, with the exception of participation in intercourse by males with SCIs and a decrease in masturbation by women with SCIs. Whether there is a similar decrease in the participation of men with SCIs in masturbation is unknown; however, if the decrease in satisfaction post-SCI is related to the lack of an interested partner, encouraging men and women with SCIs to masturbate and determine what sexual techniques will allow them to achieve pleasure may be appropriate. Furthermore, recent information about the potential of people with SCIs to obtain orgasm may indicate there is a good prognosis for improving the sexual satisfaction if appropriate treatment protocols can be developed.

TREATMENT OF ERECTILE DYSFUNCTION

Most men with SCIs will have some type of erectile dysfunction. However, although they may not have their usual psychogenic or reflex erections, many men will be able to have an erection that is adequate for penetration. Concomitantly, most men with SCIs will be on some kind of medication that will have the potential to cause a diminution in erectile function. Thus, when working with a man with an SCI, it is important to address the specific circumstances involving his erectile dysfunction and what medications he is taking.

Based on the existing knowledge of how various types of SCIs affect male sexual response, a certain percentage of males with LMN injuries affecting their sacral spinal segments should be unable to have reflex or psychogenic erections. Furthermore, a percentage of those men who are able to have some type of erection after an SCI will find them inadequate for penetration and of insufficient duration to please their partners. In the past, the only technique that was available for those men would be to teach them the technique of "stuffing" their penis into the vagina; however, much work has been done in this arena, and many techniques that now exist to treat impotence have been tested in men with SCIs.

The first technique to become available to treat erectile dysfunction was the penile prosthesis. However, this destructive technique has a high incidence of infection and extrusion after an SCI. Out of a total of 101 men with SCIs, 27 received inflatable and 74 received semirigid prostheses. Of those men, 33 men suffered serious complications including infection or extrusion of the device with necessity for surgical revision (Collins & Hackler, 1988; Golji, 1979; Light & Scott, 1981). Thus, insertion of a penile prosthesis is generally not advocated as a first-line treatment for erectile dysfunction resulting from an SCI.

Injections of combinations of medications have been used to treat impotence after an SCI. Medications tested have included phenoxybenzamine and phentolamine (both alpha-blockers); papaverine (a smooth-muscle relaxant); and prostaglandin E_1. Although success has been reported around the world with various combinations of these medications (Earle et al., 1990; Kapoor et al., 1993), the only medication approved by the U.S. Food and Drug Administration and now available for purchase in the United States in a convenient kit is prostaglandin E_1. Combined side effects reported from injection therapy with various drugs have included priapism, dysesthesia, ecchymosis, declining erectile quality, seizures, and intracorporeal fibrosis (Bodner, Lindan, Leffler, Kursh, & Resnick, 1987; Linsenmeyer, 1991; Lloyd & Richards, 1989).

Table 9–2 Quality of Orgasm—All Female Subjects

Level of Injury	Where and How Did You Stimulate Yourself to Orgasm?	Where Did You Feel the Orgasm?	What Was the Feeling Associated with the Orgasm?	How Was Your Sexual Response—Was It Similar to Your Typical Sexual Experience? Is This the Place You Are Usually Stimulated and Where You Usually Feel the Orgasm?
T-5A	Vaginal area/no vibrator	Stomach, head	Warm, tight, nice, relaxing feeling	Different/Yes
C-7C	Clitoris/with vibrator and mentally	All over	Warm, intense tingling that spreads over	Yes/Yes
C-5D	Clitoral region/with vibrator	Mostly genital, but all over	Good	Yes/Yes
C-5B	Breasts and clitoris were manually stimulated/no vibrator	In clitoral region and in head	Tingling and warm sensation	Yes/No
C-5A	Breasts, clitoris/no vibrator	Felt throbbing in vaginal area	Felt throbbing inside breasts and clitoral region	Not really/Yes
C-5D	Clitoris/no vibrator	Vaginal, pelvic area	Felt good; feels like a lot of muscle contractions/continuous for a while	Yes/Yes
C-4 to C-5A	Breasts, vagina/used vibrator	Decrease in breathing, blood pressure is slowing down, heart rate slows down, sex flush is intense then drops	Feeling of release	Yes/Yes
C-5B	Genital area/used vibrator, but not on	Genital area	Same as before; "euphoric" orgasm not same without partner	Differs/Yes
C-7A	Genital area/no vibrator	All over	Feels good; heightened then release	No/I guess

C-6B	Clitoral stimulation/distal of labia minor, crevice or ridge that goes to anterior portion of vagina—firm stimulation with both hands/used vibrator	Clitoris, labia minor, genitalia	Genitalia—focused/fantasy/relaxing/comfortable experience, was not concerned or nervous about dysreflexia; tingling, tight, some spasticity little nerve going from vagina to belly button, no sweating	No/No, very different—more intense
C-7D	"Clitoris, vagina, some thighs"/used vibrator	Head, scalp, behind knees	Tingling, dry mouth; afterward, pulsing in vagina	Yes/Yes
T-1B	Vagina, clitoris/used vibrator	Vagina, face, arms, anus	Tension and release	Same feeling/Yes
C-3 to C-4D	Clitoris, breasts/used vibrator	All over	Buildup, then release	Yes/Yes
No injury	No response	Vaginal area	Overall release, build up to peak and coming down	Yes
No injury	In vaginal area	Vaginal region	Warm, relaxing, tingling	Yes
No injury	Breasts, stroked inside of thighs, played with clitoral region	Deep inside vagina, clitoris expanded	Excitement, then contentment	No/Yes
No injury	Clitoris	Genital area, legs, back	Great, wave of sensation from clitoris and spreading all around	Yes/Just on one of them
No injury	Clitoris	Vaginal area	Wonderful, tension release, feels good	Yes/No
No injury	Clitoris	Vagina	Great	No response
No injury	Clitoris, breasts	Clitoris	Extremely pleasurable	Yes/Yes
No injury	Clitoris	Genitals	Feels good, tension release	Yes/Yes

Source: Reprinted with permission from M.L. Sipski, C.J. Alexander, and R.C. Rosen, Orgasm in Women with Spinal Cord Injuries: A Laboratory-Based Assessment, *Archives of Physical Medical Rehabilitation,* Vol. 76, pp. 1097–1102, © 1995, W.B. Saunders Co.

Another technique used extensively in men with SCIs is a vacuum that produces penile engorgement, which is followed by the application of a constricting band at the base of the penis. Although this technique is generally considered less invasive, it is sometimes considered less cosmetically appealing than other methods because the penis tends to pivot at the base where the constricting band is placed. Furthermore, distal to the band, the penis can be discolored with evidence of dilated blood vessels. Moreover, this technique is not without potential complications. Use of the constricting band is limited to 30 minutes to prevent ischemia to the penis, and individuals who are on anticoagulants or who have blood dyscrasia should not be provided with this device. Rivas and Chancellor (1994) have presented case reports of one individual with an SCI who sustained a gangrenous phallus after overnight use of a constriction device and another individual who sustained a significant phallic deformity as a result of using a vacuum constriction device while on anticoagulants. For those individuals with an SCI who are able to achieve but not sustain erections, the use of a constricting band without vacuum preparation may be sufficient to maintain an erection for the desired time; however, the user must follow the aforementioned guidelines with caution.

Other methods to remediate erectile dysfunction, such as the use of surface and oral medications, will undoubtedly be tried in men with SCIs. To date, however, these methods have not been shown to be of substantial benefit for this patient population.

BIRTH CONTROL

Although women with SCIs are capable of pregnancy, little research has examined optimal birth control methods. Nevertheless, the following methods might be appropriate. Diaphragms, cervical caps, female condoms, and contraceptive sponges may be difficult to manipulate because of decreased hand strength and loss of sensation. Some women with an SCI have used intrauterine devices (IUDs); however, potential hazards in women with SCI are a lack of sensation so that they do not notice a migration and the possibility for development of autonomic dysreflexia above the level of T-6. Furthermore, Jackson (1995) has pointed out that pelvic inflammatory disease has been associated with IUD use; women with SCIs who may have infected urinary tracts must keep this in mind. Birth control pills are often considered contraindicated because of a high risk for thrombophlebitis after an SCI; however, out of 70 women with SCIs who took birth control pills for an undetermined period of time only four developed thrombophlebitis (McCluer, 1991).

With such limited information, further research will need to be done to make more definitive recommendations about birth control pills and SCI. More recently, levonorgestrol implants surgically placed in the subcutaneous tissue of the inner upper arm have been used as a long-term contraceptive method (Moore, 1992). Levonorgestrol does not use estrogen and requires no hand manipulation, therefore it may be appropriate for women with SCIs. Another birth control method, the male condom, has the advantage of being chemical free and does not require the woman to have manual dexterity. Furthermore, if there is any doubt that the woman is involved in a mutually monogamous relationship, the male condom is the best method available to prevent sexually transmitted diseases.

MALE INFERTILITY

Male infertility and its treatment are covered in depth elsewhere in this book; therefore, discussion in this chapter is brief. Male infertility is common after an SCI mainly because of the ejaculation problems men with SCIs have in addition to low sperm counts and poor sperm motility. Bors and Comarr (1960) found that only 4% of men with complete UMN, 18% with complete LMN, 32% with incomplete UMN, and 70% with incomplete LMN reported the ability to achieve anterograde ejaculation after an SCI. For those men with SCIs who are unable to ejaculate in an anterograde fashion, an unknown number of men are thought to ejaculate in a retrograde fashion.

Diminished sperm count and motility are thought to be of multifactorial etiology with stasis, lack of temperature control, and chronic infections all considered contributory (Sipski & Alexander, 1992). Furthermore, Linsenmeyer, Pogach, Ottenweller, and Huang (1994) have shown that alterations in sperm count occur within weeks of an SCI. As a result of increased sophistication with assisted reproductive technologies, though, a decrease in sperm count has become less of a barrier to individuals who are trying to conceive.

Stimulation of ejaculation is most often performed using electrovibration and electroejaculation. Each of these techniques is discussed in detail in Chapter 24, thus discussion in this chapter is limited. Electrovibration has been reported to require integrity of the L-2 to S-1 spinal segments in addition to a return of reflex activity (Brindley, 1984). In their review of the literature on electrovibration, Beckerman, Becher, and Lankhorst (1993) noted that, of 428 patients, 60% produced an ejaculate. Because of methodological differences, they could not draw any conclusions between injury type and response rates. However, the authors observed that sperm motility and morphology were abnormal despite the generally normal semen volume.

One of the problems with obtaining an ejaculate has been determining optimum vibratory frequency and amplitude. Sonsken, Biering-Sorensen, and Kristensen (1994), however, have determined optimum stimulation parameters of 2.5 mm amplitude and 100 Hz frequency. Ohl, Menge, and Sonksen (1996) used those parameters in a series of 34 men with SCIs who were undergoing electrovibration. Results revealed 65% of patients had anterograde ejaculation. Of those patients with lesions above T-10, 81% ejaculated anterograde and 77% of those patients with hip flexion and bulbocavernosus reflexes ejaculated anterograde. Sperm counts averaged at 968 million with 26% motility. It is anticipated that, with continued use of the electrovibration parameters, future clinical studies will result in optimal results.

Electroejaculation, although more invasive, has been used more frequently in the United States than electrovibration. This technique must always be performed in a clinic and thus is more costly than electrovibration; however, it is also known to give more predictable results than electrovibration. The availability and success rates for this technique have also greatly increased since it first resulted in a live birth in 1975. Currently, optimization of live pregnancy rates is performed by combining electroejaculation with assisted reproductive technologies. Furthermore, the impact of bladder management and concomitant infections on pregnancy rates is being assessed. Ohl, Bennett, McCabe, McGuire, and Menge (1989) observed that sperm quality from electroejaculation of men who used intermittent self-catheterization was better than that of men who used other types of bladder management. This finding was confirmed by Ohl et al. (1992), who found that 44% of men with SCIs who used intermittent catheterizations achieved pregnancy with electroejaculation versus 7% of men with SCIs who used other bladder management techniques. Moreover, the pregnancy rate was 30% in the presence of sterile male urine and only 10% in the presence of infection. It is anticipated that effective counseling of newly injured males with SCIs and the continued development of assisted reproductive technologies will result in an even greater likelihood of successful procreation for men with SCIs.

Side effects of electrovibration and electroejaculation are similar. Both techniques will result in the development of autonomic dysreflexia in males with SCIs above the level of T-6 and, therefore, pretreatment with medications is appropriate. Theoretically, it is also possible that there could be damage to the skin from excessive use of vibration or burning from the use of excessive electrical stimulation. Fortunately, however, with properly performed procedures, these side effects are rarely encountered. Two other side effects may occur, however. Approximately 25% of males will report a pleasant sensation with the performance of electroejaculation (S. Seegar, personal communication, November 1, 1991). Furthermore, both techniques are known to result in a decrease in spasticity for a few hours after the procedure occurs (Halstead & Seager, 1991; Szasz & Carpenter, 1989). In addition to determination of optimum parameters for fertility, future research should definitively determine the therapeutic benefits of these techniques both from a pleasure standpoint and as a mechanism to decrease spasticity.

MENSTRUATION AND PREGNANCY

Like many other aspects of SCIs, the outlook for successful reproductive function in women has also improved. Early reports examining the impact of an SCI on menstruation indicated that a 3- to 6-month period of post-SCI amenorrhea was typical (Comarr, 1966; Cooper & Hoen, 1952; Durkan, 1968). Furthermore, it was reported that an SCI would result in an absence of dysmenorrhea (Comarr, 1966). Axel (1982) queried 38 women with SCIs in depth about their menstrual cycles and found that 58% had temporary amenorrhea for an average 5-month duration. Cycle length was unchanged in 68%, amount of flow was unchanged in 76%, and duration of flow remained the same in 60%. Of the subjects, 56% reported no change in menstrual pain; the remainder of the subjects were equally split between an increase and decrease in pain. Charlifue et al. (1992) also noted that, of 231 women with SCIs, 60% had temporary amenorrhea for an average 5-month duration.

Other issues associated with the menstrual cycle after SCI have also been addressed. Terbizan and Schneewess (1983) noted new-onset dysmenorrhea and metrorrhagia post-SCI. Autonomic dysreflexia has also occurred in association with the premenstrual syndrome in one woman with an SCI (Allen, Stover, Jackson, & Richards, 1991). Jackson (1995) pointed out, however, that, "as menstruation—normal or abnormal—may occur in the absence of ovulation, these reports tell us little about the return of normal endocrine function after SCI" (p. 14). Furthermore, Jackson (1995) reported that, of 25 women with SCIs whose hormonal levels were studied, almost two-thirds had elevations in their prolactin levels postinjury and 12% developed galactorrhea. Hypoestrogenemia was also documented. These hormonal changes, therefore, may be responsible for some of the reported menstrual cycle disturbances.

Once there is resumption of a normal ovulatory menstrual cycle, women with SCIs should have a normal ability to conceive. However, Charlifue et al. (1992) found that the postinjury pregnancy rate of 231 women with SCIs was 0.34 pregnancy per person compared with a preinjury rate of 1.3 pregnancies per person. The authors also noted that more than one-third of the women with SCIs did not wish to become pregnant largely because of the difficulty they perceived they would experience caring for children from a wheelchair. Moreover, a significant difference was noted between postinjury pregnancy rates depending on the level of injury the woman had sustained. The pregnancy rate for complete quadriplegics was 0.15; for incomplete quadriplegics, 0.42; for complete paraplegics, 0.40; and for incomplete paraplegics, 0.63. This finding supports the hypothesis that women with more significant impairments will be less apt to have children because of the difficulties associated with caring for them.

A complete discussion of the management of pregnancy in women with SCIs is beyond the scope of this chapter; the reader is referred to the excellent review by Baker and Cardenas (1996) for further information. Any discussion of pregnancy and SCI issues, however, must examine both those instances of the woman who is pregnant and sustains an SCI and the woman with an SCI who becomes pregnant. Goller and Paeslack (1972) studied 45 women who had sustained an SCI during pregnancy. Of those pregnancies, 31 produced healthy children, 5 were spontaneously aborted, 2 were induced abortions, 5 produced children with a marked disability or malformation, 1 produced a stillborn child as the result of placenta previa, and 1 resulted in a child born prematurely who died. Despite those discouraging statistics, Baker and Cardenas (1996) reported that there really are not any available data that can be used to counsel patients about the fetal impact of an SCI during pregnancy and indicate potential mechanisms for fetal trauma. Fetal death could occur from placental abruption. Furthermore, severe hypoxia or hypotension could disturb structural development of the fetus in the first trimester or cause neural problems later in pregnancy. Because of the cushioning effect of amniotic fluid, mechanical trauma to the fetus generally does not occur. Baker and Cardenas (1996) have recommended that patients be informed of a possible increased rate of fetal malformation above the baseline rate of 3% (D'Alton & DeCherney, 1993) when a pregnancy is complicated by an SCI. Furthermore, practitioners need to inform patients that, although ultrasound may detect structural damage, it may not be possible to detect all damage antenatally.

The woman with an SCI who becomes pregnant will have unique problems associated with her pregnancy because of her SCI. Medical problems include urinary tract infections because of incomplete bladder emptying and foreign bodies such as catheters and stones. Baker and Cardenas (1996) found that the majority of women with SCIs in seven combined studies had urinary infections. Anemia had previously been noted as a problem for pregnant women with SCIs (Robertson & Guttmann, 1963; Rossier, Ruffieux, & Ziegler, 1969); however, more recent reports have provided conflicting results (Baker, Cardenas, & Benedetti, 1992). Furthermore, Baker and Cardenas (1996) have pointed out that anemia is common in pregnant able-bodied women; what is more important is to have the outcomes of women with SCIs associated with specific blood counts. Increased spasticity has been noted during pregnancy (Charlifue et al., 1992; Feyi-Waboso, 1992) as have decubitus ulcers (Baker et al., 1992; Cross, Meythaler, Tuel, & Cross, 1992; Feyi-Waboso, 1992; Westgren, Hultling, Levi, & Westgren, 1993). Baker and Cardenas (1996) pointed out that SCI and pregnancy in and of themselves do not justify the use of prophylactic anticoagulation against deep vein thrombosis and pulmonary embolism. Rather, careful attention must be paid to a woman's pulmonary function because decreases resulting from the growing fetus can result in respiratory distress.

Autonomic dysreflexia is the most life-threatening complication the pregnant woman with an SCI may face. For those women at risk because of the level of their injury, the problem may occur antepartum, intrapartum, or postpartum (Baker & Cardenas, 1996). It is important to distinguish the hypertension associated with autonomic dysreflexia from preeclampsia and provide appropriate treatment. Although a variety of methods can be used to treat autonomic dysreflexia, the most common technique used has been continuous epidural anesthesia (Baker & Cardenas, 1996).

Practitioners who are managing the pregnant women with an SCI must consider the unique attributes of SCI. Women with an SCI have poor sensation and thus will not experience the same sensations during labor as able-bodied women. However, the majority of women with SCIs do perceive labor through sympathetic symptoms such as abdominal cramping, leg spasms, difficulty breathing, back pain, abdominal pain, or symptoms of autonomic dysreflexia (Wanner, Rageth, & Zach, 1987). Moreover, women below the level of T-10 should be able to experience uterine contractions, although the feeling will be different than that of able-bodied women unless their injury level is low (Baker & Cardenas, 1996).

Previously, it was thought that preterm labor was a common occurrence in the pregnant woman with an SCI; however, Baker and Cardenas (1996) have pointed out that, although the preterm labor rate may be slightly higher than the 5% to 10% rate in the general population, it is much less than that of other high-risk groups such as women who have previously had a preterm delivery. Because of the poor sensory perception of women with SCIs, however, the risks of preterm delivery are great. Hence, Baker and Cardenas (1996) have recommended instructing paraplegic women in uterine palpation to detect preterm labor, examining patients with sensation when indicated by symptoms in addition to standard pregnancy visits, and considering a more intrusive plan such as home uterine contraction monitoring in women who are unable to detect symptoms of preterm labor.

In terms of rapid labor, which was previously considered common in women with SCIs, more recent reports have indicated length of labor within the normal range (Baker et al., 1992). This perception may be the result of patients' sensory deficits, which caused them to report to the hospital in active or advanced labor (Baker & Cardenas, 1996). Finally, in terms of mode of delivery, there appears to be an increase in the rate of Caesarean section over the current U.S. rate of 25% (Baker & Cardenas, 1996). Rates in recent reports have varied from a high of 67% (Westgren et al., 1993) to a low of 18% (Hughes, Short, Usherwood, & Tebbutt, 1991); however, most reports have indicated rates in the 20% to 30% range (Baker & Cardenas, 1996).

CONCLUSION

Compared with other disabilities, a relative wealth of knowledge is available about sexuality and reproductive concerns in the individual with an SCI. Current research will serve to increase this fund of knowledge. Because of the similarities in the neurologic deficits that can occur with various disabilities, it may be useful to begin to use information from the study of people with SCIs to develop hypotheses on the sexuality concerns of people with other neurologic disabilities. It is anticipated that this area will remain a fertile ground for research and improvements in patient care.

REFERENCES

Alexander C.J., Sipski, M.L, & Findley, T.W. (1993). Sexual activities, desire, and satisfaction in males pre- and post-spinal cord injury. *Archives of Sexual Behavior 22*(3), 217–228.

Allen, J.B., Stover, S.L., Jackson, A.B., & Richards, J.S. (1991). Autonomic dysreflexia and the menstrual cycle in a woman with spinal cord injury: A case report. *Neurorehabilitation, 1,* 58–62.

American Spinal Injury Association. (1992). *International standards for neurological and functional classification of spinal cord injury—Revised 1992.* Chicago: Author.

Axel, S.J. (1982). Spinal cord injured women's concerns: Menstruation and pregnancy. *Rehabilitation Nursing, 7,* 10–15.

Baker, E.R., & Cardenas, D.D. (1996). Pregnancy in spinal cord injured women. *Archives of Physical Medicine and Rehabilitation, 77,* 501–507.

Baker, E.R., Cardenas, D.D., & Benedetti, T.J. (1992). Risks associated with pregnancy in spinal cord injured women. *Obstetrics and Gynecology, 80,* 425–428.

Beckerman, H., Becher, J., & Lankhorst, G.J. (1993). The effectiveness of vibratory stimulation in anejaculatory men with spinal cord injury. Review article. *Paraplegia, 31,* 689–699.

Bennett, C.J., Seager, S.W., Vasher, E.A., & McGuire, E.J. (1988). Sexual dysfunction and electroejaculation in men with spinal cord injury: Review. *Journal of Urology, 139,* 453–456.

Berard, E.J.J. (1989). The sexuality of spinal cord injured women: Physiology and pathophysiology. A review. *Paraplegia, 27,* 99–112.

Berkman, A.H., Weissman, R., & Frielich, M.H. (1978). Sexual adjustment of spinal cord injured veterans living in the community. *Archives of Physical Medicine and Rehabilitation, 59,* 29–33.

Bodner, D.R., Lindan, R., Leffler, E., Kursh, E.D., & Resnick, M.I. (1987). The application of intracavernous injection of vasoactive medications for erection in men with spinal cord injury. *Journal of Urology, 138,* 310–311.

Bors, E., & Comarr, A.E. (1960). Neurological disturbances of sexual function with special reference to 529 patients with spinal cord injury. *Urological Survey, 110,* 191–221.

Bregman, S., & Hadley, R.G. (1976). Sexual adjustment and feminine attractiveness among spinal cord injured women. *Archives of Physical Medicine and Rehabilitation, 57,* 448–450.

Brindley, G.S. (1984). The fertility of men with spinal injuries. *Paraplegia, 22,* 337–348.

Charlifue, S.W., Gerhart, K.A., Menter, R.R., Whiteneck, G.G., & Manley, M.S. (1992). Sexual issues of women with spinal cord injuries. *Paraplegia, 30,* 192–199.

Collins, K.P., & Hackler, R.H. (1988). Complications of penile prostheses in the spinal cord injury population. *Journal of Urology, 140,* 984–985.

Comarr, A.E. (1966). Observations of menstruation and pregnancy among female spinal cord injury patients. *Paraplegia, 3,* 263–272.

Comarr, A.E., & Vigue, M. (1978a). Sexual counseling among male and female patients with spinal cord injury and/or cauda equina injury. Part I. *American Journal of Physical Medicine, 57,* 107–122.

Comarr, A.E., & Vigue, M. (1978b). Sexual counseling among male and female patients with spinal cord injury and/or cauda equina injury. Part II. *American Journal of Physical Medicine, 57,* 215–227.

Cooper, I.S., & Hoen, T.I. (1952). Metabolic disorders in paraplegic neurologies. *Neurology, 2,* 322–340.

Cross, L.L., Meythaler, J.M., Tuel, S.M., & Cross, A.L. (1992). Pregnancy, labor and delivery post spinal cord injury. *Paraplegia, 30,* 890–892.

D'Alton, M.E., & DeCherney, A.H. (1993). Prenatal diagnosis. *New England Journal of Medicine, 328,* 114–120.

Durkan, J.P. (1968). Menstruation after high spinal cord transection. *American Journal of Obstetrics and Gynecology, 100,* 521–524.

Earle, C.M., Keogh, E.J., Wisniewski, Z.S., Tulloch, A.G.S., Lord, D.J., Watters, G.R., & Glatthaar, C. (1990). Prostaglandin E1 therapy for impotence, comparison with papaverine. *Journal of Urology, 143,* 57–59.

Erickson, R.P. (1980). Autonomic hyperreflexia: Pathophysiology and medical management. *Archives of Physical Medicine and Rehabilitation, 61,* 431–440.

Feyi-Waboso, P.A. (1992). An audit of five years' experience of pregnancy in spinal cord damaged women: A regional unit's experience and a review of the literature. *Paraplegia, 30,* 631–635.

Fitting, M.D., Salisbury, S., Davies, N.H., & Mayclin, D.K. (1978). Self-concept and sexuality of spinal cord injured women. *Archives of Sexual Behavior, 7,* 143–156.

Geiger, R.C. (1979). Neurophysiology of sexual response in spinal cord injury. *Sexuality and Disability, 2,* 257–266.

Go, B.K., DeVivo, M.J., & Richards, J.S. (1995). The epidemiology of spinal cord injury. In S.L. Stover, J.A. DeLisa, & G.G. Whiteneck (Eds.), *Spinal cord injury: Clinical outcomes from the model systems* (pp. 21–55). Gaithersburg, MD: Aspen.

Golji, J. (1979). Experience with penile prosthesis in spinal cord injury patients. *Journal of Urology, 121,* 288–289.

Goller, H., & Paeslack, V. (1972). Pregnancy damage and birth-complications in the children of paraplegic women. *Paraplegia, 10,* 213–217.

Griffith, E.R., & Trieschmann, R.B. (1975). Sexual functioning in women with spinal cord injury. *Archives of Physical Medicine and Rehabilitation, 56,* 18–21.

Guttmann, L. (1969). Clinical symptomatology of spinal cord lesions. In P.J. Vinken & G.W. Bruyn (Eds.), *Handbook of clinical neurology* (Vol. 2, pp. 178–216). Amsterdam: North Holland.

Halstead, L.S., Halstead, M.G., Salhoot, J.P., Stock, D.D., & Sparks, R.W. (1978). Sexual attitudes, behavior and satisfaction for able-bodied and disabled participants attending workshops in human sexuality. *Archives of Physical Medicine and Rehabilitation, 59,* 497–501.

Halstead, L.S., & Seager, S.W.J. (1991). The effects of rectal probe electrostimulation on spinal cord injury spasticity. *Paraplegia, 29,* 43–47.

Hohmann, G.W. (1972). Considerations in the management of psychosexual readjustment in the cord injured male. *Rehabilitation Psychology, 19,* 50–58.

Hughes, S.J., Short, D.J., Usherwood, M.M., & Tebbutt, H. (1991). Management of the pregnant woman with spinal cord injuries. *British Journal of Obstetrics and Gynaecology, 98,* 513–518.

Jackson, A.B. (1995). Medical management of women with spinal cord injury: A review. *Topics in Spinal Cord Injury Rehabilitation, 1,* 11–26.

Jackson, R. (1972). Sexual rehabilitation after spinal cord injury. *Paraplegia, 10,* 50–55.

Janos, T.M., & Hakmiller, K.L. (1975). Some effects of lesion level and emotional cues on affective expression in spinal cord patients. *Psychological Reports, 37,* 859–870.

Kapoor, V.K., Chahal, A.S., Jyoti, S.P., Mundkur, Y.J., Kotwal, S.V., & Mehta, V.K. (1993). Intracavernous papaverine for impotence in spinal cord injured patients. *Paraplegia, 31,* 675–677.

Kettl, P., Zarefoss, S., Jacoby, K., Garman, C., Hulse, C.Y., Rosley, F., Corey, R., Sredy, M., Bixler, E., & Tyson, K. (1991). Female sexuality after spinal cord injury. *Sexuality and Disability, 9,* 287–295.

Light, J.K., & Scott, F.B. (1981). Management of neurogenic impotence with inflatable penile prosthesis. *Urology, 17,* 341–343.

Linsenmeyer, T.A. (1991). Evaluation and treatment of erectile dysfunction following spinal cord injury: A review. *Journal of the American Paraplegia Society, 14,* 43–51.

Linsenmeyer, T.A., Pogach, L.M., Ottenweller, J.E., & Huang, H.F.S. (1994). Spermatogenesis and the pituitary–testicular hormone axis in rats during the acute phase of spinal cord injury. *Journal of Urology, 152,* 1302–1307.

Lloyd, L.K., & Richards, J.S. (1989). Intracavernous pharmacotherapy for management of erectile dysfunction in spinal cord injury. *Paraplegia, 27,* 457–464.

McCluer, S. (1991). Reproductive aspects of spinal cord injury in females. In J.F.J. Leyson (Ed.), *Sexual rehabilitation of the spinal cord injured patient* (pp. 181–196). Clifton, NJ: Humana Press.

Money, J. (1960). Phantom orgasm in the dreams of paraplegic men and women. *Archives of General Psychiatry, 3,* 373–382.

Moore, J.G. (1992). Contraception and sterilization. In N.F. Hacker & J.G. Moore (Eds.), *Essentials of obstetrics and gynecology* (pp. 453–467). Philadelphia: W.B. Saunders.

Ohl, D.A., Bennett, C.J., McCabe, M., McGuire, E.J., & Menge, A.C. (1989). Predictors of success in electroejaculation of spinal cord injured males. *Journal of Urology, 142,* 1483–1486.

Ohl, D.A., Denil, J., Fitzgerald-Shelton, K., McCabe, M., McGuire, E.J., Menge, A.C., & Randolph, J.F. (1992). Fertility of spinal cord injured males: Effect of genitourinary infection and bladder management on results of electroejaculation. *Journal of the American Paraplegia Society, 15,* 53–59.

Ohl, D.A., Menge, A.C., & Sonksen, J. (1996). Penile vibratory stimulation in spinal cord injured men: Optimized vibration parameters and prognostic factors. *Archives of Physical Medicine and Rehabilitation, 77,* 903–905.

Phelps, G., Brown, M., Chen, J., Dunn, M., Lloyd, E., Steanick, M.L., Davidson, J.M., & Perkash, I. (1983). Sexual experience and plasma testosterone levels in male veterans after spinal cord injury. *Archives of Physical Medicine and Rehabilitation, 64,* 47–52.

Rivas, D.A., & Chancellor, M.B. (1994). Complications associated with the use of vacuum constriction devices for erectile dysfunction in the spinal cord injured population. *Journal of the American Paraplegia Society, 17,* 136–139.

Robertson, D.N.S., & Guttmann, L. (1963). The paraplegic patient in pregnancy and labour. *Proceedings of the Royal Society of Medicine, 56,* 381–387.

Rossier, A.B., Ruffieux, M., & Ziegler, W.H. (1969). Pregnancy and labour in high traumatic spinal cord lesions. *Paraplegia, 7,* 210–216.

Sipski, M.L. (1991). Spinal cord injury: What is the effect on sexual response? *Journal of the American Paraplegia Society, 14,* 40–43.

Sipski, M.L. (1992). Unpublished observations.

Sipski, M.L., & Alexander, C.J. (1992). Sexual function and dysfunction after spinal cord injury. *Physical Medicine and Rehabilitation Clinics of North America, 3,* 811–828.

Sipski, M.L., & Alexander, C.J. (1993). Sexual activities, response and satisfaction in women pre- and post-spinal cord injury. *Archives of Physical Medicine and Rehabilitation, 74,* 1025–1029.

Sipski, M.L., Alexander, C.J., & Rosen, R.C. (1995a). Orgasm in women with spinal cord injuries: A laboratory-based assessment. *Archives of Physical Medicine and Rehabilitation, 76,* 1097–1102.

Sipski, M.L., Alexander, C.J., & Rosen, R.C. (1995b). Physiological parameters associated with psychogenic sexual arousal in women with complete spinal cord injuries. *Archives of Physical Medicine and Rehabilitation, 76,* 811–818.

Sipski, M.L., Rosen, R.C., & Alexander, C.J. (1996). Physiological parameters associated with the performance of a distracting task and genital self-stimulation in women with complete spinal cord injuries. *Archives of Physical Medicine and Rehabilitation, 77,* 419–424.

Sipski, M.L., Alexander, C.J., & Rosen, R.C. (1997). Physiologic parameters associated with psychogenic sexual arousal in women with incomplete spinal cord injuries. *Archives of Physical Medicine and Rehabilitation, 78,* 305–313.

Sjogren, K., & Egberg, K. (1983). The sexual experience in younger males with complete spinal cord injury. *Scandinavian Journal of Rehabilitation Medicine, 9,* 189–194.

Sonsken, J., Biering-Sorensen, F., & Kristensen, J.K. (1994) Ejaculation induced by penile vibratory stimulation in men with spinal cord injuries. The importance of the vibratory amplitude. *Paraplegia, 32,* 651–660.

Staas, W.E., Formal, C.S., Gershkoff, A.M., Hirschwald, J.F., Schmidt, M., Schultz, A.R., & Smith, J. (1993). Rehabilitation of the spinal cord-injured patient. In J.A. DeLisa (Ed.), *Rehabilitation medicine: Principles and practice* (pp. 886–915). Philadelphia: J.B. Lippincott.

Stroop, J.R. (1935). Studies of interference in serial verbal reactions. *Journal of Experimental Psychology, 18,* 643–662.

Szasz, G., & Carpenter, C. (1989). Clinical observations in vibratory stimulation of the penis of men with spinal cord injury. *Archives of Sexual Behavior, 18,* 461–474.

Talbot, H.S. (1955). The sexual function in paraplegia. *Journal of Urology, 73,* 91–100.

Terbizan, A.T., & Schneewess, W.D. (1983). The value of gynecological examinations in spinal cord injured women. *Paraplegia, 21,* 266–269.

Wanner, M.B., Rageth, C.J., & Zach, G.A. (1987). Pregnancy and autonomic hyperreflexia in patients with spinal cord lesions. *Paraplegia, 25,* 482–490.

Westgren, N., Hultling, C., Levi, R., & Westgren, M. (1993). Pregnancy and delievery in women with a traumatic spinal cord injury in Sweden, 1980–1991. *Obstetrics and Gynecology, 81,* 926–930.

Whipple, B., Gerdes, C.A., & Komisaruk, B.R. (1996). Sexual response to self-stimulation in women with complete spinal cord injury. *Journal of Sex Research, 33,* 231–240.

Willmuth, M.E. (1987). Sexuality after spinal cord injury: A critical review. *Clinical Psychology Review, 7,* 389–412.

Zwerner, J. (1982). Yes we have troubles but nobody's listening: Sexual issues of women with spinal cord injury. *Sexuality and Disability, 5,* 158–171.

CHAPTER 10

Multiple Sclerosis

Suzanne C. Smeltzer and C. Leith Kelley

SCOPE OF THE PROBLEM

Multiple sclerosis (MS) is a demyelinating disease of the central nervous system with the onset generally occurring during adulthood; it is estimated that approximately 350,000 people in the United States alone are diagnosed with MS (Anderson et al., 1992). The consequences of demyelination include cognitive, motor, and sensory dysfunction, depending on the areas of the brain or spinal cord involved; such dysfunction may result in a variety of alterations in sexual function in men and women.

Although the incidence of sexual dysfunction increases with the severity of disability resulting from MS, sexual dysfunction may also occur early in the course of MS and, in some cases, is the presenting symptom (Mattson, 1995). Factors considered to be predictive of sexual dysfunction in MS include exacerbation of MS; increased disease activity; long duration of disease; and depression, fatigue, spasticity, and bowel and bladder symptoms (Mattson, 1995). As in other circumstances, problems in the relationship are also predictive of sexual dysfunction.

Although it is widely acknowledged that the incidence of sexual dysfunction in MS is high, there is a paucity of research on the topic (Foley & Iverson, 1992). However, some information about sexual disorders in MS is known. It has been estimated that more than 50% of women with MS and about 75% of men with MS experience some form of sexual dysfunction during the course of this chronic disease (Mattson, Petrie, Srivastava, & McDermott, 1995; Valleroy & Kraft, 1984). Despite the prevalence of altered sexual function in MS, many people with MS are unaware that the sexual difficulties they experience may be a result of the disease. However, the frequency of sexual dysfunction in MS does not necessarily mean that a given sexual dysfunction is the result of MS. A thorough and systematic sexual history is necessary to identify the nature of sexual dysfunction and possible MS-related and non–MS-related causes of sexual dysfunction (Chancellor & Blaivas, 1994; Mattson et al., 1995). As with any sexual dysfunction, appropriate health history, physical examination, and diagnostic testing are indicated to identify the specific nature of the dysfunction and to assist in identifying treatment strategies and options (Therapeutics and Technology Assessment Subcommittee, 1995).

NATURE OF SEXUAL DYSFUNCTION

Sexual dysfunction in MS includes temporary or long-term disinterest in sex; inability to experience orgasm; difficulty engaging in sexual intercourse because of the physical changes associated with MS (e.g., spasticity, fatigue, and muscle weakness); or complete lack of erection. Sexual dysfunction in MS may be a direct result of the demyelination process in the spinal cord, more specifically the spinothalamic sensory, sympathetic, and parasympathetic pathways (Barrett, 1982), or it may coexist with cognitive dysfunction and cerebral plaques seen with brain involvement.

In addition to sexual dysfunction resulting from demyelination of the sexual pathways, problems resulting from or associated with physical symptoms, psychological factors, family responses to the diagnosis and alterations in physical status of their loved one, and treatment strategies are important factors that have been implicated in sexual disorders in MS. Fatigue, depression, anxiety, bladder and bowel incontinence, decreased sensation or dysesthesia in multiple areas of the body, muscle weakness, spasticity, tremor, and cognitive changes are not uncommon in MS and may interfere with a sexual relationship. An individual's psychological reactions to MS and changes in his or her relationship with the sexual partner may occur in response to the physical, cognitive, or emotional changes associated with this chronic illness and also may have a significant impact on sexual function. Failure of the individual with MS and his or her partner to discuss these changes is a major factor in unsatisfactory sexual relationships. Sexual dysfunction may also be an unintended side effect of medications used to treat other MS symptoms.

OVERVIEW OF SEXUAL DISTURBANCES

Although a number of gender-specific sexual dysfunctions occur in MS, many are common to both men and women. Fatigue, one of the most common and most disabling symptoms of MS, can lead to decreased participation in all activities of life, including sex. Fatigue and fear of increasing the fatigue further may result in complete abandonment of sexual activity. People with MS, especially men, may fear that the exertion of sexual activity may cause a progression of the disease. They may mistake the sedation experienced after climax to weakness, and so needlessly limit their sexual activity. The sexual partner of the person with MS may fear that sexual activity will worsen the severity of MS and thus may avoid intimate physical contact.

Decreased libido is associated with cerebral plaques and also with depression in response to the physical and lifestyle changes associated with MS. Although men with MS who have decreased libido may request that testosterone levels be measured to determine if a low testosterone level is the cause of their waning interest in sex, testosterone levels are likely to be within normal limits (Mattson, 1995). People with MS may also attribute changes in libido to a lack of interest in their specific sexual partner rather than to sexual dysfunction on their part.

Cognitive changes may have a profound effect on quality of life, including sexual function. It is estimated that some degree of cognitive impairment occurs in 43% to 65% of people with MS (Rao et al., 1991). A recent study (Rao et al., 1991) of 100 people with MS revealed greater disturbance in activities of daily living including sexual function in those people with cognitive impairment compared with those without cognitive impairment. Cognitive changes such as apathy, confusion, and diminished interest in activities can lead to major changes in relationships, including those with sexual partners. In rare circumstances, cerebral lesions may result in the development of fetishes or hypersexuality.

Sexual dysfunction also often occurs in combination with bowel and bladder dysfunction. As a result, those individuals with bowel or bladder incontinence may fear loss of bowel or bladder control during sexual activity. Hence, they may avoid sexual activity, fearing rejection or disgust on the part of their partner if soiling does occur. The partner may also fear contamination and avoid sexual contact as a result.

Muscle spasticity, which is common in MS in men and women, may be triggered during sexual activity. Spasticity of the hip adductors may be severe enough in women to be a barrier to sexual intercourse. Nighttime spasticity, frequent nightly trips to the bathroom, or nighttime incontinence can lead couples to abandon sharing the same bed and even the same bedroom to allow the healthy spouse a good night's rest. In this way, MS can impair the emotional and sexual intimacy that is fostered from a couple's sleeping together.

People with MS may fear loss of sexual attractiveness, rejection by their partner, and abandonment. Women may be unable to apply makeup because of hand tremor, poor eyesight, or impaired coordination. They may find it necessary to change from heels to flat shoes if they need to wear ankle–foot orthotic braces or if their balance is compromised by the disease. Men may be unable to shave or maintain their usual grooming and hygiene. Men who experience difficulty satisfying a sexual partner may be concerned about their partner's perception of them and may fear that their partner will be unfaithful or will abandon them. Men and women with MS without a sexual partner may isolate themselves when sexual difficulties arise, feeling that, with their sexual problems, they would be unable to find an understanding partner. Such social isolation may play a role in the development of depression, which may further affect sexual function.

In addition to the effects of physical and psychological changes on sexual function, medications used to alleviate symptoms and complications of MS may themselves affect sexual function (Table 10–1). Medications commonly prescribed for the management of MS that are known to interfere with sexual function include antidepressants, as well as antispasticity, anticholinergic, and antianxiety agents. Phenothiazines, benzodiazepines, and barbiturates as well as antispasmodics may decrease libido. Tricyclic antidepressants may interfere with erection in men and vaginal lubrication in women (Lechtenberg & Ohl, 1994). For people who receive subcutaneous interferon-β injections, painful or inflamed skin lesions on the thighs, buttocks, or abdomen may cause discomfort during sexual activity (Kelley & Smeltzer, 1994), necessitating modification of sexual positions to minimize pressure on tender areas. If the partner is unaware that MS or medications used in its treatment can cause sexual difficulties, the partner may attribute changes in the sexual relationship to lack of concern for his or her sexual needs by the person with MS or to replacement by another sexual partner.

Sexual dysfunction varies from one person to the next and within the same person. This variability and the unpredictability of symptoms of MS, including sexual dysfunction, may make it difficult for some people and their sexual partners to plan their sexual activities and to accommodate unexpected changes in sexual function. Failure of the individual with MS and his or her partner to discuss the physical and emotional changes brought about by MS is a major deterrent to a satisfactory sexual relationship and to identifying strategies to address changes in sexual function. If the sexual partners are unaccustomed to open, honest communication about their sexual desires and needs, they are unlikely to easily share information about changes in their desires and needs as a result of MS. The occurrence of changes in MS symptoms is likely to be frightening to the affected individual, family members, and sexual partners and can affect sexual function. Failure of the affected person to inform the partner of changes in physical status may lead to a misunderstanding that may undermine the sexual relationship. For example, keeping information from the sexual partner, such as that fatigue has increased in severity or that altered sensation or decreased libido has developed, is likely to result in differences in expectations, unrecognized and unmet needs, disappointment, anger, and resentment.

Family or marital stress is frequently increased in the presence of chronic and unpredictable diseases such as MS. Role reversals, decreased family income, decreased self-esteem, increased medical expenses, and the inability of the affected

Table 10–1 Sexual Problems Associated with Medications Used in Multiple Sclerosis

Drug Category	Associated Sexual Dysfunction
Antidepressants	Reduced libido, reduction of genital sensations, anorgasmia, ejaculatory disturbances, priapism (rare)
Antispasmodics	Erectile dysfunction, ejaculatory disturbances
Antianxiety agents	Erectile dysfunction, ejaculatory disturbances
Anticholinergics	Erectile dysfunction

partner to shoulder his or her share of family chores may lead to depression and loss of libido for both partners and interfere with the family and sexual relationships.

MANAGEMENT OF SEXUAL DYSFUNCTION

Certain strategies may minimize many of the difficulties experienced by men and women with MS. When fatigue is a major complaint, individuals can plan sexual activity for early morning when people with MS generally have more energy. Amantadine (Symmetrel) is a medication that may help some people with fatigue. Keeping the environment cool may also improve energy in people who are heat sensitive; however, cool temperatures may aggravate spasticity. Antispasmodics such as baclofen (Lioresal) are often prescribed to treat spasticity; however, they may contribute to sexual dysfunction. Spasticity can be managed with position changes. Because spasm of the hip adductors tends to cause the most problems, using side- or rear-entry positions may eliminate this barrier to intercourse when the female partner has spasms. Individuals also may use alternate forms of sexual activity, such as oral sex. Practitioners may suggest that individuals with MS increase the intensity or amount of stimulation with vibrators or other sexual aids when sensation or arousal is affected. Availability of mail-order catalogs enables discussion and selection of a wide variety of devices to use at home. To maintain the sexual relationship and isolate it from custodial care, it is often recommended that, if such care is needed by people severely afflicted with MS, it be performed by outside personnel to the extent possible rather than to have the sexual partner assume that care.

Because sexual dysfunction in MS often occurs in combination with loss of control of bowel and bladder function, efforts to minimize the effects of these losses of control on sexual function are important. Bladder incontinence can be managed by emptying the bladder immediately before intercourse or by withholding fluids in the hours preceding sexual activity. Position changes can decrease pressure on the bladder. In addition, for those people who are able to catheterize themselves, anticholinergics such as oxybutynin (Ditropan) can reduce bladder spasticity and incontinence. DDAVP (desmopressin acetate), a synthetic form of antidiuretic hormone or vasopressin, may reduce incontinence in some individuals by decreasing urinary output. DDAVP is given once a day, generally at night. Those people with significant lower extremity edema or hypertension would not be suitable for this medication. Although use of an indwelling urinary catheter is not recommended for long-term management of urinary incontinence, the presence of such a catheter is not a contraindication for participation in sex. An indwelling catheter can remain in place during sex: It can be folded back over the penis and both the penis and catheter covered with a condom. In women, the catheter can be taped out of the way anteriorly or laterally (Lechtenberg & Ohl, 1994).

Bowel continence is best promoted through a bowel program. For individuals with bowel incontinence, sexual activity can be planned so that it precedes intestinal stimulants such as meals or coffee. Bathing or showering together can be made part of the sexual experience and may help reassure the person with incontinence as well as his or her partner who fears contamination during sex. For example, one couple had their shower enlarged because the wife was only comfortable having sex with her incontinent husband in that environment.

If a sexual problem occurs after the initiation of a specific medication, changing the prescription, modifying the dosage, or providing a drug holiday can help determine if the dysfunction is a result of the medication. For medications that do not achieve a steady state in the bloodstream, timing sexual activity to the trough of the medication may be all that is needed.

Strategies to promote effective communication related to changes associated with MS, including sexual function, are essential. Throughout the course of MS, it is both important and appropriate for the practitioner to discuss possible alterations in sexual function. People with MS and their partners need to feel comfortable discussing sexuality and changes in sexual function with their health care providers. In addition, they may need assistance and encouragement to discuss sexual concerns between themselves. A variety of publications are available that include discussions of sexual function and are directed toward people with MS and their partners. Referral to a family or sexual therapist who is experienced with the effects of chronic illness on families is often helpful in preserving or restoring sexual relationships. Support groups often help people with MS and their family members to discuss the effects of MS on their lives and to address other relationship issues that affect sexual relationships. Local chapters of the National Multiple Sclerosis Society sponsor a variety of support groups and are often able to suggest local therapists who have experience working with MS families.

Male Sexual Dysfunction

The most frequent sexual dysfunctions reported in men with MS (Table 10–2) are inability to attain and maintain an erection, disturbed ejaculation, decreased libido, and difficulty reaching orgasm. These may exist together or separately. Of the men with MS who are between the ages of 18 and 50 years, 25% to 40% have erectile dysfunction (Lechtenberg, 1995), defined as being unable to maintain an erection long enough to satisfy a sexual partner 50% of the time. Men with inability to maintain erections may still have orgasms and ejaculate.

Treatment for erectile dysfunction associated with MS is available and may be as easy as having the man empty his bladder before sexual activity (Bering-Sorenson & Sonksen, 1992). For others, alternative treatment options may be necessary. Options are best presented to the couple whenever possible, allowing them to determine together which method of management or treatment they prefer. It is important when discussing treatment options that health care providers minimize any personal feelings they have about the available options.

At this time, several methods are available to treat inability to maintain an erection; three methods in particular enhance the engorgement of the penis and produce erection: (1) medications, (2) vacuum devices, and (3) penile implants. These methods are discussed in more detail in Chapter 22. The most common route of administration for medications to treat erectile dysfunction is by injection into the corpora cavernosa of the penis. Penile injections of a vasoactive agent such as papaverine, phentolamine, or prostaglandin E are an option for men with erectile dysfunction; however, if visual difficulties or impaired hand coordination or strength—common in MS—are present, the sexual partner needs to be trained in the technique. Furthermore, both individuals receiving these medications and their partners require training and instruction about the methods of administration and potential untoward effects. Periodic follow-up is necessary to

---

Table 10–2 Common Sexual Dysfunctions in Multiple Sclerosis

Males	*Females*
Inability to achieve/maintain an erection	Decreased libido
	Numbness or dysesthesia in the genital region
Disorders of ejaculation	
Decreased libido	Decreased vaginal lubrication
Anorgasmia	Dyspareunia
	Anorgasmia

assess for fibrosis, scarring, infection, and other complications. Administration of prostagladin E_1 into the urethra using the medicated urethral system for erection (MUSE), a new method of delivering the medication, has been found to be effective in the treatment of erectile dysfunction (Padma-Nathan et al., 1997). This route of administration is likely to be more acceptable to men and their partners than penile injections.

Yohimbine hydrocholoride (Yocon) is an orally administered alkaloid that decreases adrenergic activity but increases parasympathetic tone; the result is increased penile blood flow. In addition, yohimbine is reported to have a stimulating effect on mood and may have an aphrodisiac effect. Although not widely used, this medication may be useful in increasing penile blood flow and producing erection in men with borderline function (Chancellor & Blaivas, 1994). As with all medications, instruction about the desired action and side effects of the medications is indicated.

Vacuum devices, which are less invasive than penile injection, may be a good option for people with visual changes and hand tremor or sensory changes resulting from MS and for people who are uncomfortable with giving injections into the penis. A variety of vacuum devices are available (Chancellor & Blaivas, 1994); these devices work by creating a negative pressure or vacuum that draws blood into the corpora to create an erection. Bands or rings are placed over the penis to maintain the erection for 30 to 45 minutes. Studies have demonstrated satisfaction with these devices and preference for vacuum devices over penile injection in men with erectile dysfunction from a variety of disorders (Aloni, Heller, Keren, Mendelson, & Davidoff, 1992; Gould, Switters, Broderick, & deVere White, 1992; Moul & McLeod, 1989). Skill and comfort in using those devices safely are facilitated through training and counseling by a knowledgeable therapist.

Penile implants may be the treatment of choice in men whose erectile dysfunction cannot be effectively treated by other less invasive methods. Penile implants provide penile rigidity and allow more spontaneity in sexual activity than the other methods. However, the procedure requires surgical implantation and places the person with MS—already at risk for urinary tract infection—at increased risk for recurrent urinary tract infection that may involve the implant and necessitate its removal. Tissue erosion is also a risk, especially in those people with decreased sensation as a result of MS. Many different types of implants or prostheses are available, including inflatable prostheses and rigid and semirigid rods that are implanted in the penis. It is essential that health providers thoroughly explain the advantages and disadvantages of each type of implant and each method of treating erectile dysfunction if the person with MS and his sexual partner are to make an informed decision about treatment options. Understanding the likely benefits of treatment options can minimize unrealistic expectations on the part of the patient and partner.

Female Sexual Dysfunction

The most common forms of sexual dysfunction in women with MS (see Table 10–2) are decreased vaginal lubrication, numbness or dysesthesia in the genital region, dyspareunia, decreased libido, and impaired orgasm. Women are less likely than their male counterparts to report sexual dysfunction; however, decreased reporting by women is not attributed to differences in the number or location of lesions in the spinal cord or brain among men and women. Certainly, part of the reason a woman may not mention dysfunction relates to her ability to participate in intercourse and sexual activity despite numbness in the genital region, decreased libido, anorgasmia, or vaginal dryness. Thus, female sexual dysfunction may not outwardly affect a couple's sexual function as dramatically as an inability to sustain an erection. However, this does not mean that the woman may not be as distressed as a man is when he experiences sexual dysfunction. Another likely cause for decreased reporting of sexual dysfunction by women is related to society's view of the differences between men and women with regard to sexuality.

Decreased vaginal lubrication may be responsible for pain during intercourse and is usually easily remedied. Women need to be instructed to use a sterile water-soluble lubricant to reduce vaginal dryness without increasing the risk of urinary tract infections. Appropriate lubricants include K-Y jelly and Replens, and they are available in most pharmacies and are sold specifically for vaginal lubrication. If the woman's hand coordination is impaired, her partner can incorporate application of a vaginal lubricant into sexual activity.

Women with MS and their sexual partners may fear that sexual intercourse will be painful. The likelihood of pain occurring is increased if the woman experiences spasticity of the hip adductors. Bathing with warm water before sexual activity may reduce the spasticity. Furthermore, use of alternative positions and pillows may reduce the effects of spasticity. The woman and her partner should be encouraged to consider and explore alternative positions and ways of expressing themselves sexually. Some women with MS find satisfaction in performing oral sex for their partners, even if the satisfaction is not related solely to their own psychogenic arousal.

REPRODUCTIVE CONCERNS

Because the onset of MS frequently occurs during young adulthood, concerns about contraception, pregnancy, and childbearing are common. MS is not a contraindication to currently available contraceptives. However, some women may have difficulty inserting and removing some of the mechanical devices (e.g., diaphragm or cervical caps) because of hand tremor, lack of hand coordination, or hip adductor spasticity.

The severity of MS and the resulting disability are not usually evident until 5 years after the onset of the disease. Thus, some clinicians recommend that women wait 5 years from the time of diagnosis of MS before considering pregnancy and childbearing (Lechtenberg, 1995). However, some women have reported that they are afraid that if they wait 5 years, disease progression that may occur during that period may cause them to avoid pregnancy and childbearing altogether. Thus, they move up rather than delay their plans for pregnancy and childbearing (Smeltzer, 1994b).

Information given to women about the effect of pregnancy on MS and the influence of MS on pregnancy is often vague and contradictory (Smeltzer, 1994b). Despite evidence to the contrary (Sadovnick et al., 1994; Stenager, Stenager, & Jensen, 1994), many women with MS (and their partners and families) fear pregnancy because of the belief that pregnancy and childbearing increase the progression of the disease and the likelihood of severe disability. Women may also have concerns about their ability to cooperate or cope with labor and delivery, to breastfeed, and to adequately care for themselves, their infants, and their families because of increased MS symptoms (Smeltzer, 1994a). Because of the increased risk of exacerbation of MS postpartum, it has been recommended that women make arrangements for household help that will enable them to have adequate rest and sleep. Furthermore, medications used to treat MS may be contraindicated in pregnant women and nursing mothers (Birk, 1995); therefore, they need to be under the care of clinicians familiar with the effects of medications during pregnancy and lactation.

For the man with sexual dysfunction resulting from MS who is interested in becoming a father, there is fear that he will be unable to impregnate his mate. These fears may contribute to erosion of a man's self-esteem. In addition, the inability to father children may contribute to marital stress. Although there are techniques for harvesting semen in men who are unable to ejaculate, such techniques are costly and do not guarantee pregnancy. Although it has not been studied in people with MS, it may be easier and more cost-effective for men who have been diagnosed with MS to have semen frozen at a sperm bank at the time of diagnosis than to go through vibratory stimulation or electroejaculation at a later date.

CONCLUSION

MS has the potential to disrupt the sexual relationship of those people affected with this chronic, potentially disabling disease. Knowledgeable health care providers who believe that sexuality remains a vital part of an individual's makeup despite the onset of significant physical and psychological symptoms and alterations in lifestyle have an essential role in assisting people with MS to cope with these changes. The clinician's sensitivity to changes in family and sexual relationships and an awareness of the variety of strategies available are important if people with MS are to receive needed assistance to address these changes.

Furthermore, effective communication between the clinician and the person with MS remains the key to effective management of sexual dysfunction. Encouraging effective communication between the person with MS and his or her sexual partners is an equally important aspect of management of sexual dysfunction so that full sexual potential can be achieved.

REFERENCES

Aloni, R., Heller, L., Keren, O., Mendelson, E., & Davidoff, G. (1992). Noninvasive treatment for erectile dysfunction for the neurologically disabled population. *Journal of Sex and Marital Therapy, 18,* 243–249.

Anderson, D.W., Ellenberg, J.H., Leventhal, C.A., Reingold, S.C., Rodriquez, M., & Silberberg, D.H. (1992). Revised estimate of the prevalence of multiple sclerosis in the United States. *Annals of Neurology, 31,* 333–336.

Barrett, M. (1982). *Sexuality and multiple sclerosis.* New York: National Multiple Sclerosis Society.

Bering-Sorenson, F., & Sonksen, J. (1992). Penile erection in men with spinal cord or cauda equina lesions. *Seminars in Neurology, 12,* 98–105.

Birk, K. (1995). Reproductive issues in multiple sclerosis. *Multiple Sclerosis: Clinical Issues, 2*(3), 2 5.

Chancellor, M.B., & Blaivas, J.G. (1994). Urological and sexual problems in multiple sclerosis. *Clinical Neuroscience, 2,* 189–195.

Foley, F.W., & Iverson, J. (1992). Sexuality and MS. In R.C. Kalb & L.C. Scheinberg (Eds.), *Multiple sclerosis and the family* (pp. 63–82). New York: Demos.

Gould, J.E., Switters, D.M., Broderick, G.A., & deVere White, R.W. (1992). External vacuum devices: A clinical comparison with pharmacologic erections. *World Journal of Neurology, 10,* 68–70.

Kelley, C.L., & Smeltzer, S.C. (1994). Betaseron: The new MS treatment. *Journal of Neuroscience Nursing, 26*(1), 52–56.

Lechtenberg, R. (1995). *Multiple sclerosis fact book.* Philadelphia: F.A. Davis.

Lechtenberg, R., & Ohl, D.A. (1994). *Sexual dysfunction: Neurologic, urologic, and gynecologic aspects.* Philadelphia: Lea & Febiger.

Mattson, D.H. (1995). Sexual dysfunction in multiple sclerosis. *Multiple Sclerosis: Clinical Issues, 2*(3), 10–13.

Mattson, D.H., Petrie, M., Srivastava, D.K., & McDermott, M. (1995). Multiple sclerosis—Sexual dysfunction and its response to medications. *Archives of Neurology, 52,* 862–868.

Moul, J.W., & McLeod, D.G. (1989). Negative pressure devices in the explanted penile prosthesis population. *Journal of Urology, 142,* 729–731.

Padma-Nathan, H., Hellstrom, W.J.G., Kaiser, F.E., Labasky, R.F., Lue, T.F., Nolten, W.E., Norwood, P.C., Peterson, C.A., Shabsigh, R., Tam, P.Y., Place, V.A., & Gesundheit, N. (1997). Treatment of men with erectile dysfunction with transurethal alprostadil. *New England Journal of Medicine, 336*(1), 1–7.

Rao, S.M., Leo, G.J., Ellington, L., Nauertz, T., Bernardin, L., & Unverzagt, F. (1991). Cognitive dysfunction in multiple sclerosis. II. Impact on employment and social functioning. *Neurology, 41,* 692–696.

Sadovnick, A.D., Eisen, K., Hashimoto, S.A., Farquhar, R., Yee, I.M.L., Hooge, J., Kastrukoff, L., Oger, J.J.F., & Paty, D.W. (1994). Pregnancy and multiple sclerosis. A prospective study. *Archives of Neurology, 51,* 1120–1124.

Smeltzer, S.C. (1994a). Concerns of pregnant women with multiple sclerosis. *Qualitative Health Research, 4,* 480–502.

Smeltzer, S.C. (1994b). Concerns of pregnant women with multiple sclerosis: Reproductive decision making. In *Proceedings of the Seventh Biennial Conference of the Workshop of European Nurse Researchers* (Vol. 2, pp. 893–899). Oslo, Norway: Norsk Sykepleier Forbund.

Stenager, E., Stenager, E.N., & Jensen, K. (1994). Effect of pregnancy on the prognosis for multiple sclerosis. A 5-year follow up investigation. *Acta Neurologica Scandinavica, 90,* 305–308.

Therapeutics and Technology Assessment Subcommittee of the American Academy of Neurology. (1995). Assessment: Neurological evaluation of male sexual dysfunction. *Neurology, 45,* 2287–2292.

Valleroy, M.L., & Kraft, G. (1984). Sexual dysfunction in multiple sclerosis. *Archives of Physical Medicine and Rehabilitation, 65,* 125–128.

CHAPTER 11

Cerebrovascular Accidents

Trilok N. Monga and Anthony J. Kerrigan

Cerebrovascular accident (CVA) is the third leading cause of death and is one of the most common diseases leading to major long-term morbidity in North America. Yet little is known regarding sexual problems and sexual expression and adjustment following CVA. Most of the studies on sexuality in stroke patients have involved a small number of subjects and assessed only patients' libido and frequency of intercourse, with little reference to the broader aspects of sexual function. Furthermore, there is a lack of available information regarding sexual function in elderly stroke patients and young stroke survivors. Research is also lacking in regard to pregnancy and reproduction among those stroke patients who are in the childbearing age.

Stroke is more common in the elderly population. An 80-year-old patient who has suffered a stroke today was born in the early 20th century to parents who were born in the Victorian era. When considering sexuality issues in these patients, prevailing attitudes of the community during the past era toward sexual expressions should be considered, as should the changes in sexual behavior of an aging population. Understanding the physiologic changes of aging and sexuality in elderly people is a prerequisite to any discussion regarding sexuality in stroke patients. Since the classic work by Kinsey, Pomeroy, and Martin (1948) and Kinsey, Pomeroy, Martin, and Gebhard (1953), various investigators have studied sexual function in elderly people (Brown, Monti, & Corriveau, 1978; Freeman, 1961; Pfeiffer, Verwoerdt, & Wang, 1968; Renshaw, 1984; Starr & Weiner, 1981; Thienhaus, 1988). The subject has been recently reviewed by Kleitsch and O'Donnell (1990) and Garden and Schramm (1995).

Although sexual activity is a vital part of normal life, society tends to deny the sexuality of elderly or physically disabled people. Such people often are considered asexual. Kinsey et al. (1948, 1953) were the first to focus attention on the sexual behavior of elderly people. It is now well established that regular coitus may continue into the 7th, 8th, and even the 9th decades (Masters & Johnson, 1966). Other studies (Freeman, 1961; Newman & Nichols, 1960; Pfeiffer et al., 1968; Thienhaus, 1988) have also found that sex continues to play an important role in the lives of many elderly people. Moreover, studies on sexual function have indicated that basic physiologic responses remain essentially intact with advancing age (Masters & Johnson, 1966, 1970). In a study by Starr and Weiner (1981), 75% of the respondents reported that they felt sex was as good as or better than when they were young. Of the subjects, 76% felt that sex had a positive effect on their health, and 91% of the women indicated that they were orgasmic sometimes, most of the time, or always. The study concluded that elderly people who were sexually active and have a partner showed less decline in sexual performance. It can be concluded that, although there is a decline in sexual function, sex continues to play an important role in the lives of many elderly people.

PHYSIOLOGIC CHANGES RESULTING FROM AGING

In women, at menopause, there is a sudden decrease in estrogen levels (Exhibit 11–1). Gonadotropin and gonadotropin-releasing hormone increase, although some decline in gonadotropin levels have been reported with further aging (Quint & Kaiser, 1985). Serum testosterone levels also tend to rise after age 60 years. As

---

Exhibit 11–1 Changes in Female Subjects Resulting from Aging

Hormonal	*Physical*	*Sexual*
• Decreased serum estrogen levels	• Amenorrhea	• Loss of femininity
• Decreased progesterone levels	• Sterility	• Loss of libido
• Increased follicle-stimulating hormone	• Vaginal dryness	• Orgasmic problems
• Increased luteinizing hormone	• Vaginal stenosis	• Dyspareunia
• Increased luteinizing hormone–releasing hormone		• Loss of pleasure

Source: Adapted with permission from U. Monga, *Sexuality and Disability*, Vol. 9, No. 2, © 1995, Hanley & Belfus, Inc.

a result of reduced estrogen levels, the vaginal walls become thin and vaginal size is reduced. The amount of vaginal lubrication is often decreased during sexual arousal. Other changes that have been reported include loss of fat in the mons veneris, thinning of the labia minora, and shrinkage of the labia majora. Tone is reduced in perineal musculature. It has been reported that women who remain sexually active have less vaginal atrophy compared with sexually inactive women (Leiblum, Bachmann, Kemmann, Colburn, & Swartzman, 1983; Masters & Johnson, 1970).

In elderly women, arousal is delayed. Furthermore, there is poor vaginal lubrication, which, during intercourse, can lead to dyspareunia. Reduced skin flush and breast engorgement during arousal also has been reported (Mooradian & Greiff, 1990). The duration of stimulation needed to achieve orgasm increases. Intensity of orgasm is reduced because of a lack of tone in the perineal muscles. Furthermore, incontinence as a result of pelvic relaxation and tissue atrophy can adversely affect elderly women's sexual function. Uterine contractions that naturally occur during orgasm may be painful (Steege, 1986). Sexual desire may decrease following menopause. In addition, a decrease in coital frequency has been associated with low serum estrogen levels (Bachman, 1988).

In men, physiologic changes resulting from aging include a decline in androgen production and concentration and apparently hypothalamic–pituitary hyporesponsiveness and excessive binding of testosterone in the plasma (Exhibit 11–2). Testosterone levels decrease gradually after age 20 years; this decline is accelerated after age 60 years. Evidence has indicated that androgens play an

---

Exhibit 11–2 Changes in Male Subjects Resulting from Aging

Hormonal	*Physical*	*Sexual*
• Decreased testosterone level	• Testicular atrophy	• Loss of libido
• Increased luteinizing hormone	• Oligospermia	• Erectile difficulties
• Increased follicle-stimulating hormone	• Sperm abnormalities	• Slow response
• Increased luteinizing hormone–releasing hormone	• Pendulous scrotum	• Poor response
		• Impotency
		• Increased refractory period
		• Shorter and less intense ejaculation

Source: Adapted with permission from T.N. Monga and H.J. Ostermann, *Sexuality and Disability,* Vol. 9, No. 2, Hanley & Belfus, Inc.

important role in libido and regulate the frequency of nonerotic or reflex erections, including nocturnal penile tumescence (NPT; Davidson et al., 1983). Some authors have suggested that this change is not accompanied by a decrease in libido or in general sexual activities (Brown et al., 1978; Sjogren, Damber, & Liliequist, 1983).

All five components (libido, erection, ejaculation, orgasm, and detumescence) of normal male sexual function are variably affected. Furthermore, there apparently is a steady decline in the duration and intensity of each phase. Diminished libido may occur secondary to alterations in sensation (i.e., vision, hearing, smell, and touch) as well as changes in hormonal levels. Decreased libido in elderly people may be influenced by the negative social attitudes toward sexuality in the elderly population. In men, erections are delayed and the ability to attain erection without direct stimulation diminishes. Elderly men may need more caressing to achieve erection. Erections are not as firm as in younger men and there is a tendency to lose an erection during intercourse. Detumescence occurs more rapidly, and the refractory period increases with age. Ejaculation is shorter, less forceful, and decreased in volume.

SEXUAL FUNCTION IN STROKE PATIENTS

Various authors have reported a marked decline in many of the aspects of sexuality (Aloni, Ring, Rozenthul, & Schwartz, 1993; Aloni, Schwartz, & Ring, 1994; Boldrini, Basaglia, & Calanca, 1991; Bray, De Frank, & Wolfe, 1981; Leshner, Fine, & Goldman, 1974; Monga, Lawson, & Inglis, 1986; Niemi, Laakasonen, Kotila, & Waltimo, 1988; Sjogren, 1983; Sjogren et al., 1983). This topic has recently been reviewed (Monga, 1993; Monga & Ostermann, 1995). Overall, stroke may affect both physical and psychosocial aspects of sexuality (Exhibit 11–3). Many patients with CVAs have arousal problems. Erectile dysfunction in male patients and poor vaginal lubrication in females are also common manifestations poststroke. Others fear rejection from their partners to the extent that they withdraw from sexual encounters. Muckleroy (1977), however, stated that, although stroke patients regularly experience a change in sexual activity, this is not necessarily a major problem. Rather, it is rare for either partner to view the loss as significant.

Male Sexual Function Poststroke

The profound effect of stroke on male patients' libido has been well documented (Aloni et al., 1993; Ford & Orfirer, 1967; Fugl-Meyer & Jaasko, 1980; Goddess, Wagner, & Silverman, 1979; Kalliomaki, Markkanen, & Mustonen, 1961; Monga et al., 1986; Sadoughi, Leshner, & Fine, 1971). The earliest study (Kalliomaki et al., 1961) described sexual behavior in stroke patients younger

Exhibit 11–3 Changes in Sexual Function Following Stroke

- Diminished libido
- Poor arousal
- Erectile difficulties in males
- Poor vaginal lubrication in females
- Orgasmic difficulties
- Reduced frequency of intercourse
- Cessation of coital activity
- Premature ejaculation in males

- Absence of ejaculation in males
- Lack of or poor orgasm in females
- Reduced satisfaction with sexual activity
- Lack of enjoyment with sexual activity
- Hypersexuality

Source: Adapted with permission from T.N. Monga and H.J. Ostermann, *Sexuality and Disability*, Vol. 9, No. 2, Hanley & Belfus, Inc.

than age 60 years. The study was based on personal interviews with patients; spouses apparently were not involved in the study. According to the authors, CVA tends to diminish libido as well as the frequency of coitus.

Goddess et al. (1979), in a study of 25 stroke patients, also found a decline in libido; however, Ford and Orfirer (1967) reported that 60% of their patients had no loss of libido after CVA. In another study of elderly stroke patients (mean age at onset = 68 years), 75% of men experienced normal libido prestroke, whereas only 21% reported normal libido poststroke (Monga et al., 1986). However, no decline in libido or desire was observed by Bray et al. (1981).

Problems with achieving erections have been reported. In a study by Sjogren and Fugl-Meyer (1982), erectile difficulties were extremely common in all males with hemiplegia. Of the males studied, 64% had difficulty in achieving erections poststroke compared with 21% who reported this problem before stroke. Monga et al. (1986) reported that 73 men (94%) had normal erections before stroke compared with only 30 men (38%) who had normal responses after CVA. Similarly, Bray et al. (1981) reported that 46% ($n = 11$) of men experienced normal erections poststroke compared with 75% ($n = 18$) of men prestroke. In a study by Boldrini et al. (1991), 61% of patients did not notice any change in their ability to have an erection.

Problems with orgasm also are common in stroke patients. Although 17 men (22%) reported premature ejaculation before the onset of stroke, 57 patients (35%) had experienced premature ejaculation poststroke (Monga et al., 1986). Other studies have reported similar findings to a greater or lesser extent (Sjogren, 1980, 1983). In the study by Bray and his colleagues (1981), more male patients had problems with ejaculation poststroke compared with before the stroke; 7 of 24 men could ejaculate poststroke compared with 21 men who had normal ejaculation before stroke.

Sexuality in Male Stroke Patients

Sex, sexuality, and reproduction are all closely interwoven into the fabric of living things (Monga & Lefebvre, 1995). Thorn-Gray and Kern (1983) have described sex as a "verbal, visual, tactual and olfactory communication which expresses love and intimacy between two people" (p. 141). Although some information is available regarding physical aspects of sexual function after stroke, such as coital frequency and arousal, little is known of the broader aspects of sexuality. A few authors have attempted to study and describe sexuality in stroke patients (Lobi, Phillips, & Gresham, 1980; Sjogren & Fugl-Meyer, 1981; Trudel, Fabia, & Bouchard, 1984). There is a decline in leisure activities (Sjogren & Fugl-Meyer, 1981, 1982; Trudel et al., 1984), enjoyment with sex, and satisfaction with the level of sexual activity in the poststroke period (Monga et al., 1986). Boldrini et al. (1991), however, found no significant change in sexual satisfaction as reported by the majority of the spouses studied. Sjogren (1983) found a decline in mutual verbal and nonverbal responsiveness, a decrease in frequency of caressing and touching with intention of having sex, and a decrease in intimate caressing or foreplay following stroke. Of the men studied, 31% had ceased foreplay altogether. In addition, patients may engage in *spectatoring,* in which patients remove themselves from an active sexual role and are instead preoccupied by attempts to observe and evaluate their own and their partners' performance. Despite erectile difficulties following stroke, the participants in a recent study by Boldrini et al. (1991) reported no significant change in the time spent on foreplay activities. Rather, the majority of patients had resumed intercourse within 3 months of their stroke.

Many other authors have reported a decline in frequency of sexual activity following stroke. A majority of stroke patients may stop having intercourse completely. Sadoughi et al. (1971) studied sexual adjustment in 55 chronically ill and physically disabled patients. Of those patients, 12 had a history of stroke. Although the authors did not report the sexual problems in the various subgroups separately, 78% of the patients experienced a decline of sexual activity after the onset of their disability. In another study of 78 men, 9 men (11%) reported no coital activity before their CVA, whereas 50 men (64%) ceased all coital activity after stroke (Monga et al., 1986). Sjogren et al. (1983) noted that the decrease in frequency of intercourse appeared to be more common in males than in females. In their study, 41% of males had ceased coital activity and 31% had decreased frequency, whereas 17% of the females had ceased coital activity and 42% had decreased coital frequency. In another study by Sjogren and Fugl-Meyer (1982), changes in frequency of intercourse were related to the degree of cutaneous sensibility impairment and levels of dependence in activities of daily living, but not with degree of motor impairment. On the other hand, the degree of motor impairment was a main factor causing sexual dysfunction, according to a study by Fugl-Meyer and Jaasko (1980). Furthermore, 87% of male stroke patients studied by Boldrini et al. (1991), either ceased to have coital activity or reported decreased frequency.

Female Sexual Function Poststroke

Many females experience problems with sexual function following stroke. In a study of elderly stroke patients, 60% of the women reported normal libido prestroke, whereas only 12% of the women experienced normal libido poststroke (Monga et al., 1986). Similar findings were reported by other investigators (Aloni et al., 1993; Kalliomaki et al., 1961; Kinsella & Duffy, 1979). However, in the study by Bray et al. (1981), the patients did not report a decline in libido. Methodological differences may explain the divergent results in the studies. In the Bray et al. (1981) study, participants on average were younger than the subjects in the Monga et al. (1986) study but similar to those subjects in the Kalliomaki et al. (1961) study. Furthermore, the majority of patients in the Bray et al. (1981) study were interviewed during their rehabilitation hospitalization, whereas patients in other studies were examined as outpatients.

Problems with vaginal lubrication in women also have been reported in patients following CVA. Monga et al. (1986) reported that a majority of 35 female patients experienced problems with lubrication after their stroke. Of those patients, 63% had normal vaginal lubrication before stroke, whereas only 29% reported normal lubrication poststroke. No other investigators asked specific questions regarding lubrication.

Bray et al. (1981) reported that only 1 of 11 female patients experienced orgasm after their stroke, versus 5 of the 11 women who regularly had orgasms before their stroke. In the study by Monga et al. (1986), 27 (77%) of 35 women became anorgasmic after stroke. Other investigators have reported similar problems to a greater or lesser extent (Sjogren, 1983; Sjogren et al., 1983). Boldrini et al. (1991) reported that 14 (67%) of 21 women who were sexually active after their strokes reported no change in orgasm.

Sexuality in Female Stroke Patients

Little is known regarding the broader aspects of sexuality in female stroke patients. Masturbation and inappropriate sexual behavior has been described as a manifestation of hypersexuality (Monga, Monga, Raina, & Hardjasudarma, 1986). However, the prevalence of different means of sexual expression after stroke, such as masturbation, oral sex, and sexual fantasy, is unknown. As with male stroke patients, mutual verbal and nonverbal responsiveness declined among female stroke patients and the frequency of caressing and touching with intention of having sex also decreased (Sjogren et al., 1983). Likewise, intimate caressing or foreplay poststroke decreased. Sjogren et al. (1983) observed that 27% of 12 women had ceased foreplay altogether. In another study (Boldrini et al., 1991), no changes during foreplay were reported by 18 (86%) of 21 female patients who were sexually active after their strokes. With regard to frequency of sexual activity, Monga et al. (1986) studied 35 women of whom 29% reported no coital activity before their CVA, whereas 54% ceased all coital activity after stroke.

FERTILITY, REPRODUCTION, AND PARENTING

It has been erroneously assumed that physically disabled men and women are not interested in pursuing sexually fulfilling relationships and are unable to effectively care for newborns, and that physically disabled women are incapable of achieving pregnancy (M. Monga, 1995). The attitude as it relates to sexuality and pregnancy, in part, may reflect the paucity of available information concerning gynecological and obstetric care of these women. In a survey of 55 women with acquired and congenital disabilities, fewer than 20% had received counseling or information about sexuality following the onset of their disability (Beckmann, Gittler, Barzansky, & Beckmann, 1989). Of the respondents, only 14 (25.5%) of 55 had had a sexual history taken after their disability; 24 (45.3%) of 53 respondents indicated they would have liked information about sexuality, and 30 (55.5%) of 54 respondents indicated that they would have liked to discuss their feelings about sexuality. Concerning issues of contraception, 25 (45.5%) of 55 respondents were offered information about contraception. Although about 50% of the disabled women would have liked to have more information about sexuality and or counseling about these issues, only about 20% were offered such information and only 5% asked for it. Further, only about 30% believed that their health care provider knew enough about their disability. The authors concluded that the health care of disabled women may be improved by more extensive education of professionals in the psychosocial aspects of disability and in the area of human sexuality and communication regarding those aspects of heath care.

Because most of the attention in the literature has been paid to elderly stroke patients, the sexual needs, desires, and sexual function of young stroke survivors has been ignored. Although stroke is not uncommon in young adults, the issues of fertility, reproduction, and parenting have not been studied after stroke. Stroke during pregnancy has been reported to occur as a result of increased blood pressure. Pregnancy in general is associated with rapid physical and hormonal changes. For many women, that also means a change in their sexual feelings and behavior. Women with a physical disability including stroke may also be faced with pain, decreased mobility, and a lack of knowledge not just about the safety of sexual intercourse in pregnancy but also about how to make sex pleasurable and possible within the constraints imposed by their condition (Carty & Conine, 1988). Health care providers must consider various important factors when caring for expectant disabled women, including self-esteem, body image, fatigue, dependence or independence, and acceptance of a pregnancy. In women with disabilities, these factors may be profound, resulting in a "double dose of disequilibrium" (Carty & Conine, 1988, p. 85).

Health care providers also may need to address parenting issues with stroke patients. Monga and Ostermann (1995) reported a case of a female stroke patient who was denied custody of her child because of her disability. The patient was a 33-year-old with a history of left-sided cerebral hemorrhage, which led to right-sided hemiparesis and expressive aphasia. The patient was admitted to a rehabilitation unit for assessment of her child care abilities. Assessment indicated the patient was independent in activities of daily living, was ambulating, and performed household chores. After training, the patient also demonstrated that she could look after her baby and care for his needs. Custody of the child, however, was denied; the decision was based on the issue that, because of her aphasia, she would be unable to seek help in an emergency.

LANGUAGE DEFICITS AND SEXUALITY

Available information regarding sexual problems in aphasic patients is limited. Most of the published data either excluded aphasic patients or did not specify any issues specific to this population. Some studies have reported that impairment of language skills plays a role in sexual changes of patients following CVA (Kinsella & Duffy, 1979; Malone, 1975; Wiig, 1973). Kinsella and Duffy (1979) stressed that a sudden loss of ability to communicate effectively influenced several aspects of life, including the marital relationship. Wiig (1973) examined sexual readjustment in 100 people with aphasia and reported that the physically intact people with aphasia who had relatively good auditory comprehension and non-verbal communication ability exhibited the least problems in sexual adjustment, irrespective of expressive language ability. Wiig's findings implied that sexual readjustment was easier for aphasic patients if they could interpret other people correctly.

LONG-TERM EFFECTS OF CVA ON SEXUALITY

Few studies have been published on the long-term effects of CVA on sexuality (Hawton, 1984; Monga et al., 1986; Niemi et al., 1988; Sjogren & Fugl-Meyer,

1982; Viitanen, Fugl-Meyer, Bernspan, & Fugl-Meyer, 1988). Sjogren and Fugl-Meyer (1982), in a study on adjustment to life after stroke, reported that, although changes in coital frequency were temporally independent, changes in leisure activities were less pronounced for subjects examined later than 12 months after the stroke. They commented that subjects with previously known arterial hypertension, myocardial infarction, or diabetes mellitus had changed relatively little in their sexual function or lifestyle compared with those people without these ailments. This finding probably represents a prestroke decline in sexual function.

In a prospective long-term study of life after stroke conducted in Sweden, Viitanen et al. (1988) reported that 61% of 62 stroke patients with a follow-up of 4 to 6 years experienced a decreased general or domain-specific satisfaction with life. Twelve of these subjects (15% of the respondents) had significant decrease in four or more domain-specific aspects of life satisfaction, whereas 18% had a decrease in only one aspect. Except for contact with friends, with 85% as satisfied as before, changes in all items of domain-specific life satisfaction were significantly associated with changes in global life satisfaction. Reduced satisfaction with sex life was noted in 42 married subjects in the study.

In another study on sexual adjustment of men who have had strokes, Hawton (1984) reported that, of 50 men who were interested in sex before their strokes, 40 (80%) had noted a return of at least some of their formal interest. The interval between the onset of stroke and the interviews averaged 6.2 months ($SD = 5.4$), the shortest interval was 3 months, and in all but three patients the interviews occurred within 1 year of the stroke. This kind of experience has not been reported by other investigators (Monga et al., 1986). The authors did comment that the men who reported full return of their previous interest in sex tended to be younger than those whose interest in sex did not return or had returned partially. In the study, only two patients were older than age 70 years.

In summary, most studies have reported a decline in sexual function and decreased satisfaction with sexual activities following a CVA. However, the subjective nature of these findings is illustrated in a study by Boldrini et al. (1991) in which both the partners were interviewed separately. In 24 cases (27%), there was disagreement on answers about the frequency of intercourse; 16 of 24 patients reported a higher frequency of intercourse than their spouses, and 8 patients reported a lower frequency than their spouses. Overall, the men apparently exaggerated their sexual performance, emphasizing that the available data on sexual function in stroke patients are subjective in nature. Furthermore, most of the information regarding prestroke sexual activity may have been subject to the vagaries of memory. The focus of investigators so far has been on the physical performance aspects of sexuality; the broader areas of sexuality have not been studied.

POSSIBLE CAUSES OF SEXUAL DYSFUNCTION

Sexual dysfunction in stroke patients is complex and multifactorial in nature. There are two parameters of impairment in stroke patients: dysfunction and disfigurement. Both may vary from minor to major in terms of severity of functional loss and problems with body image and self-esteem. The sexual problems in stroke patients are rarely a consequence of "stroke" alone; rather, oftentimes they may result from a variety of associated medical conditions, such as the presence of diabetes, hypertension, or coronary artery disease. The situation is compounded by a multitude of psychosocial factors including role changes, loss of self-esteem, fear of rejection by a spouse, and poor coping skills (Exhibit 11–4). Other factors that may influence sexual function are cognitive, sensory, and motor deficits, and incontinence. However, none of these factors has been systematically investigated. Subjective loss of potency in male patients has not been objectively verified. In one study (Sjogren & Fugl-Meyer, 1981), cessation of sexual intercourse was most common among those patients who did not regain independence after their strokes.

There is controversy regarding the severity and nature of sexual dysfunction in relation to the side of lesion. It appears that the site of lesion and the structures involved influence sexual behavior to a greater degree than the side of lesion itself. Most of the understanding of the supraspinal mechanisms in sexual func-

---

Exhibit 11–4 Possible Factors Influencing Sexuality in Stroke Patients

Medical	*Psychological*
• Concomitant medical conditions	• Anxiety and fear
– Diabetes mellitus	– Of having another stroke
– Cardiovascular disease	– Of rejection by partner
– Chronic pain	– Of poor performance
– Alcoholism	– Of losing control
• Side effects of medications	– Poor coping skills
– Antihypertensives	– Mood disorders
– Antidepressants	• Changed self-image
– Tranquilizers	– Poor self-esteem
• Severity of disability	– Communication barriers
– Sensory deficits	• Relationship problems
– Spasticity	– Partner's attitudes
– Contractures	– Role changes
– Aphasia	• Cognitive deficits

tion and dysfunction has been derived from nonhuman primate experiments, with correlation to humans when possible (Boone, 1995). For example, inferomedian frontal injury may produce disinhibition and inappropriate behaviors, whereas dorsolateral frontal lesions will impair initiation of sex (Walker, 1976). It should not be surprising that sexual dysfunction is common following any significant brain insult, given the propensity of frontotemporal local contusion and diffuse brain axonal injury (Horn & Zasler, 1990). Such a dysfunction could also be explained in patients with CVA involving the frontotemporal region.

The impairment of sexual interest is reportedly more common with dominant hemispheric lesions compared with nondominant hemispheric involvement (Kalliomaki et al., 1961). The decline in libido seems to be more prevalent in subjects with dominant hemispheric lesions; however, regardless of which hemisphere is damaged, there is a substantial likelihood that libido will remain unchanged (Goddess et al., 1979). Sjogren et al. (1983) reported no significant correlation between side of lesion and any of the sexual parameters they investigated. Similarly, Boldrini et al. (1991) concluded that the side of hemispheric lesion did not play a crucial role in determining changes in sexual life after stroke. Monga et al. (1986) reported a lesser decline in sexual function among women with right-sided lesions. In the study, the sexual function of four groups (left and right hemispheric lesions in male and female patients) was compared. A single index of sexual function before and after was established. Twenty-six diabetic patients were excluded from the analysis. In 87 remaining patients, sexual function of the four groups was comparable before a CVA. Although there was a decline in sexual function for all groups after a CVA, the women with right-sided lesions had a less marked decline in index of sexual function than any of the other three groups. No significant difference in the degree of decline of sexual function was noted between men with right and left lesions. The authors concluded that the severity of cognitive deficits may contribute to this sexual decline (Monga et al., 1986). This conclusion was based on a finding previously reported by Inglis, Ruckman, Lawson, MacLean, and Monga (1982) that right-sided lesions in women did not reveal as severe cognitive deficits as the left-sided lesions in women or both right- and left-sided lesions in men.

In summary, there is no general agreement about the incidence of sexual disturbance as a function of the side of lesion. Those patients who had a higher frequency of sexual activity before their stroke were more likely to resume sexual intercourse after their stroke (Hawton, 1984).

Antihypertensives, antidepressants, and hypnotics can contribute to erectile difficulties and ejaculatory dysfunction. Sexual dysfunction, particularly erectile dysfunction, has been reported with the use of antihypertensive agents (Hagan, Wallin, & Baer, 1980). Sjogren et al. (1983), however, found no association between antihypertensive agents and sexual function. Many patients with hypertension already have pelvic vasculature insufficiency related to atherosclerotic changes

(Krane, 1986) and may have had preexisting vascular impotence. Again, little information is available regarding the role of these medications as a causative factor in sexual decline in stroke patients.

In postmenopausal female patients, low serum estrogen levels may be the cause of poor sexual function resulting from a lack of adequate lubrication and dyspareunia. However, this topic has not been studied in stroke patients. In male stroke patients, Sjogren et al. (1983) found serum testosterone values within the predicted range. They reported no relationship between serum testosterone and sexual function in those patients. Responses to stimulation with human chorionic gonadotropin also were adequate.

Autonomic nervous system dysfunction as a factor leading to sexual decline in stroke patients was suggested by Monga, DeForge, Williams, and Wolfe (1988) in their study of cardiovascular effects of exercise in stroke patients. They reported a significantly lower increase in both systolic and diastolic blood pressure with upper limb exercises compared with age- and sex-matched control subjects. No such difference was noted with lower limb exercises. They concluded that a lack of normal response may suggest an underlying autonomic dysfunction. In another study (Monga, Miller, & Biederman, 1987) involving stroke patients, autonomic nervous system function was examined and compared with an age-matched control group of normal elderly people. Abnormalities of skin temperature on the hemiparetic side compared with the normal side were noted, whereas no such findings were present in the control subjects. Similarly, abnormalities in Valsalva's maneuver and heart rate variation with change of posture were detected in some stroke patients. The abnormalities were more marked in patients who had symptoms of autonomic nervous system dysfunction. It was concluded that the findings suggest autonomic system dysfunction in stroke patients.

Alcohol also produces both long- and short-term effects on sexuality. In general, small amounts of alcohol release inhibition that leads to false perception of enhanced sexual desire and performance. Large amounts of alcohol produce erectile difficulties, and impotence results from chronic intake of alcohol, contributing to a decline in sexual performance, particularly in male stroke patients. So it is possible that some of the erectile problems observed and reported in stroke patients are the result of a history of alcohol abuse. Hawton (1984) reported that up to 80% of chronic alcoholics experienced decreased sex drive and ejaculation dysfunction.

Despite all the concomitant problems stroke patients may have, it is still likely that sexual dysfunction can be attributed to the stroke itself. Boldrini et al. (1991) examined 86 stroke patients to assess the changes in sexual life experienced after the onset of the illness. Questionnaires concerning both sexual behavior and feelings about sexuality were administered to patients and their spouses. Twenty-four couples were eliminated from analysis because of a discrepancy between husband and wife in the answers concerning sexual behavior after stroke. Authors also excluded patients who had aphasia, severe debilitating illnesses, urologic disorders, or were receiving any medication that could have caused sexual dysfunction. Yet, most of the patients in both genders reported a decline in sexual activity (frequency of intercourse). The findings suggested that most of the changes in sexual function poststroke are a direct result of stroke rather than other underlying medical conditions or medications.

One of the main factors identified in the decline in sexual function after stroke was the fear that sexual intercourse might precipitate another stroke (Monga et al., 1986). Other investigators (Boldrini et al., 1991; Sjogren et al., 1983) have also found that fear may be responsible for the decline in sexual function. Some investigators (Hawton, 1984; Renshaw, 1974) have reported that this fear of precipitating another stroke may be expressed more by the sexual partner than the patient. Another researcher (Muckleroy, 1977) disagreed that fear is a major factor in decline of sexual activity in stroke patients.

Besides fearing having another stroke or myocardial infarction, stroke patients also fear rejection by their spouse or performance failure (Monga et al., 1986). Masters and Johnson (1966, 1970), Rykken (1988), and Starr and Weiner (1981) have suggested that a major cause of sexual dysfunction in the aging male is the fear of failure, and its accompanying anxiety becomes a self-fulfilling prophesy. In time, the man will withdraw from sexual activity with his spouse altogether.

Furthermore, stroke often leads to a loss of status and a diminished self-image. Men often experience a decline in their authority within their families, which may negatively influence their relationships with their wives (Boldrini et al., 1991). Reduced self-esteem resulting from inability to perform intercourse according to expectations has been reported (Bray et al., 1981; Sjogren & Fugl-Meyer, 1981). Not surprisingly, the incidence of depression is high. The reported incidence varies from 20% to 50% (Ebrahim, Barer, & Nouri, 1987; Robinson, Bolduc, & Price, 1987; Robinson, Starr, & Price, 1984). A decrease in the frequency and firmness of erections may be a clinical manifestation of depression with a resultant decline in sex drive and desire. Beaumont (1977) reported that depressed men suffer erectile dysfunction and some depressed women have reported difficulty reaching an orgasm.

In the clinical setting, coping with the stress of stroke and its outcome is becoming increasingly recognized as necessary to preserve quality of life and sexual function. Stress is viewed as a dynamic, unfolding process rather than a static, unitary event. Stress leads to a disturbed person–environment relationship that exceeds a person's current personal resources (Lazarus, 1984). Similarly, coping is a dynamic process designed to manage the situation through regulation of distressing emotions and action to change the situation.

Sjogren et al. (1983) have contended that sexual dysfunction in the hemiplegic patient may be explained in terms of poor coping skills rather than by endocrine deficits. Among the stroke survivors they studied, there was no organic background for common sexual dysfunctions; therefore, they concluded that the dysfunctions were a result of changes in sex roles, the partner's custodial attitude, and dependency in self-care. A stroke patient may become distressed and less willing to initiate a sexual encounter while his or her spouse has to assist him or her with toileting and other self-care activities. Other investigators have also identified role change and role conflict as contributing factors that influence sexual function in stroke patients (Goldstein, Regnery, & Wellin, 1981; Kinsella & Duffy, 1979). The patient's spouse may suddenly become the wage earner, family decision maker, or household manager, and may become responsible for providing care for the stroke survivor. Social isolation, such as reduced contact with friends, fewer social interactions, and lack of time for leisure activities may add to further frustrations and influence sexual relationships with the partners. Marron (1982) cautioned that a partner's rejection of the stroke patient may reflect previous marital discord between the couple.

Although hyposexuality is common in stroke patients, some patients may present with hypersexuality. Monga et al. (1986) have described hypersexuality and deviant sexual behavior as a poststroke complication. Symptoms in hypersexual patients were similar to those described in Klüver-Bucy syndrome. Klüver and Bucy (1939) described the following behavior changes as a result of bilateral lobectomies in rhesus monkeys: increased sexual activity, marked changes in dietary habits, and antisocial behavior. Hypersexuality has been described in both animals and humans with temporal lobe lesions and seizures (Blumer & Walker, 1967; Falconer, Hill, Meyer, Mitchell, & Pond, 1955; Savard & Walker, 1965). Andy and Velamati (1978) demonstrated that temporal lobe or limbic system seizures may induce hypersexuality in the early stages of seizure development. In addition, patients described by Monga et al. (1986) had involvement of temporal lobe lesions. However, in two cases, the lesion was extended into the frontal lobe, and a history of seizure activity was present. Management of these patients is more difficult and rehabilitation outcomes tend to be poor because partners have difficulty accepting and coping with such a problem.

MANAGEMENT

Physical Assessment

It is clear that poor sexual function in stroke patients is multifactorial and the traditional organic versus psychogenic approach to sexual dysfunction in these patients is a gross oversimplification. Most of the sexual problems encountered by stroke patients result from a complex interaction of psychological and physical factors. Attempts should be made to assess and delineate the extent to which various factors may be playing a role in the severity of sexual dysfunction.

A physical assessment should include a medical history comprising details of past and present medical conditions, history of any surgical procedures, drug usage, endocrine function, and other neurologic deficits or diseases that may influence sexual function (Exhibit 11–5). Because vascular disease is one of the major causes of impotence in patients older than age 40 years, a prestroke history of erectile difficulties will be important in an overall patient assessment. If the patient gives a history of erectile difficulties during sexual intercourse, it is helpful to evaluate erections during nondemanding situations, such as masturbation, nocturnal and early morning erections, and during fantasy. Furthermore, low penile brachial pressure has been reported in patients who have erectile problems and is an indicator of a major future vascular event (Morley, Korenman, Kaser, Mooradian, & Viosca, 1988). It is also important to examine penile sensitivity in elderly stroke patients because it may be a factor in their sexual behavior (Edwards & Husted, 1976).

Health care providers should note diseases that may adversely affect sexuality (e.g., diabetes mellitus, renal failure, or chronic obstructive pulmonary disease). They also should take a detailed history of medications, drug abuse, and exces-

---

Exhibit 11–5 Physical Assessment

In Male and Female Patients

- Complete history
- Diabetes mellitus
- Renal failure
- Coronary artery disease
- Chronic alcoholism
- Drug abuse
- Current medications
- Prestroke/poststroke
  – Marital adjustment
  – Sexual function
  – Psychological function
- Cognitive skills
- Functional status
- Need for current medications
- Preferences for sexual expression

In Selected Patients

- Neuropsychological assessment
- Psychiatric consultation

In Selected Male Patients

- Urology consultation
- Nocturnal penile tumescence
  – Doppler flow studies
- Arteriography
  – Pharmacocavernosometry
  – Pudendal artery angiography
  – Somatosensory evoked potential
  – Sacral latency

In Selected Female Patients

- Gynecological examination
- Referral to endocrinologist

Source: Adapted with permission from T.N. Monga and H.J. Ostermann, *Sexuality and Disability*, Vol. 9, No. 2, Hanley & Belfus, Inc.

sive alcohol consumption. CVA is a dynamic process and, as such, the assessment of physical deficits, cognitive function, and emotional status should be carried out regularly and frequently during the acute and subacute stages of the vascular event. Special note should be made regarding severity of sensory loss, degree of muscle weakness, muscle tone, extent of cognitive deficits, and level of family support. Whether the person has a history of bladder and bowel incontinence needs to be documented. The degree of functional limitations in self-care activities and changes in physical appearance are important to assess because they may predict the severity of impact on emotional response and sexuality.

In the elderly male patient with urinary incontinence and an enlarged prostate, a careful urologic assessment should be made. In patients who are unable to achieve satisfactory erections and have a strong desire to remain sexually active, practitioners need to consider further investigations. A referral to a urologist may be in order for those patients. Investigations that might help to delineate the underlying pathophysiology include urodynamics, penile biothesiometry, dorsal nerve somatosensory evoked potentials (SSEP), and NPT. However, the absence of NPT should not lead to the conclusion that the dysfunction is wholly or even partially organic in nature, because it could be the result of an underlying depression. Moreover, there is a paucity of information regarding the value of urodynamics, penile biothesiometry, dorsal nerve SSEP, and NPT in the diagnosis of impotence in stroke patients. Measurement of serum testosterone level may not be of much help either in diagnosis or management of the patient, because the relationship between testosterone levels and sexuality in older men has been found to be modest (Brown et al., 1978).

Psychological Assessment

A stroke is a significant and traumatic event in an individual's life, affecting the well-being of not only the stroke patient but also the immediate family (Schulz, Rompkins, & Rau, 1988). The subsequent physical impairments and disabilities are invariably accompanied by significant psychosocial consequences, although health care professionals may downplay or even ignore these psychosocial problems.

Negative emotional reactions are common following stroke. According to Anderson (1982), the reaction of each patient is shaped by his or her premorbid personality, the individual's manner of coping with stress, support of family and friends, and the cognitive deficits created by stroke itself. It is likely every area of a relationship with a significant other may be strained following stroke. Feibel, Berk, and Joynt (1979) have described social isolation, decreased community involvement, lifestyle alterations, disruption of family function, major depression, anxiety, and anger following stroke.

Considering the scope of emotional reactions, it is recommended that assessment include an in-depth interview of both partners (together and separately). Attempts should be made to determine sexual history, sexual behavior, and sexual function before the onset of stroke, because a person's sexual relationships before stroke is one of the predictors for poststroke sexual function. Practitioners should note any psychosocial disorders (e.g., depression or anxiety) and other factors that may interfere with sexual function. During the interview, practitioners should determine how the couple has been coping with stresses resulting from stroke, with special reference to sexuality-related concerns. Interviewing spouses separately provides insight into the partners' preferences about methods of sexual expression. Such interviewing also may help to unmask concerns about the nondisabled partner's perceived extramarital relationships. Sometimes it is possible that both partners do not desire sexual activity as part of the relationship. The interviewer should explore fears, anxiety, and self-image concerns that may interfere with successful arousal and sexual behavior.

Of stroke survivors, 20% to 50% suffer from depression within 6 months poststroke (Ebrahim et al., 1987; Robinson et al., 1984, 1987). It is difficult to diagnose depression in stroke patients because many of the vegetative symptoms of depression (e.g., sleep and appetite disturbances, fatigue, or psychomotor retardation) may themselves be a physical manifestation of stroke or, for that matter, many other medical conditions. However, a significant decrease in the frequency and firmness of night erections occur in patients suffering from depression (Morley et al., 1988). Furthermore, depression may lead to further psychosocial problems and declines in physical and sexual function. Thus, it is important to consider a past and present history of depression. The validity of applying *Diagnostic and Statistical Manual of Mental Disorders* criteria to stroke patients has been questioned because some of the criteria rely on verbal responses (Primeau, 1988; Ross, Gordon, Hibbard, & Egelko, 1986). Assessments of depression based on self-report inventories have similar limitations.

Other behavioral problems also need to be assessed, including irritability, loss of self-control, lower frustration tolerance, emotional lability, and reduced initiative. These problems all may lead to difficulties in family adjustment and sexual dysfunction.

TREATMENT

It is important to prevent and minimize the residual physical, psychological, and social problems resulting from stroke through appropriate interventions in a timely manner (Exhibit 11–6). Although sexual education for the patient is viewed as an essential component of total rehabilitation for patients with a spinal cord injury, this is not the case for patients with CVAs. Many of the problems with sexual function can be prevented by integrating information on sexual function into a comprehensive stroke rehabilitation program. The information could be included in the existing stroke education materials or through structured stroke groups.

Opinions differ regarding the best time at which this aspect of care should be discussed. Some health providers believe that discussion should occur early in the course of recovery to possibly reduce patient anxiety. However, at the time of diagnosis and during the early period of recovery, the patient and family are more concerned about survival, recovery, and suffering rather than sexual function, so perhaps sexuality-related questions should be addressed at the time of follow-up. U. Monga (1995) has suggested that each case should be handled individually. It is the authors' (T.N. Monga and A.J. Kerrigan) opinion that discussion about sexuality should not be delayed but, rather, be offered early during the recovery from stroke. The most appropriate time might be when the patient is going home for a weekend pass or sooner, if the patient mentions concerns regarding sexual function. Most patients welcome an open and honest discussion of this topic as well as suggestions (Exhibit 11–7).

Exhibit 11–6 Management Approaches

In Male and Female Patients	*In Selected Patients*

• Provide general counseling
  – Remove communication barriers
  – Reassure regarding
  – Acceptance
  – Performance
  – Safety
  – Remove anxiety
  – Improve coping skills
  – Suggest alternative positions
• Improve functional status
  – Retrain cognitive functioning
  – Improve perceptual deficits
  – Train in self-care activities
  – Improve social skills
  – Advise on adaptive equipment
  – Advise on bladder management
• Modulate medications
• Treat depression
	• Provide psychotherapy
	• Provide sex therapy
	  – Behavior modification
	
	In Selected Male Patients
	
	• Testosterone supplement
	• Trial of yohimbine
	• Penile prostheses
	  – Vacuum constrictive devices
	  – Corpus cavernosa injection
	
	In Selected Female Patients
	
	• Estrogen replacement
	• Water-based vaginal creams
	• Vaginal dilators

In the literature, there is some controversy about who should provide sex education and counseling. Some researchers believe that physicians should discuss sexuality-related issues during the course of history taking or during routine rounds. Others have suggested that nursing staff are more trained in dealing with psychosocial and sexual problems (Burgener & Logan, 1989). It really does not matter who starts the initial discussion; however, there should be an identified team member who is responsible for providing counseling on a regular basis. This team member should know about the sexual problems as well as possible interventions to recommend. Sexual counseling and discussion should not be left in the hands of staff members who feel uncomfortable discussing sexual issues with disabled people. Conine and Evans (1982) have pointed out that stroke patients will discuss sexual concerns with people with whom they feel comfortable. The assessment should include prestroke relationship issues, sexual interactions, and sexual attitudes toward various expressions of sexuality. It is important to determine the areas of psychosocial responsibilities (e.g., wage earner, homemaker) that may have undergone the most change.

Staff Education

It is important for patients to differentiate between sexuality and physical sexual performance. Sexuality may be influenced, but cannot be destroyed, by illness and environmental factors. Patients need to understand that, although physical intimacy is desirable, there are other means of sexual expression that will provide satisfaction and pleasure (U. Monga, 1995). Health care providers should reassure stroke patients and their partners that, in many cases, the physiologic sexual responses remain normal following stroke. However, because of sensory and motor disturbances, adaptive changes in sexual behavior and expression may be necessitated.

Exhibit 11–7 Topics for Patient and Family Education

- Stroke and its prognosis
- Treatment goals
- Preventive measures
- Expected treatment outcome
- Importance of family involvement in the rehabilitation process
- Impact of stroke on sexuality
- Impact of medications on sexuality
- Adjustment to role changes
- Sexual rehabilitation

As reported in some studies, poor sexual function is correlated with lower functional status in activities of daily living, meaning those patients who are not independent in self-care activities report more sexual problems and decline in coital frequency (Sjogren & Fugl-Meyer, 1982). Dependency leads to a vicious cycle of poor self-esteem, poor relationships, and poor sexual function that leads to further depersonalization and decline in functional status. Therefore, attempts should be made to improve the patient's functional status and make him or her as independent as possible.

Practitioners must emphasize the importance of various means of sexual expression, such as hugging, kissing, caressing, and providing verbal affection, to couples. Furthermore, they should assess the need for marital counseling and provide counseling, if necessary. Sjogren (1983) has emphasized the importance of role changes and increased dependency in self-care as major factors that contribute to a decline in frequency of intercourse because they interfere with positive attitudes toward sexuality. Once the problem of custodial care has been identified, then it is possible to facilitate alternative ways of providing care to maintain the previous relationship and sex roles. If depression has been diagnosed, the patient should be treated effectively by psychotherapy or, if needed, medication.

Several other concerns need to be addressed, including problems with self-image, self-esteem, communication barriers between the partners, problems related to sensory perceptual deficits, weakness, contractures, and bowel and bladder incontinence. Practitioners also need to address patient fears about having another stroke or a heart attack, about rejection, and about performance. Survivors and partners may be uncertain when to resume sexual activity; they may feel that waiting longer would be safer or better for them. On the contrary, resuming sexual activity early, as soon as the patient feels interested and comfortable, may minimize the likelihood of psychological complications (Finger, 1993).

Permission-giving is a fundamental intervention (Herring, 1985); hence, practitioners should provide reassurance that concerns and questions following stroke are normal. Furthermore, patients should be reassured regarding the safety of exercises and intercourse. No data are available to indicate that sexual intercourse will or may precipitate another stroke; moreover, exercises within limits of fatigue have been found to be safe (Monga et al., 1988). Practitioners should ask their patients to seek medical advice if patients experience any shortness of breath, chest pain, or dizziness during sexual intercourse. Furthermore, clinicians need to be cautious when prescribing unsupervised exercises in which the patient will be using the upper limbs.

Positioning

Clinicians should provide information on alternate sexual positions for couples in which one partner has residual physical impairments. Conine and Evans (1982) and Fugl-Meyer and Jaasko (1980) have suggested methods for enhancing sexual performance in male hemiplegics. The hemiplegic patient should lie on the affected side so that the unaffected arm is free to caress the partner. In this position, with a pillow wedged behind the male's back, a rear entry is easiest. The female partner may need encouragement to increase her active participation. The spouse should be advised to focus kissing and caressing on those parts of the patient's body where sensation is intact and comfortable. If intercourse in the side-lying, rear-entry position is acceptable, the patient should be advised not to fall asleep in this position, which would compromise circulation to the involved extremity. A painful shoulder may make this position uncomfortable. If this position is impossible, the affected partner can remain supine during intercourse while the other partner can adopt a top-superior position.

In some female patients, hip adductor spasticity may impede smooth intromission. However, the position of rear vaginal entry requires only minimal hip abduction. Abduction of the hip can be facilitated with hip and knee flexed. The female hemiplegic patient may also enjoy coitus in the supine position, lying nearly at a right angle to her partner with her knees flexed over his thighs; he faces her side-lying and penetrates her from below (Conine & Evans, 1982). Costello (1981) also has recommended that stroke patients assume a mutual side-lying or supine position with their partners to facilitate intercourse. Patients with shoulder pain should avoid the side-lying position; instead, they should adopt a supine position. The partner may need to be reminded that the patient may neglect stimuli from the affected side because of perceptual and sensory deficits.

McCormick, Riffer, and Thompson (1986) have schematically outlined several alternate positions for couples in which the male is hemiplegic (Figure 11–1). The authors reported that, in their study, the neurologic difficulty made it virtually impossible for the males to assume the superior coital position, which was frustrating and demoralizing for the husbands and left the wives unsure about how they should respond. Various coital positionings were discussed with the couples using stick-figure drawings that were sufficiently abstract to avoid offending patient sensitivities. The wives and their husbands reported that the discussion of sexuality and poststroke sexuality provided them with encouragement.

In Figure 11–1, position **A** is a male-superior position for which a considerable upper body strength is required, along with body balance. Positions **B** and **C** are two female-astride coital positions, which allow the male stroke patient to lie down and provide the female with more control of the act. Positions **D** and **E** are coital positions with the stroke patient sitting in a wheelchair that has removable armrests. Positions **F** and **G** can be used by male patients with adequate body balance and good lower body strength. Position **H** reveals how the female can lie on her back with the male perpendicular to her body trunk. Unfortunately, it is unclear from the study how many couples changed their coital positions and were satisfied with the newly adapted positions.

Medical/Surgical Management

The most frequent cause of erectile dysfunction in a medical outpatient population is the use of medications (Slag et al., 1983). However, surprisingly little has been written about this topic (Morley et al., 1988). Antihypertensive agents appear to interfere with normal sexuality more than any other drug group. Medications may need to be adjusted or changed to drugs with fewer side effects on sexual function. Prazosin and calcium channel blockers may have the lowest incidence of sexual side effects (Kochar, Zeller, & Itskovitz, 1979; Pitts, 1975). Clinicians should discourage empirical use of antidepressants and tranquilizers. In addition, they should take a history of nonprescription illicit drug use because marijuana, cocaine, and heroin are associated with sexual problems. If spasticity interferes with sexual performance, the patient could try dantrolene sodium to relieve the increased tone.

Although there appears to be no significant relationship between the level of testosterone and the severity of sexual problems, in some selected patients who have low serum testosterone levels, treatment with testosterone may be considered. However, the role of testosterone and yohimbine has not been studied in stroke patients. Oral forms of testosterone are ineffective and increase serum lipids and produce liver damage. Furthermore, testosterone therapy may stimulate the growth of an occult prostate cancer. When indicated, intramuscular testosterone is given once a month.

Although noninvasive and invasive devices such as vacuum devices and penile implants are growing in popularity, the role and need for these devices has not been studied in stroke patients. Self-injection therapy with papaverine, phentolamine, or prostaglandin E_1 in stroke patients also has not been reported. See Chapter 22 for further discussion on impotence treatment.

In female patients, clinicians should make an effort to identify causes leading to arousal difficulties and anorgasmia. Furthermore, they must elicit a history of prestroke sexual function. Psychological causes, similar to those experienced by male patients, include changes in self-image, anxiety, depression, and fear of rejection by a partner. Endocrinologic assessment should be carried out to delineate any underlying hormonal changes. If indicated, the clinician should refer the patient to a gynecologist. Nonestrogen topical lubricants, suppositories, and vaginal moisturizers may be used in the management of female patients with painful coitus.

Reproduction and Parenting

In young stroke patients, counseling needs to include questions regarding contraceptive options, pregnancy, labor, delivery, and parenting. There is a paucity of information regarding labor, delivery, and parenting, however. Clinicians should be aware that oral contraceptives are contraindicated because of the increased

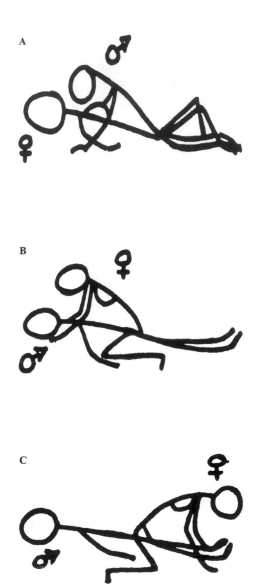

continues

Figure 11–1 Coital positioning for stroke-surviving couples. *Source:* Reprinted from *Rehabilitation Nursing*, 18(6), 384–387, with permission of the Association of Rehabilitation Nurses, 4700 W. Lake Avenue, Glenview, IL 60025-1485. Copyright © 1986. Association of Rehabilitation Nurses.

Figure 11–1 continued

continues

Figure 11–1 continued

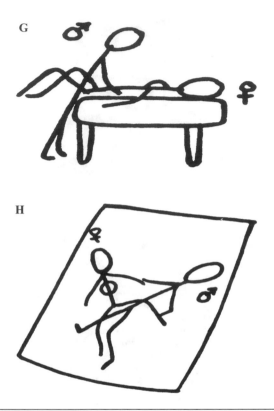

risk of thromboembolism. Furthermore, patients may experience difficulty inserting a diaphragm because of poor coordination and balance. Use of condoms may be the most practical means of contraception; however, its use may require partner cooperation.

In summary, many options, suggestions, and recommendations have been put forward as far as treatment and management of the stroke survivor is concerned; however, no information is available to support that these approaches are effective in managing sexual dysfunction. Further research is needed regarding the outcomes of various treatment approaches, including sexual counseling.

CONCLUSION

A marked decline in many aspects of sexuality after stroke has been reported. Common problems include declines in libido, coital frequency, vaginal lubrication, and orgasm in women and poor or lack of erection and ejaculation in men. Patients experience lack of enjoyment and poor satisfaction with sexual activity during the poststroke period. This decline appears to be multifactorial in nature. Furthermore, the major factors influencing sexuality comprise poor coping skills; psychosocial adjustment to the impairment; role changes; changes in partners' sexual interest; fear of having another stroke; and, to a certain extent, the severity of sensory, perceptual, and cognitive deficits.

The first step in management is a complete assessment of the patient's medical, functional, and psychosocial status. Clinicians must conduct an in-depth interview with both partners to determine sexual history and behavior before and after stroke, followed by appropriate interventions. Interventions should focus on providing relevant information, education, reassurance, an adjustment of medications, counseling regarding coping skills, suggestions for alternate positioning, and a means of sexual expression and satisfaction.

REFERENCES

Aloni, R., Ring, H., Rozenthul, N., & Schwartz, J. (1993). Sexual function in male patients after stroke: A follow-up study. *Sexuality and Disability, 11*(2), 121–128.

Aloni, R., Schwartz, J., & Ring, H. (1994). Sexual function in post-stroke female patients. *Sexuality and Disability, 12*(3), 191–199.

Anderson, T.P. (1982). Rehabilitation of patients with completed stroke. In E.J. Kottke, G.K. Stillwell, & J.F. Lehmann (Eds.), *Krusen's handbook of physical medicine and rehabilitation* (pp. 583–603). Philadelphia: W.B. Saunders.

Andy, O.J., & Velamati, S. (1978). Temporal lobe seizures and hypersexuality. *Applied Neurophysiology, 41*, 13–28.

Bachman, G.A. (1988). Sexual dysfunction in postmenopausal women: The role of medical management. *Geriatrics, 43*, 79–83.

Beaumont, G. (1977). Sexual side of clomipramine (Anafranil). *Journal of Internal Medicine Research, 5*, 37–44.

Beckmann, C.R.B., Gittler, M., Barzansky, B.M., & Beckmann, C.A. (1989). Gynecologic health care of women with disabilities. *Obstetrics and Gynecology, 74*, 75–79.

Blumer, D., & Walker, A.E. (1967). Sexual behavior in temporal lobe epilepsy. *Archives of Neurology, 16*, 37–43.

Boldrini, P., Basaglia, N., & Calanca, M.C. (1991). Sexual changes in hemiparetic patients. *Archives of Physical Medicine and Rehabilitation, 72*, 202–207.

Boone, T.B. (1995). The physiology of sexual function in normal individuals. In T.N. Monga (Ed.), *Sexuality and disability* (pp. 313–324). Philadelphia: Hanley & Belfus.

Bray, G.P., De Frank, R.S., & Wolfe, T.L. (1981). Sexual functioning in stroke patients. *Archives of Physical Medicine and Rehabilitation, 62*, 286–288.

Brown, W.A., Monti, P.M., & Corriveau, D.P. (1978). Serum testosterone and sexual activity and interest in men. *Archives of Sexual Behavior, 7*, 97–103.

Burgener, S., & Logan, G. (1989). Sexuality concerns of the post-stroke patient. *Rehabilitation Nursing, 14*(4), 178–181.

Carty, E.A., & Conine, T.N. (1988). Disability and pregnancy: A double dose of disequilibrium. *Rehabilitation Nursing, 13,* 85–87.

Conine, T.A., & Evans, J.H. (1982). Sexual reactivation of chronically ill and disabled adults. *Journal of Allied Health, 11(4),* 261–270.

Costello, S.P. (1981). The sexual recovery of stroke patients. *Sexual Medicine Today, 5,* 6–11.

Davidson, J.M, Chen, J.J., Crapo, L., Gray, G.D., Greenleaf, A.J., & Catania, J.A. (1983). Hormonal changes and sexual function in aging men. *Journal of Clinical Endocrinology and Metabolism, 57,* 71–77.

Ebrahim, S., Barer, K.D., & Nouri, F. (1987). Affective illness after stroke. *British Journal of Psychiatry, 15,* 52-56.

Edwards, A.E., & Husted, J.R. (1976). Penile sensitivity, age and sexual behavior. *Journal of Clinical Psychology, 32,* 697–700.

Falconer, M.A., Hill, D., Meyer, A., Mitchell, W., & Pond, D.A. (1955). Treatment of temporal lobe epilepsy by temporal lobectomy: Survey of findings and results. *Lancet, 1,* 827–835.

Feibel, J.H., Berk, S.S., & Joynt, R.J. (1979, April). Unmet needs of stroke survivors. *Neurology, 29,* 592.

Finger, W.W. (1993). Prevention, assessment and treatment of sexual dysfunction following stroke. Sexual counseling for people with disabilities [Special issue]. *Sexuality and Disability, 11(1),* 39–56.

Ford, A.B., & Orfirer, A.P. (1967). Sexual behavior and chronically ill patient. *Medical Aspects of Human Sexuality, 1,* 51–61.

Freeman, J.T. (1961). Sexual capacities in aging male. *Geriatrics, 16,* 37–43.

Fugl-Meyer, A.R., & Jaasko, L. (1980). Post-stroke hemiplegia and sexual intercourse. *Scandinavian Journal of Rehabilitation Medicine, 7,* 158–166.

Garden, F.H., & Schramm, D.M. (1995). The effects of aging and chronic illness on sexual function in older adults. In T.N. Monga (Ed.), *Sexuality and disability* (pp. 463–474). Philadelphia: Hanley & Belfus.

Goddess, E.D., Wagner, N.N., & Silverman, D.R. (1979). Post-stroke sexual activity of CVA patients. *Medical Aspects of Human Sexuality, 13(3),* 16–29.

Goldstein, V., Regnery, G., & Wellin, E. (1981). Caretaker role fatigue. *Nursing Outlook, 29(1),* 24–30.

Hagan, M.J., Wallin, J.D., & Baer, R.M. (1980). Anti-hypertension therapy and male sexual dysfunction. *Psychosomatics, 21(3),* 234–237.

Hawton, K. (1984). Sexual adjustment of men who had strokes. *Journal of Psychosomatic Research, 28,* 243–249.

Herring, B.E. (1985). Sexual changes in patients and partners following stroke. *Rehabilitation Nursing, 10,* 28–30.

Horn, L.J., & Zasler, N.D. (1990). Neuroanatomy and neurophysiology of sexual function. *Journal of Head Trauma Rehabilitation, 5,* 1–13.

Inglis, J., Ruckman, M., Lawson, J.S., MacLean, A.W., & Monga, T.N. (1982). Sex differences in cognitive effects of unilateral brain damage. *Cortex, 18,* 257–275.

Kalliomaki, J.L., Markkanen, T.K., & Mustonen, V.A. (1961). Sexual behavior after cerebral vascular accident: Study on patients below age 60 years. *Fertility and Sterility, 12,* 156–158.

Kinsella, G.H., & Duffy, F.D. (1979). Psychosocial readjustment in the spouses of aphasic patients: A comparative survey of 79 subjects. *Scandinavian Journal of Rehabilitation Medicine, 11,* 129–132.

Kinsey, A.C., Pomeroy, W.B., & Martin, C.E. (1948). *Sexual behavior in the human male.* Philadelphia: W.B. Saunders.

Kinsey, A.C., Pomeroy, W.B., Martin, C.E., & Gebhard, P.H. (1953). *Sexual behavior in the human female.* Philadelphia: W.B. Saunders.

Kleitsch, E.C., & O'Donnell, P.D. (1990). Sex and aging. In F.P. Maloney & K.M. Means (Eds.), *Rehabilitation and the aging population* (pp. 121–135). Philadelphia: Hanley & Belfus.

Klüver, H., & Bucy, P.C. (1939). Preliminary analysis of functions of temporal lobes in monkeys. *Archives of Neurology and Psychiatry, 42,* 979–1000.

Kochar, M., Zeller, J., & Itskovitz, H. (1979). Prazosin in hypertension with and without methyldopa. *Clinical Pharmacology and Therapeutics, 25,* 143–148.

Krane, R. (1986). Sexual function and dysfunction. In P. Walsh, R.F. Gittes, A.D. Perlmutter, & T.A. Stamey (Eds.), *Campbell's urology* (5th ed., pp. 700–735). Philadelphia: W.B. Saunders.

Lazarus, R.S. (1984). *Stress, appraisal and coping.* New York: Springer.

Leiblum, S., Bachmann, G., Kemmann, E., Colburn, D., & Swartzman, L. (1983). Vaginal atrophy in the postmenopausal women: The importance of sexual activity and hormones. *Journal of the American Medical Association, 249,* 2195–2198.

Leshner, M., Fine, H.L., & Goldman, A. (1974). Sexual activity in older stroke patients. *Archives of Physical Medicine and Rehabilitation, 55,* 578–579.

Lobi, M.L.C., Phillips, T.F., & Gresham, G.E. (1980). Psychosocial disability in physically restored long term stroke survivors. *Archives of Physical Medicine and Rehabilitation, 61,* 56–71.

Malone, P.E. (1975). A preliminary investigation of changes in sexual relations following strokes. In R. Brookshire (Ed.), *Clinical aphasiology: Proceedings of conference.* Minneapolis, MN: BBK.

Marron, K.R. (1982). Sexuality with aging. *Geriatrics, 37,* 135–138.

Masters, W.H., & Johnson, V.E. (1966). *Human sexual response.* Boston: Little, Brown.

Masters, W.H., & Johnson, V.E. (1970). *Human sexual inadequacy.* Boston: Little, Brown.

McCormick, G.P., Riffer, D.J., & Thompson, M.M. (1986). Coital positioning for stroke afflicted couples. *Rehabilitation Nursing, 11*(2), 17–19.

Monga, M. (1995). Fertility and pregnancy in disabled women. In T.N. Monga (Ed.), *Sexuality and disability* (pp. 503–522). Philadelphia: Hanley & Belfus.

Monga, T.N. (1993). Sexuality post stroke. In R. Teasell (Ed.), *Long term consequences of stroke* (pp. 225–236). Philadelphia: Hanley & Belfus.

Monga, T.N., DeForge, D.A., Williams, J., & Wolfe, L.A. (1988). Cardiovascular responses to acute exercise in patients with cerebrovascular accident. *Archives of Physical Medicine and Rehabilitation, 69,* 937–940.

Monga, T.N., Lawson, J.S., & Inglis, J. (1986a). Sexual dysfunction in stroke patients. *Archives of Physical Medicine and Rehabilitation, 67,* 19–22.

Monga, T.N., & Lefebvre, K.A. (1995). Sexuality: An overview. In T.N. Monga (Ed.), *Sexuality and disability* (pp. 299–312). Philadelphia: Hanley & Belfus.

Monga, T.N., Miller, T., & Biederman, H.J. (1987). Autonomic nervous system dysfunction in stroke patients. *Archives of Physical Medicine and Rehabilitation, 68,* 630.

Monga, T.N., Monga, M., Raina, M.S., & Hardjasudarma, M. (1986b). Hypersexuality in stroke. *Archives of Physical Medicine and Rehabilitation, 67,* 415–417.

Monga, T.N., & Ostermann, H.J. (1995). Sexuality and sexual adjustment in stroke patients. In T.N. Monga (Ed.), *Sexuality and disability* (pp. 345–360). Philadelphia: Hanley & Belfus.

Monga, U. (1995). Sexuality in cancer patients. In T.N. Monga (Ed.), *Sexuality and disability* (pp. 417–442). Philadelphia: Hanley & Belfus.

Mooradian, A.D., & Greiff, V. (1990). Sexuality in older women. *Archives of Internal Medicine, 150,* 1033–1038.

Morley, J.E., Korenman, S.G., Kaser, F.E., Mooradian, A.D., & Viosca, S.P. (1988). Relationship of penile brachial pressure index to myocardial infarction and cerebrovascular accidents in older men. *American Journal of Medicine, 84,* 445–448.

Muckleroy, R.N. (1977). Sex counseling after stroke. *Medical Aspects of Human Sexuality, 11*(12), 115–116.

Niemi, M.L., Laakasonen, R., Kotila, M., & Waltimo, O. (1988). Quality of life 4 years after stroke. *Stroke, 19,* 1101–1107.

Newman, G., & Nichols, C.R. (1960). Sexual activities and attitudes in older persons. *Journal of the American Medical Association, 173,* 33–35.

Pfeiffer, E., Verwoerdt, A., & Wang, H.S. (1968). Sexual behavior in aged men and women. 1. Observation on 254 community volunteers. *Archives of General Psychiatry, 19,* 753–758.

Pitts, N.E. (1975). A clinical evaluation of Prazosin, a new antihypertensive agent. *Postgraduate Medicine, 58,* 117–127.

Primeau, F. (1988). Post-stroke depression: A critical review of the literature. *Canadian Journal of Psychiatry, 33,* 757–765.

Quint, A.R., & Kaiser, F.E. (1985). Gonadotrophin determinations and thyrotropin releasing hormone and luteinizing hormone-releasing hormone testing in critically ill postmenopausal women with hypothyroxinemia. *Journal of Clinical Endocrinology and Metabolism, 60,* 464–471.

Renshaw, D.C. (1974). Stroke and sex. In A. Comfort (Ed.), *Sexual consequences of disability* (pp. 121–131). Philadelphia: Stickley.

Renshaw, D.C. (1984). Geriatric sex problems. *Journal of Geriatric Psychiatry, 17,* 123–148.

Robinson, R.G., Bolduc, P.L., & Price, T.R. (1987). Two years longitudinal study of post-stroke mood disorders: Diagnosis and outcome at one and two years. *Stroke, 18,* 837–843.

Robinson, R.G., Starr, L.B., & Price, T.R. (1984). A two year longitudinal study of mood disorders following stroke: Prevalence and duration at six months follow-up. *British Journal of Psychiatry, 144,* 256–262.

Ross, R.D., Gordon, W.A., Hibbard, M., & Egelko, S. (1986). The dexamethasone suppression test, post-stroke depression and validity of DSM-III based diagnostic criteria. *American Journal of Psychiatry, 143,* 1200–1201.

Rykken, D.E. (1988). Sex in the later years. In P. Silverman (Ed.), *The elderly as modern pioneers* (Vol. 19, pp. 158–182). Bloomington: Indiana University Press.

Sadoughi, W., Leshner, M., & Fine, H.L. (1971). Sexual adjustment in chronically ill and physically disabled population: Pilot study. *Archives of Physical Medicine and Rehabilitation, 52,* 311–317.

Savard, R., & Walker, E. (1965). Changes in social functioning after surgical treatment for temporal lobe epilepsy. *Social Worker, 10,* 87–95.

Schulz, R., Rompkins, C.A., & Rau, M.T. (1988). A longitudinal study of psychosocial impact of stroke on primary support persons. *Psychological Aging, 3,* 131–141.

Sjogren, K. (1980). Leisure after stroke. *Internal Rehabilitation Medicine, 7*(Suppl.), 140.

Sjogren, K. (1983). Sexuality after stroke with hemiplegia. II. With special regard to partnership adjustment and to fulfillment. *Scandinavian Journal of Rehabilitation Medicine, 15,* 63–69.

Sjogren, K., Damber, J.E., & Liliequist, B. (1983). Sexuality after stroke with hemiplegia. I. Aspects of sexual function. *Scandinavian Journal of Rehabilitation Medicine, 15,* 55–61.

Sjogren, K., & Fugl-Meyer, A.R. (1981). Sexual problems in hemiplegia. *International Rehabilitation Medicine, 3*(11), 28–31.

Sjogren, K., & Fugl-Meyer, A.R. (1982). Adjustment to life after stroke with special reference to sexual intercourse and leisure. *Journal of Psychosomatic Research, 26*(4), 409–417.

Slag, M.F., Morley, J.E., Elson, M.K., Trence, D.L., Nelson, C.J., & Nelson, A. (1983). Impotence in medical clinic outpatients. *Journal of the American Medical Association, 249,* 1736–1740.

Starr, B.D., & Weiner, M.B. (1981). *The Starr-Weiner report on sex and sexuality in the mature years.* New York: McGraw-Hill.

Steege, J.F. (1986). Sexual function in the aging women. *Clinical Obstetrics and Gynecology, 29,* 462–469.

Thienhaus, O.J. (1988). Practical overview of sexual function and advancing age. *Geriatrics, 43,* 63–67.

Thorn-Gray, B., & Kern, L. (1983). Sexual dysfunction associated with physical disability: A treatment guide for the rehabilitation practitioner. *Rehabilitation Literature, 44,* 138–144.

Trudel, L., Fabia, J., & Bouchard, J.P. (1984). Quality of life of 50 carotid endarterectomy survivors: A long term follow-up study. *Archives of Physical Medicine and Rehabilitation, 65,* 310–312.

Viitanen, M., Fugl-Meyer, K.S., Bernspan, B., Fugl-Meyer, A.R. (1988). Life satisfaction in long term survivors after stroke. *Scandinavian Journal of Rehabilitation Medicine, 20,* 17–24.

Walker, A.E. (1976). The neurological basis of sex. *Neurology India, 24*(1), 1–13.

Wiig, E.H. (1973). Counseling the adult aphasic for sexual readjustment. *Rehabilitation Counseling Bulletin, 17*(2), 110–119.

CHAPTER 12

Traumatic Brain Injury

M. Elizabeth Sandel

Sexual function after traumatic brain injury is a relatively unexplored area of research and clinical practice. A decline in sexual function often occurs after brain injury, but little research evidence exists to establish reasons for this decline. Researchers have described disinhibited sexual behaviors after brain injury, but the etiologies for these alterations in behavior are also poorly understood. Furthermore, health care professionals have an inadequate understanding of the anatomic correlates for the various manifestations of sexual dysfunction in the general population as well as in brain-injured survivors. Relevant animal literature has suggested varying consequences of brain lesions on sexual behavior, but extrapolation to humans has been largely speculative. Moreover, human studies in traumatic brain injury have not established clear links between pathophysiology or the effects of impairments on sexual function. Also unclear are the effects of interpersonal issues and the stigma of disability, of communicative or cognitive impairments, and of asssociated depression on sexual function. This chapter provides theoretical and practical approaches to maintaining sexual function after traumatic brain injury, with the perspective that further research may alter these approaches.

LIMITATIONS OF CLINICAL RESEARCH

Researchers have used various instruments to determine aspects of sexual function after brain injury (Table 12–1). However, they have not agreed on the instrument that is most effective for evaluating sexual function in the brain-injured population. In addition, research studies have not always provided the psychometric properties of the instruments used. As a result, cross-study comparisons have been difficult.

Table 12–1 Sexuality Inventories

Instrument	Reference Using Instrument
Derogatis Interview for Sexual Function (Derogatis, 1987)	Sandel, Williams, DellaPietra, & Derogatis (1996)
Golombok-Rust Inventory of Sexual Satisfaction (Rust & Golombok, 1985)	O'Carroll, Woodrow, & Maroun (1991)
Self-Evaluation of Sexual Behavior and Gratification	Garden, Bontke, & Hoffman (1990)
Sexual Interaction Inventory	Garden, Bontke, & Hoffman (1990)
Sexual Performance Evaluation	Rosenbaum & Najenson (1976)
General Rehabilitation Assessment Sexuality Profile (GRASP)	Kreutzer & Zasler (1989)
Psychosexual Assessment Questionnaire	Kreutzer & Zasler (1989)
Sexuality Questionnaire: Survivor	Davis & Schneider (1990)

For the most part, research in traumatic brain injury has consisted of results on small populations that were not well characterized. Studies have varied in the reporting of injury type, severity, and level of cognitive or physical function, medication use, and coexistence of depression or other mood disturbances. Furthermore, most published studies have not included female subjects.

BRAIN INJURY AND SEXUAL FUNCTION: A LITERATURE REVIEW

Sexual Function Disorders: Incidence and Prevalence in Brain Injury

The percentage of subjects who have reported sexual dysfunction after brain injury has ranged greatly, probably largely because of the heterogeneity of populations studied. For example, erectile dysfunction in brain-injured men has been reported at a rate of 4% to 71% across studies (Davis & Schneider, 1990; Garden et al., 1990; Kosteljanetz et al., 1981; Kreutzer & Zasler, 1989; Meyer, 1955; Walker & Jablon, 1961). Specifically, in their survey of 67 brain-injured men, Davis and Schneider (1990) found that only 4% reported difficulty with erection. In their study of 739 male subjects with brain injury, Walker and Jablon (1961) found that only 8.1% reported erectile dysfunction. Garden et al. (1990) documented that 36% of a sample of 11 men reported erectile dysfunction and a decline in the frequency of sexual activity. Moreover, Kosteljanetz et al. (1981) found that 42% of a sample of 19 men with postconcussive disorder reported erectile dysfunction. Kreutzer and Zasler (1989), in their study of 21 brain-injured males, found that 57% of the sample reported decreased ability to maintain an erection. In contrast, Meyer (1955), in a survey of 100 male survivors of traumatic brain injury, found that 71% reported erectile dysfunction.

Sexual Function Following Mild Brain Injury

The studies that have focused on patients with mild brain injury have provided inconsistent findings. Kosteljanetz et al. (1981) studied a group of 19 male patients, the majority of whom reported sexual dysfunction (53% reported reduced libido; 42%, erectile dysfunction). Intellectual impairment correlated with reports of sexual dysfunction. In addition, reduced spermatogenesis was suggested by increased plasma concentrations of follicle-stimulating hormone (FSH) in 37% of patients. In contrast, Oddy, Humphrey, and Uttley (1978) studied 50 brain-injured adults (with periods of posttraumatic amnesia less than 24 hours) at 6 or more months after injury. Half of the 12 married patients reported an increase in frequency of sexual intercourse and half reported a decrease. None of the spouses reported problems after the sixth month postinjury.

Sexual Behavior Disorders

Descriptions of sexual behavior disorders after traumatic brain injury exist chiefly as case reports or anecdotal discussions, not large-scale studies (Lusk & Kott, 1982; Miller, Cummings, McIntyre, Ebers, & Grodes, 1986; Sabhesan & Natarajan, 1989; Weinstein, 1974, 1981; Weinstein & Kahn, 1961). Such descriptions have been consistent with animal research describing similar behaviors in animals (Doane, 1986; MacLean, 1975). Disinhibition, which is associated with orbitofrontal injury, presents the underlying pathophysiologic substrate leading to so-called "hypersexual" or "inappropriate" behaviors. These behaviors are usually described in the context of interpersonal contacts, but also may be manifested as perseverative behaviors, such as excessive masturbation. It is unclear to what extent these behaviors represent response to injury in the form of reduced inhibitions, loss of self-esteem, or other psychological consequences of the injury.

Impact of Brain Injury on Family and Relationships

The effects of traumatic brain injury on relationships within the family, including spousal relationships, has been explored in a large number of studies in the United States and abroad. Thomsen (1984) studied severely brain-injured Danish patients and demonstrated that family members were more disturbed by intellectual deficits than by physical impairments. In addition, the relationships between single adult patients and mothers were better than between patients and spouses. In the Rosenbaum and Najenson (1976) study of severely brain-injured veterans in Israel, wives endorsed the questionnaire item "dislikes physical contact with husband" with high frequency within the sample. The researchers used a mood inventory to assess the relationship between mood disturbance and sexual function; mood disturbance in a spouse was associated with decreased levels of sexual activity. Lezak (1978) noted a high frequency of altered libido in brain-injury survivors and emphasized that emotional adjustment of family members, including spouses, occurred only after they accepted the permanence of the deficits. For some partners, this adjustment culminated in divorce, separation, or placement in a long-term care facility. Sexual function and marital adjustment also were studied in a small group of married couples (11 men and 4 women with brain injuries) by Garden et al. (1990). Intercourse frequency declined, more for couples in which the husband rather than the wife was brain injured, and orgasm in female spouses also showed a significant decline. Using measures of anxiety and depression for both partners, Kreutzer and Zasler (1989) found a significant number of mental health problems in the population. O'Carroll et al. (1991) also examined the psychosocial and sexual sequelae of 36 male brain-injured patients during follow-up no more than 4 years after injury. Half of the men scored within the dysfunctional range on psychosexual profiles. Their major complaint was decreased frequency of sexual intimacy, but they also reported emotional distress (61%), anxiety (25%), and depression (22%). Findings did not correlate with severity of insult; age and time following injury were related to the degree of dysfunction.

Anatomy and Physiology of Sexual Function: Animal Studies

To better understand how traumatic brain injury affects sexual function, it is necessary to examine the various physiologic systems involved. The following discussion is based on animal studies. The reticular activating system of the pons and midbrain provides input for initiation and maintenance of arousal and alertness and, hence, contributes to human sexual response. Injury to brain stem motor or sensory systems, then, may alter sexual arousal and responsiveness (Boller & Frank, 1982). These pathways connect with frontal and limbic structures, which play a role in sexual behaviors and affective responses. The brain stem carries afferent and efferent messages from sensory and motor systems, which then connect with cortical and subcortical structures. Injury to these systems may influence the general level of arousal and thus impair sexual function at a fundamental level.

Other structures with important roles in the generation of sexual and reproductive behaviors, the thalamus and hypothalamus, are interconnected with frontal and limbic structures. Sensory systems from the genitalia and other erogenous zones relay information to the thalamus. Stimulation of the thalamus produces erection in animals, and stimulation of the basal ganglia may result in species-specific sexual behaviors (MacLean, 1975).

The hypothalamus is a crucial structure in the elaboration of the human sexual response. Some of the information the hypothalamus receives is in the form of neuronal messages, but other information arrives in the form of chemical messages, including gonadal steroids. In addition, the hypothalamus synthesizes and secretes hormones of its own, many of which exert influences over sex and reproduction. Gonadotropin-releasing hormone stimulates the release of FSH and luteinizing hormone (LH), which regulate the menstrual cycle in women and testosterone secretion in men. In adults, hypothalamic injury can lead to sexual dysfunction or amenorrhea. In children, such injury can lead to precocious puberty (Blendonohy & Philip, 1991; Klachko, Winer, & Burns, 1968; Shaul, Towbin, & Chernausek, 1985). The supraoptic nucleus of the hypothalamus synthesizes oxytocin, a hormone involved in lactation, birthing, and orgasm. Naloxone, an opiate antagonist, prevents the release of oxytocin, suggesting that the release at orgasm is controlled, at least in part, by the endorphin system (Fabbri et al., 1989; Goldstein, 1986).

The medial preoptic area of the hypothalamus plays a role in sexual behavior. Lesions in this area produce a reduction or elimination of copulatory behavior. Stimulation of the medial preoptic area elicits mounting and other sexual behaviors. This area receives neuronal inputs from other brain regions, including the olfactory system, and the cerebral cortex, including the visual cortex. The preoptic area has high concentrations of androgen and estrogen receptors, as well as the enzyme that converts androgens to estrogens. Manipulating androgens and androgen receptors in this region affects copulatory behavior. Stimulation of the dorsomedial nucleus of the hypothalamus generates ejaculation in animals. This nucleus may receive input from the medial preoptic area. In addition, the ventromedial nucleus of the hypothalamus appears to play a role in "female" sexual behaviors. In female rats and monkeys, lesions in this area result in the elimination or reduction of "female" sexual behaviors, including lordosis and "presenting." This nucleus is also strongly influenced by sex hormones, in particular estrogen and progesterone, at least in the female rat. In primate females, androgens (secreted by the adrenal gland) are more important in the maintenance of libido than behavior but perhaps are also involved in generating sexual behaviors (LeVay, 1993).

The frontal lobes are clearly involved in the regulation of sexual behaviors. Hypersexual behaviors occur after injury to the frontal lobes, particularly the orbitofrontal surfaces. These effects may be caused by lesions of the limbic and paralimbic systems. In the case of dorsolateral frontal injury, when attention and initiation impairments are primary, libido or sexual assertiveness may be impaired.

Damage to frontal structures may also lead to an inability to fantasize (Horn & Zasler, 1990). The role of the olfactory system is unclear, but recent research has indicated that anosmia may not significantly affect sexual function (Goldberg & Wise, 1990).

Stimulation of the septal complex and amygdala produce erections and, in the case of the septal region, preorgasmic sensations of pleasure. Stimulation of the hippocampus, a mesial temporal structure, results in erection in animals, and damage may lead to sexual dysfunction (MacLean, 1975). Lesions of the piriform cortex, which interconnects with the olfactory cortex, produce hypersexual responses in animals. Stimulation of the cingulate gyrus produces sexual hallucinations and erections (Heath, 1964). Ablation of the anterior temporal poles also results in hypersexual and exploratory behaviors with hyperorality—the Klüver-Bucy syndrome (Klüver & Bucy, 1939; Lilly, 1983; Mesulum, 1985). Temporal lobe seizures can be manifested by genital sensations and other sexual phenomena, with hypersexual or hyposexual behavior during both ictal and interictal periods. Endocrine disturbances, common in men and women with temporal lobe epilepsy, result in decreased libido, impotence, and menstrual and reproductive disorders (Herzog, Russell, Vaitokaitis, & Geschwind, 1982; Herzog, Seibel, Schomer, Vaitokaitis, & Geschwind, 1986).

Severity of Injury, Time since Injury, and Locus of Lesion: Human Studies

Current research concerning relationships between severity and locus of lesion to sexual dysfunction has been inconclusive. Bond (1976) noted that the level of sexual activity among brain-injured patients was unrelated to severity as measured by the duration of posttraumatic amnesia or the level of cognitive or physical impairment. Yet, Walker and Jablon (1961) found that sexual dysfunction was related only to the severity, but not the locus, of injury. Kosteljanetz et al. (1981) observed a correlation between cognitive deficits and sexual dysfunction in a group of postconcussive disorder patients. In a survey of 100 male survivors of traumatic brain injury, Meyer (1955) found that decline in erectile function was related to the location and severity of injury. Kreutzer and Zasler (1989) and O'Carroll et al. (1991) found that age and time since injury were related to measures of psychosexual dysfunction, but severity of injury was not. In regard to the production of hypersexual behaviors, Miller et al. (1986) found evidence that injury to certain structures, such as medial basal–frontal injury or diencephalic injury, was associated with hypersexuality and limbic injury was associated with changes in sexual preference in a population of eight patients.

A study by Sandel et al. (1996) examined sexual function in a group of 52 male and female outpatients with severe traumatic brain injuries (the average length of posttraumatic amnesia was 54 days). Sexual function was reduced below levels reported in healthy populations, but only significantly so on two subscales (Orgasm, and Drive and Desire) of the Derogatis Interview for Sexual Function (Derogatis, 1987). No correlations were found with brain injury severity, cognitive measures, or the clinical examination. However, location of injury was related to sexual function in that patients with frontal lobe lesions reported an overall higher level of sexual satisfaction and function than those individuals without frontal lesions. Patients with frontal lobe lesions reported more sexual cognitions and fantasies and a higher overall satisfaction with sexual function.

Time since injury may be related to sexual dysfunction. In the Sandel et al. (1996) study, time since injury was inversely related to scores on the Arousal Scale. That is, the more recently injured subgroup reported higher levels of sexual function. This finding may also represent the effects of orbitofrontal lesions, which commonly produce a disinhibition syndrome, underlining a possible role for injured frontal lobe or limbic systems in hypersexual states in the early recovery period after injury. Or, perhaps, this effect represents the development of depression after injury, suggested in a study by O'Carroll et al. (1991). In that study, time since injury was related to measures of psychosexual dysfunction. A majority (61%) of patients reported degrees of emotional distress that fell within the range of psychiatric diagnosis of depression, anxiety, or other psychiatric disorder. Both subjects and partners had evidence of depression (22% and 6%, respectively) or anxiety (25% and 18%, respectively).

Right hemisphere injuries also correlated with higher scores on reports of sexual arousal and sexual experiences. Patients with right hemisphere lesions were found to have higher sexual arousal and more sexual experiences compared with other brain-injured patients in the same cohort. Those findings were unrelated to injury severity (Sandel et al., 1996). Contradictory findings regarding site of injury have been published in studies of stroke survivors. Some studies have reported a greater decline in sexual function after right hemisphere stroke in women (Monga, Monga, Raina, & Hardjasudarma, 1986), in men and women (Coslett & Heilman, 1986) or after left hemisphere stroke (Goddess, Wagner, & Silverman, 1979; Kalliomaki, Markkanen, & Mustonen, 1961). In other studies, locus of lesion did not correlate with changes in sexual function (Boldrini, Basaglia, & Calanca, 1991; Sjogren, 1983; Sjogren, Damber, & Liliequist, 1983). Increased libido or hypersexuality has been reported after right hemisphere stroke (Goddess et al., 1979) and after temporal lobe stroke (Monga et al., 1986).

Of related interest, a study (Cohen & Rosen, 1976) of electroencephalographic activity from the right and left hemisphere in six subjects (four males and two females) at the moment of orgasm documented a dissociation between the hemispheres. The right hemisphere showed activation during periods of erection and orgasm, whereas the left hemisphere was relatively inactive. In the study, no subject showed increased amplitude over the left parietal region during orgasm.

Studies of traumatic brain-injured survivors have not always included women, or have had few female subjects. However, the few that have collected data on male and female subjects (Garden et al., 1990; O'Carroll et al., 1991; Sandel et al., 1996) did not establish clear gender differences on reports of sexual dysfunction. Gender differences in outcome have been reported in some studies of survivors of stroke. A decline was found in both genders in one study (Boldrini et al., 1991) but the perceived emotional effects were reported at higher levels in men. A decline in sexual function occurred in women but not in men with right hemisphere strokes in one study (Monga et al., 1986). In other studies (Sjogren, 1983; Sjogren et al., 1983), no difference was reported between women and men who survived strokes.

In addition, studies of depression after stroke and traumatic brain injury have suggested that lesions to the left brain may be more likely to result in depression than right brain lesions (Silver, Hales, & Yudofsky, 1990). Perhaps depression and sexual function in those populations have a common neurophysiologic and neuroanatomic basis. Perhaps lesions in the frontal and right hemispheres do not interfere with sexuality as much as lesions in other parts of the brain. Rather, frontal and right hemisphere lesions, which have been associated with disinhibition and lack of insight into deficits, may contribute to a distorted sense of reality in brain-injured populations. Frontal lobe and right hemisphere patients tend to be less inhibited and less aware of socially appropriate behavior. Perhaps they were more willing to report sexual arousal and experience. Also, insight may be impaired in those anatomic subgroups, and this lack of insight may contribute to a distorted sense of reality. Those individuals may not realize the extent to which their sexual function has deteriorated. Interviews with partners and spouses may further clarify these issues in future studies.

In summary, the etiology of sexual disorders after brain injury is still unclear. Localization of the lesion, severity of the cerebral insult, gender, or other clinical factors may be important. Furthermore, medication may inhibit responsiveness or affect libido ("Drugs That Cause Sexual Dysfunction," 1983). In addition, role shifts, the stigmatization of disability, and dependency may predispose people with brain injury or stroke to problems with intimate relationships (Sjogren, 1983). The spouse may be identified as a parental figure rather than a truly equal partner (Kinsella & Duffy, 1980), communication may affect the relationship and lead to sexual dysfunction, or fear of precipitating a medical complication may inhibit sexual interest or response (Monga et al., 1986).

Endocrinologic Disturbances after Traumatic Brain Injury

The endocrinologic effects of brain injury result in disruptions of sexual and reproductive function. Endocrinologic disturbances, such as posttraumatic hypopituitarism with permanent hypogonadotropic hypogonadism, may occur after adult brain injury (Edwards & Clark, 1986; Kosteljanetz et al., 1981). A more recent study (Clark, Raggatt, & Edwards, 1988) has suggested that hypogonadotropic hypogonadism may be more frequent than usually recognized after severe brain injury; in that study, 88% of men with severe head injury had subnormal testosterone levels at 7 to 10 days postinjury, and 3 to 6 months later, 24% of a smaller sample still had low testosterone levels with loss of libido and impotence. To evaluate pituitary–gonadal function, Lee, Zasler, and Kreutzer (1994) conducted a prospective study of 21 men with severe brain injury in acute inpatient rehabilitation. Of the men, 14 (67%) had abnormally low testosterone levels.

Sexual and reproductive consequences of brain injury on children and adolescents include both hypogonadotropic hypogonadism and precocious puberty. Klachko and associates (1968) reported the case of a 39-year-old male with hypopituitarism following severe brain injury at age 4 years. The epiphyses remained open, but he gained a height of more than 5 feet despite low growth hormone levels. His genitalia were infantile, the testes small, and no pubic hair was present. Another report of precocious puberty after traumatic brain injury in childhood include a case of accelerated growth of pubic hair and estrogenization of the vaginal mucosa, which occurred within 5 months of the accident (Shaul et al., 1985). In another report, two girls, ages 3 years and 5 years, with precocious puberty exhibited breast development, pubic hair, and changes in vaginal mucosa consistent with estrogenization (Blendonohy & Philip, 1991). The proposed mechanism is destruction of inhibitory neuronal pathways into the hypothalamus, with premature activation of gonadotropin-releasing hormone from the arcuate nucleus.

Temporal Lobe Seizures and Sexual and Reproductive Function

Approximately 20% of patients with posttraumatic epilepsy have temporal lobe seizures (Jennett & Teasdale, 1981). Temporal systems exert a modulatory influence on the hypothalamic regulation of the pituitary. Temporal lobe seizures usually arise from limbic structures such as the amygdala and affect the hypothalamic–pituitary–gonadal axis through effects on dopamine. Because dopamine is a prolactin-inhibitory hormone within this system, decreases in dopamine result in hyperprolactinemia (Herzog et al., 1982).

Up to 58% of males with temporal lobe seizure disorders are impotent or hyposexual and up to 40% of females have menstrual irregularities and reproductive dysfunction, including anovulatory cycles, hypogonadotropic hypogonadism, premature menopause, and polycystic ovarian syndrome (Herzog et al., 1986). Estrogens lower the seizure threshold, and seizure frequency can increase in females at the time of menses and during pregnancy. The hypogonadotropic hypogonadism with amenorrhea seen in temporal lobe seizure patients is associated with low LH levels. Because no hypothalamic disorder has been described, this abnormality may occur because of limbic discharges that result in altered secretion of gonadotropin–releasing hormone (Herzog et al., 1986). Premature menopause also occurs. In polycystic ovarian syndrome, also associated with temporal lobe seizures, LH is elevated along with prolactin, and FSH is depressed (Herzog et al., 1986).

Men with temporal lobe epilepsy and hypogonadism, unlike those with isolated hypogonadism, may have no improvement in libido or potency when parenteral testosterone is given. However, treatment of the epilepsy first, followed by neuroendocrine treatment (bromocriptine or pergolide for hyperprolactinemia, and testosterone for hypogonadism) is sometimes effective (Spark & Wills, 1984).

ASSESSMENT

Interview and Physical Examination

When interviewing brain-injured survivors, the clinician should ask questions that focus on the following areas of concern: pre-injury and postinjury medical and psychiatric problems, current medications, pre-injury and postinjury sexual and reproductive function and relationships, birth control, and safer sex practices. The examiner may provide education during the course of the history-taking session, but should reinforce the teachings later with further elaboration and written materials (Griffith & Lemberg, 1993; Haseltine, Cole, & Gray, 1993; Kroll & Klein, 1992; National Head Injury Foundation, 1996). Furthermore, the examiner must be comfortable discussing all aspects of sexuality, including alternative forms of sexual expression and alternative lifestyles (Mapou, 1990). A nonjudgmental style is essential; staff training that focuses on attitudinal issues as well as education is recommended for physicians (Ducharme & Gill, 1990). The partner or spouse should be present for a portion of the interview (Allgeier & Allgeier, 1991; Cole, 1965), especially if the brain-injured person has memory deficits, and to help provide insight into relationship issues as well.

During the assessment, the clinician also should inquire about the medications the patient is taking. The most common cause of erectile dysfunction in medical populations is medication. Frequently implicated are antihypertensive agents; antipsychotic drugs; antidepressants (although some may have beneficial effects); anxiolytics; and sedatives. Drug-related effects on sexual function are usually reversible on discontinuation of the offending drug.

General questionnaires and interview formats have been designed for the assessment of sexual function in general or medically impaired populations; these instruments have been used in various studies of disabled populations (see Table 12–1). The Derogatis Interview for Sexual Function (Derogatis, 1987) collects information from men and women (two versions) by self-report in the five domains: Fantasy, Arousal, Experience, Orgasm, and Drive and Desire. A General Sexual Satisfaction Score is obtained as well as a total score. The Golombok-

Rust Inventory of Sexual Satisfaction (Rust & Golombok, 1985), also a self-report scale, provides male and female scores (two versions) in the categories of Vaginismus, Anorgasmia, Impotence, Premature Ejaculation, Non-Sensuality, Avoidance, Dissatisfaction, Infrequency, and Non-Communication, as well as a total score. These instruments have been standardized and normed.

Several instruments have been developed to assess sexual function in patients with traumatic brain injury (see Table 12–1). The GRASP instrument assesses sexual history, sexual physical examination results, and results of clinical diagnostic testing. The Psychosexual Assessment Questionnaire was tested on men in heterosexual relationships (Kreutzer & Zasler, 1989). Davis and Schneider (1990) have recommended an open-format sexuality questionnaire for survivors of traumatic brain injury. Garden and associates (1990) used an instrument for men and women in their sample. Most instruments have been designed for male patients or wives of male patients. Most studies have not used standardized, normed instruments.

In addition to interviewing patients, the clinician should complete a general physical examination with a focused assessment of the several areas to identify impairments that may influence communication, positioning, movement, oral ability, and sensory awareness. These areas are aphasia; dysarthria; aprosody; neglect; visual–perceptual deficits; and deficits in attention, concentration, and memory. The examiner should also identify facial scars, oral and facial movement, olfactory function, and visual and hearing impairments. He or she must also evaluate range of motion, especially in the proximal lower extremities. Movement of the limbs and trunk, coordination and motor planning ability, and sensation are crucial portions of the examination. Examination of the genitalia and rectal area must be completed and, in women, should include a breast examination and Papanicolau test and pelvic examination (Zasler & Horn, 1990).

Laboratory Screening

As part of the assessment of sexual function, the practitioner should screen for endocrinologic disorders. Hypopituitarism, which is an infrequent consequence of brain injury, may be manifested by low levels of growth hormone, thyroxine, cortisol, or hypogonadism. Isolated hypogonadism is more common after brain injury and is characterized by low sperm count, low serum levels of testosterone, and inappropriately low levels of LH and FSH. Hypogonadism can be caused by primary gonadal failure as well as secondary failure at a central level. In addition, Klinefelter's syndrome may be a cause of low testosterone in a patient with brain injury, by coincidence; the disorder occurs relatively frequently (1 in 500 men). Because protein-bound testosterone can be increased by thyroid hormone therapy and cirrhosis and decreased by hypothyroidism and obesity, free testosterone levels or sex steroid–binding globulin may give a more accurate picture of inadequate gonadal function.

In women, hypogonadism is characterized by low serum levels of estradiol and inappropriately low serum levels of LH and FSH. Laboratory assessment for women includes FSH, LH, prolactin, estradiol, and dehydroepiandrosterone (tested in the early follicular phase). The gonadotropin-releasing hormone test is useful in distinguishing hypothalamic from pituitary causes of hypogonadism, although this test is not infallible. The clomiphene citrate–provocative test can be used to evaluate the gonadal axis. Single determinations of any of these levels may not accurately reflect the function of this system; three samples should be obtained 20 minutes apart and combined for a single measurement. In men, the assessment should include three samples of FSH, LH, prolactin, and free testosterone (Abboud, 1986).

TREATMENT OF SEXUAL DISORDERS

Pharmacotherapy for Males and Females

Because there are no studies of pharmacologic treatment of hyposexual desire disorders or sexual response disorders in people with traumatic brain injuries, the following review of the literature focuses on medications that *may* have potential benefit, given theoretical considerations, for this population (see Table 12–2 for a review of options). In addition, the study populations in these pharmacologic trials often are heterogeneous, with both healthy individuals and people with comorbidities included. Only one of the pharmacologic studies reviewed included female patients. Clearly, more research is needed before conclusions can be reached about what medications may be useful in any population of individuals with sexual disorders, and, in particular, in those individuals with brain injuries.

Hormonal agents, antidepressants, dopaminergic agents, opiate antagonists, and alpha-adrenergic blocking agents have been investigated for the treatment of hypoactive sexual dysfunction in non–brain-injured patients. Only testosterone and yohimbine have been officially approved for such use by the Food and Drug Administration.

Hormones

O'Carroll (1991), who reviewed the results of investigations of sexual desire disorders in non–brain-injured women, described hypoactive sexual desire as *the* "major female psychosexual dysfunction" (p. 610). There is little evidence in women (without brain injuries) that sexual desire disorders can be traced to hormonal inadequacies, unless they are hypogonadal. However, hypogonadal women

Table 12–2 Potential Drug Therapy for Sexual Dysfunction in Brain Injury

Drug	Indication	Dose/Frequency	Mechanism	Side Effects
Testosterone	↓ Libido ↓ Arousal (?)	200 mg IM biweekly (?)	Central effect	Fluid retention Hypertension Gynecomastia Acne
Yohimbine	Impotence	5.4 mg (1 tablet 3 times/day)	Alpha blocker	Tachycardia Hypertension Nausea Dizziness
Naltrexone	↓ Arousal Impotence	24–50 mg/day	Endorphin antagonist	Nausea, vomiting Liver enzyme elevations Headaches
Bupropion	↓ Libido ↓ Arousal	225–450 mg/day (3 times/day)	↑ Dopamine	Menstrual distur- bances Insomnia Seizures (at high doses)

Source: Reprinted with permission from L.J. Horn and N.D. Zasler, *Medical Rehabilitation of Traumatic Brain Injury*, p. 564, © 1996, Hanley & Belfus, Inc.

do demonstrate an increase in sexual interest following androgen replacement (Sherwin & Gelfand, 1987).

In men, testosterone can also increase sexual interest with pretreatment levels in the normal range (O'Carroll & Bancroft, 1984). Testosterone injections biweekly for 6 weeks in a group of 20 eugonadal men with low libido, when compared with placebo, resulted in an increase in frequency of sexual thoughts. However, no effect was observed in men with erectile dysfunction. Men with hyposexual sexual desire disorder may benefit from testosterone injections even if serum levels are within the normal range.

Human chorionic gonadotropin was used as a treatment in men with erectile failure (45 cases) or lack of sexual desire (6 cases; Buvat, Lemaire, & Buvat-Herbaut, 1987). The treatment period was 1 month with twice weekly injections of 5,000 IU or placebo in a double-blind design. Of the patients treated, 47% had a "good result" compared with 12% of the placebo group. The researchers, though, did not separate the cases of erectile failure from low sexual interest or fully define a *good result*.

Antidepressants and Dopaminergic Agents

Antidepressants have been noted to cause a variety of sexual side effects, but a few, including a number of serotonin-reuptake inhibitors and bupropion (a dopamine-reuptake inhibitor), have been observed to improve sexual function. Trazodone and fenfluramine appeared to improve libido in a number of case reports, although both have also been associated with sexual dysfunction (Gartrell, 1986; Mathews, Whitehead, & Kellet, 1983; Stevensen & Solyom, 1990; Sullivan, 1987), as has fluoxetine (Zajecka, Fawcett, Schaff, Jeffries, & Guy, 1991). Bupropion treatment may improve libido in individuals with hypoactive sexual desire disorders. In a study (Crenshaw, Goldberg, & Stern, 1987) of 60 female and male outpatients with psychosexual dysfunction (sexual aversion, inhibited sexual desire, inhibited sexual excitement, or inhibited orgasm), 12 weeks of double-blind treatment with bupropion (225 to 450 mg/day) resulted in significant improvement in sexual function in the treatment group; only 3% of placebo-treated patients reported improvement, compared with 63% for the medicated group.

Other dopaminergic agents have a potential role in the treatment of sexual dysfunction. Apomorphine, a short-acting dopamine receptor agonist that decreases prolactin secretion, stimulates growth hormone production, and induces erections, improved erectile function in seven out of nine male subjects; benztropine, a cholinergic agent, had no effect on erection (Lal, 1988; Lal, Ackman, Thavundayil, Kiely, & Etienne, 1984). In another study (Danjou, Alexandre, Warot, Lacomblez, & Puech, 1988), apomorphine induced erections in 10 healthy men with impotence. In 10 male patients with Parkinson's disease and erectile dysfunction, treatment with levodopa resulted in slight-to-moderate increases in spontaneous erections at night, although increase in libido was reported in only 2 patients, and erections were not sustainable for sexual intercourse (Benkert, Crombach, & Kockott, 1972).

These preliminary studies suggest a crucial role for dopaminergic systems in sexual dysfunction. Because mesocortical/mesolimbic dopaminergic systems may be particularly vulnerable to traumatic brain injury, sexual dysfunction in this population may be associated with decreased activity in these neurotransmitter systems.

Other Pharmacologic Agents

Opioids also may play a role in the treatment of sexual dysfunction. Naloxone potentiated apomorphine-induced penile erections in rats; methyl naloxone, which does not cross the blood–brain barrier, was ineffective (Berendsen & Gower, 1986). In a small study (Goldstein, 1986) involving 7 men, 25 to 50 mg/day led to full return of erectile function as well as nocturnal penile tumescence in 6 patients. In a study (Fabbri et al., 1989) of 30 male patients, aged 25 to 50 years, with idiopathic erectile dysfunction, naltrexone, an opiate antagonist, increased "sexual performance" in 11 out of 15 treated patients. There were no significant side effects. Furthermore, LH, FSH, and testosterone were unaffected, suggesting a central effect.

Yohimbine, an alpha-adrenoceptor blocker, has been investigated in a number of studies of sexual dysfunction (Danjou et al., 1988; Morales et al., 1987; Reid, Morales, & Harris, 1987; Riley, Goodman, & Kellet, 1989; Sondra, Mazo, & Chancellor, 1990; Susset et al., 1989). No specific studies have been published that have examined sexual dysfunction in patients with brain injuries using either yohimbine or opioid.

Treatment of Erectile Dysfunction

Self-injection of papaverine (a smooth muscle relaxant) or papaverine with phentolamine (an alpha-adrenergic blocking agent) is a treatment modality for men who are impotent because of neurologic causes or vasculogenic causes. Nearly all patients with neurogenic impotence and 60% to 70% of patients with vasculogenic impotence respond to intracavernous injections (Sidi & Chen, 1989). However, patients have developed priapism, fibrosis of erectile tissues, hematomas, vasovagal reflex, and chemical hepatitis after such injections (Levine et al., 1989). Intracavernous injection of prostaglandin E_1 has been recommended more recently; results are promising, although painful erection occurs in up to 20% of patients, a problem that is, perhaps, related to concentration or neuropathy (Ishii et al., 1989; Stakl, Hasun, & Marberger, 1988). The mechanism of action of papaverine—with or without phentolamine—and prostaglandin E_1 is through increased arterial inflow as a result of vasodilatation and decreased venous outflow by occluding draining venules, probably through relaxation of smooth muscle in the corpus cavernosum. Injection unilaterally results in bilateral effects through cross-circulation (Donatucci & Lue, 1992). No studies have been done, though, on the injection treatment approach for patients with brain injury. Other alternatives for the treatment of impotence include vacuum constriction devices, vascular reconstruction, and arterial and venous surgery, which are reviewed elsewhere in this book.

Men with erectile disorders choose prosthetic surgery less frequently because other alternatives are available. When they have elected such surgery, though, they have reported a patient–partner satisfaction rate of almost 90% as a result of the surgery (Benson & Boileau, 1987). The two major categories of penile prostheses are semirigid and inflatable. Complications of surgery include mechanical failure, infection, pain, and perforation, but the rate of complications is now lower because of technological advances (Benson & Boileau, 1987). No reports exist on the use of prosthetic surgery and prostheses in men after brain injury, though. Theoretically, either injection or prosthetic surgery may be appropriate with impotence resulting from neurologic causes.

Nonpharmacologic Treatment for Women

Because women's sexuality has been inadequately addressed in both animal and human research, little can be offered beyond commonsense approaches. If lubrication is a problem, then the woman with brain injury can use lubricants. Other components of the sexual response continuum, including engorgement, elevation, and elongation of the vagina and clitoral erection, are not influenced by lubrication alone. Oral–genital stimulation and the use of vibrators may be helpful, but no clinical research has been done in substantiating their effectiveness in women with a neurogenically induced sexual arousal disorder. Dyspareunia and vaginismus may be consequences in women with sexual dysfunction after brain injury, but these disorders also have not been studied in this population.

Education, Counseling, and Therapy for Patients and Their Families

For many individuals and couples, key issues are education and counseling. Often a lack of education results in problems in establishing healthy intimate, sexual relationships. Communication with a physician or counselor, with permission to discuss issues of intimacy and sexuality, will decrease anxiety and promote greater likelihood that couples will be able to begin to communicate with each other. Recent books (Griffith & Lemberg, 1993; Haseltine et al., 1993; Kroll & Klein, 1992) written for the lay community will be useful to some patients and their partners. Other publications (Blackerby, 1990; Garden et al., 1990; McCormick, Riffer, & Thompson, 1986; Medlar, 1993; Neistadt & Freda, 1987) address education and counseling programs and services for people with brain injury. Both verbal and nonverbal communication is important in establishing the basis for intimate physical communication. Safer sex practices include a careful selection of partners, mutual screening as necessary, use of condoms, use of spermicides, avoidance of anal penetration (or use of condoms if this choice is made). Suggestions for positioning for stroke patients may also be useful for brain-injury survivors with hemiparesis (McCormick et al., 1986).

Furthermore, sexual therapy may help some brain-injured survivors or their partners. Therapeutic techniques focus on various strategies to improve sexual relationships in couples who may have sexual desire or arousal disorders. These techniques require the intervention of therapists with specific education and training in sex therapy as well as in the effects of traumatic brain injury on physical, cognitive, communicative, visual–perceptual, and psychosocial function.

Staff Education

Education of staff is important to encourage consistent responses to individuals who display inappropriate social behaviors. Practitioners will need to redirect the inappropriate behaviors and educate patients about more appropriate behaviors. Furthermore, they may find it helpful to address issues of self-esteem directly. Wesolowski and Burke (1988) have outlined treatment approaches using behavioral modification techniques, including self-monitoring, feedback with reinforcement, and dating skills training. Similarly, Zencius, Wesolowski, Burke, and Hough (1990) have presented three cases in which a variety of techniques were used, including scheduled feedback; self-monitoring; private self-stimulation; dating skills training; and the use of a scheduled period when the target behavior (inappropriate touching) was permitted under supervision. These techniques were effective in eliminating (in two cases) or reducing (in one case) the inappropriate behaviors.

Sexually aggressive behaviors, including violent ones, after brain injury are rare. Brain-injured people are more often at risk as victims of sexual abuse or violence by others (Cole, 1986). Case reports of aggressive sexual behaviors after brain injury, though, can usually be traced to disinhibition. Medroxyprogesterone or other antiandrogens such as cyproterone (a progesterone derivative), which produce decreases in serum testosterone levels, have been used to treat sexual offenders (Berlin & Meinecke, 1981; Boller & Frank, 1982; Emory, Cole, & Meyer, 1995; Freund, 1980). These interventions have not been thoroughly studied in brain-injured patients, however.

FERTILITY AND REPRODUCTIVE ISSUES

Women's Issues

Female reproductive dysfunction after brain injury has been largely unstudied. Amenorrhea is a frequently observed phenomenon after injury. Hypopituitarism following head trauma results in amenorrhea, among other clinical signs (Weiss, 1977), but many cases of amenorrhea after brain injury are not associated with hypopituitarism. Infertility evaluations should include hormonal assays including LH, FSH, prolactin, thyroid function studies, and total testosterone. Low concentrations of LH, FSH, and testosterone suggest hypopituitary or hypothalamic injury, and a releasing hormone stimulation test is required for diagnosis. Hypothalamic ovulatory dysfunction can be treated with clomiphene citrate, menotropins (human menopausal gonadotropins or LH and FSH), or gonadotropin-releasing hormone (Shane, 1993).

Infertility in Males

In males, hypothalamic–pituitary failure can be treated with menotropins, human chorionic gonadotropin, or gonadotropin-releasing hormone. Testosterone promotes virilization and may enhance sexual function, but has no effect on spermatogenesis (Shane, 1993).

Drugs with Teratogenic Potential

Women who have sustained traumatic brain injuries are at risk for seizures and may require ongoing treatment for seizure disorders. Hence, if they are considering pregnancy, they should be made aware of the teratogenic potential of some drugs. The absolute risk of major malformations in newborns exposed to antiepileptic drugs in utero is 7% to 10%, which is 3% to 5% higher than for the general population (Lindhout & Omtzigt, 1992). Barbiturates and phenytoin are associated with congenital heart malformations as well as craniofacial anomalies, which are characteristic of fetal hydantoin syndrome. This syndrome, further characterized by prenatal and postnatal growth deficiencies, mental retardation, and limb defects, and less often microcephaly, ocular defects, hypospadias, and hernias, can be caused by other epileptic agents (Buehler, Delimont, van Waes, & Finnell, 1990). In addition, valproate and carbamazepine are associated with spina bifida aperta and hypospadias (Buehler et al., 1990; Rosa, 1991). High daily dosage, high serum concentration, low folate levels, and polytherapy are additional risk factors (Lindhout & Omtzigt, 1992). Furthermore, infants of epileptic mothers may develop hemorrhagic disorders, apparently as the result of a deficiency in vitamin K–dependent factors (Werler, Shapiro, & Mitchell, 1993).

A reported 40% of epileptic women are at increased risk of seizures during pregnancy, labor, and delivery, although 50% likely will have no change, and 10% likely will have a decrease in seizures (Dalessio, 1985). In one study (Schmidt et al., 1983), 68% of pregnancies in which seizure frequency increased were associated with noncompliance with the treatment recommendations. During pregnancy, levels decline over time. This decline can result from emesis, decreased absorption, increased plasma volume, increased liver metabolism, and increased renal clearance. However, hormone changes may lead to increased seizures, and protein binding may be altered. Therefore, monitoring is necessary.

Women with seizure disorders may plan to nurse their infant. Practitioners should consider that transmission rates of anticonvulsants in breast milk vary:

valproate, 5% to 10%; phenytoin, 30%; phenobarbital, 40%; carbamazepine, 45%; primadone, 60%; and ethosuximide, 90% (Briggs, Freeman, & Yaffe, 1994).

The International League Against Epilepsy (Commission on Genetics, 1993) has published guidelines for the care of women with epilepsy who may become pregnant. Recommendations include counseling concerning the risk of seizures, bleeding, and toxemia to the pregnant women; counseling concerning malformations, prematurity, seizures, and developmental disorders in the fetus and infant; ultrasound evaluation for neural tube defects, heart malformations, and craniofacial anomalies; amniotic fluid analysis of alpha-fetoprotein (for neural tube defects) and discussion of options for termination of pregnancy; careful choice of anticonvulsants and the monitoring of anticonvulsant levels, both during pregnancy (when decreases occur) and after delivery (when increases occur); a diet with adequate amounts of folate; and adequate sleep. Most studies have recommended 4 mg of folate to prevent neural tube defects (Czeizel & Dudas, 1992; Werler et al., 1993; Yerby, 1987).

Despite the risks, 90% of women with seizure disorders will deliver normal babies. Because the teratogenicity of anticonvulsant medications is associated with elevated levels of oxidative metabolites, an enzymatic marker may be useful in determining risk. Low enzymatic activity was found in 4 of 19 fetuses, and high risk for fetal hydantoin syndrome was predicted, which was confirmed postnatally (Buehler et al., 1990).

Contraception

Options for contraception are generally not limited by medical considerations in brain-injured women. However, oral hormonal contraception can increase the risk of venous thrombosis. Poor patient compliance because of memory difficulties or impulsivity may challenge effectiveness of oral contraception. More preferable, if the patient desires, might be the long-acting injectable techniques or more permanent solutions such as vasectomy or tubal ligation. Consider that subdermal delivery of the synthetic progestin levonorgestrel has a failure rate of 4 to 5 per 1,000 users per year, compared with 20 to 50 per 1,000 users per year for oral contraceptives; for people taking phenytoin or carbamazepine, pregnancy rates are higher (Patel & Bontke, 1990; "Subdermal Progestin Implant," 1991). Two excellent sources of information concerning reproduction for people with traumatic brain injury are Haseltine et al. (1993) and Rogers and Matsumura (1991).

CONCLUSION

A comprehensive approach to assessment and treatment of sexual function after traumatic brain injury is required, with consideration given to physical, physiologic, endocrinologic, cognitive, communicative, visual–perceptual, and psychosocial factors that influence the capacity for establishing and maintaining intimate, sexual relationships. Future research likely will focus on investigations of the relationship between depression and sexual dysfunction and on the use of pharmacologic strategies to enhance sexual function in the population of people with traumatic brain injury.

The identification of subpopulations at risk for sexual dysfunction will be helpful in prevention and treatment of sexual dysfunction. Clinicians are urged to use existing psychological and psychosexual inventories in routine clinical practice to address sexual function and to refer patients for appropriate evaluation and treatment. Identification of comorbidities and medication side effects is crucial. Furthermore, treatment of depression with pharmacologic agents must be undertaken with an understanding of the potentially deleterious as well as beneficial effects of these agents on sexual function. Rehabilitation clinicians must also address reproductive issues, including contraception and infertility, at appropriate intervals following acute care.

REFERENCES

Abboud, C.F. (1986). Laboratory diagnosis of hypopituitarism. *Mayo Clinic Proceedings, 61,* 35–48.

Allgeier, W.E., & Allgeier, A.R. (1991). *Sexual interactions* (3rd ed.). Lexington, MA: Heath.

Benkert, O., Crombach, G., & Kockott, G. (1972). Effect of L-dopa on sexually impotent patients. *Psychopharmacology, 23,* 91–95.

Benson, G.S., & Boileau, M.A. (1987). The penis: Sexual function and dysfunction. In J. Y. Gillenwater, J.T. Grayhack, S.S. Howards, & J.W. Duckett (Eds.), *Adult and pediatric urology* (pp. 1407–1447). Chicago: Yearbook Publishers.

Berendsen, H.H.G., & Gower, A.J. (1986). Opiate-androgen interactions in drug-induced yawning and penile erections in the rat. *Neuroendocrinology, 42,* 185–190.

Berlin, F.S., & Meinecke, C.F. (1981). Treatment of sexual offenders with antiandrogenic medication: Conceptualization, review of treatment, and preliminary findings. *American Journal of Psychiatry, 138,* 601–607.

Blackerby, W.F. (1990). A treatment model for sexuality disturbance following brain injury. *Journal of Head Trauma Rehabilitation, 5,* 73–82.

Blendonohy, P., & Philip, P. (1991). Precocious puberty in children after traumatic brain injury. *Brain Injury, 5,* 63–68.

Boldrini, P., Basaglia, N., & Calanca, M.C. (1991). Sexual changes in hemiparetic patients. *Archives of Physical Medicine and Rehabilitation, 72,* 202–207.

Boller, F., & Frank, E. (1982). *Sexual dysfunction in neurologic disorders: Diagnosis, management and rehabilitation.* New York: Raven Press.

Bond, M.R. (1976). Assessment of the psychosocial outcome of severe head injury. *Acta Neurochirurgica, 34,* 57–70.

Briggs, G.G., Freeman, R.K., & Yaffe, S.J. (1994). *Drugs in pregnancy and lactation: A reference guide to fetal and neonatal risk* (4th ed.). Baltimore: Williams & Wilkins.

Buehler, B.A., Delimont, D., van Waes, M., & Finnell, R.H. (1990). Prenatal prediction of risk of the fetal hydantoin syndrome. *New England Journal of Medicine, 322,* 1567–1572.

Buvat, J., Lemaire, A., & Buvat-Herbaut, M. (1987). Human chorionic gonadotropin treatment of nonorganic erectile failure and lack of sexual desire: A double-blind study. *Urology, 30,* 216–219.

Clark, J., Raggatt, P., & Edwards, O. (1988). Hypothalamic hypogonadism following major head injury. *Clinical Endocrinology, 29,* 153–165.

Cohen, H.D., & Rosen, R.C. (1976). Electroencephalographic laterality changes during human sexual orgasm. *Archives of Sexual Behavior, 5,* 189–199.

Cole, S. (1986). Facing the challenges of sexual abuse in persons with disabilities. *Journal of Sexuality and Disability, 7,* 71–89.

Cole, T.M. (1965). *Sexual history-taking: Adults with a prior history of sexual relations with another person.* Framingham, MA: National Head Injury Foundation.

Commission on Genetics, Pregnancy and the Child, International League Against Epilepsy. (1993). Guidelines for the care of women of childbearing age with epilepsy. *Epilepsia, 34,* 588–589.

Coslett, H.B., & Heilman, K.M. (1986). Male sexual function: Impairment after right hemisphere stroke. *Archives of Neurology, 43,* 1036–1039.

Crenshaw, T.L., Goldberg, J.P., & Stern, W.C. (1987). Pharmacologic modification of psychosexual dysfunction. *Journal of Sex and Marital Therapy, 13,* 239–252.

Czeizel, A.E., & Dudas, I. (1992). Prevention of the first occurrence of neural tube defects of periconceptual vitamin supplementation. *New England Journal of Medicine, 327,* 1832–1835.

Dalessio, D.J. (1985). Seizure disorders and pregnancy. *New England Journal of Medicine, 312,* 559–563.

Danjou, P., Alexandre, L., Warot, D., Lacomblez, L., & Puech, A.J. (1988). Assessment of erectogenic properties of apomorphine and yohimbine in man. *British Journal of Clinical Pharmacology, 26,* 733–739.

Davis, D.L., & Schneider, L.K. (1990). Ramifications of traumatic brain injury for sexuality. *Journal of Head Trauma Rehabilitation, 5,* 31–37.

Derogatis, L.R. (1987). *Derogatis Interview for Sexual Function.* Baltimore: Clinical Psychometric Research.

Doane, B.K. (1986). Clinical psychiatry and the physiodynamics of the limbic system. In B.K. Doane & K.E. Livingston (Eds.), *The limbic system: Functional organization and clinical disorders* (pp. 302–304). New York: Raven Press.

Donatucci, C.F., & Lue, T.F. (1992). The combined intracavernous injection and stimulation test. *Journal of Urology, 148,* 61–62.

Drugs that cause sexual dysfunction. (1983). *The Medical Letter,* pp. 73–76.

Ducharme, S., & Gill, K.M. (1990). Sexual values, training, and professional roles. *Journal of Head Trauma Rehabilitation, 5,* 38–45.

Edwards, O.M., & Clark, J. (1986). Post-traumatic hypogonadism: Six cases and a review of the literature. *Medicine, 65,* 281–290.

Emory, L.E., Cole, C.M., & Meyer, W.J. (1995). Use of depo-provera to control sexual aggression in persons with traumatic brain injury. *Journal of Head Trauma Rehabilitation, 10,* 47–58.

Fabbri, A., Jannini, E.A., Gnessi, L., Moretti, C. Ulisse, S., Franzese, A., Lazzari, R., Fraioli, F., Frajese, G., & Isidori, A. (1989). Endorphins in male impotence. Evidence for naltrexone stimulation of erectile activity in patient therapy. *Psychoneuroendocrinology, 14,* 103–111.

Freund, K. (1980). Therapeutic sex drive reduction. *Acta Psychiatrica Scandinavica, 62*(Suppl. 287), 5–37.

Garden, F.H., Bontke, C.F., & Hoffman, M. (1990). Sexual functioning and marital adjustment after traumatic brain injury. *Journal of Head Trauma Rehabilitation, 5,* 52–59.

Gartrell, N. (1986). Increased libido in women receiving trazodone. *American Journal of Psychiatry, 143,* 781–782.

Goddess, E.D., Wagner, N.N., & Silverman, D.R. (1979). Post-stroke sexual activity of CVA patients. *Medical Aspects of Human Sexuality, 13,* 16–30.

Goldberg, R.L., & Wise, T.N. (1990). The importance of the sense of smell in human sexuality. *Journal of Sex Education and Therapy, 16,* 236–241.

Goldstein, J.A. (1986). Erectile failure and naltrexone. *Annals of Internal Medicine, 105,* 799.

Griffith, E.R., & Lemberg, S. (1993). *Sexuality and the person with traumatic brain injury: A guide for families.* Philadelphia: F.A. Davis.

Haseltine, F., Cole, S., & Gray, D.B. (Eds.). (1993). *Reproductive issues for persons with physical disabilities.* Baltimore: Brookes.

Heath, R.G. (1964). Pleasure response of human subjects to direct stimulation of the brain: Physiologic and psycho-dynamic considerations. In R.G. Heath (Ed.), *The role of pleasure in behavior.* New York: Harper & Row.

Herzog, A., Russell, V., Vaitokaitis, J.L., & Geschwind, N. (1982). Neuroendocrine dysfunction in temporal lobe epilepsy. *Archives of Neurology, 39,* 133–135.

Herzog, A., Seibel, M., Schomer, D., Vaitokaitis, J.L., & Geschwind, N. (1986). Reproductive endocrine disorders in women with partial seizures of temporal lobe origin. *Archives of Neurology, 43,* 341–346.

Horn, L.J., & Zasler, N.D. (1990). Neuroanatomy and neurophysiology of sexual function. *Journal of Head Trauma Rehabilitation, 5,* 1–13.

Ishii, N., Watanabe, H., Irisawa, Y., Kawamura, S., Suzuk, K., Chiba, R., Tokiwa, M., & Shirai, M. (1989). Intracavernous injection of prostaglandin E_1 for the treatment of erectile impotence. *Journal of Urology, 141,* 323–325.

Jennett, B., & Teasdale, G. (1981). *Management of head injuries.* Philadelphia: F.A. Davis.

Kalliomaki, J.L., Markkanen, T.K., & Mustonen, V.A. (1961). Sexual behavior after cerebral vascular accident: Study on patients below age 60 years. *Fertility and Sterility, 12,* 156–158.

Kinsella, G.H., & Duffy, F.D. (1980). Attitudes toward disability by spouses of stroke patients. *Scandinavian Journal of Rehabilitation Medicine, 12,* 73–76.

Klachko, D.M., Winer, N., & Burns, T.W. (1968). Traumatic hypopituitarism occurring before puberty: Survival 35 years untreated. *Journal of Clinical Endocrinology and Metabolism, 28,* 1768–1772.

Klüver, H., & Bucy, P.C. (1939). Preliminary analysis of functions of temporal lobes in monkeys. *Archives of Neurology and Psychiatry, 42,* 979–1000.

Kosteljanetz, M., Jensen, T., Norgard, B., Lunde, I., Jensen, P.B., & Johnsen, S.G. (1981). Sexual and hypothalamic dysfunction in the postconcussional syndrome. *Acta Neurologica Scandinavica, 63,* 169–180.

Kreutzer, J.S., & Zasler, N.D. (1989). Psychosexual consequences of traumatic brain injury: Methodology and preliminary findings. *Brain Injury, 3,* 177–186.

Kroll, K., & Klein, E.L. (1992). *Enabling romance: A guide to love, sex, and relationships for the disabled.* New York: Harmony Books.

Lal, S. (1988). Apomorphine in the evaluation of dopaminergic function in man. *Progress in Neuro-Psychopharmacology and Biological Psychiatry, 12,* 117–164.

Lal, S., Ackman, D., Thavundayil, J.X., Kiely, M.E., & Etienne, P. (1984). Effect of apomorphine, a dopamine receptor agonist, on penile tumescence in normal subjects. *Progress in Neuro-Psychopharmacology and Biological Psychiatry, 8,* 695–699.

Lee, S.C., Zasler, N.D., & Kreutzer, J.S. (1994). Male pituitary dysfunction following severe traumatic brain injury. *Brain Injury, 8,* 571–577.

LeVay, S. (1993). *The sexual brain.* Boston: MIT Press.

Levine, S.B., Althof, S.E., Turner, L.A., Risen, C.B., Bodner, D.R., Kursh, E.D., & Resnick, M.I. (1989). Side effects of self-administration of intracavernous papaverine and phentolamine for the treatment of impotence. *Journal of Urology, 141,* 54–57.

Lezak, M.L. (1978). Living with the characterologically altered brain injured patient. *Journal of Clinical Psychiatry, 39,* 592–598.

Lilly, R. (1983). The human Klüver-Bucy syndrome. *Neurology, 33,* 1141–1145.

Lindhout, D., & Omtzigt, J.G. (1992). Pregnancy and teratogenicity. *Epilepsia, 33,* S41–S48.

Lusk, M.D., & Kott, J.A. (1982). Effects of head injury on libido. *Medical Aspects of Human Sexuality, 16,* 22–30.

MacLean, O. (1975). Brain mechanisms of primal sexual functions and related behavior. In M. Sandler & G. Gessa (Eds.), *Sexual behavior: Pharmacology and biochemistry* (pp. 1–11). New York: Raven Press.

Mapou, R.L. (1990). Traumatic brain injury rehabilitation with gay and lesbian individuals. *Journal of Head Trauma Rehabilitation, 5,* 67–72.

Mathews, A., Whitehead, A., & Kellet, J. (1983). Psychological and hormonal factors in the treatment of female sexual dysfunction. *Psychological Medicine, 13,* 83–92.

McCormick, G.P., Riffer, D.J., & Thompson, M.M. (1986). Coital positioning for stroke afflicted couples. *Rehabilitation Nursing, 11,* 17–19.

Medlar, T.M. (1993). Sexual counseling and traumatic brain injury. *Sexuality and Disability, 11,* 57–71.

Mesulum, M. (1985). *Principles of behavioral neurology.* Philadelphia: F.A. Davis.

Meyer, J.E. (1955). Die Sexuellen storungen der Hirnverletzten. *Archiv fur Psychiatrie und Zeitschrift Neurologic, 193,* 449–469.

Miller, B., Cummings, J., McIntyre, H., Ebers, G., & Grodes, M. (1986). Hypersexuality or altered sexual preference following brain injury. *Journal of Neurology, Neurosurgery, and Psychiatry, 49,* 867–873.

Monga, T.N., Monga, M., Raina, M.S., & Hardjasudarma, M. (1986). Hypersexuality in stroke. *Archives of Physical Medicine and Rehabilitation, 67,* 415–417.

Morales, A., Condra, M., Owen, J.A., Surridge, D.H., Fenemore, J., & Harris, C. (1987). Is yohimbine effective in the treatment of organic impotence? Results of a controlled trial. *Journal of Urology, 137,* 1168–1172.

National Head Injury Foundation. (1996). *Information packet on sexuality.* Framingham, MA: Author.

Neistadt, M.E., & Freda, M. (1987). *Choices: A guide to sex counseling with physically disabled adults.* Malabar, FL: Robert E. Kreiger.

O'Carroll, R.E. (1991). Sexual desire disorders: A review of controlled treatment studies. *Journal of Sex Research, 28,* 607–624.

O'Carroll, R.E., & Bancroft, J. (1984). Testosterone therapy for low sexual interest and erectile dysfunction in men: A controlled study. *British Journal of Psychiatry, 145,* 146–151.

O'Carroll, R.E., Woodrow, J., & Maroun, F. (1991). Psychosexual and psychosocial sequelae of closed head injury. *Brain Injury, 5,* 303–313.

Oddy, M., Humphrey, M., & Uttley, D. (1978). Subjective impairment and social recovery after closed head injury. *Journal of Neurology, Neurosurgery, and Psychiatry, 41,* 611–616.

Patel, M., & Bontke, C. (1990). Impact of traumatic brain injury on pregnancy. *Journal of Head Trauma Rehabilitation, 5,* 60–66.

Reid, K., Morales, A., & Harris, C. (1987). Double-blind trial of yohimbine in treatment of psychogenic impotence. *Lancet, 2,* 421–423.

Riley, A.J., Goodman, R.E., & Kellet, J.M. (1989). Double-blind trial of yohimbine hydrochloride in the treatment of erection inadequacy. *Sexual and Marital Therapy, 4,* 17–26.

Rogers, J.G., & Matsumura, M. (1991). *Mother-to-be: A guide to pregnancy and birth for women with disabilities.* New York: Demos.

Rosa, F.W. (1991). Spina bifida in infants of women treated with carbamazapine in pregnancy. *New England Journal of Medicine, 324,* 674–677.

Rosenbaum, M., & Najenson, T. (1976). Changes in life patterns and symptoms of low mood as reported by wives of severely brain-injured soldiers. *Journal of Consulting and Clinical Psychology, 44,* 881–888.

Rust, J., & Golombok, S. (1985). The Golombok-Rust Inventory of Sexual Satisfaction (GRISS). *British Journal of Clinical Psychology, 24,* 63–64.

Sabhesan, S., & Natarajan, M. (1989). Sexual behavior after head injury in Indian men and women. *Archives of Sexual Behaviors, 18,* 349–356.

Sandel, M.E., Williams, K.S., DellaPietra, L., & Derogatis, L.R. (1996). Sexual functioning following traumatic brain injury. *Brain Injury, 10,* 719–728.

Schmidt, D., Canger, R., Avanzini, G., Battino, D., Cusi, C., Beck-Mannagetta, G., Koch, S., Ratting, D., & Janz, D. (1983). Change of seizure frequency in pregnant epileptic women. *Journal of Neurology, Neurosurgery and Psychiatry, 46,* 751–755.

Shane, J.M. (1993). Evaluation and treatment of infertility. *Clinical Symposia, 45,* 2–32.

Shaul, P., Towbin, R., & Chernausek, S. (1985). Precocious puberty following severe head trauma. *American Journal of Diseases of Children, 139,* 467–469.

Sherwin, B., & Gelfand, M. (1987). The role of androgen in the maintenance of sexual function in oopherectomised women. *Psychosomatic Medicine, 149,* 397–409.

Sidi, A.A., & Chen, K.K. (1989). Clinical experience with vasoactive intercavernous pharmacotherapy for treatment of impotence. *World Journal of Urology, 5,* 156–159.

Silver, J.M., Hales, R.E., & Yudofsky, S.C. (1990). Psychopharmacology of depression in neurologic disorders. *Journal of Clinical Psychiatry, 51*(1), 33–39.

Sjogren, K. (1983). Sexuality after stroke with hemiplegia. II. With special regard to partnership adjustment and fulfillment. *Scandinavian Journal of Rehabilitation Medicine, 15,* 63–69.

Sjogren, K., Damber, J.E., & Liliequist, B. (1983). Sexuality after stroke with hemiplegia. I. Aspects of sexual function. *Scandinavian Journal of Rehabilitation Medicine, 15,* 55–61.

Sondra, L.P., Mazo, R., & Chancellor, M.D. (1990). The role of yohimbine for the treatment of erectile impotence. *Journal of Sex and Marital Therapy, 16,* 15–21.

Spark, R.F., & Wills, C.A. (1984). Hypogonadism, hyperprolactinaemia, and temporal lobe epilepsy in hyposexual men. *Lancet, 1*(8374), 413–417.

Stakl, W., Hasun, R., & Marberger, M. (1988). Intracavernous injection of prostaglandin E_1 in impotent men. *Journal of Urology, 141,* 66–68.

Stevensen, R.W.D., & Solyom, L. (1990). The aphrodisiac effect of fenfluramine: Two case reports of a possible side effect to the use of fenfluramine in the treatment of bulimia. *Journal of Clinical Psychopharmacology, 10,* 69–71.

Subdermal progestin implant for long-term contraception. (1991). *The Medical Letter, 33*(839), 17–20.

Sullivan, G. (1987). Increased libido with trazodone. *American Journal of Psychiatry, 144,* 967.

Susset, J.G., Tessier, C.D., Wincze, J., Bansal, S., Malhotra, C., & Schwacha, M.G. (1989). Effect of yohimbine hydrochloride on erectile impotence: A double-blind study. *Journal of Urology, 141,* 1360–1363.

Thomsen, I.V. (1984). Late outcome of severe blunt head trauma: A 10–15 year second follow-up. *Journal of Neurology, Neurosurgery and Psychiatry, 47,* 260–268.

Walker, A.E., & Jablon, S. (1961). *A follow-up study of head wounds in World War II.* (Veteran's Affairs Medical Monograph). Washington, DC: Department of Veterans Affairs.

Weinstein, E.A. (1974). Sexual disturbances after brain injury. *Medical Aspects of Human Sexuality, 8,* 10–16.

Weinstein, E.A. (1981). Effects of brain damage on sexual behavior. *Medical Aspects of Human Sexuality, 15,* 162–164.

Weinstein, E.A., & Kahn, R.L. (1961). Patterns of sexual behavior following brain injury. *Psychiatry, 24,* 69–78.

Weiss, S. (1977). Hypopituitarism following head trauma. *American Journal of Obstetrics and Gynecology, 127,* 678–679.

Werler, M.M., Shapiro, S., & Mitchell, A.A. (1993). Periconceptual folic acid exposure and risk of neural tube defects. *Journal of the American Medical Association, 269,* 1292–1293.

Wesolowski, M.D., & Burke, W.H. (1988). Behaviour management techniques. In P.M. Deutsch & K. Fralish (Eds.), *Innovations in head injury rehabilitation.* New York: Matthew Bender.

Yerby, M.S. (1987). Problems and management of the pregnant woman with epilepsy. *Epilepsia, 28,* S29–S36.

Zajecka, J., Fawcett, J., Schaff, M., Jeffries, H., & Guy, C. (1991). The role of serotonin in sexual dysfunction: Fluoxetine-associated orgasm dysfunction. *Journal of Clinical Psychiatry, 52,* 66–68.

Zasler, N.D., & Horn, L.J. (1990). Rehabilitative management of sexual dysfunction. *Journal of Head Trauma Rehabilitation, 5,* 14–24.

Zencius, A., Wesolowski, M.D., Burke, W.A., & Hough, S. (1990). Managing hypersexual disorders in brain injured clients. *Brain Injury, 4,* 175–181.

CHAPTER 13

Neuromuscular Diseases

John R. Bach and Joan L. Bardach

Neuromuscular disorders include those diseases in which the nerve or innervated muscle is affected, causing varying degrees of movement dysfunction. Most neuromuscular diseases are inherited disorders. Some, like polymyositis, are acquired. Some can be inherited or apparently acquired. For example, for about 10% of patients with amyotrophic lateral sclerosis (ALS), the condition is inherited with autosomal dominant inheritance. Most patients, however, develop ALS sporadically as adults.

Taken as a whole, neuromuscular diseases are common: the incidence is greater than 1 per 1,000 in the population (Bach, 1996). ALS alone affects 1 per 1,800 in the population; Duchenne-type muscular dystrophy (DMD), 1 per 3,000 males; spinal muscular atrophy (SMA), 1 per 5,000; myotonic dystrophy, 13 per 100,000; myasthenia gravis, 1 per 10,000; and Becker's muscular dystrophy, 1 per 25,000.

DISORDERS DEFINED

Because of the pathology of these disorders, their effects on sexual function and sexuality are primarily the result of nongenital causes. This chapter first describes the multiple disorders under the category neuromuscular diseases whose effects on sexual functioning are generally similar. Then the chapter discusses issues related to sexuality. Because of the large number of disorders, the discussion is limited to the most common disorders (Exhibit 13–1).

Typically, children with DMD have an onset of muscle weakness before age 4 years. They have a relentless, progressive, fairly symmetrical, and predictable pattern of extremity contractures, muscle weakness, and wasting. Ambulation may never be quite normal. The ability to run, which is normally achieved by age 24 months, is always impaired and may never develop. Of DMD children, 15% can occasionally walk until age 15 years (Brooke et al., 1983; Hoffman et al., 1988). In addition, 90% of DMD children develop scoliosis by age 17 years (McDonald

Exhibit 13–1 Common Progressive Neuromuscular Conditions

1. Myopathies
   - Muscular dystrophies
     - Dystrophinopathies: Duchenne-type and Becker's muscular dystrophies
     - Other muscular dystrophies: limb-girdle, Emery-Dreifuss, fascioscapulo-humeral, congenital, childhood autosomal recessive, and myotonic dystrophy
   - Non-Duchenne myopathies
     - Congenital and metabolic myopathies such as acid maltase deficiency
     - Inflammatory myopathies such as polymyositis
     - Diseases of the myoneural junction such as myasthenia gravis
2. Neurologic disorders
   - Spinal muscular atrophies
   - Motor neuron diseases
   - Poliomyelitis
   - Neuropathies
     - Hereditary motor neuropathies including familial hypertrophic interstitial polyneuropathy
     - Guillain-Barré syndrome
   - Disorders of supraspinal tone such as Friedreich's ataxia

et al., 1995), which continues to progress throughout life (Lord et al., 1990; Miller, Moseley, & Koreska, 1984). Furthermore, the lifespan of DMD patients is short-ened and most patients die of pulmonary failure before age 25 years (Bach & Lieberman, 1993).

The onset of Becker's muscular dystrophy is from age 5 years to age 25 years. The genetics, evaluation, and management principles are basically the same as for DMD but the disease course is much milder. Ambulation is lost more than 20 years after onset. Significant contractures, scoliosis, and ventilatory failure are uncommon and, except for those people with fatal cardiomyopathy, lifespan is usually normal.

Myotonic dystrophy usually presents between ages 20 years and 50 years with some combination of myotonia, hand weakness, gait difficulties, poor vision, pto-sis, weight loss, erectile dysfunction, and hypertrichosis (excessive hair growth). Systemic manifestations may include cataracts, gonadal atrophy and other endo-crine anomalies, cardiomyopathy, chronic alveolar hypoventilation, bony changes, abnormalities of serum immunoglobulins, and frontal baldness (in the male). Dys-arthria can result from facial muscle weakness and myotonia. Mental deficits are especially pronounced for congenital myotonic dystrophy patients. Ankle and occasionally other musculotendinous contractures also develop along with more severe weakness and wasting of the limbs.

Polymyositis, an inflammatory myopathy, occurs most commonly in females in their fifties or sixties. Furthermore, the incidence is about four times as great among black women (Kagen, 1988). Progression of the disease may be rapid with symmetric, predominantly proximal muscular weakness unless early treatment is initiated. Neck muscle weakness is also common. Muscular atrophy is not severe and deep tendon reflexes are relatively spared. Creatinine kinase, an enzyme detected in the bloodstream, is elevated during disease progression but may otherwise be normal. There may be skin changes or other manifestations of collagen disease. Spontaneous remissions occur. When diagnosed in a timely manner, corticosteroid therapy and occasionally immunosuppressives can halt and often reverse muscle weakness.

Motor neurons are severely involved in the SMAs, poliomyelitis, and ALS. The SMAs are usually inherited as autosomal recessive disorders, with rare cases having autosomal dominant inheritance (Brooke, 1986). They range in severity from severe generalized paralysis requiring ventilatory support at birth to relatively mild, slowly progressive conditions presenting in a person's twenties or thirties. These disorders have been further classified into infantile SMA type 1, with onset between birth and age 6 months and in which the developmental milestones of rolling, sitting, and walking are not achieved; chronic infantile SMA type 2, with onset up to age 2 years (both SMA types are also known as Werdnig-Hoffmann disease); and chronic proximal SMA type 3 (also known as Kugelberg-Welander disease), with onset from age 2 years to 17 years and occasionally later (Paern & Wilson, 1973). Weakness usually begins in the distal musculature, tends to be asymmetrical, and may progress rapidly (Namba, Aberfeld, & Grob, 1970). Of chronic infantile SMA patients, 80% with an onset of symptoms between age 6 months and 24 months achieve early developmental milestones then lose the ability to ambulate before adulthood (Barois, Estournet, Duval-Beaupere, Bataille, & Leclair-Richard, 1989). Musculotendinous contractures and especially scoliosis are invariably present in type 1 and type 2 patients and are of primary consideration in management. Acute ventilatory failure can occur at birth for severe type 1 patients or, more likely, between age 4 years and 30 years for others. The type 3 variety can range in severity from being comparable with DMD to having onset and moderate progression beginning in a person's twenties or thirties. Although patients with SMA type 1 rarely survive to adulthood, patients with type 2 and type 3 often do.

More than 500,000 people were estimated to be afflicted with poliomyelitis in the United States from 1928 to 1962 (U.S. Department of Commerce, 1975). With senescence and progressive loss of function of remaining anterior horn cells, postpolio survivors are experiencing late-onset sequelae often known as the postpolio syndrome. The postpolio syndrome refers to late-onset muscle weakness in combination with musculoskeletal symptoms, fatigue, and increased functional difficulties (Halstead, 1991). Dysphagia may become a problem; furthermore, an increasing number of postpoliomyelitis patients require ventilatory assistance (Bach & Alba, 1991).

ALS is a disease of unknown etiology of both upper and lower motor neurons. Of cases, 5% to 10% are genetically transmitted by way of an autosomal dominant pattern. ALS most often presents in middle age but can begin before age 30 years. The patient's first complaints are usually of muscle cramps and weakness; however, fatigue, dyspnea, slurred speech, dysphagia, and even vocal cord paralysis can be among the presenting symptomatology. In ALS, the neurologic highlight is that flaccid paralysis and atrophy can coexist with cramps, fasciculations, and spasticity. The length and severity of the disease is highly variable. An estimated 15% to 20% of all ALS patients have a relatively benign course, with a greater than 5-year survival rate (Mulder & Howard, 1976); however, the duration of ALS can be as short as less than 1 year. Some individuals may live up to 10 years (Gilgoff, Baydur, Bach, Prentice, & Hsu, 1992), with, and occasionally without, ventilator use; however, the average survival rate without ventilatory support is 3 to 4 years.

The most common hereditary peripheral neuropathy is Charcot-Marie-Tooth disease, an autosomal dominant disorder with variable penetrance. Symmetric distal greater than proximal weakness and sensory involvement is the hallmark of the disease. Consequently, ankle deformities are usually the only significant contractures that occur with this condition. Weakness is slowly progressive and most patients remain functional throughout most of their adult life. Occasionally generalized weakness can become severe and lead to total disability.

Acute postinfectious polyneuropathy or the Guillain-Barré syndrome is an acquired inflammatory segmental demyelinating disease. Of cases, 67% give a history of preceding viral infection, immunizations, surgery, or diseases affecting the immunologic system (Lisak, 1988). Sensory loss is usually slight and is absent in one-third of patients (Lisak, 1988). Ascending weakness and parasthesias begin in the hands and feet. The condition usually progresses for 1 to 2 weeks and, at its worst point, severe quadriparesis and respiratory failure requiring ventilatory support occurs in 20% to 30% of cases. Electromyography and nerve conduction studies will reveal severe nerve conduction slowing and can be used to prognosticate neurologic recovery. Recovery is variable, but usually takes 3 to 6 months. Residual weakness may range from mild ankle dorsiflexion weakness to, on rare occasions, essentially complete paralysis necessitating permanent ventilatory support.

Myasthenia gravis is characterized by muscle weakness in voluntary muscles following repetitive activation or prolonged tension, with recovery after a period of inactivity. The modal age of onset is about 20 years (Simpson, 1988). The onset is usually sudden but may be insidious. Diagnosis is made on the basis of history and physical examination, which often includes severe bulbar and respiratory muscle weakness in addition to electromyographic findings, evidence of decremental evoked action potential amplitudes during repetitive supramaximal stimulation, response to administration of anticholinesterases, and the presence of antireceptor site antibodies in the bloodstream. Patients respond well to currently available treatments including corticosteroid therapy, anticholinesterase administration, and plasmaphereses.

Overall, neuromuscular diseases encompass a broad spectrum of clinical disorders. However, individuals with neuromuscular diseases usually have progressive muscular weakness, atrophy, and musculotendinous contractures that can result in severe physical disability. Pediatric conditions can also result in severe scoliosis and can have a profound effect on the social awareness, development, and maturation of the affected individual. Even when not considered to be progressive, patients with neuromuscular diseases like SMA weaken with age as they experience senescent loss of remaining functioning neural and muscular tissues. In many cases, this loss leads to total dependence for activities of daily living and ventilator dependence.

IMPACT ON SEXUAL FUNCTION

Unfortunately, little information has been presented in the medical literature regarding the sexual function of people with neuromuscular diseases. Gonadal atrophy has been noted in males with myotonic dystrophy (Church, 1967), and some males with Duchenne-type muscular dystrophy have been noted to have small testicles, underdeveloped genitalia, and gynecomastia (Lundberg, 1966); however, the impact of these disorders on sexual response has not been studied. Thus, based on pathophysiology, most patients are assumed to have potential to be sexually aroused, have erections or vaginal lubrication, and experience orgasms.

The psychological aspects of these disabilities, the associated physical disabilities, and the limitations imposed on their social function, however, must affect the sexuality of individuals with neuromuscular diseases. Individuals with neuromuscular diseases have psychosocial and psychosexual needs similar to able-bodied people. Although solutions to sexual difficulties depend on the particular physical needs and psychological attitudes of individual patients and their partners, general sexuality education provided through established guidelines is useful for all patients and their significant others.

To assess the specific sexual difficulties and needs of patients with neuromuscular disorders, Anderson and Bardach (1983) interviewed 40 patients with neuromuscular diseases; patient ages ranged from 19 to 74 years. The researchers addressed the individuals' sexual function, including activities in which they participated, positions for intercourse, living situation, vocational status, social activities, and activities of daily living capabilities. In addition, a physical therapist evaluated each individual to delineate physical limitations for sexual activities and to devise alternatives. Sexual function was evaluated by assessing sexual knowledge, early sexual experiences, and current sexual practices and problems. Of the males interviewed, 93% reported they currently masturbated, compared with 38% of the females. Although subjects were queried about their participation in numerous other sexual activities, no information was obtained about the subjects' current practices. Subjects were grouped based on the age of onset of their neuromuscular disorder and its rate of progression, which were found to be critical determinants of patients' sexual practices and problems.

Childhood Onset

The young individual who experiences a progressive loss of muscle power since birth or early childhood reaches adolescence with severe obstacles to fulfilling sexual interests and needs. Early onset together with rapid progression results in more severe physical limitations, loss of privacy, and constricted psychosocial and psychosexual development. Some children never attain physical independence. These factors, and the resulting negative body image, further hamper sexual expression. Parents' and society's attitudes toward their sexuality are often repressive and overprotective and can contribute to inhibition and feelings of inadequacy. These young individuals miss out on the usual opportunities to learn about "sex" from friends. Even the reading of erotic literature and masturbation are often prevented, perhaps as much from a lack of privacy as from physical disability. Social isolation resulting from limited opportunities for socialization can be a barrier to the establishment of peer relationships. Furthermore, social isolation can contribute to withdrawal, decreased sense of personal autonomy, low self-esteem, and immaturity, all of which can limit the probability of finding a sexual partner and developing satisfying sexual relationships. Both parents and attendants should be aware of the effect of these limitations on what are essentially normal desires.

Parents often need help in acknowledging the sexuality of their disabled child. Many cannot imagine how their child could have a life independent of them for physical care. As with parents of nondisabled children, there might be excessive concern about the child being "hurt" or "exploited." Parental concerns are unique to particular situations as well as to ethnic, socioeconomic, and religious backgrounds. Overprotective parents and society at large can project to disabled individuals that they cannot get married or that it would be a bad idea to marry. It is important that parents are provided with a realistic view of the capabilities of their child with a neuromuscular disease.

Often, patients may view health care professionals as parental figures. Inadvertently, a health care professional may then lapse into the role of an overprotective, critical, judgmental, or omniscient parent. Like parents, the health care professional who works with patients with neuromuscular disorders must be educated and may also need to examine his or her own attitudes concerning the sexuality of disabled patients.

Adult Onset

Adult patients with neuromuscular disorders often need encouragement to discuss sexual function. They need to feel that it is as important as any other topic discussed during an evaluation. Individuals with adult-onset neuromuscular disorders experience a disruption in lifestyle that results in emotional stress. These individuals may have once had vocational, social, and interpersonal sexual experiences more typical of the nondisabled population. As physical limitations increase, these individuals often need assistance in activities of daily living and they have restrictions on sexual activity. In addition, bodily changes are often accompanied by a loss of self-esteem and depression. Psychological and physical factors place stress on ongoing emotional and sexual relationships. The need to modify sexual activity can result in further stress.

This vicious cycle emphasizes the need for education about the impact of neuromuscular disease on sexual function. It is important to address sexual issues up front to potentially avoid future problems. Furthermore, patients must be given permission to ask questions about sexual difficulties. If a satisfactory sexual relationship is to be achieved, changes in attitudes may be necessary; for example, redefining the male role in terms of being the more physically active.

Ideally, a sexual history including any history of sexually transmitted diseases should be routinely included either as part of a medical or a nursing examination, or as part of a psychosocial evaluation by a social worker or psychologist for all patients with neuromuscular diseases. Too often clinicians omit this aspect of the medical history, not only because of their discomfort in discussing sexual issues but also because they fail to assume that the person with a neuromuscular disease may have had sexual contact. The physical or occupational therapist evaluation should include questions regarding the patient's ability to assume and maintain positions used during sexual activity and should include a range of motion assessment for the patient's ability to use contraceptive devices such as condoms or diaphragms. Health care professionals who are knowledgeable and comfortable with the topic of sexuality should assess the patient and provide the information.

Another hazard to maintaining healthy sexuality in individuals with neuromuscular diseases involves the choosing of a caregiver. The intensity of sexual feelings among couples can change drastically when one partner has to shift between the roles of caregiver and lover. Counseling may be useful to address this difficulty as well as for support for the person who is mourning the loss of physical abilities. Individual counseling can provide time for each sexual partner to express his or her likes, dislikes, and expectations; where pertinent, the health care provider can explain the effect of aging on erections, vaginal lubrication, and other sexual activities to eliminate worries and misunderstandings. Furthermore, the provider can discuss the effects of physical deformities and cardiopulmonary function on sexual response and provide appropriate counseling about techniques and conditioning.

Adult disabled people, like able-bodied people, also may be concerned about pleasuring a partner. Individuals who wish to have sexual intercourse may be unable to move adequately or assume the necessary positions. Clinicians should provide specific suggestions on appropriate positions for weak males or females. Devices such as the rocking bed ventilator (J. H. Emerson Company, Cambridge, MA) can facilitate sexual intercourse for patients who are unable to move on their own and can also provide ventilatory support if needed. Also, nonintercourse sexual activities can be emphasized. Patients should strongly consider using water-soluble vaginal lubricants, devices like vibrators, and modified positioning, which can facilitate sexual activity. Patients with musculotendinous contractures that impede sexual activity may require physical therapy and possibly surgical interventions.

Health care professionals should give their patients clear and simple explanations using models, films, diagrams, and illustrations, as necessary (Anderson & Bardach, 1983). They also should make available group discussions in which disabled individuals can voice concerns about sexual function. By talking about sexual matters in a group, disabled individuals learn from each other and can become more assertive in voicing their concerns to health care professionals. Peer support from group participation can also be helpful for developing interpersonal communication skills fundamental to establishing satisfying relationships. The sharing of concerns with peers might also serve to relieve some anxiety about their own attitudes and bodies and how they function, once they realize that others have similar concerns.

Someone with a physical disability may have to work hard at building self-esteem to seek out socialization opportunities and to be more assertive in social interactions. It might be useful for disabled individuals to make contacts with community agencies and charitable organizations that sponsor recreational activities. In Romano's (1976) teachings, the disabled individual identifies difficult social situations—for example, being stared at in public—and develops hierarchies of responses to the situations ranging from being very passive to very assertive. With the guidance of a counselor, the individual can practice any particular response. Self-confidence increases as the individual learns more effective social skills to handle different situations.

Because of the physical limitations imposed by neuromuscular diseases, individuals eventually become restricted by the need for assistance in many or all activities of daily living, which leads to invasion of privacy, both psychologically and physically. The person may become dependent on parents or attendants for, for example, the purchase of reading materials as well as for all social interaction. Parental attitudes and attitudes of the disabled person and attendant alike are instrumental in helping or hindering the achievement of sexual satisfaction through autoerotic activities. The parent or care provider might feel awkward on discovering bedclothes or personal clothing stained or stiffened by ejaculate, perhaps from a wet dream, but should handle the situation in a neutral tone. In a group living situation or institution, staff, too, must recognize the need for privacy. A policy might be sought to set up "social rooms" or "privacy rooms."

For all patients, cost and limited availability of transportation, the presence of environmental obstacles, societal attitudes, and social isolation can be barriers to the establishment of peer relationships and the sense of personal autonomy. As a result, the probability of finding a sexual partner is decreased.

Another barrier to effective sexual function is that parents and care providers may misunderstand the potential and ultimate capabilities of severely disabled individuals to function both socially and vocationally. These topics were addressed in a recent survey (Bach & Barnett, 1996) that assessed the marital status, satisfaction with life, and related issues concerning sexual function of severely disabled ventilator users with neuromuscular diseases. The respondents to the survey were 621 ventilator users with neuromuscular diseases. All respondents lived in the community, all individuals were wheelchair users, and 585 were unable to walk and depended on attendant care for virtually all activities of daily living. Of the respondents, 313 were males with a mean age of 46.5 years and 306 were females with a mean age of 52.2 years. Two individuals whose gender was not indicated had an average age of 41 years. Of the respondents, 380 had had poliomyelitis; 60, DMD; 35, non-Duchenne myopathies; 27, spinal cord injury; 13, ALS; 5, myasthenia gravis; 5, severe kyphoscoliosis; 5, polymyositis; 2, Charcot-Marie-Tooth disease; 1, SMA; 1, polyneuropathy; and 87, other disorders. The 621 ventilator users had depended on ventilatory support for a mean of 21.1 years and, at the time of the survey, had used their ventilators a mean of 15.7 hours per day (Bach & Barnett, 1996).

Furthermore, of the respondents, 277 ventilator users—157 males and 120 females—had not married. Also, 186 individuals—97 males and 89 females—were married before requiring ventilatory support and remained married and lived with their spouses. These 186 respondents included 4 individuals who were widowed before requiring ventilatory support and later remarried while using support and also two males who were divorced before requiring support and remarried while on aid. These 186 individuals had been using ventilatory support for a mean of 22.7 years and required 13.7 hours of support per day. In addition, 20 other individuals were married before requiring ventilatory aid and were subsequently widowed. Furthermore, 36 individuals—10 males and 26 females—were married before requiring ventilatory support and had been divorced and remained divorced while using ventilatory aids. An additional 60 individuals—32 males and 28 females—married for the first time as severely disabled ventilator users and continued to live with their spouses. Of the respondents, 42 did not respond to this question. Of the 284 patients who were married before onset of ventilator dependence, 16.2% ($n = 46$) were divorced subsequently and had not remarried over a mean period of 22.7 years (individual ages were 28 to 51 years) of ventilator use. This group became ventilator users at the mean age of 28 years. The general nondisabled population has a divorce rate of 30% for people married at age 28 years (National Center for Health Statistics, 1989).

At first, it might seem surprising that so many patients with little or no use of their arms or legs and with little or no ability to breathe without use of respirators would have so many apparently successful marriages. Clearly important were independence in community living and attendant care and the ability to self-direct one's personal affairs, despite severe physical disability.

In another survey (Campbell, Converse, & Rodgers, 1976) to assess the quality of life of severely disabled patients with neuromuscular diseases who require ongoing ventilatory assistance, the only major life domain associated with quality of life with which the majority of severely disabled individuals were dissatisfied was with their sexual lives. Interestingly, in the survey of semantic differentials concerning how the patients perceived their lives, the major deficiencies were the feeling of "being tied down" and that life was "hard." Exploring sexuality, however, requires confidence that goals can be attained with considerable effort, curiosity, sexual energy, and opportunity, among other attributes. Many of these traits are suppressed or hampered both by the weakness associated with the patient's disease and by limitations imposed by society.

The ability to explore sexual relationships is virtually impossible in long-term care institutions or when the patient has little or no control over his or her attendent care services. Without appropriate personal care services, the severely disabled individual has little freedom to function socially, the most important prerequisite for successful sexual function. A good model of patient-managed home attendant care services (Concepts of Independence, Inc.) has been operating in New York City since 1979; it permits self-directed clients themselves to hire, train, direct, and dismiss their own personal care attendants, thus eliminating part of the problem (Schnur & Holland, 1987).

Fertility

Fertility is an often neglected aspect of managing individuals with neuromuscular diseases. Patients with childhood-onset diseases are often not expected to survive into adulthood or not to want to pass on their condition to following generations. However, practitioners must consider the advisability of individuals with autosomal dominant or sex-linked disorders to bear children in view of genetic rights. Most adult-onset conditions occur later in life and are rapidly progressive, thereby possibly making procreation difficult. Nevertheless, successful pregnancies are beginning to be reported more frequently in patients with neuromuscular diseases.

Myotonic dystrophy is the one neuromuscular condition that is common—essentially static—and in which survival into adulthood is common and fertility has been considered. In a study of 41 families with 235 myotonic dystrophy–affected patients (Passos-Bueno, Cerqueira, Vainzof, Marie, & Zatz, 1995), an excess of male offspring was observed. The frequency of patients who did not reproduce was similar for males and females; however, female patients had on average 25% fewer children than male patients. Indeed, males with myotonic dystrophy had more children than females with the condition during the period of observation. In another study, Dao, Mathieu, Bouchard, and DeBraekeleer (1992) studied 373 patients for number of children, age at marriage, ages at the time of birth of the first and last child, interval between the marriage and the birth of the first child, and interval between consecutive births. The mean number of children born to patients with gonadal atrophy and to control individuals in the community did not differ.

Fertility issues also have been addressed as they relate to SMA. Successful pregnancies in the presence of SMA types I and II have been reported internationally and in the United States. For example, five women with SMA type II successfully delivered eight children (Carter, Bonekat, & Milio, 1994). Problems during their pregnancies included recurrent urinary tract infections, progressive worsening of pulmonary function, dyspnea, wheelchair and seating problems, and musculoskeletal and low back pain. Seven of the eight pregnancies culminated in a Caesarean section. All patients had normal uterine contractility, and no disease progression was noted in any patient. Recommendations included pelvic assessment for shape and size to determine the delivery mode and possible contraindication of spinal or epidural anesthesia because of spinal deformity.

In 12 women with SMA type III, 18 births were documented, of which 4 were by Caesarean section (Carter et al., 1994). Of these women, 3 were first diagnosed with the disease during pregnancy. Other complications included increases in muscle weakness during pregnancy up to the level of wheelchair dependence in one woman. Seven women had marked increases in muscle strength postpartum; however, in 5 women, strength did not return until a few months postpartum.

Most babies were healthy, except for two—from different families—who were later diagnosed with the disease. Those two babies probably inherited the disease because of an infrequent dominant mode of transmission that can occur in any SMA (Rudnik-Schoneborn, Zerres, Ignatius, & Rietschel, 1992; Wilson & Williams, 1992).

Although it is not necessarily appropriate to extrapolate the information gleaned from a population of individuals with myotonic dystrophy and SMA to patients with other neuromuscular disorders, it appears that, when the opportunity becomes available, patients with neuromuscular diseases can succeed in having children. However, genetic counseling should be considered. Moreover, the physiologic constraints of the woman's disability must be appropriately managed during pregnancy.

CONCLUSION

A recent study found that of the major issues that concern quality of life and life satisfaction in severely disabled ventilator users, the only issue in which the majority of subjects reported dissatisfaction was their sex lives (Bach & Barnett, 1996). Health care professionals should seek ways to assist patients in finding greater fulfillment and life satisfaction. This begins by investigating a patient's sexuality and discussing options for permitting greater sexual expression both with the patient as well as with care providers and significant others. Such attention on the part of the care provider can play a fundamental role in the rehabilitation of severely disabled individuals with neuromuscular conditions.

REFERENCES

Anderson, F., & Bardach, J.L. (1983). Sexuality and neuromuscular disease: A pilot study. *International Journal of Rehabilitation Medicine, 5,* 21–26.

Bach, J.R. (1996). Neuromuscular and skeletal disorders leading to global alveolar hypoventilation. In J.R. Bach, Jr. (Ed.), *Pulmonary rehabilitation: The obstructive and paralytic conditions* (pp. 257–273). Philadelphia: Hanley & Belfus.

Bach, J.R., & Alba, A.S. (1991). Pulmonary dysfunction and sleep disordered breathing as post-polio sequelae: Evaluation and management. *Orthopedics, 14,* 1329–1337.

Bach, J.R., & Barnett, V. (1996). Psychosocial, vocational, quality of life and ethical issues. In J.R. Bach, Jr. (Ed.), *Pulmonary rehabilitation: The obstructive and paralytic conditions* (pp. 395–411). Philadelphia: Hanley & Belfus.

Bach, J.R., & Lieberman, J.S. (1993). Rehabilitation of the patient with disease affecting the motor unit. In J.A. DeLisa (Ed.), *Rehabilitation medicine: Principles and practice* (pp. 1099–1110). Philadelphia: J.B. Lippincott.

Barois, A., Estournet, B., Duval-Beaupere, G., Bataille, J., & Leclair-Richard, D. (1989). Amyotrophie spinale infantile. *Revue Neurologique (Paris), 145,* 299–304.

Brooke, M.H. (1986). *A clinician's view of neuromuscular diseases* (2nd ed.). Baltimore: Williams & Wilkins.

Brooke, M.H., Fenichel, G.M., Griggs, R.C., Mendell, J.R., Moxley, R., Miller, J.P., Province, M.A., & the CIDD Group. (1983). Clinical investigation in Duchenne dystrophy: 2. Determination of the "power" of therapeutic trials based on the natural history. *Muscle and Nerve, 6,* 91–103.

Campbell, A., Converse, P.E., & Rodgers, W.L. (1976). *The quality of American life: Perceptions, evaluations and satisfactions.* New York: Russell Sage Foundation.

Carter, G.T., Bonekat, W., & Milio, L. (1994). Successful pregnancies in the presence of spinal muscular atrophy: Two case reports. *Archives of Physical Medicine and Rehabilitation, 75,* 229–231.

Church, S.C. (1967). The heart in myotonia atrophica. *Archives of Internal Medicine, 119,* 176–181.

Dao, T.N., Mathieu, J., Bouchard, J.P., & DeBraekeleer, M. (1992). Fertility in myotonic dystrophy in Saguenay-Lac-St-Jean: A historical perspective. *Clinical Genetics, 42,* 234–239.

Gilgoff, I.S., Baydur, A., Bach, J.R., Prentice, W., & Hsu, J.D. (1992). Tracheal intermittent positive pressure ventilation for patients with neuromuscular disease. *Journal of Neurological Rehabilitation, 6,* 93–101.

Halstead, L.S. (1991). Post-polio sequelae: Assessment and differential diagnosis for post-polio syndrome. *Orthopedics, 14,* 1209–1217.

Hoffman, E.P., Fischbeck, K.H., Brown, R.H., Johnson, M., Medori, R., Loike, J.D., Harris, J.B., Waterston, R., Brooke, M., Specht, L., Kupsky, W., Chamberlain, J., Caskey, C.T., Shapiro, F., & Kunkel, L.M. (1988). Characterization of dystrophin in muscle-biopsy specimens from patients with Duchenne's or Becker's muscular dystrophy. *New England Journal of Medicine, 318,* 1363–1368.

Kagen, L.J. (1988). Polymyositis and dermatomyositis. In W.A. Katz (Ed.), *Diagnosis and management of rheumatic diseases* (pp. 482–493). Philadelphia: J.B. Lippincott.

Lisak, R.P. (1988). The immunology of neuromuscular disease. In J.N. Walton (Ed.), *Disorders of voluntary muscle* (5th ed., pp. 345–371). London: Churchill Livingstone.

Lord, J., Behrman, B., Varzos, N., Cooper, D., Lieberman, J.S., & Fowler, W.M. (1990). Scoliosis associated with Duchenne muscular dystrophy. *Archives of Physical Medicine and Rehabilitation, 71,* 13–17.

Lundberg, P.O. (1966). Observations on endocrine function in ocular myopathy. *Acta Neurologica Scandinavica, 42,* 39–61.

McDonald, C.M., Abresch, R.T., Carter, G.T., Fowler, W.M., Johnson, E.R., Kilmer, D.D., & Sigford, B.J. (1995). Duchenne muscular dystrophy. *American Journal of Physical Medicine and Rehabilitation, 74,* S62–S69.

Miller, F., Moseley, C., & Koreska, J. (1984). Treatment of spinal deformity in Duchenne muscular dystrophy. *Proceedings of Scoliosis Research Society* (p. 99). Orlando, FL.

Mulder, D.W., & Howard, F.M. (1976). Patient resistance and prognosis in amyotrophic lateral sclerosis. *Mayo Clinic Proceedings, 51,* 537–541.

Namba, T., Aberfeld, D.C., & Grob, D. (1970). Chronic proximal spinal muscular atrophy. *Journal of the Neurological Sciences, 11,* 401–423.

National Center for Health Statistics, U.S. Public Health Service. (1989).*Vital statistics of the United States, 1985. Volume III. Marriage and divorce.* DHHS Publication No. (PHS) 89-1103. Washington, D.C.: U.S. Government Printing Office.

Paern, J.H., & Wilson, J. (1973). Acute Werdnig-Hoffman disease. *Archives of Diseases of Childhood, 48,* 425–430.

Passos-Bueno, M.R., Cerqueira, A., Vainzof, M., Marie, S.K., & Zatz, M. (1995). Myotonic dystrophy: Genetic, clinical, and molecular analysis of patients from 41 Brazilian families. *Journal of Medical Genetics, 32,* 14–18.

Romano, M. (1976). Social skills training with the newly handicapped. *Archives of Physical Medicine and Rehabilitation, 57,* 302–303.

Rudnik-Schoneborn, S., Zerres, K., Ignatius, J., & Rietschel, M. (1992). Pregnancy and spinal muscular atrophy. *Journal of Neurology, 239,* 26–30.

Schnur, S., & Holland, I. (1987). Concepts—A unique approach to personal care attendants. *Rehabilitation Gazette, 28,* 10–11.

Simpson, J.A. (1988). Myasthenia gravis and myasthenic syndromes. In J.N. Walton (Ed.), *Disorders of voluntary muscle* (5th ed., pp. 628–665). London: Churchill Livingstone.

U.S. Department of Commerce, Bureau of the Census. (1975). *Historical statistics of the United States: Colonial times to 1970, bicentennial edition, part 1* (Vol. 8). Washington, DC: U.S. Government Printing Office.

Wilson, D.R., & Williams, K.P. (1992). Spinal muscular atrophy and pregnancy. *British Journal of Obstetrics and Gynaecology, 99,* 516–517.

CHAPTER 14

Arthritis and Other Connective Tissue Diseases

Scott Nadler

Individuals with arthritis may suffer not only from pain, joint stiffness, fatigue (Blake, Maisiak, Alarcon, & Brown, 1987), and decreased libido resulting from use of steroids and other drugs (Conine & Evans, 1982), but also the loss of mobility, disturbed body image (Pigg & Schroeder, 1984), and depression (Lipe, Longstreth, Bird, & Linde, 1990). Sexual dysfunction in arthritic patients may be difficult to manage for four main reasons. First, the nature of sexual dysfunction is difficult to diagnose because it oftentimes is complicated by the underlying medical condition. Second, intervention is elusive because of fluctuating physical and emotional factors. Third, chronic illness places special stresses on patients' sexual partners and their relationship. Fourth, sexual disorders in arthritic patients get low priority because most of the focus is on the disease itself (Blake, 1988). Clinicians managing arthritic patients must consider these issues and develop a comprehensive treatment approach.

EVALUATION

The evaluation process is extremely important, not only to assess limitations secondary to pain and loss of motion, but also to assess functional limitations. The history must characterize the types of pain suffered, including the location, duration, intensity, and factors that worsen or improve the pain. Clinicians should also assess the types of medication used, duration of effect, side effects, and onset time. Furthermore, they should explore the limitations on activities of daily living, including sexual function, in detail. A review of systems must include the effects of fatigue, weakness, and diseases of other organ systems such as cardiovascular, pulmonary, and genitourinary. The review also should include an assessment of psychosocial functioning, in which the clinician would monitor for depression, personality or anxiety disorders, and high stress levels (Ducharme, Gill, Biener-Bergman, & Fertitta, 1993).

The physical examination must include an assessment of joint range of motion and presence of inflammation, atrophy, or deformity. The examiner should address muscle strength and flexibility because asymmetrical loss of either may lead to additional functional limitations. Furthermore, the examiner should undertake an intensive evaluation of the peripheral nervous system because compression of the spinal cord, nerve roots, or peripheral nerves (i.e., carpal tunnel syndrome or cubital tunnel syndrome) are more common findings in arthritic patients.

Clinicians also should assess the peripheral vascular system because vasculitis may occur with systemic lupus erythematosus (SLE), scleroderma, and rheumatoid arthritis (RA). The examiner must also evaluate the mouth and genitalia for ulceration, irritation, and discharge, which are commonly seen, depending on the rheumatic condition (e.g., Behçet's, Reiter's, or Sjögren's syndrome). Any or all of these conditions can lead to pain or to limitation of sexual function (Cole & Cole, 1990).

Osteoarthritis

Osteoarthritis (OA) is the most common arthritic condition present in society. The prevalence of OA increases with age, becoming universal in people older than age 75 years. It is more frequent in men before age 45 years and in women after age 55 years (Gilliland, 1988b). The disorder is characterized by a progressive deterioration and loss of articular cartilage accompanied by new bone formation, with thickening of the joint capsule and surrounding tissues. OA is divided into a primary generalized condition characterized by involvement of three or more joints and a secondary form resulting from traumatic, systemic, or congenital disorders. The progressive loss of cartilage leads to joint space narrowing, loss of motion, and secondary irritation of tendons and the peripheral nerves or nerve roots. The lack of synovial inflammation present in OA makes this condition less painful, although still relatively incapacitating.

The effects of OA on sexual function are many. Diffuse involvement of the hands can make masturbation difficult both individually and with a partner. Loss of range of motion of the hips, especially abduction and external rotation, can cause significant difficulties with sexual activity (Currey, 1970). The loss of motion, which causes the hip to assume an adducted position, can make both the man-on-top and woman-on-top positions difficult and painful. Knee involvement, especially narrowing of the space between the patella and the femur, can lead to significant discomfort with repetitive knee flexion or pressure on the patella with the woman on all fours or the man on his knees. Low back pain is commonly encountered in the osteoarthritis patient. Positions that require excessive spinal extension and rapid twisting of the back tend to increase muscle spasm. For both females and males with back pain, the supine position is most comfortable (Buckwalter, Wernimont, & Buckwalter, 1982b). In addition, peripheral nerve entrapment or irritation can occur with excessive wrist extension or elbow flexion, respectively.

Rheumatoid Arthritis

RA is a chronic, multisystem disease characterized by a persistent inflammatory synovitis of the peripheral joints. Associated with inflammation is cartilage destruction, bone erosion, and resultant joint deformity. RA is a polyarthritis that has many systemic sequelae including fatigue, generalized weakness, anorexia, and weight loss along with more severe problems affecting the vasculature, heart, and lungs. The course of RA is variable and may be relatively benign in 15% of RA patients or relentlessly progressive with marked deformity in 10% of patients (Lipsky, 1988). Moreover, RA can be quite disabling, but life expectancy is only minimally shortened.

Sexual problems may occur in both men and women with RA, although published studies on this topic are few and numbers of subjects are small. Gordon, Beastall, Thomson, and Sturrock (1986) studied 31 males with RA aged 19 to 60 years. Of those subjects, 33% admitted periods of erectile dysfunction and 50% noted decreased libido during the time they suffered from arthritis. Nine out of 10 men with erectile dysfunction also acknowledged a decreased sex drive.

Yoshino and Uchida (1981) studied 91 married women with RA; 83.5% had been married for more than 11 years. More than half of the subjects reported a decreased desire for sex since their disease onset. More than 50% also complained of arthralgia during intercourse and 22% reported their arthritis symptoms were sometimes aggravated the day after intercourse. Although approximately 60% of respondents noted mutual dissatisfaction with their sexual relationship, 73.6% reported their illness had no impact on their relationship, 7.7% reported improvement, 8.8% did not respond, and only 9.9% reported dissatisfaction increased since the onset of their illness. Based on this information, it is uncertain whether this group of subjects generally suffered from a high level of sexual dissatisfaction or whether their arthritis was the main cause of sexual dissatisfaction. However, Bhadauria et al. (1995) studied another sample of 17 women with RA and 6 with SLE and found similar significant decreases in sexual satisfaction 1 year postdisease onset compared with 1 year predisease onset. Furthermore, frequency of sexual intercourse and a desire for sexual intercourse also significantly decreased 1 year postdisease onset. Joint pains and fatigue affected sexual performance in 56% and 61% of subjects, respectively. Overall, these studies have suggested a number of issues, including that joint stiffness and contractures may limit sexual expression in RA, but pain may be the most serious limitation (Buckwalter et al., 1982b).

The decreased desire for and satisfaction with sexual activity in people with RA is often the result of pain or joint ankylosis, but also may be the result of psychological factors. The development of a chronic disease with associated disability can undoubtedly lead to depression, altered self-esteem, and relationship problems, all of which may affect sexuality. Men and women with RA may show aversion to sexual interaction, and the more severe their disability, the more likely they will be less sexually motivated (Elst et al., 1984). Attending only to the physical aspects of the patient's problems thus will limit the impact of any treatment approach (Moore, 1994).

Overall, treatment of RA includes a synchrony of therapeutic modalities including drugs, rehabilitation, joint surgery, and attention to psychosocial issues. Many of the same difficulties that exist with osteoarthritis are present in RA, but more persistent attention is required with RA. With regard to sexual difficulties, people with RA should avoid positions that put prolonged pressure on painful inflamed joints. Individuals with RA may pre-medicate or consider the use of a hot bath, hot pack, and so forth, before sexual activity (Buckwalter et al., 1982a, 1982b). After sexual activity is completed, patients may place ice packs over more seriously involved joints to decrease inflammation. Clinicians treating individuals with RA may suggest these prophylactic techniques and should consider a more comprehensive program to improve joint stability and strengthen weakened muscles. In a severe attack, splinting of the involved area will predictably reduce synovial inflammation.

The use of medications in the treatment of RA is an important area to address. Many side effects caused by the use of corticosteroids may individually or as a whole affect sexual expression. Side effects include acne, truncal obesity, hirsutism, and a buffalo hump or moon face. Corticosteroids are also known to cause osteoporosis, which can predispose patients to fractures (Katz, 1985). The immunosuppressives used to treat various cancers and connective tissue diseases are also known to have serious side effects on the bladder (e.g., cyclophosphamide) and to cause oral–genital ulceration (e.g., gold). In addition, erectile dysfunction has been found to be more common in arthritic patients who take methotrexate (Blake, Maisiak, Koplan, Alarcon, & Brown, 1988; Salmon, 1987). Other common medications that can impact on sexual function are covered elsewhere in this book. The clinician treating the RA patient must monitor for these side effects and modify treatment accordingly.

Systemic Lupus Erythematosus

SLE is a devastating disease that affects the entire body. Antibodies are produced that attack cells in the blood, brain, kidney, joints, muscle, and so on. Common clinical manifestations include aching pain of the muscles, joints, and tendons, and variable muscle weakness within the musculoskeletal system along with resultant fatigue, malaise, anorexia, and weight loss. Other systemic conditions add to the overall debilitating effects of SLE: involvement of the heart, blood vessels, lungs, and kidneys, along with anemia and so forth (Hahn, 1988).

Because of the systemic nature of the condition, the SLE patient has a multitude of issues related to sexual function compared with controls. One study (Curry, Levine, Conty, Jones, & Kurit, 1994) compared 100 women with SLE with 71 disease-free controls through structured interviews and psychometric scales. SLE patients were found to have a higher rate of abstention, lower frequency of sexual activity, poor sexual adjustment, and diminished vaginal lubrication. Bhadauria et al. (1995) also noted diminished sexual desire, satisfaction, and frequency in a group of SLE patients 1 year postdisease onset. Furthermore, the greater the severity of subjects' disease, the greater their impairment in sexual function (Curry et al., 1994).

In adolescents with SLE, the role of health care providers is to promote the establishment of normal psychosocial development—developing a positive body image, sexual identity, independence, and acquiring of formal thought processes (Fuller & Hartley, 1991). Any interference with the accomplishment of the normal developmental sequence can have harmful effects on psychosocial and sexual function.

Patients with SLE, however, can function normally despite problems with self-image, sexual function, and lifestyle. Stein, Walters, Dillon, and Schulzer (1986) demonstrated that SLE was not a barrier to marriage or a primary cause of divorce: 40% of 14 female and 6 male subjects married after disease onset and only 12.3% had a history of divorce. Disease severity, premorbid sexual adjustment, and relationship quality have all been found to be predictors of sexual outcomes in patients with SLE. The clinician managing the SLE patient must therefore consider the combination of interpersonal, psychological, and medical conditions that may affect overall function (Curry, Levine, Jones, & Kurit, 1993).

Ankylosing Spondylitis

Ankylosing spondylitis (AS) is a progressive inflammatory disease involving the articulations of the spine, hip, shoulder, sacroiliac joints, and adjacent soft tissues. The disease occurs more commonly in men between the ages of 15 and 40 years and is rare after age 50 years. Hip pain, indistinguishable from OA and nocturnal back pain, stiffness of the spine, and tenderness of the sacroiliac and costosternal joints are common findings (Gilliland, 1988a). Sexual function in the AS patient may be limited secondary to pain, loss of motion, or psychosocial factors (Elst et al., 1984). Gordon et al. (1986) studied 33 males with ages ranging from 22 to 55 years and found that 13% had periods of erectile dysfunction and 39% had periods of decreased libido. In another study of 345 patients with chronic arthritis as a result of RA, OA, AS, or gout, Brown, Dare, Smith, and

Meyers (1987) discovered the most common problems encountered were pain (65%), stiffness (61%), and sexual difficulties in 31%. Clinicians should routinely provide sexual education to assist AS patients in understanding their limitations and ways to improve their sexual function.

Progressive Systemic Sclerosis

Progressive systemic sclerosis (PSS) is a multisystem disorder characterized by inflammatory, vascular, and fibrotic changes of the skin, gastointestinal tract, heart, lungs, and kidneys. It typically begins with the onset of intermittent vasoconstriction of the arteries and arterioles of the fingers, toes, and occasionally the face brought on by stress, temperature, and vibration. This vascular phenomenon, termed Raynaud's phenomenon, is usually a presenting complaint. Later findings include joint swelling, thickening of the skin and connective tissues, and ulceration. The patient with PSS will suffer from many systemic problems relating to the fibrosis within connective tissue and the polyarthritis that resembles RA.

Sexual function in patients with PSS, like that of patients with arthritis, may be affected by immobility, fatigue, and diminished self-esteem. Moreover, both women and men with PSS have been found to have other sexual difficulties, possibly related to the uniqueness of this disease. Bhadauria et al. (1995) compared 60 women with PSS with an age- and disease-duration–matched control group of women with RA and SLE. Women with PSS reported a decrease in the frequency of sexual intercourse and sexual satisfaction 1 year postinjury compared with 1 year before the injury. Women with PSS also reported a decrease in desire for sexual activity. Furthermore, women with PSS had a greater frequency of dyspareunia, vaginal dryness, ulcerations, and fissures after disease onset. Skin tightness, esophageal reflux symptoms, contractures, and muscle weakness caused problems during coitus in more PSS patients than controls, and PSS patients noted a decrease in the number and intensity of orgasms. Changes in position, use of lubricants, and the consumption of light meals prior to coitus were techniques used to improve sexual performance in women. Erectile dysfunction has also been observed in men with PSS. One-third to one-half of men reportedly have erectile problems (Lally & Jimenez, 1981, 1990; Simeon et al., 1994) as a result of vascular changes that limit penile blood flow (Saad & Behrendt, 1996).

Other Disorders

Other rheumatologic disorders known to impact on sexual function include Behçet's disease and Sjögren's syndrome. Behçet's disease is a syndrome characterized by three of the following symptoms: recurrent oral ulcers, genital aphthous ulcers, cutaneous vasculitis, uveitis, synovitis, and meningoencephalitis

(O'Duffy, 1989). Oral ulcers are present in virtually 100% of patients and, like genital ulcers, are painful. Dyspareunia can occur in conjunction with vulvar ulcers. Furthermore, although not specifically studied, it follows that sexual activity may be limited by the desire to avoid stimulation of painful ulcers.

Sjögren's syndrome can occur in primary or secondary forms (Whaley & Alspaugh, 1989). Primary Sjögren's syndrome comprises dry eyes with or without enlargement of the lacrimal glands and dry mouth with or without salivary gland enlargement. Secondary Sjögren's syndrome occurs when the preceding conditions occur as a result of another connective tissue disease. Theoretically, dry mouth in these patients may cause sexual problems such as difficulty with kissing or performance of oral sex, although this issue has not been studied.

TREATMENT STRATEGIES

As part of the program to treat sexual dysfunction in the patient with arthritis, the clinician must address all aspects of the person's function. Treatment strategies may involve education, pain management, exercise, rehabilitation principles, and psychological interventions.

Education

Education of patients with arthritis regarding the impact of their illness on sexual response and function is paramount. Furthermore, the clinician can tactfully give the patient permission to discuss sexual concerns through a basic, patient-oriented approach. Brochures such as those offered by the Arthritis Foundation offer useful diagrams showing positions for intercourse with various painful joints (Figures 14–1 through 14–7). Highlighting recommended positions in this fashion often makes them easier for the patient to understand.

Pain

Pain is a subjective feeling that causes an objective or measurable degree of disability. It may be a significant cause of sexual difficulties (Currey, 1970) and may adversely affect sexual function and overall enjoyment (Yoshino & Uchida, 1981). Understanding and treating the patient with pain is the cornerstone of effective intervention (Voiss, 1993). The clinician must perform a complete history, taking into account frequency, intensity, and duration of pain in addition to the effects on sexual activity. The physical examination should emphasize the degree of joint limitation secondary to pain and effects on functional activities. Many screening tools are available to assess pain. The McMaster Toronto Arthritis Patient Preference Disability Questionnaire (MACTAR; Alpiner, Oh, Hinderer,

Figure 14–1 Both partners lying on side. The man enters from behind. The woman can have a pillow between her knees. This position is good if the woman has hip problems. *Source:* From the information sheet, "Living and Loving: Information about Sexuality and Intimacy," Arthritis Information. Used by permission of the Arthritis Foundation. For more information, please call the Arthritis Foundation's information line at 800-283-7800.

Figure 14–2 The woman lies on her back, knees together, with pillow under hips and thighs. Notice that the man is supporting his own body weight on his hands and knees. This position can be used if the woman has hip or knee problems or is unable to move her legs apart. *Source:* From the information sheet, "Living and Loving: Information about Sexuality and Intimacy," Arthritis Information. Used by permission of the Arthritis Foundation. For more information, please call the Arthritis Foundation's information line at 800-283-7800.

Figure 14–3 Side position with partners facing each other. This position can be used if the man has back problems. Notice that in the positions illustrated in Figures 14–3 and 14–7, the woman must provide most of the hip movement. *Source:* From the information sheet, "Living and Loving: Information about Sexuality and Intimacy," Arthritis Information. Used by permission of the Arthritis Foundation. For more information, please call the Arthritis Foundation's information line at 800-283-7800.

Figure 14–4 The woman lies on her back with knees flexed. This position can be used if the woman's tendons or muscles are severely shortened or shrunken. *Source:* From the information sheet, "Living and Loving: Information about Sexuality and Intimacy," Arthritis Information. Used by permission of the Arthritis Foundation. For more information, please call the Arthritis Foundation's information line at 800-283-7800.

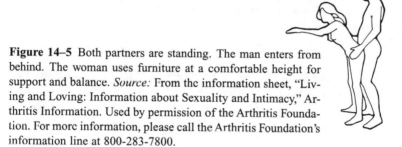

Figure 14–5 Both partners are standing. The man enters from behind. The woman uses furniture at a comfortable height for support and balance. *Source:* From the information sheet, "Living and Loving: Information about Sexuality and Intimacy," Arthritis Information. Used by permission of the Arthritis Foundation. For more information, please call the Arthritis Foundation's information line at 800-283-7800.

Figure 14–6 The woman is kneeling, her upper body supported by furniture (and pillows, if preferred). Her knees can be supported by a pillow. This position may be helpful if the woman has hip problems. This position is not good if shoulders are involved or if either partner has had recent knee surgery. *Source:* From the information sheet, "Living and Loving: Information about Sexuality and Intimacy," Arthritis Information. Used by permission of the Arthritis Foundation. For more information, please call the Arthritis Foundation's information line at 800-283-7800.

Figure 14–7 The man lies on his back. He may use pillows for support. The woman can support her own body weight on her elbows and her knees. This position can be used if the man has hip or knee problems. *Source:* From the information sheet, "Living and Loving: Information about Sexuality and Intimacy," Arthritis Information. Used by permission of the Arthritis Foundation. For more information, please call the Arthritis Foundation's information line at 800-283-7800.

& Brander, 1995), though, may be the best available tool to assess the impact of pain on sexual activity because the patients themselves define functional parameters of clinical importance. On completion of the assessment phase of pain in the arthritis patient, the clinician may devise a more definite treatment plan.

Exercise

Exercise may be a valuable tool in the overall management of the arthritic patient with sexual dysfunction. Exercise may help those patients with impaired body image, loss of confidence, depression, and mobility issues. Decreases in general stress symptomatology including anxiety, depression, and anger have been found to occur following a single exercise session in normal individuals (Berger, Friedmann, & Eaton, 1988; Steptoe & Cox, 1988). Exercise for patients with arthritis can increase and maintain range of motion, and increase both strength and endurance. Furthermore, increases in strength can have dramatic effects on overall function because a transfer of stress from the involved joints to overlying musculature may help to significantly decrease the inflammatory response. The clinician managing the exercise program must be ready to modify the program, because exercise may be harmful in an acutely inflamed joint (Grootveld, Henderson, Farrell, Blake, & Purkes, 1991).

Typical exercise programs include pool therapy with water temperature approximately 85°F. The warm water not only provides a feeling of weightlessness, unloading the joints, but also analgesia. In addition, bicycle ergometry is preferable to running on treadmills because less stress is placed on the joints (Hicks, 1994).

Of all patients with arthritic hips, 67% to 85% have some mechanical sexual disability (Currey, 1970; Yoshino & Uchida, 1981). It is important, then, to maintain range of motion, especially abduction/external rotation in the female and hip extension in the male. Neither pain, stiffness, flexibility, nor loss of motion of the knee should mechanically limit intercourse (Hicks & Gerber, 1988). The loss of motion of the knee, however, may limit various positions. Furthermore, increased mechanical stress may further increase joint dysfunction. Strengthening exercises, then, may be beneficial. In individuals with inflamed joints, isometric strengthening appears to place less stress on the joints (Merritt & Hander, 1983) and is not associated with increasing joint inflammation (Jayson & Dixon, 1970). Isometric strengthening of the quadriceps should be encouraged initially, followed by short arc squats and high-seat cycling. Overall, the practitioner should encourage flexibility of the muscles of the hip and knee along with an appropriate home exercise program to decrease stress to the involved joints. In addition, general conditioning exercises may improve cardiovascular function and endurance (Hicks & Gerber, 1988).

The arthritic patient without a significant inflammatory component will also benefit from isotonic strengthening exercises. This strengthening should be performed in a concentric (shortening) manner and progressed as tolerated to eccentric (lengthening) strengthening. Overall, exercise will improve the arthritic patient's level of function, self-image, and well-being (Ekblom, Lovgren, Alderin, Fridstrom, & Satterstrom, 1975), perhaps subsequently improving feelings of sexual attractiveness and desire secondary to improved body image and improving sexual function with improved physical condition.

Rehabilitation Principles

A comprehensive rehabilitation program will be a useful adjunct to the management of sexual dysfunction in the arthritic patient. Pain control, exercise, modalities, orthotics, and other assistive devices are all appropriate means for improving function. The main goal of rehabilitation intervention is to decrease incapacity, improve overall function, and maximize quality of life. The arthritic patient with sexual dysfunction presents a unique situation to the rehabilitation team. The team must identify the multitude of issues surrounding the dysfunction, including those secondary to medication, physical limitations, and the psychosocial realm. The individual disciplines can then attack those problem areas within their domain in a coordinated, directed, and goal-oriented program.

Modalities can be useful to the arthritic patient to decrease pain and to improve mobility and function. Some modalities are quite useful in people with sexual dysfunction. Arthritis in the hands may severely interfere with the early stages of lovemaking, especially caressing and manual stimulation (Yoshino & Uchida, 1981). Splinting, then, may be especially beneficial. Patients may use small ring splints to reduce the deformity and discomfort caused by swan-neck or boutonnière deformities. Cock up wrist splints are useful for pain secondary to carpal tunnel syndrome, carpal–carpal, or carpal–metacarpal inflammation. Physical deformity leading to altered cosmetic appearance can be a major factor and may lead to impaired body image, but overall benefit in function and pain must be weighed against this effect.

Compression gloves have been shown to decrease finger joint pain, morning stiffness, and nighttime throbbing and to improve the overall sense of well-being (Culic, Battagalia, Widerman, & Schmid, 1979). Patients may remove the gloves during times of intimacy to allow for caressing and mutual masturbation. Other modalities useful for the hands include the home use of paraffin or hot packs, which may also improve hand function. Capsaicin topical ointment applied to the hands of OA patients has been shown to decrease pain and tenderness as well (McCarthy & McCarty, 1992).

Various heating modalities including hot packs and hot soaks are useful for the larger joints of the body including the shoulder, hips, and knees. Before sexual activity, heating these joints may decrease pain and improve range of motion. Ice has been shown in some RA patients to decrease pain and stiffness and may be preferable to heat treatment (Kirk & Kersley, 1968). This author prefers to prescribe ice treatments after sexual activity is completed to decrease the likelihood of an inflammatory response. Furthermore, most sexual partners prefer a warm body, as opposed to a cold one. Clinicians also may attempt a trial of transcutaneous nerve stimulation (TENS) to decrease pain. TENS has been used successfully for RA of the hands (Mannheimer, Staffan, & Carlsson, 1978), OA of the knees (Lewis, Lewis, & Starrock, 1984), and AS when patients have back pain (Gemignani, Olivieri, Raju, & Pasero, 1985). The use of TENS, although somewhat controversial, should be tried when other treatments have failed or are contraindicated (Nicholas, 1994).

Referral to other rehabilitation professionals will assist in improving the overall sexual function of the patient with arthritis. The occupational therapist may assist the arthritic patient with techniques to improve upper extremity function and ability to perform activities of daily living. Joint protection teaches the patient to avoid prolonged periods in the same position, thus minimizing stress and maintaining range, strength, and good joint alignment. Techniques include instruction in the use of adaptive equipment (reachers, buttonhooks, velcro closures, and so on); appropriate splinting during inflammatory phases; and the use of rest and activity modification to avoid overuse. Energy conservation, including proper posture, rest, and conditioning, combined with avoiding overuse and fatigue are also stressed (Hicks & Gerber, 1988).

Psychological Interventions

The psychological impact of arthritis must not be minimized. Patients with arthritis, in addition to coping with pain, may have to deal with both losses in function and in physical attractiveness because of the disease; medication side effects; and the reactions of friends, spouse, and family (Hicks & Gerber, 1988). RA and joint-diseased patients constitute an important segment of the large number of patients with chronic conditions who experience prominent depression (Alarcon & Glover, 1994). Anxiety is also commonly seen in patients with arthritic conditions (Baum, 1982). Besides depression and anxiety, loss of self-esteem, inability to perform an expected role, restricted opportunities, and physical separation all contribute to the psychosocial dilemma facing the arthritic patient (Lim, 1995). Clinicians use various strategies to treat psychosocial dysfunction including classic psychotherapy, cognitive or behavioral therapy, education and support groups, and medications. The goal of psychological support is to educate both patient and family on the disease process and life stressors, and to train all involved in coping strategies.

SEXUAL FUNCTION AFTER JOINT REPLACEMENT

Degenerative joint disease may cause significant limitations on a patient's sexuality. In one study (Currey, 1970), two-thirds of patients with arthritis reported that this limitation was most commonly secondary to hip pain and immobility rather than a loss of libido. A consideration in performing joint replacement should thus be its impact on sexual function. In one report (Stern et al., 1991), 81% of patients related a history of not being instructed by their surgeon regarding when they could resume sexual intercourse after total hip replacement surgery. The reluctance of physicians to discuss such issues remains a problem. Currey (1970) performed a mail survey of 202 patients who had undergone hip replacement. Of the 121 respondents, 57% had some relief of sexual difficulty after surgery, whereas only 34% reported complete or considerable improvement. Stern et al. (1991) reported that 65% of patients in their study were without problems after total hip replacement. One difficulty reported in those studies is that patients did not receive adequate information in the postoperative period.

Because resumption of sexual activity after joint replacement appears to be an issue that both surgeons and patients are reluctant to discuss, health care providers should distribute educational tools such as booklets and pamphlets to the preoperative patient. These materials should clearly outline any or all limitations on function and suggested time frames for resumption of activity.

In general, most patients should be able to resume sexual intercourse between 1 and 2 months postoperatively after total hip replacement. Stern et al. (1991) reported that 55% of patients had resumed sexual intercourse within 1 to 2 months after hip replacement, with males slightly earlier than females. At this time, the surgical wound, hip musculature, and joint capsule should be well healed, reducing instability and the risk for dislocation. Practitioners should make the postoperative hip patient aware of preferred sexual positions. In males, the missionary position is preferred because no excess motion is required of the hip joint. In females, the side-lying position with the nonoperative hip down and operative side supported by pillows helps to prevent the hip from adducting or rotating internally (positions of instability).

Joint replacement of the knees, shoulders, hands, and so forth may cause difficulty with sexual performance in the acute postoperative period. Overall mobility, however, should not be compromised as in patients with hip replacement. Nevertheless, proper sexual positioning to decrease stress across the operative joint is recommended.

FERTILITY

The ability to procreate is an important part of life. The fertile years can be a difficult time for individuals with arthritis because the effects of RA are most commonly encountered in women of childbearing age (Pritchard, 1992). Females with RA compared with controls were demonstrated to have a decreased fertility rate (Nelson et al., 1993). The potential causes of decreased fertility have been variously described, including insufficient progesterone secretion, antibodies to spermatazoa, antibodies to the ovary, or impairment in the hormonal control of ovulation (Cohen & Speroff, 1991; Pritchard, 1992; Schlaghecke, Kornely, Wollenhaupt, & Specker, 1992; Shulman, 1986). Women with PSS have also been found to have a higher incidence of surgical menopause than the general population (Bhadauria et al., 1995), which can also result in decreased fertility. Further studies need to be performed to enable researchers to quantify and understand the pathogenesis of decreased fertility in women with RA and other disorders.

Males with connective tissue diseases may have decreased fertility secondary to fatigue, immobility, erectile dysfunction, and decreased libido. There also may be hormonal changes associated with the development of arthritis in males. Lower serum testosterone has been demonstrated in males with RA compared with controls. Carrabba et al. (1985) demonstrated similar findings in males with SLE, in which testosterone levels were significantly lower compared with a healthy control group.

CONCLUSION

Sexual dysfunction in the arthritic patient is a common entity that clinically, for the most part, has been avoided. The physician managing sexual dysfunction must be cognizant of its existence and perform the appropriate focused history and physical. He or she must address the impacts of medications, systemic disease consequences, psychologic factors, and age on the person's sexual function. Furthermore, the practitioner should enlist a comprehensive multidisciplinary approach focused on improving the overall function of the patient with arthritis. Further research is needed to better understand the impact of various arthritic conditions on sexual response and fertility and to develop ways to improve function.

REFERENCES

Alarcon, R.D., Glover, S.G. (1994). Assessment and management of depression in rheumatoid arthritis. *Physical Medicine and Rehabilitation Clinics of North America, 5*(4), 837–858.

Alpiner, N., Oh, T.H., Hinderer, S.R., & Brander, V.A. (1995). Rehabilitation in joint and connective tissue diseases: Systemic diseases. *Archives of Physical Medicine and Rehabilitation, 76,* 32–39.

Baum, J. (1982). A review of the psychological aspects of rheumatic disease. *Seminars in Arthritis and Rheumatism, 11,* 352–361.

Berger, B.G., Friedmann, E., & Eaton, M. (1988). Comparison jogging, the relaxation response and group interaction for stress reduction. *Journal of Sports Exercise Psychology, 10,* 431–447.

Bhadauria, S., Moser, D.K., Clements, P.J., Singh, R.R., Lachenbruch, P.A., Pitkin, R.M., & Weiner, S.R. (1995). Genital tract abnormalities and female sexual function impairment in systemic sclerosis. *American Journal of Obstetrics and Gynecology, 172,* 580–587.

Blake, D.J. (1988). Sexual disorders among patients with arthritis. *Internal Medicine, 9,* 173–182.

Blake, D.J., Maisiak, R., Alarcon, G.S., & Brown, S. (1987). Sexual quality of life of patients with arthritis compared to arthritis-free controls. *Journal of Rheumatology, 14,* 570–576.

Blake, D.J., Maisiak, R., Koplan, A., Alarcon, G.S., & Brown, S. (1988). Sexual dysfunction among patients with arthritis. *Clinical Rheumatology, 7*(1), 50–60.

Brown, G.M., Dare, C.M., Smith, P.R., & Meyers, O.L. (1987). Important problems identified by patients with chronic arthritis. *South African Medical Journal, 72,* 126–128.

Buckwalter, K.C., Wernimont, T., & Buckwalter, J.A. (1982a). Musculoskeletal conditions and sexuality (part I). *Sexuality and Disability, 4*(3), 131–142.

Buckwalter, K.C., Wernimont, T., & Buckwalter, J.A. (1982b). Musculoskeletal conditions and sexuality (part II). *Sexuality and Disability, 5*(5), 195–207.

Carrabba, M., Giovine, C., Cheallard, M., Angelini, M.R.I., Ambrosi, B., & Travaglini, P. (1985). Abnormalities of sex hormones in men with systemic lupus erythematosus. *Clinical Rheumatology, 4*(4), 420–425.

Cohen, I., & Speroff, L. (1991). Premature ovarian failure update. *Obstetrical and Gynecological Survey, 46,* 156–162.

Cole, T.M., & Cole, S.S. (1990). Rehabilitation of problems of sexuality in physical disability. In F.J. Kottke, J.F. Lehman, & G.K. Stillwell (Eds.), *Krusen's handbook of physical medicine and rehabilitation* (4th ed., pp. 958–1008). Philadelphia: W.B. Saunders.

Conine, T.A., & Evans, J.H. (1982). Sexual reactivation of chronically ill and disabled adults. *Journal of Allied Health, 11,* 261–270.

Culic, D.D., Battagalia, M.C., Widerman, B.S., & Schmid, F.R. (1979). Efficacy of compression gloves in rheumatoid arthritis. *American Journal of Physical Medicine and Rehabilitation, 58,* 278–284.

Currey, H.L.F. (1970). Osteoarthritis of the hip joint and sexual activity. *Annals of the Rheumatic Diseases, 29,* 488–493.

Curry, S.L., Levine, S.B., Conty, E., Jones, P.K., & Kurit, D.M. (1994). The impact of systemic lupus erythematosus on women's sexual functioning. *Journal of Rheumatology, 21,* 2254–2260.

Curry, S.L., Levine, S.B., Jones, P.K., & Kurit, D.M. (1993). Medical and psychosocial predictors of sexual outcome among women with systemic lupus erythematosus. *Arthritis Care Research, 6,* 23–30.

Ducharme, S., Gill, K., Biener-Bergman, S., & Fertitta, L. (1993). Sexual functioning: Medical and psychological aspect. In J.A. DeLisa (Ed.), *Rehabilitation medicine: Principles and practice* (2nd ed., pp. 763–782). Philadelphia: J.B. Lippincott.

Ekblom, B., Lovgren, O., Alderin, M., Fridstrom, M., & Satterstrom, G. (1975). Effect of short-term physical training on patients with rheumatoid arthritis. *Scandinavian Journal of Rheumatology, 4,* 80–86.

Elst, P., Sybesma, T., Van der Stadt, R.J., Prins, A.D., Muller, W.H., & den Butter, A. (1984). Sexual problems in rheumatoid arthritis and ankylosing spondylitis. *Arthritis and Rheumatism, 27,* 217–270.

Fuller, C., & Hartley, B. (1991). Systemic lupus erythematosus in adolescents. *Journal of Pediatric Nursing, 6,* 251–257.

Gemignani, G., Olivieri, I., Raju, G., & Pasero, G. (1985). Transcutaneous electrical nerve stimulation on ankylosing spondylitis: A double-blind study. *Arthritis and Rheumatism, 28,* 288–289.

Gilliland, B.C. (1988a). Ankylosing spondylitis. In E. Braunwald, K.J. Issebacher, R.G. Petersdorf, J.D. Wilson, J.B. Martin, & A.S. Fauci (Eds.), *Harrison's principles of internal medicine* (pp. 1428–1436). New York: McGraw-Hill.

Gilliland, B.C. (1988b). Degenerative joint disease. In E. Braunwald, K.J. Issebacher, R.G. Petersdorf, J.D. Wilson, J.B. Martin, & A.S. Fauci (Eds.), *Harrison's principles of internal medicine* (pp. 1456–1458). New York: McGraw-Hill.

Gordon, D., Beastall, G.H., Thomson, J.A., & Sturrock, R.D. (1986). Androgenic status and sexual function in males with rheumatoid arthritis and ankylosing spondylitis. *Quarterly Journal of Medicine, 231,* 671–679.

Grootveld, M., Henderson, E.B., Farrell, A., Blake, D.R., & Purkes, H.G. (1991). Oxidative damage to hyaluronate and glucose in synovial fluid during exercise of the inflamed rheumatoid joint. *Biochemical Journal, 273,* 459–467.

Hahn, B.H. (1988). Systemic lupus erythematosus. In E. Braunwald, K.J. Issebacher, R.G. Petersdorf, J.D. Wilson, J.B. Martin, & A.S. Fauci (Eds.), *Harrison's principles of internal medicine* (pp. 1418–1423). New York: McGraw-Hill.

Hicks, J.E. (1994). Exercise in rheumatoid arthritis. *Physical Medicine and Rehabilitation Clinics of North America, 5,* 701–728.

Hicks, J.E., & Gerber, L.H. (1988). Rehabilitation of the patient with arthritis and connective tissue disease. In J.A. DeLisa (Ed.), *Rehabilitation medicine: Principles and practice* (pp. 765–794). Philadelphia: J.B. Lippincott Co.

Jayson, M.I.V., & Dixon, A.St.J. (1970). Intraarticular pressure in rheumatoid arthritis of the knee. III. Pressure changes during joint use. *Annals of the Rheumatic Diseases, 29,* 401–408.

Katz, W.A. (1985). Modern management of rheumatoid arthritis. *American Journal of Medicine, 79,* 24–31.

Kirk, J.A., & Kersley, G.D. (1968). Heat and cold in the physical treatment of rheumatoid arthritis of the knee: A controlled clinical trial. *Annals of Physical Medicine, 9,* 270–274.

Lally, E.V., & Jimenez, S.A. (1981). Impotence in progressive systemic sclerosis. *Annals of Internal Medicine, 95,* 150–153.

Lally, E.V., & Jimenez, S.A. (1990). Erectile failure in systemic sclerosis. *New England Journal of Medicine, 322,* 1398.

Lewis, D., Lewis, B., & Starrock, R.D. (1984). Transcutaneous electrical nerve stimulation in osteoarthritis: A therapeutic alternative? *Annals of the Rheumatic Diseases, 43,* 47–49.

Lim, P.A.C. (1995). Sexuality in patients with musculoskeletal diseases. *Physical Medicine and Rehabilitation: State of the Art Reviews, 9*(2), 401–415.

Lipe, H., Longstreth, W.T., Bird, T.D., & Linde, M. (1990). Sexual function in married men with Parkinson's disease compared to married men with arthritis. *Neurology, 40,* 1347–1349.

Lipsky, P.E. (1988). Rheumatoid arthritis. In E. Braunwald, K.J. Issebacher, R.G. Petersdorf, J.D. Wilson, J.B. Martin, & A.S. Fauci (Eds.), *Harrison's principles of internal medicine* (pp. 1423–1428). New York: McGraw-Hill.

Mannheimer, C., Staffan, L., & Carlsson, C.A. (1978). The effect of transcutaneous electrical nerve stimulation on joint pain in patients with rheumatoid arthritis. *Scandinavian Journal of Rheumatology, 7,* 13–16.

McCarthy, G.M., & McCarty, D.J. (1992). Effect of topical capsaicin in the therapy of painful osteoarthritis of the hands. *Journal of Rheumatology, 19,* 604–607.

Merritt, J.L., & Hander, G.G. (1983). Passive range of motion, not isometric exercise, amplifies acute urate synovitis. *Archives of Physical Medicine and Rehabilitation, 64,* 130–131.

Moore, C.P. (1994). Rheumatic disorders. In R.M. Harp, G.H. Kraft, & W.C. Stolov (Eds.), *Disease and disability: A contemporary rehabilitation approach to medical practice* (pp. 190–196). New York: Demos.

Nelson, J.L., Koepsell, T.D., Dugowson, C.E., Voight, L.F., Daling, J.R., & Hansen, J.A. (1993). Fecundity before disease onset in women with rheumatoid arthritis. *Arthritis and Rheumatism, 36*(1), 7–14.

Nicholas, J.J. (1994). Physical modalities in rheumatological rehabilitation. *Archives of Physical Medicine and Rehabilitation, 75,* 994–1001.

O'Duffy, J.D. (1989). Behçet's disease. In W.N. Kelley, E.D. Harris, S. Ruddy, & C.B. Sledge (Eds.), *Textbook of rheumatology* (pp. 1209–1214). Philadelphia: W.B. Saunders.

Pigg, J.S., & Schroeder, P.M. (1984). Frequently occurring problems of patients with rheumatic disease. The ANA outcome standards for rheumatology nursing practice. *Nursing Clinics of North America, 19*(4), 697–708.

Pritchard, M.H. (1992). An examination of the role of female hormones and pregnancy as risk factors for rheumatoid arthritis, using a male population as a control group. *British Journal of Rheumatology, 31*(6), 395–399.

Saad, S.C., & Behrendt, A.E. (1996). Scleroderma and sexuality. *Journal of Sex Research, 33,* 215–220.

Salmon, S.E. (1987). Drugs and the immune system. In B.G. Katzung (Ed.), *Basic and clinical pharmacology* (pp. 702–718). East Norwalk, CT: Appleton & Lange.

Schlaghecke, R., Kornely, E., Wollenhaupt, J., & Specker, C. (1992). Glucocorticoid receptors in rheumatoid arthritis. *Arthritis and Rheumatism, 35,* 740–744.

Shulman, S. (1986). Sperm antigens and autoantibodies: Effects on fertility. *American Journal of Reproductive Immunology and Microbiology, 10,* 82–89.

Simeon, C.P., Fonollosa, V., Vilardell, M., Ordi, J., Solans, R., & Lima, J. (1994). Impotence and Peyronie's disease in systemic sclerosis. *Clinical and Experimental Rheumatology, 12,* 464.

Stein, H., Walters, K., Dillon, A., & Schulzer, M. (1986). Systemic lupus erythematosus: A medical and social profile. *Journal of Rheumatology, 13,* 570–576.

Steptoe, A., & Cox, S. (1988). Acute effects of aerobic exercise on mood. *Health Psychology, 7,* 329–340.

Stern, S.H., Fuchs, M.D., Ganz, S.B., Classi, P., Sculco, T.P., & Salvati, E.A. (1991). Sexual function after total hip arthroplasty. *Clinical Orthopaedics and Related Research, 269,* 228–235.

Voiss, D.V. (1993). The problem patient with pain: From myth to mayhem. *Physical Medicine and Rehabilitation Clinics of North America, 4*(1), 27–40.

Whaley, K., & Alspaugh, M.A. (1989). Sjögren's syndrome. In W.N. Kelley, E.D. Harris, S. Ruddy, & C.B. Sledge (Eds.), *Textbook of rheumatology* (pp. 999–1019). Philadelphia: W.B. Saunders.

Yoshino, S., & Uchida, S. (1981). Sexual problems of women with rheumatoid arthritis. *Archives of Physical Medicine and Rehabilitation, 62,* 122–123.

CHAPTER 15

Diabetes and Amputation

Margaret C. Tilton

DIABETES MELLITUS: GENERAL PRINCIPLES

Approximately 16 million Americans have *diabetes mellitus*, a serious disorder that affects the ability of the body to produce or properly respond to insulin. *Insulin* is a protein pancreatic hormone secreted by the B cells of the islets of Langerhans. It allows blood sugar to enter the cells of the body to be used for energy. Without insulin, liver, muscle, and fat tissues, which act as the energy stores for the body, are unable to take up absorbed nutrients; rather, they continue to deliver glucose, amino acids, and fatty acids into the bloodstream. Alterations in fat metabolism lead to the accumulation of ketones, which are normal intermediates in lipid metabolism, but which in abnormally high concentrations are toxic (Karan & Forsham, 1994).

Diabetes mellitus is a complex disease affecting multiple organ systems, with varying clinical presentations. It is best viewed as a syndrome, rather than as a disease in the classic sense. It is a clinical entity that may be manifested by any or all of a host of symptoms and laboratory abnormalities. Disorders of glucose metabolism are the hallmark of the syndrome, are easy to quantify, and have been the focus of therapeutic intervention in diabetes. Table 15–1 shows the classifications of diabetes mellitus.

IDD is most common in young people, but occurs occasionally in nonobese adults. There is a virtual absence of circulating insulin with failure of the pancreatic B cells to respond to all insulinogenic stimuli. Hence, treatment with exogenous insulin is necessary to compensate for the inability of the body to respond to elevated blood sugar levels with its own insulin production. Development of IDD probably depends on genetic predisposition in the presence of an inciting infectious or toxic environmental insult to the pancreatic B cells. An autoimmune mechanism is responsible in which the immune system mistakenly identifies pancreatic B cells as foreign proteins and, consequently, produces autoantibodies to them.

Table 15–1 Classifications of Diabetes Mellitus

Type and Prevalence	Ketosis	Autoimmune Mechanism	Genetic Association	Treatment
Insulin-dependent diabetes (IDD, type I) mellitus: 10–20% of all diabetics	Marked	Usually present at onset	Yes	Insulin, diet
Non–insulin-dependent diabetes (NIDD, type II) mellitus: 80–90% of all diabetics; NIDD nonobese: 15% of NIDD patients	Absent	Absent	No	Diet alone or with oral hypoglycemic or insulin
NIDD obese: 85% of NIDD patients	Absent	Absent	No	Weight reduction, diet with oral hypoglycemic or insulin

NIDD occurs predominantly in adults but may occasionally occur in childhood. In contrast to IDD, NIDD is not associated with ketosis and has no autoimmune basis. At least 85% of NIDD diabetics are obese and have an insensitivity to endogenous insulin that correlates with the presence of the predominantly abdominal distribution of fat. In these patients, chronic overeating leads to eventual desensitization of insulin receptors, a process that is often reversible when overfeeding is corrected and storage depots become less saturated.

Clinical features common to both types of diabetes include thirst, polyuria, blurred vision, paresthesias, and fatigue, all of which are manifestations of hyperglycemia and the hyperosmolar state it creates. In IDD, weight loss despite normal appetite initially results because of depletion of water, glycogen, and triglyceride stores; later, it results from reduced muscle mass. Lowered plasma volume produces postural hypotension; loss of muscle protein and serum potassium are responsible for generalized weakness. Ketoacidosis adds to the dehydration and hyperosmolality by producing anorexia, nausea, and vomiting.

In NIDD, the onset of hyperglycemia is often gradual, with an initial relatively asymptomatic period. Generalized itching and symptoms of vaginitis may be the presenting complaint in women and erectile dysfunction may be the presenting complaint in men. Nonobese NIDD patients have no characteristic physical findings, but obese diabetics of both sexes have a centripetal distribution of fat, with more fat on the abdomen, chest, neck, and face, and relatively less fat on the hips and thighs.

Chronic complications of both types of diabetes include ophthalmologic, renal, neurologic, cardiovascular, dermatologic, and bone and joint complications, and characteristic infections. Of most significance to sexual function are abnormalities in the autonomic nervous system, which can affect multiple phases of the male and female sexual response. Accelerated atherosclerosis of large vessels and microangiopathic changes of smaller vessels may also be responsible for sexual dysfunction in diabetic individuals.

MALE SEXUALITY

Diabetes has the potential for significant impact on every aspect of male sexuality and sexual function. Its effect on male sexual performance has been studied quite extensively and a considerable body of literature has emerged, with conflicting data and conclusions.

Libido

Libido is a complex phenomenon dependent on many psychosocial, cultural, situational, and biologic parameters. There is some degree of controversy regarding to what extent libido is affected by the physiologic milieu of diabetes mellitus, but the consensus is that male libido is relatively unaffected by diabetes. The experience of sexual desire is obviously subjective; studies of libido in diabetic men, by necessity, have relied on self-report and cannot be objectively confirmed or quantified. Researchers generally consult the extensive work by Kinsey, Pomeroy, and Martin (1948) on male sexual behavior for comparison with normal populations.

In a study of 314 men with diabetes (Schoffling, Federlin, Ditschuneit, & Pfeiffer, 1963), all of whom had developed the disease before age 60 years, 160 patients had observed sexual dysfunction after periods ranging from months to years following the discovery of diabetes. Of those 160 individuals, one-half reported a decrease in libido. In another group of 7 male diabetics with impotence, ranging in age from 20 to 44 years, and with duration of diabetes 1 to 15 years, only 3 reported difficulty with libido. All of these men had evidence of depression on psychological testing and all had neuropathy. By comparison, of the 4 impotent men with preserved libido, 2 were depressed and 3 had neuropathy (Faerman et al., 1972). Jensen (1981) studied 80 diabetic males. Of those males, 44% reported some sexual dysfunction and 31% reported decreased libido, compared with only 1 of the 40 men in the nondiabetic control group who reported decreased libido. Loss of interest in sex is likely to be a psychological reaction to impotence. Loss of libido in the absence of erectile dysfunction does not seem to occur.

Erectile Function

Evidence is strongest for a link between diabetes and erectile dysfunction. Impotence is the most common sexual dysfunction reported by men with diabetes, occurring in up to 50% of patients. It is at least three to five times more prevalent among diabetics than among the general population. Furthermore, these figures may well be underestimates because much sexual dysfunction in diabetic men goes unreported and many impotent men in the general population may be undiagnosed diabetics.

Chronology is important in determining whether impotence is reversible. Poor glycemic control is associated with impotence, which resolves when metabolic control is reattained. This temporary dysfunction is probably on a histochemical basis, involving sorbitol and water accumulation in autonomic nerve fibers. When erectile dysfunction evolves more slowly, becoming chronic, it is more likely organic and the result of permanent changes in the autonomic nerve fibers of the corpora cavernosa.

The strongest association with erectile dysfunction in diabetic men is the presence of autonomic neuropathy (Buvat et al., 1985; Ellenberg, 1971a, 1977a; Faerman, Jadzinsky, & Podolsky, 1980; Melman, Henry, Felten, & O'Connor, 1980). Indeed, impotence has been shown to occur in virtually all patients with other manifestations of diabetic autonomic neuropathy (Baum, Neiman, & Lewis, 1988; Faerman ct al., 1980; Melman et al., 1980). The presence of peripheral diabetic neuropathy is also associated with impotence possibly because of its common association with autonomic neuropathy (Kolodny, Kahn, Goldstein, & Barnett, 1974).

The significant role of neuropathy in diabetic impotence was confirmed by neurologic and urologic evaluation of 45 impotent diabetic men and 30 men with diabetes and intact erectile function (Ellenberg, 1971a). Of the 45 impotent subjects, 37 had neurogenic bladder abnormalities and 38 had neuropathy. In contrast, of the nonimpotent diabetics, only 3 had bladder involvement and 6 had neuropathy. In the same article, the author reported results of his survey of 200 diabetic men, which showed the same association: 59% were impotent and, of those men, 82% had neuropathy. Of the 41% of responders who were nonimpotent only 12% had neuropathy.

Histologic studies of autonomic nerve fibers of the corpora cavernosa at autopsy in five impotent diabetic males revealed anatomic changes consistent with autonomic neuropathy (Faerman, Glocer, Fox, Jadzinsky, & Rapaport, 1974). These changes were not found in the control group of nondiabetic, nonimpotent males. Another histologic study of these nerve fibers in 16 impotent male diabetics revealed anatomic integrity and a reduction in the normally dense concentration of the neurotransmitter norepinephrine (Melman et al.,1980).

Not all investigators agree that autonomic neuropathy is solely responsible for most cases of impotence in men with diabetes. In one study (Buvat et al., 1985), 52 diabetic males (of whom 48 were IDD) aged 21 to 55 years were questioned about their sexual function. All subjects were hospitalized for diabetes-related problems at the time of their participation in the study. The authors did not speculate on what effect their acute illnesses may have had on their responses. In addition, the requirement for hospitalization for diabetes-related complications suggests that the subjects may have had poorer than average control over their hyperglycemia. One-half of the men reported erectile impotence for at least 6 months and one-half reported normal function. The nonimpotent diabetic subjects had a significantly greater urine flow rate compared with the impotent subjects. A decrease in urine flow rate, an indirect measure of autonomic nervous system function, was not associated with prostatic hypertrophy. In addition, the Minnesota Multiphasic Personality Inventory (MMPI) was administered to the impotent group and found to be abnormal in 60% of the subjects. (A major design flaw was that the nonimpotent group did not take the MMPI.) Impotent men with normal MMPI scores often had abnormalities on arterial examination. Hence, the authors concluded that at least two factors may be necessary to produce impotence in a diabetic man: autonomic neuropathy and either psychogenic or arterial factors.

Especially in the older age group, arterial occlusive disease may be a cause of impotence. Occlusion of the terminal aorta (Leriche's syndrome) or of the common or internal iliac arteries may preclude penile vascular engorgement adequate for erection. *Microangiopathy*—atherosclerosis of smaller vessels, as indicated by the presence of nephropathy and retinopathy—is less clearly associated with erectile dysfunction in diabetic men. One study involving histopathologic autopsy study of impotent and nonimpotent diabetic men (Faerman et al., 1974) found no correlation between impotence and diabetic microangiopathy. In two larger studies of diabetic men with and without impotence (Buvat et al., 1985) erectile dysfunction was positively associated with microangiopathic changes.

Although it would seem logical that a positive relation would exist among impotence, age, and duration of diabetes, data are conflicting on this point. In the nondiabetic population, the prevalence of impotence clearly increases with age, with a sharp increase after age 60 years. The majority of studies of diabetic males have found a similar increase with age (Ellenberg, 1971b; Schoffling et al., 1963), with a sharp increase in cumulative incidence of impotence occurring earlier, at about age 50 years (Schoffling et al., 1963). In a study of 52 males with IDD, one-half with impotence and one-half without, mean ages were not significantly different (45 years in the impotent group and 37 in the nonimpotent group; Buvat et al., 1985). Several studies have shown no significant correlation between duration of diabetes and impotence (Ellenberg, 1971a, 1971b; Kolodny et al., 1974).

Hormonal factors appear to play little, if any, role in the development of sexual dysfunction in diabetic men. Impotent diabetic males have been shown to have normal plasma concentrations of testosterone, normal steroid biosynthesis by testicular tissue, and normal testicular histology and cellular morphology (Faerman et al., 1972). As expected, treatment of impotent diabetic men with testosterone has been ineffective (Ellenberg, 1971a).

Evaluation and Treatment of Erectile Dysfunction

Evaluation of a patient with diabetes mellitus and a history suggestive of organic impotence should consist, at a minimum, of a complete blood count, urinalysis, serum testosterone level, penile Doppler study, and an objective assessment of penile engorgement such as that provided by a Rigi-Scan device (Podolsky, 1982). If the history or physical examination suggests peripheral neuropathy, especially involving the second to fourth sacral nerve roots, comprehensive urodynamic studies should be performed to assess the sacral reflex arc, which is the common innervation of the bladder and the erectile tissue of the penis (Baum et al., 1988).

The most useful approach to the assessment and treatment of impotence in diabetic men is the biopsychosocial model (Meisler, Carey, Lantinga, & Krauss, 1989), which focuses not on identifying a single etiologic factor but, rather, on the interplay of predisposing, precipitating, and maintaining factors. For example, neuropathy is a predisposing factor that, together with the precipitating factor of a single episode of random erectile failure and the maintaining factor of performance anxiety, may result in a pattern of continuing dysfunction. Addressing only one of these factors will decrease the likelihood of therapeutic success.

Some men equate masculinity with erectile potency and are likely to experience severe loss of self-esteem with the inability to achieve erection. Practitioners should encourage those individuals and their sex partners to explore alternative methods for providing each other sexual pleasure and release. Lack of adequate penile tumescence for intercourse does not preclude orgastic ability. For those couples who feel that coitus is essential for their sexual expression, treatment of impotence is appropriate. This topic is discussed in detail in Chapter 22.

Orgasm

In men with diabetes mellitus, effects on ejaculation or orgasm are much less frequent than effects on erection and libido. Ejaculation results when impulses from the sympathetic nervous system reach the testes, epididymis, and vas deferens. Autonomic neuropathy appears to have a more pronounced effect on the parasympathetic nervous system, whose fibers control the erectile response. Orgastic and ejaculatory capacity usually continue even when the ability to achieve erection has been long absent. In a study of 80 diabetic men (Jensen, 1981), whereas 27 reported erectile dysfunction and 25 noted decreased libido, only 5 described any orgastic dysfunction. Of those 5 individuals, 3 had premature ejaculation and 2 had retarded ejaculation.

Another fairly frequent abnormality experienced at orgasm by diabetic men is *retrograde ejaculation,* the propulsion of seminal fluid through the posterior urethra retrograde into the urinary bladder. Retrograde ejaculation occurs because of dysfunction of the internal vesical sphincter as a result of diabetic neuropathy. The patient is aware of orgasm but there is no apparent ejaculate (Faerman et al., 1980).

Frequency of Activity

As the frequency of erectile dysfunction increases in diabetic men, the frequency of sexual activity can be expected to diminish as well. Jensen (1981) studied 80 males with IDD. Of those men, 46% reported coital activity once or twice a month or less frequently. By comparison, only 20% of controls reported sexual frequency of one to two times per month or less. Similarly, frequency of masturbation was lower in diabetic males than in controls, with 82.5% of the diabetic group reporting masturbation less than or equal to one to two times monthly, a frequency reported by only 45% of the control group.

The discrepancy between sexual desire and coital activity in couples in which the man was diabetic was found to be actually less than in couples where the man was not diabetic (Jensen, 1985). Whereas about 55% of diabetic men reported that their sexual desire was greater than their frequency of intercourse, 65% of nondiabetic men reported such a discrepancy. Of the nondiabetic men, 5% indicated that their frequency of intercourse exceeded their desire for it. None of the diabetic men reported they felt this way. Of the nondiabetic men, 30% and 45% of the diabetic men reported that their desire for sex and frequency of activity matched.

Satisfaction

Little research has focused on the effects of diabetic sexual dysfunction on satisfaction within sexual relationships. Although erectile dysfunction is estimated to occur in at least 50% of diabetic men, it cannot be assumed that this will directly correlate with dissatisfaction with their sex lives. If sex practices change in men with diabetes, the change may be the result of fatigue, medical comorbidities associated with diabetes, different sensations, psychological concerns, or any combination of these factors.

Among the emotions with an inhibitory effect on expression of sexuality are anxiety, fear, guilt, anger, and shame. A man may experience erectile dysfunction on the basis of organic factors but have the problem compounded by concerns about his sexual performance. As a result of such concerns, he may be less able to enjoy the sensory experience of intercourse because he constantly monitors the state of his penis. Such "spectatoring" may be amenable to techniques of sex therapy including genital stimulation with proscription of intercourse and concentration on feelings and sensations or on erotic fantasies during sexual activity.

Schmitt and Neubeck (1985) surveyed 77 men, aged 30 to 85 years (mean 51.6 years), to determine the effects of sexual function problems on marital relationships. Of this group, 64% controlled their diabetes with insulin, 15% were on oral medication, and 21% controlled their diabetes with diet alone. Furthermore, 81% were married or cohabitating, 10% were widowed or recently divorced, and 9% were single and never married. Of the men, 64% experienced some degree of erectile dysfunction; 71% of those men reported "severe" erectile difficulties (defined as inability to get an adequate erection 75% to 100% of the time). Of the 45 men in marital relationships who reported erectile dysfunction, 58% reported a negative effect on the relationship. Among the reported effects were a decline in sexual and nonsexual affection, refusal of the wife to participate in sexual activity with her spouse, withdrawal of the husband from sexual activity, and initiation of an extramarital sexual relationship by the husband or wife. Six couples experimented with different sexual techniques, usually involving more oral and manual stimulation. One couple divorced and another contemplated divorce because of the man's impotence.

Of the 42% of relationships in which erectile difficulties were present but not reported to have a negative impact, three common characteristics emerged. The men and their wives seemed to understand the etiologic connection between diabetes and erectile dysfunction, the problem was viewed as a problem of the couple—not just of the man—and all couples had a free and open style of communication about sexual matters.

Fertility

Men with diabetes experience a lower than expected rate of pregnancy among their female partners. Several explanations for this phenomenon have been proposed, any or all of which may be operational in any given individual. Besides the obvious association with inability to achieve erection and inability to impregnate, there are two other proposed mechanisms for the decreased fertility observed in this group: endocrine abnormalities and retrograde ejaculation.

Although most investigators have not found evidence of endocrine dysfunction in diabetic males (Ellenberg, 1971a; Kolodny et al., 1974), one study of diabetic men with impotence (Schoffling et al., 1963) found that two-thirds of the subjects had decreased urinary levels of gonadotropin. In those men, size of the testes and prostate were frequently less than normal. In addition, sperm counts were often low and there was an increased percentage of abnormal or dead sperm. Urinary levels of 17-ketosteroids were elevated, except for the fraction containing metabolites of testosterone. One-third of the men had low sperm counts and half had decreased fructose in the semen, indicating androgen deficiency. Testicular biopsy in 24 men demonstrated thickened basement membrane in the tubules along with abnormal spermatogenesis. Some men in this group were treated with chorionic gonadotropin and testosterone and later succeeded in impregnating their partners.

Semen volume decreases gradually in some diabetic men, so that eventually they may experience "dry orgasm" (Jensen, 1985). Analysis of the semen quality of 19 diabetic men (all of whom had diabetes for at least 12 years) revealed that 9 of the subjects produced no seminal fluid externally, despite normal orgasmic sensation (Klebanow & MacLeod, 1960). In 6 of those men, spermatozoa were found in the urine, but in a lesser quantity than associated with retrograde ejaculation. When ejaculation was present, semen quality in diabetic men controlled with insulin did not indicate serious disruption in spermatogenesis, although in half the subjects, somewhat diminished sperm motility was noted.

The clinician can confirm retrograde ejaculation by examining urine obtained after orgasm, which will reveal a large number of motile sperm. Treatment of retrograde ejaculation has been attempted by masturbation with a full bladder (Templeton & Mortimer, 1982). In the case study reported (Templeton & Mortimer, 1982), anterograde ejaculate was obtained with this method from a diabetic man who otherwise had only retrograde ejaculation. Although this method may not be effective in all patients, it is worth trying because it obviates problems with osmolality and acidity inherent in postmasturbation urine centrifugation to obtain a sperm specimen.

In a study of pregnancy outcomes (Babbott, Rubin, & Ginsburg, 1958), 167 diabetic men were interviewed and compared with a control group of nondiabetic men. There were no significant differences in the two populations with respect to number of conceptions, premature births, stillbirths, live births, sex ratio of off-spring, or birth weights. The partners of diabetic men, however, did demonstrate a significantly higher incidence of spontaneous abortion.

FEMALE SEXUALITY

The relationship between diabetes and female sexuality has been obscured by inappropriate comparisons with male sexuality. Although correlations exist be-tween the stages of sexual response in males and females (desire in both, erection in males and lubrication in females, and orgasm in females and orgasm plus ejacu-lation in males), it cannot be assumed that effects of diabetes on male sexuality will have an equivalent in female sexuality. As is true of the study of sexuality in general, there has been a paucity of objective experimental investigations into female sexuality and diabetes, compared with a relatively large literature on male sexuality. In the past, discussions of the effect of diabetes on female sexuality have almost exclusively involved fertility and reproductive health, essentially equating female sexual function with reproduction.

A few studies have concerned diabetic female sexuality (Ellenberg, 1977b; Jensen, 1981; Kolodny, 1971) but they are less than optimal and provide incon-sistent findings. Most researchers have relied on patient responses to question-naires. Few studies have used objective measurements of psychophysiologic response to erotic stimuli (Geer, Morokoff, & Greenwood, 1974; Slob, Koster, Radder, & Van der Werff ten Bosch, 1990). Unlike male sexual function in diabe-tes, in which erectile dysfunction clearly predominates, in female sexual func-tion, diabetes has been found to be associated with numerous, more varied, sexual concerns. There is a great need for standardized, controlled scientific investiga-tion into the female sexual response cycle.

The diagnosis of diabetes may have a very different impact on sexuality de-pending on the female patient's developmental stage. In childhood, poor diabetic control may be associated with delays in development including delayed menarche. An altered body image compared with peers can have a profound impact on the preadolescent female. Diabetes diagnosed during adolescence can make even more difficult the normal tasks of formation of personal and sexual identities, emanci-pation from parents, and exploration of vocational roles. In the adult years, con-cepts of sexuality evolve with marriage, reproduction, menopause, and old age. Development of diabetes during any of these periods further complicates the on-going process of sexual self-redefinition (Dunning, 1993).

Libido

Studies of libido in diabetic women, as with studies of libido in any group, are hampered by an inability to directly measure; instead, researchers must rely on self-reported, subjective data. In general, research on sexual desire uses different methods to define and measure libido, making comparisons among studies difficult. Hypoactive sexual desire is reported to be characteristic of diabetic women in some studies, but the prevalence is probably not much different from that in the general population (Spector, Leiblum, Carey, & Rosen, 1993).

Jensen (1981) found that 27% of female diabetic patients reported sexual dysfunction, compared with 25% of age-matched controls. The most frequently reported dysfunction in both groups was decreased libido. Another study (Schreiner-Engel, Schiavi, Vietorisz, Eichel, & Smith, 1985) found more sexual dysfunction in diabetic females compared with age-matched controls, with lower desire one of the difficulties experienced most often.

A study of 81 women with diabetes (Newman & Bertelson, 1986), all of whom used insulin, consisted of interviews and standardized questionnaires dealing with sexual function. The study did not include a control group of normal women. Of the women studied, 38 were diagnosed with sexual dysfunction; 17 of those women reported decreased sexual desire. More diabetic than nondiabetic women have been reported to experience sexual aversion, an extreme form of libido dysfunction (Young, Koch, & Bailey, 1989). In another study of 48 diabetic women (Campbell, Redelman, Borkman, McLay, & Chisholm, 1989), one-half reported one or more sexual dysfunctions, including decreased libido. In 17 of those patients, however, the dysfunction was present at the time of onset of diabetes.

Lubrication

Lubrication in women is analogous to erection in men as the initial physiologic indicator of the sexual response, the stage usually described as excitement. With sexual stimulation, there is marked dilation of the arteries and venous plexus surrounding the outer vagina. The increased vascular load results in a transudate, which coalesces in the form of a fluid, that is, vaginal lubrication. Because sexual dysfunction in male diabetics is primarily that of vasocongestion leading to erection, it has long been assumed that sexual dysfunction of diabetic women would be related to vasocongestion and lubrication associated with sexual arousal. Data have not consistently supported this assumption. Women with diabetes are more susceptible to vaginal infections, which can result in decreased lubrication, vaginal discharge, odor, itching, and tenderness. Urinary tract infections associated with vaginitis may add to their discomfort.

In a clinical and questionnaire study of 48 diabetic women, one-half reported one or more sexual dysfunctions, including inadequate lubrication, but no relationship existed between the presence of sexual dysfunction and duration of the disease, presence of neuropathy or other clinical complications, or recent control of diabetes (Campbell et al., 1989).

Two studies that did not distinguish between NIDD and IDD women (Leedom, Feldman, Procci, & Zeidler, 1991; Whitley & Berke, 1984) found that those women with neuropathy were more likely to have both decreased arousal and decreased lubrication. Along with lack of lubrication with intercourse and masturbation, all diabetic subjects were more likely than controls to report pain with intercourse. Those with duration of diabetes 6 years or more reported vaginal dryness almost six times more often than the group with diabetes for a shorter period (Whitley & Berke, 1984).

Jensen (1981) found that 25% of diabetic women reported inadequate lubrication, but noted that the problem did not necessarily result in sexual dysfunction, perhaps because a lack of lubrication is relatively easily compensated for. In his 6-year follow-up study of the same group of diabetic women, Jensen (1986) found that the number of women complaining of decreased lubrication had increased. In a study of 125 diabetic (including IDD and NIDD) women (Kolodny, 1971), 44 were nonorgasmic and only 6 reported any problem with lubrication. In contrast, in the nondiabetic control group in the Kolodny study, all of the nonorgasmic women reported difficulty with vaginal lubrication.

Obesity, which is common in women with NIDD, may have a beneficial effect on lubrication. There is an increased availability of estrogen, which is stored in fatty tissue. This hormonal environment reduces the likelihood of postmenopausal vaginal atrophy and decreased lubrication.

Two recent studies have provided physiologic data about arousal in women with diabetes mellitus. Albert and Wincze (1990) compared five women with IDD and five age-matched controls while they were viewing erotic videos. Results indicated that the diabetic women displayed significantly lower levels of vaginal blood flow than did the able-bodied subjects. However, the authors did not control for the presence of neuropathy in their subjects with IDD. Slob et al. (1990) used labia minora temperature to compare women with IDD and able-bodied, age-matched controls in the degree of vaginal responsiveness during the viewing of an erotic video. The women with diabetes were free from neuropathy and microangiopathy, and the authors hypothesized that this is why those diabetic women did not exhibit sexual dysfunction, whereas the subjects in the Albert and Wincze (1990) study did. However, the use of temperature-based methods to evaluate vaginal blood flow are potentially insensitive and not as well-established as vaginal plethysmography; therefore, it is recommended that women with IDD and varying combinations of neuropathy and microangiopathy be evaluated in a laboratory setting. It should be determined whether the vaginal pulse amplitude responses of women with diabetes mellitus are diminished and what associations with diabetic neuropathy or microangiopathy are present.

Orgasm

Along with libido and lubrication, orgasm has been widely studied as an indicator of sexual responsiveness in diabetic women. Some investigators have reported significantly greater secondary orgasmic failure in women with diabetes compared with women without diabetes (Campbell et al., 1989; Kolodny, 1971; Zrustova, Rostlaplil, & Kabrhelova, 1978), whereas others have shown no significant difference in orgasmic function between diabetic and nondiabetic women (Ellenberg, 1977b; Jensen, 1981). No clear consensus has emerged, and all studies have been limited by the subjective nature of self-reported data.

Kolodny (1971) studied 100 hospitalized nondiabetic controls and 125 women with IDD and NIDD between the ages of 18 and 42 years, who were hospitalized for complications of diabetes. Of the women with diabetes, 35% were nonorgasmic. Most of them (91%) had at one time been able to achieve orgasm. All experienced orgasmic dysfunction after the onset of their diabetes, gradually losing orgasmic capacity over 6 to 12 months. In contrast, only 6% of the nondiabetic group was nonorgasmic, and none of these women had ever experienced orgasm. Although this study is notable, questions about sexual function are not ideally asked during an acute illness requiring hospitalization, an obvious problem with the study design.

Moreover, Zrustova et al. (1978) found that 33% of a group of diabetic women were unable to achieve orgasm; in all subjects, loss of sexual responsiveness occurred after the development of diabetes mellitus. The same investigators performed necropsy examination of clitoral nerves and found characteristic changes of autonomic neuropathy in young diabetic women, whereas similar changes were found only in the most elderly subjects of the nondiabetic control group at autopsy.

Ellenberg (1977b) studied 100 diabetic women aged 20 to 74 years and found no significant differences in orgasmic ability among the diabetic women with and without neuropathy, compared with the general population of nondiabetic women. In this group, there was a correlation between libido and capacity for orgasm, with none of the women who had lost orgasmic function retaining libido. Leedom et al. (1991), who did not differentiate between IDD and NIDD women, found that subjects with neuropathy experienced significantly more symptoms of sexual dysfunction, including orgasmic dysfunction, than those without neuropathy. Confounding factors in that study included more depression and longer duration of diabetes among the women with neuropathy.

In a study of a population of people with diabetes over time (Faerman et al., 1972), the female diabetic patients surveyed 6 years apart showed about the same pattern of sexual dysfunction, despite presumed progression of the disease. This finding was similar to that for the male diabetics in the group. Orgasmic dysfunction was relatively uncommon at baseline (10%) and at 6 years (14%).

Frequency of Activity

Most studies on diabetes and female sexuality have not addressed frequency of sexual activity. Jensen (1981), in his study of 80 female and 80 male patients with IDD (mean age of males was 35.8 years; mean age of females, 35.3 years; mean duration of diabetes, 15 years), did examine the frequency of coitus and masturbation. The diabetic group and the control group showed no difference in age at first coitus, which was 17 years. Among diabetic women, 95% masturbated once or twice a month or less, whereas all diabetic women reporting sexual dysfunction reported a masturbation frequency of once or twice a month or less. This was not different from the masturbation frequency of the control group, in which 95% engaged in masturbation once or twice a month or less. Coital activity occurring as infrequently as one to two times per month or less was reported in 31% of diabetic women and only 15% of the control group.

Satisfaction

Women may be more likely than men to focus on the subjective interpersonal quality of their sexual relationships, being less concerned with specific complaints of inadequate physiologic response during sexual activity. However, research into the effects of diabetes on female sexuality has almost exclusively emphasized the physiologic response and paid little attention to the issue of overall satisfaction. The presence of altered sexual function does not necessarily correlate with loss of sexual satisfaction.

Young et al. (1989) found no difference in marital satisfaction between diabetic and nondiabetic women. However, the women in the diabetic group described themselves as moderately healthy with few complications, and their view of themselves as healthy may have protected them from the marital discord that can result from assumption of the sick role. In contrast, low levels of marital satisfaction have been found to correlate with sexual dysfunction in diabetic women (Newman & Bertelson, 1986; Schreiner-Engel et al., 1985). Compared with controls, 15 women with NIDD and 35 women with IDD had lower sexual desire and overall sexual function (Schreiner-Engel et al., 1985).

In a popular culture that idealizes thinness, obesity may have a negative impact on body image and feelings of sexual attractiveness. Women with NIDD are often obese. In addition to their own feelings of sexual unattractiveness and dissatisfaction with their bodies, they may experience reduced sexual interest on the part of their partners, particularly if the weight gain occurred after the relationship was established (Spector et al., 1993). An exception to this association has been found among African American women with diabetes, in whom there is a significant positive relationship between body mass index and sexual satisfaction (Watts, 1994). This finding suggests that obesity, in the African American cultural context, is not a deterrent to expression and enjoyment of sexuality.

Fertility and Pregnancy

Diabetes presents challenges in the areas of contraception, fertility, successful pregnancy outcome, and long-term health of the children of women with diabetes. Excellent control of blood glucose levels before and during pregnancy is critical for the health of the diabetic woman and her developing child. Gestational diabetes is a type of the disease that occurs during pregnancy, usually resolves with delivery, but tends to develop into NIDD in later years. Gestational diabetes is most common in women older than age 30 years who are overweight and have a family history of NIDD.

Traditionally, women with diabetes have been advised to use barrier methods of contraception and have not been considered candidates for oral contraceptive use, because of the increased risk of complications. Women who have had gestational diabetes and who want to use oral contraception should receive only combination estrogen–progestin formulations with the lowest dose of progestin available to avoid raising their risk of developing NIDD. Monitoring of blood pressure, blood glucose, and cholesterol levels should be performed three to four times a year in these women (Kjos, 1996).

Although fertility in the diabetic female is only slightly subnormal, the chance of pregnancy in a diabetic woman resulting in a live birth is decreased (Williams, 1981). Women with diabetes must develop excellent control of their blood glucose levels before conception to reduce the risk of miscarriage and birth defects often associated with diabetic pregnancies, as well as development of diabetes complications. Women who already have neuropathy, nephropathy, or retinopathy warrant particularly close monitoring during pregnancy. *Gastroparesis* (slowed stomach emptying resulting from autonomic neuropathy) is especially problematic during pregnancy because it can lead to excessive vomiting and the need for intravenous nutrition. Among women with kidney disease, it is essential to control both blood glucose and blood pressure to optimize the pregnancy outcome. The choice of antihypertensive drugs is critical because some can adversely affect the fetus or glucose control. Women with severe kidney disease may need multiple medications to control their hypertension during pregnancy. Among women with retinopathy, it is important to identify and treat any abnormal blood vessels in the eye before conception. If blood glucose control is optimized and neovascularization is treated before pregnancy, retinopathy usually does not progress during pregnancy (Kitzmiller, 1996).

If blood sugar is poorly controlled, the embryo is subject to a hostile metabolic environment from the moment of conception. Gestational diabetes develops later during pregnancy, subjects the fetus to a shorter period of potential metabolic derangement, and will not affect organ development in the embryonic period. Both categories of diabetes, however, can cause *macrosomia* (increased fetal size and weight, potentially complicating delivery) and birth defects, including congenital heart disease, kidney disease, poorly developed colon, and central nervous system and spinal deformities (Hare, 1994). In the neonatal period, infants of diabetic mothers are likely to have metabolic derangements, including abnormally low levels of blood glucose, magnesium, and calcium. Respiratory distress syndrome is more likely to develop in these infants, even when full term, because of delayed lung maturation (Moya, 1985).

Exposure to maternal diabetes by the fetus may present long-term health problems that are not manifest until later in childhood or even into adulthood. Children of diabetic mothers tend to be overweight, have impaired glucose tolerance, and have elevated blood pressure, factors that predispose to the development of cardiovascular disease in adulthood. Furthermore, if the mother's diabetes was poorly controlled during pregnancy, there may be increased risk of learning disabilities in the child (Silverman, 1996).

Further discussion of the issues of pregnancy and diabetes is beyond the scope of this book. For more information, health care providers and people with diabetes should contact the American Diabetes Association, a voluntary health organization supporting diabetes research, information, and advocacy. It has an affiliate office in every state and can be accessed on the Internet at http://www.diabetes.org.

AMPUTATION

The loss of a limb is divided into two broad categories: congenital and acquired. Acquired amputation may be the result of disease, tumor, or trauma. The exact prevalence of amputation is unknown, but the National Center for Health Statistics estimated that, in 1990, there were 1,232,000 people in the United States with major limb loss (Leonard & Meier, 1993). Approximately 160,000 amputations are performed annually in the United States, with the majority involving the lower extremity. Levels of amputation are now classified according to skeletal structures affected: below knee is known as *transtibial*; above knee, *transfemoral*; below elbow, *transradial*; above elbow, *transhumeral*; through the joint, *disarticulation*.

In the upper limb, trauma is the leading cause of acquired amputation (approximately 75%) and occurs most often in men aged 15 to 45 years (Leonard & Meier, 1993). Disease and tumor are responsible for equal numbers of the remaining surgical amputations. In the lower limb, complications of vascular disease and diabetes account for 75% of all acquired amputations; trauma (20%) and tumor (5%) account for the remainder. In the pediatric age group, tumor is the most common cause of upper and lower limb amputations.

Psychological adaptation to amputation has been described as proceeding through four predictable stages (Bradway, Malone, Racy, Leal, & Poole, 1984). The first is the preoperative stage, when the patient begins to realize that the loss of a limb is a possibility. Grief is a universal reaction to this news. The patient may have questions about future functional capabilities as well as concerns about pain, general health, and body image. The second stage begins in the immediate postoperative period with the patient's first realization that the limb is no longer present. The third stage is a transitional one that, for many patients, occurs during inpatient rehabilitation. The amputee may experience denial, grieve for the lost limb, and experience difficulty interacting with friends and relatives. This is a preparatory phase for reintegration back into the community with a new disability. The fourth stage begins with the patient's return home. Out of the hospital environment, there may be an abrupt decrease in supportive help.

Health care providers should seek out the amputee's sexual concerns at each of these four stages. Patients will vary in their readiness to discuss sexual issues. It is important for members of the treatment team to implicitly grant permission for discussion by bringing up the subject of sexuality and not waiting for the patient to initiate questions. Evidence suggests that few amputees receive any information or advice from health care providers about how amputation may affect their sexuality. A recent study of the impact of amputation on sexuality (Williamson & Walters, 1996) indicated that fewer than 10% of participants received information on sexuality. Those who reported having received information were more likely to be well-educated white males who may well have initiated the discussion with direct and pertinent questions. One factor that probably contributes to the lack of discussion of sexuality is the advanced age of many amputees. People older than age 60 years account for 85% of all amputations. Societal views of aging individuals often involve a denial of the importance of sexuality in their lives and their interest in continuing sexual activity. Research has not supported this perception. Rather, it has indicated that substantial numbers of men and women report sexual interest, availability, and activity with a partner into older adulthood (Hallstrom & Samuelsson, 1990; Mulligan & Palguta, 1991; O'Donohue, 1987; Schover, 1989).

In the early postoperative period, residual limb pain and incomplete healing may be problematic. *Neuromas* (proliferation of the transected end of a nerve) may become quite painful when involved in scar tissue and may be subject to tension and pressure from the prosthesis or during the course of sexual contact. Phantom limb sensations are universal in acquired amputation and have been described in congenitally limb-deficient individuals as well. The health care provider should explain to the patient that these sensations are normal and expected, and that their natural course is to disappear gradually over time. Phantom limb pain, that is, the perception of noxious sensation in the amputated portion of the limb, is fortunately less common. It can be mild and intermittent or severe and virtually constant. Successful treatment depends on early diagnosis and aggressive intervention with physical modalities and pharmacologic therapy. As with any chronic pain condition, the presence of phantom limb pain can significantly interfere with sexual interest and activity.

Loss of motion also can be problematic for amputees engaging in sexual activity. Preservation of the knee joint is helpful in maintaining balance in coital positions. For transfemoral amputees, positioning with pillows can help maintain stability (Buckwalter, Wernimont, & Buckwalter, 1982). Individuals with an upper limb amputation may have difficulty with supporting the upper body in some positions. They may prefer a side-lying position for intercourse, thereby permitting free movement of their intact arm.

Adults with amputation also may experience depression, which may persist for many years. On a standardized depression inventory (Rybarczyk, Nyenhuis, Nicholas, Cash, & Kaiser, 1995), 28% of amputees (an average of 17 years postamputation) scored in the clinically depressed range. Perceived social stigma, low social support, and poor body image all independently correlated with depression in those patients.

Regardless of the reason for amputation, amputees must deal with the deficiency of a limb and loss of body wholeness. Furthermore, if the amputation was necessary because of a malignancy, the amputee likely will be concerned about possible recurrence. Treatment by either chemotherapy or radiation may have transient or permanent effects that can impact sexuality (Shell, 1989). Similarly, with diabetes or vascular disease, there is always the possibility of progression of the disease and future need for more extensive amputation.

Successful prosthetic use with an optimal functional outcome helps to restore an intact body image and a sense of mastery of the environment, both of which are integral to expression of sexuality. Resumption of usual sexual activity also reinforces feelings of attractiveness and wholeness, which can contribute to better integration of the prosthesis into the amputee's daily life.

Male Sexual Response

Little has been written about sexuality following amputation. Individuals with amputations secondary to diabetes or arterial occlusive disease may have concomitant sexual dysfunction as a result of the underlying disease. The amputation itself interferes with sexual function because it affects physical comfort and positioning, but, much more fundamentally, it affects psychological health. The few studies on amputation and sexuality have focused on frequency of and satisfaction with sexual activity (Kegel, Carpenter, & Burgess, 1978; Reinstein, Ashley, & Miller, 1978; Williamson & Walters, 1996). One survey (Medhat, Huber, & Medhat, 1990), which compared sexual adjustment between transtibial and transfemoral amputees (but did not make a comparison with a control group of individuals without amputation), found no significant difference in sexual desire between the two groups.

In a study of 39 male amputees (Reinstein et al., 1978), all of whom had fairly recent amputations and who were independent prosthetic users, 77% reported a substantial decrease in frequency of sexual intercourse. The decrease in frequency of sexual activity was greater in men who were unmarried, in those experiencing phantom pain, and in those with amputation at the transfemoral level. Perhaps surprisingly, no relationship was found between decreased sexual activity and the etiology of amputation, although it might be expected that men with coexisting diabetes or vascular disease would have more sexual difficulty. Furthermore, there was no change postamputation in the frequency of masturbation or oral–genital sex, or in the incidence of homosexual or extramarital sexual activity. When comparing frequency of sexual activity between transtibial and transfemoral amputees, Medhat et al. (1990) found no significant difference between the groups; however, they also did not compare those amputees with nonamputees.

In a recent study of 51 male and 25 female amputees (Williamson & Walters, 1996), more than 75% of respondents reported that their sexual activities were at least somewhat restricted since their amputation, with 10% reporting cessation of sexual activity since amputation. Nevertheless, more than 60% described their current sexual activity level as either "very active" or "moderately active." One-third were at least somewhat dissatisfied with the frequency of sex since amputation. In general, older amputees were less likely to be unhappy with their frequency of sexual activity. Interestingly, of the only seven individuals who had been provided with advice about sexual activity after amputation, none felt that their amputation had greatly restricted sexual activity.

Level of limb loss appears to be significant in those amputees who have reported sexual difficulty after amputation. A survey by Kegel et al. (1978) examined level of activity in 131 people with lower limb amputation. The authors found that sexual activity was not a serious problem for those patients: 65% reported no change in their sexual function as a result of amputation. Of those surveyed, 20% either did not answer or felt the question did not apply to them (e.g., children and elderly widowers living alone). The 15% who said they were affected included 8% of transtibial, 22% of transfemoral, and 35% of bilateral amputees. Unfortunately, the authors provided no details on the nature of the impact on sexuality.

When questioned about the satisfaction with the *quality* of sexual activity since amputation, more than 20% were to some degree dissatisfied (Williamson & Walters, 1996). This is fewer than the 30% who reported some degree of dissatisfaction with the *frequency* of their sexual activity. In the study, age was found to be significantly correlated with decreased satisfaction with sexual quality.

Unlike diabetes with its multiple systemic effects, the state of limb deficiency as a result of amputation would be expected to have no direct effect on either erectile or orgasmic capacity. However, those patients with diabetes, vascular disease, or who are elderly may have erectile dysfunction because of these other causes. Indirect psychosocial effects certainly are operative and may also interfere with ability to attain erection and orgasm. Medhat et al. (1990) did find that transfemoral amputees were more likely to have problems achieving orgasm than transtibial amputees.

Male Fertility

A review of the literature reveals no discussion of amputation and male fertility. Again, although no metabolic reason for alteration in fertility may exist in this population, it cannot be assumed that men with amputation have the same reproductive experience as men without this impairment. Research is needed in this area, as in many neglected areas of disability and sexuality.

Female Sexual Response

Not unexpectedly, in keeping with the relative dearth of knowledge of female sexual function, even less information exists about female sexuality in the context of amputation than exists about male sexuality. Studies that have examined male and female sexual response have tended to have more male subjects because of the demographics of amputation, with more men than women affected. Perhaps even more than their male counterparts, women experiencing amputation have apprehension about their body image and attractiveness. Depending on the woman's style of dress, the prosthesis may be more apparent to the casual observer; consequently, the female amputee may feel she is constantly "on display."

One survey (Medhat et al., 1990) of sexual adjustment in amputees found that only 38% of female amputees reported a decreased frequency of sexual intercourse, compared with 77% of male amputees. This finding may be due in part to the distribution of levels of amputation in the two groups. Of the 21 female amputees, 13 had transtibial amputation; 4, transfemoral; and 4, bilateral. Among the 39 males, 19 were transtibial amputees; 13, transfemoral; 2, hip disarticulation; and 5, bilateral. Thus, a greater percentage of the male group had higher levels of multiple amputation, which has been correlated with more sexual difficulty. In their article on marital–sexual adjustment of amputees, Mourad and Chiu (1974) made the following statement, which reflects the then-prevalent thinking on female sexuality, and probably still represents the beliefs of many people: "Because of the female's relatively passive role in sexual acts, there are very little physical difficulties they will experience. We are often amazed by the rare incidence of marital difficulty after amputation."

Except for the highest levels of amputation, such as the transpelvic or translumbar, amputation in the female does not significantly interfere with sexual activity in the supine, prone, or side-lying positions. Standing or kneeling postures for sexual activity can be achieved either by wearing the prosthesis or by using the upper limbs and pillows for balance and positioning. In the supine position, the amputee may use pillows as needed to maintain a level pelvis. Hip flexion contracture in the transfemoral amputee may interfere with prone positioning. In the transpelvic amputee, there may be extra folds of skin. A compression sock can be used to mold these skinfolds into a hiplike shape. An area of the sock can then be removed to allow exposure of the genitals (Buckwalter et al., 1982).

Female Fertility and Pregnancy

Menstruation and fertility are unaffected by amputation except at the high and extremely infrequently performed transpelvic or translumbar level. This radical surgery involves loss of the pelvic organs. Upper limb amputation has implications in terms of contraception use. The female amputee with upper limb involvement may need assistance to insert a diaphragm or to check on intrauterine device placement. With concomitant vascular disease or diabetes, oral contraceptives may be relatively or absolutely contraindicated (Campion, 1990).

Research is needed in the area of female reproductive function in amputation; to date, no studies have addressed this issue. In the absence of such studies, health care providers have only extrapolations from other populations that do not necessarily reflect the reproductive experience of women with amputation.

CONCLUSION

Diabetes and amputation have potentially profound effects on every level of human sexual function. Although clinical studies are few in number and often limited in design, they do indicate a need for vigilance on the part of the health care provider to anticipate, recognize, prevent, educate about, and treat sexual dysfunction in this population at risk.

REFERENCES

Albert, A., & Wincze, J.P. (1990). *Sexual arousal in diabetic females: A psychophysiological investigation.* Unpublished manuscript, Brown University, Providence, RI.

Babbott, D., Rubin, A., & Ginsburg, S.J. (1958). Reproductive characteristics of diabetic men. *Diabetes, 7*(1), 33–35.

Baum, N., Neiman, M., & Lewis, R. (1988). Evaluation and treatment of organic impotence in the male with diabetes mellitus. *Diabetes Educator, 14*(2), 123–129.

Bradway, J.K., Malone, J.M., Racy, J., Leal, J.M., & Poole, J. (1984). Psychological adaptation to amputation: An overview. *Orthotics and Prosthetics, 38*(3), 46–50.

Buckwalter, K.C., Wernimont, T., & Buckwalter, J.A. (1982). Musculoskeletal conditions and sexuality (part II). *Sexuality and Disability, 5*(5), 195–207.

Buvat, J., Lemaire, A., Buvat-Herbaut, M., Guidu, J.D., Bailleul, J.P., & Fossati, P. (1985). Comparative investigations in 26 impotent and 26 nonimpotent diabetic patients. *Journal of Urology, 133,* 34–38.

Campbell, L.V., Redelman, M.J., Borkman, M., McLay, J.G., & Chisholm, D.J. (1989). Factors in sexual dysfunction in diabetic female volunteer subjects. *Medical Journal of Australia, 151,* 550–552.

Campion, M.J. (1990). First steps in deciding to start a family. In M.J. Campion (Ed.), *The baby challenge: A handbook on pregnancy for women with a physical disability* (pp. 3–14). London: Tavistock/Routledge.

Dunning, P. (1993). Sexuality and women with diabetes. *Patient Education and Counseling, 21,* 5–14.

Ellenberg, M. (1971a). Impotence in diabetes: The neurologic factor. *Annals of Internal Medicine, 75,* 213–219.

Ellenberg, M. (1971b). Sex and diabetes: A comparison between men and women. *Diabetes Care, 2*(1), 4–8.

Ellenberg, M. (1977a). Diabetic neuropathy: Present and future trends. In J.S. Bajaj (Ed.), *Diabeta* (pp. 643–648). Amsterdam: Excerpta Medica.

Ellenberg, M. (1977b). Sexual aspects of the female diabetic. *Mount Sinai Journal of Medicine, 44,* 495–499.

Faerman, I., Glocer, L., Fox, D., Jadzinsky, M.N., & Rapaport, M. (1974). Impotence and diabetes: Histological studies of the autonomic nervous fibers of the corpora cavernosa in impotent diabetic males. *Diabetes, 23*(12), 971–976.

Faerman, I., Jadzinsky, M., & Podolsky, S. (1980). Diabetic neuropathy and sexual dysfunction. In S. Podolsky (Ed.), *Clinical diabetes: Modern management* (pp. 306–316). New York: Appleton-Century-Crofts.

Faerman, I., Vilar, O., Rivarola, A., Rosner, J.M., Jadzinsky, M.N., Fox, D., Perez Lloret, A., Bernstein-Hahn, L., & Saraceni, D. (1972). Impotence and diabetes: Studies of androgenic function in diabetic impotent males. *Diabetes, 21*(1), 23–30.

Geer, J.H., Morokoff, P., & Greenwood, P. (1974). Sexual arousal in women: The development of a measurement device for vaginal blood volume. *Archives of Sexual Behavior, 3*(6), 559–564.

Hallstrom, T., & Samuelsson, S. (1990). Changes in women's sexual desire in middle life: The longitudinal study of women in Gothenberg [Sweden]. *Archives of Sexual Behavior, 19*(3), 259–267.

Hare, J.W. (1994). Diabetes and pregnancy. In C.R. Kahn & G.C. Weir (Eds.), *Joslin's diabetes mellitus* (pp. 889–899). Philadelphia: Lea & Febiger.

Jensen, S.B. (1981). Diabetic sexual dysfunction: A comparative study of 160 insulin treated diabetic men and women and an age-matched control group. *Archives of Sexual Behavior, 10*(6), 493–504.

Jensen, S.B. (1985). Sexual relationships in couples with a diabetic partner. *Journal of Sex and Marital Therapy, 11*(4), 259–270.

Jensen, S.B. (1986). Sexual dysfunction in insulin-treated diabetics: A six-year follow-up study of 101 patients. *Archives of Sexual Behavior, 15*(3), 271–283.

Karan, J.H., & Forsham, P.H. (1994). Pancreatic hormones and diabetes mellitus. In F.S. Greenspan & J.D. Baxter (Eds.), *Basic and clinical endocrinology*. Norwalk, CT: Appleton & Lange.

Kegel, B., Carpenter, M.L., & Burgess, E.M. (1978). Functional capabilities of lower extremity amputees. *Archives of Physical Medicine and Rehabilitation, 59,* 109–120.

Kinsey, A.C., Pomeroy, W.B., & Martin, C.E. (1948). *Sexual behavior in the human male.* Philadelphia: W.B. Saunders.

Kitzmiller, J.L. (1996, June). *Recommendations for pregnant diabetic women with complications.* Paper presented at the 56th annual scientific sessions of the American Diabetes Association, San Francisco, CA.

Kjos, S.L. (1996, June). *Contraceptive guidelines for women with diabetes.* Paper presented at the 56th annual scientific sessions of the American Diabetes Association, San Francisco, CA.

Klebanow, D., & MacLeod, J. (1960). Semen quality and certain disturbances of reproduction in diabetic men. *Fertility and Sterility, 11,* 255–261.

Kolodny, R.C. (1971). Sexual dysfunction in diabetic females. *Diabetes, 20*(7), 557–559.

Kolodny, R.C., Kahn, C.B., Goldstein, H.H., & Barnett, D.M. (1974). Sexual dysfunction in diabetic men. *Diabetes, 23*(4), 306–309.

Leedom, L., Feldman, M., Procci, W., & Zeidler, A. (1991). Symptoms of sexual dysfunction and depression in diabetic women. *Journal of Diabetic Complications, 5*(1), 38–41.

Leonard, J.A., Jr., & Meier, R.H., III. (1993). Upper and lower extremity prosthetics. In J.A. DeLisa (Ed.), *Rehabilitation medicine: Principles and practice* (2nd ed., pp. 507–508). Philadelphia: J.B. Lippincott.

Medhat, A., Huber, P.M., & Medhat, M.A. (1990). Factors that influence the level of activities in persons with lower extremity amputation. *Rehabilitation Nursing, 15*(1), 13–18.

Meisler, A.W., Carey, M.P., Lantinga, L.J., & Krauss, D.J. (1989). Erectile dysfunction in diabetes mellitus: A biopsychosocial approach to etiology and assessment. *Annals of Behavioral Medicine, 11*(1), 18–27.

Melman, A., Henry, D.P., Felten, D.L., & O'Connor, B. (1980). Effect of diabetes upon penile sympathetic nerves in impotent patients. *Southern Medical Journal, 73*(3), 307–317.

Mourad, M., & Chiu, W.S. (1974, February). Marital-sexual adjustment of amputees. *Medical Aspects of Human Sexuality,* 47–57.

Moya, F.R. (1985). Infants born to diabetic mothers. *Medical Aspects of Human Sexuality, 19,* 30–40.

Mulligan, T., & Palguta, R. (1991). Sexual interest, activity, and satisfaction among male nursing home residents. *Archives of Sexual Behavior, 20*(2), 199–204.

Newman, A.S., & Bertelson, A.D. (1986). Sexual dysfunction in diabetic women. *Journal of Behavioral Medicine, 9*(3), 261–270.

O'Donohue, W.T. (1987). The sexual behavior and problems of the elderly. In L. Carstensen & B. Edelstein (Eds.), *Handbook of clinical gerontology* (pp. 66–75). New York: Pergamon.

Podolsky, S. (1982). Diagnosis and treatment of sexual dysfunction in the male diabetic. *Medical Clinics of North America, 66*(6), 1389–1395.

Reinstein, L., Ashley, J., & Miller, K.H. (1978). Sexual adjustment after lower extremity amputation. *Archives of Physical Medicine and Rehabilitation, 59,* 501–504.

Rybarczyk, B., Nyenhuis, D.L., Nicholas, J.J., Cash, S.M., & Kaiser, J. (1995). Body image, perceived social stigma, and the prediction of psychosocial adjustment to leg amputation. *Rehabilitation Psychology, 40*(2), 95–110.

Schmitt, G.S., & Neubeck, G. (1985). Diabetes, sexuality, and family functioning. *Family Relations, 34,* 109–113.

Schoffling, K., Federlin, K., Ditschuneit, H., & Pfeiffer, E.F. (1963). Disorders of sexual function in male diabetics. *Diabetes, 12*(6), 519–527.

Schover, L.R. (1989). Sexual problems in chronic illness. In S.R. Leiblum & R.C. Rosen (Eds.), *Principles and practice of sex therapy: Update for the 90s* (2nd ed., pp., 319–351). New York: Guilford Press.

Schreiner-Engel, P., Schiavi, R.C., Vietorisz, D., Eichel, J.D., & Smith, H. (1985). Diabetes and female sexuality: A comparison study of women in relationships. *Journal of Sex and Marital Therapy, 11*(3), 165–175.

Shell, J. (1989). Sexual rehabilitation of the amputee. *Oncology Nursing Forum, 16*(1), 105–106.

Silverman, B.L. (1996, June). *Lifetime risks for offspring of diabetic women.* Paper presented at the 56th annual scientific sessions of the American Diabetes Association, San Francisco, CA.

Slob, A.K., Koster, J., Radder, J.K., & Van der Werff ten Bosch, J.J. (1990). Sexuality and psychophysiological functioning in women with diabetes mellitus. *Journal of Sex and Marital Therapy, 16*(2), 59–69.

Spector, I.P., Leiblum, S.R., Carey, M.P., & Rosen, R.C. (1993). Diabetes and female sexual function: A critical review. *Annals of Behavioral Medicine, 15*(4), 257–264.

Templeton, A., & Mortimer, D. (1982). Successful circumvention of retrograde ejaculation in an infertile diabetic man. *British Journal of Obstetrics and Gynaecology, 89,* 1064–1065.

Watts, R.J. (1994). Sexual function of diabetic and nondiabetic African American women: A pilot study. *Journal of the National Black Nurses Association, 7*(1), 50–59.

Whitley, M., & Berke, P. (1984). Sexuality and diabetes. In N.F. Woods (Ed.), *Human sexuality in health and illness* (pp. 328–340). St. Louis, MO: C.V. Mosby.

Williams, R.H. (Ed.). (1981). *Textbook of endocrinology.* Philadelphia: W.B. Saunders.

Williamson, G.M., & Walters, A.S. (1996). Perceived impact of limb amputation on sexual activity: A study of adult amputees. *Journal of Sex Research, 33*(3), 221–230.

Young, E.W., Koch, P.B., & Bailey, D. (1989). Research comparing the dyadic adjustment and sexual functioning concerns of diabetic and nondiabetic women. *Health Care for Women International, 10,* 377–394.

Zrustova, M., Rostlaplil, J., & Kabrhelova, A. (1978). Sexual disorders in diabetic women. *Csekoslovak Gynekologika, 43,* 277–281.

CHAPTER 16

Cardiac and Pulmonary Disease

Todd P. Stitik and Barbara T. Benevento

Because participation in a sexual relationship is an important determinant of most adults' quality of life, any condition that disrupts sexuality can have an important far-reaching effect on a patient. Of all the chronic cardiac conditions, coronary artery disease (CAD) is most known for its potential to interfere with sexual function. As a result of improved medical and surgical management of CAD, life expectancy after an acute myocardial infarction (MI) has increased over the past decade (Blocker, 1995). Thus, CAD now has the ever-increasing capability of leading to premature cessation of a couple's sexual relationship. Fortunately, the effects of CAD on sexuality as well as potential treatment strategies of sexual dysfunction are now being explored in some detail. Yet, many myths concerning this issue still exist and some are still widespread.

ALTERED SEXUAL FUNCTION WITH CARDIAC DISEASE

Although researchers have generally agreed that sexual activity—at least initially—tends to decline after an acute cardiac event, the literature on the eventual return to sexual activity is encouraging. Studies have estimated the return to sexual activity in several different ways. Specifically, some studies have examined the frequency of intercourse by quantifying the number of sexual encounters, others have looked at the percentage of patients resuming sexual activity, whereas others have described the average time to return to sexual activity. Some studies have reported on a combination of these measures.

Frequency of sexual activity has been examined in both males and females. Several studies involving large patient groups consisting of men who were status post-MI showed that 40% to 70% had both diminished frequency and quality of sexual activity (Blocker, 1995). As is true for almost all aspects of heart disease, statistics on the return to sexual activity by women after an acute MI have traditionally been limited compared with those for men. For example, as recently as 1993, only one study (Papadopoulos, Beaumont, Shelley, & Larrimore, 1983) focused exclusively on women. The authors of that study found that, of 130 women who had suffered an MI, 44% demonstrated decreased frequency of intercourse, frequency did not change in 27%, and another 27% became completely abstinent. Pooled data from other studies has shown that frequency of sexual activity after an MI is quite similar to that of the male population (Papadopoulos, Larrimore, Cardin, & Shelley, 1980). A study of 107 post-MI males found that, although 53% had resumed previous levels of intercourse, 43% showed a decline, and only 4% had an increase in sexual activity (Amsterdam, Amsterdam, Riggs, DeMaria, & Mason, 1977).

Not only is it important to know frequency of sexual activity post-MI, but it is important to know when activity resumes. Another interview study of 100 married male veterans, at 6 months postdischarge after an MI (Mehta & Krops, 1979) reported that 30% of the men had not resumed intercourse and 24% had not resumed any shared sexual activity. A descriptive survey of 20 women and 42 men who were sexually active before an acute MI (Hamilton & Seidman, 1993) was undertaken to determine when people resumed sexual activity post-MI. Findings indicated that all subjects resumed sexual activity after an average of 8 weeks. In another prospective randomized clinical trial on the effect of adding a teaching–counseling program to a traditional exercise-based cardiac rehabilitation program compared with both a traditional program and a control group (Froelicher, Kee, Newton, Lindskog, & Livingston, 1994), it was found that, of 219 male and 39 female patients who returned to sexual activity, most did so by 12 weeks.

A classic study by Hellerstein and Friedman (1970) examined several measures of sexual function. By 1 year post-MI, the return to sexual activity was found to be approximately 80% of what it was before the illness and most study patients reported at least some sexual encounters. Of the patients who returned to sexual activity, 42% returned to the same level of intercourse, whereas 58% showed some decline in activity. Of that 58%, however, 25% reported an improvement in the actual quality of sexual performance. Those patients who resumed having sex did so at roughly the 14-week postevent mark. Papadopoulos (1978) also studied the time to return to intercourse and the percentage of patients returning. He found that 25% of patients returned to sexual activity from 2 weeks to 12 months after the event. He also pointed out an interesting trend of earlier return to sexual activity. Specifically, before 1970, the average time to return was 16 weeks, whereas after 1970, it had diminished to 8 to 9 weeks.

Even before the cardiac patient is overtly aware of his or her disease, sexual dysfunction might be present at a level that is higher than that in the general population. In an interview of 131 male cardiac patients, two-thirds reported significant sexual dysfunction before their cardiac event. Premorbid problems included impotence (64%), decreased frequency of intercourse (28%), and premature ejaculation (8%; Wabrek & Burchell, 1980). In another survey involving 100 female MI patients (Abramov, 1976), 64% suffered from premorbid "frigidity" compared with 24% in the control group. These findings bring up an interesting "chicken versus the egg" analogy: Was the sexual dysfunction present the result of coronary disease even before it overtly manifested, or did the stress associated with the sexual dysfunction contribute to the development of CAD? The answer to this question is unknown.

Once the patient's CAD has manifested, sexual dysfunction occurs for any one of a number of reasons. Several studies have attempted to identify the etiologies and quantify them. According to Hellerstein and Friedman (1970), the reasons for decreased sexual activity include loss of interest or desire (39%); spouse's reluctance to cooperate (25%); depression (21%); and anxiety about recurrence of CAD, coital death, or cardiovascular symptoms commonly associated with sexual activity after an MI (18%). In a Veterans' Administration survey (Mehta & Krop, 1979), 100 male patients who were veterans were interviewed 6 months after their acute MI. Reasons for not resuming intercourse included inability to maintain or obtain an erection (39%), chest pain (28%), lack of physical fitness (28%), lack of desire (19%), fear of another heart attack (16%), boredom (15%), depression (14%), change in opportunity (10%), physician's advice (10%), self-advice (10%), and partner's decision (2%).

Some of these factors have been examined in detail. For example, Blocker (1985) noted that, after an MI, patients tend to suffer from three psychologic disturbances: denial, anxiety, and depression, each of which is capable of influencing a patient's sexual function. Denial is usually the patient's initial psychological response and does not tend to interfere with the patient's sexual function because it serves more as a defense mechanism than as a barrier. Studies have documented sexually aggressive behavior in male coronary care unit patients toward staff at an incidence of up to 20% (Cassem & Hackett, 1971; Gentry, Foster, & Harey, 1972). This behavior is believed to be part of the denial response as well as an attempt on the patient's part to regain control over his life. However, this initial sexually aggressive behavior usually ceases because denial tends to dissipate with time. Denial lasts for 13 to 14 days in fewer than 5% of patients (Masters & Johnson, 1966). Anxiety, on the other hand, will develop into a chronic condition in 10% to 20% of patients (Blocker, 1995). Anxiety tends to be proportionate to the severity of the CAD symptoms and is influenced by the patient's premorbid psychological makeup. A major potential source of this anxiety is fear of death resulting from another cardiac event. Anxiety can have a major impact on the patient. Some medical authorities believe that postinfarct impotence is largely secondary to anxiety (Conine & Evans, 1982). In contrast, some patients seem to blame the impotence on their cardiac condition. Depression is perhaps the most clearly established underlying psychological cause for sexual dysfunction (Cassem & Hackett, 1973). Furthermore, it can have a long-standing effect and tends to become chronic in 10% of patients.

Studies have been performed on the psychological disturbances after an MI. For example, a survey of 100 males (Mehta & Krop, 1979) found that 34% developed some degree of new psychological symptoms. Specifically, 18% manifested reactive depression, whereas 16% developed anxiety neuroses. In contrast, studies on psychological reactions specifically in female patients after an MI are less common. In the Abramov (1976) survey, nearly two-thirds of the 100 female cardiac patients surveyed reported sexual "frigidity" and dissatisfaction post-MI compared with nearly one-fourth in the control group.

In addition to psychological etiologies, sexual dysfunction also occurs for physiologic reasons. For example, CAD often has a direct detrimental effect on cardiac function by diminishing cardiac reserve. Although intercourse has not been shown to place a greater physiologic demand on the hearts of patients who have undergone an acute MI compared with those who have not (Hellerstein & Friedman, 1970), diminished cardiac reserve can simply make the patient physically less able to perform. In addition, angina may accompany cardiac dysfunction, making it more difficult for the post-MI patient to function sexually because of fear of a recurrence as well as the obvious discomfort because of pain. Angina during sexual activity has been documented in both males and females; however, a descriptive survey of 20 women and 42 men who were sexually active before an acute MI (Hamilton & Seidman, 1993) reported more episodes of chest pain during sexual activity in women than in men. Interestingly, angina usually occurs in post-MI patients during the resolution stage of sexual activity, rather than during orgasm when energy demand is at its peak (Conine & Evans, 1982), perhaps, in part, because orgasm lasts for only a short period.

In addition to angina, other potential sources of pain exist during intercourse. For example, if coronary artery bypass grafting (CABG) was performed, sternal incisional pain will occur for at least the first several weeks postoperatively, but usually subsides within 6 to 8 weeks (Blocker, 1995). However, in some patients, this pain will be more prolonged and, thus, can cause a long-term disruption of a couple's sexual interactions.

Side effects from various cardiac medications also may contribute to sexual dysfunction. Perhaps no other group of medications has been studied in as great detail for their effects on sexual function than those used by patients with chronic cardiac conditions such as CAD, hypertension, or congestive heart failure (CHF). Of the commonly used antihypertensive medications, many are believed to be capable of producing adverse effects on sexual activity (Smith & Talbert, 1986). In contrast, other less frequently used medications such as hydralazine and minoxidil have not been shown to cause problems with sexual function. It is unknown whether calcium channel blockers are capable of causing erectile dysfunction by exerting relaxant effects on penile tissue (Seidl et al., 1991), but this topic is worthy of study given the widespread use of calcium channel blockers in the treatment of hypertension and as adjunctive medications for angina and certain types of arrhythmias.

Other classes of cardiac medications such as digoxin and diuretics also have known side effects on sexual function (Jain, Shamoian, & Mobarak, 1987; Thompson, 1986). A side effect of digoxin and triamterene that can lead to sexual dysfunction in a less obvious way is gynecomastia, which may result in embarrassment and psychological stress among males, perhaps discouraging these men from participating in a sexual relationship. In women, cardiac medications have also been known to exert side effects that diminish sexual function. The same medications that can cause erectile dysfunction in men can also diminish lubrication in women (Mann, Abbott, Gray, Thiebaux, & Belzer, 1982). Furthermore, those medications that disrupt ejaculation in men may also delay or inhibit orgasm in women (Shen & Sata, 1983). Females with cardiac disease have been advised to avoid oral contraceptives because of potential blood pressure increases (Conine & Evans, 1982). In contrast, other cardiac medications such as prophylactic nitroglycerin and perhaps nifedipine can be specifically used to help with sexual function by preventing angina or variant (vasospastic) angina, respectively, during intercourse.

Although CAD can and does occur in younger individuals, it is still largely a disease of middle age and older individuals. Irrespective of one's cardiac status or medication use, advanced age can adversely affect sexuality and can compound the previously discussed problems. It has been shown that men in their fifties were more susceptible to sexual dysfunction than those in their sixties or those in the 30- to 40-year-old age group (Seidl et al., 1991). Hence, these men are prone to a disease that can interfere with their sexual function at a time in their lives when they may already be having significant premorbid problems with sexual function.

Male Sexual Function

Certain aspects of sexual dysfunction after an MI are unique to males. These problems can be grouped into two main categories: erectile failure and premature ejaculation (Scalzi, 1982). Some controversy exists, however, about their frequency. Specifically, researchers have suggested that ejaculatory problems are rare, whereas problems involving erections, orgasms, and object-related libido are more common (Sjogren & Fugl-Meyer, 1983). Others have indicated that premature ejaculation is quite common but did not support this claim with statistics (Scalzi, 1982). In terms of impotence, several studies involving large groups of patients have shown that impotence occurs in 10% to 15% of men who have experienced an MI (Tardif, 1989). The etiology of this impotence, however, is unknown. Some researchers have suggested that postinfarct impotence is largely secondary to patient anxiety, despite the claim by some patients that their impotence has resulted from their cardiac condition (Conine & Evans, 1982).

Female Sexual Function

All of the general disorders of female sexual function have been described in the female coronary patient as well as in the otherwise healthy patient (Novak & Novak, 1962). These disorders include primary anorgasmia, secondary anorgasmia, dyspareunia, sexual aversion, and vaginismus. Insufficient data are available at this time to reasonably estimate whether there is an increased prevalence in subjects with cardiac disease compared with the able-bodied population.

DEATH DURING SEXUAL ACTIVITY

Ueno (1963) analyzed 5,559 cases of sudden death after an MI in Japan and estimated that 0.6% occurred during sexual activity. Silber and Katz (1980) studied Americans and similarly found that 0.5% of postcoronary deaths occurred during sexual activity. Most recently, Muller, Mittleman, Maclure, Sherwood, and Tofler (1996) studied 1,774 patients with MI, of which 858 were sexually active in the prior year. Of those patients, 3% reported sexual activity in the 2 hours preceding onset of their MI. The risk of triggering MI after sexual activity was similar in those patients with and without a history of preexisting cardiac disease or MI. Furthermore, sexual activity was thought to contribute to the etiology of MI in 0.9% of cases.

Risk factors for sudden cardiac death after an MI have been studied. Ueno (1963) reported that 80% of the sudden cardiac deaths during sexual activity occurred in middle-aged males who were involved with a younger woman as part of an extramarital affair. In contrast, only 20% of the 0.6% cases of sudden death occurred in men engaged in sex with their spouse. Silber and Katz (1980) explored etiologies for death during sexual activity and found that death usually resulted from ventricular fibrillation, asystole, or a ruptured ventricle. Other researchers have suggested that sudden death after an MI primarily results from arrhythmias (Derogatis & King, 1981). The whole issue of arrhythmias during sex has been examined in some detail. Most studies have reported that arrhythmias occur during work and sex at similar rates (Derogatis & King, 1981). Only one study reported a higher incidence of arrhythmias associated with sex than with work (Johnson & Fletcher, 1979).

Some investigators have proposed that post-MI coital death does not usually occur because of cardiac reasons. One study reported that most of the deaths actually result from cerebral hemorrhage rather than cardiac dysrhythmias (Blocker, 1995). Another investigator pointed out that not all of the deaths during intercourse occurred because of "natural causes." Rather, some have involved accidental fatal strangulation in an attempt to enhance orgasm by compromising the carotid circulation (Massie, 1969).

Whatever the chances, many CAD patients seem to fear dying during sexual activity. This fear can create psychological turmoil, particularly in male patients who might be faced with a conflict between their desire to reassert their masculine role and their fear of injury or death from sexual activity (Dafoe & Koshal, 1993). In an attempt to quantitate this phenomenon, Papadopoulos (1978) reported that fear, including fear of death during intercourse, was reported by 51% of female post-MI patients and by 34% of male post-MI patients studied. In another interview of 107 male MI patients, 43% reported fear of resuming sexual activity (Amsterdam et al., 1977). Two other groups of post-MI patients who were surveyed most frequently mentioned fear of another heart attack or death as their major concern regarding return to sexual activity (Hamilton & Seidman, 1993; Walbroehl, 1984).

Fear can also involve the patient's sexual partners. In one survey (Papadopoulos et al., 1980), 92% of the wives of spouses who had suffered an MI feared that their post-MI husbands would have angina or another MI during sex. Male sexual partners of female cardiac patients also admit to fear that their partner will die during sex. Moreover, impotence has been known to occur in these men as a result of this fear (Conine & Evans, 1982). In one study of 130 post-MI female patients (Papadopoulos, 1978), fear of resumption of intercourse was present in more than 50% of female patients and in 44% of their husbands.

Practitioners should educate cardiac patients that the relative risk of MI during sexual activity is low and is similar in people with and without a history of cardiac disease. Furthermore, the Muller et al. (1996) data have revealed that regular exercise can decrease and perhaps eliminate the slight possibility of MI during intercourse. Thus, practitioners should advise their patients to enroll in a regular exercise program as a preventative measure against sustaining cardiac problems during intercourse.

CARDIAC-RELATED DISORDERS

Patients with hypertension but no other forms of cardiac disease may face certain obstacles to normal sexual function. In addition to the side effects of various cardiac medications, hypertension might have an adverse effect on the sexual function of elderly women (Mooradian & Greiff, 1990). The proposed mechanism is diminished vulvovaginal blood flow resulting from severe arteriosclerosis. This theory, however, has not been subjected to any studies.

In addition to incisional pain, other effects of CABG on sexuality have been discussed in the literature. Thurer (1982) administered the Structured and Scaled Interview to Assess Maladjustment to seven males and three females before CABG, 4 months after the surgery, and 4 years after the surgery. Furthermore, the participants' physical status was graded using the New York Heart Association Functional Classification. Thurer (1982) found that the patients' physical condition improved significantly but the majority of patients reported worsened sexual relations; therefore, CABG was not shown to improve long-term sexual adjustment. Papadopoulos, Shelley, Piccolo, Beaumont, and Barnett (1986) interviewed 134 males who had undergone CABG about the effects of the surgery on their sexuality. They found that sexual dissatisfaction before surgery was a poor prognosticator for return to sexual activity, whereas a closer emotional relationship predicted a return to sex. In addition, CABG patients did better than patients who had suffered MIs, and most CABG patients who were sexually active before surgery returned to sexual activity postsurgery. Of the CABG patients studied by Papadopoulos et al. (1986), 39% were found to decrease their frequency of sexual activity, 17% of the patients and 35% of the partners expressed fear of resumption, and 23% had symptoms during coitus. The average time for return to sexual activity was 8 weeks. A small number of patients indicated that the quality of sex improved but an equal number reported that it deteriorated. To the deterioration in quality, the authors hypothesized that CABG patients who were sexually dissatisfied before surgery used the surgery as an excuse not to resume sexual activity.

Two other studies examined sexual function after heart surgery other than CABG (Frank, Heller, & Kornfeld, 1972; Heller, Frank, Kornfeld, Malu, & Bowman, 1974). The Frank et al. (1972) study was a retrospective study of approximately 800 open-heart surgery patients. The majority reported unchanged sexual relations, whereas 36% reported improved relations and 15% reported worsened relations. The Heller et al. (1974) study concluded that, after open-heart surgery, patients generally began to experience impaired sexual function at the 1-year mark.

The sexual function of patients who have undergone percutaneous transluminal coronary angioplasty (PTCA) has also been studied. One report (Gundle, Reeves, Tate, Raft, & McLaurin, 1980) compared 32 male PTCA patients with 15 male CABG patients. The study revealed improved sexual performance at 6 months in the PTCA group; however, by 15 months, the difference had become negligible. Before the PTCA, the main symptom in patients was angina. Because angina was often relieved by the procedure, the men were able to continue with their usual sex life shortly after the procedure. In contrast, even though CABG also relieved angina, this patient group did not do as well initially perhaps because CABG leads to initial psychosocial maladaptation.

Another smaller, but ever-increasing group of patients are cardiac transplantation patients. Data on these patients are extremely limited, likely because of the small population size and because successful cardiac transplantation is a comparatively new technique. The only data uncovered by a Medline literature search was a description of a personal communication with Baylor College of Medicine/ The Methodist Hospital Transplant Center (Blocker, 1995). The author stated that "no man and few women were sexually active prior to cardiac transplant. The transplant patients were sexually dysfunctional because of chest pain and breathlessness, which precluded any physical stress. A small percentage of the postcardiac transplant patients are capable of being sexually active; some have been able to indulge in competitive sports" (cited in Blocker, 1995, p. 389). A likely reason for sexual dysfunction in those patients is the use of immunosuppressive medications (Blocker, 1995).

TREATMENT OF SEXUAL DYSFUNCTION IN CARDIAC PATIENTS

Cardiac Physiology during Sexual Activity

Masters and Johnson (1966) are probably most known for their studies of the correlates of sexual response. According to their studies, peak heart rates during orgasm have ranged from 110 to 180-plus beats per minute in males and females. Blood pressure elevations in males were observed to range from 20 to 50 mmHg in diastolic pressures and 40 to 100 mmHg in systolic pressures, whereas females were noted to have 20 to 40 mmHg elevations in diastolic pressures and 30 to 80 mmHg in systolic pressures. Some researchers have cautioned that, when interpreting data regarding blood pressure changes, researchers should consider that blood pressure recordings during exercise bike riding or other physical exercise for a given workload might not correlate with those recordings during intercourse. The explanation for this phenomenon is that exercise can cause elevated blood pressure readings in the arms but not central pressures, whereas intercourse may also cause an increase in central aortic blood pressure (Rowell, Brengelmann, Blackman, Bruce, & Murray, 1968). Besides intercourse, other sexual activities such as masturbation also have been investigated. A 1975 pilot study (Wagner, 1975) was performed to determine if masturbation, as an alternative to intercourse, would cause smaller changes in heart rate. The study found that a maximum heart rate of 130 beats per minute was within the limits required for masturbation. Thus, if the patient can safely tolerate this heart rate, then he or she should be cleared to resume this activity.

Energy requirements during sex also have been studied and have been expressed in terms of metabolic equivalents (METS), external workload performed, and oxygen consumption. Orgasm requires 4 to 6 METS for 10 to 15 seconds, whereas the first two stages of the sexual response cycle (excitement and plateau) and the resolution stage requires 3 to 4 METS (Cohen, 1986). The average requirement for the entire act is 3.7 METS (Cole, Levin, Whitley, & Young, 1979). Furthermore, in the specific patient population of middle-aged married men, requirements do not generally exceed 4 METS (Skinner, 1986). In terms of external workloads, approximately 600 kilometers per minute (6 to 8 kcal/min) is required (Hellerstein & Friedman, 1970). Oxygen consumption, also known as oxygen uptake, averages 16.3 mL oxygen per min/kg during intercourse (Seidl et al., 1991), which is less than the average of 22.3 mL oxygen per min/kg required to perform the Master two-step exercise (Seidl et al., 1991). A Master two-step exercise is the number of trips a person can make in 3 minutes on an apparatus consisting of two 9-inch high, 10-inch deep, and 20- to 24-inch wide steps. One trip is defined as ascending to the top and walking down the other side. Thus, if a patient is able to safely perform the Master test, then he or she should be able to safely return to sexual activity.

The position in which a couple engages in intercourse also appears to influence energy requirements. For example, the missionary position for healthy young men consumes 3.3 to 5.5 METS for the few seconds of orgasm (Johnson & Fletcher, 1979). Familiarity also seems to play a role. Classic teaching is that the energy requirement is less for a familiar position, regardless of the actual position, than that needed for an unfamiliar position (Bohlen, Held, Sanderson, & Patterson, 1984). Tasks that require amounts of energy equivalent to those used in sexual activity include scrubbing a floor (Cole et al., 1979), walking on a treadmill at 3 miles/hr at 5% grade (Blocker, 1995), and climbing two flights of stairs at a rate of 20 steps in 10 seconds (Hellerstein & Friedman, 1969). Although the energy expenditure was equivalent during stair climbing as compared with sex, blood pressure was significantly higher in patients during stair climbing (Underhill, Woods, Silvarajan, & Halpenny, 1982). This finding is further support for those researchers and practitioners who take the position that sexual activity is not as physiologically demanding as was initially believed.

Safe Return to Sexual Activity

Various methods of determining safe return to sexual activity have been proposed. Hellerstein and Friedman (1970) studied 48 male post-MI patients who were monitored with a Holter for 24 to 48 hours as outpatients. During this period, 14 of the men engaged in sexual intercourse with their spouses. Based on heart rate responses, it was found that the energy cost of intercourse was similar to that of exercising at 6 to 8 METS (for example, quickly ascending two flights of stairs). Therefore, the authors proposed that if a patient is able to rapidly ascend two flights of stairs without symptoms of cardiac dysfunction, then he or she is advised that it is safe to resume sexual activity with the usual partner.

The ability of the two-flight test to serve as an accurate predictor of cardiovascular function, however, is controversial. Siewicki and Mansfield (1977) found that, at a stair climbing rate of at least 20 steps in 10 seconds (two steps per second), the mean pressure rate product averaged out to be within the normal range reported for sexual activity. Hence, the myocardial oxygen requirement is similar to that required for sexual activity. However, Elster and Mansfield (1977) reported that, because during the test the patient does not reach actual levels of exertion compared with sex, the test can only be used to make a rough estimate of those levels.

A major potential shortcoming of the two-flight test is its inability to detect silent ischemia. The frequency of silent ischemia in CAD patients during sexual activity is an important issue examined in a study on CAD outpatients (Drory, Shapira, Fisman, & Pines, 1995). In that study, 88 males with an average age of 52 years (range, 36 to 66 years) were enrolled in a cardiac rehabilitation program and underwent ambulatory electrocardiogram (ECG) monitoring. The study showed silent ischemia was more common than symptomatic ischemia during sex and that one-third of the patients had ischemia during sex. All of the patients who had ischemia during sex also had a positive exercise stress test (EST), whereas patients with a negative EST did not have ischemia during sex. Furthermore, the time to mean peak heart rate was shorter during the EST than during coitus. The conclusion was that return to sexual activity in patients with CAD can be predicted based on the results of a true EST. In addition, the authors hypothesized that, because all ischemic episodes during sex were associated with an increase in heart rate, heart rate reduction and improved exercise tolerance should be a goal of therapy.

Craig, Ewart, Taylor, Reese, and DeBisk (1975) examined the issue of whether the combination of the patient's knowledge of the results of an EST as well as actual counseling could influence the resumption of sexual activity. They found that frequency of sexual activity was increased by this combination. In addition, compared with other activities such as running, climbing, and walking, sexual activity and lifting objects showed the greatest proportional increases.

Another suggestion to evaluate a patient's readiness for resumption of sexual activity has been to actually record a patient's ECG during sex (Eliot & Miles, 1975), which, in a sense, would serve as a "sexercise tolerance test." Physiologic data obtained using this method can assist the physician to modify counseling of the patient (Scalzi & Dracup, 1978).

Although researchers have generally agreed that there are many physical and psychological benefits from participation in a cardiac rehabilitation program, it is unclear whether enrollment in an exercise program has a beneficial effect on a person's return to sexual activity. The physiologic effects of exercise as they specifically pertain to sexual activity have been studied. For example, a study of

16 men who participated in a 16-week bicycle ergometer training program 12 to 15 weeks after an MI, found improved aerobic conditioning as well as a reduction in peak coital heart rate (Stein, 1977). The author suggested that an aerobic training program should be undertaken in part to reduce the incidence of angina during intercourse. Kavanagh and Shepard (1977) questioned 161 patients who attended an exercise rehabilitation program 3 years after an MI. Sexual activity was increased or unchanged in only one-half of the patients. The other one-half had angina or premature ventricular beats, or a more passive role in sexual activity. Those patients also were more depressed and attended the training programs less frequently.

In another report, Stern and Cleary (1981) studied 784 men who had MI fewer than 3 years earlier. Subjects were enrolled in a 6-week low-level exercise program. The study showed that a low-level exercise program increased mean work capacity and improved psychosocial, sexual, and vocational function. Those patients with infarcts fewer than 6 months before the study showed greatest improvement. Roviaro, Holmes, and Holmsten (1984) studied 28 males who had either had an MI or had undergone CABG. The subjects were assessed before treatment, 3 months after treatment began, and 7 months after treatment began. Treatment involved a 3-month exercise-based cardiac rehabilitation program versus a control group (i.e., no cardiac rehabilitation). The group enrolled in the exercise-based program had an absolute increase in sexual activity (3.28 to 4.02 times per month), whereas the controls showed an absolute decrease in sexual activity (3.34 to 2.94 times per month). The cardiac rehabilitation program apparently led to improved psychosocial function as reflected by the increase in sexual activity.

Patient Counseling

Sexuality counseling is often overlooked in cardiac patients (Amsterdam et al., 1977; Bloch, Maeder, & Haissly, 1975; Cohen, 1986; Krop, Hall, & Mehta, 1979; Mitchell, 1982; Tuttle, Cook, & Fitch, 1964). This deficiency largely occurs because physicians or nurses fear embarrassing patients (Cohen, 1986). When they do offer counseling, they sometimes use vague statements that may increase a patient's feelings of insecurity, confusion, and depression, feelings the patient is already experiencing in response to the MI. Another reason why counseling is not as prevalent as it should be is the admission from physical and occupational therapists that their training did not prepare them to deal with their patients' physical problems as they pertain to sexual activity (Conine, Christie, Hammer, & Smith-Minton, 1980).

Three studies in particular illustrate the frequency of sexual counseling given to cardiac patients. Tuttle et al. (1964) found that two-thirds of male patients who had suffered an MI received no advice for returning to sexual activity, whereas the remaining one-third only received vague and nonspecific advice. Of those patients, 65% reported a reduction in the frequency of intercourse and 10% noted permanent impotence. Krop, Hall, and Mehta (1979) interviewed 100 married male veterans at the time of discharge after an MI and found that only 36% of them had discussed return to sexual activity with their physicians, although 66% of them had expressed concerns about resumption of sex to their caregivers. Amsterdam et al. (1977) studied 107 male MI patients and found that 80% were instructed by physicians regarding the return to physical activity, but only 4% were counseled about resuming sexual activity. Interestingly, 54% of the patients asked the physician about this topic, but physicians initiated this discussion with only 21% of patients. Of these patients, 43% feared that resumption of sexual activity would worsen their cardiac condition.

The problem is not just confined to male patients. In a study of 130 women (Papadopoulos et al., 1983), only 45% received advice regarding sexual activity after their MIs. The paucity of counseling actually seems to be worse in female patients. In a descriptive survey of 20 women and 42 men who were sexually active before an acute MI (Hamilton & Seidman, 1993), the women received less counseling than the men. Furthermore, it appears that the decision of whether to counsel women who have had an MI has often been made on the basis of marital status, despite the findings in one report (Baggs & Karch, 1987) that, of the 58 women surveyed, many of the married women were not sexually active, whereas many sexually active women were not married. Furthermore, even though widows were much less likely to be sexually active, they nonetheless indicated that they believed information regarding return to sexual activity should have been offered to them. Another possible reason for the apparent inequality in sexual counseling between men and women is that, because heart disease tends to occur in women at a later age in life, the medical profession may still be under the misconception that those women are no longer sexually active or even interested in sex (Baggs & Karch, 1987).

The effectiveness of counseling has also been examined. Although some researchers have suggested that sexual counseling and therapy is effective for treating the sexual dysfunction that develops in cardiac patients (Cohen, Wallsten, & Wallsten, 1980; Scalzi, 1982), only one study (Bertie, King, Reed, Marshall, & Ricketts, 1979) has supported this premise. In that study, an exercise and counseling group had a 76% return to sexual activity, whereas the exercise-only group had a 38% return. Other studies that have examined the effectiveness of education offered through inpatient cardiac rehabilitation programs to improve rates of return to sexual activity have been unable to demonstrate efficacy (Caplan, Robinson, French, Caldwell, & Shinn, 1976; Marston, 1970). In one study (Froelicher et al., 1994), 258 patients (219 men and 39 women) were enrolled in a prospective randomized clinical trial and were divided into three groups. In one group, a teaching–counseling program was added to a traditional exercise-based cardiac rehabilitation program; a second group was enrolled in a traditional cardiac rehabilitation program; and the third group was the control group. Rates of return to sexual activity were not significantly different among the groups. Two other studies also have come to essentially this same conclusion (Stern & Cleary, 1982; Stern, German, & Kaslow, 1983).

Part of the difficulty in demonstrating the effectiveness of counseling may be the lack of knowledge about the optimal time to provide counseling. It is unclear whether patients actually benefit from counseling begun in the acute-care situation (Caplan et al., 1976; Marston, 1970). Intuitively, it seems as though patients might not be able to retain information in that environment because of the stressors involved with hospitalization. One study examined the ability of patients to increase their knowledge base in response to counseling in the acute-care setting (Steele & Ruzicki, 1987). In that study, 38 CABG inpatients were enrolled in a phase I program and took a knowledge acquisition test to determine whether they were able to learn specific content. The material included instruction about the resumption of sexual activity postoperatively and symptom recognition indicative of activity intolerance. The patients scored a combined 76% preoperatively and 84% postoperatively. These findings suggest that patients are able to absorb general information about sexual function that is presented to them while they are in acute care. The implication is that, perhaps, sexual counseling should begin right away before misconceptions develop, particularly about return to sexual activity.

Other generalizations about appropriate timing for counseling can be made. For instance, because questions and concerns about sex are generally resolved within 3 to 4 months after an MI, sexual counseling should begin before this time (Cohen et al., 1980). Some researchers have even advocated that sexual counseling should begin as soon as the patient is stable (Egnew & Jones, 1984); however, the clinician should not force patients to talk about sex (Cole et al., 1979). Some patients who are interested will hint to their caregivers by making statements such as, "I wonder if I'll ever be whole again?" "When can I get back to my usual activity?" "How is all this going to affect my life?" (Cohen et al., 1980). Other clues include patient actions such as aggressive sexual behavior, particularly by male patients toward female nurses in the intensive care unit (Cohen et al., 1980).

Varied opinions exist about which professionals should actually do the counseling. Nurses are probably in the best position to provide the initial counseling because of their early and close interpersonal contact with patients (Baggs & Karch, 1987). In addition, excellent quality counseling programs, specifically designed for nurses, have been developed (Baggs, 1986; Bloch et al., 1975; Cohen & Lemberg, 1978; Cole, 1979; Comoss, Burke, & Swails, 1979; Hogan, 1980;

Moore, Folk-Lighty, & Nolen, 1977; Murillo-Rhode, 1980; Okoniewski, 1979; Puksta, 1977; Scalzi, 1982; Scalzi & Dracup, 1978; Segev & Schlesinger, 1981; Woods, 1975). Although physicians are also well situated to provide this service, certain barriers that exist between the physician and patient need to be solved before the physician can truly become an effective counselor (Green, 1975). For example, some patients are embarrassed to bring up issues pertaining to sexuality with their physicians, and some physicians are uncomfortable discussing sexuality. These attitudes can create a communication gap regarding sexuality between the patient and physician. Moreover, many physicians and nurses are faced with an information gap pertaining to sex and cardiac disease (Bramble, 1978; Green, 1975; Hellerstein & Friedman, 1969; Picconi, 1977).

Recommendations for counselors of patients with cardiac disease abound (Seidl et al., 1991). Counselors should avoid vague or nebulous remarks such as "take it easy" or "it's OK to have sex as long as it isn't strenuous" (Egnew & Jones, 1984, p. 110). Furthermore, counselors must be careful not to impose their moral standards on the patient (Cole et al., 1979). Discussions should be clear and frank, and counselors must not assume that, once the topic has been discussed, it is forever resolved for that patient (Cole et al., 1979). Sexual counseling should also include the spouse (Egnew & Jones, 1984), and sexuality should be placed in the context of other problems (Cole et al., 1979). The overall goal is to provide the patient with the information he or she needs to make a personal choice pertaining to sexual activity (Scalzi & Dracup, 1978).

Counselors should use the PLISSIT (*p*ermission, *l*imited *i*nformation, *s*pecific *s*uggestions, and *i*ntensive *t*herapy) model (Annon, 1976) when discussing sexuality with patients. The permission phase involves informing patients that their thoughts, feelings, and behaviors pertaining to sexuality are normal. It essentially gives them permission to learn more about the possibility of sexual activity after a cardiac event. Moreover, it gives patients permission to ask questions about their sexual function. The limited information level involves the provision of a limited amount of material pertaining to sexuality and the impact of cardiac disease. Specific suggestions may include giving the patient information on positions that require less energy expenditure or on timing their use of medications and sexual activity. Intensive therapy should be provided when complex sexual issues such as marital and other problems arise in conjunction with cardiac disease.

Recommendations for Resumption of Sexual Activity

Timing and Environment for Sexual Activity

Specific suggestions for sexual activity in patients with cardiac disease begin with the timing of sexual activity. Sex may be best in the morning with rest periods before and after (Griffith, 1973; Masur, 1979). For those patients who report angina shortly after waking in the morning, it has been suggested that foreplay is especially important to gradually raise the heart rate (Conine & Evans, 1982). Patients should avoid sexual intercourse after a heavy meal (Abbott & McWhirter, 1978; Conine & Evans, 1982; Griffith, 1973; Masur, 1979; Scalzi, 1982; Semmler & Semmler, 1974), when fatigued (McCauley, Choromanski, Wallinger, & Liu, 1984; Scalzi, 1982), during emotional outbursts (McCauley et al., 1984), or for at least 3 hours after consuming alcoholic beverages (Abbott & McWhirter, 1978; Griffith, 1973; Masur, 1979; Scalzi, 1982; Semmler & Semmler, 1974). They also should avoid intercourse when under time pressure (Scalzi, 1982).

Furthermore, emotional stress during sex such as that associated with secretive or anxiety-producing conditions should also be avoided (Griffith, 1973; Masur, 1979; Semmler & Semmler, 1974). An example of an anxiety-producing condition is when sex occurs during an extramarital affair, particularly in an unfamiliar environment. This circumstance can cause a profound and sometimes deadly increase in cardiac workload (Silber & Katz, 1980).

Advice regarding environmental factors in which the sexual act occurs also includes the avoidance of temperature extremes (Abbott & McWhirter, 1978; Griffith, 1973; Masur, 1979; Semmler & Semmler, 1974) and after a very hot or cold bath (Blocker, 1995). Sex may also be best in a cool environment to minimize cardiac workload (Blocker, 1995).

Positioning

Many recommendations have been made about positioning during sexual activity. Practitioners have counseled male patients to avoid the prone position using arm extension to support the upper body weight during intercourse because of the potential large increases in blood pressure. Instead, those patients have been advised to use the prone-on-elbows position, which only requires shoulder girdle contraction to maintain stability (Conine & Evans, 1982). A topic of great controversy has been the male-on-top position versus the male-on-bottom position. It has long been held that males with CAD should use the male-on-bottom position because it is a more passive position that is less physiologically demanding. Nemec, Mansfield, and Kennedy (1976), however, studied 10 male patients aged 24 to 40 years with a Holter monitor and automatic blood pressure cuff on during sexual activity. Subjects monitored their blood pressure at rest, intromission, orgasm, and 30, 60, and 120 seconds after orgasm for five episodes of sexual intercourse. The first encounter was to orient the subject and his partner to the equipment, and then the next four times, the subjects alternated male-on-top and male-on-bottom positions. No difference in the mean maximum heart rate or blood pressure was noted in the two different positions. Specifically, for the male-on-top position, peak heart rates averaged 114 beats per minute and peak mean blood pressures averaged 163/81. In contrast, for the male-on-bottom position, peak heart rates averaged 117 beats per minute and peak mean blood pressures averaged 161/77. The side-by-side position has also been suggested as an alternative by some researchers (Abbott & McWhirter, 1978; Griffith, 1973; Semmler & Semmler, 1974; Wagner, 1975), as has the use of a low wide chair (Abbott & McWhirter, 1978; Griffith, 1973; Semmler & Semmler, 1974).

Awareness of Symptoms and the Disease Effects

Patients should be counseled to report certain symptoms to their physician (Scalzi, 1982). Besides angina, these symptoms include a rapid heart rate or breathing pattern that persists for 7 to 10 minutes after orgasm, a feeling of extreme fatigue after orgasm, and the development and persistence of other sexual difficulties. Prophylactic nitroglycerin to prevent angina from occurring during intercourse should be considered (Abbott & McWhirter, 1978; Eliot & Miles, 1975; Koller, Kennedy, Butler, & Wagner, 1972; Semmler & Semmler, 1974; Wagner, 1975). For post-CABG patients, allowing at least 4 weeks postdischarge for the sternum to heal before engaging in sex is recommended to prevent pain from the healing sternal wound (Blocker, 1995; Dafoe & Koshal, 1993).

Besides face-to-face counseling, clinicians should teach cardiac patients about the effects of their disease on sexuality, using various educational tools such as printed material, audiotapes, and other audiovisual aids (Scalzi, 1982). These tools are extremely important, especially when patients have not received counseling. In those cases, couples would otherwise be forced to rely on their own knowledge, which may very well be interspersed with myths and misconceptions (Scalzi & Dracup, 1978). Although educational materials have improved over the years in that they are more specific in their recommendations, they still can be somewhat vague (Gulanick, MiJa, & Holm, 1991). One can only imagine the confusion and anxiety that a statement such as "take it easy during recovery" would cause in an educational pamphlet given to a patient who had suffered an MI and was concerned about return to sexual activity (Gulanick et al., 1991). Continued improvements in and easier access to quality patient educational material should help to reinforce effective counseling.

Once patients are able to return to their usual sexual routine and pattern, practitioners should remind them that, contrary to what some patients may want to believe, sexual activity alone is an inadequate source of physical exercise. Both exercise and return to normal psychological and social functioning are necessary to bring cardiac patients up to their maximum potential (Roviaro et al., 1984).

ALTERED SEXUAL FUNCTION WITH PULMONARY DISEASE

Similar to patients with cardiac disease, patients with chronic pulmonary diseases may experience difficulty with sexual function. Unfortunately, there is a paucity of research on this topic and, therefore, there are no statistics that can indicate what percentage of patients with chronic respiratory disease have a problem with sexual function and how that compares with the general population (Plummer, 1984). Regardless, sexual dysfunction is an important topic. Moreover, there is an increasing prevalence of chronic pulmonary disease especially in older patients. Because chronic obstructive pulmonary disease (COPD) is both the most common and most intensely studied of the chronic pulmonary diseases in terms of its effect on sexuality, it is used in this chapter as the representative example for chronic pulmonary disease in general. Although COPD patients may be classified into one of two categories—emphysema and chronic bronchitis—there is often enough overlap between the two conditions to make the distinction unclear. Thus, in the discussion that follows, *COPD* is used to represent both conditions.

The effects of COPD on sexual function have not been well studied and thus are uncertain (Fletcher & Martin, 1982). Anecdotal reports have associated sexual dysfunction with pulmonary disease (Agle & Baum, 1977; Kass, Updegraff, & Muffly, 1972). However, Hanson (1982), in a survey of 128 patients, found that, although the patients as a whole reported an adverse effect, some said that sexual expression was improved with COPD because of the increased need for physical comfort. Another prospective study of 20 male COPD patients (Fletcher & Martin, 1982) suggested that sexual dysfunction worsened as COPD worsened and that impotence could be associated with COPD. These suggestions also supported the authors' previous impression that the severity of sexual dysfunction seemed to coincide with the severity of the pulmonary disease as assessed by pulmonary function tests, arterial blood gases, and exercise tests. Other data also have supported the notion of a direct correlation (Fletcher & Martin, 1982). In contrast, it has been reported that in early COPD, sexual dysfunction appears to be uncommon and actually seems to be more related to marital conflict and psychological problems than to COPD per se (Kass et al., 1972). The Fletcher and Martin (1982) study disputed the relationship between COPD and sexual dysfunction, showing that there was no direct correlation between severity of COPD and degree of sexual impairment. These data are probably conflicting because it is difficult to completely exclude other causes of male sexual dysfunction in this population, such as diabetes mellitus, peripheral autonomic nerve dysfunction, depression, androgen deficiency, hyperprolactinemia, luteinizing hormone level disturbances, and follicle-stimulating hormone level disturbances, all of which can contribute to sexual dysfunction (Fletcher & Martin, 1982).

Potential barriers to sexual expression experienced by COPD patients generally involve dyspnea leading to diminished activity tolerance (Hahn, 1989). Sexual activity in particular can be difficult because the sexual act often requires an increase in respiratory rate to the 40 to 60 breaths per minute range. Consequently, the COPD patient has difficulty achieving full exhalation because obstruction to exhalation is already present. This difficulty may also occur with certain sexual positions. For example, if the patient is on the bottom, dyspnea can be exacerbated by the pressure of the partner's chest (Rabinowitz & Florian, 1992). Dyspnea can be so severe that anxiety and fear develop, leading to the development of a vicious cycle: As the COPD patient's disease progresses, he or she becomes increasingly dyspneic with exertion. As a result, the patient experiences performance anxiety during sexual activity, which leads to further dyspnea. In addition to dyspnea, bronchospasm leads to coughing, which tends to be frequent and can lead to embarrassment. Coughing can also diminish a male patient's erection (Hahn, 1989), making the sexual act more difficult and, perhaps, leading to further embarrassment. The patient may become depressed, which tends to foster noncompliance with medications and other aspects of treatment. Improper treatment then causes a worsening of the condition. Depression per se can also lead to worsening of the COPD by way of hypoxemia resulting from hypoventilation (Dudley, Wermuth, & Hague, 1973).

Adverse side effects on sexuality caused by medications used by COPD patients have been examined (Jain et al., 1987). As a result of improved medical treatment, COPD patients tend to live longer, and are therefore on more medications with a concomitant greater risk of medication side effects (Thompson, 1986). The medications most commonly used to treat COPD include theophylline, bronchodilators, and corticosteroids. Although these medications do not directly cause sexual dysfunction, their side effects can interfere with patients' interest in sex, especially by making them feel irritable and unattractive. As a result of the associations between COPD and hypertension, heart failure due to an underlying pulmonary disorder (cor pulmonale), and depression, COPD patients tend to be placed on antihypertensives, diuretics, digoxin, and antidepressants. These medications can all cause adverse sexual side effects (Jain et al., 1987; Thompson, 1986).

Erectile dysfunction in male COPD patients can generalize so that it does not just occur during coughing episodes. By factoring out other potential causes of impotence, it has been demonstrated that there is an association between COPD and impotence (Fletcher & Martin, 1982). Male COPD patients tend to have significant decreases in serum testosterone levels, thus leading to diminished libido (Semple, Beastall, Watson, & Hume, 1980; Semple et al., 1984). Decreased serum testosterone is believed to be a reflection of hypoxemia, the use of high-dose glucocorticoids, and possibly also the stress of chronic disease (Mooradian & Greiff, 1990). As the sexual activity of COPD patients is studied in further detail, the physiologic reasons for impotence may become more apparent. Impotence can also secondarily occur in the male partners of female COPD patients because the male fears hurting his partner (Rabinowitz & Florian, 1992).

Psychological barriers to sexual performance in COPD patients also exist. Sexual self-image changes (i.e., role reversals leading to gender identity disturbances) have been identified in both men and women (Hahn, 1989). Kravetz (cited in Plummer, 1984) has described the emasculation of male COPD patients. Males have said that they felt "less a man" because of their inability to continue performing traditional male tasks such as yard work, throwing out the garbage, and so forth. This lack of self-esteem can lead to fear of sexual rejection by the partner; furthermore, these fears can have some basis because the female partner may actually no longer find the male to be sexually attractive as a result of his loss of male identity (Thompson, 1986). Women, on the other hand, have reported that their being "poor wives" since their COPD may make it impossible for them to continue to perform the traditionally female tasks of housecleaning and meal preparation. In addition, women with COPD may feel they are sexually unattractive because they have developed a barrel chest as a consequence of their chronic pulmonary condition (Conine & Evans, 1982). Kravetz (cited in Plummer, 1984) has also reported the feeling of diminished sexual attractiveness in female COPD patients. In either gender, embarrassment can also stem from halitosis associated with chronic pulmonary infections (Thompson, 1986). Embarrassment, of course, can create a formidable psychological barrier.

Sexual dysfunction in chronic pulmonary disease has been studied in COPD patients almost to the exclusion of other chronic pulmonary conditions. However, patients with cystic fibrosis might also have sexual dysfunction. Cystic fibrosis is an inherited multisystem disorder characterized by abnormal endocrine gland function. The most common cause of death in these patients is pulmonary disease. One study (Levine & Stern, 1982) involved 30 married male and female cystic fibrosis patients. The study found that 57% reported no or only occasional problems in the four stages of sexual function, whereas 30% had complained of serious sexual problems. Data are otherwise quite scarce on the sexual consequences of other chronic pulmonary conditions; therefore, practitioners should use similar treatment principles as for COPD.

TREATMENT OF SEXUAL DYSFUNCTION IN COPD PATIENTS

The issue of energy expenditure during sexual activity has been studied less intensely for COPD patients than it has for cardiac patients. Activities of equivalent energy expenditure compared with coitus for most COPD patients are walking briskly on level terrain for 4 to 6 minutes (Hahn, 1989), walking up and down two flights of stairs or walking briskly around a city block (Wise, 1983), and climbing a flight of stairs (Thompson, 1986). Using a male and a female subject, one study of sexual response (Bartlett & Bohr, 1956) revealed that hyperventilation was present during both the arousal and orgasm phases of intercourse. In addition, minute volume increased markedly, but the effect on tidal volume was varied and depended on the respiratory rate.

Education about Disease Effects and Counseling

As with cardiac disease patients, the issue of counseling and education about the impact of pulmonary disease on sexual function is important. Many patients seem to appreciate when the physician asks about sexual issues (Thompson, 1986). Alternatively, any one of a variety of health care professionals is in a position to establish enough of a rapport with the patient to counsel the patient. These professionals include the intensive care unit nurses (Campbell, 1987), respiratory therapists (Plummer, 1984), social workers, or professional sex therapists. As such, it has been recommended that counselors not discuss the more personal aspects of a patient's sexuality until the counselor and patient have developed a trusting relationship (Campbell, 1987). In addition, the counselor should always make an attempt to try and include the sexual partner in counseling sessions (Campbell, 1987). To help establish rapport, a good question to begin with is, How are your breathing problems affecting your sexual relations? (Hahn, 1989, p. 195). Particularly if these discussions are being held in the acute-care hospital, discussions should be held in privacy (Campbell, 1987). From the beginning, the counselor needs to explain that some dyspnea during sex is normal and that sexual activity is not too stressful to the heart and will not lead to damage to the lungs or other organ systems. Patients may have this misconception. Other common myths that must be dispelled include the following: disabled patients are asexual; an erection is absolutely necessary to satisfy a sexual partner; and an orgasm is needed for a female to be sexually satisfied (Plummer, 1984). Counselors are also urged to listen actively and help the patient to problem solve by coming to his or her own conclusions.

Counselors should help patients set attainable goals (Campbell, 1987) and should encourage them to talk about any nervousness during sexual activity. Other general issues that should be raised include masturbation as a form of sexual pleasure (Rabinowitz & Florian, 1992) and the need for sexual partners to diminish anxiety by sometimes agreeing ahead of time to just "play around" rather than to have intercourse (Hahn, 1989). Besides anxiety, COPD patients should be evaluated for depression, which can then be treated to improve their sexual function (Thompson, 1986). Depression is often a cause of sexual dysfunction in general and in COPD patients in particular (Timms, 1982).

Specific treatment strategies for sexual dysfunction in COPD have been developed. First, practitioners should instruct patients to avoid sex during a pulmonary infection. As a prelude to a sexual encounter, patients should be instructed to plan ahead (Hahn, 1989). Proper planning actually starts the night before: patients are instructed to get a good night's rest before sex (Rabinowitz & Florian, 1992) but to avoid sex right after awakening because of the accumulation of secretions during sleep (Campbell, 1987). On the day of the sexual encounter, patients are to wait 2 to 3 hours after heavy meals before having sex (Campbell, 1987) and to avoid physical exertion (Hahn, 1989; Rabinowitz & Florian, 1992) before sexual activity. Choosing a familiar environment is important to keep anxiety to a minimum, thus preventing hyperventilation, which results in dyspnea (Campbell, 1987). Creating the proper atmosphere is also important; patients may be told to relax before and after intercourse with music. Moreover, a couple may take a bath or shower together, or create a candlelight setting with soft background music (Thompson, 1986). In addition, practitioners should instruct patients to prepare the room by placing a box of tissues nearby for removal of coughing secretions to avoid interruptions. Placing a firm mat on the floor and having sex on the mat may also be preferable to a soft mattress during sex (Hahn, 1989). Alternatively, a waterbed to help provide a rhythmic rocking motion, thus decreasing energy expenditure, may be used (Campbell, 1987; Hahn, 1989). The use of an inhaler or cough drop before sex can help to prevent bronchospasm and its sequelae (Hahn, 1989). Because oxygen use in general can help with a patient's exercise tolerance, patients are instructed to tape oxygen tubing in place for the side-lying position (Hahn, 1989); in general, proper taping and the use of tubing extensions allows greater mobility (Thompson, 1986). Just before actually engaging in sex, the patient should remove any unnecessary clothes to relieve the feeling of being closed in (Hahn, 1989). The patient should also consider pursed-lip diaphragmatic breathing before intercourse (Campbell, 1987). Although touching and caressing are never discouraged, the couple is to avoid prolonged kissing and the performance of oral sex before intercourse if those practices typically result in dyspnea (Hahn, 1989). During actual intercourse, special breathing techniques (especially pursed-lip breathing during expiration) can be helpful (Thompson, 1986).

Positioning and Handling of Symptoms

Consideration should be given to positions for intercourse, especially avoiding those that put pressure on the chest (Rabinowitz & Florian, 1992). Specifically, it is believed that the side-lying position allows for easier breathing and easier use of oxygen (Figures 16–1 and 16–2), whereas the seated position allows the patient to lean forward and thus ease breathing (Thompson, 1986; Figure 16–3). Another reason for encouraging the upright position is to maximize ventilation/perfusion; a rocking chair is especially useful because it also achieves maximum movement with a minimum amount of muscular activity (Campbell, 1987). The lateral position with the woman turned away or the woman with her chest supported by the bed and the male entering from behind (Figure 16–4) are also comfortable positions (Mooradian & Greiff, 1990).

Patients should be encouraged to adjust the rate and intensity of intercourse to their breathing needs (Hahn, 1989). They should be counseled to use coughing interruptions as a time to pause and enjoy longer foreplay (Hahn, 1989). If pulmonary symptoms develop during sex, the couple should stop coitus but continue to talk and caress to maintain the intimate feeling that has developed (Campbell,

Figure 16–1 Side-lying position for female patient. *Source:* Reprinted with permission from J.R. Bach, *Pulmonary Rehabilitation: The Obstructive and Paralytic Conditions,* © 1996, Hanley & Belfus, Inc.

Figure 16–2 Side-lying position for male patient. *Source:* Reprinted with permission from J.R. Bach, *Pulmonary Rehabilitation: The Obstructive and Paralytic Conditions,* © 1996, Hanley & Belfus, Inc.

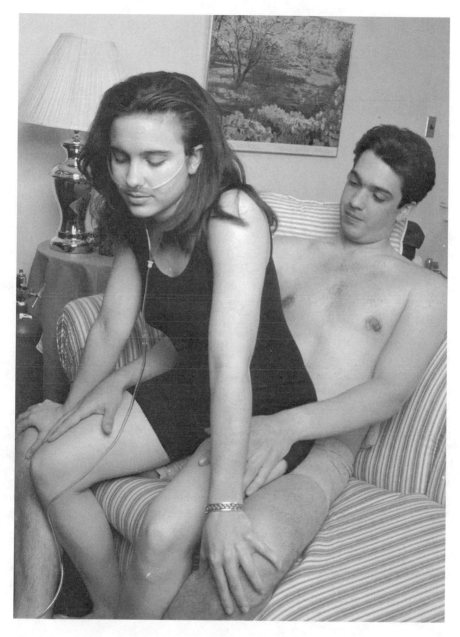

Figure 16–3 Seated position. *Source:* Reprinted with permission from J.R. Bach, *Pulmonary Rehabilitation: The Obstructive and Paralytic Conditions,* © 1996, Hanley & Belfus, Inc.

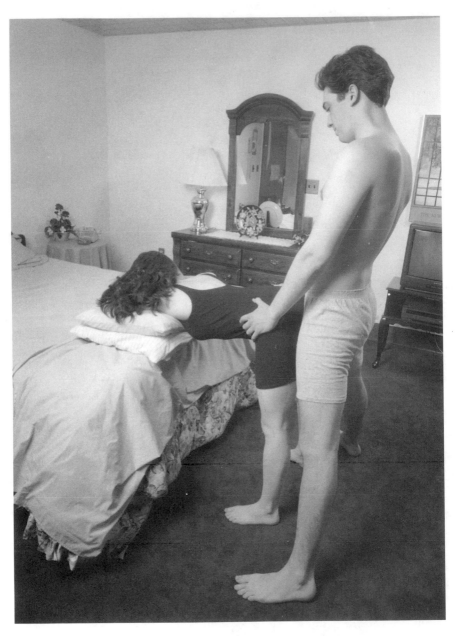

Figure 16–4 Female with chest supported by bed. *Source:* Reprinted with permission from J.R. Bach, *Pulmonary Rehabilitation: The Obstructive and Paralytic Conditions,* © 1996, Hanley & Belfus, Inc.

1987). They may even need to assume a more passive role during sexual activity (Campbell, 1987), thus allowing their partner to be more active.

In addition to the advice given to patients, practitioners should review some topics with the patient's partner. Practitioners should explain to those partners of patients who are still physically capable of engaging in intercourse that it is unlikely that the partner will cause the patient physical harm as long as the couple adheres to the principles described. In contrast, for partners of very ill patients, alternate sexual practices such as masturbation should be encouraged.

INFERTILITY WITH CARDIAC OR PULMONARY DISEASE

Male Infertility

The major group of male cardiac or pulmonary patients who have problems with infertility is that of men with cystic fibrosis. Bilateral absence or atrophy of the vas deferens is nearly universal in males with cystic fibrosis (Kaplan et al., 1968), and semen analysis reveals azoospermia in virtually all adult males with cystic fibrosis (Stern et al., 1983). Because of the high incidence of genetic mutations in men with cystic fibrosis and a carrier frequency of 1:25 in females, screening for cystic fibrosis mutations is recommended before assisted reproductive techniques are undertaken (Dodge, 1995).

Female Infertility

Fertility is generally an important aspect of female sexuality in most situations. However, as opposed to other patient populations, the topic of fertility usually is of minor consequence in females with CAD because of the older age of this patient population. In addition to increasing androgen levels, the comfort of no longer having to worry about birth control is one of the reasons why women tend to become more interested in sex as they age (Cohen, 1986). Thus, it seems unjust to older women with CAD that the fear of becoming pregnant has been replaced by the fear of death from heart disease.

Female infertility is also generally not a problem for younger women with cardiac or pulmonary disease, including women with cystic fibrosis, who have been reported to have normal pregnancies (Durieu et al., 1995). Moreover, women with congenital or acquired heart disease and cardiac transplantation (Jordan & Pugh, 1996) have been known to carry pregnancies to term. Issues to consider in the woman with cardiac disease include the risk–benefit relationship of use of anticoagulants for women with heart valve replacements (Rothlin et al., 1995) and that, compared with the general population, women with cardiac disease have reportedly had more frequent instrumental vaginal deliveries, Caesarean sections, and low-birth-weight babies (Chia, Yeoh, Viegas, Lim, & Ratnam, 1996). Furthermore, women with cardiac disease and concomitant pulmonary hypertension have been shown to have more low-birth-weight babies than women with cardiac disease alone (Tahir, 1995). However, no differences were noted in perinatal mortality, rate of prematurity, or mode of delivery. Considering these issues, it has been recommended that pregnant women with preexisting heart disease be managed at a tertiary care center (Chia et al., 1996).

REFERENCES

Abbott, M.A., & McWhirter, D.P. (1978). Resuming sexual activity after myocardial infarction. *Medical Aspects of Human Sexuality, 12*(6), 18–28.

Abramov, L.A. (1976). Sexual life and sexual frigidity among women developing acute myocardial infarction. *Psychosomatic Medicine, 38*, 418–425.

Agle, D.P., & Baum, G.L. (1977). Psychologic aspects of chronic obstructive pulmonary disease. *Medical Clinics of North America, 61*, 749–757.

Amsterdam, E.A., Amsterdam, G.L., Riggs, K., DeMaria, A.N., & Mason, D.T. (1977). Sexual counseling and sexual activity after myocardial infarction: Patient attitudes and physician response. *Clinical Research, 25*, 86A.

Annon, J.S. (1976). The PLISSIT model: A proposed conceptual scheme for behavioral treatment of sexual problems. *Journal of Sex Education Therapy, 2*, 1–15.

Baggs, J. (1986). Nursing diagnosis: Potential sexual dysfunction after myocardial infarction. *Dimensions of Critical Care Nursing, 5*, 178–181.

Baggs, J.G., & Karch, A.M. (1987). Sexual counseling of women with coronary heart disease. *Heart and Lung, 16*(2), 154–159.

Bartlett, R.G., & Bohr, V.C. (1956). Physiological responses during coitus in the human. *Federation Proceedings, 15*, 10.

Bertie, J., King, A., Reed, N., Marshall, A.J., & Ricketts, C. (1979). Benefits and weakness of a cardiac rehabilitation programme. *Journal of the Royal College of Physicians, 26*, 147–151.

Bloch, A., Maeder, J., & Haissly, J. (1975). Sexual problems after myocardial infarction. *American Heart Journal, 90*, 536–537.

Blocker, W.P. (1985). Cardiac rehabilitation. In L. Halstead & M. Grabois (Eds.), *Medical rehabilitation* (pp. 181–192). New York: Raven Press.

Blocker, W.P., Jr. (1995). Coronary heart disease and sexuality. *Physical Medicine and Rehabilitation: State of the Art Reviews, 9*, 387–399.

Bohlen, J.G., Held, J.P., Sanderson, M.O., & Patterson, R.P. (1984). Heart rate, rate pressure product and oxygen uptake during four sexual activities. *Archives of Internal Medicine, 144*, 1745–1748.

Bramble, K. (1978). Myocardial infarction patients and sexual counseling. *Communicating Nursing Research, 11*, 78–79.

Campbell, M. (1987). Sexual dysfunction in the COPD patient. *Dimensions of Critical Care Nursing, 6*(2), 70–74.

Caplan, R., Robinson, E., French, J., Caldwell, J., & Shinn, M. (1976). *Adhering to medical regimens*. Ann Arbor: Institute for Social Research, University of Michigan.

Cassem, N.H., & Hackett, T.P. (1971). Psychiatric consultation in a coronary care unit. *Annals of Internal Medicine, 75,* 9–14.

Cassem, N.H., & Hackett, T.P. (1973). Physiological rehabilitation of myocardial infarction patients in the acute phase. *Heart and Lung, 2,* 382–388.

Chia, Y.T., Yeoh, S.C., Viegas, O.A., Lim, M., & Ratnam, S.S. (1996). Maternal congenital heart disease and pregnancy outcome. *Journal of Obstetric and Gynecologic Research, 2,* 185–191.

Cohen, B.D., Wallsten, B.S., & Wallsten, K.A. (1980). Sex counseling in cardiac rehabilitation. *Archives of Physical Medicine and Rehabilitation, 140,* 38–41.

Cohen, J.A. (1986). Sexual counseling of the patient following myocardial infarction. *Critical Care Nurse, 6*(6), 18–29.

Cohen, N.H., & Lemberg, L. (1978). Cardiac rehabilitation in the coronary care unit: Part 1. *Heart and Lung, 7,* 667–670.

Cole, C.M. (1979). A treatment strategy for post-myocardial sexual dysfunction. *Sexuality and Disability, 2,* 122–129.

Cole, C.M., Levin, E.M., Whitley, J.O., & Young, S.H. (1979). Brief sexual counseling during cardiac rehabilitation. *Psychological Aspects of Critical Care, 8*(1), 124–129.

Comoss, P.M., Burke, E.A.S., & Swails, S.H. (1979). *Cardiac rehabilitation.* Philadelphia: J.B. Lippincott.

Conine, T.A., Christie, G.M., Hammer, G.K., & Smith-Minton, M.F. (1980). Sexual rehabilitation of the handicapped: The roles and attitudes of health professionals. *Journal of Allied Health, 9,* 260–267.

Conine, T.A., & Evans, J.H. (1982). Sexual reactivation of chronically ill and disabled adults. *Journal of Allied Health, 11*(4), 261–270.

Craig, K., Ewart, C., Taylor, C., Reese, L., & DeBisk, R.F. (1975). Effects of early post myocardial infarction exercise testing on self-perception and subsequent physical activity. *American Journal of Cardiology, 51,* 1076–1080.

Dafoe, W.A., & Koshal, A. (1993). Noncardiologic complications of coronary artery bypass surgery and common patient concerns. In F.J. Pashkow & W.A. Dafoe (Eds.), *Clinical cardiac rehabilitation: A cardiologist's guide* (pp. 183–195). Baltimore: Williams & Wilkins.

Derogatis, L., & King, K.M. (1981). The coital coronary: A reassessment of the concept. *Archives of Sexual Behavior, 10,* 325–335.

Dodge, J.A. (1995). Male fertility in cystic fibrosis. *Lancet, 346,* 587–588.

Drory, Y., Shapira, I., Fisman, E., & Pines, A. (1995). Myocardial ischemia during sexual activity in patients with coronary artery disease. *American Journal of Cardiology, 75,* 835–837.

Dudley, D.L., Wermuth, C., & Hague, W. (1973). Psychosocial aspects of care in the chronic obstructive pulmonary disease patient. *Heart and Lung, 2,* 389–393.

Durieu, I., Bellon, G., Vital-Durand, D., Calemard, L., Morel, Y., & Gilly, R. (1995). La mucouiscidose a l'age adulte [Cystic fibrosis in adults]. *Presse Medicale, 39,* 1882–1887.

Egnew, T.R., & Jones, J.M. (1984). Teaching psychosocial aspects of coronary care. *Journal of Family Practice, 18*(1), 107–113.

Eliot, R.S., & Miles, R.R. (1975). Advising the cardiac patient about sexual intercourse. *Medical Aspects of Human Sexuality, 9*(6), 49–50.

Elster, S.E., & Mansfield, L.W. (1977). Stair climbing as a test of readiness for resumption of sexual activity after a heart attack. *Circulation, 56,* 102.

Fletcher, E.C., & Martin, R. (1982). Sexual dysfunction and erectile impotence in chronic obstructive pulmonary disease. *Chest, 81,* 413–421.

Frank, K.A., Heller, S.S., & Kornfeld, D.S. (1972). A survey of adjustment to cardiac surgery. *Archives of Internal Medicine, 130,* 735–738.

Friedman, J.M. (1978). Sexual adjustment of the postcoronary male. In J. LoPicolo & L. LoPicolo (Eds.), *Handbook of sex therapy.* New York: Plenum Press.

Froelicher, E.S., Kee, L.L., Newton, K.M., Lindskog, B., & Livingston, M. (1994). Return to work, sexual activity, and other activities after acute myocardial infarction. *Heart and Lung, 23*(5), 423–435.

Gentry, W.D., Foster, S., & Harey, T. (1972). Denial as a determinant of anxiety and perceived health status in the coronary care unit. *Psychosomatic Medicine, 34,* 39–43.

Green, A.W. (1975). Sexual activity and the postmyocardial infarction patient. *American Heart Journal, 89,* 246–252.

Griffith, G.C. (1973). Sexuality and the cardiac patient. *Heart and Lung, 2,* 70–73.

Gulanick, M., MiJa, K., & Holm, K. (1991). Resumption of home activities following cardiac events. *Progress in Cardiovascular Nursing, 6*(1), 21–28.

Gundle, M.J., Reeves, B.R., Tate, S., Raft, D., & McLaurin, L.P. (1980). Psychosocial outcome after coronary artery surgery. *American Journal of Psychiatry, 137,* 1591–1594.

Hahn, K. (1989). Sexuality and COPD. *Rehabilitation Nursing, 14,* 191–195.

Hamilton, G.A., & Seidman, R.N. (1993). A comparison of the recovery period for women and men after an acute myocardial infarction. *Heart and Lung, 22,* 308–315.

Hanson, E.I. (1982). Effects of chronic lung disease on life in general and on sexuality: Perceptions of adult patients. *Heart and Lung, 11,* 435–441.

Heller, S., Frank, K., Kornfeld, D., Malu, J., & Bowman, S. (1974). Psychological outcomes following open heart surgery. *Archives of Internal Medicine, 134,* 908–914.

Hellerstein, H.K., & Friedman, E.H. (1969). Sexual activity and the postcoronary patient. *Medical Aspects of Human Sexuality, 3*(3), 70–96.

Hellerstein, H.K., & Friedman, E.H. (1970). Sexual activity and the post coronary patient. *Archives of Internal Medicine, 125,* 987–999.

Hogan, R.M. (1980). *Human sexuality: A nursing perspective.* New York: Appleton-Century-Crofts.

Jain, H., Shamoian, C., & Mobarak, A. (1987). Sexual disorders in the elderly. *Medical Aspects of Human Sexuality, 21*(3), 14–28.

Johnson, B.L., & Fletcher, B.F. (1979). Dynamic electrocardiographic recording during sexual activity in recent post myocardial infarction and revascularization patients. *American Heart Journal, 98,* 736–741.

Jordan, E., & Pugh, L.C. (1996). Pregnancy after cardiac transplantation: Principles of nursing care. *Journal of Obstetric, Gynecologic, and Neonatal Nursing, 2,* 131–135.

Kaplan, E., Shwachman, H., Perlmuter, A.D., Rule, A., Khaw, K.T., & Holsclaw, D.S. (1968). Reproductive failure in males with cystic fibrosis. *New England Journal of Medicine, 279,* 65–69.

Kass, I., Updegraff, K., & Muffly, R.B. (1972). Sex in chronic obstructive pulmonary disease. *Medical Aspects of Human Sexuality, 63,* 33–42.

Kavanagh, T., & Shepard, R.J. (1977). Sexual activity after myocardial infarction. *Canadian Medical Association Journal, 116,* 1250–1253.

Koller, R., Kennedy K.W., Butler, J.C., & Wagner, N.N. (1972). Counseling the coronary patient on sexual activity. *Postgraduate Medicine, 51*(4), 133–136.

Krop, H., Hall, D., & Mehta, J. (1979). Sexual concerns after myocardial infarction. *Sexuality and Disability, 2,* 91–97.

Levine, S.B., & Stern, R.C. (1982). Sexual function in cystic fibrosis: Relationship to overall health status and pulmonary disease severity in 30 married patients. *Chest, 81*(4), 422–428.

Mann, K.V., Abbott, E.C., Gray, J.D., Thiebaux, H.J., & Belzer, E.G. (1982). Sexual dysfunction with beta-blocker therapy: More common than we think? *Sexuality and Disability, 5,* 67–77.

Marston, M. (1970). Compliance with medical regimens: A review of the literature. *Nursing Research, 19,* 312–323.

Massie, E. (1969). Sudden death during coitus—fact or fiction? *Medical Aspects of Human Sexuality, 3*(6), 22–26.

Masters, W.H., & Johnson, V.E. (1966). *Human sexual response.* Boston: Little, Brown.

Masur, F.T. (1979). Resumption of sexual activity following myocardial infarction. *Sexuality and Disability, 2,* 98–114.

McCauley, K., Choromanski, J.D., Wallinger, C., & Liu, K. (1984). Learning to live with controlled ventricular tachycardia: Utilizing the Johnson model. *Heart and Lung, 13*(6), 633–638.

Mehta, J., & Krop, H. (1979). The effect of myocardial infarction on sexual functioning. *Sexuality and Disability, 2,* 115–121.

Mitchell, M.E. (1982). Sexual counseling in cardiac rehabilitation. *Journal of Rehabilitation, 48*(4), 15–18.

Mooradian, A.D., & Greiff, V. (1990). Sexuality in older women. *Archives of Internal Medicine, 150,* 1033–1038.

Moore, K., Folk-Lighty, M., & Nolen, M.J. (1977). The joy of sex after a heart attack. *Nursing, 7*(6), 52–55.

Muller, J.E., Mittleman, M.A., Maclure, M., Sherwood, J.B., & Tofler, G.H. (1996). Triggering myocardial infarction by sexual activity: Low absolute risk and prevention by regular physical exertion. *Journal of the American Medical Association, 275,* 1405–1409.

Murillo-Rhode, I. (1980). Sexual problems of the post coronary patient. *Imprint, 27,* 32–33.

Nemec, E., Mansfield, L., & Kennedy, J.W. (1976). Heart rate and blood pressure responses during sexual activity in normal males. *American Heart Journal, 92,* 274–277.

Novak, E., & Novak, E.R. (1962). Problems of sex life. In L. Parsons & S. Sommers (Eds.), *Gynecology* (pp. 571–577). Baltimore: Williams & Wilkins.

Okoniewski, G.A. (1979). Sexual activity following myocardial infarction. *Cardiovascular Nursing, 15,* 1–4.

Papadopoulos, C. (1978). A survey of sexual activity after myocardial infarction. *Cardiovascular Medicine, 3,* 821–826.

Papadopoulos, C., Beaumont, C., Shelley, S.I., & Larrimore, P. (1983). Myocardial infarction and sexual activity of the female patient. *Archives of Internal Medicine, 143,* 1528–1530.

Papadopoulos, C., Larrimore, P., Cardin, S., & Shelley, S.I. (1980). Sexual concerns and needs of the postcoronary patient's wife. *Archives of Internal Medicine, 140,* 38–41.

Papadopoulos, C., Shelley, S.I., Piccolo, M., Beaumont, C., & Barnett, L. (1986). Sexual activity after coronary bypass surgery. *Chest, 190*(5), 681–685.

Picconi, J. (1977). Human sexuality: A nursing challenge. *Nursing 77, 7,* 72D, 72F, 72G, 72M.

Plummer, J.K. (1984). Psychosocial factors in pulmonary rehabilitation. In J.A. O'Ryan & D.G. Burns (Eds.), *Pulmonary rehabilitation from hospital to home* (pp. 162–165). Chicago: Yearbook Publishers.

Puksta, N.S. (1977). All about sex . . . after a coronary. *American Journal of Nursing, 77,* 602–605.

Rabinowitz, B., & Florian, V. (1992). Chronic obstructive pulmonary disease—Psychosocial issues and treatment goals. *Social Work in Health Care, 16*(4), 60–86.

Rothlin, M.E., Egloff, L., Fleisch, M., Hirzel, H.O., Siebenmann, R., Studer, M., & Tartini, R. (1995). [Acquired heart diseases and pregnancy]. *Schweizerische Medizinische Wochenschrift, 7*, 304–310.

Roviaro, S., Holmes, D.S., & Holmsten, R.D. (1984). Influence of a cardiac rehabilitation program on the cardiovascular, psychological and social functioning of cardiac patients. *Journal of Behavioral Medicine, 7*(1), 61–81.

Rowell, L.B., Brengelmann, G.L., Blackman, J.R., Bruce, R.A., & Murray, J.A. (1968). Disparities between aortic and peripheral pulse pressures induced by upright exercise and vasomotor changes in man. *Circulation, 37*, 954–964.

Scalzi, C.C. (1982). Sexual counseling and sexual therapy for patients after myocardial infarction. *Cardiovascular Nursing, 18*, 13–17.

Scalzi, C.C., & Dracup, K. (1978). Sexual counseling of coronary patients. *Heart and Lung, 7*(5), 840–845.

Segev, U., & Schlesinger, Z. (1981). Rehabilitation of patients after acute myocardial infarction: An interdisciplinary family-oriented program. *Heart and Lung, 10*, 841–847.

Seidl, A., Bullough, B., Haughey, B., Scherer, Y., Rhodes, M., & Brown, G. (1991). Understanding the effects of a myocardial infarction on sexual functioning: A basis for sexual counseling. *Rehabilitation Nursing, 16*(5), 255–264.

Semmler, C., & Semmler, M. (1974). Counseling the coronary patient. *American Journal of Occupational Therapy, 28*, 609–614.

Semple, P.D., Beastall, G.H., Watson, W.S., & Hume, R. (1980). Serum testosterone depression associated with hypoxia in respiratory failure. *Clinical Science, 58*, 105–106.

Semple, P.D.A., Beastall, G.H., Brown, T.M., Stirling, K.W., Mills, R.J., & Watson, W.S. (1984). Sex hormone suppression and sexual impotence in hypoxic pulmonary fibrosis. *Thorax, 39*, 46–51.

Shen, W.W., & Sata, L.S. (1983). Inhibited female orgasm resulting from psychoactive drugs. *Journal of Reproductive Medicine, 28*, 497–499.

Siewicki, B.J., & Mansfield, L.W. (1977). Determining readiness to resume sexual activity. *American Journal of Nursing, 77*, 604.

Silber, E.N., & Katz, L.V. (1980). *Cardiac activity and sexual response.* New York: Macmillan.

Sjogren, K., & Fugl-Meyer, A. (1983). Some factors influencing quality of sexual life after myocardial infarction. *International Rehabilitative Medicine, 5*, 197–201.

Skinner, J.B. (1986). Sexual relations and the cardiac patient. In M.L. Pollock & D.H. Schmat (Eds.), *Heart disease and rehabilitation* (pp. 583–589). New York: Wiley.

Smith, P., & Talbert, R. (1986). Sexual dysfunction with antihypertensive and antipsychotic agents. *Clinical Pharmacology, 5*, 373–384.

Steele, J.M., & Ruzicki, D. (1987). An evaluation of the effectiveness of cardiac teaching during hospitalization. *Heart and Lung, 16*(3), 306–317.

Stein, R.A. (1977). The effect of exercise training on heart rate during coitus in the post myocardial infarction patient. *Circulation, 55*, 738–840.

Stern, M., & Cleary, P. (1981). National Exercise and Heart Disease Project: Psychosocial changes observed during a low-level exercise program. *Archives of Internal Medicine, 141*, 1463–1467.

Stern, M.J., & Cleary, P. (1982). The National Exercise and Heart Disease Project: Long-term psychosocial outcome. *Archives of Internal Medicine, 142*, 1093–1097.

Stern, M.J., German, P.A., & Kaslow, L. (1983). The group counseling vs. exercise therapy study: A controlled intervention with subjects following myocardial infarction. *Archives of Internal Medicine, 143,* 1719–1725.

Tahir, H. (1995). Pulmonary hypertension, cardiac disease and pregnancy. *International Journal of Gynaecology and Obstetrics, 51,* 109–113.

Tardif, G.S. (1989). Sexual activity after a myocardial infarction. *Archives of Physical Medicine and Rehabilitation, 70,* 763–766.

Thompson, W.L. (1986). Sexual problems in chronic respiratory disease: Achieving and maintaining intimacy. *Postgraduate Medicine, 79,* 41–52.

Thurer, S.L. (1982). The long-term sexual response for coronary bypass surgery: Some preliminary findings. *Sexuality and Disability, 5,* 208–212.

Timms, R.M. (1982). Sexual dysfunction and chronic obstructive pulmonary disease. *Chest, 81*(4), 398–399.

Tuttle, W.B., Cook, W.L., & Fitch, C. (1964). Sexual behavior in post myocardial infarction patients. *American Journal of Cardiology, 13,* 140.

Ueno, M. (1963). The so-called coition death. *Japanese Journal of Legal Medicine, 17,* 330–340.

Underhill, S., Woods, S., Silvarajan, E., & Halpenny, C.J. (1982). *Cardiac nursing.* Philadelphia: J.B. Lippincott.

Wabrek, A.J., & Burchell, R.C. (1980). Male sexual dysfunction associated with coronary heart disease. *Archives of Sexual Behavior, 9,* 69–75.

Wagner, N.N. (1975). Sexual activity and the cardiac patient. In R. Green (Ed.), *Human sexuality: A health practitioner's text* (pp. 172–179). Baltimore: Williams & Wilkins.

Walbroehl, G. (1984). Sexual activity and the post coronary patient. *American Family Physician, 29,* 175–177.

Wise, T.N. (1983). Sexual dysfunction in the medically ill. *Psychosomatics, 24*(9), 787–801.

Woods, N.F. (1975). *Human sexuality in health and illness.* St. Louis, MO: C.V. Mosby.

CHAPTER 17

Cancer

Tracey L. Waldman and Barbara Eliasof

"It's cancer." Those words reverberate as the patient and his or her partner sit staring in shock at the physician who is already outlining statistics and treatment options in an often stoic fashion.

Cancer is a devastating disease that threatens a person's physical and emotional well-being. As the patient is forced to face his or her mortality, survival is at the forefront of concerns and the immediate needs are physical. As the shock subsides, other facets of one's personal existence emerge and an attempt at normalization begins. One area of interest that has received little attention has been the sexual concerns of cancer patients. Health care professionals are responsible for assisting patients through their process of adaptation and also for incorporating all issues, inclusive of sexuality, that affect an individual's quality of life. Nonetheless, many oncology professionals continue to be reluctant to broach the topic of sex with their patients; therefore, these clients are left feeling confused and alone with no one to turn to for help.

Sexual function is affected in individuals following a cancer diagnosis from both a physical and emotional perspective. The primary sexual organs and their neurovascular supply may be injured by the disease process itself. In addition, treatment options such as chemotherapy, radiation therapy, surgery, and hormone manipulation may yield similar impairments. An individual's emotional response and stage of life at which the diagnosis occurs also have an impact on sexual function.

These factors all pinpoint the need for health care professionals who work with cancer patients to conduct a thorough psychosocial assessment that includes questions about premorbid sexual function. In addition, education must be provided regarding potential physical side effects, fertility concerns, and reproductive options that may require initiation before the onset of cancer treatment.

It is impossible to cover all facets of sexuality as they relate to numerous cancer diagnoses and treatments. This chapter, therefore, provides an overview of the physical and psychological repercussions on sexuality in relation to various cancer types. In addition, it outlines possible effects on fertility and offers options for reproductive potential following treatment. The chapter also suggests guidelines for health care professionals who are assisting cancer patients through the course of their disease.

CANCER AND THE MALE PATIENT

Prostate

Prostate carcinoma is the most common form of cancer diagnosed in males; approximately 244,000 new cases were reported in the United States in 1995 (American Cancer Society [ACS], 1995). This alarming statistic represents a significant increase from the 73,000 new cases identified a mere 6 years earlier (Auchincloss, 1989). This escalation in diagnosis may be attributed to several factors, including an ever-increasing elderly population (the median age of diagnosis is 70 years), advanced screening techniques, and a heightened awareness among individuals as the result of greater media exposure. Although older men may experience sexual dysfunctions related to other medical conditions such as diabetes and hypertension or resulting from medication side effects, they still have interests and desires as sexual beings.

Current treatment options for carcinoma of the prostate include a prostatectomy (accomplished through transurethral perineal or transabdominal approaches); radiation therapy (external and interstitial implant); hormonal therapy; and bilateral orchiectomy (removal of testes). Each treatment, as well as the diagnostic workup, may produce substantial sexual changes. Several individual factors may influence the physical effects on sexuality such as "preoperative potency, neurovascular bundle preservation, age and clinical stage" (ACS, 1995, p. 706). In addition, men may experience anxiety in response to the threat to their basic needs and safety while they struggle with feelings of loss and emasculation.

A radical prostatectomy is a therapeutic treatment option for early stage prostate cancer. This procedure includes the removal of the entire prostate, seminal vesicles, and vas deferens. The two most common side effects of a radical prostatectomy are impotence and incontinence. Studies have demonstrated that nearly 100% of males experience erectile dysfunction following this procedure and that a mere 10% to 15% of those men will regain erectile function in time (Perez, Fair, & Ihde, 1989). However, nerve-sparing radical prostatectomies result in a more optimistic outcome (Quinlan, Epstein, Carter, & Walsh, 1991). Brender and Walsh (1992) have reported that, on average, 69% of men with potency preoperatively will regain this level of function. The preservation of both neurovascular bundles results in a 76% return of erectile capacity, whereas the preservation of only one bundle reduces this figure to 60%. In addition, retrograde ejaculation is prevalent in men following both transurethral and transabdominal resections (Perez et al., 1989).

Radiation therapy is another therapeutic treatment option for early prostate cancer in cases in which the individual is not a good surgical candidate. In addition, this approach is used for more extensive disease (Waxman, 1993). This method of treatment is either delivered on a daily basis, over the course of weeks, by way of an external beam or through the surgical implant of radiation seeds. Survival rates for irradiation versus surgery are similar with localized prostate cancer (Held, Osborne, Volpe, & Waldman, 1994; Helgason, Frederikson, Adolfsson, & Steineck, 1995). In patients with more advanced stages of disease, external beam radiation is preferred because treatment may be applied to a larger field. The extent of sexual dysfunction following radiation therapy is influenced by the size of the field to which radiation is administered, damage to the pelvic vascular bed, sympathetic nerve damage, testicular damage from radiation scatter, and decreased testosterone levels (Perez et al., 1989). The effects of the treatment may result in impotence, urethral strictures, urinary incontinence, prostatitis, diarrhea, cystitis, edema of the lower extremities, and bone marrow suppression. Furthermore, ejaculatory pain may result from irradiation to the posterior urethra and a reduction in semen flow (Heinrich-Rynning, 1987). These side effects have an understandably profound impact on an individual's desire to engage in sexual activity as well as in his ability to perform.

Internal beam radiation therapy, otherwise known as brachytherapy, is being used in the treatment of early stage prostate cancer. Its efficacy in controlling later stage cancer and bulkier tumors remains questionable. However, the internal implant appears to result in a lower incidence of sexual difficulties, with a 15% rate of erectile dysfunction (Porter & Forman, 1993). Overall, the use of this procedure has not been well defined and, as further research is made available, the efficacy, advantages, and disadvantages of this treatment option may become clearer (Greenberg, Petersen, Hansen-Peters, & Baylinson, 1990).

Hormonal therapy is primarily used for the management of metastatic disease. The purpose of hormonal manipulation is to attempt to interfere with the cancer cells that are sensitive to or that depend on androgens for growth. There are varying methods through which to facilitate this process including surgery (orchiectomy) or the use of pharmacological agents (i.e., estrogen or luteinizing hormone–releasing hormone analogs). All options result in a decrease in testosterone of up to 90% to 95%. In addition, flutamide is often used to interfere with the adrenal production of testosterone. This combination of total androgen blockage results in slower progression of disease and an improved survival time. Side effects of hormonal therapies include decreased libido, hot flashes, cardiovascular complications, increase in bone pain, urinary dysfunction, impotence, vomiting, and nausea. Hormonal therapy may have a more profound effect on sexual function than either radical prostatectomy or radiation therapy because of its central effect on the brain in reducing desire and arousability (Litwin et al., 1995; Taylor, 1991).

Testicular

Although testicular cancer is rare, accounting for an estimated 7,100 new cases per year, it is the most common form of cancer in men between the ages of 15 and 35 years (ACS, 1995). Increasing interest has emerged among researchers because of the curability of this disease as well as the developmental stage of life at which men are affected. Fertility and sexuality are of primary concern to many of those individuals.

Testicular cancer presents itself in either of two forms, the pure seminomas or nonseminomas. A pure seminoma is radiosensitive, and treatment consists of removal of the diseased testicle (bilateral disease is rare) followed by radiation therapy of the lymph nodes. Should the patient fail to respond to this treatment, chemotherapy is used. A nonseminoma is treated with an orchiectomy followed by chemotherapy. For bulkier tumors, a retroperitoneal lymphadenectomy (RL) may be necessary with the nonseminoma form (Krebs, 1993). An RL has a devastating impact on both fertility and sexuality because the paraaortic sympathetic nerves that innervate these functions are severed. Retrograde ejaculation results in a decreased volume of ejaculation in nearly 100% of cases (Krebs, 1993). Anterograde ejaculation may return spontaneously over the years following surgery or with the assistance of sympathomimetic medication. Nerve-sparing procedures may diminish the effects when possible. Usually desire, erection, and orgasm remain unchanged after treatment for testicular carcinoma. However, in cases in which chemotherapy is necessary, a decreased sex drive is typical in response to side effects that include nausea, diarrhea, fever, weakness, and fatigue.

The psychological impact of testicular carcinoma often produces a significant effect on sexual desire and may lead to sexual avoidance. Couples therapy may be indicated to work through the anxieties over treatment, infertility options, and psychosocial concerns. Because the majority of men are affected during the developmental stage in which they are beginning both their career and family, infertility concerns may be primary. Options of sperm banking should be discussed before the onset of therapy (see the section *Fertility in Men with Cancer*).

Penile

Penile carcinoma accounts for only 1% of diagnosed cancer in males and typically occurs in men older than age 50 years (Andersen & Lamb, 1995). Despite this low incidence, the impact on sexuality from both a physical and psychological perspective may be devastating. When small lesions are present, treatment options include a partial penectomy, radiation therapy, or topical chemotherapy, as opposed to total penectomy with perineal urethrostomy for more advanced stages of the disease. In the case of a partial penectomy, the ability for ejaculation and orgasm remains. In addition, erectile capacity is maintained, although the quality of the erection is influenced by the amount of remaining penile tissue and the patient's premorbid capacity. Although the ability to have an erection is obviously eliminated when a total penectomy is performed, this loss does not have to result in a complete absence of the sexual experience. Arousal may occur with stimulation to other erotically sensitive areas (i.e., mons, scrotum, perineum, and anus) and ejaculation may occur through the perineal urethrostomy. Penile prostheses have been successfully implanted: "A Mayo Clinic study reported a successful placement rate of 90% to 95% and an 8% mechanical failure rate in the three year study period of patients with penile implants. Eighty-nine percent of subjects and mates felt satisfied with function and appearance" (Krebs, 1993, p. 700). Although new technology provides hope of normalization for patients with penile cancer, oncology professionals must recognize the psychological needs of those individuals and assist them in coping with alterations in body image and sexual identity.

CANCER AND THE FEMALE PATIENT

Breast

Breast cancer is the most prevalent site of cancer in women, with more than 182,000 new cases diagnosed yearly (ACS, 1995). Treatment options usually begin with a surgical procedure followed by radiation, chemotherapy, or hormonal therapy. Treatment choices vary depending on the stage of disease, a person's age, and other variables that differentiate the various forms of breast cancer. In some cases, women may experience a modified radical mastectomy and axillary node dissection, whereas in other cases, a lumpectomy and axillary node dissection followed by radiation is the treatment of choice. Many studies have explored the effects of mastectomy versus lumpectomy on sexuality in women. Findings have varied, which, in part, may be attributed to vast individual differences among patients (Kaplan, 1992; Schover et al., 1995).

When breast cancer cells are receptive to estrogen, hormonal manipulation may be necessary. Women may be treated with the antiestrogen compound tamoxifen, which may result in temporary or permanent menopause. Chemotherapy may trigger menopause as well. In either case women may experience soreness, dryness, shrinking of the vagina, hot flashes, mood swings, and a decrease in sexual desire (Kaplan, 1992). Relief of these side effects may be provided by the application of estrogen cream. In addition, studies are presently being conducted worldwide to examine the benefits of using oral estrogen replacement to minimize postmenopausal symptoms in women with breast cancer (Lamb, 1995).

Although breast cancer does not physically impair the ability to engage in sexual activity, the impact of the diagnosis and treatment regime directly affect a woman's sexual identity and ability to perform. The breast has become a symbol of femininity, nurturance, and of one's ability to be a "good mother" in American society. Today, women may make choices in relation to either breast-sparing surgery or reconstruction. These interventions have been shown to have less of a detrimental effect on a woman's self-concept and identity as a sexual being. However, disruption in sexual activity, including orgasmic difficulties and reduced frequency of intercourse, have been reported by up to 39% of women, regardless of the treatment used (Lamb, 1991).

A women's sense of self and the strength of her support system will provide a barometer for how she will cope with the challenge she must face over the course of treatment. Overall, the psychological effect of this disease may far outweigh the physical ramifications. It is therefore the responsibility of health care providers to address the sexual concerns of this population.

Ovarian and Endometrial

Ovarian cancer is the third most frequently diagnosed gynecological malignancy (ACS, 1995). Sexual dysfunction before the diagnosis of ovarian or endometrial cancer may be the catalyst that motivates women to seek medical attention. Patients present with complaints of postcoital bleeding and pelvic pain that interfere with sexual enjoyment. Weight loss, change in bowel function, anorexia, abdominal pain, and increased abdominal girth are symptoms frequently associated with this type of cancer. Although those symptoms may interfere with sexual function, they are typically mild in onset and are associated with later stage disease (Lamb, 1991).

The treatment for ovarian cancer entails surgical interventions including total abdominal hysterectomy, bilateral oophorectomy, and debulking of the tumor followed by chemotherapy, or radiation. This intensive treatment regimen, extending over a long period, has a profound negative effect on the patient's physiologic and psychological well-being, as well as on relationship dynamics.

Surgical removal of the ovaries causes the abrupt onset of menopause. This sudden hormonal shift results in an exacerbation of numerous symptoms associated with menopause such as hot flashes and mood swings. In addition, loss of childbearing capacity is an additional stress to those women in the procreational stage of life. Adjuvant chemotherapy is frequently prescribed to women follow-ing surgery for ovarian cancer. In addition to the stressors mentioned, side effects of chemotherapy such as alopecia, weight loss, fatigue, bone marrow depression, and anorexia have a devastating impact on a woman's sense of body image and sexuality.

In the case of advanced pelvic cancer, a pelvic exenteration may be the treat-ment of choice. This surgery involves removal of the bladder, vagina, uterus, rec-tum, and associated structures. Urinary and fecal evacuation must be rerouted through ostomies. Obviously, sexual function is severely impaired both physi-cally and psychologically. Studies (Auchincloss, 1989; Vera, 1981) have found that the majority of women have reported no sexual activity following this radical procedure.

Overall, gynecological cancers have a tremendous impact on sexual function in women. However, with aggressive counseling and psychosocial support, a nor-malization of sexual function is possible. Patients with emotional, marital, and social health appear to have a better chance of obtaining a positive outcome.

Cervical

Excluding in situ disease, treatment options for cervical cancer include a radi-cal hysterectomy, radiation therapy, or a combination of the two. During the first 6 months following treatment, the effects on sexual function between surgery and radiation approaches have not been found to be different (Schover, Fife, & Gershenson, 1989), perhaps because of the aggressiveness and significant side effects of those treatments. A higher incidence of sexual dysfunction has been found in patients treated with radiation therapy over time resulting from fibrosis, pain of penetration, decreased lubrication, and vaginal stenosis. Those side ef-fects may be minimized through the use of vaginal dilators and lubricants. Psychoeducational support of the patient and significant other should include counseling on alternative positions for intercourse to minimize discomfort.

Vulva

Gynecological cancers in general are the most common type of malignancy diagnosed in women following breast, lung, and colorectal, with 73,000 new cases yearly. Carcinoma of the vulva accounts for 1% of gynecological cancers and is most commonly diagnosed in postmenopausal women (ACS, 1995). Treatment for preinvasive disease may involve surgical excision (simple vulvectomy) of the affected area, wide local excision, the application of 5-fluorouracil cream topi-cally, or laser therapy. Studies have demonstrated that the more aggressive proce-dures have devastating physical and psychological ramifications that lead to a negative impact on a woman's body image and sexual well-being (Lamb, 1995). Although cosmetic alterations with fewer radical treatments are minor in comparison, it is essential that health care providers be aware that the effect on self-esteem and feelings of sexuality is often great (Andersen & Hacker, 1983).

In the case of a simple vulvectomy, studies have shown that sexual function, including the capacity for orgasm, is not necessarily affected (Cartwright-Alcarese, 1995). However, when the clitoris is removed, the degree of sexual impairment is more substantial. It has been found that women may continue to experience sexual pleasure and desire following a radical vulvectomy because adrenal androgens and ovarian hormone function are unaffected. However, some studies (Cartwright-Alcarese, 1995) have shown that a number of patients become nonorgasmic in part because of the psychological distress associated with this type of cancer. Further studies examining the impact on desire and motivation are warranted.

Vaginal

Primary cancer of the vagina is extremely rare and is generally diagnosed at an early stage with a high cure rate (Krebs, 1993). Treatment options vary among surgery, radiation, and chemotherapy based on the stage of the disease. The options may result in abnormalities or the need for reconstruction of the vagina. Sexual dysfunction may occur in the form of shortening and narrowing of the vagina, dryness, and dyspareunia. One study (Hubbard & Shingleton, 1985) showed a return of orgasmic sensations, if the clitoris was left intact, in 30% to 70% of patients who had reconstruction following a total vaginectomy.

CANCER IN BOTH SEXES

Colorectal

Cancer of the colon or the rectum (also called colorectal cancer) affects more than 138,000 men and women yearly. It is the most common cancer that affects both sexes and typically strikes older age groups (ACS, 1995). The mainstay of treatment for colorectal cancer involves an anterior resection, an abdominoperineal resection (APR), pelvic lymphadenectomy, chemotherapy, or radiation therapy. The surgical options result in different degrees of sexual impairment; however, desire is maintained regardless of surgery type because of the continued presence of testosterone.

When an APR is performed, there is significant parasympathetic nerve damage that results in a negative effect on erection and ejaculation. Erectile dysfunction is reported in 50% to 100% of patients following surgery (Grunberg, 1986). This is not necessarily the case with an anterior resection, in which the extent of the surgery will correlate with the degree of erectile impairment. Disruption in ejaculation ability is reported in 50% to 75% of patients who undergo an APR (Dobkin & Broadwell, 1986). Additionally, an APR requires a colostomy, which involves the creation of a stoma and use of an external appliance. After adjustment to the initial diagnosis, treatment plan, and stoma, male patients whose erectile function has not normalized with time may consider the option of a penile prosthesis.

There is a paucity of research on the physiologic effects on sexuality in women. Sexual ramifications such as genital numbness, dyspareunia, and a reduction in sexual desire have been identified (Lamb, 1991). However, the literature has found numerous psychological effects including impairments in body image and sexual avoidance linked to embarrassment from odor and fecal leakage. Research has suggested that sexuality in both sexes is impaired beyond the physical limitations necessitated by the colostomy: "Feelings of depression, anger with no one to blame, and being mutilated are common. Fears of becoming repugnant or being helplessly unable to keep clean must also be addressed" (Auchincloss, 1989, p. 390).

Bladder

Bladder cancer accounts for 2% of malignant tumors, with a greater incidence in males than females (ACS, 1995). Standard treatment involves surgery often followed by radiation therapy. The stage and subsequent treatment of the disease will regulate the extent of sexual dysfunction experienced. Erectile impotence nears 100% in cases in which a radical cystectomy was performed because of nerve damage. However, sexual desire remains unaffected because testosterone production is not disrupted. In addition, orgasm is experienced but ejaculation is retrograde. Transurethral resection, intravesicle chemotherapy, or fulguration used to treat more superficial bladder cancers do not usually result in organic sexual dysfunctions in men (Schover, von Eschenbach, Smith, & Gonzales, 1984).

In women, a radical cystectomy involves a total abdominal hysterectomy, bilateral oophorectomy, and removal of the anterior vaginal wall. This procedure can impair innervation of the perineum, resulting in numbness, a decrease in estrogen, narrowing of the vagina, impaired lubrication, and painful intercourse. Patients can be counseled to use lubricants and vaginal dilators and should receive specific instructions on how to relax pubococcygeal muscles (Kegel exercises) and what positions will make intercourse less painful. Painful intercourse has been reported by both men and women following repeated cystoscopies that result in diminished desire. Women who are able to resume sexual activity following the treatments report an ability to achieve orgasm (Lamb, 1991). Similar to the effects discussed with colorectal cancer, sexual difficulties arise as a result of the necessity of a stoma and ileal conduit to facilitate urinary voiding. Patients experience a deterioration in body image and self-esteem. Patients may use creative methods to minimize embarrassment including bathing before sexual activity and covering the appliance (Shipes, 1987). A new surgical procedure currently under examination, continent diversion, provides a pouch internally for urine and allows the patient to provide self-catheterizations and avoid the presence of an obvious device.

Other Cancers

Other cancer sites with obvious significance to both self-image and sexuality have received less attention in the literature. Head and neck cancer and its treatments, for example, are often severely disfiguring and have a profound effect on a person's body image. Extensive defects often result following aggressive treatment of those cancers as a result of the removal of vast areas of bony and soft tissues from around the head and neck. Speech and swallowing may also be affected. In addition, sexual function may be impaired as a result of treatments (e.g., chemotherapy or irradiation). These patients need tremendous assistance in overcoming feelings that they are repulsive to others and are no longer of sexual appeal.

FERTILITY AND CANCER

Fertility in Women with Cancer

After overcoming the initial shock of a cancer diagnosis and coping with the fears ignited by having a life-threatening illness, fertility concerns often become salient in women of pre-childbearing and childbearing years. The ability to become pregnant following cancer treatment varies among women and is influenced by both individual differences among patients and treatment options.

Although the use of chemotherapy often achieves the sought after outcome of cancer cure, this form of therapy also produces short- and long-term toxicities in patients, resulting in temporary or permanent sterility. This reproductive dysfunction may be a result of hormonal alterations or direct effects that create ovarian fibrosis and follicle destruction, which lead to ovarian ablation.

Age is a primary factor in predicting fertility potential following treatment. Studies have shown (Lamb, 1995) that older women are more likely to experience an accelerated onset of menopause. Pubertal and prepubertal girls, on the other hand, are less likely to experience ovarian damage as a result of chemotherapy. Women younger than age 35 years are able to tolerate a higher dose of chemotherapy than older women, without resulting infertility (Krebs, 1993). Treatment-related factors including type of drug, single versus multiple use of agents, length of therapy, and time since cessation of therapy also play an essential role in reproductive dysfunctions (Lamb, 1995).

Two interventions that may minimize gonadal toxicity resulting from cytoxic chemotherapy regimens have been identified. First, the substitution of drugs that have not been linked to gonadal toxicity may be considered. In addition, the efficacy of using oral contraceptives during treatments to protect the ova and suppress gonadal activity has been studied with controversial results (Lamb, 1995). Further research examining the risks versus benefits of such actions is warranted.

Radiation therapy may also interfere with sexual function and fertility primarily because of ovarian failure. Female reproduction depends on follicular maturation and ovum release, which are altered by this form of treatment. Temporary or permanent sterility is related to age and dose, and also to the amount of tissue exposed to radiation. Studies (Granai, Amado, & Goldstein, 1991; Horning, Hoppe, & Kaplan, 1981), however, have shown that movement of the ovaries out of the field of radiation (ovariopexy) either to the iliac crests or behind the uterus may preserve fertility even when high doses of radiation are being applied.

In vitro fertilization and embryo transfer may be options for females who have experienced infertility as a result of immunologic infertility, endometriosis, or absent and damaged fallopian tubes. Other reproductive options, which yield a successful pregnancy outcome of approximately 40%, include the use of cryopreserved oocytes and zygotes (Abdalla, Barber, & Kirkland, 1989; Levran, Dor, & Rudak, 1991; Seibel, 1988). In addition, egg donation and surrogacy may provide hope for women who are not able to use alternative reproductive techniques. It is essential that reproductive counseling be initiated with the patient and her partner before the onset of therapy. Counseling is especially critical in patients who may choose to reap the benefits of cryopreserved oocytes.

Fertility in Men with Cancer

Men who are diagnosed with cancer often voice similar concerns to those of women in terms of their reproductive potential following treatment. Unfortunately, many men will be subfertile or infertile at the time of diagnosis (Schover, 1988). Scar tissue or damage to the pelvic nerve and lymph glands secondary to cancer-related surgical procedures may result in infertility as well. It is essential that oncology professionals educate patients and their partners about the techniques available to assist them in achieving parenthood following treatment.

The effect of chemotherapy on male fertility is determined by the dose and class of chemotherapeutic agent used. A higher probability of reproductive dysfunction has been found in men undergoing higher doses of chemotherapy and those exposed to alkylating agents. Those treatments cause injury to the germinal epithelium lining of seminiferous tubule (Monga, 1995). When possible, chemotherapeutic agents that do not correlate as highly with infertility should be used.

Similar to the effects of radiation therapy on fertility in women, male fertility is influenced by age, dose, exposure time, and site of treatment. When the testes are exposed to radiation, the sperm count begins to decrease and, depending on the dosage, may result in temporary or permanent sterility (Krebs, 1993). However, men who receive radiation to the abdominal or pelvic region may regain partial or full sperm production depending on the amount of injury to the testes. When possible, attempts should be made to protect testes from radiation damage through the use of lead shields. In addition, when infertility is a result of abnormal hormone production, the use of hormone manipulation may lead to a successful return of sperm production (Gradishar & Schilsky, 1988).

Before the initiation of any of the preceding interventions, the practitioner should discuss semen storage for use in artificial insemination with those patients who desire to procreate in the future. Semen storage provides the patient with protection from the antifertility and mutagenic effects of cancer treatments. This option may not be appropriate for all patients for several reasons. Many men may be infertile or subfertile at the time of diagnosis. In addition, because sperm banking must be completed before the initiation of treatment, men with rapidly progressing disease frequently do not have the option of delaying interventions until the completion of the cryopreservation process. In addition, this procedure is extremely costly, and approximately 25% of frozen sperm die per year. However, pregnancy rates as high as 45% have been reported following the use of this technique (American Society for Reproductive Medicine, 1995).

Both men and women have significant fear regarding reproductive capabilities following cancer treatments. Although reproductive options have advanced and have provided new hope for cancer survivors, most options are expensive, stressful, and involve the potential inclusion of another individual in the pregnancy process (i.e., a surrogate). In addition, all of the options involve the risk that time, money, and emotions will be exhausted only to result in failed attempts at obtaining pregnancy following cancer treatment. Judicious counseling can be of immense value to individuals and couples at a time when they are faced with the uncertainties of a cancer diagnosis. They are suddenly thrown into the health care system and are asked to make decisions regarding treatment options while struggling simultaneously with issues of life versus death.

PSYCHOSOCIAL FACTORS INFLUENCING SEXUALITY

The emotions that come in to play following a diagnosis of cancer cover the entire affective spectrum, ranging from disbelief to profound sadness. Many of these painful emotions, including anxiety and depression, have a direct impact on an individual's sexual function. Diminished self-concept and body image as well as role changes are a few common ramifications created by the toll that a cancer diagnosis takes on an individual. It is essential to keep in mind that difficulties can occur at any phase in cancer care from the point of diagnosis, through treatment, during recovery periods, and ongoing.

Although men and women may experience different types of cancer treatments, the psychological effects are universal. An affective response is evoked by both the reality of disfigurement following treatment as well as a person's self-perception. Situational depression and anxiety are often experienced as individuals have difficulty coping and adapting to their new body. Clinical interviews have indicated that up to 25% of hospitalized cancer patients meet the criteria for a clinical depression (Lamb, 1991). Patients may go through an expected period of grief and mourning over the multiple losses they have experienced. During this time, their sexual desire is diminished, and even if normal sexual function is possible from a physiologic perspective, psychological distress may interfere in erection, premature ejaculation, lubrication, and orgasm.

In terms of body image, patients often describe themselves as damaged goods who feel mutilated and deformed as a result of treatment. They may feel that these deformities (e.g., mastectomy) are as repulsive to others as they are to them. In turn, they have difficulty believing that others could find them sexually attractive and fear rejection and abandonment. These concerns are exacerbated in individuals with ostomies who also may worry about odor, leakage, and the appearance of the stoma and appliance. However, self-esteem may be negatively affected, with or without overt changes to one's body (Foltz, 1987).

The experience of cancer is a devastating blow to a person's sense of competence and ability in all areas. The numerous roles (e.g., husband, wife, parent, homemaker, or breadwinner) the patient fulfilled before the cancer diagnosis are temporarily and often permanently affected by cancer and treatments. This loss of control may also be true for patients who must deal with issues of sexual intimacy. The experience of loss of control in one's life, in and of itself, lowers their sense of sexual competence. It may be difficult for men or women to see themselves as a sexual partner when they are unable to fulfill their role as breadwinner or caregiver. In addition, cancer patients are dealing with new bodies that have different sensations and functions. In many cases, they can tolerate only certain positions, and when intercourse is impossible, they must achieve enjoyment through alternate methods. As a result of this failure to perform, individuals may find themselves in a pattern of sexual avoidance.

People who are in existing relationships may experience this crisis as a test that will result in a strengthening or breakup of the couple. However, individuals who are single may withdraw from social and sexual contacts for fear of rejection and embarrassment. All of these factors pinpoint the essential need for health care professionals to be aware that sexuality is a basic human need for these patients and significantly affects their quality of life.

ASSESSMENT AND INTERVENTION MODEL

As in the general population, the sexual needs and concerns of cancer patients vary. A person's sexual health can best be determined by the inclusion of this topic in an initial psychosocial assessment. This session should begin with a thorough sexual history including questions regarding relationship status, frequency of intercourse, prior dysfunctions, and an understanding of how important sexuality is in the patient's life. Various authors have suggested asking questions such as: Has being ill interfered with your being a (husband, father, wife, mother)? Has your illness changed your sense of self? Has your illness interfered with your sexual desire? (Lamb & Woods, 1981). The presentation of this type of assessment should be done by a professional with whom the patient has established trust. One way to increase this trust is to begin with less threatening, open-ended questions and to actively listen to the patient's individual worries. If the patient has a partner, he or she should also be an active part of both the initial assessment and intervention plan.

One model used successfully with cancer patients is the Annon (1974) PLISSIT model, which provides four levels of intervention. The first three levels involve brief therapy and the fourth is more intensive: *p*ermission, *l*imited *i*nformation, *s*pecific *s*uggestions, and *i*ntensive *t*herapy.

The practitioner should initiate the permission level during the initial assessment and continue it during both the preoperative and postoperative periods. During the permission level, the patient and partner are given permission to express sexual concerns, including their sexuality while they are undergoing and recovering from treatment as well as their lack of sexual appetite or sexual desire during that time. The permission phase establishes an environment in which a health care professional accepts and validates sexual communication and concerns in an unconditional manner. During this period, the patient and partner's experiences are normalized and fears that their experiences are uncommon are eased. The patient and partner are encouraged to share their experiences and feelings with one another, although they are often reluctant to discuss such issues.

Limited information is the second level of treatment in the PLISSIT model. This level incorporates the permission level and also provides the patient and partner with factual information regarding aspects of sexuality and fertility that are influenced by the disease. At times, the practitioner must present and explain basic information on "normal" human sexuality to the individual or couple and also clarify myths, questions, fears, and misconceptions. Furthermore, the health care professional will address common anxieties about contagion and an acceleration of tumor growth as a result of sex. The process is once again normalized for the individual or couple because they are informed of the appropriateness of sexual activity at this point and their concerns about present and future abilities (e.g., erectile dysfunction, ejaculation, and orgasm) are addressed.

Once the phases of permission and limited information are accomplished, some patients require specific suggestions to tackle their problems—the third level of intervention. Before initiating specific suggestions for alternatives to increase sexual satisfaction, however, the practitioner should obtain a thorough sexual problem history. This history will help provide the clinician with a clear picture about the problems that preceded the cancer diagnosis. Such issues may need to be treated in a different manner because they may be related to other medical conditions and preexisting relationship conflicts. In addition, this assessment should include questions regarding the couple's values and beliefs as they relate to sexuality. Furthermore, a requirement during this level is the patient's clearly stated goal, which the health care professional can assist the patient to achieve. For example, common concerns focus on difficulties with arousal before and comfort during sexual activity. The health care provider may inform the couple of methods to decrease discomfort, such as alternative positions while engaging in intercourse. In addition, problem solving related to difficulties with arousal may include the substitution of alternative methods to achieve sexual pleasure (e.g., oral stimulation or digital stimulation). During this level, the importance of open communication between the couple is identified. It is essential that the patient and his or her partner be able to discuss their emotional responses to the cancer, their fears, and their concerns. They must be able to identify their sexual needs for their partner to feel fulfilled following sexual activity.

If the patient or couple are dissatisfied with the achievements made during the first three phases, the fourth level of intensive therapy may be warranted. During this level, the practitioner should refer the couple to a psychologist, counselor, sex therapist, physician, or nurse trained in this specialty. Working with a specialist will allow the couple to work through both long-standing sexual and marital problems as well as newly emerged difficulties on an ongoing basis. This level also covers such interventions as the insertion of a penile prosthesis or the provision of other intensive medical therapies to remediate sexual dysfunction.

CONCLUSION

As individuals with a cancer diagnosis have begun to experience more "disease-free" survival time, more attention is being directed toward quality of life issues for these patients. Regardless of a person's age, sexual expression continues to be an essential component that factors into his or her quality of life. It is obvious that a cancer diagnosis and its treatments have a devastating effect on a person as a sexual being, from both a physiologic and a psychological perspective. Nonetheless, the study of sexual dysfunctions among patients remains relatively new and has focused predominantly on the physical repercussions. However, the increasing attention to sexual dysfunctions in these patients is encouraging.

The urgency for health care professionals to identify and evaluate sexual difficulties with their patients in the clinical setting in which the cancer treatment is prescribed should be apparent. Unfortunately, the majority of health care providers seem to shy away from discussions regarding the patient's sexuality because of their own discomfort with the topic. Patients are often left without information, thus feeling isolated and abandoned. Providing the patient with an environment in which to express sexual concerns may assist people in leading the fullest life possible and increase their self-confidence as sexual beings.

With continuing research and an increase in the willingness of oncology professionals to overcome their own anxieties and undertake this responsibility, sexual dysfunctions among these patients may be successfully identified and treated more often. Only awareness of these concerns will allow professionals to assist patients to experience the quality of life they deserve.

REFERENCES

Abdalla H.I., Barber, R.J., & Kirkland A. (1989). Pregnancy in women with premature ovarian failure using tubal and intrauterine transfer of cryopreserved zygotes. *British Journal of Obstetrics and Gynaecology, 96*, 1071–1075.

American Cancer Society. (1995). *Cancer facts & figures—1995*. New York: Author.

American Society for Reproductive Medicine. (1995). Fertility after cancer treatment: A guide for patients. *(Patient Information Series)*. Birmingham, AL: Author.

Andersen, B.L., & Hacker, N.F. (1983). Psychosexual adjustment after vulvar surgery. *Obstetrics and Gynecology, 62*, 457–462.

Andersen, B.L., & Lamb, M.A. (1995). Sexuality and cancer. In R. Lanhard, W. Lawrence, & G. Murphy (Eds.), *American cancer textbook of clinical oncology* (pp. 700–711). New York: American Cancer Society.

Annon, J. (1974). *The behavioral treatment of sexual problems, I*. Honolulu: Kapiolani Health Services.

Auchincloss, S.S. (1989). Sexual dysfunction in cancer patients: Issues in evaluation and treatment. In J.C. Holland & J.H. Rowland (Eds.), *Handbook of psychooncology: Psychological care of the patient with cancer* (pp. 383–413). New York: Oxford University Press.

Brender, C., & Walsh, P. (1992). Prostate cancer: Evaluation and radiotherapeutic management. *CA: A Cancer Journal for Clinicians, 42*, 223–240.

Cartwright-Alcarese, F. (1995). Addressing sexual dysfunction following radiation therapy for a gynecologic malignancy. *Oncology Nursing Forum, 22*(8), 1227–1232.

Dobkin, K.A., & Broadwell, D.C. (1986). Nursing considerations for the patient undergoing colostomy surgery. *Seminars in Oncology Nursing, 2*, 249–255.

Foltz, A.T. (1987). The influence of cancer on self concept and quality of life. *Seminars in Oncology Nursing, 3*, 303–312.

Gradishar, W.J., & Schilsky, R.L. (1988). Effects of cancer treatment on the reproductive system. *Critical Reviews in Oncology and Hematology, 8*(2), 153–171.

Granai, C.O., Amado, P.M., & Goldstein, A.S. (1991). The effects of cancer therapy on fertility. *Clinical Advances in Oncology Nursing, 3,* 1, 3, 7–9.

Greenberg, S., Petersen, J., Hansen-Peters, I., & Baylinson, W. (1990). Interstitially implanted I125 for prostate cancer using transrectal ultrasound. *Oncology Nursing Forum, 17,* 849–854.

Grunberg, K.J. (1986). Sexual rehabilitation of the cancer patient undergoing ostomy surgery. *Journal of Enterostomal Therapy, 13,* 148–152.

Heinrich-Rynning, T. (1987). Prostatic cancer treatments and their effects on sexual function. *Oncology Nursing Forum, 14*(6), 37–41.

Held, J.L., Osborne, D.M., Volpe, H., & Waldman, A.R. (1994). Cancer of the prostate: Treatment and nursing implications. *Oncology Nursing Forum, 21*(9), 1517–1529.

Helgason, A.R., Fredrikson, M., Adolfsson, J., & Steineck, G. (1995). Decreased sexual capacity after external radiation therapy for prostate cancer impairs quality of life. *International Journal of Radiation Oncology, Biology, Physics, 32*(1), 33–39.

Horning S.J., Hoppe R.T., & Kaplan H.S. (1981). Female reproductive potential after treatment for Hodgkin's disease. *New England Journal of Medicine, 304,* 1377–1382.

Hubbard, J.L., & Shingleton, H.M. (1985). Sexual function of patients after cancer of the cervix treatment. *Clinical Obstetrics and Gynecology 12,* 247–264.

Kaplan, H.S. (1992). A neglected issue: The sexual side effects of current treatments for breast cancer. *Journal of Sex and Marital Therapy, 18*(1), 3–19.

Krebs, L.U. (1993). Sexual and reproductive dysfunction. In S.L. Groenwald, M. Goodman, M.H. Frogge, & C.H. Yarbro (Eds.), *Cancer nursing: Principles and practice* (pp. 697–719). Boston: Jones and Bartlett.

Lamb, M. (1991). Alterations in sexuality and sexual functioning. In S.B. Baird, R. McCorkle, & M. Grant (Eds.), *Cancer nursing: A comprehensive textbook* (pp. 831–849). Philadelphia: W.B. Saunders.

Lamb, M.A. (1995). Effects of cancer on the sexuality and fertility of women. *Seminars in Oncology Nursing, 11*(2), 120–127.

Lamb, M., & Woods, N.F. (1981). Sexuality and the cancer patient. *Cancer Nursing, 4,* 137–144.

Levran, D., Dor, J., & Rudak, E. (1991). Pregnancy potential of human oocytes—The effect of cryopreservation. *New England Journal of Medicine, 323,* 1153–1156.

Litwin, M.S., Hays, R.D., Fink, A., Ganz, P.A., Leake, B., Leach, G.E., & Brook, R.H. (1995). Quality-of-life outcomes in men treated for localized prostate cancer. *Journal of the American Medical Association, 273*(2), 129–135.

Monga, U. (1995). Sexuality in cancer patients. *Physical Medicine and Rehabilitation: State of the Art Reviews, 9*(2), 417–442.

Perez, C.A., Fair, W.R., & Ihde, D.C. (1989). Carcinoma of the prostate. In V.T. DeVita, S. Hellman, & S. Rosenberg (Eds.), *Cancer principles and practice of oncology* (3rd ed., pp. 1023–1058). Boston: Jones & Bartlett.

Porter, A., & Forman, J. (1993). Prostate brachytherapy: An overview. *Cancer, 71,* 953–958.

Quinlan, D.M., Epstein, J.I., Carter, B.S., & Walsh, P.C. (1991). Sexual function following radical prostatectomy: Influence of preservation of neurovascular bundles. *Journal of Urology, 145,* 998–1002.

Schover, L.R. (1988). *Sexuality & cancer: For the man who has cancer, and his partner.* New York: American Cancer Society.

Schover, L.R., Fife, M., & Gershenson, D.M. (1989). Sexual dysfunction and treatment for early stage cervical cancer. *Cancer, 63*, 204–212.

Schover, L.R., von Eschenbach, A.C., Smith, D.B., & Gonzales, J. (1984). Sexual rehabilitation of urologic cancer patients: A practical approach. *CA: A Cancer Journal for Clinicians, 34*(2), 66–73.

Schover, L.R., Yetman, R.J., Tuason, L.J., Meisler, E., Esselstyn, C.B., Hermann, R.E., Grundfest-Broniatowski, S., & Dowden, R.V. (1995). Partial mastectomy and breast reconstruction. *Cancer, 75*, 54–64.

Seibel, M.M. (1988). A new era in reproductive technology: In vitro fertilization, gamete intrafallopian transfer, and donated gametes and embryos. *New England Journal of Medicine, 318*, 828–834.

Shipes, E. (1987). Sexual functioning following ostomy surgery. *Nursing Clinics of North America, 22*, 303–310.

Taylor, R. (1991). Endocrine therapy for advanced stage D prostate cancer. *Urologic Nursing, 11*(3), 22–26.

Vera, M.I. (1981). Quality of life following pelvic exenteration. *Gynecological Oncology, 12*, 355–366.

Waxman, E.S. (1993). Sexual dysfunction following treatment for prostate cancer: Nursing assessment and interventions. *Oncology Nursing Forum, 20*(10), 1567–1571.

CHAPTER 18

Sexual Development of Children and Adolescents

Donald Kewman, Seth Warschausky, Lisa Engel,
and William Warzak

The development of sexuality involves a complex interaction between the psychosocial consequences of chronic disease and disability and the direct physiologic effects of medical conditions and treatments. Other chapters in this book describe the physiologic effects of different disabilities on sexual function and reproduction in detail. For that reason, this chapter concentrates on the psychological and behavioral aspects of sexual expression in children and adolescents. Children with chronic physical conditions constitute 10% to 20% of the population (Wallander & Thompson, 1995), with about 1% to 2% with severe physical disability (Gortmaker & Sappenfield, 1984). Furthermore, 10% of children and adolescents experience serious chronic physical disorders or disease by age 18 years (Neinstein & Katz, 1986a). This chapter focuses on children and adolescents with physical handicaps and chronic diseases, and makes limited reference to youths with mental handicaps or with visual or hearing impairment.

In efforts to characterize psychosocial and sexual development, some authors have distinguished between children and adolescents with significant body disfigurement or a conspicuous disability versus those with a concealable disfigurement or disability. For example, Blos and Finch (1974) have described the greater difficulty individuals with conspicuous disabilities may have with the development of sexuality. Another important dichotomy is the degree to which the medical condition affects cognitive or behavioral function, which may dramatically affect socialization and the ability to form peer relationships. Early onset of disability (before age 3 years) versus later-onset disability (after age 18 years) also has been shown to influence the nature and frequency of sexual expression (DeHaan & Wallander, 1988), again probably a function of social development. The chapter authors contend that these variables affect the degree to which adolescents are successful in forming peer relationships. Furthermore, the evidence presented in this chapter highlights the importance of the ability to form relationships with peers as a critical mediator of sexual adjustment for children and adolescents with disabilities and chronic illness.

PSYCHOSEXUAL DEVELOPMENT

Numerous studies have indicated the increased risk of psychosocial dysfunction in children with disabilities (e.g., Dorner, 1976; Guralnick & Weinhouse, 1984; Lavigne & Faier-Routman, 1992). Typically, psychosocial factors have a greater effect on the development of sexuality than the person's physical condition (Evans & Conine, 1985). Cole (1981) has termed these effects "isolation from intimacy" (p. 3). In addition to the secondary effects of psychological problems, the risk of developing social isolation has been associated with limited accessibility to peer activities and overly protective parenting (Greydanus, Demarest, & Sears, 1985; Yarkony & Anderson, 1996). Evidence has suggested that the long-term effects of isolation differ from those of rejection. Decades of research on social stigma of disability have highlighted the extent to which children are subject to stigmatization from a very early age (Centers & Centers, 1963; Sigelman & Begley, 1987), despite efforts to "mainstream" such youngsters and promote greater community integration.

Factors associated with disability will have different effects on different stages of psychosexual development. In what has been termed the "magnification phenomenon" (Woodhead & Murph, 1985, p. 175), the early effects of disability can be magnified in the succession of developmental stages. In addition, acquired disabilities will have different effects depending on the child's developmental stage at the time of onset. A congenital disability will be integrated into ongoing sexual development and maturation; sexual adjustment will be shaped by the experience of disability. A disabling injury that occurs in childhood or adolescence, however, may disrupt beliefs and expectations regarding future sexual roles and sexual function (T. Cole & S. Cole, 1982). Cole (1981) has made the distinction between deficits in early development versus the need to redefine aspects of the self with later-onset disability.

Disability may have complex effects on the development of gender or sex identity. Among children without disability, there has been debate in the literature about the age at which children attain gender constancy, with a range from approximately age 3 years to 7 years given (Serbin, Powlishta, & Gulko, 1993). Clearly, there are environmental effects on sex-typed preferences; for example, children whose mothers are engaged in less traditional sex-typed tasks are less sex-typed in their own preferences (Serbin et al., 1993). Findings have suggested that children with disabilities and chronic diseases may have mothers who are necessarily in more traditional roles because the children frequently need a "full-time" parent caregiver (Warschausky, Engel, Augenstein, & Nelson, 1995); hence, those children may exhibit less sex-role flexibility than would normally emerge in middle childhood. In addition, evidence exists of more cross-sex friendships in children with disabilities (Bohnert, Parker, & Warschausky, in press), again with potential implications for sex-typing and flexibility—that is, cross-sex friendships may influence development of less rigid sex-typing and greater role flexibility.

The effects of disability on development of sexuality may be identifiable from birth. Investigators have placed great emphasis on the prerequisites of sexuality such as emotional responsiveness (Robinault, 1978). Development of emotional responsiveness is predicted in part by mother–infant interactions in the course of being held and fed (Stern, 1977). Infants with disabilities may have altered patterns of interactions with their mothers because of physical abnormalities and medical treatment or may have altered responses to contact as a result of cognitive, motor, or sensory impairment, thus constraining pleasurable mother–infant interaction (Battle, 1974). Parents may diminish or alter their interactions with the infant with disabilities in response to real or perceived aspects of the child's condition. The persisting effects of parents' perceptions of vulnerability or fragility of the infant on parent–child interactions that then affect development have been termed the "vulnerable child syndrome" (Green & Solnit, 1964, p. 58). This syndrome, in which parents have difficulty supporting age-appropriate development of independence, has been the focus of renewed interest in recent years (Thomasgard & Metz, 1995).

In middle childhood, development of sexuality includes acquiring sexual language. Peers, rather than parents, typically facilitate the acquisition of this information (Woodhead & Murph, 1985). As a result of relative social isolation from peer contacts, children with physical disabilities may have limited opportunities to develop an understanding of sexual terminology (Cole & Cole, 1983). The demands on parents of children with disabilities are so great that it is typical to neglect parenting tasks related to sexuality education (Capell & Capell, 1981).

In early adolescence, parents' and child's concerns about sexual development may become more prominent. In the nondisabled population, there are complex interactions between social development and the onset of puberty. For example, males with early maturation have been shown to have social advantages through high school, but as adults, they tend to be less creative and independent (Clausen, 1975; Livson & Peskin, 1980). Evidence has indicated that pubertal maturation may have direct effects on sexual behavior, as well. Udry, Talbert, and Morris (1986), for example, found that androgenic hormones were related to sexual interest and motivation in girls. Testosterone levels in boys have been associated with sexual activity, including intercourse (Udry, Billy, Morris, Groff, & Raj, 1985).

Physical conditions and medical interventions can have both direct effects on puberty and indirect effects on adolescent sexual development. Puberty can be either delayed or accelerated by illness, condition, or medications (McAnarney, 1985; Woodhead & Murph, 1985). Diverse conditions such as spina bifida, cerebral palsy (CP; Blum, Resnick, Nelson, & St. Germaine, 1991), spinal cord injury (Warschausky, Engel, Kewman, & Nelson, 1996), and blindness result in increased risk of altered adolescent sexual development. Indirect risk factors for delayed sexual development include general social isolation (Cromer et al., 1990; Dorner, 1977; McAndrew, 1979), social competence deficits (Lavigne & Faier-Routman, 1992), the effects of therapeutic regimens on social activity, parental constraints on increasing independence (McAnarney, 1985), lack of knowledge about sexuality, lack of understanding about one's own sexual or reproductive capabilities, and parental doubts regarding adolescent capabilities and potential (Hayden, Davenport, & Campbell, 1979). Middle-to-late adolescence is the period during which most individuals first have sexual intercourse (Woodhead & Murph, 1985). Normal adolescent experimentation may be either limited or attenuated by insecurity or self-esteem issues in the population with disabilities (McAnarney, 1985). Coupey and Cohen (1984), in a discussion of sex differences in adolescents' ability to overcome obstacles associated with their physical conditions as well as the nature of those obstacles, indicated that girls experience less disruption of their relationships.

If onset of disability occurs during the adolescent period, psychosocial effects apparently can be particularly devastating with secondary effects of adjustment reactions on psychosexual development. This topic is discussed quite extensively in the spinal cord–injury literature (Dewis, 1989; Kewman, Warschausky, & Engel, 1995; Rutledge & Dick, 1983; Trieschmann, 1988; Warschausky et al., 1996). Issues may arise related to losing independence that are particularly relevant to youths for whom independence was the previous developmental focus (Mulcahey, 1991). Comparisons to one's premorbid self may be especially difficult and disruptive to adjustment (Kempton, 1988). Some authors (Evans & Conine, 1985; Greydanus et al., 1985) have described the difficulties adolescents with disabilities face in dealing with the age-appropriate preoccupation with appearance and body image. Adolescents with chronic illnesses and disabilities must cope with coming to terms with a body image that incorporates their physical abnormalities.

Body Image

The illness or disability and its treatment may result in alterations in the child or adolescent's body, for example, short stature in renal disorders and cystic fibrosis (CF), delayed or precocious puberty, or alopecia in collagen vascular disease or as a result of chemotherapy (Selekman & McIlvain-Simpson, 1991). Children and adolescents react to these changes in a variety of ways. According to Offer, Ostrov, and Howard (1984), males are more sensitive than females to impairment of their bodies.

The literature has suggested that adolescents with spinal cord injuries compare their bodies unfavorably with those of their able-bodied peers and reject themselves (Mulcahey, 1991), or go to great lengths to cover up their disabilities with clothing and to hide injury-related symptoms such as pain and fatigue (Dewis, 1989). Adolescents with CF also become adept at disguising their illness-related thinness with clothing and hairstyles (Boyle, di Sant'Agnese, Sack, Millican, & Kulczycki, 1976). One-half of the subjects in a study conducted by Coffman, Levine, Althof, and Stern (1984) reported feeling unattractive because of CF-related body characteristics such as extreme thinness, shortness, clubbed fingers, or stained teeth. More than one-half of the subjects with CF in a study by Boyle et al. (1976) drew male and female figures with almost no differences in body characteristics. The subjects' drawings showed other body distortions, as well.

Accessibility

Accessibility issues also become barriers to interacting and learning from peers informally (Cole & Cole, 1993; Daniels, 1981; McKown & English, 1986). Adolescents with disabilities may lack easily available opportunities to interact with other adolescents outside of school, even if they are not lacking in social skills. For instance, if a teenager has to be catheterized, transferred into an electric wheelchair, assisted into a van, and delivered to a friend's home or public event where further assistance is needed to get into and out of the building, spontaneity, social experiences, and risk taking may be inhibited (Cole & Cole, 1993).

Abuse

The occurrence of physical or sexual abuse can also have a dramatic effect on the development of sexuality in people with disability and chronic disease (Sullivan & Scanlan, 1987). Finkelhor, Hotaling, Lewis, and Smith (1990) found that 27% of women and 16% of men in the general population reported at least one experience of childhood sexual abuse. Children and adolescents with cognitive or physical disabilities or chronic diseases may depend more on others for personal care that involves opportunities for caregivers to engage in intimate touching or sexual acts. For this and other reasons, the incidence of abuse is believed to be higher in this population (American Nurses' Association, 1979; Cohen & Warren, 1987; Tharinger, Horton, & Millea, 1990). Glaser and Bentovim's (1979) data have suggested that, after age 5 years, children with handicaps are three times more likely to be abused. Baladerian (1991) reported that the rates for sexual abuse of developmentally disabled children may be even greater than those of the general population of children with disabilities. Chamberlain, Rauh, Passer, McGrath, and Burket (1984) reported that one-third of mildly retarded and one-fourth of moderately retarded female youths had been victims of rape or incest. Chapter 28 addresses the issue of sexual abuse in more depth.

Acquisition of Knowledge and Attitudes

The literature widely reflects the importance of peer influence on the sexual knowledge and attitudes of a child with a disability (Cole & Cole, 1993; Evans & Conine, 1985; McKown & English, 1986; Renshaw, 1985; Robinault, 1978). Evans and Conine (1985) reported that school-age children rely on peers for discussion of sexual ideas and to develop social skills. A child's disability often interferes with making friends and forming a peer group. The authors suggested that the child with chronic illness can be best assisted in forming friendships by encouraging the child to engage in age-appropriate activities in which he or she can share with others and by allowing the child privacy when with friends.

McKown and English (1986) and Cole and Cole (1993) have emphasized the importance of peer feedback to the adolescent's developing sense of sexual identity. Adolescents with disabilities need opportunities to interact with peers to engage in social experimentation that leads to adult social and sexual satisfaction. Socially isolated adolescents with chronic illnesses may have even greater difficulty forming a sense of sexual identity and may eventually doubt their rights to be sexual people (McKown & English, 1986). Sexual information is generally learned without oversight from parents and is greatly and dramatically influenced by peers and the media. Limited contact with peers may leave children with disabilities or chronic illness lacking in knowledge about sex education and sexual behavior (Robinault, 1978). Adolescents with disabilities often lack the sexual knowledge and the social skills necessary to become responsible sexual partners (Blum, 1984). Another difficult issue for children and adolescents with chronic illnesses and disabilities is the lack of role models (Thornton, 1981). These children know few others with chronic illnesses and they are likely never to have been exposed to adults with a disability or chronic illness who have made good sexual and social adjustments to life. If these children see only able-bodied and healthy adolescents and adults relating sexually, they may question if sexuality is or should be a part of their own lives.

Contraception and Reproduction

Adolescents with chronic illnesses and disabilities frequently lack knowledge regarding many specific areas of sexuality affected by their disease or disability. Studies (Cromer et al., 1990; Haefner & Elkins, 1991) have found that many youths with disabilities express an interest and expectation that they will marry, yet few have inquired or have been provided information related to sexual and reproductive function. For instance, many adolescents with disabilities do not know how their disabilities affect reproduction. Nolen, Desmond, Herlich, and Hardy (1986) conducted a study in which a standardized questionnaire was used to assess knowledge of their disease in 28 patients with CF who ranged in age from 10 to 21 years. The results showed that patients understood the nature of their disease and treatment, but were less knowledgeable about genetic implications and effects on reproduction. Younger CF patients showed less knowledge regarding genetics and reproduction than did older patients. Female patients showed better knowledge of the disease including genetic and reproductive aspects than did the male patients. Of the patients aged 13 years and older, 83% said that they had thought about having children, yet 39% of these older patients were unaware of the health risks that pregnancy can cause in women with CF. Of the patients, 75% indicated no knowledge that almost all males with CF are sterile.

Different populations of chronically ill teenagers may have different perceptions of their fertility, which may or may not be accurate. Cromer et al. (1990) studied sexual knowledge and attitudes in adolescents with CF and myelomeningocele as well as in an able-bodied control group using a sexual knowledge questionnaire and a structured interview. They found that 50% of boys with CF and 75% of boys with myelodysplasia thought they could impregnate a girl. Significantly more girls with CF and myelodysplasia thought they would have medical complications as a result of pregnancy than did the girls in the control group. Although 50% of adolescents with myelodysplasia and 75% of those with CF thought that they were at greater risk of transmitting their illness genetically, the majority of those adolescents said they wished to have children. All the adolescents in the study had sex education in school and, yet, the knowledge of reproductive issues was significantly lower in the adolescents with myelodysplasia and CF than in the control group. This disparity remained even when researchers controlled the data for level of intelligence quotient (IQ).

Although authors seem to agree that adolescents with disabilities and chronic illnesses should be well informed about contraception as well as the health risks of pregnancy to the chronically ill woman and the unborn child, little has been published about these adolescents' knowledge and attitudes about contraception (Robinault, 1978). Such information is particularly important because of the increased risk of morbidity and mortality for pregnant women with many illnesses and disabilities (Neinstein & Katz, 1986a, 1986b). Neinstein and Katz have touted the importance of knowledgeable and sympathetic family planning counseling to patients' adjustment to their illness. They have emphasized that lack of information or misinformation may be life-threatening, yet it is difficult for the female adolescent with a chronic illness to place high priority on the use of contraception if she is more concerned about her chronic health condition. They have recommended sensitively addressing this issue when discussing the risks of pregnancy and contraception.

The use of contraception by adolescents depends on various factors including their perception of risk of pregnancy or sexually transmitted disease (STD), cognitive ability to plan and use measures, and physical capabilities to use different techniques. Barrier methods may be safe for all teenagers, but dexterity or cognitive problems may limit their use, and failure rates for barrier methods with the general teenage population is twice the adult rate (Neinstein & Katz, 1986a). Unfortunately, oral contraceptives may worsen certain heart conditions; change seizure threshold; interact with antiseizure medications to increase the risk of pregnancy; and, in girls with CF, decrease pulmonary status (Neinstein & Katz, 1986a). Enhanced passage or poor absorption of gastrointestinal contents caused by some chronic conditions can decrease oral contraceptive effectiveness (Hanker, 1990). Concerns with contraceptive safety or effectiveness may discourage their use in some populations of teenagers with chronic disease or disability. In mentally impaired teenagers, among whom poor planning and decision making may affect use of oral or barrier methods, the largest number in the Chamberlain et al. (1984) sample used injectable medroxyprogesterone acetate. Of the developmentally disabled youths in their study, 48% used contraception. They found a meager 32% 1-year continuation rate for oral contraceptives and a high rate of pregnancy for sexually active adolescents with disabilities.

STDs

Few studies have been published regarding the attitudes and knowledge of adolescents with chronic disease and disability regarding STD or contraception, despite acknowledgment of their importance (Cole & Cole, 1993; Kahn, 1994; Robinault, 1978; Thornton, 1981). One exception is the literature regarding the attitudes and knowledge of adolescents with hemophilia regarding acquired immune deficiency syndrome (AIDS). Overby, Lo, and Litt (1989) studied a population of adolescents with hemophilia with a human immunodeficiency virus antibody positivity rate of 70% to 90%. The factual knowledge of AIDS in 26 patients with hemophilia, aged 13 to 19 years old, was tested using a questionnaire developed for the study. Subjects showed a high degree of factual knowledge of the causes, history, transmission, and prevention of AIDS. However, subjects also reported that they were not following safer sex precautions consistently. A number of the subjects said they had not informed their partners about their hemophilia for fear of being rejected. Safer sex was not fashionable, required planning, and could reduce sexual pleasure. The adolescents also spoke of attitudes of invulnerability or fatalism regarding their risk of acquiring AIDS.

Knowledge and Attitudes Regarding Sexual Behavior

In exploring the knowledge and attitudes of adolescents with disabilities toward sexual function, it is helpful to consider that just because teenagers are sexually active does not mean they are knowledgeable regarding sexual issues (Kahn, 1994). College students with disabilities and their able-bodied counterparts have been the subjects of several studies of knowledge and attitude toward sexual function. Swartz (1993) compared the sex knowledge of deaf and hearing college freshmen using the Sex Knowledge and Attitude Test (SKAT) and the researcher's Sex Knowledge Inventory (SKI). After controlling for various factors, deaf students showed the greatest knowledge deficits in anatomy and physiology. Swartz discussed the possible reasons for this significant disparity, for example, sex education for deaf students lags behind that for hearing students. Furthermore, schools for deaf people and schools in which deaf children are mainstreamed often have other priorities for their students, including remedial language courses and speech therapy, in addition to core academic classes. Swartz added that sex education is likely to be taught verbally in mainstreamed classrooms in which there may be no interpreter. Even when an interpreter is present, the language that deals with sex may have to be finger spelled rather than signed, thus impeding comprehension and retention. Deaf students may also have difficulty understanding the language used in sex education textbooks.

DeHaan and Wallander (1988) compared the sexual knowledge and attitudes of college women with early- versus late-onset physical disability and a control group of nondisabled college students. Contrary to one hypothesis of the study, women from the early-onset disability group had no less knowledge about sex and were no more conservative in their sexual attitudes than women who had late-onset or no disability. The researchers hypothesized that the women's education helped them compensate for the early lack of sexual information. They also found that greater sexual knowledge and more liberal attitudes toward heterosexual sex and masturbation were related to greater frequency of sexual expression. Sexual attitudes and knowledge were not related to satisfaction with one's sexuality, however.

Religion

The literature contains almost no mention of the relationship between religion and sexual knowledge or attitudes for children and adolescents with chronic disease or disability. One exception is Evans and Conine's (1985) warning of potential conflict between parents' religious or moral values and those of the health care team. For example, masturbation may be considered sinful by some families, whereas practitioners in general believe it is a healthy activity that may promote psychosexual development. The same is true of early childhood play in which children compare or explore the genitals of same-sex or opposite-sex playmates. If parents disapprove of such experiences, heath care professionals are still obliged to explain the normalcy of such behavior while acknowledging the family's values.

SEXUAL BEHAVIOR AND ACTIVITY

Pleasuring and Masturbation

Developmentally, the early forms of overt genital sexual expression involve self-exploration and pleasuring. No studies have documented the degree to which these behaviors may be affected by different disabilities in children. Nevertheless, it is obvious that lack of sensation, severe motor impairment, or limb deficiency will reduce or alter a child's exploration of his or her genitals or other parts of the body for pleasure. Furthermore, disease processes that are associated with pain or loss of physical stamina may affect the desire for or gratification from self-pleasuring. In addition, dependency on others for self-care including bathing, dressing, undressing, toileting, and menstrual hygiene, as well as the use of diapers, urinary appliances, and braces, may reduce opportunities for genital exploration and self-pleasuring. Both disease processes and treatment may have a negative effect on sexual interest, enjoyment, and expression. For instance, brain tumors or endocrine disorders may either increase or decrease libido. Chemotherapy, other medications, or radiation may have profound negative effects on sexual desire and activity (Greydanus et al., 1985). Despite these obstacles, children and adolescents with disabilities will often find creative ways to derive sexual pleasure. Blos and Finch (1974) described a case of a child with bilateral limb deficiency who learned to masturbate while lying on his stomach. In contrast, Dorner (1977) reported that only one-third of teenage boys with spina bifida reported masturbating, whereas three-quarters of the total sample had genital sensation. In the general population, 82% of boys masturbate by age 15 years (Kinsey, Pomeroy, & Martin, 1948).

Sex Play

The first sexual behavior with peers may be comparison or comments regarding sexual body parts. Another early form of sexual behavior may be physical exploration through touching or play. No studies were found that discussed the degree to which children with handicaps engaged in preadolescent or early adolescent genital "sex play" with same-sex or opposite-sex peers. Early studies (Kinsey, Pomeroy, Martin, & Gebhard, 1953) of the general population found that sex play occurred in approximately 12% of children at age 5 years, and 35% of boys and a smaller number of girls at age 13 years. The incidence in children with chronic disease or disability may be less in individuals with fewer peer relationships or for whom mobility is restricted by the medical condition.

Dating

As children move into adolescence, hand-holding, kissing, and dating are initial forms of overt sexual behavior with peers. Several studies have contrasted different groups of adolescents with chronic disease or disability compared with normal groups based on these measures. Frauman and Sypert (1979) pointed out that holding hands and hugging may be more difficult in people with neurologic or rheumatoid disease. Blum et al. (1991) found a low frequency of dating among congenitally disabled youths with spina bifida (14.7%) and CP (23.8%); most dated infrequently, and approximately 7% of those with disabilities had a steady boyfriend or girlfriend. Steinbock and Zeiss (1977) reported that people with CP expressed concern regarding their ability to engage in a range of sexual activities. DeHaan and Wallander (1988) compared a group of young adults who had various disabilities before age 3 years with a late-onset group (after age 18 years) and a group of nondisabled young adults. Those people disabled before age 3 years reported less frequency of self-pleasuring (less than once per month) and dating or kissing (never or a few times per year). They also reported lowest satisfaction with the frequency of sexual expression and greater discrepancy between current and desired enjoyment of sex.

In Dorner's (1977) sample of British teenagers with spina bifida, aged 13 to 19 years, only 11% were dating a member of the opposite sex at the time they were interviewed. Only 29% of the total sample reported any prior relationship in which there was some physical contact. Just one incidence of intercourse was acknowledged in the sample of 63 teenagers. Mobility limitations seemed be associated with less sexual activity for boys; however, girls were more concerned with their ability to conceive babies than pleasurable genital sensations, which was reportedly absent in 71% of the girls.

In a more recent study that compared 13- to 21-year-old youths with spina bifida versus CF and normal control subjects, Cromer et al. (1990) reported significant differences between the groups. Of youngsters with spina bifida, 67% had gone on a date without their parents, whereas 80% of those with CF and 88% of controls had dated without parents. Youths with myelomeningocele had dated significantly fewer people than those with CF or controls and had fewer dates with the same person. Twenty-five percent of youths with spina bifida and 40%

of youths with CF reported previous sexual activity compared with 60% of controls. All control subjects and those youths with CF thought they would eventually become sexually active, whereas 73% of the youths with spina bifida thought they would. Anderson and Duffey (1978) studied a sample of adolescents with diabetes and CF and found satisfactory sexual adjustment. Although childhood diabetes, CF, and spinal bifida are early-onset disorders, diabetes and CF are less conspicuous and do not involve neurologic or mobility impairment. Therefore, they may have less effect on psychosocial development and sexual expression. Youths with myelomeningocele in the Cromer et al. (1990) study indicated that their disability made it harder to get to know new people. However, it was not the degree or severity of disability in the Cromer et al. study that was related to level of social activity or sexual history, but more likely other factors having to do with social competence and early social development.

Kokkonen, Saukkonen, Timonen, Serlo, and Kinnunen (1991) studied a Finnish sample of young adults (aged 19 to 26 years; mean age, 22.3 years) with either CP or spina bifida. Of the group, 50% with CP had hemiplegia and 25% had mental impairment. One-half of the sample had not dated as compared with 11% of controls. In the group with disabilities, 54% reported no sexual experience compared with 15% of controls. Dating started later in the disabled group.

Cognitive Impairment

The incidence of sexual activity in mentally impaired teenagers who do not have serious mobility or genital–urinary problems is probably higher than in people with other disabilities, but appears to vary in relation to degree of cognitive impairment. Chamberlain et al. (1984) reported that about 50% of mildly retarded, 32% of moderately retarded, and 9% of severely retarded females aged 11 to 23 years in their sample had experienced sexual intercourse. In an institutionalized sample of severely retarded adults aged 10 to 33 years (West, 1979), masturbation was the most common sexual behavior observed, although sex play in prepubertal and postpubertal residents was also a common occurrence. Apart from aggression, these were often the only spontaneous cooperative social behaviors observed between the severely disabled residents.

In the early stages of recovery from a traumatic brain injury, agitation and disinhibition often result in sexual self-stimulation and arousal in settings where others may incidentally observe the behavior. In the later stages of recovery following return to the community, some youths with traumatic brain injuries may continue to exhibit disinhibited or socially inappropriate sexual behaviors such as masturbation in public, inappropriate touching of others, or inappropriate use of sexually explicit language (Kahn, 1994). Kahn has suggested that adolescents with traumatic brain injuries may engage in promiscuous or aggressive sexual behavior in part because of difficulty perceiving, interpreting, and responding to subtle interpersonal cues. Particular sensory disabilities or cognitive deficits also may interfere with the perception of subtle social cues such as facial expressions or voice intonation, which provide information relevant to socially acceptable and unacceptable sexual behavior (Schuster, 1986; Warzak, Evans, & Ford, 1992). In addition, cognitive deficits may interfere with the ability to monitor one's own behavior, leading to behavioral excess or deficiency, intended or otherwise, thereby complicating the ability of others to interpret the intentions of the individual with a disability (Warzak & Kilburn, 1990).

Developmentally disabled and other disabled youths such as those with acquired brain injuries have an increased likelihood of coming to the attention of authorities because of their sexual behavior, yet they less commonly commit other offenses. Day (1994) reported on a sample of 47 such people who had been involved in 191 sexual incidents that came to the attention of authorities. Of the sample, 32% were under age 20 years. The mean IQ was 59.5 (range, 43 to 82). The majority of the offenses were characterized as minor, such as attempts to kiss, cuddle, pinch a person's bottom, fondle breasts outside of clothing, or make remarks about underwear or clothing. Rarely was force used and the offender usually desisted when objections were raised. Approximately 6% of the offenses were deemed serious. The group of offenders was notable for their lack of social competence as well as that only one had a significant mobility impairment (marked gait disturbance). Of the offenders, 63% were described as shy, immature, isolated, and withdrawn. Furthermore, 25% were rated as sexually naive, and 58% admitted to no heterosexual experience before the first incident that came to the attention of authorities.

Same-Sex and Transgender Preferences and Behavior

The degree of homosexual behavior or same-sex sexual preference among children and adolescents with chronic disease or disability has received little attention in the literature. There is no evidence that the incidence of homosexuality is markedly different when compared with the nondisabled population (West, 1979). The prevalence of transgender identification among youths with chronic disease or disability also is unknown. In addition, there is no evidence that it is significantly different from the general population; however, fewer youths with disabilities may act on their preferences with cross-dressing, hormonal treatment, or surgery because of cost, accessibility, or concerns about further stigmatization (S. Cole, personal communication, March 22, 1996).

THEORETICAL FRAMEWORK

The authors of this chapter believe that a developmental model of sexuality that has social competence with peers as the primary variable mediating the relationship between disability and sexual adjustment is most consistent with the existing literature. Furthermore, several important variables moderate this process for youths with chronic illness or disability: early versus later onset, cognitive impairment, conspicuousness of disability, and mobility or motor impairment (Figure 18–1).

One must carefully evaluate the reports of differences in patterns of sexual expression in different populations. For instance, Cromer et al. (1990) proposed that studies of sexual function in youths with chronic disease or disability may include a higher participation rate of sexually active adolescents with higher social adaptation because they and their parents were less likely to feel threatened by the content of such studies compared with those youths who refused to participate. This selection bias may overestimate the actual numbers of youths who are engaging in various sexually related behaviors, but likely still offers insights into differences between populations of youths with different disabilities.

SEXUALITY EDUCATION AND THERAPY

Although youths with disabilities are similar in many ways to their unimpaired peers, the challenges imposed by their disability often pose obstacles to emerging

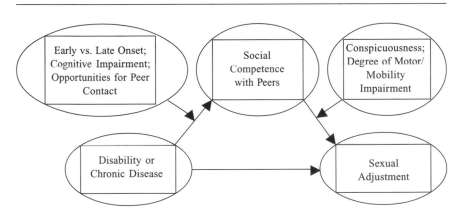

Figure 18–1 This complex partial mediating model shows social competence mediating the relations between disability or chronic disease and sexual adjustment with onset, cognitive impairment, conspicuousness, and motor/mobility impairment as moderating variables.

sexuality that others do not face (Warzak, Kuhn, & Nolten, 1995). Facilitating the sexual adjustment of these individuals is unfortunately often ignored until inappropriate sexual behavior, potentially the result of many factors, forces others to attend to this aspect of development. Many factors, including the kind of disability and the age at which it occurs, are relevant in this regard. Perhaps the most significant obstacle to effective adjustment is simply a lack of information about sexuality. This lack of knowledge is often more detrimental to satisfactory sexual adjustment than other psychological sequelae that accompany disability (Cole, 1988). Access to relevant information is affected by circumstances as varied as limited mobility and subsequent inability to obtain materials to a lack of available information specific to particular disabilities. In some cases, providers do not educate their adolescent patients because they fail to anticipate issues related to sexual maturation and sexual function. In addition, surveys have indicated that some institutional staff believe that individuals with disabilities will have little or no opportunity to engage in interpersonal sexual behavior and require no preparation for this eventuality (Malloy & Herold, 1988). Unless staff are thoroughly supported administratively, they may fear repercussions for broaching sensitive and potentially charged subject matter; the result is limited educational opportunities and support of only the lowest level of innocuous interpersonal sexual behavior (Knight, 1989). In other cases, parents may be reluctant to provide information to their children for fear of nurturing premarital sexual activity and exposing their children to the risks attendant to sexual activity, such as pregnancy, sexual exploitation, and STDs (Manikam & Hensarling, 1990; Peuschel & Scola, 1988). In addition, an individual's own anxiety about the subject matter or cognitive communication deficits may limit the ability to engage in dialogue about sexuality with peers, parents, or providers and may limit understanding of community standards and the consequences of sexual behavior (Giami, 1987).

Educational Approaches

Early efforts to educate youths with disabilities tended to focus on hygiene and warnings about potential risks associated with sexual behavior, serving more to control students than to instruct them (Daniels, Cornelius, Makas, & Chipouras, 1981). Recent curricula have focused primarily on youths with developmental disabilities, with fewer resources allocated to other sorts of impairment that may compromise sexual adjustment and sexual function. Nevertheless, some of these curricula can be adapted to the needs of youths with other disabilities and chronic diseases. For example, the Life Horizons curriculum (Kempton, 1988) accommodates those youths with sensory deficits and those youths with developmental disabilities of varying severity, in part, through extensive use of slides and visual aids. Different modules inform participants about the physiologic, psychological, and social aspects of sexuality, and the materials may be presented at the pace to accommodate participants' needs. An assessment of sexual knowledge is also available through this curriculum. The Circles curriculum (Champagne & Walker-Hirsch, 1982) provides a concrete and systematic approach to presenting factual information as well as helping students with developmental delays learn appropriate social sexual behavior while fostering prevention of abuse and STDs.

Other training models use the PLISSIT approach (Annon, 1976; programs that provide *p*ermission, *l*imited *i*nformation, *s*pecific *s*uggestions, and *i*ntensive *t*herapy) to address specific sexuality issues and the Developmental Skills-Based Approach (Keller & Buchanan, 1984). The Developmental Skills-Based Approach emphasizes an intensive individualized therapy involving an assessment of individual needs and capacities, facilitation of knowledge and skills for sex adjustment, and implementation of a plan jointly developed by the student and provider.

Sex education programs must be tailored to accommodate individual limitations, including general developmental level and cognitive, sensory, and social skills deficits. Deficits related to impaired attention, retention, and recall; language delays; and limited ability to deal effectively with abstract concepts are common among these populations (Warzak et al., 1992). Simple language, audiovisual materials, and repetition are needed to promote retention and retrieval of sex education facts. Structured settings with few distractions may be required. Behavioral strategies that promote skills acquisition and compliance with appropriate interpersonal behavior may facilitate the development of an appropriate sexual repertoire (Warzak & Kilburn, 1990).

Educators should assess the student's level of sexual information and current sexual repertoire. For some students, physical maturational variables may be directly related to their disability and may be an additional curriculum factor (Rosen, 1991). General educational curricula should address pregnancy prevention and prevention of STDs, especially because many birth control methods do not provide protection against STDs. Essential health and hygiene skills, such as menstrual hygiene training, are basic curriculum elements, particularly among those students with cognitive deficits and developmental delays (Epps, Prescott, & Horner, 1990; Epps, Stern, & Horner, 1990). Contraceptive methods requiring planning and judgment may be unsuitable for individuals whose cognitive processes are very immediate and concrete. Other techniques may require manual dexterity incompatible with particular disabilities. Issues related to community values and standards of conduct should be included, as appropriate. Educators also must actively identify and correct misinformation. Some sources of information, such as television, may provide a distorted view of social sexual behavior and complicate rather than facilitate sexual adjustment (Kempton, 1988). Furthermore, parents must be informed of the nature of the proposed curriculum, lest they have objections or concerns, especially related to moral or religious values, that staff do not adequately address (Cromer et al., 1990).

Social Skills Training

Individuals with characteristics that set them apart often become socially isolated and may be deprived of the social environment within which appropriate sexual development and sexual adjustment occur (Yarris, 1992). Their attempts to engage in interpersonal sexual behavior may be awkward, ineffective, or inappropriate (Cole, 1981). Social skills training, consisting of a rationale, modeling, behavioral rehearsal, feedback, and reinforcement (Kelly, 1982), has been successful in remediating social skills deficits across many different populations, including those with disabilities (Yarris, 1992).

Of particular relevance are programs that focus on teaching assertive behavior to individuals who have difficulty recognizing situations appropriate to initiating sexual behavior, refusing unwanted sexual behavior, or requesting safer sex behavior from an appropriate and willing partner (Duggan-Ali, 1992; Howard, 1985; Sobsey & Doe, 1991; Warzak & Page, 1990). Most assertiveness training programs in this area have focused on unimpaired populations and have emphasized information, communications skills, and contraceptive issues (Committee on Adolescence, 1987; Flaherty, Marecek, Olsen, & Wilcove, 1983; Schinke, 1984; Shendell, 1992). Those programs have met with limited success (Dawson, 1986; Melton, 1988). Few programs have been geared toward working with individuals with disabilities and few have specifically targeted sexual behavior refusal skills. Yet, unlike other contraceptive strategies, refusal skills are portable and require no advanced planning once learned, underscoring their potential benefit.

Warzak and Page (1990) extrapolated refusal skills technology from the addictive behavior literature and applied it to sexually active adolescents with disabilities. The researchers conducted individual needs assessments and identified behavioral deficits. Warzak and colleagues (Warzak, Grow, Poler, & Walburn, 1995) also assessed specific contexts in which problematic sexual behavior occurred, an important consideration given the situational specificity of assertiveness (Eisler, Hersen, Miller, & Blanchard, 1975). However, the behavioral components of refusal were not empirically cross-validated. Cross-validation studies of the behavioral components of sexual refusal skills have only recently been explored (Grow, Warzak, & Kramer, 1994). More work is needed in this area before effective strategies can be confidently developed for sexual behavior refusal within any population, including youths with disabilities.

Parents as Educators

The family is the child's first sex educator (Woodhead & Murph, 1985). Parents can initiate a healthy sexual identity in their child with a disability by demonstrating unconditional acceptance of the child's body (Selekman & McIlvain-Simpson, 1991). Sadly, parents may expend their emotional energy coping with their own issues around their child's illness or disability and may have little energy left to cope with their child's psychosexual development (Woodhead & Murph, 1985). The child's increased dependency may complicate the parents' ability to recognize and acknowledge the child's emerging sexuality (Evans & Conine, 1985). The adolescent's emerging sexuality indicates an overall shift toward independence. This change may have a profound impact on the parents, who have spent much of their adult lives caring for the child and may view themselves primarily as caregivers.

During adolescence, sexual maturation may increase youths' motivation to form closer bonds with peers and distance themselves from parents (Frauman & Sypert, 1979). For parents, sexual maturation of their disabled children may be the catalyst for a profound grief reaction (Pattullo, 1975), as parents realize that the transition to adult urges and reproductive potential by their children is not accompanied by a commensurate increase in potential for community integration or independent living.

Parents are likely to have limited knowledge about sexuality and no knowledge about sexuality and disability. They may be unsure about what their children know or should know about sex. Parents may also fear that early sexual knowledge may result in inappropriate sexual behavior. To the contrary, experts have suggested that sexual behavior results from curiosity about the unknown (Robinault, 1978). Thus, it is important for health care professionals to initiate discussions regarding sexuality and disability with children and their parents (Evans & Conine, 1985). For children growing up with a disability, health professionals need to encourage parents to avoid overprotection and to validate the child's sexuality. Professionals need to give parental guidance on how to actively promote positive self-regard and body image as well as to increase opportunities for peer interactions (S. Cole & T. Cole, 1982).

It is critical for youngsters to be aware that their disease or disability may result in the development of secondary sexual characteristics, including menarche, to occur earlier or later than usual. Because of their history, adolescents with disabilities and chronic diseases are prone to interpret physical changes as pathologic manifestations of their disease or disability. Patullo (1975) has pointed out that it is important for teenagers to be taught that menstruation, ejaculation, or nocturnal emissions are normal and not a manifestation of their disease or disability. Handicapped adolescents who have fewer contacts with able-bodied peers may depend more on instruction from parents and health professionals regarding basic sexual information such as menstrual hygiene and contraception (Evans & McKinlay, 1988).

One of the chief tasks of adolescence is separation and individuation from one's parents. Adolescents with a chronic illness will likely have more difficulty than their healthy peers because of their limited ability to experiment and to take increased responsibility for themselves. Anxiety around the child's illness and treatment makes the normal adolescent issues of gaining independence and experimenting even greater challenges (Greydanus et al., 1985). The parent and health care professional can assist the child in moving toward greater independence by training the child to administer all possible medications and treatments for which others have previously taken responsibility. The professional may also encourage parents to allow the adolescent greater privacy and decision making (such as at medical exam visits or time alone in their bedroom), explaining that the failure to do so can lead to depression and noncompliance with treatment regimens, which can become life-threatening (Evans & Conine, 1985; Greydanus et al., 1985).

REFERENCES

American Nurses' Association. (1979). *A report on the hearings on the unmet health needs of children and youth*. Kansas City, MO: Author.

Anderson, A., & Duffey, M. (1978). *The achievement of selected developmental tasks of early adolescence by well and chronically ill adolescents*. Unpublished master's thesis, University of Michigan, Ann Arbor.

Annon, J. (1976). *The behavioral treatment of sexual problems: Brief therapy*. New York: Harper & Row.

Baladerian, N.J. (1991). Sexual abuse of people with developmental disabilities. *Sexuality and Disability, 9*(4), 323–336.

Battle, C.V. (1974). Disruptions in the socialization of a young, severely handicapped child. *Rehabilitation Literature, 35,* 130–140.

Blos, P., & Finch, S. (1974). Sexuality and the handicapped adolescent. In J.A. Downey & N.L. Low (Eds.), *The child with disabling illness* (pp. 521–540). Philadelphia: W.B. Saunders.

Blum, R.W. (1984). Sexual health needs of physically and intellectually impaired adolescents. In R.W. Blum (Ed.), *Chronic illness and disabilities in childhood and adolescence* (pp. 127–141). Orlando, FL: Grune & Stratton.

Blum, R.W., Resnick, M.D., Nelson, R., & St. Germaine, A. (1991). Family and peer issues among adolescents with spina bifida and cerebral palsy. *Pediatrics, 88,* 280–285.

Bohnert, A., Parker, J., & Warschausky, S. (in press). Friendship adjustment in children following TBI. *Developmental Neuropsychology.*

Boyle, I.R., di Sant'Agnese, P.A., Sack, S., Millican, F., & Kulczycki, L.L. (1976). Emotional adjustment of adolescents and young adults with cystic fibrosis. *Journal of Pediatrics, 88*(2), 318–326.

Capell, B., & Capell, J. (1981). Being parents of children who are disabled. In D.G. Bullard & S.E. Knight (Eds.), *Sexuality and physical disability: Personal perspectives* (pp. 80–86). St. Louis, MO: C.V. Mosby.

Centers, L., & Centers, R. (1963). Peer group attitudes towards the amputee child. *Journal of Social Psychology, 61,* 127–132.

Chamberlain, A., Rauh, J., Passer, A., McGrath, M., & Burket, R. (1984). Issues in fertility control for mentally retarded female adolescents: I. Sexual abuse and contraception. *Pediatrics, 73,* 445–450.

Champagne, M.P., & Walker-Hirsch, L.W. (1982). Circles: A self-organization system for teaching appropriate social/sexual behavior to mentally retarded/developmentally disabled persons. *Sexuality and Disability, 5*(3), 172–177.

Clausen, J. (1975). The social meaning of differential physical and sexual maturation. In S. Dragastin & G. Elder (Eds.), *Adolescence and the life cycle* (pp. 25–46). New York: Wiley.

Coffman, C.B., Levine, S.B., Althof, S.E., & Stern, R.C. (1984). Sexual adaptation among single young adults with cystic fibrosis. *Chest, 86*(3), 412–418.

Cohen, S., & Warren, R.D. (1987). Preliminary survey of family abuse of children served by United Cerebral Palsy centers. *Developmental Medicine and Child Neurology, 29*(1), 12–18.

Cole, S. (1981). Disability/ability: The importance of sexual health in adolescence: Issues and concerns of the professional. *SIECUS Report, 9*(5/6), 3–4.

Cole, S. (1988). Women, sexuality, and disabilities. *Women and Therapy, 7,* 277–294.

Cole, S., & Cole, T. (1982). How physical disabilities affect sexual health. *Medical Aspects of Human Sexuality, 16,* 136–151.

Cole, S., & Cole, T. (1983). Disability and intimacy: The importance of sexual health. In G.W. Albee, S. Gordon, & H. Leitenberg (Eds.), *Promoting sexual responsibility and preventing sexual problems* (pp. 297–305). Hanover, NH: University Press of New England.

Cole, S., & Cole, T. (1993). Sexuality, disability, and reproductive issues through the lifespan. *Sexuality and Disability, 11*(3), 189–205.

Cole, T., & Cole, S. (1982). Rehabilitation of problems of sexuality in physical disability. In F.J. Kottke, G.K. Stillwell, & J.F. Lehman (Eds.), *Krusen's handbook of physical medicine and rehabilitation* (pp. 899–905). New York: W.B. Saunders.

Committee on Adolescence. (1987). Role of the pediatrician in management of sexually transmitted diseases in children and adolescents. *Pediatrics, 79,* 454–456.

Coupey, S., & Cohen, M. (1984). Special considerations for the health care of adolescents with chronic illness. *Pediatric Clinics of North America, 31,* 211–219.

Cromer, B.A., Enrile, B., McCoy, K., Gerhardstein, M.J., Fitzpatrick, M., & Judis, J. (1990). Knowledge, attitudes and behavior related to sexuality in adolescents with chronic disability. *Developmental Medicine and Child Neurology, 32,* 602–610.

Daniels, S., Cornelius, M., Makas, E., & Chipouras, S. (1981). Sexuality and disability: The need for services. *Annual Review of Rehabilitation, 2,* 83–112.

Daniels, S.M. (1981). Critical issues in sexuality and disability. In D.G. Bullard & S.E. Knight (Eds.), *Sexuality and physical disability* (pp. 5–11). St. Louis, MO: C.V. Mosby.

Dawson, D.A. (1986). The effects of sex education on adolescent behavior. *Family Planning Perspectives, 18*(4), 162–170.

Day, K. (1994). Male mentally handicapped sex offenders. *British Journal of Psychiatry, 165,* 630–639.

DeHaan, C.B., & Wallander, J.L. (1988). Self-concept, sexual knowledge and attitudes, and parental support in the sexual adjustment of women with early- and late-onset physical disability. *Archives of Sexual Behavior, 17*(2), 145–161.

Dewis, M.E. (1989). Spinal cord injured adolescents and young adults: The meaning of body changes. *Journal of Advances in Nursing, 14*, 389–396.

Dorner, S. (1976). Adolescents with spina bifida: How they see their situation. *Archives of Disease in Childhood, 51*, 439–444.

Dorner, S. (1977). Sexual interest and activity in adolescents with spina bifida. *Journal of Child Psychology and Psychiatry, 18*, 229–237.

Duggan-Ali, D. (1992). Social skills and assertiveness training integrated into high school sexuality education curriculum. In I.G. Fodor (Ed.), *Adolescent assertiveness and social skills training* (pp. 219–233). New York: Springer.

Eisler, R.M., Hersen, M., Miller, P.M., & Blanchard, E.B. (1975). Situational determinants of assertive behavior. *Journal of Consulting and Clinical Psychology, 43*, 330–340.

Epps, S., Prescott, A., & Horner, R. (1990). Social acceptability of menstrual-care training methods for young women with developmental disabilities. *Education and Training in Mental Retardation, 25*(1), 33–44.

Epps, S., Stern, R., & Horner, R. (1990). Comparison of simulation training on self and using a doll for teaching generalized menstrual care to women with severe mental retardation. *Research in Developmental Disabilities, 11*, 37–66.

Evans, J., & Conine, T. (1985). Sexual habilitation of youngsters with chronic illness or disabling conditions. *Journal of Allied Health, 24*(1), 79–87.

Evans, A.L., & McKinlay, I.A. (1988). Sexual maturation in girls with severe mental handicap. *Child: Care, Health & Development, 14*, 59–69.

Finkelhor, D., Hotaling, G., Lewis, I.A., & Smith, C. (1990). Sexual abuse in a national survey of adult men and women: Prevalence, characteristics, and risk factors. *Child Abuse and Neglect, 14*(1), 19–28.

Flaherty, E.W., Marecek, J., Olsen, K., & Wilcove, G. (1983). Preventing adolescent pregnancy: An interpersonal problem solving approach. *Prevention in Human Services, 2*(3), 49–63.

Frauman, A.C., & Sypert, N.S. (1979). Sexuality in adolescents with chronic illness. *Maternal and Child Nursing, 4*, 371–375.

Giami, A. (1987). Coping with the sexuality of the disabled: A comparison of the physically disabled and the mentally retarded. *International Journal of Rehabilitation Research, 10*(1), 41–48.

Glaser, D., & Bentovim, A. (1979). Abuse and risk to handicapped and chronically ill children. *Child Abuse and Neglect, 3*(2), 565–575.

Gortmaker, S., & Sappenfield, W. (1984). Chronic disorders: Prevalence and impact. *Pediatric Clinics of North America, 31*, 3–18.

Green, M., & Solnit, A.J. (1964). Reactions to the threatened loss of a child: A vulnerable child syndrome. *Pediatrics, 34*, 58–66.

Greydanus, D.E., Demarest, D.S., & Sears, J.M. (1985). Sexuality of the chronically ill adolescent. *Medical Aspects of Human Sexuality, 19*, 36–52.

Grow, C.R., Warzak, W.J., & Kramer, J.J. (1994). *Identifying behavioral components of a competent sexual refusal.* Poster session presented at the annual meeting of the American Psychological Association, Los Angeles, CA.

Guralnick, M.J., & Weinhouse, E. (1984). Peer-related social interactions of developmentally delayed young children: Development and characteristics. *Developmental Psychology, 20,* 815–827.

Haefner, H.K., & Elkins, T.E. (1991). Contraceptive management for female adolescents with mental retardation and handicapping disabilities. *Adolescent and Pediatric Gynecology, 3,* 820–824.

Hanker, J.P. (1990). Gastrointestinal disease and oral contraception. *American Journal of Obstetrics and Gynecology, 163*(6), 2204–2207.

Hayden, P.W., Davenport, S.L.H., & Campbell, M.M. (1979). Adolescents with myelodysplasia: Impact of physical disability on emotional maturation. *Pediatrics, 64,* 53–59.

Howard, M. (1985). Postponing sexual involvement among adolescents: An alternative approach to prevention of sexually transmitted diseases. *Journal of Adolescent Health Care, 6*(4), 271–277.

Kahn, L. (1994). Adolescents with brain injury: Issues of sexuality. *i.e. Magazine, 2*(3), 34–37, 44.

Keller, S., & Buchanan, D.C. (1984). Sexuality and disability: An overview. *Rehabilitation Digest, 15,* 3–7.

Kelly, J. (1982). *Social skills training.* New York: Springer.

Kempton, W. (1988). *Sex education for persons with disabilities that hinder learning: A teacher's guide.* Santa Monica, CA: James Stanfield.

Kewman, D.G., Warschausky, S.A., & Engel, L. (1995). Juvenile rheumatoid arthritis and neuromuscular conditions: scoliosis, spinal cord injury, and muscular dystrophy. In M.C. Roberts (Ed.), *Handbook of pediatric psychology* (pp. 384–402). New York: Guilford Press.

Kinsey, A.C., Pomeroy, W.B., & Martin, C.E. (1948). *Sexual behavior in the human male.* Philadelphia: W.B. Saunders.

Kinsey, A.C., Pomeroy, W.B., Martin, C.E., & Gebhard, P.H. (1953). *Sexual behavior in the human female.* Philadelphia: W.B. Saunders.

Knight, S.E. (1989). Sexual concerns of the physically disabled. In B.W. Heller, L.M. Flohr, & L.S. Zegans (Eds.), *Psychosocial interventions with physically disabled persons* (pp. 183–199). New Brunswick, NJ: Rutgers University Press.

Kokkonen, J., Saukkonen, A., Timonen, E., Serlo, W., & Kinnunen, P. (1991). Social outcome of handicapped children as adults. *Developmental Medicine and Child Neurology, 33,* 1095–1100.

Lavigne, J.V., & Faier-Routman, J. (1992). Psychological adjustment to pediatric physical disorders: A meta-analytic review. *Journal of Pediatric Psychology, 17*(2), 133–157.

Livson, N., & Peskin, H. (1980). Perspectives on adolescence from longitudinal research. In J. Adelson (Ed.), *Handbook of adolescent psychology* (pp. 47–98). New York: Wiley.

Malloy, G., & Herold, E. (1988). Factors related to sexual counseling of physically disabled adults. *Journal of Sex Research, 24,* 220–227.

Manikam, R., & Hensarling, D.S. (1990). Sexual behavior. In J.L. Matson (Ed.), *Handbook of behavior modification with the mentally retarded* (pp. 503–521). New York: Plenum.

McAnarney, E.R. (1985). Social maturation: A challenge for handicapped and chronically ill adolescents. *Journal of Adolescent Health Care, 6*(2), 90–101.

McAndrew, I. (1979). Adolescents and young people with spina bifida. *Developmental Medicine and Child Neurology, 21,* 619–629.

McKown, J.M., & English, B.A. (1986). Disabled teenagers: sexual identification and sexuality counseling. *Sexuality and Disability, 7*(1/2), 17–27.

Melton, G.B. (1988). Adolescents and prevention of AIDS. *Professional Psychology: Research and Practice, 19*(4), 403–408.

Mulcahey, M.J. (1991). Returning to school after a spinal cord injury: Perspectives from four adolescents. *The American Journal of Occupational Therapy, 46,* 305–312.

Neinstein, L.S., & Katz, B. (1986a). Contraceptive use in the chronically ill adolescent female: Part I. *Journal of Adolescent Health Care, 7*(2), 123–133.

Neinstein, L.S., & Katz, B. (1986b). Contraceptive use in the chronically ill adolescent female: Part II. *Journal of Adolescent Health Care, 7*(5), 350–360.

Nolen, T., Desmond, K., Herlich, R., & Hardy, S. (1986). Knowledge of cystic fibrosis in patients and their parents. *Pediatrics, 77,* 229–235.

Offer, D., Ostrov, E., & Howard, K.I. (1984). Body image, self-perception, and chronic illness in adolescence. In R.W. Blum (Ed.), *Chronic illness and disabilities in childhood and adolescence* (pp. 59–73). Orlando, FL: Grune & Stratton.

Overby, K.J., Lo, B., & Litt, I.F. (1989). Knowledge and concerns about acquired immunodeficiency syndrome and their relationship to behavior among adolescents with hemophilia. *Pediatrics, 83,* 204–210.

Pattullo, A.W. (1975). The socio-sexual development of the handicapped child. A preventive care approach. *Nursing Clinics of North America, 10*(2), 361–372.

Peuschel, S.M., & Scola, P.S. (1988). Parents' perception of social and sexual functions in adolescents with Down's syndrome. *Journal of Mental Deficiency, 32,* 215–220.

Renshaw, D.C. (1985, February). How handicapped teens cope with friendship, love and sex. *PTA Today,* pp. 21–22.

Robinault, I.P. (1978). *Sex, society, and the disabled: A developmental inquiry into roles, reactions, and responsibilities.* Hagerstown, MD: Harper & Row, Inc.

Rosen, D.S. (1991). Pubertal growth and sexual maturation for adolescents with chronic illness or disability. *Pediatrician, 18,* 105–120.

Rutledge, D.N., & Dick, G. (1983). Spinal cord injury in adolescence. *Rehabilitation Nursing, 8*(6), 18–21.

Schinke, S.P. (1984). Preventing teenage pregnancy. In M. Hersen, R.M. Eisler, & P.M. Miller (Eds.), *Progress in behavior modification* (pp. 31–64). Orlando, FL: Academic Press.

Schuster, C.S. (1986). Sex education of the visually impaired child. *Journal of Visual Impairment and Blindness, 80,* 675–680.

Selekman, J., & McIlvain-Simpson, G. (1991). Sex and sexuality for the adolescent with a chronic condition. *Pediatric Nursing, 17*(6), 535–538.

Serbin, L.A., Powlishta, K.K., & Gulko, J. (1993). The development of sex typing in middle childhood. *Monographs of the Society for Research in Child Development, 58*(2)(232), 1–99.

Shendell, M.B. (1992). Communication training for adolescent girls in junior high school setting: Learning to take risks in self-expression. In I.G. Fodor (Ed.), *Adolescent assertiveness and social skills training* (pp. 205–218). New York: Springer.

Sigelman, C.K., & Begley, N.L. (1987). The early development of reactions to peers with controllable and uncontrollable problems. *Journal of Pediatric Psychology, 12*(1), 99–115.

Sobsey, D., & Doe, T. (1991). Patterns of sexual abuse and assault. *Sexuality and Disability, 3,* 243–259.

Steinbock, E.A., & Zeiss, A.M. (1977). Sexual counseling for cerebral palsied adults: Case report and further suggestions. *Archives of Sexual Behavior, 6*(1), 77–83.

Stern, D. (1977). *The first relationship: Infant and mother.* Cambridge, MA: Harvard University Press.

Sullivan, P.M., & Scanlan, J.M. (1987). Therapeutic issues. In J. Garbino, P.E. Brookhouses, & K.J. Authier (Eds.), *Special children, special risks: The maltreatment of children with disabilities.* (pp. 127–159). New York: Aldine deGruyter.

Swartz, D.B. (1993). A comparative study of sex knowledge among hearing and deaf college freshmen. *Sexuality and Disability, 11*(2), 129–147.

Tharinger, D., Horton, C.B., & Millea, S. (1990). Sexual abuse and exploitation of children and adults with mental retardation and other handicaps. *Child Abuse and Neglect, 14*(3), 301–312.

Thomasgard, M., & Metz, W.P. (1995). The vulnerable child syndrome revisited. *Developmental and Behavioral Pediatrics, 16,* 47–53.

Thornton, V.A. (1981). Growing up with cerebral palsy. In D.G. Bullard & S.E. Knight (Eds.), *Sexuality and physical disability* (pp. 26–31). St. Louis, MO: C.V. Mosby.

Trieschmann, R.B. (1988). *Spinal cord injuries: Psychological, social, and vocational rehabilitation.* New York: Demos.

Udry, J.R., Billy, J.O.G., Morris, N.M., Groff, T.R., & Raj, M.H. (1985). Serum androgenic hormones motivate sexual behavior in adolescent boys. *Fertility and Sterility, 43,* 90–94.

Udry, J.R., Talbert, L.M., & Morris, N.M. (1986). Biosocial foundations for adolescent female sexuality. *Demography, 23*(2), 217–230.

Wallander, J.L., & Thompson, R.J. (1995). Psychosocial adjustment of children with chronic physical conditions. In M.C. Roberts (Ed.), *Handbook of pediatric psychology* (pp. 124–141). New York: Guilford Press.

Warschausky, S., Engel, L., Augenstein, K., & Nelson, V.S. (1995, August). *Family adjustment to the home care of a ventilator assisted child.* Paper presented at the annual meeting of the American Psychological Association, New York City.

Warschausky, S., Engel, L.E., Kewman, D.K., & Nelson, V. (1996). Psychosocial factors in the rehabilitation of the child with a spinal injury. In R.R. Betz & M.J. Mulcahey (Eds.), *The child with a spinal cord injury.* Chicago: American Association of Orthopaedic Surgeons.

Warzak, W.J., Evans, J., & Ford, L. (1992). Working with the traumatically brain injured patient: Implications for rehabilitation. *Journal of Comprehensive Mental Health Care, 2,* 115–130.

Warzak, W.J., Grow, C., Poler, M., & Walburn, J.N. (1995). Enhancing refusal skills: Identifying contexts which place adolescents at risk for unwanted sexual activity. *Journal of Developmental and Behavioral Pediatrics, 16*(2), 98–100.

Warzak, W.J., & Kilburn, J. (1990). Behavioral approaches to activities of daily living. In D.E. Tupper & K.D. Cicerone (Eds.), *The neuropsychology of everyday life: Vol. 1. Assessment and basic competencies* (pp. 285–305). New York: Martinus Nijhoff.

Warzak, W.J., Kuhn, B.R., & Nolten, P.W. (1995). Obstacles to the sexual adjustment of children and adolescents with disabilities. In G.A. Rekers (Ed.), *Handbook of child and adolescent sexual problems* (pp. 81–100). New York: Lexington.

Warzak, W.J., & Page, T. (1990). Teaching refusal skills to sexually active adolescents. *Journal of Behavior Therapy and Experimental Psychiatry, 21,* 133–140.

West, R.R. (1979). The sexual behaviour of the institutionalised severely retarded. *Australian Journal of Mental Retardation, 5*(5), 11–13.

Woodhead, J., & Murph, J.R. (1985). Influence of chronic illness and disability on adolescent sexual development. *Seminars in Adolescent Medicine, 1,* 171–176.

Yarkony, G.M., & Anderson, C.J. (1996). Sexuality. In R.R. Betz & M.J. Mulcahey (Eds.), *The child with a spinal cord injury.* Chicago: American Association of Orthopaedic Surgeons.

Yarris, S. (1992). Assessment of social skills of physically disabled adolescents. In I.G. Fodor (Ed.), *Adolescent assertiveness and social skills training* (pp. 183–200). New York: Springer.

Treatment Concerns

CHAPTER 19

Sexuality Education and the Team Approach

Kathleen L. Dunn

SEXUALITY EDUCATION IN THE REHABILITATION ENVIRONMENT

Importance

In today's rehabilitation environment with shortened length of stays and the expectation to provide maximal physical and functional improvement in minimal time and at minimal cost, it would be easy for some inpatient rehabilitation facilities to put off providing sexuality education and counseling. Some may consider this a "frill" or an issue that can easily wait for the outpatient phase of care (Strauss, 1991). The costs associated with services that may not be reimbursable or that require extra staff or other resources may be seen as prohibitive and unnecessary for the goals of physical rehabilitation, which emphasizes activities of daily living; mobility; bowel and bladder management; and speech, language, and behavioral management. Some administrators may fear that sexuality education and counseling may expose the institution to public relations problems or liability issues, especially in conservative communities or religious group–sponsored institutions. Often, it takes a crisis related to the lack of a sexuality philosophy, policies and procedures, or staff or patient education to stimulate action in developing a program (Strauss, 1991). Rehabilitation professionals may perceive this reluctance (or even prohibition) from administration and use it as an excuse for avoiding the issue (Cornelius, Chipouras, Makas, & Daniels, 1982). The literature (Conine, 1984; Ducharme & Gill, 1990; Finger, 1993a, 1993b; Gender, 1992; Kempton & Kahn, 1991; Medlar, 1993; Sawyer & Allen, 1983; Strauss, 1991) has documented the poor preparation of most health care providers in the area of sexuality.

Sexuality and disability are two of the major taboos in Western society (Eisenberg & Rustad, 1976). Rehabilitation professionals are also a product of our society, which traditionally has viewed disabled people paternally as unable or disinterested in developing intimate relationships, especially through marriage or parenting. The disability becomes generalized to all aspects of the entire person (Medlar & Medlar, 1990). Furthermore, disabled people have been encouraged to remain in this childlike state of helplessness and asexuality (Conine, 1984). This is particularly true of children who are disabled at an early age, when taboos regarding the discussion of the disability and sexuality go hand in hand in an attempt to protect the child and deal with the parents' discomfort with the long-term implications of those subjects (Rousso, 1993). Common reactions of laypeople and most health care professionals to sexual behavior or questions from people with disabilities may include disbelief (How could they be sexual?); revulsion or disgust (anything but "normal" sexual activity is a perversion); active suppression (strict enforcement of prohibitions, segregation by sex, punishment, no provision for privacy, and so on); avoidance (if we do not discuss it, it will not happen; it is not my job); or resigned tolerance (we do not like it, but will look the other way as long as it is kept quiet; Cornelius et al., 1982). Clinicians who are insufficiently trained tend to pathologize sexual behavior of patients and emphasize eradication and control of behavior rather than provide education and counseling (Medlar, 1993). Unprepared staff may be overwhelmed by a lack of knowledge or skills in addition to cultural taboos, personal discomfort, and embarrassment (Conine, 1984). As a result, staff may react with anger, denial, lack of empathy, moralizing, or lack of objectivity, and become overly restrictive, overly protective, and judgmental (Ducharme & Gill, 1990).

Nurses' attitudes about sexuality have been extensively studied (Ducharme & Gill, 1990; Medlar & Medlar, 1990; Novak & Mitchell, 1988; Wilson & Dibble, 1993). Nursing students are less knowledgeable and more conservative than other students regarding sexuality (Medlar & Medlar, 1990). In rehabilitation nurses, increased religiosity has been correlated with decreased knowledge about sexuality and more conservative sexual values, regardless of years of rehabilitation experience (Wilson & Dibble, 1993). Nursing historically started in religious orders in which nurses were viewed as pure and asexual; purity, modesty, self-sacrifice, and humility were valued. Furthermore, early nurses were not allowed to marry. Nursing was concerned with cleanliness and hygiene, and sex was seen as "dirty." Nursing faculty were unprepared to teach this content themselves, so it was ignored or limited to only certain necessary topics (e.g., reproduction). Sexuality was seen as a private issue for the patient and not as a nursing concern. In addition, most nurses were women, and interest in or discussion of sexuality was considered unladylike (Gender, 1992). Although other health care professions have been studied less extensively, many of them have similar origins, traditions, and cultures (Issacson & Delgado, 1974; Novak & Mitchell, 1988). Historically, sexual counseling as an art and science emerged in the 1960s with the research and treatment programs developed by Masters and Johnson. The application of this knowledge to people with disabilities was slower and more controversial, but paralleled the development of the disability rights movement (Ducharme, 1993; Kempton & Kahn, 1991). In the early 1970s Ted Cole and his colleagues developed the first formal program for sexuality awareness and comfort training for both professionals and people with disabilities (Cole, Chilgren, & Rosenberg, 1973). Various Sexual Attitude Reassessment (SAR) programs, presented throughout the United States, emphasized developing comfort with both personal sexuality and other people's sexuality. Techniques for counseling or for establishing sexuality education and counseling programs in rehabilitation facilities were not included in the SAR programs (Ducharme, 1993). During the 1980s, increasing social conservatism regarding sexuality and sexual values was somewhat offset by increasing awareness of the importance of proper education about the prevention of the human immunodeficiency virus or acquired immune deficiency syndrome (Finger, 1993a) and sexual abuse (Kempton & Kahn, 1991), but the frequency of SAR programs or other formal programs for the practicing professional declined, partially because of a lack of funding. In addition, trends in the literature have emphasized the impact of disability on physical sexual function, with limited information provided on therapeutic strategies for treating or managing other issues of sexuality with clients (Finger, 1993b). Although health care professionals are more aware of the importance of sexuality issues to their clients, they continue to feel ill equipped to address those needs.

In a 1988 survey of 129 rehabilitation professionals (Ducharme & Gill, 1990), 79% reported that sexuality was as important as other major aspects of rehabilitation, but only 9% indicated they were comfortable addressing sexuality, and 51% addressed it only if the patient or family first brought up the subject. Furthermore, of the respondents surveyed, 41% attributed their discomfort to a lack of preparation and experience. In another study of rehabilitation nurses and occupational therapists (Novak & Mitchell, 1988), 55% of the registered nurses (RNs) and 58% of the occupational therapists (OTs) consistently approached their patients about the topic. Of those professionals who did not counsel patients regarding sexuality, 70% of OTs and 90% of RNs said the reasons included "someone else does it" or not believing they were prepared (OTs, 22%; RNs, 28%). Because of role ambiguity and overlap and territoriality issues on the team, some team members may be reluctant to address sexuality for fear of invading another team member's "territory." Consequently, sexuality issues frequently fall between the cracks (Conine, 1984).

In a survey of 268 people with spinal cord injury following initial rehabilitation (Tepper, 1992), only 45% received any sexual counseling or education during their initial rehabilitation. Of those people, 48% indicated that their needs were met. Only 24% were directly offered services, 8% reported no interest, and

9% refused services. Of the respondents, 77% reported they needed more information following discharge, but only 29% received such information. Although those people injured between 1982 and 1992 were three times more likely to have received services than those people injured earlier, men remained twice as likely to have received sexuality information or counseling than women. Of the services received, 57% received written materials, 42% had group discussions or classes, 39% were shown videos or films, 18% had group counseling, and 20% had peer counseling. Only 27% received individual or couples counseling. Length of stay and type of rehabilitation facility were not factors in services received. Of the respondents, 17% indicated that the topic should be addressed immediately after injury; 30%, within 1 to 5 weeks; 19%, from 6 to 10 weeks; 8%, 11 to 15 weeks; and 8%, more than 15 weeks after injury.

In another study of spinal cord–injured persons (White, Rintala, Hart, & Fuhrer, 1994), 66% of men received sexuality education and counseling, whereas 37% of the women reported receiving such intervention. Of those women, only 31% reported that the information was helpful. Areas of concern were ranked differently by men and women: men ranked not satisfying partner, fear of sexual disease, urinary accidents, not enough personal satisfaction, and feeling sexually attractive as their top five concerns. Women ranked urinary accidents, bowel accidents, not satisfying partner, feeling sexually unattractive, and feeling that others find them sexually unattractive as their top five concerns. Topics of interest also differed: men ranked methods for achieving sexual satisfaction, helping partners cope emotionally with limitations, fertility, coping emotionally with changes, and exploration of values and attitudes as their top five topics. Women ranked coping emotionally with changes, helping partners cope emotionally with limitations, methods for achieving sexual satisfaction, exploration of values and attitudes, and birth control as their top five topics. It is interesting that the interpersonal and self-esteem aspects of sexuality ranked so high in contrast to the usual focus in many rehabilitation sexuality programs of emphasis on physiologic changes, sexual function, and management of physical problems (Tepper, 1992).

An earlier study (Cornelius et al., 1982) found that the services and information desired by disabled people included social skills training, general sexual education, sexuality and disability issues, access to reading materials, access to audiovisual materials, and group discussions. Also desired were individual counseling, group counseling, couples or family counseling, sex therapy, genetic and contraceptive counseling, and obstetrical/gynecological/genitourinary care.

Consumers of rehabilitation services are increasingly demanding sexuality education and counseling services, although they often still are reluctant to approach rehabilitation professionals directly for this information. With increased societal openness regarding sexual matters and increased acceptance of the normalization of disabled people, rehabilitation clients are less likely to tolerate sexual dissatisfaction (Conine, 1984). Consumer demand may interest administrators in supporting sexuality programs in an era of increased attention to patient satisfaction and competitive marketing. In addition, health care professionals and administrators must examine the milieu of a program and its impact on the patient's psychosocial adaptation to his or her disability. Although the effect of such a program is less easily measured, it may indirectly have measurable outcomes. Sexually nonfunctioning clients are more likely to be depressed, anxious, and overwhelmed by the rehabilitation process (Conine, 1984). Sexual identity, self-concept, and self-worth are so strongly linked that if one is impaired, the other aspects of the personality may suffer (Drench, 1992). True rehabilitation needs to deal with physical and medical problems, as well as the interpersonal, social, and psychological crises that occur. At the core of psychological well-being is a feeling of sexual adequacy (Conine, 1984). Disabled people have reported that loneliness and isolation from friends and family are more problematic than their physical rehabilitation problems (Strauss, 1991). Furthermore, impaired sexual function has a direct adverse effect on medical, psychological, and vocational rehabilitation for people with chronic illness and disability (Shrey, Kiefer, & Anthony, 1979).

Problems in sexual adjustment can be prevented through early education, information, and suggestions for sexual function. Integration of sexual counseling into the rehabilitation program normalizes patient concerns and gives the patient permission to question and express them (Finger, 1993a). Having a satisfying sexual life makes people want to take better physical care of themselves, improves their ability to relate to others, and increases productivity (Trieschmann, 1988). Thus, provision of sexuality services may ensure better outcomes in more measurable areas such as mobility and activities of daily living.

A sexuality program is useless unless it is offered by staff to all patients (Cornelius et al., 1982). Staff who do not approach patients are unaware of the numbers of patients who have these concerns but are fearful of asking for help. Staff who are not properly educated expect the patient to introduce the topic. Patients should not leave the rehabilitation setting without receiving at least basic information regarding their disability and how it may affect their sexuality (Hoeman, 1996) as well as information on accessing more information or further services. Total rehabilitation needs to include sexual rehabilitation (Drench, 1992). A rehabilitation program that does not include and offer these services risks the ability of the program to honestly market comprehensive rehabilitation services, as would neglect of activities of daily living training or pressure ulcer prevention. Sexual counseling services are required by many certifying organizations such as the Commission on Accreditation of Rehabilitation Facilities (1997) and by professional standards of care such as those of the Association of Rehabilitation Nurses (American Nurses Association and Association of Rehabilitation Nurses, 1994). In areas with managed care, the opportunity for rehabilitation professionals to provide education and counseling to patients and significant others may be lost after brief inpatient admissions of 2 to 6 weeks, which makes early intervention much more important for the patient. In addition, the development of health care provider attitudes, skills, and knowledge in sexuality and disability must be expanded beyond the traditional rehabilitation center to include primary care providers, community clinics, subacute rehabilitation programs, skilled nursing facilities, board-and-care and residential facilities, and home care agencies. The acute inpatient rehabilitation center should advocate for expanded sexuality services and can provide a model for program development as well as a resource for professional education and referral for higher level or more complex services.

Establishment of a Sexuality Program

What must be done to establish or improve sexuality programs in a rehabilitation center or other health care institutions? Care must be taken to ensure that consumers are aware of services available, that there are positive staff attitudes, and that staff have appropriate knowledge and skills. The program must be both physically and financially accessible to consumers, provide alternative accommodations for special client needs, and have administrative support (Cornelius et al., 1982). A poorly planned program may find itself hampered by only lukewarm or token support from administrators, with services provided in a haphazard way, and may be actively sabotaged (Zejdlik, 1992).

Assessment and Planning

Key members of the rehabilitation team and administrators must be involved in the initial planning for a sexuality program. Clinicians who have attended formal sexuality courses during their basic or graduate-level education are most likely to be knowledgeable in this area (Wilson & Dibble, 1993) and can play a key position in finding a sympathetic administrator to help champion the cause. A minimum of 2 years should be planned to develop a comprehensive program (Ducharme, Cole, & Medlar, 1993).

Initially, a systems needs assessment should be conducted and a program proposal written, ideally by an interdisciplinary group of rehabilitation clinicians. However, these tasks may be impossible in smaller institutions or new facilities. An excellent guideline for this process is *Who Cares? A Handbook on Sex Education and Counseling Services for Disabled People* (Cornelius et al., 1982). The importance of including the following topics in any assessment and proposal is stressed.

What Is the Mission of the Institution? If the program will be a comprehensive rehabilitation program that will provide inpatient and outpatient care to all disability groups, the needs for services will be different than for a diagnosis-specific program, long-term or residential care facility, or outpatient clinic.

How Does This Program Relate to Institutional Philosophy, Goals, and Purposes? Issues such as comprehensiveness, holistic view of the patient or client, family-centered care, and so forth lend themselves readily to the integration of sexuality services.

What Are the Characteristics of the Client Population Served (or Solicited)? This section needs to include demographic information such as disability types, age, sex, socioeconomic factors, and culture. In addition, length-of-stay information, payers, and methods of access to services and information should be included.

What Are Our Staff Resources and Composition? This section should include information on staff mix, current training and expertise, traits and current attitudes, who will need what level of education, who will provide what services, what further education and training is needed, and any anticipated increase in staff costs. A staff survey using a variety of tools may prove helpful in providing factual data for this section. Plans for orientation of new staff and ongoing inservice education should be included. Backup resources for staff on vacation or leave with specialty responsibilities needs to be addressed as well (Zejdlik, 1992).

What Are Our Existing Policies and Politics? During the initial stages, planners must identify where there is administrative and staff support or resistance (both overt and covert) and also must address strategies for dealing with resistance. Some strategies that may be considered include asking consumers or other agencies for letters of support describing the need for services, or sponsoring a workshop by a well-known expert in the field. If the existing written policies are prohibitive or restrictive, they need to be analyzed for potential or actual negative impact on the institution, staff, or clients.

What Will Be the Need for Budget and Financial Considerations? Emphasis should be placed on fiscal impact of improved marketability, patient satisfaction, and improved patient functional outcomes instead of more difficult to measure issues such as improved quality of life or self-esteem (Ducharme et al., 1993). Planners may address how to decrease institutional liability by educating staff in the management of clients' sexually inappropriate or risky behavior or inappropriate behavior in staff–patient interactions. Budget items need to include the initial and ongoing costs for trainers or outside consultants, educational time for staff, educational materials for staff and patients, and audiovisual equipment or aids such as sexual organ models. In a fee-for-service system, methods of billing for sexuality services for clients and potential for actual reimbursement must be addressed. In a managed care or capitated system, increases in revenues or mitigating costs also must be addressed, especially for any needed outside services. Planners also should explore sponsorship of underfunded clients or programs by foundations, grants, or service groups.

What Is the Size of the Organization? This section needs to include data such as numbers of clients served, space availability, scheduling, and staffing flexibility. If the organization is part of a larger health care network, resources that may be shared should also be analyzed.

What Is Our Location and Access? What provisions will be made for clients with special needs such as wheelchair transportation, wheelchair access, sign language interpretation, low vision aids, and provisions for nonverbal clients (Ziff, 1986)? Will a privacy or conjugal visit room be provided, and, if so, under what conditions? How will clients be informed of services available and what other agencies will need to be included as part of a marketing plan or referral system? Will provision of services require a physician's order or a referral from another professional or case manager, or will self-referral be sufficient?

What Legal or Ethical Issues Must Be Addressed? This section is especially important if the agencies deal with minors or clients with guardians or conservators. How the agency will deal with consent or prohibition in these cases must be addressed. Consent forms should also be included in the proposal (Ducharme et al., 1993). In some jurisdictions, certain services, such as sexually transmitted disease (STD) information or sexual abuse prevention training, may be required for certain types of agencies. Some agencies may be prohibited from providing birth control or abortion information because of religious affiliation or legislated requirements. How will explicit materials be handled? In residential or long-term facilities, special attention must be given to the provision for client privacy/noninterference with consensual behaviors, rights related to age-appropriate sexual behavior and roles, and acceptance of nontraditional sexual orientation and behaviors (Cornelius et al., 1982). If they do not exist, a staff sexual ethics code or policies on patient protection from sexual abuse or exploitation and management of any violations must be addressed and developed (Ducharme et al., 1993).

What Specific Services Are Proposed? This section is based on the preceding assessment and should be as specific as possible. A broad overview (Haffner, 1990) of services that need to be considered include those that provide clients with information: human growth and development, reproduction, family life, childbirth, parenthood, sexual response cycle, effects of disability, management of disability-specific problems, masturbation, sexual orientation, contraception, abortion, sexual abuse, and prevention of STDs. Development of sexual values is also needed: questioning and exploring sexual values; impact of family, culture, and religion; clarification of personal values; positive body image; increased self-esteem; insights about relationships with others; and help defining personal responsibilities to others. In addition, development of skills should be included: communication; decision making; assertiveness; refusal skills; ability to create satisfying relationships; and use of sexual devices, techniques, and aids. Development of responsibility also must be addressed: abstinence, resistance to peer or other pressure for sexual involvement, use of contraception, prevention of STDs, and resistance to sexual abuse or exploitation. Considerations also need to include what services will be provided on-site or in-house and what services must be obtained by outside referral or consultation. If outside referrals will be used, what consideration is made for selecting other providers who are also knowledgeable and skilled in a particular area? For example, if on-site obstetrical care for women with spinal cord injuries will not be provided, how will the program identify and access providers who are knowledgeable about the special needs of this population and willing to provide services? Will such identification be done by contract or through more informal referral arrangements? What costs may be involved? Who will make referrals?

What Is the Implementation Plan? Timelines for the development of policies, staff training and evaluation, and implementation of client services should be presented in a manner that is realistic but meets client and institutional needs. Most institutions will support a well-defined program of reasonable cost that increases quality and competitiveness of their rehabilitation program (Neistadt & Freda, 1987).

Staff Education and Training

Planning also needs to include specific content for staff education, teaching methods to use, and who will teach the course. Guidelines (Ducharme et al., 1993) for planning in this area include the following.

Establishment of an Interdisciplinary Sexuality Committee. This committee can act as a steering committee for the program and should largely comprise clinicians who provide direct care and have previous education or interest in sexuality services. Client or peer representation is also strongly encouraged. This committee will be responsible for planning the staff educational content and methods, planning ongoing staff education, implementing and evaluating programs and services, and providing input to administration regarding policies and procedures. When possible, committee members should be involved in writing the original proposal.

Needs Assessment. The sexuality committee should conduct a baseline assessment to assess current staff attitudes, knowledge, and skills in providing client sexuality services. It is encouraged that all levels of staff be included in this assessment, including administrators; clinicians; and support staff such as secretarial, dietary, and janitorial staff. Tools may be selected that already have determined validity and reliability such as the Sexual Attitude and Information Questionnaire (SAIQ; Brockway & Steger, 1980; Brockway et al., 1978) or may be developed in-house. It may also be helpful to assess current practice patterns regarding initiation of the topic with clients, which clients are offered services, range of education and counseling services currently provided to clients, and so forth. This information can be particularly helpful later when evaluating the impact of education programs on practice. Assessment of the needs of present or past clients is also encouraged and should be coordinated by the sexuality committee. Assessment can be done using surveys, patient satisfaction tools, focus groups, telephone interviews, or informal interviews with individuals in clinics and wards. The committee should also conduct an appropriate literature review related to the special needs of specific disability groups or populations. When dealing with a pediatric or adolescent population, or with clients with intellectual impairments, parental involvement in the needs assessment process as well as the planning of services is crucial (Hoeman, 1996; McDermott, Kelly, & Spearman, 1994; National Information Center for Children and Youth with Disabilities, 1992; Pender & Hingburger, 1991; Ragg & Rowe, 1991; Rousso, 1993; Watson & Rogers, 1980).

Selection of Models and Philosophy. The sexuality committee can help develop conceptual models and a program philosophy. Issues that must be addressed before the start of staff educational programs include who should provide sexuality education and counseling services. Some centers choose to delegate this responsibility to only specific disciplines or people, whereas others choose to hold all staff accountable for at least a baseline competence and initiation of the topic with patients. Training for all staff should be mandatory, regardless of which model is selected (Novak & Mitchell, 1988). A philosophy may include a sexuality program mission statement or list of values statements or program assumptions (Goddard, 1988). Use of models and a philosophy provide a structure around which to design both education programs for staff and intervention programs for clients.

Course Formats

The literature has presented several models for implementation of staff education. Perhaps the oldest and most frequently cited is SAR (Cole et al., 1973; Cornelius et al., 1982; Ducharme, 1992; Halstead, Halstead, Salhoot, Stock, & Sparks, 1977). Originally developed for medical students in San Francisco by the National Sex and Drug Forum, SAR was further developed by Cole and his colleagues to specifically address general issues related to sexuality as well as those specific to disability. SAR is designed for both people with disabilities and their partners as well as health care professionals and educators. The goals of SAR are to reduce too hasty or emotional reactions to sexual stimuli by desensitization and education, and then to resensitize participants to a more gentle, humanistic, and professional understanding of the sexuality of self and others. Originally, SAR was an intensive 2½-day experience; the first 10 hours were devoted to desensitization with progressively more explicit and controversial content using slides, films, panels, and speakers, interspersed with small group (12 to 14 people) discussion and sharing of feelings. The members of the small groups were usually consistent to generate more trust and risk taking among members. The remainder of the course included explicit content as well, but focused more on issues specific to disability (Cole et al., 1973). Evaluation revealed that 95% of attendees reported SAR was helpful for their work, 74% felt it should be required for professional training in sexuality, and 76% reported they were more able to talk openly about sexuality issues with clients (Ducharme, 1992). The strengths of the model include the focus on the individual's personal sexual experiences, feelings, and attitudes, the dispelling of sexual myths and stereotypes, and its applicability to a variety of participants. The weaknesses of the approach are that the leaders must be highly skilled, there can be significant costs for the explicit media, controversy may exist over the use of explicit materials, a large space is needed to accommodate the small groups, and the model is time intensive (Cornelius et al., 1982). In addition, although professionals became more aware of their own anxieties and comfort levels regarding sexuality topics, the actual impact on quality of practice or initiation of sexual counseling with clients was more difficult to assess (Trieschmann, 1988). More recently, the concept of "mini-SARs" of 4 to 8 hours have been popular because of the reduced time and resources needed (Ducharme et al., 1993).

The sexual health model or sexual clinician model involves intensive training of only a select team of clinicians who provide most sexuality services (Miller, Szasz, & Anderson, 1981; Zejdlik, 1992). In addition to providing specialized services to clients on a referral basis, the clinicians are usually also responsible for staff education about sexuality. In some settings, this job is combined with another job (such as urologic nurse), whereas in others, the clinician deals only with sexuality issues for a large group of patients. An advantage of this approach is a high level of expertise and experience; a disadvantage is that the patient generally has no prior relationship with the provider in which to develop respect and trust, which must occur for effectiveness in more sensitive areas of counseling or education.

Another unique model is the sexuality program provided by the Massachusetts Rehabilitation Commission Statewide Head Injury Program (SHIP; Ducharme et al., 1993). This program provides services to SHIP-sponsored day treatment, residential, and supported employment programs for people with brain injury. The program is administered at the state level by a steering committee. An advisory committee that comprises professionals, consumers, and nationally recognized experts develops and approves educational materials, content, format, and programs for both providers and clients. Each facility has a core committee made up of its own staff. The statewide program is responsible for orienting the administration of the facility to sexuality issues, selecting and training core committee members, providing staff training, and assisting with and evaluating patient education and counseling programs. Evaluation includes needs assessments and pre-training and posttraining evaluation forms and questionnaires. Because the brain-injured population has special needs related to socially appropriate sexual behavior, the Sexually Related Occurrence Data Collection tool (Ducharme et al., 1993) is used at facilities to collect data on sexual behaviors that occur after training. These data serve as the basis for further problem solving and education with core committee members by consultants from the statewide program.

A similar program is available in South Carolina for use with developmentally disabled clients. Called STEPS (Socialization, Training, Education, and Parenting Services), this program is administered by the state Department of Disabilities and Special Needs (McDermott et al., 1994). STEPS coordinators (social workers, human services workers, nurses, and psychologists) receive an initial 40 hours of training with quarterly follow-up inservices in the use of a structured client curriculum of 30 lesson plans that address issues such as body functions and hygiene, self-esteem and assertiveness, refusal skills, contraception and STD prevention, pregnancy, nutrition, and parenting skills. Coordinators provide services to clients (22 in a caseload) in private homes, institutional setting, and schools, and in groups or individually. Goals are individually negotiated with the client and family. Similar models could also be used with other populations served either by government agencies, consumer-oriented organizations, or health care institutions in a large network.

A number of formats can be selected for staff education regarding sexuality. Probably the most successful will be a combination of several methods (Cornelius et al., 1982), both for variety and to meet the needs of varying learning styles and baseline knowledge. In addition, different program behavior objectives may be better met using different approaches. Knowledge building regarding anatomy and physiology, growth and development, or disability-specific problems and the dispelling of sexual myths may be most appropriately addressed through structured readings, group lectures, and discussions. Attitudes, increased awareness, and comfort with sexual topics are generally inappropriate for discussion in large groups or in lecture format. Techniques for teaching this content may include desensitization with explicit materials or language plus small group discussion, exploration of personal values and beliefs in small groups with instructor guidance, use of special assessment tools and exercises, and role playing. Panel presentations by professionals and clients with learner participation may also be helpful. Furthermore, skills in active listening, assessment, history taking, and interpersonal communication may be developed by instructor modeling and role playing with feedback in typical situations and using audiovisual media. Practice with models may also be helpful. The addition of independent study with reading materials, computer-assisted learning, and workbooks for self-assessment also has great potential as a supplement to other methods, but should not replace interaction with peers and skilled instructors. Advantages of having several class sessions with time in between (every other week for several weeks, and so on) over the intensive course are that the increased opportunities may allow the students to practice with their newly learned knowledge and skills and bring problems encountered back to class for help in resolution, and there may be more time for individual contemplation of issues, values, and feelings among participants (Cornelius et al., 1992; Medlar & Medlar, 1990). Ideally, instructors should be familiar with the participants and be already trusted, respected members of the team. Course instructors also need to be knowledgeable regarding the content, proficient in interpersonal skills, and sensitive to the group's concerns and feelings (Drench, 1992).

Course Content

The content of the course should be based on the needs assessment, but the literature has provided guidance on topic areas that should be addressed (Bosshart & Ernst, 1991; Finger, 1993b; Finger, Stack Hall, & Peterson, 1992; Gender, 1992; Hoeman, 1996; Medlar, 1993; Novak & Mitchell, 1988; Strauss, 1991).

Knowledge-Based Content. This content should include sexual anatomy and physiology, the reproductive cycle, normal growth and development related to sexuality, the human sexual response cycle, birth control or contraception technology, and methods for the prevention of STDs. It also should include special issues related to children, adolescents, or elderly people, and disability-specific effects, concerns, and methods for managing problems such as spasticity; bowel and bladder dysfunction; cognitive impairment; impulse control; disinhibition; contractures; phantom sensation; spatial neglect or visual field cuts; visual, communicative, or hearing impairments; erectile dysfunction; or infertility. The impact of culture, religion, and values, and the dispelling of myths and stereotypes related to both sexuality and disability should be presented. In addition, staff need to be educated about the sexuality patient or family education and counseling program being implemented or revised, including the philosophy, models, policies and procedures, responsibilities, referral methods, and appropriate use of educational tools including explicit media and other resources available (Ducharme et al., 1993).

Attitudes and Values Training. This training should include desensitizing sexual images and words; developing awareness of one's own beliefs, values, and attitudes; making changes in beliefs and attitudes based on new information or exposure to different perspectives; and developing sensitivity to patients' and other perspectives. In addition, issues related to role boundaries and sexual ethics need to be presented and discussed (Brown, 1992; Ducharme et al., 1993; Edelwich & Brodsky, 1991). In the rehabilitation setting, boundary issues are especially common between patients and staff because of special circumstances. Most rehabilitation care requires extensive touching as the result of the patient's initial dependence or to provide the required service. There is a prolonged length of stay or professional contact over weeks or months, and patients and staff are often alone in private areas together. The nature of rehabilitation itself, which usually is generated by a crisis with frequent, intense feelings generated in patients, hopes raised or shattered, and dreams and plans changed can result in a special bond created with the provider. Patients, who may be especially vulnerable emotionally—fearing that no one will ever find them attractive again—may test these feelings with staff. In addition, intimate and sometimes sexually stimulating topics are addressed on a daily basis. Clients may misperceive staff's genuine caring and concern as something more. Staff can become more than an empathetic guide and become the patient's rescuer, fantasy partner, or sexual object.

Neophyte staff are especially vulnerable to developing inappropriate relationships with patients to fulfill their own unmet needs, such as power, control, affection, or recognition. The rescuer singles the patient out for special time, perhaps visiting on his or her day off or taking the patient on pass. The rescuer may buy the patient gifts or give the patient special privileges, rescuing the patient from distressful crises and the "misunderstanding" of the patient by other team members (Brown, 1992). These relationships do not need to be physically intimate to be dangerous. If the staff person allows the relationship to continue, and then must end it, he or she only reinforces the patient's negative self-statements, feelings of worthlessness, and rejection by the world in general. The patient's fragile new self-image and weakened ego strength can be seriously damaged. Moreover, the staff person may become alienated from peers and isolated at a time when he or she needs guidance and assistance to understand the danger of the situation. It is essential that policies be established and enforced and staff be trained in ways to avoid these pitfalls (Brown, 1992; Edelwich & Brodsky, 1991; Medlar, 1993).

Areas of particular concern related to boundary violations that should be addressed in policy include physical contact (hugs, kissing, and so on); social contact (taking a client on a pass or going on a date); extra therapy or privileges; money (loans, free services or gifts, or the hiring of patients for personal work or at the institution); socialization with former patients; and excessive staff self-disclosure of personal information. Because of the often intermittent, long-term relationship between people with disabilities and rehabilitation agencies, it is recommended that any individual social contact with former patients be done only with the knowledge and consent of the professional's supervisor (Edelwich & Brodsky, 1991).

Skills Training. This training should address effective and active listening, interviewing and assessment skills, facilitation of communication, values clarification skills, recognition of covert and overt patient cues for readiness, how to initiate the topic of sexuality with clients, and how to deal with inappropriate sexual behavior. Depending on the program goals, selected psychomotor skills may also need to be taught, such as the methods for training patients in the use of sexual devices, positions, or techniques. Discussion and modeling of the personal qualities of a good sexuality counselor such as compassion, a sense of humor, patience, perceptiveness, integrity, and flexibility are also valuable (Hoeman, 1996).

Program Implementation

One of the issues that must be addressed in implementing a sexual education and counseling program is who should provide the services. In some settings, only certain people or disciplines are authorized to provide any sexual counseling. This regulation can be over-restrictive and counterproductive. Patients should be free to approach anyone on the professional staff with whom they feel trust, comfortable, and have respect regarding the discussion of sensitive issues (Conine, 1984; Cornelius et al., 1982; Drench, 1992). Often, this source of sexuality information is not the traditional figure such as a physician or psychologist. In inpatient rehabilitation programs, patients frequently establish especially close bonds to their nurse or therapist because of the intensity of contacts and intimacy and type of care. This contact helps the client to develop a comfort level that facilitates frank and open discussion. Nurses often assist patients through other emotional crises related to their disability and have officially sanctioned "touch" privileges. In addition, nurses frequently have responsibilities related to intimate care of patients, such as bowel or bladder care or bathing, that can create a sense in the patient that the nurse may be a resource for other intimate information and counseling (Finger et al., 1992; Hoeman, 1996; Novak & Mitchell, 1988). In some settings, this degree of intimacy may also be developed with a recreation therapist, speech pathologist, life skills trainer, or other team member. In addition, in an inpatient setting, every patient comes into contact with a nurse, frequently as the first contact with a team member. Not every patient will have a psychologist, or even be allowed this contact, depending on the payer and funding, an issue that must be considered, given the current climate of patient-focused care and the blurring of traditional boundaries between disciplines.

PLISSIT Model

An extensively used model for implementation of sexuality education counseling is the PLISSIT model developed by Annon (1976). PLISSIT stands for *p*ermission, *l*imited *i*nformation, *s*pecific *s*uggestions, and *i*ntensive *t*herapy. It has the advantage of utility in a wide variety of settings or service models and with a wide variety of disciplines. Furthermore, it lends itself readily to an interdisciplinary team approach for sexual education and counseling.

Instead of identifying which disciplines should provide which type of services, the PLISSIT model revolves around the intensity of client needs and types of interventions, as well as the provider's preparation and comfort level with different levels of education and skill. It can be a valuable model to build into both staff training and the provision of sexual education and counseling services in the clinical setting.

Permission

At this level, the provider gives both overt and covert messages to the patient that sexuality is O.K. and sex is spoken here (Lemon, 1993). For example, the provider may provide privacy with the patient's partner for intimate activity or for discussion of feelings or questions, assist the patient to dress or groom attractively, serve as an active empathetic listener, let the patient know that his or her concerns are normal and not unusual or perverse, assist the patient to deal with anger or grief over losses, help the patient to identify strengths (Dittmar, 1989), offer appropriate reassurance, and validate the patient's concerns. The provider also offers more information when the patient is ready. The provider may provide permission through his or her responses to the patient's questions, but more effectively will introduce the topic in a nonthreatening manner to elicit the patient's hidden fears and concerns. Permission can be a powerful tool to help patients deal with the basic issues of self-esteem, personal worth, and body image.

Permission can be given using different approaches (Cornelius et al., 1982). The gradual approach is used when assessing the patient's overall status by working from very general to specific topics and from less to more threatening topics. The gradual approach could be done while collecting a general health or social history by asking about work, friends, family, significant others, and then the sexual partner, or by asking about developmental milestones such as growing up and peer relationships and eventually about social skills and intimacy. The strong possibility approach allows the provider to more directly address sexuality, but in general terms such as, "Many people with amputations have concerns about their sexual attractiveness. Is this a concern of yours?" This approach emphasizes the normalcy and naturalness of the patient's concerns and reassures the patient that he or she is not a freak for having such thoughts. A provider can also use a multiple problem approach in early contacts with the patient by listing services provided by the agency or topics to be addressed during rehabilitation, including sexuality education and counseling. This approach allows patients to hear that sexuality is considered a normal part of the program and gives them permission to choose which programs, including sexuality, they want for themselves at this time or in the future. The direct approach may occasionally work, but is more likely to offend or threaten patients; thus, it should be used only judiciously. This approach might include asking a patient, "How is your love life?" or "Are you having any sexual problems?" In many settings, all levels of staff, professional and ancillary, are expected to have sufficient knowledge, skills, and comfort with sexual topics to function within the permission level.

Limited Information

At the next level, the provider provides general and basic education, which usually includes factual information such as anatomy and physiology of the genitals or reproduction, the dispelling of myths, general ways that problems have been resolved by others with similar disabilities or functional problems, general information on prevention of STDs, contraception, and sexual effects of medications or anticipated surgical procedures. At this level, it is important that the provider know his or her own limitations in knowledge, skill, or comfort, and refers the patient to others when these limits are exceeded by the patient's needs. For example, a clinician may be comfortable discussing topics such as orgasm with a heterosexual couple, but not with a homosexual partner. In that case, the provider should refer the patient and partner to another clinician who is more comfortable with homosexuality. Limited information must always be linked with permission, both in giving it to the patient to elicit interest and in obtaining permission from the patient to discuss selected topics. Many agencies encourage or require all professional staff (e.g., RNs, OTs, and so on) to maintain competence at the limited information level. This competence must be fostered by the provision of appropriate education to these staff by the agency.

Specific Suggestions

At this level, the professional assists the patient to identify specific concerns or needs related to the patient's sexual expression, sexual function, or relationships. The professional then assists the patient by setting specific individualized goals or suggesting or providing individualized and specific ways to resolve a problem or explore it in more depth. Topics might include specific relationship problems; methods for achieving sexual satisfaction or satisfying the partner; change in behavior (managing disinhibition or memory problems, and so on); issues of arousal; erectile dysfunction; ejaculation; management of bowel and bladder problems; management of sexual effects of medications or surgical interventions; specific positions to use or avoid; or choices related to parenting or contraception. Generally the professional functioning at the specific suggestion level should have additional education, expertise, and experience in sexuality and disability beyond that provided to all staff. This education can be provided through graduate-level courses in sexuality, additional conferences or workshops, additional readings, by working with a mentor or preceptor, or by fulfilling the requirements for specialty certification (e.g., American Association of Sex Educators, Counselors, and Therapists). The professional functioning at this level must also be aware of his or her limitations in comfort, skills, or knowledge and must be prepared to refer the patient to other providers who may be better prepared to address selected specific suggestions or go on to the next level.

Intensive Therapy

This level is the least frequently needed in the rehabilitation setting, but it is critical that the agency either provide intensive therapy or have the resources for obtaining this level of service when indicated. Intensive therapy includes psychotherapy; intensive or prolonged marital or relationship counseling; counseling and therapy for battering, sexual abuse, or rape; surgical or invasive procedures (penile prosthesis or injection therapy, or abortion) or medical management of infertility; childbirth; hormonal imbalances; or severe behavioral or psychiatric problems. Provision of services at this level usually requires a psychologist, psychiatric or maternal–child clinical nurse specialist or nurse practitioner, or specialty physician with additional training, certification, or credentials. Ideally, referral resources should also be knowledgeable about the special needs related to the person's disability, or work closely with the professional making the referral to ensure that the needs are being met and coordinated with the therapy planned. Intensive therapy usually requires a longer time commitment by the both the provider and patient (Goddard, 1988). Plans should be made to avoid disrupting the therapeutic relationship as much as possible during a transition from inpatient to outpatient care.

The PLISSIT model provides the practitioner with a structure for identifying his or her own current level of appropriate practice as well as for assisting the professional in identifying areas for future professional growth. The sexuality committee may be a valuable resource for knowledge, comfort, and skill building on an individual level. The author of this chapter worked in a setting where monthly meetings of the committee were divided into two parts. The first dealt with committee business such as planning education programs or policy development. The second half involved educational programs for committee members at or desiring to move to the specific suggestions level, such as a formal didactic speaker, a journal article review, the learning and practicing of a new technique, or case presentations. Case presentations were particularly helpful in identifying options for management, and often became sources for problem solving with both inpatients and outpatients. Mentoring and precepting opportunities also became available as a result of these meetings.

Evaluation

An important component of an established sexuality education and counseling program that is often neglected is evaluation. In a national study of OTs and RNs who provided sexuality counseling for people with spinal cord injury, only 28% of the OTs and 37% of the RNs conducted follow-up interviews with patients to assess effectiveness, patient satisfaction with services, or the need for further services (Novak & Mitchell, 1988). Research methodology for this program component is lacking for both the complete range of staff development outcomes and for evaluation of patient outcomes. The SAIQ has been used the most for staff education outcome evaluation, but fails to measure actual change in practice patterns or effectiveness of staff following training (Brockway & Steger, 1980). Recommendations have been made that patients receive at least one follow-up contact 6 months after an intervention and ideally be followed for 2 years to assess effectiveness and to intervene, if necessary (Andamo, 1980). Follow-up can be informal, asking the patient if goals have been achieved, how effective suggested modifications are, whether the patient has resumed or increased sexual activity, and if sexual devices are used, or follow-up can be formal, using surveys and questionnaires (Spica, 1989). Unfortunately, unless such follow-up is a part of a research study or quality management project it rarely occurs. In the Tepper (1992) study of National Spinal Cord Injury Association members, 77% of the respondents indicated they needed more information after discharge from their initial rehabilitation setting. Only 29% of the respondents reported receiving any information following discharge. It would be interesting to determine if this low percentage could be generalized to the spinal cord–injured population at large, because people who join consumer organizations are generally more assertive in ensuring that their needs are met and are more proactive in their adjustment to their injury. Little evaluation research of sexuality services provided during rehabilitation has been conducted using people with disabilities other than spinal cord injury. Nothing has been published from nontraditional rehabilitation settings such as family planning clinics, home health agencies, or subacute rehabilitation programs. These deficiencies need to be corrected.

Further research and the development of valid and reliable evaluation tools are therefore needed for sexuality education and counseling. Tools are also needed to evaluate the outcomes of staff and professional education programs. In this era of reductions in staff and budgets, accurate measurement of outcomes is extremely important to justify continuation of programs such as sexual counseling within most rehabilitation settings.

REFERENCES

American Nurses Association and Association of Rehabilitation Nurses. (1994). *Standards and scope of rehabilitation nursing practice*. Kansas City, MO: Author.

Andamo, E.M. (1980). Treatment model: Occupational therapy for sexual dysfunction. *Sexuality and Disability, 3*(4), 26–38.

Annon, J. (1976). The PLISSIT model: A proposed conceptual scheme for the behavioral treatment for sexual problems. *Journal of Sex Education and Counseling, 2*, 1–15.

Bosshart, H.T., & Ernst, J.L. (1991). Current practices in sex education and counseling with the spinal cord injured population: How well are we doing? [Special issue: Sexuality and Disability]. *SCI Psychosocial Process, 66–69*.

Brockway, J.A., & Steger, J.C. (1980). Sexual attitude and information questionnaire: Reliability and validity in a spinal cord injured population. *Sexuality and Disability, 3*(4), 49–60.

Brockway, J.A., Steger, J.C., Berni, R., Ost, V.V., Williamson-Kirkland, T.E., & Peck, C.L. (1978). Effectiveness of a sex education and counseling program for spinal cord injured patients. *Sexuality and Disability, 1*(2), 127–136.

Brown, J.F. (1992). Another ethical issue without a resolution . . . for some. *SCI Psychosocial Process, 5*(2), 42–43.

Cole, T.M., Chilgren, R., & Rosenberg, P. (1973). A new programme of sex education and counseling for spinal cord injured adults and health care professionals. *Paraplegia, 11*(2), 111–124.

Commission on Accreditation of Rehabilitation Facilities. (1997). *Standards manual and interpretive guidelines for medical rehabilitation*. Tucson, AZ: Author.

Conine, T.A. (1984). Sexual rehabilitation: The roles of allied health professionals. In D.W. Kruger (Ed.), *Rehabilitation psychology* (pp. 81–87). Rockville, MD: Aspen.

Cornelius, D.A., Chipouras, S., Makas, E., & Daniels, S.M. (1982). *Who cares? A handbook on sex education and counseling services for disabled people* (2nd ed.). Baltimore: University Park Press.

Dittmar, S. (Ed.). (1989). *Rehabilitation nursing: Process and application*. St. Louis, MO: C.V. Mosby.

Drench, M.E. (1992). Impact of altered sexuality and sexual function in spinal cord injury. *Sexuality and Disability, 10*(1), 3–14.

Ducharme, S. (1992). Developing training programs for sexuality and disability: A personal perspective. *Sexuality and Disability, 10*(3), 193–203.

Ducharme, S. (1993). From the editor. *Sexuality and Disability, 11*(1), 1–2.

Ducharme, S., Cole, S., & Medlar, T. (1993, June). *Developing effective staff training for sexuality and disability*. Paper presented at the 70th annual meeting of the American Congress of Rehabilitation Medicine, Denver, CO.

Ducharme, S., & Gill, K.M. (1990). Sexual values, training, and professional roles. *Journal of Head Trauma Rehabilitation, 5*(2), 38–45.

Edelwich, J., & Brodsky, A. (1991). *Sexual dilemmas for the helping professional* (revised and expanded). New York: Brunner/Mazel.

Eisenberg, M.G., & Rustad, L.C. (1976). Sex education and counseling program on a spinal cord injury service. *Archives of Physical Medicine and Rehabilitation, 57*(3), 135–140.

Finger, W.W. (1993a). Preface to the special issue on sexual counseling for people with disabilities. *Sexuality and Disability, 11*(1), 3–5.

Finger, W.W. (1993b). Prevention: Assessment and treatment of sexual dysfunction following stroke. *Sexuality and Disability, 11*(1), 39–56.

Finger, W.W., Stack Hall, E., & Peterson, F.L. (1992). Education in sexuality for nurses. *Sexuality and Disability, 10*(2), 71–79.

Gender, A.R. (1992). An overview of the nurse's role in dealing with sexuality. *Sexuality and Disability, 10*(2), 81–89.

Goddard, L.R. (1988). Sexuality and spinal cord injury. *Journal of Neuroscience Nursing, 20*(4), 240–244.

Haffner, D.W. (1990). *Sex education 2000: A call to action.* New York: Sex Information and Education Council of the U.S.

Halstead, L.S., Halstead, M.M., Salhoot, J.T., Stock, D.D., & Sparks, R.W. (1977). A hospital-based program in human sexuality. *Archives of Physical Medicine and Rehabilitation, 58*(9), 409–412.

Hoeman, S.P. (Ed.). (1996). *Rehabilitation nursing: Process and application* (2nd ed.). St. Louis, MO: C.V. Mosby.

Issacson, J., & Delgado, H.E. (1974). Sexual counseling for those with spinal cord injuries. *Social Casework, 55,* 622–627.

Kempton, W., & Kahn, E. (1991). Sexuality and people with intellectual disabilities: A historic perspective. *Sexuality and Disability, 11*(1), 99–100.

Lemon, M.A. (1993). Sexual counseling and spinal cord injury. *Sexuality and Disability, 11*(1), 73–97.

McDermott, S., Kelly, M., & Spearman, J. (1994). Evaluation of a family planning program for individuals with mental retardation. *Sexuality and Disability, 12*(4), 307–317.

Medlar, T.M. (1993). Sexual counseling and traumatic brain injury. *Sexuality and Disability, 11*(1), 57–71.

Medlar, T., & Medlar, J. (1990). Nursing management of sexuality issues. *Journal of Head Trauma Rehabilitation, 5*(2), 46–51.

Miller, S., Szasz, G., & Anderson, L. (1981). The sexual health care clinician in an acute spinal cord injury unit. *Archives of Physical Medicine and Rehabilitation, 62*(7), 315–320.

National Information Center for Children and Youth with Disabilities. (1992). *Sexuality education for children and youth with disabilities.* Washington, DC: Author.

Neistadt, M.E., & Freda, M. (1987). *Choices: A guide to sex counseling with physically disabled adults.* Malabar, FL: Robert E. Krieger.

Novak, P.P., & Mitchell, M.M. (1988). Professional involvement in sexuality counseling for patients with spinal cord injuries. *American Journal of Occupational Therapy, 42*(2), 105–112.

Pender, G., & Hingburger, D. (1991). Sexuality: Dealing with parents. *Sexuality and Disability, 9*(2), 123–130.

Ragg, D.M., & Rowe, W. (1991). The effective use of group in sex education with people diagnosed as mildly developmentally disabled. *Sexuality and Disability, 9*(4), 337–352.

Rousso, H. (1993). Special considerations in counseling clients with cerebral palsy. *Sexuality and Disability, 11*(1), 99–100.

Sawyer, H.W., & Allen, H.A. (1983). Sexuality and spinal cord injured individuals: A challenge for counselors and trainers. *Journal of Applied Rehabilitation Counseling, 14*(4), 14–17.

Shrey, D.E., Kiefer, J.S., & Anthony, W.A. (1979). Sexual adjustment counseling for persons with severe disabilities: A skill-based approach for rehabilitation professionals. *Journal of Rehabilitation, 45*(2), 28–33.

Spica, M.M. (1989). Sexual counseling standards for the spinal cord injured. *Journal of Neuroscience Nursing, 21*(1), 56–60.

Strauss, D. (1991). Biopsychosocial issues in sexuality with the neurologically impaired patient. *Sexuality and Disability, 9*(1), 49–67.

Tepper, M.S. (1992). Sexual education in spinal cord injury rehabilitation: Current trends and recommendations. *Sexuality and Disability, 10*(1), 15–31.

Trieschmann, R.B. (1988). *Spinal cord injuries: Psychological, social, and vocational rehabilitation* (2nd ed.). New York: Demos.

Watson, G., & Rogers, R.S. (1980). Sexual instruction for the mildly retarded and normal adolescent: A comparison of educational approaches, parental expectations, and pupil knowledge and attitudes. *Health Education Journal, 39,* 88–95.

White, M.J., Rintala, D.H., Hart, K., & Fuhrer, M.J. (1994). A comparison of the sexual concerns of men and women with spinal cord injuries. *Rehabilitation Nursing Research, 3*(2), 55–61.

Wilson, P.S., & Dibble, S.L. (1993). Rehabilitation nurses' knowledge and attitudes toward sexuality. *Rehabilitation Nursing Research, 2*(2), 69–74.

Zejdlik, C. (1992). *Management of spinal cord injury* (2nd ed.). Boston: Jones and Bartlett.

Ziff, S.F. (1986). Symbolic sexual vocabulary for the severely speech impaired. *Sexuality and Disability, 7*(1–2), 3–14.

CHAPTER 20

Ethical Concerns

Craig J. Alexander

Relationships between health care personnel and patients, at times, can be confusing, especially in settings where professionals from a variety of health care disciplines have differing amounts of training and experience. Specifically, sexuality and related ethical concerns are sensitive, important issues in health care. Because most clinical ethics research has focused on dilemmas in critical care medicine (Scofield, 1993), the topic of sexual relationships between professionals and patients warrants increased attention. For instance, what extenuating circumstances justify having sexual relations with a patient? Do these situations vary among professional disciplines? Are there any exceptions to these circumstances? For example, is it acceptable to have relations with a former patient after a specified period? Is it acceptable once the former patient is in treatment with another professional? Is it acceptable to have a platonic relationship with a patient of the same sex? What if a provider accidentally meets a patient? Does that make fostering a personal relationship more acceptable? What if a provider runs into a former patient years later? Should mature individuals decide for themselves if a relationship is acceptable? It is not uncommon for a health care professional to marry a patient and have an apparently successful and happy marriage. After all, any two people can fall in love. Professionals working in health care need to address these and other questions. Each provider must come to an understanding about the limits and boundaries he or she must observe with patients in terms of physical contact, social contact, financial dealings, and self-disclosure.

ETHICAL CODES

Codes of ethical behavior that help guide and direct the conduct of health care professionals vary in how they address the issue of therapist–patient relations. The two disciplines that have addressed this issue in the most detail are psychiatry and psychology. The American Psychological Association (APA) for many years held close to the belief that "once a patient, always a patient," prohibiting dual relationships and sexual involvement with patients forever. However, the psychology code of ethics was recently revised (APA, 1992) to prohibit sexual relations between therapists and patients for at least 2 years after termination of treatment. After that point, the burden of proof falls on the psychologist to demonstrate that no exploitation occurred as a result of their relationship. On the other hand, professional boundaries in general medical practice are not as well defined (Gabbard & Nadelson, 1995). Physicians are expected to refrain from sexual involvement with their patients. However, the American Medical Association Council on Ethical and Judicial Affairs (1991) allows for sexual relations between former patients and physicians if there is no exploitation of trust, knowledge, emotions, or influence derived from the previous professional relationship. Within medicine, however, the field of psychiatry has been most active and vocal in developing standards on the topic of sexual relations between physician and patient. Immediately following APA's change in position on the subject, the discipline of psychiatry placed an absolute ban on sex with former patients, with no exceptions (Gabbard, 1994).

What about other key disciplines? How do their codes of ethics address this issue? The code of ethics for nurses (American Nurses Association, 1985) includes the protection, promotion, and restoration of health along with the prevention of illness and the alleviation of suffering. Nurses make clinical judgments and decisions using universal moral principles such as respect for the person, autonomy, and beneficience. No specific mention is made regarding patient–staff relations. Furthermore, ethical principles of the American Physical Therapy Association (1991), American Speech and Hearing Association (1994), American Therapeutic Recreation Association (1990), and the American Occupational Therapy Association (1994) do no specifically mention sexual relations with patients. The code of ethics of the National Association of Social Workers (1997) forbids sexual activities with clients under any and all circumstances. No mention, however, is made regarding former clients.

Clearly, a code of ethics for any discipline cannot be all encompassing and address every specific situation. A code is intended to serve as a guide for judicious appraisal of conduct. Each of the association's codes previously mentioned do consider the primacy of patients' interests. The issue of patient–staff relationships is critical, though. When not specifically addressed in the code of ethics, however, the individual provider must judge whether a sexual relationship with a patient may be harmful. Sexuality is an important part of life and continues to be a need well into old age. Disability and illness might affect sexuality but do not eliminate its importance. In some cases, illness or disability can profoundly affect one's self-esteem and sense of sexuality. When this occurs, who will the patient turn to? Usually, a patient will talk with whomever they feel closest, frequently, the provider with whom they spend the most time and who has "hands-on" contact with the patient, such as nurses and therapists. It is not surprising then that patient–staff boundary issues might be a concern. To compound this matter, many nurses and therapists are young and have limited experience to confront these difficult situations. Clearly, the codes of ethics of various disciplines need to explicitly address the issue of patient–staff relations.

INCIDENCE OF PATIENT–STAFF SEXUAL INVOLVEMENT

Health care providers are probably aware of individuals within their own setting who have become personally involved with one or more of their patients. However, what does the research show to be the incidence of patient–staff relationships? How much of a problem are these relationships? Research methodology in this area has taken one of two approaches: (1) directly ask the therapist to report his or her sexual involvement or (2) indirectly ask patients or therapists of any knowledge of such activities. In either case, these methods might result in underreporting of sexual misconduct (if it is perceived as such).

Several research studies have addressed this issue among physicians. In 1973, Kardener, Fuller, and Mensh surveyed 1,000 male physicians including gynecologists; psychiatrists; and internal medicine, surgery, and general practice physicians. They received a return rate of 46%. Results showed that between 5% and 13% of the sample acknowledged engaging in erotic behavior with their patients. Moreover, 19% indicated that sexual contact might actually be beneficial to patients. Benefits outlined by the physicians included improved sexual maladjustments, demonstration that there was no physical cause for the patient's absence of sex drive, and the relief of sexual frustration in a widow or divorcee. In a survey of 500 female physicians, Perry (1976) found that only 1 reported erotic contact with a patient. However, many of the individuals acknowledged practicing "nonerotic touching." Gartrell, Herman, Olarte, Feldstein, and Localio (1986) sampled 5,574 psychiatrists and received a 26% return rate. Of the respondents, 7% of the male and 3% of the female psychiatrists acknowledged sexual contact with patients. Gartrell, Milliken, Goodson, Thiemann, and Lo (1992) sampled more than 10,000 family practice, internal medicine, gynecology, and surgery physicians and had a 19% return rate. Of the respondents, 10% of males and 4% of females reported sexual contact with patients.

The issue of sexual involvement is not unique to America. The College of Physicians and Surgeons of British Columbia (1992) surveyed 2,082 physicians from all specialties, receiving almost a 70% return rate. Of the respondents, 4% of males and 0.3% of females acknowledged having had sex with patients. In addition, 8.1% of males and 4.3% of females reported sexual contact with former patients. Lamont and Woodward (1994) surveyed 792 Canadian gynecologists and received a 78% return rate. Of the respondents, 3% of males and 1% of females indicated sexual contact with patients. In the Netherlands, Wilbers, Veensstra, van de Wiel, and Schultz (1992) surveyed 975 gynecologists and ear, nose, and throat physicians. Of the 74% of physicians responding, 4% of males and 4% of females acknowledged sexual contact with their patients.

Other professional disciplines have also been studied. Pope (1994) pooled data from eight national studies, with a total of 5,148 participants from psychology, psychiatry, and social work. Summarizing the findings, Pope (1994) reported that 6.8% of the male therapists and 1.6% of the female therapists engaged in sex with a patient. Significant gender differences were found. Males were four times more likely to be offenders. No differences were found among the professional disciplines. Parsons and Wincze (1995) questioned all licensed mental health therapists in Rhode Island regarding sexual exploitation. Psychologists, psychiatrists, social workers, marriage and family therapists, and mental health counselors were asked if they had treated clients who had been involved sexually with a previous therapist between 1989 and 1991. They received 331 returns for a 49% response rate. Of the therapist, 26% ($n = 86$) reported treating at least one patient who acknowledged having sexual involvement with a previous therapist. Similar to previous research, male psychologists and psychiatrists were most likely to be perpetrators and female clients, the victims. The most common sexual behaviors reported in rank order were fondling, vaginal intercourse, and suggestive behavior. Almost all the therapists agreed that sexual involvement with clients was detrimental to the patient. Incidents of nonsexual misconduct also were reported, and included planned social encounters with patients and altered health claims.

Other studies have examined the issue of sexual relations among multidisciplinary rehabilitation professionals and patients. Alexander, Sipski, and Findley (1993) reported that 38% of their sample of 39 spinal cord–injured males acknowledged "sexual activity" with health care personnel. In addition, Sipski and Alexander (1993) reported that 16% of 25 spinal cord–injured females acknowledged "sexual activity" with health care personnel. As a follow-up to those findings, Sipski and Alexander (1994) surveyed 395 rehabilitation professionals from a wide range of disciplines on whether they had participated in sexual relations with patients. Of the individuals surveyed, 37% responded. The median age of the respondents was 43 years; 52% of the respondents were male; 5%, homosexual; and 70%, married. Subjects completed an anonymous and confidential questionnaire. The questionnaire addressed issues such as knowledge of sexual ethics, sexual behavior with patients, awareness of others' behavior with patients, the extent of the relationship and source of information, education received about sexuality, and whether the discipline had a code of ethics addressing the area of sexual relationships with patients.

Results indicated that 45% of respondents acknowledged no formal training in the area of sexuality. Moreover, 63% of respondents indicated no formal training in the area of sexual ethics. However, on a scale from 1, least comfortable, to 10, most comfortable, the median level of reported comfort discussing sex with patients was an 8. Despite the lack of formal training, most individuals indicated they felt extremely comfortable discussing sexuality with their patients. Respondents claimed to discuss sex with an average of one out of every three of their patients. A breakdown of respondents into individual disciplines revealed that occupational therapists least frequently discussed sex with their patients, whereas psychologists most frequently reported discussing sex with their patients. In response to the question, Is it ethical for staff and patients to have sexual relations, 90% indicated "No," 2% indicated "Yes," and 8% indicated "Sometimes."

Six subjects (4.1%) reported they had been involved in a sexual relationship with a patient. Five of those subjects reported one relationship and one reported having been involved in two relationships with patients. Of the six subjects who acknowledged their involvement with patients, two reported their profession as occupational therapy, one as a physical therapist, one as a nurse, one as a psychologist, and one reported the discipline as vocational rehabilitation. Three subjects reported they had masters' degrees and three had a doctorate in philosophy. All six subjects were heterosexual, 50% were male, and 50% were female. Subjects were asked to describe the circumstances of their relationships. Four subjects noted they became involved with the patient while they were actively treating the patient; two noted their involvement began after the therapeutic relationship. Five subjects reported they met the patient as a direct result of providing patient care; one subject met the patient out of the hospital. The psychologist noted that the involvement with the patient was restricted to a brief hug at the end of a therapy session. Another subject noted that the relationship lasted 2 weeks and the involvement was limited to hugging and kissing. Two subjects noted their relationships with patients lasted several months and that they had intercourse with the patient. One of those subjects had been involved with two patients. The remaining two individuals reported they had married the patients with whom they had developed relationships.

Because of the small sample size of subjects in each particular discipline, subjects were asked to indicate whether they had knowledge of other health care professionals who were personally involved in a relationship with a patient and to indicate the source of their knowledge. Of the respondents, 58% indicated they were aware of such relationships. The other professionals reported most often were nurses (25% of cases) and physical therapists (23%). This is not surprising because individuals practicing in those professions have the most direct hands-on contact with rehabilitation patients. Moreover, 36% of nurses and 20% of physical therapists surveyed indicated that their discipline does not have a code of ethics regarding sexual behavior with patients. An additional 43% of nurses and 30% of physical therapists were uncertain if the code of ethics in their discipline addressed sexual behavior with patients.

Clearly, these data suggest that sexual contact between professional health care providers and patients does occur in a variety of settings with individuals from various disciplines. Prior research has indicated that, with the physician or psychologist population, most of this erotic contact occurs between male professionals and female patients. However, in a female-dominated profession such as rehabilitation, erotic contact between female professional caregiver and male patients may be more common. Research also points to a lack of knowledge and training among health care professionals and a false sense of confidence regarding issues inherent in the professional–patient relationship. These issues apparently are not routinely addressed in the academic and clinical training of most health care professionals. Moreover, there are dramatic differences in the ethical codes among disciplines on this subject matter. Some disciplines, for example, psychology, address the issue of professional–patient relationships in detail, whereas, other disciplines barely address this issue at all. In addition, most institutional codes of ethics do not address the issue of patient–staff relationships. Thus, there is a strong need for a multidisciplinary code of ethics within the field of rehabilitation that addresses the issue of patient–staff relations.

In addition to a code of ethics, staff members need better education on the issues involved in relationships with patients. For example, understanding that developing feelings of attraction and aversion toward patients is normal. Furthermore, working closely with patients in rehabilitation can result in strong personal reactions. In a 12-part series of articles addressing ethical issues in physical medicine and rehabilitation, Jennings (1993) addressed the importance of the therapeutic relationship between patient and health care provider in the overall healing process. In addition, Purtilo and Meier (1993) suggested that, because of the long-term nature of the therapeutic relationship inherent in rehabilitation, developing a closeness and even a friendship is not unusual. However, there is a difference between feelings and actions. Acting on feelings is a choice. To refrain from acting unprofessionally is a responsibility that all health care providers have.

Research has demonstrated that at least six categories of sexually exploitive therapists exist (Schoener & Gonsiorek, 1989). One category is the uninformed or naive therapist. This individual is oftentimes a paraprofessional who is unaware of professional boundary issues and responsibilities. The therapist's unprofessional behavior may indicate poor social judgment or a deficiency in training. The neurotic or socially isolated therapist, another category, suffers from significant personal problems and tends to be overinvested in work. This therapist becomes easily overinvolved with patients, which can lead to sexual relations. Another category is the healthy or situational breakdown therapist, usually a one-time offender who reacts to stressful situations and is aware of the wrongdoing. Another type of therapist might be labeled an impulsive or compulsive character disorder. This individual is frequently careless, demonstrates poor judgment, and may sexually harass staff members as well as patients. Another category is the therapist with sociopathic or narcissistic personality disorder. This individual tends to be self-centered and deliberately exploit others through intimidation. In another category, the therapist with more severe problems such as psychoses or borderline personalities has a poor orientation to reality.

Edelwich and Brodsky (1991) have pointed out that the therapeutic relationship is a form of seduction involving a myriad of emotions, openness, and trust. The therapist may use this seduction for positive or negative outcomes. Edelwich and Brodsky described various types of seduction. Either the professional or the patient may initiate seduction within a professional–patient relationship. When patients attempt to seduce the caregiver, they may develop sexual fantasies involving their therapist. Oftentimes patients will indicate a preference for a therapist of one sex or another. Patients may discuss their sexual experiences with the therapist. Or, patients may inquire about the therapist's sexual life. These are common forms of sexual seduction. In addition, extracurricular contact between patient and therapist can signal a seduction, for example, when the patient spends excessive time after hours with a therapist. The patient's body language to the therapist may also indicate an alternative agenda.

Patients attempt to seduce caregivers for many reasons. They may be attempting to gratify their own sexual desire. Or, they may engage in seduction to divert attention from the real treatment issues. Seduction also can result in manipulation and can undermine the therapist's therapeutic objectivity. Seduction will compromise the therapist's position of authority, power, and expertise within the professional–patient relationship. Patients also may try to seduce the therapist to improve their status among their peers. Patients might brag about their "conquest" with the therapist. Seduction also can result in increased attention and gratification to which a patient may have become accustomed (Edelwich & Brodsky, 1991). It is important to realize and acknowledge clinicians are vulnerable to patient seductions.

When a clinician senses a problem relationship with a patient, the clinician may do the following: acknowledge his or her feelings; separate his or her personal feelings from dealings with the patient, confide in a supervisor or peers, set limits while giving the patient a safe space for self-expression, express nonsexual caring, confront the issue straight on, and explore the patient's behavior therapeutically. The clinician should avoid making the patient's problem his or her own problem, focusing his or her problems on the patient, rejecting the patient, being drawn into answering personal questions about himself or herself, and referring the patient to somebody else without attempting to first confront the issue head-on (Edelwich & Brodsky, 1991).

LIABILITIES FOR PATIENTS AND CAREGIVERS

Numerous factors argue against sexual relationships with patients or former patients. Evidence has indicated that erotic contact between professional and patient results in harmful effects. For example, Taylor and Wagner (1976) reported that 47% of their sample of patients who had experienced erotic contact with a professional caregiver evidenced negative effects. More recently, Bouhoutsos, Holroyd, Lerman, Forer, and Greenberg (1983) reported ill effects in 90% of individuals who experienced erotic contact with health care professionals. Some of the ill effects reported were increased depression, loss of motivation, impaired social adjustment, significant emotional disturbance, suicidal feelings, and increased substance use.

Gabbard (1994) has delineated numerous reasons why the uniqueness of a therapeutic relationship does not lend itself to sexual involvement. First, a therapeutic relationship necessarily involves an inherent power imbalance. The close, caring, and personal relationship can create an artificial and dependent situation. Moreover, a therapist may have access to patients' innermost emotions and needs, leaving a patient vulnerable to possible exploitation and abuse. This sexual exploitation may not even be a purposeful or conscious effort on the therapist's part. Rather, a therapist may engage in sexual relationships with patients for his or her own self-gratification and self-esteem needs. Such therapists tend to have a high need for control, and the inherent power imbalance fulfills a need. A therapist may also engage in rationalization thinking that his or her relationship reflects a complete dedication to the patients, or even worse, that the therapist is doing the patient a favor. Furthermore, because therapists are required to maintain records on their patients for a specified period, there is a real possibility that they may have to relinquish those records or testify about a patient. Another issue to consider is transference, that is, displaced feelings from past providers onto the therapist. It is common that, following initial termination from therapy, patients will more than likely contact the therapist again in the future for continuing treatment needs, including both physical and emotional therapy needs. Once a therapist becomes a lover, future therapeutic work is no longer objectively possible.

Clinicians must understand the extent of this problem and what they stand to lose by becoming sexually involved with patients. For example, developing a relationship with a patient takes up much personal time along with a tremendous amount of energy. Clinicians may put their job and career in jeopardy, and, possibly, their marriage and family. Furthermore, the legal liabilities inherent in this dangerous circumstance would not be pleasant. As Perr (1989) has reported, "Complaints concerning psychologists' sexual involvement with clients are the leading cause of lawsuits. Sexual involvement by psychiatrists with patients now constitutes the second leading cause of all professional practice litigation" (p. 212).

CONCLUSION

Clinicians need to acknowledge that sexuality is an important and sensitive aspect of all of our lives. A goal of treatment might be to help patients regain a healthy sense of their own sexuality. Thus, clinicians will want to address the area of sexuality with patients; however, they must recognize the limits of their involvement with patients in the area of personal relationships. Crossing the line between having a professional relationship and a personal relationship with patients can be damaging to both clinician and patient. Educational inservice programs on this issue should be routinely provided in health care, both on a departmental level and on an institutionwide level.

REFERENCES

Alexander, C.J., Sipski, M.L., & Findley, T.W. (1993). Sexual activities, desire and satisfaction in males pre- and post-spinal cord injury. *Archives of Sexual Behavior, 22*(3), 217–228.

American Medical Association, Council on Ethical and Judicial Affairs. (1991). Sexual misconduct in the practice of medicine. *Journal of the American Medical Association, 266,* 2741–2745.

American Nurses Association. (1985). *ANA Nursing Code of Ethics.* Washington DC: Author.

American Occupational Therapy Association. (1994) *AOTA Code of Ethics.* Bethesda, MD: Author.

American Physical Therapy Association. (1991). *APTA Code of Ethics.* Paterson, VA: Author.

American Psychological Association. (1992). Ethical principles of psychologists and code of conduct. *American Psychologist, 47,* 1597–1611.

American Speech and Hearing Association. (1994). ASHA code of ethics. *ASHA Magazine, 35*(3), 1–2.

American Therapeutic Recreation Association. (1990). *ATRA Code of Ethics.* Hattiesburg, MS: Author.

Bouhoutsos, J., Holroyd, J.C., Lerman, H., Forer, B.R., & Greenberg, M. (1983). Sexual intimacy between psychotherapists and patients. *Professional Psychology: Research and Practice, 14,* 185–196.

College of Physicians and Surgeons of British Columbia, Committee on Physician Sexual Misconduct. (1992). *Crossing the boundaries: The report of the Committee on Physician Sexual Misconduct.* Vancouver, British Columbia: Author.

Edelwich, J., & Brodsky, A. (1991). *Sexual dilemmas for the helping professional.* New York: Brunner/Mazel.

Gabbard, G.O. (1994). Reconsidering the American Psychological Association's policy on sex with former patients: Is it justifiable? *Professional Psychology: Research and Practice, 25*(4), 329–335.

Gabbard, G.O., & Nadelson, C. (1995). Professional boundaries in the physician–patient relationship. *Journal of the American Medical Association, 273,* 1445–1449.

Gartrell, N., Herman, J., Olarte, S., Feldstein, M., & Localio, R. (1986). Psychiatrist–patient sexual contact: results of a national survey, I: Prevalence. *American Journal of Psychiatry, 143,* 1126–1131.

Gartrell, N.K., Milliken, N., Goodson, W.H., Thiemann, S., & Lo, B. (1992). Physician–patient sexual contact: Prevalence and problems. *Western Journal of Medicine, 157,* 139–143.

Jennings, B. (1993). Healing the self: The moral meaning of relationships in rehabilitation. *American Journal of Physical Medicine and Rehabilitation, 72*(6), 401–404.

Kardener, S.H., Fuller, M., & Mensh, I.N. (1973). A survey of physicians' attitudes and practices regarding erotic and nonerotic contact with patients. *American Journal of Psychiatry, 130,* 1077–1081.

Lamont, J.A., & Woodward, C. (1994). Patient–physician sexual involvement: A Canadian survey of obstetrician–gynecologists. *Canadian Medical Association Journal, 150,* 1433–1439.

National Association of Social Workers. (1997). *NASW Code of Ethics.* Washington, DC: Author.

Parsons, J.P., & Wincze, J.P. (1995). A survey of client–therapist sexual involvement in Rhode Island as reported by subsequent treating therapists. *Professional Psychology: Research and Practice, 26*(2), 171–175.

Perr, I.N. (1989). Medicolegal aspects of professional sexual exploitation. In G.O. Gabbard (Ed.), *Sexual exploitation in professional relationships* (pp. 211–228). Washington, DC: American Psychiatric Press.

Perry, J.A. (1976). Physicians' erotic and nonerotic physical involvement with patients. *American Journal of Psychiatry, 133,* 838–840.

Pope, K.S. (1994). *Sexual involvement with therapists: Patient assessment, subsequent therapy, forensics.* Washington, DC: American Psychological Association.

Purtilo, R.B., & Meier, R.H. (1993). Team challenges: Regulatory constraints and patient empowerment. *American Journal of Physical Medicine and Rehabilitation, 72*(5), 327–330.

Schoener, G.R., & Gonsiorek, J.C. (1989). Assessment and development of rehabilitation plans for the therapist. In G.R. Schoener, J.H. Milgrom, J.C. Gonsiorek, E.T. Luepker, & R.M. Conroe (Eds.), *Psychotherapists' sexual involvement with clients: Intervention and Prevention* (pp. 401–420). Minneapolis: Walk-In Counseling Center.

Scofield, G.R. (1993). Ethical considerations in rehabilitation medicine. *Archives of Physical Medicine and Rehabilitation, 74,* 341–346.

Sipski, M.L., & Alexander, C.J. (1993). Sexual activities, response and satisfaction in women pre- and post-spinal cord injury. *Archives of Physical Medicine and Rehabilitation, 74,* 1025–1029.

Sipski, M.L., & Alexander, C.J. (1994). *Sexual relations among rehabilitation professionals and patients.* Unpublished manuscript.

Taylor, B.J., & Wagner, N.N. (1976). Sex between therapists and clients: A review and analysis. *Professional Psychology, 7,* 593–601.

Wilbers, D., Veensstra, G., van de Wiel, H.B.M., & Schultz, W. (1992). Sexual contact in the doctor–patient relationship in the Netherlands. *British Medical Journal, 304,* 1531–1534.

CHAPTER 21

Disability and the Lesbian, Gay Man, or Bisexual Individual

S. Chris Saad

Between 2% and 22% of the population engages in sexual activity with the same gender or with both genders (Garber, 1995). Hence, it is reasonable to assume that a comparable percentage of people with chronic illnesses and disabilities are lesbians, gay men, or bisexuals. Because clinicians likely will encounter clients who are not heterosexual, they will want to familiarize themselves with issues endemic to gay men, lesbians, and bisexuals. This chapter provides professionals with information about the gay man, lesbian, or bisexual disabled or chronically ill client. Because the issues surrounding disability and illness are dealt with comprehensively elsewhere in this book, the main focus of this chapter is on sexual orientation.

Of the gay men and lesbian population, 11% have disabilities; however, this figure does not include people with human immunodeficiency virus (HIV; O'Toole & Bregante, 1992). As many as 50% of the gay men in large cities such as New York and San Francisco may be infected with HIV (Abramson & Pinkerton, 1995). Therefore, a large portion of this chapter is devoted to discussion of issues associated with HIV and acquired immune deficiency syndrome (AIDS).

PSYCHOLOGICAL ISSUES

Initial Issues

People with HIV and their partners encounter many problems specific to HIV and AIDS. Sexual partners of those with HIV sometimes have difficulty bringing themselves to go for an HIV test. The clinician can help by providing pretest counseling. The test should be done at an anonymous test site to ensure that results will not be given to employers, health insurance carriers, or others (Silverstein & Picano, 1992). In addition, issues around death and dying surface in relationships in which one or both partners have AIDS or other terminal illnesses. Healthy partners may end relationships because they cannot bear to watch their partners die (Loulan, 1984; Nichols, 1989). Conversely, healthy partners may crave closeness in the form of sexual intimacy (Loulan, 1984).

Inhibited Desire

People with HIV may respond to their diagnoses by denying their sexual interest (Denenberg, 1993). Furthermore, sexual activity becomes associated with death and dying (Behrendt & George, 1996; Nichols, 1989). Lesbians and gay men may come to view HIV as a punishment for sexual activity and therefore repress their sexual desires (Nichols, 1989). Nichols described the case of a gay man with AIDS who was afraid of going to hell after he died because of his sexual orientation. People with HIV often repress desire because they are afraid of infecting others (Nichols, 1989; Pakenham, Dadds, & Terry, 1996). These individuals often find information about safer sex and disease transmission helpful (Barrows & Halgin, 1988; Nichols, 1989). For women, inhibited desire may stem from other factors. Lesbian–feminist analyses of women's sexuality have often focused on exploitation issues such as rape (Nichols, 1989) as have analyses of disabled women's sexuality. This focus on victimization may be damaging to the disabled lesbian's sexual desire. Inhibited desire can result from internalized homophobia or the feeling that it is intrinsically better to be heterosexual than homosexual or bisexual (McCormick, 1994). The therapist can help the client develop a positive sense of self as a lesbian, gay man, or bisexual individual.

Inhibited desire is also an issue for people with chronic illnesses because depression, loss of self-esteem, fatigue, stress, pain, and so forth detract from sexual desire. Sometimes a couple may be so busy coping with the illness and managing day-to-day activities that there is simply no time or energy left for intimacy (Schover, 1989). As a consequence of the combination of sexual orientation and illness issues, a gay or lesbian couple in which one or both partners is chronically ill may have very little sex.

Stigma

Stigma is a particular problem for people who are both homosexual and disabled. Of the deaf and hard-of-hearing gay men in a Swartz (1995) study, 30% to 40% reported wishing they were heterosexual. However, 81% of the hard-of-hearing and deaf gay men reported being happy with their current "love lives" and nearly 100% reported being happy with their sex lives. These seemingly discrepant findings may indicate that deaf gay men get pleasure and joy from their relationships but encounter societal stigma.

Gay and lesbian couples encounter the same problems faced by heterosexual couples, but there are the added issues of homophobia and societal stigma (George & Behrendt, 1987; Marsiglio, 1993; Storms, 1978). Gay and lesbian couples are disadvantaged by lack of social support, which can create stress in the relationships. When one partner becomes ill or disabled, a relationship that may have been kept secret is brought into public view. The couple must cope not only with the illness but with health providers' and family members' reactions to homosexuality. The healthy partner does not have the legal rights of a heterosexual spouse and therefore may be excluded from visitation and decision making (Barrows & Halgin, 1988; Rolland, 1994). In one highly publicized case, lesbian Sharon Kowalski was hit by a drunk driver and permanently disabled. Her long-term partner, Karen Thompson, was denied any role in Sharon's care (Appleby, 1994; O'Toole & Bregante, 1992).

When there is a health crisis, heterosexuals often turn to their parents as well as their sexual partners for support and assistance. If ill gay men and lesbians are not open about their orientation with their parents or if the parents do not accept homosexuality, they cannot count on parents as an added source of support (McDaniel, 1995). As a result, the sexual partner of the gay man or lesbian who is ill may feel overwhelmed. The therapist should suggest alternative avenues for obtaining support.

However, sometimes support is unavailable even within the gay male and lesbian communities. People with disabilities are often excluded from the gay community (McDaniel, 1995; Thompson, 1994). When the author of this chapter interviewed several gay men and lesbians in 1992, all the men complained about the *looksism,* or discrimination on the basis of perceived good looks, in the gay bars. Clients may need assistance in recognizing that sexual desirability does not depend solely on physical perfection (Schover, 1989).

Looksism is less of a problem for lesbians. Indeed, there is a recognition that many body types are beautiful in the lesbian community (McCormick, 1994). Still, women with illnesses and disabilities do report feeling unwelcome at lesbian events (McDaniel, 1995). Sometimes other lesbians assume that disabled women are asexual; other times, the events are simply inaccessible. One mobility-impaired woman interviewed by Appleby (1994) commented that she felt more disabled than usual at lesbian events because so many of the events were inaccessible. Because most lesbian events are planned with small budgets (Appleby, 1994), a lack of accessibility results.

Often the disability community accepts homosexuality whereas the lesbian and gay men communities do not accept disability (Appleby, 1994). The obvious exception is that gay men who have HIV or AIDS usually have a large cohort of peers who also have HIV. In his study of gay men with HIV, Schwartzberg (1993) found that 74% of the men interviewed indicated that having HIV had strengthened their sense of community. Even in this population, between 25% (Pakenham et al., 1996) and 37% (Schwartzberg, 1993) viewed their HIV as separating them from others who did not have HIV. (Some of the men in Schwartzberg's study viewed their illnesses as both strengthening their sense of community and isolating them from others who did not have HIV.) Some people with other disabilities, such as gay people who are deaf, also band together to form their own communities (Swartz, 1995).

Women with HIV are especially fearful of stigma because they do not have a community of peers with HIV as gay men do (Perez, 1992). Stigma is also a particular problem for people with emotional illnesses (Loulan, 1984). They may become isolated because they keep their illnesses a secret to avoid discrimination (Perez, 1992).

Unlike members of other minority groups, such as Jews or African Americans, homosexuals and people with disabilities are often the only minority group members in their families of origin (Hillyer, 1993). As gay men or lesbians with disabilities, the clients may feel doubly alienated from their families and from society as a whole. Although many members of racial and religious minority groups learn that the roadblocks they encounter result from racism or other institutionalized oppression, gay men and lesbians with disabilities often believe that these roadblocks are somehow their own fault. Similarly, Jews and African Americans are commonly taught by their families to feel pride about their minority group membership; disabled homosexuals, however, are generally instructed to try to appear as much like the majority group (able-bodied heterosexuals) as possible (Hillyer, 1993).

"Passing" and "Coming Out"

Chronically ill people and gay men and lesbians often pretend to be someone other than who they are. Gay men, lesbians, and bisexuals may pretend to be heterosexual to avoid stigma (Barrows & Halgin, 1988), whereas many chronically ill individuals may avoid stigma by "passing" as able-bodied (Belgrave, 1990; O'Toole & Bregante, 1992). The prevalent assumptions that all people are able-bodied until proven otherwise and that all people are heterosexual until proven otherwise makes passing easy for chronically ill gay men and lesbians whose medical conditions are not self-evident (Anderson & Wolf, 1986). Those gay men and lesbians with visible disabilities cannot choose to pass as able-bodied; they may therefore decide to pass as heterosexual because they are already stigmatized as the result of their disabilities (Appleby, 1994). The main benefit of passing is obvious: passing allows a person to avoid social stigma and discrimination (Hillyer, 1993).

Bisexuals frequently pass as homosexuals because they encounter discrimination within the lesbian and gay communities (McCormick, 1994). Lesbians and gay men frequently do not recognize that bisexuality is a true sexual orientation; they accuse bisexuals of being gay men or lesbians and afraid to make their true orientation known (Nichols, 1989).

Some individuals pass temporarily; they "come out," or make their illnesses and sexual orientations known after the person knows them and is less likely to stereotype them (Hillyer, 1993). Deciding when to tell a person one is dating that one has a chronic illness is a particularly worrisome problem for people who are not in relationships (Flapan, 1993; Pakenham et al., 1996).

Ill lesbians and gay men frequently pass selectively; they pass in certain situations to save their energy for instances in which they need to come out for political or personal reasons (Hillyer, 1993). They may pass with their sexual partners in that they may pretend they are not feeling fatigue or pain. This kind of passing is motivated by a wish to protect the partner from distress (Lessing, 1984).

Because of discomfort or misplaced delicacy, the chronically ill lesbian or gay man's able-bodied, heterosexual associates may encourage the person to pass (Kleinman, 1988). When abled-bodied and heterosexual people pretend they do not notice the ill lesbian's or gay man's "secret," they are implying that illness and homosexuality are unmentionable (Hillyer, 1993).

There are many drawbacks to passing. Many people pass to conserve energy, but keeping secret an integral part of one's identity expends an enormous amount of energy. In addition, those people who pass often feel isolated and demoralized (O'Toole & Bregante, 1992). Furthermore, when a person must be constantly vigilant to avoid revealing evidence of illness and sexual orientation, obsession about the illness and sexual orientation may become the central focus of his or her life. Passing can be harmful to the chronically ill lesbian or gay man's health. In trying to conceal the illness, the person may skip medical treatments, not take medicine, and neglect to rest (Hillyer, 1993). Furthermore, lesbians or gay men who are open about their true identities may have higher self-esteem than those who remain in the closet (McCormick, 1994).

Couples may seek therapy if the partners have different approaches to passing. For example, McCormick (1994) described a lesbian couple in which one partner was completely open about her sexual orientation and the other partner pretended they were just casual friends when among others. As a result, the open partner distanced herself from the relationship.

Those people who decide not to pass must "come out," or make their ill or homosexual status known. Unlike their healthy gay men and lesbian counterparts, chronically ill gay men and lesbians have two coming out tasks: disclosing their health status and disclosing their sexual orientation. One woman interviewed by Appleby (1994) found it much easier to be out as a lesbian than to be out as a disabled person; she felt she encountered less stigma for her lesbianism.

The professional may wish to explore the benefits and drawbacks of coming out and of passing with the client or the couple in terms of disability as well as of sexual orientation. The therapist should be cognizant that the client who passes has good reasons for doing so, as does the client who comes out.

Clients also may have difficulty coming out because they have personal identity issues. Masculinity may be a particular issue for disabled gay men. It has traditionally been part of gay male culture to be "hypermasculine," wearing leather and denim and developing a muscular physique (Nichols, 1989). Males with chronic physical problems may have difficulty reconciling their male status with their disabled status and therefore may feel they are unable to participate in this masculine culture. Whereas maleness implies strength and independence in our culture, disability implies weakness and dependence. Disabled men cope with this dichotomy in several ways. Many may redefine masculine behavior, for example, by defining independence as giving directions to one's personal care attendant. Others may continue to subscribe to their pre-illness definitions of masculinity and therefore may refuse help or may participate in wheelchair sports. Another group of males with disabilities may cope by completely rejecting the popular concept of masculinity (Gerschick & Miller, 1994).

Femininity is not a concern for many lesbians, who traditionally have rejected stereotypical feminine roles on the grounds that such roles are oppressive. Many younger lesbians, however, are "lipstick lesbians" who present typically feminine persona (Nichols, 1989). In any case, lesbians, like heterosexual women, base self-image as women on the body's appearance and function. Self-image therefore becomes damaged in certain situations such as when cervical cancer causes sterility (Anderson & Wolf, 1986) or when breast cancer necessitates mastectomy.

The therapist can help couples come to terms with an ill or disabled partner's changed appearance. The ill or disabled partner may benefit from counseling aimed at increasing self-esteem and improving body image, and both partners can benefit from suggestions on how to accommodate the changed body part. The disabled partner can "introduce" the able-bodied partner to the changed body part. The able-bodied partner can stroke or caress that body part, recognizing it as part of the loved one. Members of couples in which a partner has a catheter or ostomy may each need time alone with the therapist to discuss feelings about the appliance. Such couples will also need practical advice about managing the appliance during sex (Lessing, 1984).

PHYSIOLOGIC ISSUES

Although most gay men and lesbians with chronic illnesses and disabilities work out their own solutions to the sexual difficulties that result from their health problems, some may need or desire therapy. Lesbians generally complain of fewer sexual problems than gay men. Dyspareunia is obviously not a problem, and lesbians experience less vaginismus and anorgasmia than heterosexual women. The most commonly reported sexual problem among lesbians is infrequent intercourse (McCormick, 1994; Nichols, 1995).

There can be sexual problems specific to the disability in homosexuals. HIV can lead to diminished sexual desire for physiologic reasons, because it can cause decreased testosterone levels (Nichols, 1989). Other illnesses such as end-stage renal disease and certain cancers inhibit sexual desire. Certain medications, such as antihypertensives, also adversely affect sexual desire (Loulan, 1984; Schover, 1989). Joint pain, stiffness, and muscle weakness can also curtail sexual enjoyment and limit a person's ability to masturbate himself or herself or the partner (Bhadauria et al., 1995; McCormick, 1994). Some creativity is required to solve the problems caused by limited dexterity (McCormick, 1994). A person can use his or her thumbs, wrists, or backs of hands to touch himself or herself or the partner. Use of auxiliary materials such as vibrators, dildos, creams, and lotions often enhance sexual pleasure. Partners can help unroll condoms onto the erect penis or a dildo. If disease prevention is a concern, it is essential that people with limited manual dexterity ask sexual partners to handle condoms and dental dams if they themselves cannot manage (Saad & Behrendt, 1996).

When pain or stiffness make it difficult for people to engage in "traditional" lesbian or gay male sexual behaviors such as oral sex, the professional may need to help the client explore alternate sexual activities. Loulan (1984) described a woman who avoided sex altogether because it was painful for her to separate her legs to receive cunnilingus. She found that discussing the situation and working with her partner to find a more comfortable position was beneficial. It can be helpful to experiment with positions in a nonsexual situation in which both partners are fully clothed (Loulan, 1984).

The professional may wish to discuss specific techniques for remaining sexually active. Some creativity might be required. For instance, the therapist can suggest that fatigued clients hold their partners while the partners masturbate (Lessing, 1984). Discussing these issues may seem overwhelming to both partners. The therapist can help create a supportive space in which to talk. It is beneficial to discuss these issues in a nonsexual situation such as therapy (Loulan, 1984). It is important for the clinician to initiate such discussions, because other health care providers may initiate discussions about sexuality only with heterosexual, married people, making it necessary for gay men and lesbians to initiate such conversations themselves (Saad & Behrendt, 1996).

PRACTICALITY ISSUES

Concerns about the practicalities of day-to-day living often arise in therapy. Lesbian couples typically earn less money than gay male and heterosexual couples.

As a result, when one member of a lesbian couple becomes ill with a serious condition such as cancer, there may not be adequate health insurance to cover treatment (McDaniel, 1995). Furthermore, most members of same-gender couples are not covered by their partners' health insurance policies. Disabled women also tend to have low incomes (Asch & Fine, 1995). Lesbians with illness and disabilities are therefore among the lowest earners in our society (O'Toole & Bregante, 1992).

Financial issues are also a problem for gay men with illnesses and disabilities. Gay male couples frequently have high incomes and no dependents to support (Nichols, 1989). Because disabled and ill men generally have lower incomes than their able-bodied peers, they may not have the financial means to participate in the more costly aspects of gay male culture such as attending operas and plays. In a recent study (Pakenham et al., 1996), 65% of symptomatic gay and bisexual men with HIV, compared with none of the gay and bisexual men not infected with HIV, indicated that employment concerns were a problem. Similarly, 45% of symptomatic HIV-infected gay and bisexual men and none of the noninfected men indicated that financial concerns were a problem.

Gay men and lesbians who want children generally encounter many barriers, particularly gay men and lesbians with illnesses or disabilities. Their only means of having a child may be through heterosexual intercourse, because the avenues of adoption and reproductive technologies may be unavailable to them (Denenberg, 1993; Rand, Graham, & Rawlings, 1982).

Practical matters are particularly difficult for lesbians and gay men with cognitive disabilities, and lesbians and gay men with physical or cognitive disabilities are sometimes sexually exploited (Swartz, 1995; Thompson, 1994). Of the deaf gay men studied by Swartz (1995), 29% reported that their first homosexual experiences involved force. Their perpetrators were usually hearing teachers or other caregivers at residential schools for the deaf. Most of the gay men with learning disabilities interviewed by Thompson (1994) described being the receptive partner for anal intercourse as painful, yet those men did not see any alternatives other than simply waiting until the inserter was done. Those men did not often act as the inserters themselves. Other learning disabled men described physically abusive sexual encounters. Those men often agreed to sex in return for attention from nondisabled men, money, cigarettes, or other small tokens (Thompson, 1994).

Safer sex is also problematic for gay men and lesbians with cognitive impairments. Even when the person understands safer sex guidelines, there may be no awareness that these guidelines must be applied in that person's own situation (Thompson, 1994). People with cognitive impairments often need to be shown how to use condoms or other barriers (Thompson, 1994).

RECOMMENDATIONS FOR HEALTH CARE PROFESSIONALS

Staff working with the cognitively impaired people are often reluctant to provide information about sexuality beyond contraception and safer sex guidelines

(Appleby, 1994; Thompson, 1994). Similarly, only 20% to 30% of special education teachers reported having received preservice or inservice training about sexual orientation issues (Foley & Dudzinski, 1995). Thus, most disabled youths are unlikely to have had the opportunity to discuss these issues in sexuality education classes. Professionals should therefore be aware that gay men, lesbians, and bisexuals with disabilities may have unanswered questions (O'Toole & Bregante, 1992). Of the gay and bisexual men with HIV studied by Pakenham et al. (1996), 28% reported that accessing information was a problem for them. Professionals should provide opportunities for asking questions.

The professional should be cognizant that gay male and lesbian norms differ from heterosexual norms. It is not unusual for gay male couples to be nonmonogamous (Barrows & Halgin, 1988; Nichols, 1989), and gay men often engage in alternative forms of sexual expression such as telephone sex or "jerk-off" parties. The lesbian community is divided in its attitude toward sexual expression. Some lesbians view sex similarly to their gay male counterparts: these women are frequently nonmonogamous and they explore many avenues of sexual expression. Other lesbians emphasize the warm, gentle, relational aspects of sex, valuing closeness more than genital stimulation or orgasm (Nichols, 1989). It is important for the therapist to become familiar with those aspects of lesbian and gay male culture. Care should be taken to avoid the assumption that homosexual sexuality replicates heterosexual sexuality. If couples initiate sex therapy because of issues around nonmonogamy, sex therapists must examine their own values around this issue (Nichols, 1989).

Unlike heterosexual clients, who frequently begin sex therapy because they are experiencing dysfunction, the lesbian or gay client often initiates therapy because of sexual identity issues. The client may have exclusively homosexual feelings but be unable to come to terms with a homosexual orientation (Nichols, 1989). Homosexual identity formation involves several stages: individuals progress through confusion about their sexual orientation, comparison of different orientations, tolerance of their homosexuality, acceptance of their sexual orientation, pride in being a gay male or lesbian, and finally, identity synthesis (Cass, 1984). The individual who is in the process of exploring a gay male, lesbian, or bisexual identity does not necessarily progress through these stages in order (McDonald, 1982).

The client also may be having trouble making sense of an attraction to both genders. The previously heterosexual client may have trouble accepting a homosexual or bisexual identity in part because such an identity can lead to loss of employment, family, friends, and life plans. The previously gay or lesbian client may have trouble accepting a bisexual identity because this identity can lead to loss of support in the homosexual community (Nichols, 1989). The therapist should be aware that sexual orientation is not an either–or proposition. Rather, sexual orientation is a fluid continuum ranging from exclusively heterosexual to exclusively homosexual, with many points in between (McConaghy, 1987).

People with sexual identity issues often seek out a heterosexual therapist because a lesbian, gay male, or bisexual therapist may seem threatening. The therapist must be more positive about homosexuality and bisexuality than the client. Professionals can introduce clients to gay male or lesbian culture (Barrows & Halgin, 1988; Nichols, 1989) and use bibliotherapy to help build a positive lesbian, gay male, or bisexual identity (Barrows & Halgin, 1988). Furthermore, the therapist should affirm the client's choices whether or not the client chooses to act on the homosexual feelings (Nichols, 1989). It is therefore necessary for professionals to examine their own attitudes about homosexuality before counseling lesbian, gay male, or bisexual clients (Barrows & Halgin, 1988).

The professional should also be aware that not all people who engage in sexual behaviors with same-gender partners identify as homosexual or bisexual (Lever, Kanouse, Rogers, Carson, & Hertz, 1992; McCormick, 1994; Thompson, 1994). Similarly, not all people who identify as homosexual or bisexual actually engage in sexual behaviors with the same gender (McCormick, 1994; Thompson, 1994). Rather than asking about sexual orientation, the professional can ask if the client has engaged in sexual activity with men, women, or both (Denenberg, 1993). It is important for professionals to examine their own assumptions and stereotypes. Care should be taken to avoid the all too common assumption that there is no need to ask disabled women about their sexual orientation because disabled women are all heterosexual, if sexual at all (Asch & Fine, 1995; Lessing, 1984; O'Toole & Bregante, 1992). The professional can also ask about the client's attractions and fantasies, because many people who are attracted to the same gender do not act on these attractions (Nichols, 1989). It is important for professionals to ask clients about their HIV status, because clients may not initially volunteer the information that they are infected with HIV (Behrendt & George, 1996).

In addition, the therapist should know that alcoholism and drug use are particular problems in the lesbian and gay male communities. Deevey and Wall (1992) estimated that at least 30% of lesbians are alcoholic. Kus (1991) estimated that between 20% and 33% of the gay male population is addicted to alcohol or drugs. Alcoholism is a method of coping with the self-hatred that is the consequence of the shaming messages with which gay men and lesbians are bombarded (Deevey & Wall, 1992). Kus (1988) discussed the importance of internalized homophobia as a contributor to alcoholism in gay men. Five recovering alcoholic lesbians and gay men interviewed in 1992 discussed this phenomenon (Saad, 1992):

K. came out as a lesbian in 1978. She continued drinking to ease the pain of having to keep her lesbianism a secret and of being different.

Coming to terms with his sexual identity was a long and painful process for A. He used drugs and alcohol to numb the pain and to help him deny his homosexuality. "If the thought that I might be gay entered my mind, I'd take a pill or take a drink right away."

D. came out when he was 19 years old. He reported that he experienced extremely low self-esteem when he was an active alcoholic. He could not face his shame about his homosexuality. D.'s involvement with Mormonism contributed to this shame. Because he felt so much shame, his behavior was very self-destructive. "I drank like a pig," D. said.

J. began drinking at age 10 years, in part to numb the pain of being a lesbian. Ironically, being drunk ultimately prolonged J.'s process of coming to accept her lesbianism.

B. believes he drank to get numb because he felt so much shame over his homosexuality.

The most striking factor of those interviews was that all five subjects began drinking before reaching adulthood. All five interviewees also attributed their alcoholism to a combination of growing up in an alcoholic home and drinking to numb the pain of being gay.

When lesbian and gay male alcoholics and addicts become sober, however, they often find it difficult to resume sexual activity. For those people, sexual activity has become inexorably linked with drinking or drug use (Loulan, 1984). The professional should help the client learn how to express sexuality while sober.

Another recommendation for the clinician is that he or she should be aware that disabled women are generally unused to health care providers' initiating discussions pertaining to sexuality beyond mentioning the need for contraception (Loulan, 1984; O'Toole & Bregante, 1992). A woman may be taken aback and reluctant to disclose her lesbianism or bisexuality for fear that she will encounter stigma (O'Toole & Bregante, 1992). It can be helpful for the provider to establish rapport before broaching sexual issues.

RECOMMENDATIONS FOR FUTURE RESEARCH

Professionals may have trouble locating specific information pertaining to disabled lesbians, gay men, and bisexuals. For example, a review of the literature indicated that all existing studies about the effects of spina bifida on sexuality exclusively explored autosexual (masturbatory) and heterosexual activity (Cromer et al., 1990; Dorner, 1977). No inquiries into homosexual orientation or activity in adolescents or adults with spina bifida were available. Research in this area needs to be conducted.

Furthermore, the paucity of materials about disabled lesbians is particularly extreme (O'Toole & Bregante, 1992) and reflects that most research on homosexuality has focused on men (Blackwood, 1986), as has most research on illness and disability. For example, most existing research about scleroderma has emphasized women's ability to reproduce (Black, 1990; Czirjak, Bokk, Csontos, Lorincz, & Szegedi, 1989; Friedman, Bernstein, & Kitzmiller, 1991; Silman, 1992; Varner, 1991). Three-quarters of the people with scleroderma are women, yet a disproportionate amount of the literature has addressed the effects of scleroderma on male sexuality (Ahmed, 1990; Johnson, 1981; Lally & Jimenez, 1990; Ordi et al., 1990; Schover, 1989).

When a disability does not impair a woman's ability to bear children, it appears that little is written about the effect of that disability on female sexual function. In a patriarchal culture, childbearing ability rather than sexual pleasure is seen as the most important issue regarding female sexuality. More research needs to be conducted to determine the sexual effects of disabilities, such as spinal cord injuries, that do not impair women's childbearing ability (McCormick, 1994).

Research on the transmission of HIV between women and on the prevalence of HIV and AIDS among lesbians is also lacking. Data about whether woman-to-woman transmission of HIV is a serious risk are scarce (Kennedy, Scarlett, Duerr, & Chu, 1995). Published statistics tend to underestimate the numbers of lesbian and bisexual women who have HIV and AIDS. Research needs to be conducted to determine the frequency of woman-to-woman transmission of HIV and to determine the problems and issues faced by lesbians and bisexual women with HIV and AIDS (Warren, 1993).

CONCLUSION

Professionals working with people who have disabilities or illnesses should not make assumptions about the sexual orientation of their clients. Professionals should ask whether clients engage in sexual behavior with men, women, or both. Professionals should not assume that those clients who do engage in sexual behaviors with partners of the same gender face the same issues as heterosexual clients. Gay male, lesbian, and bisexual clients may have values about relationships, sexuality, and monogamy that differ from those of most heterosexuals. These people often encounter issues around coming out and may face societal stigma. Therapists can help by creating an environment that is supportive to people of various sexual orientations, explicitly discussing sexual issues, and providing practical suggestions.

REFERENCES

Abramson, P.R., & Pinkerton, S.D. (1995). *With pleasure: Thoughts on the nature of human sexuality*. New York: Oxford University Press.

Ahmed, S. (1990). Scleroderma and impotence: Response to nitroglycerin applied to the fingers and penis. *Southern Medical Journal, 83,* 1495.

Anderson, B.J., & Wolf, F.M. (1986). Chronic physical illness and sexual behavior: Psychological issues. *Journal of Counseling and Clinical Psychology, 54,* 168–175.

Appleby, Y. (1994). Out in the margins. *Disability and Society, 9*(1), 19–32.

Asch, A., & Fine, M. (1995). Beyond pedestals: Revisiting the lives of women with disabilities. In M. Fine (Ed.), *Disruptive voices: The possibilities of feminist research* (pp. 139–171). Ann Arbor: University of Michigan Press.

Barrows, P.A., & Halgin, R.P. (1988). Current issues in psychotherapy with gay men: Impact of the AIDS phenomenon. *Professional Psychology: Research and Practice, 19*(4), 395–402.

Behrendt, A.E., & George, K.D. (1996). Sex therapy for gay and bisexual men. In L. Diamant & R.D. McAnulty (Eds.), *The psychology of sexual orientation, behavior, and identity: A handbook* (pp. 220–236). Westport, CT: Greenwood Press.

Belgrave, L.L. (1990). The relevance of chronic illness in the everyday lives of elderly women. *Journal of Aging and Health, 2,* 475–500.

Bhadauria, S., Moser, D.K., Clements, P.J., Singh, R.R., Lachenbruch, P.A., Pitkin, R.M., & Weiner, S.R. (1995). Genital tract abnormalities and female sexual function impairment in systemic sclerosis. *American Journal of Obstetrics and Gynecology, 172,* 580–587.

Black, C.M. (1990). Systemic sclerosis and pregnancy. *Bailliere's Clinical Rheumatology, 4,* 105–124.

Blackwood, E. (1986). Breaking the mirror: The construction of lesbianism and the anthropological discourse on homosexuality. *Journal of Homosexuality, 11*(3–4), 1–17.

Cass, V. (1984). Homosexual identity formation: Testing a theoretical model. *Journal of Sex Research, 20*(2), 143–167.

Cromer, B.A., Enrile, B., McCoy, K., Gerhardstein, M.J., Fitzpatrick, M., & Judis, J. (1990). Knowledge, attitudes, and behavior related to sexuality in adolescents with chronic disability. *Developmental Medicine and Child Neurology, 32,* 602–610.

Czirjak, L., Bokk, A., Csontos, G., Lorincz, G., & Szegedi, G. (1989). Clinical findings in 61 patients with progressive systemic sclerosis. *Acta Dermato-Venereologica, 69,* 533–536.

Deevey, S., & Wall, L.J. (1992). How do lesbian women develop serenity? *Health Care for Women International, 13,* 199–208.

Denenberg, R. (1993). Applying harm reduction to sexual and reproductive counseling: A health provider's guide to supporting the goals of people with HIV/AIDS. *SIECUS Report, 22*(1), 8–12.

Dorner, S. (1977). Sexual interest and activity in adolescents with spina bifida. *Journal of Child Psychology and Psychiatry and Related Disciplines, 18,* 229–237.

Flapan, M. (1993). Why suffer emotionally more than necessary? *The Beacon, 1,* 6–16.

Foley, R.M., & Dudzinski, M. (1995). Human sexuality education: Are special educators prepared to meet the educational needs of disabled youth? *Journal of Sex Education and Therapy, 21*(3), 182–191.

Friedman, S.A., Bernstein, M.S., & Kitzmiller, J.L. (1991). Pregnancy complicated by collagen vascular disease. *Obstetrics and Gynecology Clinics of North America, 18,* 213–236.

Garber, M. (1995). *Vice versa: Bisexuality and the eroticism of everyday life.* New York: Simon & Schuster.

George, K.D., & Behrendt, A.E. (1987). Therapy for male couples experiencing relationship problems and sexual problems. *Journal of Sex Research, 14*(1–2), 77–88.

Gerschick, T.J., & Miller, A.S. (1994). Gender identities at the crossroads of masculinity and physical disability. *Masculinities, 2,* 34–55.

Hillyer, B. (1993). *Feminism and disability.* Norman: University of Oklahoma Press.

Johnson, W.R. (1981). *So desperate the fight: An innovative approach to chronic illness.* New York: Institute for Rational Living.

Kennedy, M.B., Scarlett, M.I., Duerr, A.C., & Chu, S.Y. (1995). Assessing HIV risk among women who have sex with women: Scientific and communication issues. *Journal of the American Medical Women's Association, 50,* 103–107.

Kleinman, A. (1988). *The illness narratives: Suffering, healing, and the human condition.* New York: Basic Books.

Kus, R.J. (1988). Alcoholism and non-acceptance of gay self: The critical link. *Journal of Homosexuality, 15,* 25–41.

Kus, R.J. (1991). Sobriety, friends, and gay men. *Archives of Psychiatric Nursing, 5,* 171–177.

Lally, E.V., & Jimenez, S.A. (1990). Erectile failure in systemic sclerosis. *New England Journal of Medicine, 322,* 1398.

Lessing, J. (1984). Sex and disability. In J.A. Loulan (Ed.), *Lesbian sex* (pp. 151–158). San Francisco: Spinsters/Aunt Lute.

Lever, J., Kanouse, D., Rogers, W., Carson, S., & Hertz, R. (1992). Behavior patterns and sexual identity of bisexual males. *Journal of Sex Research, 29*(2), 141–167.

Loulan, J.A. (1984). Specific issues on sex and disability. In J.A. Loulan (Ed.), *Lesbian sex* (pp. 275–288). San Francisco: Spinsters/Aunt Lute.

Marsiglio, W. (1993). Attitudes toward homosexual activity and gays as friends: A national survey of heterosexual 15–19 year old males. *Journal of Sex Research, 30*(1), 12–17.

McConaghy, N. (1987). Heterosexuality/homosexuality: Dichotomy or continuum? *Archives of Sexual Behavior, 16*(5), 411–424.

McCormick, N.B. (1994). *Sexual salvation: Affirming women's sexual rights and pleasures.* Westport, CT: Praeger.

McDaniel, J. (1995). *The lesbian couples' guide: Finding the right woman and creating a life together.* New York: HarperCollins.

McDonald, G. (1982). Individual differences in the coming out process for gay men: Implications for theoretical models. *Journal of Homosexuality, 8*(1), 47–60.

Nichols, M. (1989). Sex therapy with lesbians, gay men, and bisexuals. In S.R. Leiblum & R.C. Rosen (Eds.), *Principles and practice of sex therapy* (pp. 269–297). New York: Guilford Press.

Nichols, M. (1995). Sexual desire disorder in a lesbian–feminist couple: The intersection of therapy and politics. In R.C. Rosen & S.R. Leiblum (Eds.), *Case studies in sex therapy* (pp. 163–175). New York: Guilford Press.

Ordi, J., Selva, A., Fonollosa, V., Vilardell, M., Jordana, R., & Tolosa, C. (1990). Peyronie's disease in systemic sclerosis. *Annals of the Rheumatic Diseases, 49,* 134–135.

O'Toole, C.J., & Bregante, J.L. (1992). Lesbians with disabilities. *Sexuality and Disability, 10*(3), 163–172.

Pakenham, K.I., Dadds, M.R., & Terry, D.J. (1996). Adaptive demands along the HIV disease continuum. *Social Science and Medicine, 42*(2), 245–256.

Perez, E. (1992). Why women wait to be tested for HIV infection. In Sex Information and Education Council of the United States (Ed.), *HIV/AIDS: SIECUS Reprint Series 3* (pp. 28–29). New York: Sex Information and Education Council of the United States.

Rand, C., Graham, D., & Rawlings, E. (1982). Psychological health and factors the court seeks to control in lesbian mother custody trials. *Journal of Homosexuality, 8*(1), 27–39.

Rolland, J.S. (1994). In sickness and in health: The impact of illness on couples' relationships. *Journal of Marital and Family Therapy, 20*(4), 327–347.

Saad, S.C. (1992). [Gay and lesbian alcoholics]. Unpublished raw data.

Saad, S.C., & Behrendt, A.E. (1996). Scleroderma and sexuality. *Journal of Sex Research, 33*(3), 215–220.

Schover, L.R. (1989). Sexual problems in chronic illness. In S.R. Leiblum & R.C. Rosen (Eds.), *Principles and practice of sex therapy* (pp. 319–351). New York: Guilford Press.

Schwartzberg, S.S. (1993). Struggling for meaning: How HIV-positive gay men make sense of AIDS. *Professional Psychology: Research and Practice, 24,* 483–490.

Silman, A.J. (1992). Pregnancy and scleroderma. *American Journal of Reproductive Immunology, 28,* 238–240.

Silverstein, C., & Picano, F. (1992). *The new joy of gay sex.* New York: HarperCollins.

Storms, M. (1978). Attitudes toward homosexuality and femininity in men. *Journal of Homosexuality, 3*(3), 257–263.

Swartz, D.B. (1995). Cultural implications of audiological deficits on the homosexual male. *Sexuality and Disability, 13*(2), 159–181.

Thompson, D. (1994). The sexual experiences of men with learning disabilities having sex with men—Issues for HIV prevention. *Sexuality and Disability, 12*(3), 221–242.

Varner, M.W. (1991). Autoimmune disorders and pregnancy. *Seminars in Perinatology, 15,* 238–250.

Warren, N. (1993). Out of the question: Obstacles to research on HIV and women who engage in sexual behaviors with women. *SIECUS Report, 22*(1), 13–16.

CHAPTER 22

Management of Erectile Dysfunction

David A. Rivas and Michael B. Chancellor

People with chronic illness and disability, especially those people with neurologic lesions, such as traumatic spinal cord injury, commonly experience difficulty with either attaining phallic erection or maintaining the erect state to experience satisfactory intercourse. To more clearly understand the impaired mechanism of sexual response in people with chronic disability, such as neurologic impairment, it is important to first comprehend the physiology of sexual excitation and function in people without disability. This chapter concentrates on the physiologic response to sexual excitation that culminates in phallic erection suitable for vaginal penetration and of adequate duration for each participant to achieve sexual gratification. The chapter also discusses the etiology of sexual dysfunction and proposes specific therapeutic management strategies that can enable people with altered sexual function to accomplish satisfying and fulfilling sexual intercourse.

ERECTILE APPARATUS

Components

The structure of the male penis may be considered to comprise two functional areas: the body and the root. The root of the phallus provides anchoring essential for control during sexual intercourse. The support of the phallic root is provided from two suspensory ligaments. The fundiform ligament of the penis is simply a continuation of the anterior rectus sheath inferiorly, where it fuses in the midline to form the linea alba. The true suspensory ligament of the phallus may provide greater support because it is attached to the bony and cartilaginous prominence of the symphysis pubis.

Externally, loosely connected skin provides protection of the internal structures, but is compliant in character to allow significant engorgement of the erectile bodies, resulting in phallic enlargement and rigidity. At its distal aspect, the phallic skin folds over on itself to form the prepuce. This preputial foreskin is often surgically excised for cosmetic and hygienic reasons—a circumcision. Contained within the skin of the phallus are three erectile bodies—two corpora cavernosae and the corpus spongiosum—as well as investing fascia, vascular structures, nerves, and the urethra.

The urethra itself is completely invested by the central erectile body, the corpus spongiosum. This structure comprises three distinct sections. In proximity to the apex of the prostate gland, the corpus spongiosum is contained circumferentially for several centimeters by the bulbospongiosus muscle, which not only provides support, but also is responsible for seminal expulsion at the time of ejaculation. In the midportion of the urethra, the corpus spongiosum comprises mainly of spongy vascular sinuses that augment the penile diameter during the erect state. At its most distal aspect, the spongy tissue of the corpus spongiosum expands in a conical configuration to cover the distal aspects of the paired corpora cavernosae, forming the glans penis. The spongy erectile tissue of the corpus spongiosum becomes engorged during penile erection, although providing little to the rigidity associated with tumescence. This rigidity is established because blood is entrapped in the paired corpora cavernosae. These tubular structures are found posterior to, and to either side of, the corpus spongiosum. These three erectile bodies function together as an erectile unit, although their vascular supply and drainage are somewhat distinct. The vascular tributaries and neurologic structures that facilitate tumescence are contained within a tough layer of fascia which circumferentially envelopes the entire erectile unit.

The corpora cavernosae are paired structures that serve to entrap the blood essential for erection. They are fused in the midline, posterior to the corpus spongiosum, where sinusoids enable the free exchange of blood between the two structures. More proximally, the corpora cavernosae diverge to allow ligamentous attachment to either side of the pubic arch, extending proximally to the level of the ischial tuberosity and establishing a firm anchor for the erect phallus. The erectile tissue of these two bodies comprises a spongy network of endothelial lined lacunae. These lacunae function to allow engorgement with blood with a pressure approximating the systemic blood pressure. It is the containment of blood by these structures at this pressure that is most important in establishing the structural rigidity essential for vaginal penetration during sexual intercourse (Aitken, Causey, Joseph, & Young, 1978).

Blood Supply

Blood is supplied to the many components of the phallus by many vessels derived from the iliac arteries. Although the skin and superficial structures may receive vascular supply from the branches of the external iliac arteries, the chief blood supply to the erectile bodies is derived from the internal iliac arteries through the paired internal pudendal arteries. The bulbar and urethral arteries are responsible for supplying blood to the corpus spongiosum, the urethral structures, and the glans penis more distally. Although the internal pudendal arteries branch primarily to the bulbar and urethral arteries, they continue as the cavernosal artery. These paired cavernosal arteries each penetrate their respective corpus cavernosum near its insertion onto the pubic arch proximally, but continue centrally through the length of the corporal body. The final branch of each internal pudendal artery is that of the dorsal artery of the penis. This vessel runs posterior to the corporal structures throughout their length, yielding blood supply by way of superficial circumflex branches to the corpora cavernosae, and terminating in arterioles that contribute blood supply to the glans penis.

Venous Drainage

The corpora cavernosae return venous blood through emissary veins, which penetrate the tough tunica albuginea, which compose the corporal walls. The corporal blood passes through both cavernous veins and circumflex veins. This venous blood drains into the deep dorsal vein of the phallus, which passes under the symphysis pubis to form the retropubic preprostatic venous Santorini's plexus. Alternatively, cavernosal venous blood may drain through alternate venous structures into vessels of the deep pelvis that empty into the internal iliac veins. The superficial dorsal veins of the penis provide drainage from the penile skin and superficial structures to empty into the saphenous system.

Innervation

As a result of psychological or tactile erotic stimulation, the activity of the autonomic nervous system increases. This increase in activity, and especially the increase in parasympathetic autonomic tone, is conducted to the erectile bodies by way of the cavernous nerves, which induce a dramatic increase in arterial inflow to the structures of the deep pelvis, including the erectile structures of the phallus (Wagner, 1992). The parasympathetic component to these cavernous nerves emanates from the spinal segments S-2 to S-4, whereas a sympathetic contribution arises from the hypogastric plexus. The autonomic nerves form a plexus, the prostatic plexus, which lies immediately adjacent to the prostate and rectum. As the nerves course lateral to the prostate and urethra, they begin to divide and emanate from the pelvis. The nerves initially send branches to the crura of the corpora, then course dorsally to contribute fibers that coalesce to develop the dorsal nerves of the penis, providing additional innervation to the more distal aspects of the corpora. Penile sensory nerves are believed to be branches of the pudendal nerve, fibers of which also contribute to the dorsal nerve of the penis (Tanagho, 1992).

HUMAN SEXUAL RESPONSE

The sexual responses of the male and female involve a complex series of neurologically mediated phenomena that occur within a hormonal milieu. It is essential that each aspect of the erectile structure, including the corporal bodies themselves, the nervous pathways, and blood supply, remain intact and functional. Moreover, it is the interaction among the components of the erectile structure that enable erection, and these components are governed primarily by hormonal responses. Clearly, the physiology of penile erection depends on a series of complex interactions involving the vascular, hormonal, and neurogenic systems of the body (Abber & Lue, 1987).

In the male, the response to sexual stimulation, whether psychogenic or tactile, progresses from the development of phallic rigidity to glandular secretion, seminal emission, and eventually orgasm and ejaculation. The female sexual response is believed to be analogous to that of the male, in which stimulation initially causes engorgement of the external genitalia and vaginal lubrication, and with continued excitation, ultimately, the rhythmic contraction of the pelvic floor musculature that is perceived as orgasm (Masters & Johnson, 1966). Although the sexual response may be viewed as an essentially reflex phenomenon, it is well known that alterations in either the psychological, structural, or physiologic components that contribute to a satisfactory sexual experience can have a profound effect on the outcome of sexual interaction (Benard & Lue, 1990).

Physiology of Sexual Response

Satisfactory sexual intercourse depends on rigidity of the phallus adequate for vaginal penetration. This level of rigidity must be maintained throughout intercourse for both partners to escalate their level of sexual excitation to the point at which seminal emission and ejaculation occurs in the male and rhythmic pelvic floor muscular contraction occurs in the female, such that each achieves sexual gratification and that delivery of the ejaculate is effective in reaching the uterine cervix if conception is desired.

Phallic erection may be initiated by psychogenic impulses (Maclean & Ploog, 1962). Although emanating from the cerebrum, these impulses are mediated by the hypothalamus and limbic system, then conducted through the thoracolumbar spinal cord to the sacral erection centers (Bors & Comarr, 1960). Alternatively, erection may result as a reflex phenomenon in response to direct tactile stimulation of the phallus or other erogenous zones.

Phallic sensory impulses are conducted to the sacral spinal cord through the dorsal nerve of the penis initially, then the pudendal nerve. The reflex arc in the sacral cord involves synapses with parasympathetic nuclei. This results in the generation of parasympathetic efferent impulses, which then travel through the pelvic plexus and are conducted to the erectile structures by way of the cavernosal nerves (Weiss, 1972). This parasympathetic outflow is essential to the initiation of the erectile response, which begins with accentuated blood flow to the corporal structures. As a result of vascular smooth muscle relaxation in the internal pudendal artery, blood flow though the penile artery increases. Dilatation of this artery, which divides into the cavernosal, bulbar, urethral, and dorsal arteries of the penis (Henderson & Roepke, 1933), allows a dramatically increased delivery of blood to the erectile mechanism.

Parasympathetic stimulation induces cholinergic and nonadrenergic, noncholinergic relaxation of the smooth muscle–lined cavernous sinuses contained in the corporal structures of the phallus. The helicine arterioles, which branch from the cavernosal arteries, selectively shunt penile blood flow to the erectile apparatus, filling the lacunar spaces of the cavernosal bodies as a direct result of decreased peripheral resistance of these arteries. Continued filling of the lacunar spaces with blood results in the compression of the subtunical venules within the cavernosal bodies, which usually serve to provide venous outflow. As these venules become compressed by the expanding lacunae, venous outflow is significantly reduced. As vascular inflow is accentuated in the face of impaired venous return, the pressure within the corporal structures becomes markedly elevated. It is this entrapment of blood with escalating pressure that brings about the elongation, dilatation, and rigidity recognized as tumescence and phallic erection. The vascular phenomenon of erection eventually stabilizes, with the intracorporal pressure approximating that of the systolic blood pressure, when continued arterial inflow is minimal as a result of blood trapping by the veno-occlusive mechanism. Continued parasympathetic outflow enables ongoing phallic rigidity throughout intercourse (Smith & Bodner, 1993).

Sexual Climax and Detumescence

As sexual sensory and psychogenic excitation increases during intercourse, the climax of the sexual interaction culminates in an accentuated sympathetic outflow from the T-11 to L-2 spinal segments. These impulses exit the sympathetic chain to the hypogastric plexus, traversing the hypogastric nerve. The sympathetic outflow courses through the pelvis in nerves sharing parasympathetic conduction to reach the genital structures. It is this sympathetic outflow that controls not only the signals responsible for causing ejaculation, but induces the events that bring about detumescence (Root & Bard, 1947).

Initially, the sympathetic outflow synapses with adrenergic neurons on the bladder neck, vas deferens, seminal vesicles, epididymis, and prostate to cause seminal emission. This complex process occurs as a result of smooth muscle contraction, in which spermatozoa in the vas deferens are driven into the ampulla of the vas, and further contraction of the ampulla, seminal vesicles, and prostate result in delivery of seminal fluid into the posterior urethra. The smooth muscle of the bladder neck simultaneously contracts, preventing retrograde seminal flow into the urinary bladder (Bors & Comarr, 1960). After the initial seminal emission has been delivered to the posterior urethra, the rhythmic contraction of the bulbocavernosus, ischiocavernosus, and pelvic floor musculature causes the antegrade expulsion of semen from the posterior urethra to the urethral meatus, recognized as ejaculation.

The sympathetic outflow also has a direct effect on the smooth muscle sinusoids within the corporal bodies, inducing contraction of the lacunar spaces. With the contraction of smooth muscle sinusoids responsible for engorgement of the corporal bodies, entrapped blood is forced into the emissary veins, resulting in decreasing rigidity. The decrease in intracorporal volume allows relaxation of the angulation and compression of these emissary veins, further promoting venous outflow and lowering intracorporal pressure, which eventually decreases outflow resistance and enables complete detumescence (de Tejada, Goldstein, & Krane, 1988).

ERECTILE DYSFUNCTION IN NEUROLOGIC DISEASE

As can be ascertained from the description of the sexual response, neurologic function is imperative to the development of phallic erection. Any process that disturbs the propagation of neurologic impulses will impair erectile ability (Siroky & Krane, 1979). Organic factors that affect the function of cerebral cortical transmission, such as cerebrovascular accidents, demyelinating disease, or trauma to the higher centers will have a significant impact on the development of psychogenic erections (Brock & Lue, 1992). Disturbances in the thoracolumbar segments likewise can impair sympathetic outflow and not only reduce the capacity for psychogenic erection, but also significantly reduce the capacity for seminal emission and ejaculation in the male, or their correlates in the female (Sipski, 1991b).

Those people with lesions of higher centers of the central nervous system may suffer from the inability to achieve psychogenic sexual function, although those individuals may retain the ability to engage in sexual intercourse if reflex erectile activity is preserved through functional, intact sacral segments and reflex arcs. Alternatively, people with lesions of the lower centers of the central nervous system may be unable to achieve phallic erection through tactile stimulation and reflex mechanisms, but may retain the ability to obtain penile rigidity through visual and other erotic stimuli through impulses from the higher centers transmitted through the autonomic nervous system (de Groat & Booth, 1984).

ERECTILE DYSFUNCTION AFTER SPINAL CORD INJURY

The phase of spinal shock that follows acute injury to the spinal cord commonly results in the complete inability to achieve phallic erection. This total erectile failure will generally resolve slowly as the patient emerges from spinal shock, although the timing and extent of the recovery of erectile function depends on several factors. The completeness and level of spinal injury will determine not only the potential for recovery, but also the method by which phallic erection may be initiated (Strasberg & Brady, 1988). Consideration of the patient's emotional status is critically important in the sexual rehabilitation of patients with such a sudden and incapacitating condition as spinal cord injury (Sipski, 1991a). The health care provider must convey to the patient a significant emphasis on the potential for recovery of function and must incorporate this emphasis into any rehabilitation program. Without the proper motivation and encouragement, an individual's sexual identity and performance may never be restored (Alexander, 1991).

Sexual dysfunction may occur in up to 75% of men after suffering traumatic spinal cord injury (Stone, 1987). However, historical data are often skewed. Even though what is perceived as normal erectile function may not be evident, up to 80% of spinal cord–injured males are able to attain some element of penile rigidity, depending on the level and completeness of injury. In those men with complete spinal cord lesions, the potential for recovery of sexual function is generally believed to be less than the potential of those men with incomplete lesions (Chapelle, Durand, & Lacert, 1980), who may indeed attain the recovery of erectile function suitable for vaginal penetration and satisfactory sexual relations.

In patients with upper motor neuron lesions above the level of the sacral reflex arc, the potential for recovery of reflexogenic erections should not be underestimated. Comarr (1970) studied 115 patients with upper motor neuron lesions and found that 92% were able to achieve reflexogenic erection to some extent. Although the reflex erections of this population may be of short duration and unsuitable for sexual gratification of the patient or his partner, augmentation of the sexual response with modern therapy is often capable of restoring a satisfactory sexual experience.

In those individuals with lower motor neuron lesions, injury to the sacral reflex arc effectively blocks the impulses generated from tactile stimulation of the genital region from inducing penile rigidity. However, psychogenic erection may be attainable from impulses generated from higher centers through alternative erotic stimulation and transmitted by way of the autonomic nervous system, although in the Comarr (1970) study, this was possible in only 26% of patients. Direct injury to the cauda equina markedly impairs pudendal nerve–mediated sensation; therefore, reflex erection in this patient group would not be expected (Comarr, 1971) and may not occur even with incomplete injury.

PSYCHOLOGICAL CONSIDERATIONS OF THE PATIENT

Chronic disability forces the individual to confront a significant alteration in lifestyle. Those people with chronic disability suffer from dramatic adjustments in their perception of body image and capabilities. Commonly, thwarted expectations for future achievement often negatively influence sexual desire and performance. If an individual can be educated and counseled effectively to adjust to the dramatic alterations in lifestyle and expectations, sexuality can often be preserved. Although the means to engage in sexual activity may be different, the concept that sexual activity is not only possible, but also enjoyable, is exceedingly important, and must be reinforced (Alexander, 1991).

Sexual rehabilitation of patients with not only neurologic lesions but other forms of chronic disability is best undertaken and achieved with greatest success in a multidisciplinary fashion. It is important to include the patient's sexual partner in the rehabilitation program so that all of the couple's fears, problems, and potential conflicts that may develop in the course of therapy are addressed promptly and to each person's satisfaction. The patient should feel comfortable and be permitted to raise the topic of sexual dysfunction with the clinician. The clinician should then provide limited information and specific suggestions with regard to altered sexual function so that the patient is better able to understand the nature of sexual dysfunction. As the patient gains greater understanding of the nature of the dysfunction, the clinician can initiate intensive therapy to restore function (Linsenmeyer, 1991).

It is important to consider not only physiologic changes, but also psychological alterations, in people with disability and chronic illness. Although a physiologic lesion may have a significant impact on a person's ability to achieve phallic erection adequate for satisfactory intercourse, psychological factors can have an equally negative effect on sexual function. Many patients with erectile dysfunction and neurologic lesions may be treated as though they have true organic erectile dysfunction. Although such a treatment regimen may be effective in restoring sexual function, it is possible that this subgroup of patients may be equally well managed with less invasive forms of treatment aimed at psychological etiologies for decreased libido and sexual performance.

THERAPEUTIC APPROACH

It is important to obtain a thorough medical history before initiating therapy for patients with sexual dysfunction. Often, an effective therapeutic regimen will be most readily developed when all medical factors are considered. In particular, the clinician must note any medical conditions or medications that are known to adversely affect libido or sexual performance. Those patients with documented endocrinologic abnormalities, for example, may respond best to hormonal manipulation therapy, whereas an older male with significant cardiovascular disease may suffer from a vasculogenic etiology for his erectile dysfunction, which may preclude certain therapeutic alternatives. The clinician must review the patient's current medical regimen because pharmacologic therapy often imparts an adverse effect on erectile function. The use of beta-adrenergic blockade, central nervous system depressants, and tricyclic anticholinergic therapy, for example, are known to negatively affect blood flow to the corporal structures, thus impairing erectile activity.

General urologic health is an important consideration before addressing erectile dysfunction. It is essential to elicit a history of recurrent genitourinary conditions, such as infections, calculi, or urethral strictures, which tend to identify those patients who require adjunctive therapy before treatment of neurogenic impotence (Brock & Lue, 1992). Significant neurogenic lower urinary tract dysfunction may profoundly affect an individual's overall health, resulting in recurrent illness and potentially significant morbidity, and even death. The clinician should evaluate such dysfunction completely and institute an effective treatment regimen before considering the treatment of erectile dysfunction.

Once the clinician has completely evaluated the psychological, pharmacologic, and physiologic factors that can impair the erectile response, and those factors have been treated, the clinician can initiate a formal therapeutic regimen for erectile dysfunction. He or she may use several different approaches to enhance or restore sexual function in people with disability and chronic illness. Establishing the proper hormonal milieu for erection to occur is of primary concern. The clinician should quantify a serum testosterone level to rule out the possibility that hormonal imbalance, whether of benign or malignant nature, may be a contributing factor to an individual's decreased sexual function. Once adequate androgenous hormone levels are ensured, attention can then be turned toward augmenting the erectile response.

Initially, the clinician may use different forms of stimulation therapy. Stimulation therapy may be targeted toward psychogenic erections. The use of erogenous zone development, erotic visual or audio aids, and even olfactory stimulation may facilitate psychogenic erection. Alternatively, reflex erectile activity may be pursued. At times, those patients who are unresponsive to manual stimulation may respond to vibratory stimulation. Should these methods fail, minimally invasive techniques are often effective in restoring erectile function. Certain medications have been found to significantly augment the filling and engorgement of the corporal bodies with blood, including the application of systemic alpha-adrenergic blocking agents and the direct application of intracorporal vasoactive agents. Use of vacuum-assisted corporal engorgement also augments this process. Alternatively, if conservative, less invasive measures fail, phallic erection can be achieved with the use of a surgically placed intracorporal penile prosthesis.

Oral Pharmacologic Therapy

Alpha-Adrenergic Agonists

Yohimbine is an alkaloid agent that blocks presynaptic alpha-2 adrenergic receptors. This medication mainly affects the peripheral autonomic nervous system, resulting in a relative decrease in adrenergic activity while increasing parasympathetic tone. The pharmacologic result is that of augmenting the physiologic shunting of blood to the corporal bodies. By affecting the alteration of impaired penile blood flow, those patients with borderline erectile function may be able to regain their erectile function. Yohimbine is administered as a 5.4-mg tablet taken orally 3 times daily. This medication may improve the erectile response in patients with an altered shunting mechanism; however, Smith and Bodner (1993) have pointed out there is no evidence to support the use of yohimbine or other psychotropic agents in this patient population.

Another potentially effective agent that acts on alpha-1 and alpha-2 adrenergic receptors is that of phentolamine. This agent has been commonly used for intracorporal injection therapy, although a recent clinical trial has suggested its efficacy when orally administered immediately before intercourse. Zorgniotti and Lizza (1993) in a study of more than 100 patients with impotence reported that an oral dose of 25 to 50 mg produced erection adequate for vaginal penetration in 42% of the patients. The majority of the patients who responded to this agent were believed to have nonspecific, psychogenic, or mild vascular impotence, and side effects of nasal congestion, palpitations, and dizziness were noted. This form of therapy is still under investigation and therefore is not recommended.

L-arginine

Nitric oxide has been demonstrated to mediate the relaxation of vascular smooth muscle in the corporal sinuses, resulting from increased cyclic adenosine monophosphate (cAMP) and cyclic guanosine monophosphate (cGMP). L-arginine is an amino acid precursor to the formation of nitric oxide, and, for this reason, Zorgniotti and Lizza (1994) attempted a limited trial of high doses of the medication (2,800 mg) in 15 men over a 2-week period. Of the 15 men, 6 reported a significant improvement in their erections. Further investigation of this agent is being conducted.

UK-92,480

Recent investigations have revealed that, although nitric oxide may be required for physiologic phallic erection, manipulation of its second messenger, cGMP, may be effective in improving erectile function. Several investigators in the United Kingdom have used an orally administered investigational agent, UK-92,480, as a selective inhibitor of type 5 (cGMP-specific) phosphodiesterase to treat erectile dysfunction. This agent is theorized to decrease the catabolism of cGMP in the corpora cavernosae, thereby enhancing the erectile response.

The medication may be administered as a 10-, 25-, 50-, or 75-mg oral dose either immediately before sexual activity or as a daily regimen. Recent investigations have concluded that UK-92,480 is safe and effective in improving erectile duration and rigidity of phallic erection in 70% to 90% of patients tested (Boolell, Gepi-Attee, Gingell, & Allen, 1996; Eardley et al., 1996; Gingell et al., 1996).

Serotoninergic Receptor Agonists

Serotonin is known to have a centrally mediated inhibitory effect on libido, although serotonin agonists have demonstrated a peripheral action of facilitating erectile function. Trazodone, often used in the treatment of affective disorders, was found incidentally to be associated with the development of priapism in men and women (Pescatori, Engleman, & Davis, 1993). Part of its effect may be attributed to a peripheral alpha-adrenergic blockade (Saenz de Tajada et al., 1991). The agent is usually administered as a 100- or 200-mg dose at bedtime. Reports have indicated up to a 60% response when used as monotherapy. There is some suggestion that a synergistic response may be achieved with the use of yohimbine.

Topical Pharmacologic Therapy

Several different agents have been topically applied to the glans penis and phallic shaft in efforts to augment the erectile response. These topical agents may indeed increase intracorporal nitric oxide levels.

Nitroglycerin Paste

Nitroglycerin and its derivatives are well-known vasodilating agents. Topical nitroglycerin paste, administered for the treatment of cardiovascular disease states, has proven to be well absorbed. For this reason, and its documented property of nitric oxide donation, the administration of nitroglycerin directly to the phallus was used to enhance corporal engorgement and held promise for the treatment of erectile dysfunction. In a laboratory investigation of the effect of topical nitroglycerin on erectile function in the rat, however, limited effects were noted using intracorporal cavernosometry (Rivas, Chancellor, Huang, & Salzman, 1995).

A randomized placebo-controlled study by Claes and Baert (1989) in a group of 26 men with vasculogenic erectile dysfunction revealed a return to satisfactory sexual function in 12 using nitroglycerin plasters (10 mg/24 hr). Meyhoff, Rosenkilde, and Bodker (1992) treated 10 patients with various etiologies of impotence in a non–double-blind study using a penile application of nitroglycerin (Transderm-Nitro) plaster (10 mg/24 hr). Only 4 of the 10 patients achieved satisfactory erections. Sonksen and Biering-Sorensen (1992) tested topical nitroglycerin (Transderm-Nitro, 10 mg/24 hr) in 17 spinal cord–injured men who had previously responded to intracavernosal papaverine injections. Of the 17 men, 5 reported an erection with rigidity adequate for vaginal penetration using the nitroglycerin plasters. The overall inferior results, associated with the side effects of hypotension and headache, have not encouraged its widespread use.

Minoxidil

Minoxidil was first used orally as an antihypertensive agent because it induces vasodilatation by a direct relaxation of arterial smooth muscles (Clissold & Heel, 1987). The use of minoxidil as a topical transcutaneous facilitator of erection may be justified because vasorelaxation has proved to occur, in an experimental model, by way of the promotion of potassium conductance and inhibition of calcium entry through voltage-dependent calcium channels in vascular smooth muscles (Leblanc, Wilde, Keef, & Hume, 1989). The medication may be applied as a 2% solution sprayed onto the penile glans and shaft.

In a placebo-controlled trial of 33 men with organic impotence, Cavallini (1991) determined minoxidil applied topically to the glans penis to be more effective than nitroglycerin or placebo in improving penile diameter and rigidity as measured with Rigi-Scan. A follow-up study by Radomsky, Herschorn, and Rang-aswamy (1994) failed to demonstrate clinical efficacy of the transcutaneous application of minoxidil for the treatment of erectile dysfunction in 21 patients, 8 of whom were determined to have neurogenic impotence. One patient in the study did respond to minoxidil, but since has not required treatment to achieve satisfactory penile erection. Chancellor, Rivas, Panzer, Freedman, and Staas (1994), who recently completed a clinical trial of minoxidil in 18 spinal cord–injured male patients, noted that no patient achieved an erection adequate for intercourse with topical minoxidil.

Although the pharmacologic action of minoxidil should encourage phallic erection, limited tissue absorption may account for the minimal effects noted in clinical trials. Indeed, when steps are taken to enhance penetration into the corporal bodies, an increase in intracorporal pressure may occur. In a laboratory investigation of erection therapy in the rat, Rivas et al. (1995) found that, when the 2% minoxidil was applied either to a degloved phallus or to the mucous membrane of the urethra, a statistically significant increase in intracorporal pressure resulted. Further clinical research into the effect of minoxidil when applied to such surfaces with enhanced absorptive capability, such as the urethral mucosa, may indeed demonstrate efficacy of this agent.

Prostaglandins

The vasodilatory effects of the prostaglandins have been well documented in the literature. Prostaglandin F_1 (PGE_1) has been used successfully to treat erectile dysfunction, although its application is through intracorporal injection. The limited absorption of prostaglandins applied topically to the skin of the phallus has stimulated interest in determining whether these agents may demonstrate absorption sufficient to produce the erect state if absorbed through the mucous membrane of the urethra. Wolfson, Pickett, Scott, DeKernion, and Rajfer (1993) studied the use of prostaglandin E_2 (PGE_2) applied intraurethrally in 20 men with erectile dysfunction. A prostaglandin ointment was created by blending a crushed 20- or 40-mg PGE_2 suppository, 10 cc of 2% lidocaine jelly, and 40 cc of surgical lubricant. Of the cream, 2 mL, containing either 67 or 134 mg of the PGE_2–jelly–lubricant was instilled intraurethrally and the urethra occluded for 5 minutes. Of the 20 participants, 70% responded to the treatment and 30% developed penile erection with rigidity deemed adequate for intercourse.

In a more recent investigation into the intraurethral application of PGE_1, 1,511 adult men and their partners participated in a double-blind, placebo-controlled multicenter study (Padma-Nathan et al., 1996). Those patients were exposed to the application of increasing doses of a tiny pellet of PGE_1 (125, 250, 500, or 1000 μg) placed intraurethrally until satisfactory erection was noted. The patients then were allowed to use the optimum dose in their homes for a 3-month trial. The treatment was well tolerated: 65% of patients reported the ability to engage in sexual intercourse, although 11% of patients documented penile pain with intraurethral PGE$_1$ use.

Intraurethral PGE$_1$ suppositories were approved by the Food and Drug Administration (FDA) and became available with a doctor's prescription in January 1997. Each suppository is preloaded into an individual, one-time-use sterile applicator. Four dosages are available: 125, 250, 500, and 1000 μg. Proper dose determination by a physician is essential, however, to avoid side effects and minimize the potential for priapism with this method of achieving erection.

After evaluation by a physician, the patient is tested with the lowest dosage application, and the effect on tumescence is recorded. If deemed adequate for intercourse with regard to engorgement, rigidity, and duration of erection, the patient is given a prescription for this dosage. If the erection is judged unsuitable, the patient returns on subsequent days, receiving increasing doses of PGE$_1$ until a satisfactory result is noted by the physician. The suppository dosage required for that individual patient is then prescribed for home use.

Intracavernosal Injection Therapy

Intracavernosal injection therapy is widely accepted as an effective treatment for the restoration of erectile function in men with impotence of varying etiologies. Although less successful in men with significantly impaired penile arterial flow, such as after aortic aneurysm repair, intracorporal injection can be highly effective in producing a natural erection in patients with psychogenic or neurogenic erectile dysfunction. The medications injected into the corporal bodies act directly on the sinusoidal smooth muscle to induce relaxation and enhance corporal filling.

In patients without erectile dysfunction, parasympathetic outflow, produced by sexual stimulation, induces the relaxation of the smooth muscle within the lacunae of the corporal sinusoids. With intracorporal therapy, a small volume, often less than 1 mL, of a vasoactive agent is injected directly into one of the paired corporal bodies using a 27-gauge needle. The medication spreads to both corporal bodies through intercommunicating channels, inducing relaxation of the lacunar smooth muscle and encouraging filling of the lacunar spaces with blood. As the corporal spaces fill, the emissary veins that usually provide venous drainage of the corporal structures become angulated and compressed. The erection that develops can be remarkably natural in size and rigidity. The duration of the erection is directly proportional to the dose of the agent administered (Wein, Malloy, & Hanno, 1987); overdosage can result in the development of priapism.

Patients with spinal cord injury may be exquisitely sensitive to the application of these drugs. A denervation supersensitivity is proposed to account for this sensitivity, which must be considered before the initiation of intracorporal injection (Benard & Lue, 1990). Therefore, intracorporal injection therapy in patients with spinal cord injury is usually instituted with a fraction of the dose of pharmacologic agent anticipated to be effective. Subsequent doses are gradually increased until an erection suitable for intercourse is achieved with a duration of 30 to 60 minutes (Wyndaele, de Meyer, de Sy, & Claessens, 1986).

Until recently, this form of treatment was not approved by the FDA. Although effective, patients were using papaverine and rigitine without federal approval. The use of these agents has been significantly curtailed by withdrawal from the market of available injectable preparations. In their place, PGE$_1$ has become available in unit-dose packaging containing PGE$_1$, diluent fluid, a sterile syringe, and alcohol skin-preparation pads. The packaging is a hard plastic case that can be locked with its own plastic hub to ensure proper safe disposal (Figure 22–1).

Most recently, a study of the efficacy and safety of intracavernosally injected PGE$_1$ was conducted in 683 men with erectile dysfunction of varying etiology (Linet & Ogrinc, 1996). The participants of the study reported the ability to engage in sexual intercourse after 94% of injections. Satisfaction with intercourse made possible by the PGE$_1$ injections was confirmed by 87% of the men and by 86% of their sexual partners. Although penile pain may have been encountered by 50% of participants at some time during the 6-month study, only 11% of the

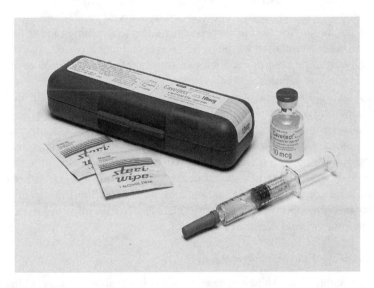

Figure 22–1 PGE$_1$ self-injection kit. Courtesy of Pharmacia & Upjohn, Kalamazoo, Michigan.

injection episodes were associated with penile pain. Although prolonged erections occurred in 5% of patients, priapism occurred in only 1%, penile fibrosis in 2%, and hematoma or ecchymosis in 8%. Overall, the investigators concluded that PGE_1 intracorporal self-injection was effective in the treatment of erectile dysfunction, with tolerable side effects.

Complications

Before initiating this form of therapy, patients must be fully aware of the significant risks they incur. The clinician should obtain a formal, signed consent to the administration of intracorporal agents before initiating treatment (Wein et al., 1987). A possible adverse effect of intracavernosal therapy, attributed to chronic administration, is scarring of the tunica albuginea, which may result in permanent curvature of the erect phallus (Lakin, Montague, Vanderbrug, Tesar, & Schover, 1990). Another primary risk of this form of treatment is the development of priapism, a prolonged erection that results in the development of intracorporal acidosis and that may impair future erectile response.

In cases in which priapism does occur, the patient must seek medical attention immediately. An initial form of treatment for this condition involves the aspiration of blood from each corporal body. An alpha-adrenergic agonist, such as phenylephrine or epinephrine, may be injected to promote contraction of the corporal smooth muscle and restore venous drainage from the system (Lue & Tanagho, 1987). An initial dosage of 0.5 mg phenylephrine in 2 mL of saline may be effective in achieving detumescence, but repeated injections every 15 minutes may be required to maintain the flaccid state. If repeated up to five times and still ineffective, large-bore cannulation of the cavernosal structures must be undertaken to continually clear the cavernosae of blood using an irrigation solution of epinephrine in physiologic saline solution (Wein et al., 1987).

Persistent priapism refractory to this alpha-adrenergic therapy indicates that a surgical shunting of blood is needed to effect detumescence. Although these emergent shunts are thought to close spontaneously after several days, a persistently patent shunt may further impair erectile function. Factors that predispose to the development of priapism include a supersensitivity to the medication, an excessive single dose of the medication, or repeated injections undertaken because of an inadequate erectile response. Patients are advised to limit the frequency of intracorporal injection therapy to every other day to minimize the risks associated with intracorporal therapy (Benard & Lue, 1990).

Selection of the Pharmacologic Agent

Drugs that have been shown to be effective as intracorporal agents in the treatment of erectile dysfunction include papaverine, with its direct smooth muscle inhibition, and phentolamine, which produces smooth muscle relaxation through its alpha-adrenergic blocking effects. Therapy may be initiated with papaverine alone; however, in patients who require high doses of this single agent, a mixture of papaverine and phentolamine has been effective (Nellans, Ellis, & Kramer-Levien, 1987). Recently, the application of prostaglandins has demonstrated increased efficacy and decreased morbidity in contrast to papaverine or phentolamine. Decreased penile discomfort in patients with intact sensation, decreased tunical scarring, and decreased incidence of priapism have contributed to their popularity (Waldhauser & Schramek, 1988). PGE_1 is most widely used, although the application of PGE_2 is currently under investigation. The cost of the prostaglandins is considerably higher than other agents, which, before FDA approval, restricted their widespread use to some extent.

Patient Selection

Whether the etiology of erectile dysfunction is psychogenic, neurogenic, vasculogenic, or hormonal, almost any patient may be effectively treated using intracorporal injection therapy. The patient must have adequate visual acuity and manual dexterity to be able to prepare and self-administer the intracorporal agent, although his sexual partner may often be trained to administer the injections if the patient is unable to do so. Those patients with significant abdominal, pubic, and perineal adipose tissue may encounter significant difficulty in injecting the medication directly into the corporal bodies. In such cases, the phallus is often retracted or an abdominal pannus obstructs a clear view of the penile shaft. Furthermore, those patients currently treated with anticoagulant therapy should avoid intracorporal injections because significant penile hematomas have formed when such patients have used intracorporal injection to induce erection.

Patient Education

It is best to begin a self-injection program with a thorough discussion of the physiologic process that results in erection. The patient should be fully cognizant of the erectile mechanism and the action of the medication that induces erection. The patient should understand the reason for his erectile dysfunction and how the medication will work to overcome altered physiology. A full explanation of the pertinent anatomy, including anatomical drawings and photographs, greatly enhances the self-injection education process.

Self-education publications and video programs on videocassette that are available can further strengthen the educational process; the patient can review the information repeatedly in the clinic or at home until the patient has achieved adequate understanding. The patient must fully understand the risks of therapy, including penile scarring and discomfort, caused by the injection itself, and the potential for priapism. The clinician should provide the patient with instructions regarding the methods to treat priapism and emphasize to the patient the urgency of immediate medical attention. The patient should provide an emergency contact so that he will be able to receive treatment promptly if priapism does occur.

Once the patient fully understands the erectile mechanism and the principles underlying artificial erection achieved through intracorporal self-injection, an initial practical demonstration can be undertaken in the office setting. The patient should be comfortable, because anxiety and excessive sympathetic tone may impair the effect of the pharmacologic agent. The patient's sexual partner can often play a supportive role and improve understanding and learning of the self-injection technique. The initial injection should be of a low dose and serve mainly as an instructional endeavor. The patient must realize that it is best to begin with a first injection with minimal risk of priapism, and expect that erection may well not occur beforehand, so that he does not become disappointed by a minimal effect.

Self-Injection Office Visits

The patient must begin his trial of self-injection therapy under close observation with a series of self-injection office visits. Because PGE_1 is the only agent currently approved for self-injection treatment, the patient is given a prescription for a self-injection kit, which he brings with him to the office visit. It is best if the physician monitors the patient while the patient prepares the medication for himself, correcting any errors in the process and reminding him of the principles of sterile technique. The patient mixes 1 mL of diluent with the PGE_1 powder in its vial, shakes the mixture gently until it has dissolved completely, then withdraws the solution into the provided syringe.

In general, the patient manually extends the phallic shaft and clearly examines it so that he may contemplate the anatomy and decide the best site for injection. The clinician should remind the patient to avoid any superficial veins that may result in hematoma formation. The easiest injection site is that of the superolateral aspect of one of the corporal bodies. The patient prepares the site with an alcohol wipe and introduces the needle until it is felt to penetrate the tough tunica albuginea of the corpus cavernosum. Proper intracorporal position of the needle tip is confirmed by the appearance of blood within the barrel of the syringe as the plunger is drawn back lightly. An initial injection of 2.5 μg, 0.25 mL of a 10 mg/mL solution, is usually a safe first-injection dosage. After the patient injects this volume of the solution, he withdraws the needle and is instructed to apply firm pressure to the injection site.

The clinician then monitors the size and rigidity of the phallus for 10 minutes to judge the effect of the medication. It is preferable for the patient to return for at least three self-injection practical visits to ensure that he is performing the technique properly. During the visits, the patient will gradually increase the dose of each injection until an erection adequate for intercourse is achieved. The usual effective dose varies greatly from patient to patient. Those patients with spinal cord injury may respond to as little as 1 or 2 μg, whereas those patients with vascular disease may require up to 40 μg to attain a rigid erection.

Once the proper dose is reached, the patient is given a prescription for his specific dose, with instructions regarding the need to alternate the site of injection and to perform self-injection no more than every other day. The clinician must caution the patient that if an injection of the proper dose does not result in a usable erection, he must avoid the temptation to reinject himself, because reinjection could result in priapism. The patient should be evaluated after 1 month to determine his success with treatment and discuss any potential problems. Once he has successfully mastered his treatment regimen, 6-month reevaluation visits are mandatory to monitor for adverse effects of self-injection.

Intracorporal "Cocktail" Mixtures

In some individuals, PGE_1 alone may be inadequate to achieve an adequate erection. In such cases, the injection mixture may be augmented with papaverine or phentolamine. Before the introduction and acceptance of PGE_1 as the drug of choice for self-injection therapy, patients often initiated self-injection with papaverine alone. This medication is supplied in a 10-mL vial containing a papaverine solution of 30 mg/mL. Self injection would be initiated with 0.25 mL and the dose of each injection would be gradually increased up to 1.0 mL, or 30 mg. If this dose did not produce sufficient erection, the patient would be initiated on a regimen of combined papaverine and phentolamine. This cocktail combination is produced by the injection of 10 mg of phentolamine directly into the 10-mL vial of 30 mg/mL papaverine, so that each milliliter of the cocktail would contain 1 mg phentolamine and 10 mg papaverine. As before, the initial injection dose would be minimized at 0.25 mL, then increased gradually with each injection until a satisfactory erection occurred. If this mixture is administered up to 1 mL per injection and erection still is not realized, prostaglandin may be added to each injection, and the dose gradually titrated upward until therapeutic efficacy is demonstrated.

Vacuum-Assisted Erection

Many patients are opposed to the use of self-injection therapy. Although intracorporal self-injection causes the development of a more natural-appearing erection, certain patients do not feel comfortable with the use of hypodermic needles and syringe. The risks of penile pain, penile curvature and deformity, hematoma formation, and especially priapism are simply felt to be too great for some individuals to accept. An alternative and less invasive means of achieving corporal filling to develop penile rigidity is the use of vacuum pressure. Specialized devices have been developed that are effective in developing a negative pressure within the phallus, essentially sucking blood into the corporal bodies. Once the corporal bodies are filled with blood and the phallus is erect, the trapping of blood within the corporal bodies is accomplished with the application of a tightly-fitting latex ring applied to the base of the penis.

Vacuum Erection Device

Vacuum erection devices (VEDs) consist of a cylindrical, hard plastic tube of adequate length and diameter to contain the erect phallus. At the end of the tube, a small port leads to the vacuum-generating pump. For those individuals with adequate manual dexterity, a manual pump activated by repeated squeezing motions generates the negative pressure required for corporal filling (Figure 22–2). Other devices use a piston-type of arrangement to generate the vacuum. For patients with poor manual dexterity, because of arthritis or neurologic lesions, devices are available that create the vacuum with a small, battery-powered pump (Figure 22–3). These pumps are directly attached to the end of the penile vacuum tube, so that the entire relatively compact apparatus can be operated with one hand with the touch of a single button that activates the vacuum.

Figure 22–2 Hand-pump VED. Courtesy of Osbon Medical Systems, Augusta, Georgia.

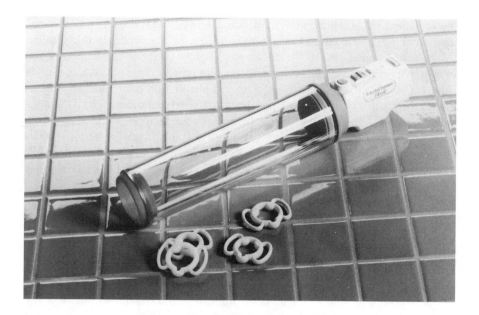

Figure 22–3 Battery-operated VED, useful for people with impaired dexterity. Courtesy of Osbon Medical Systems, Augusta, Georgia.

Patient Education

Patients must first be educated about the mechanism of erection and informed regarding the principles of vacuum-assisted erection. They must be cautioned regarding the risks of personal injury attributed to application of excessive vacuum; for example, significant penile hematoma has resulted from improper usage of VEDs. VEDs are relatively safe and effective for the majority of patients, although those patients who are receiving anticoagulant therapy are at much higher risk of penile hematoma injury and should not use a VED. Once the patient understands the principle behind vacuum-assisted erection, it is important that he be properly instructed regarding device usage.

Although fairly simple to understand and use, many patients initially experience difficulty if not educated about the proper technique. Medically approved devices are available to individuals with a prescription and order form signed by a licensed physician. The devices are dispensed as a kit that contains the vacuum tube, vacuum-generating pump, a selection of corporal body constriction rings of varying diameters, a carrying case that can easily accommodate the device components, and a self-instruction videocassette. After minimal training with viewing of patient education literature, videotape, and personal instruction, most patients find the devices are easy to use and effective in establishing penile rigidity.

The actual application of the device begins with a liberal lubrication of the internal aspect of the cylindrical penile vacuum tube with a water-soluble lubricant. This eases the application to the flaccid phallus and minimizes skin irritation as the phallus becomes engorged during vacuum generation. The patient attaches a small cone to the base of the tube; this cone facilitates stretching of the corporal constriction ring over the vacuum tube so that it can be in proper position for displacement onto the base of the phallus when erection has been achieved. The patient then places the tube over the flaccid phallus, with the slight angulation of the constriction ring adjusted to align with the urethra (Figure 22–4). This bulge of the constriction ring is specifically designed to relieve pressure on the urethra while maintaining corporal compression and permitting seminal ejaculation with increased comfort. The VED may be applied in the standing, sitting, or supine position.

The patient must press the base of the tube firmly against the skin surrounding the base of the phallus so that a hermetic seal is generated. Pubic hair at the base of the phallus may interfere with achieving this airtight seal, and therefore the patient may need to shave the base of the phallus. The patient then gradually applies the vacuum with manual pumping or the one-touch battery-operated vacuum pump. As blood is pulled into the corporal bodies, the phallus gradually enlarges until a full erection is achieved (Figure 22–5). Once adequate rigidity is established, the patient transfers the elastic corporal constriction band from the

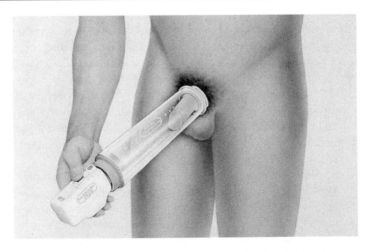

Figure 22–4 Initial placement of the VED. Courtesy of Osbon Medical Systems, Augusta, Georgia.

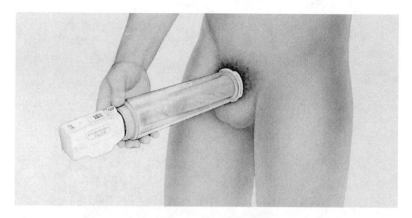

Figure 22–5 Erection induced by vacuum generation. Courtesy of Osbon Medical Systems, Augusta, Georgia.

base of the vacuum tube to the base of the penis (Figure 22–6). A proper fit of this constrictive ring is essential to prevent egress of the intracorporal blood and to maintain the phallic erection. The patient should experiment with the different rings supplied with the device until he identifies the ring that is the most suitable at constricting the corpora but not the urethra.

Constriction Band Treatment

A population of men exists who are able to achieve a rigid erection on demand, but are unable to maintain the erection perhaps because of a "venous leak" phenomenon or as a result of neurologic lesions that do not provide adequate neural output to maintain rigidity. In these individuals, accentuated, incompetent corporal veins are ineffective at containing the intracorporal blood; therefore, erections are short lived. In such patients able to achieve spontaneous erection but unable to maintain rigidity of sufficient duration for acceptable intercourse, the use of the constriction band alone is often effective in allowing maintenance of the phallic erection. The elastic bands and an application cone are sold separately from the vacuum pump expressly for this purpose. For these individuals, erection is established in the usual manner, then the patient applies the corporal constriction ring promptly before detumescence occurs, without the use of the vacuum pump (Nadig, Ware, & Blumoff, 1986).

Patient Satisfaction

The VED has been proven to be an acceptable form of treatment for many patients with organic impotence. Not all patients are entirely pleased with the

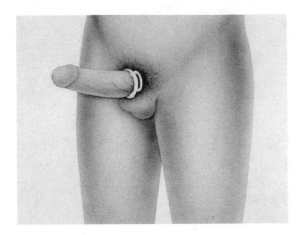

Figure 22–6 Erection maintained by constriction band. Courtesy of Osbon Medical Systems, Augusta, Georgia.

erection produced by this system, however. One major problem that affects the popularity of VEDs is that the system is somewhat cumbersome to use. Some patients may find that the different components, bulky nature of the device, slippery feel of the lubricants, and time required to apply the vacuum and constrictive band significantly interfere with the spontaneity of their sexual experience.

A more technical consideration of vacuum-assisted erection is that it establishes penile rigidity only in those portions of the corporal bodies distal to the elastic compression band. Those portions of the corpora cavernosae proximal to the constriction band, which anchor the phallus to the pubic arch, remain flaccid. The result is a hingelike effect at the base of the penis, which can interfere with control of the penis during intercourse, allowing the phallus to be repeatedly displaced from the vagina.

Another reason for dissatisfaction with the VED relates to the relative ischemia generated by impaired penile blood flow caused by the constriction band. The male patient may complain of pain, which may result from poor blood flow, and may perceive the excessively tight band itself as extremely uncomfortable. Female partners have reported that the phallus feels slightly cooler during intercourse and that this sensation is disruptive to enjoying satisfactory intercourse (Turner et al., 1990).

Potential Complications

Vacuum-assisted erection devices maintain an erect phallus through corporal trapping of blood. Because the blood is prevented from exiting the corporal bodies, fresh arterial blood supply is also significantly reduced. The relative ischemia produced by this system should not be considered dangerous, as long as the system is used properly. Clinicians must caution patients and ensure they understand fully that application of the erectile constriction band is contraindicated for greater than 30 minutes. Penile injury, including the necrosis of penile skin and injury to the erectile mechanism, may result in tissue loss and permanent penile deformity. In addition, patients must understand that subcutaneous bruising has been reported with the use of this device, likely because of excessive vacuum application. Therefore, the system must always be applied correctly, and vacuum applied judiciously, to avoid inadvertent penile injury. Patients who are receiving anticoagulants should avoid VED use altogether (Rivas & Chancellor, 1994).

Penile Revascularization

Michal, Kramer, and Pospidal (1973) first described the use of a penile revascularization procedure, in which the inferior epigastric artery was anastomosed directly to the corporal body. Since that time, other investigators have used revascularization surgery to augment the erectile response, but the results have been poor: success rates have approximated 35%. In later trials, Michal, Kramer, and Pospidal (1980) used an anastomosis of the inferior epigastric artery to the dorsal penile artery with an improvement in 10 of 18 patients. At about the same time, Virag, Zwang, and Demange (1983) were using an anastomosis of the inferior epigastric artery to the deep dorsal penile vein, suggesting that the increased pressure in this system would increase intracorporal pressure. They continued with modifications of this procedure, including ligation of the vein proximally, but reported only a 60% success rate.

Crespo, Bove, and Farrell (1987) used a vein graft between the femoral artery and the cavernosal arterial supply to improve erectile function, and reported improvement in 22 of 45 patients. Other investigators, such as McDougal and Jeffery (1983), Goldstein (1986), and Furlow and Fisher (1988), attempted penile revascularization procedures, all with mixed results.

Clearly, those patients who wish to consider penile revascularization surgery should undergo an extremely thorough evaluation that should include a medical and social history, physical examination, hormonal evaluation, and nocturnal penile tumescence testing. If the studies indicate true organic impotence, duplex doppler ultrasonography of the phallus with blood flow augmentation using intracorporal pharmacotherapy may help identify those patients with truly isolated, impaired penile blood flow who may be candidates for pelvic angiography. If angiography confirms occlusion of the pudendal vessels supplying the corporal bodies, the patient may be a candidate for revascularization surgery (Sharaby, Benet, & Melman, 1995). The patient, however, must understand that, although surgery of this type appears to be promising, historical data have suggested that durable efficacy has not yet been demonstrated. A consensus conference on impotence by the National Institutes of Health (1993) recommended that revascularization surgery have a limited role in the treatment of organic impotence and suggested that such procedures remain limited to medical centers with experienced personnel.

Penile Prosthesis

A certain subset of patients with erectile dysfunction find that neither intracorporal self-injection nor vacuum-assisted erection provides a phallic erection suitable for satisfactory intercourse. For such patients, more invasive therapy may produce a better outcome. The surgically implanted penile prosthesis provides penile rigidity with much greater spontaneity than the VED, of greater duration when compared with either vacuum- or injection-assisted erection, and with suitable cosmetic and aesthetic appearance than other forms of treatment.

A surgically implanted prosthetic device, however, should not be viewed as a panacea. Patients and their partners may be disappointed with the size, rigidity, and texture of the prosthesis-induced erection. The devices themselves, especially inflatable–deflatable devices, are known to suffer mechanical failures that require reoperation and device replacement. A prosthetic device carries with it the risk of device infection, which can be painful and develop into serious illness if not treated promptly; hence, device explantation may be required (Carson, 1989). As a foreign body, the pressure exerted on the genital structures may predispose to tissue erosion, which ultimately may result in spontaneous extrusion of the prosthetic cylinders.

Therefore, it is essential that the clinician approach the subject of penile prosthetic placement comprehensively with the patient, and often his partner, so that the patient and partner will develop a realistic set of expectations before surgery. The patient must fully understand all potential complications of prosthesis placement and he must be willing to accept the risks of the device, particularly the need for another operation in the event of device failure, erosion, or infection.

Prosthetic Device Types

Many different types of penile prosthetic devices have been developed for establishing penile rigidity. The devices first developed were rigid tubes of synthetic material that provided a permanently erect posture to the phallus. Later devices were developed with a malleable core or hinge, which permitted manipulation of the penis to help conceal the phallus when an erection was not needed (Figure 22–7). Further development of the concept of penile prosthetics resulted in inflatable devices.

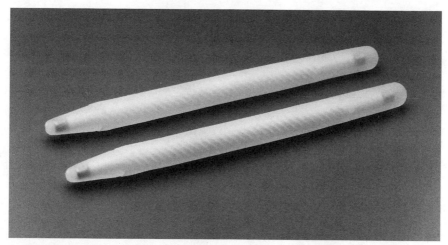

Figure 22–7 Malleable penile prosthesis. Courtesy of American Medical Systems, Inc., Minnetonka, Minnesota.

The most commonly used prosthesis today, the inflatable penile prosthesis, affords concealability when an erection is not desirable, but inflates the phallus to a cosmetic erection with rigidity adequate for vaginal penetration. Some inflatable devices consist only of two erectile cylinders that are surgically implanted within the paired corporal bodies. Each of the cylinders contains a fluid reservoir, usually at the base, an inflation pump, usually at the tip, and an expansile chamber in the middle of the cylinder (Figure 22–8).

With manual pumping of the device at the tip of each corporal body, the self-contained fluid is transferred from the reservoir at the rigid base of the cylinder to the expansion chamber. As the chamber fills, the corporal bodies become extended and more rigid, although the diameter of the phallus does not increase greatly. After intercourse has been completed, gentle pressure on a relief valve and compression of the expansion chamber of the cylinders permits transfer of fluid back into the self-contained reservoirs, and detumescence.

These self-contained devices are attractive because no tubing or connectors are required and separate placement of the pump mechanism within the scrotum and reservoir within the abdominal cavity is avoided. Because of the limited size of the reservoir, the erection obtained by these devices may not equal that of a multicomponent device with a much larger reservoir and expansile intracorporal cylinders.

The moving parts, valves, and pump mechanisms of inflatable penile prostheses have been known to develop problems with regular use. Therefore, the most popular devices, multicomponent inflatable prostheses, have been continually

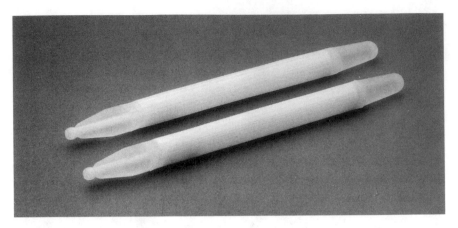

Figure 22–8 Self-contained inflatable penile prosthesis. Courtesy of American Medical Systems, Inc., Minnetonka, Minnesota.

refined over the past decade in response to reports of device failure. These devices consist of a reservoir of fluid that is placed intraabdominally during surgery, a pump mechanism that most commonly is placed within the scrotum to provide accessibility, and two cylinders that are placed within the corporal bodies themselves (Figure 22–9). All components communicate with each other by connection tubing that traverses the perineal region (Figure 22–10; Linsenmeyer, 1991). As with the self-contained devices, the erection is developed through filling of the cylinders within the paired corpora cavernosae. Because the cylinders occupy the entire volume of the corporal bodies, their filling provides a full, usable erection adequate for intercourse.

The erection attained with an inflatable prosthesis, however, is usually not of the length and girth that the patient may have enjoyed before the development of erectile dysfunction, because the corporal bodies do not expand to the point achieved with a natural filling of blood. Another factor relating to the somewhat lesser size of the prosthesis-induced erection is that vascular engorgement of the phallus does not occur; therefore, the central corpus spongiosum remains unaltered. Because the glans and central structures of the phallus are less pronounced than a physiologic erection, some patients complain of a less than adequate erection.

Patient Satisfaction and Device Failure

Despite what is deemed an acceptable erection suitable for intercourse, a review of the literature revealed that satisfaction rates approximate 75% for people with an implantable inflatable penile prosthesis. One factor that may contribute

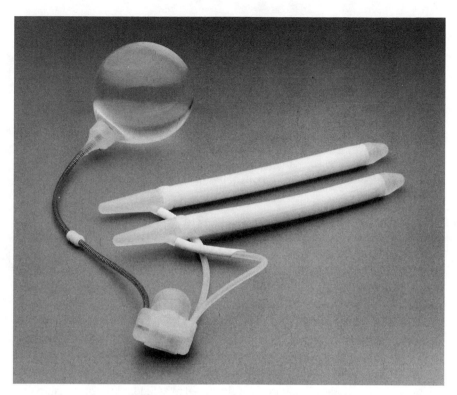

Figure 22–9 Multicomponent inflatable penile prosthesis. Courtesy of American Medical Systems, Inc., Minnetonka, Minnesota.

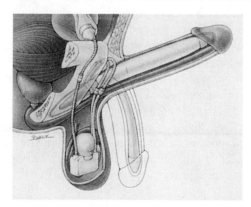

Figure 22–10 Implanted multicomponent inflatable penile prosthesis. Courtesy of American Medical Systems, Minnetonka, Minnesota. Illustration by Michael Schenk.

to dissatisfaction, either of the patient or his partner, is the perception that the attained erection is shorter or of inadequate girth than the patient or partner previously had experienced. Also contributing to patient dissatisfaction is the perception that the sensation of orgasm may be altered, and possibly significantly prolonged, after penile prosthesis placement. Approximately 25% of patients may complain of altered orgasm and ejaculation and up to 10% of patients may feel their prosthetic erection is of inadequate rigidity to enjoy intercourse (Lewis, 1995).

Technical considerations may account for dissatisfaction among some patients. Because proper function of the device depends on proper filling and emptying of the reservoir and corporal cylinders, encapsulation of the device components can result in inferior performance. As the body reacts to the foreign bodies, scars may form. As a scar matures, contraction of the scar capsule may entrap the components, preventing expansion of either of the cylinders, which results in impaired erection, or preventing expansion of the reservoir, which impedes detumescence.

Another set of problems results from failure of the device components themselves. The corporal cylinders, generally composed of a silicone-based material, may become attenuated in certain areas. As the wall of the cylinders weakens, aneurysmal dilatation can result in penile deformity, curvature, and angulation. Progression of localized weakness within the cylinder wall will eventually result in extravasation of the expansion fluid and total device failure. Another source of device failure is extravasation of the expansion fluid from the connection tubing. With continued refinement, the connection tubing has been continually reinforced, especially at stress points, to combat this problem. The insertion point of the tubing into the cylinders is commonly reinforced to avoid kinking and ensure free flow of the expansion tubing. Initially, connection tubing had been made with internal connectors secured with nonabsorbable suture material. Refinements of these connectors has resulted in the development of quick-connect devices of synthetic material, which not only speed the implantation procedure, but minimize stress imposed on the tubing and theoretically reduce the incidence of connection disruption. The pumps themselves are vitally important to proper device function. These pumps depend on an internal series of valves that maintain pressure and allow drainage at appropriate times. With continued development, the pump systems have been improved with respect to reliability.

Considering the potential shortcomings, refinement of the many types of devices available has contributed to a constantly improving profile of device durability. Although previous reports documented a disappointing rate of device failure, currently available inflatable penile prostheses can be expected to have a mechanical failure rate approximating 5% (Lewis, 1995).

Infection

As a surgically implanted foreign body, the patient contemplating penile prosthesis placement must accept the risk that implantation of the device could result in infection. At the time of surgery, the perineal and genital region receive a thorough cleansing with antimicrobial scrub for at least 10 minutes. The surgical field is then prepared with the liberal application of a topical antimicrobial skin cleanser, such as chlorhexidine gluconate, or a local anti-infective, such as povidone-iodine. Immediately before surgery, systemic parenteral antimicrobial agents are administered, such as a cephalosporin, vancomycin, and an aminoglycoside, to minimize the risk of infection. The device itself is often soaked in an antimicrobial solution, and the corporal bodies are liberally irrigated with an antimicrobial agent before device insertion. Systemic antimicrobials are commonly administered postoperatively to ensure that all steps have been taken to avoid infection resulting from device implantation.

Despite these extensive steps in fighting against infection, the infection rate of an implantable penile prosthesis has historically ranged from 0.6% to 8.9% (Carson & Robertson, 1988). In cases in which a device must be replaced, the rate of infection resulting from implantation of the new device tends toward the upper aspect of this range (Quesada & Light, 1993). In patients with spinal cord injury, the rate of infection resulting from prosthesis implantation is much higher. Rossier and Fam (1984) experienced a 16.5% infection rate of prostheses implanted into their spinal cord–injured patients.

Most commonly, the presentation of infection resulting from device implantation occurs within the first several months after surgical placement. The literature, however, has documented that a prosthetic device may become contaminated long after device implantation with episodes of transient bacteremia (Carson & Robertson, 1988). Therefore, it is currently recommended that patients with a prosthetic implant be treated with antimicrobial prophylaxis before instrumentation that could cause bacteremia, including dental procedures. In cases in which device infection occurs, it is often necessary to remove the entire device to effect eradication of the infection. Although removal may result in corporal fibrosis and scarring, salvage surgery may result in an 80% success rate with the placement of a new device (Lewis & McLaren, 1987).

Special Considerations in Patients with Neurologic Disease

The implantation of a prosthetic device in patients with neurologic disease should not be undertaken without serious consideration. Patients with chronic neurogenic vesical dysfunction are often subject to the development of recurrent urinary tract infections. The proximity of such an infection places the device at risk. Implantable prosthetic devices of any type are susceptible to becoming colonized and infected with microorganisms. Once this occurs, device removal may be required to effect resolution of the infection. In patients who are predisposed to developing infections, especially an infection in proximity to the implanted device, the risk of infection resulting from prosthesis implantation is significant (Kaufman, Lindner, & Raz, 1982). Therefore, it is essential to address lower urinary tract function and institute effective therapy before prosthesis placement. In patients who are continually troubled with recurrent urinary tract infection despite adequate treatment of lower urinary tract dysfunction, surgical placement of a prosthetic device may be contraindicated.

A separate consideration for patients with neurologic impairment is the potential for tissue erosion by the prosthetic device. The foreign body of the prosthesis cylinders or pump may induce a pressure necrosis of overlying tissues. This development is especially common in patients with impaired sensation, because undue pressure or trauma to the genital structures, accentuated by the relatively unyielding foreign body, will often not be appreciated (Rossier & Fam, 1984). Such trauma to the genitals need not be excessive to provide tissue injury of significant magnitude to induce prosthetic erosion. The pressure of tight-fitting clothing, bodily position, or another foreign body, such as an indwelling catheter, may be adequate—when applied chronically—to result in significant complications. Although penile prostheses have been successfully implanted in patients with significant neurologic impairment, the clinician must consider that device to be at high risk of requiring removal, unless the patient is extremely cautious and responsible with the care and treatment of the device. In a study by Kabalin and Kessler (1988), 25% of the of penile prostheses implanted into spinal cord–injured men required explantation because of either infection or erosion of the device.

In the past, the rigid and semirigid devices were considered to be more durable. Previous noninflatable devices required revision for device failure less often than inflatable penile prostheses because they do not depend on moving parts, pumps, or fluid, which can extravasate and incapacitate the device. In contrast, the risk of noninflatable devices may be greater than that of inflatable devices, because the pressure on the corporal structures is constant. Although the noninflatable device itself may be more durable, in patients with impaired sensation, the risk of device loss may be greater in that this constant pressure may increase the risk of pressure necrosis and spontaneous extrusion. Currently, the modern, refined inflatable prostheses appear to have more acceptable durability and may be preferred. This preference may be accentuated by considering that, in the nonerect state, the risk of pressure-induced tissue erosion is somewhat lessened.

CONCLUSION

The mechanism of sexual function is well understood by clinicians familiar with chronic disability and neurologic disease. Those afflicted with disability should be evaluated, and the options for restoration of sexual function should be discussed. The patient may then feel free to select the method of management that best suits his lifestyle and personal preferences. In the era of newer and more effective treatment modalities, the rehabilitation of sexual function is attainable in the vast majority of affected individuals. The restoration of sexual function should become an integrated component of an impaired individual's total rehabilitation program.

REFERENCES

Abber, J.C., & Lue, T.F. (1987). Evaluation of impotence. *Problems in Urology, 1,* 476–486.

Aitken, J.T., Causey, G., Joseph, J., & Young, J.Z. (1978). *Manual of human anatomy.* London: Churchill Livingstone.

Alexander, C.J. (1991). Psychological assessment and treatment of sexual dysfunctions after spinal cord injury. *Journal of the American Paraplegia Society, 14,* 127–131.

Benard, F., & Lue, T.F. (1990). The roles of urologist and patient in autoinjection therapy for erectile dysfunction. *Contemporary Urology, 2,* 21–26.

Boolell, M., Gepi-Attee, S., Gingell, C., & Allen, M. (1996). UK-92,480: A new oral treatment for erectile dysfunction. A double-blind, placebo-controlled crossover study demonstrating dose response with RigiScan and efficacy with outpatient diary. *Journal of Urology, 155,* 495A.

Bors, E., & Comarr, A.E. (1960). Neurological disturbances of sexual function with specific reference to 529 patients with spinal cord injury. *Urology Survey, 10,* 191–196.

Brock, G., & Lue, T.F. (1992). Impotence: A patient's goal-directed approach. *Monographs in Urology, 3,* 99–110.

Cavallini, G. (1991). Minoxidil versus nitroglycerin: A prospective double-blind controlled trial in transcutaneous erection facilitation for organic impotence. *Journal of Urology, 146,* 50–53.

Carson, C.C. (1989). Infections in genitourinary prosthesis. *Urology Clinics of North America, 16,* 139–147.

Carson, C.C., & Robertson, C.N. (1988). Late hematogenous infection of penile prosthesis. *Journal of Urology, 139,* 50–52.

Chancellor, M.B., Rivas, D.A., Panzer, D.E., Freedman, M.K., & Staas, W.E. (1994). Prospective comparison of topical minoxidil to vacuum constriction device and intracorporal papaverine injection in the treatment of erectile dysfunction due to spinal cord injury. *Urology, 43,* 365–369.

Chapelle, P.A., Durand, J., & Lacert, P. (1980). Penile erection following complete spinal cord injury in man. *British Journal of Urology, 52,* 216–217.

Claes, H., & Baert, L. (1989). Transcutaneous nitroglycerin therapy in the treatment of impotence. *Urologia Internationalis, 44,* 309–312.

Clissold, S.P., & Heel, R.C. (1987). Topical minoxidil: A preliminary view of its pharmacodynamic properties and therapeutic efficacy in alopecia areata and alopecia androgenetica. *Drugs, 33,* 107–109.

Comarr, A.E. (1970). Sexual function among patients with spinal cord injury. *Urologia Internationalis, 25,* 134–168.

Comarr, A.E. (1971). Sexual concepts in traumatic cord and cauda equina lesions. *Journal of Urology, 106,* 375–380.

Crespo, E.L., Bove, D., & Farrell, C. (1987). Microvascular surgery technique and follow-up. *Vascular Surgery, 21,* 277–281.

de Groat, W.C., & Booth, A.M. (1984). Autonomic systems to the urinary bladder and sexual organs. In P.J. Dyck, P.K. Thomas, E.H. Lambert, & R. Bunge (Eds.), *Peripheral neuropathy* (pp. 285–299). Philadelphia: W.B. Saunders.

de Tejada, I.S., Goldstein, I., & Krane, K.J. (1988). Local control of penile erection: Nerves, smooth muscle, and endothelium. *Urology Clinics of North America, 15,* 9–22.

Eardley, I., Morgan, R.J., Dinsmore, W.W., Pearson, J., Wulff, M.B., & Boolell, M. (1996). UK-92,480: A new oral therapy for erectile dysfunction. A double-blind, placebo controlled trial with treatment taken as required. *Journal of Urology, 155,* 495A.

Furlow, W.L., & Fisher, J. (1988). Deep dorsal vein arterialization: Clinical experience with a new technique for penile revascularization. *Journal of Urology, 139,* 298A.

Gingell, C.J.C., Jardin, A., Olsson, A.M., Dinsmore, W.W., Osterloh, I.A., Kirkpatrick, J., Cuddigan, M., & the Multicenter Study Group. (1996). UK-92,480: A new oral treatment for erectile dysfunction. A double-blind, placebo-controlled, once daily dosage response study. *Journal of Urology, 155,* 495A.

Goldstein, I. (1986). Arterial revascularization procedures. *Seminars in Urology, 4,* 252–257.

Henderson, V.E., & Roepke, M.H. (1933). On the mechanism of erection. *American Journal of Physiology, 106,* 441–443.

Kabalin, J.N., & Kessler, R. (1988). Infectious complications of penile prosthesis surgery. *Journal of Urology, 139,* 953–955.

Kaufman, J.J., Lindner, A., & Raz, S. (1982). Complications of penile prosthesis surgery for impotence. *Journal of Urology, 128,* 1192–1193.

Lakin, M.M., Montague, D.R., Vanderbrug, M.S., Tesar, L., & Schover, L.R. (1990). Intracavernous injection therapy: Analysis of results and complications. *Journal of Urology, 143,* 1138–1141.

Leblanc, N., Wilde, D.W., Keef, K.D., & Hume, J.R. (1989). Electro-physiological mechanisms of minoxidil sulfate-induced vasodilation of rabbit portal vein. *Circulation Research, 65,* 1102–1105.

Lewis, R.W. (1995). Long-term results of penile prosthetic implants. *Urology Clinics of North America, 22,* 847–855.

Lewis, R.W., & McLaren, R. (1987). Reoperation for penile prosthesis implantation. *Problems in Urology, 7,* 381–401.

Linet, O.I., & Ogrinc, F.G. (1996). Efficacy and safety of intracavernosal alprostadil in men with erectile dysfunction. *New England Journal of Medicine, 334,* 873–877.

Linsenmeyer, T.A. (1991). Evaluation and treatment of erectile dysfunction following spinal cord injury: A review. *Journal of the American Paraplegia Society, 14,* 43–51.

Lue, T.F., & Tanagho, E.A. (1987). Physiology of erection and pharmacological management of impotence. *Journal of Urology, 137,* 829–836.

Maclean, P.D., & Ploog, D.W. (1962). Cerebral representation of penile erection. *Journal of Neurophysiology, 25,* 29–31.

Masters, W.H., & Johnson, V.E. (1966). *Human sexual response.* Boston: Little, Brown.

McDougal, W.S., & Jeffery R.F. (1983). Microscopic penile revascularization. *Journal of Urology, 129,* 517–521.

Meyhoff, H.H., Rosenkilde, P., & Bodker, A. (1992). Non-invasive management of impotence with transcutaneous nitroglycerin. *British Journal of Urology, 69,* 88–90.

Michal, V., Kramer, R., & Pospidal, J. (1973). Direct arterial reanastomosis on corporal cavernosa penis in therapy of erectile impotence. *Rozhledy v Chirurgii, 52,* 587–589.

Michal, V., Kramer, R., & Pospidal, J. (1980). Vascular surgery in the treatment of impotence: Its present possibilities and prospects. *Czechoslovak Medicine, 3,* 213–215.

Nadig, P.W., Ware, J.C., & Blumoff, R. (1986). Noninvasive device produces an erection-like state. *Urology, 27,* 126–131.

National Institutes of Health. (1993). NIH consensus conference: Impotence. NIH Consensus Development Panel on Impotence. *Journal of the American Medical Association, 270,* 83–92.

Nellans, R.E., Ellis, L.R., & Kramer-Levien, D. (1987). Pharmacological erection: Diagnosis and treatment applications in 69 patients. *Journal of Urology, 138,* 52–54.

Padma-Nathan, H., Auerbach, S.M., Barada, J.H., Burnett, A.L., Costabile, R.A., Ferrigni, R.G., Gillenwater, J.Y., Hellstrom, W.J.G., Lue, T.F., Patterson, D.E., Romas, N.A., Shabsigh, R., Young, P.R., Gesungheit, N., Spivack, A.P., Place, V.A., & the VIVUS-MUSE Study Group. (1996). Multicenter, double-blind, placebo-controlled trial of transurethral alprostadil in men with chronic erectile dysfunction. *Journal of Urology, 155,* 496A.

Pescatori, E., Engleman, J.C., & Davis, G. (1993). Priapism of the clitoris: A case report following trazodone use. *Journal of Urology, 149,* 1557–1559.

Quesada, E.T., & Light, J.K. (1993). The AMS 700 inflatable penile prosthesis: Long-term experience with the controlled expansion cylinder. *Journal of Urology, 149,* 46–48.

Radomsky, S.B., Herschorn, S., & Rangaswamy, S. (1994) Topical minoxidil in the treatment of male erectile dysfunction. *Journal of Urology, 151,* 1225–1226.

Rivas, D.A., & Chancellor, M.B. (1994). Complications associated with the use of vacuum constriction devices for erectile dysfunction in the spinal cord injured population. *Journal of the American Paraplegia Society, 17,* 137–140.

Rivas, D.A., Chancellor, M.B., Huang, B., & Salzman, S.K. (1995). Erectile response to topical, intraurethral, and intracorporal pharmacotherapy in a rat model of spinal cord injury. *Journal of Spinal Cord Medicine, 18,* 245–250.

Root, W.S., & Bard, P. (1947). The mechanism of feline erection through sympathetic pathways with some remarks on sexual behavior after de-afferentation of the genitalia. *American Journal of Physiology, 150,* 80–84.

Rossier, A.B., & Fam, B.A. (1984). Indication and results of semirigid penile prostheses in spinal cord injury patients: Long-term followup. *Journal of Urology, 131,* 59–62.

Saenz de Tajada, I., Ware, J.C., Blanco, R., Pittard, J.T., Nadig, P.W., Azadzoi, K.M, Krane, R.J., & Goldstein, I. (1991). Pathophysiology of prolonged penile erection associated with trazodone use. *Journal of Urology, 145,* 60–64.

Sharaby, J.S., Benet, A.E., & Melman, A. (1995). Penile revascularization. *Urology Clinics of North America, 22,* 821–832.

Sipski, M.L. (1991a). The impact of spinal cord injury on female sexuality, menstruation, and pregnancy: A review of the literature. *Journal of the American Paraplegia Society, 14,* 122–126.

Sipski, M.L. (1991b). Spinal cord injury: What is the effect on sexual response? *Journal of the American Paraplegia Society, 14,* 40–43.

Siroky, M.B., & Krane, R.J. (1979). Physiology of male sexual dysfunction. In R.J. Krane & M.B. Siroky (Eds.), *Clinical neuro-urology* (pp. 45–62). Boston: Little, Brown.

Smith, E.M., & Bodner, D.R. (1993). Sexual dysfunction after spinal cord injury. *Urology Clinics of North America, 20,* 535–542.

Sonksen, J., & Biering-Sorensen, F. (1992). Transcutaneous nitroglycerin in the treatment of erectile dysfunction in spinal cord injured. *Paraplegia, 30,* 554–557.

Stone, A.R. (1987). The sexual needs of the injured spinal cord patient. *Problems in Urology, 3,* 529–536.

Strasberg, P.D., & Brady, S.M. (1988). Sexual functioning of persons with neurologic disorders. *Seminars in Neurology, 8,* 141–146.

Tanagho, E.A. (1992). Anatomy of the lower urinary tract. In P.C. Walsh, A.B. Retik, T.A. Stamey, & E.D. Vaughan (Eds.), *Campbell's urology* (pp. 40–69). Philadelphia: W.B. Saunders.

Turner, L.A., Althof, S.E., Levine S.B., Tobias, T.R., Kursh, E.D., Bodner, D., & Resnick, M. (1990). Treating erectile dysfunction with external vacuum devices: Impact upon sexual, psychological and marital functioning. *Journal of Urology, 144,* 79–82.

Virag, R., Zwang, G., & Demange, H. (1983). Vasculogenic impotence: A review of 92 cases with 54 surgical operations. *Vascular Surgery, 15,* 9–14.

Wagner, G. (1992). Aspects of genital physiology and pathology. *Seminars in Neurology, 12,* 87–95.

Waldhauser, M., & Schramek, P. (1988). Efficiency and side effects of prostaglandin E_1 in the treatment of erectile dysfunction. *Journal of Urology, 140,* 525–527.

Wein, A.J., Malloy, T.R., & Hanno, P.M. (1987). Intracavernosal injection programs—Their place in management of erectile dysfunction. *Problems in Urology, 1,* 496–506.

Weiss, H.D. (1972). The physiology of human penile erection. *Annals of Internal Medicine, 76,* 793–796.

Wolfson, B., Pickett, S., Scott, N.E., DeKernion, J.B., & Rajfer, J. (1993). Intraurethral prostaglandin E_2 cream: A possible alternative treatment for erectile dysfunction. *Urology, 42,* 73–75.

Wyndaele, J.J., de Meyer, J.M., de Sy, W.A., & Claessens, H. (1986). Intracavernous injection of vasoactive drugs: One alternative for treating impotence in spinal cord injury patients. *Paraplegia, 24,* 271–275.

Zorgniotti, A.W., & Lizza, A.F. (1993). "On demand" oral drugs for erection on impotent men. *Journal of Urology, 147,* 308A.

Zorgniotti, A.W., & Lizza, A.F. (1994). Effect of large doses of nitric oxide precursor L-arginine on erectile failure. *International Journal of Impotence Research, 6,* 33–34.

CHAPTER 23

Management of Other Male Sexual Dysfunctions

Stanley H. Ducharme and Kathleen M. Gill

For many years, male sexual dysfunction was a subject people tended to avoid and deny. The shame and embarrassment regarding disorders of a sexual nature prevented most men from seeking either a comprehensive assessment or treatment. Although some sexual education was available in most rehabilitation centers, treatment for the various dysfunctions was scarce and generally unavailable. Over the past two decades, however, this situation has begun to change rather drastically. Recent interest in the topic, media coverage, and sexual treatment options have dramatically changed. For example, frank discussions of topics such as impotence, homosexuality, condom use, acquired immune deficiency syndrome (AIDS), and premature ejaculation have become commonplace in the media. This openness of once taboo topics has encouraged individuals with sexual dysfunctions to communicate with their partners and health care professionals about these subjects. Men and their sexual partners are increasingly likely to make a medical or psychological appointment and to seek treatment for sexual difficulties that may have existed before the disability or have appeared as a result of the disability. Yet, because of a lack of medical knowledge regarding male sexual function, it may still be difficult for men with sexual dysfunctions to locate professionals with specific knowledge regarding treatment.

The occurrence of a sexual dysfunction is relatively common among men. More than 10 million men are estimated to have a sexual dysfunction and at least 52% of men older than age 40 years have a specific sexual dysfunction, according to a Massachusetts male aging study (Feldman, Goldstein, & Hatzichristou, 1994). Among men with disabilities, this number is considerably higher. Some authors have suggested that virtually all men with disabilities such as spinal cord injury, multiple sclerosis, and traumatic head injury are affected in the sexual realm by the onset of a disability (Ducharme & Gill, 1995). Disabilities, such as diabetes, may initially not cause disturbances but ultimately create significant sexual problems as the result of progressive physical changes that can impair erections or ejaculations. Other disabilities, such as amputations, cancer, hip replacements, cerebral palsy, and chronic pain can create sexual difficulties by affecting body image, self-esteem, and other psychological functions. Ultimately, the psychological disturbances can manifest themselves in alterations in physical function as well.

The types of male sexual dysfunctions are decreased libido, ejaculatory disturbances, and erectile dysfunctions. Other less common male sexual dysfunctions include priapism and Peyronie's disease. Many male sexual dysfunctions result from psychological issues such as relational problems, depression, anxiety, low self-esteem, or stress. Physical factors such as the effects of medications on the body, testosterone levels, neurologic disturbances, and circulatory problems can also significantly affect male sexual function. Although erectile difficulties may be the most common of the male sexual dysfunctions, this particular problem is discussed in detail in Chapter 22. Instead, this chapter discusses other male sexual dysfunctions that may be present in men with a physical disability. From the onset, it is important to point out that there is a paucity of literature on male sexual dysfunctions, other than erectile dysfunctions, for men with a disability. Typically, these male dysfunctions tend to go undiagnosed and untreated among these men.

PREMATURE EJACULATION

Definition

From the perspective of research, premature ejaculation (PE), what defines it, what causes it, and why treatment works remains controversial. A recent review article (Rosen & Leiblum, 1995) recognized premature ejaculation among the most frequent male sexual dysfunctions. Although incidence and success rates have declined since the introduction of Masters and Johnson's treatments in the 1970s, clinical experience with PE has demonstrated that it can be confidently resolved with psychological interventions that integrate cognitive–behavioral, systems, and dynamic approaches (McCarthy, 1989; Zilbergeld, 1992). In addition, pharmacotherapy is being investigated as an adjunct to traditional behavioral therapy.

For men with disabilities, problems with PE tend to predate the onset of the disability. Rarely are the problems seen as a consequence of the disability itself, except when certain organic factors such as prostate or urinary bladder infections are involved. Such factors are detectable by sperm culture and may be treated with appropriate antibiotics or antiinflammatory drugs. Because these organic disorders can contribute to ejaculatory dysfunctions, they should be explored in the initial diagnostic workup (Tordjman, 1993). More often, however, ejaculation for men with disabilities will be absent or retrograde into the bladder, as is seen in men in whom nerve conduction is impaired by diabetes, trauma, demyelination, or other circumstances.

The assessment of PE is complicated by a lack of a precise definition. Also called "early" or "rapid" ejaculation, PE has been defined as latency-to-ejaculation that is less than the norm, lack of ejaculatory control, and inability to postpone ejaculation during pelvic thrusting. These definitions contain tacit assumptions that are neither necessary nor useful: that it is the man's responsibility to last long enough to please the partner or his responsibility to bring the partner to orgasm through intercourse. Many women are not orgasmic from intercourse alone, and the authors' clinical work demonstrates that increasing latency-to-ejaculation does not increase the rate of women who become orgasmic from intercourse. Contemporary models of successful sexual interaction view satisfaction as the couple's joint responsibility. Thus, a practical definition of PE is a lack of satisfaction with the latency or circumstances of ejaculation. Given this more broad definition, men with disabilities rarely have decreased latencies that are dissatisfying to either partner. Again, both partners must assume responsibility for mutual pleasuring through sharing, communication, and exploration of mutual sexual needs and desires.

Men may present themselves with problems of ejaculating before, or immediately on, entering the vagina, or as soon as any thrusting occurs. In addition to causing the man distress because of his lack of ejaculatory control, this rapid ejaculation is often not as satisfying as an ejaculation that accompanies a longer period of sexual arousal. Ejaculation that occurs without erection is also typically experienced as frustrating and unpleasurable. For men with disabilities, therefore, a positive experience with ejaculation is often paired with the male's ability to achieve and maintain a satisfying erection. If the quality of his erection is poor, a man may tend to find the ejaculation is dissatisfactory, both before and after onset of disability.

The partner's satisfaction may also be affected either because of the limited duration or type of stimulation provided to her. Men with or without disabilities who have problems with PE may tend to avoid intimacy for fear of failure and may report some decrease in libido. As a result, it is not uncommon for the partner to attribute some form of rejection, disinterest, withdrawal, anger, or lack of attractiveness to the PE. The partner may inadvertently or purposely convey pressure to the male, which will tend to maintain and strengthen the symptom. High anxiety combined with high levels of arousal facilitates rapid ejaculation. Despite the popular notion that ideal sexual activity should be prolonged, average latencies-to-ejaculation are within minutes of premature latencies. A shift in attitude from sole reliance on intercourse for satisfaction is an important component of the standard behavioral treatment for PE. Because intercourse may be more difficult—because of erectile difficulties—for men with disabilities, this shift may occur more easily in the disabled male population, who may rely more on manual and oral stimulation if they are sexually active.

Thus far, the descriptions have focused on heterosexual couples; problems with PE are widely represented among homosexual couples as well, and the principles of treatment apply to patients who ejaculate rapidly with oral, manual, or anal stimulation by the male partner. These couples may find it more difficult, however, to receive adequate treatment because of the stigma of being homosexual. Many psychotherapists or physicians may feel uncomfortable providing treatment when moral or ethical considerations may be involved. Often, this prejudice is unconscious and may be denied by the helping professional but shown in more passive–aggressive remarks. For couples in which one partner has a disability, there is a double stigmatization that often results in inadequate sexual education during rehabilitation, lack of privacy for the couple, and poor treatment options (Ducharme & Gill, 1995).

Another assumption that has not been proven true is that there is a higher incidence of PE among men who have sustained a cerebral insult such as traumatic head injury or cerebrovascular accident. Presumably, these men are seen as being hypersexual. This theory is in line with more traditional psychoanalytic theories that blame ejaculatory control on an exacerbated sex drive and fail to recognize that brain injury often results in hyposexuality rather than hypersexuality. What may be described as hypersexuality in the men is frequently more a function of disinhibition and other cognitive disturbances rather than increases in libido.

Other issues in defining PE deal with the circumstances under which it occurs. Clinicians distinguish between global versus situational occurrences, that is, whether the PE occurs on all occurrences of masturbation, partner stimulation, and intercourse, or only with intercourse; whether PE occurs with one partner but not others; or whether PE occurs after a period of normal ejaculatory control (called secondary PE), in contrast to a lifelong primary PE. There are also individual differences in ejaculatory latencies that appear to be constitutional; in addition, a wide variety of psychological factors and systems issues in the relationship can interfere with ejaculation latency and increased enjoyment (Spark, 1991). Psychological issues, especially anxiety, are often present early after disability and can further interfere with the couple's sexual function. Even if ejaculation has been spared after the disability, anxiety can mask the perceptions that should alert the man to the imminence of ejaculation. The man may confuse the signals of imminent ejaculation with the signals of ejaculation itself. This situation can be further complicated if there are sensory changes in the genital area that cause additional confusion, anxiety, and apprehension.

Treatment

The basic behavioral treatment for PE capitalizes on the observation that increasing the frequency of sexual contact naturally increases latency-to-ejaculation. In addition, frequent sexual contact provides a gradual increase in the intensity of the stimulation, with the man delaying ejaculation by pausing or squeezing the tip or base of the penis. Other approaches may include decreasing emphasis on penetration and intercourse. In these cases, the couple is requested to use oral and manual techniques to increase the man's latency-to-ejaculation. Such treatments are appropriate for both men with disabilities as well as able-bodied men. The therapy includes the partner whenever possible because the context of the relationship in which the behavioral practice occurs is vitally important to therapy outcome. If relational difficulties or anxiety after disability is involved, a cooperative team approach is even more critical. The therapy specifically directs the couple to work as a team in identifying what is emotionally and physically satisfying to each partner. Often, the degree of satisfaction may have changed after the disability. This cooperative atmosphere facilitates compliance with experiential homework exercises designed to increase both latency and pleasure. The atmosphere, as well as specific training in relaxation, reduces anxiety and allows the male to focus on sensation rather than performance. Specific cognitive–behavioral interventions teach the man to challenge self-defeating patterns of thinking that also detract from the sensual experience and contribute to the dysfunction. Furthermore, a program of generalization and maintenance is recommended to help continue improved sexual function after termination of treatment. This program may include a request to continue specific behavioral techniques such as the squeeze exercise to equip the couple to restart training at any time, should the ejaculatory dysfunction recur (LoPiccolo, 1992).

Typically, at some point in the treatment plan, a couple presenting with problems with PE can expect to be asked to complete homework assignments designed to identify their sexual needs and to communicate those needs to each other. Such communication is often more difficult than initially perceived, especially if one partner has a disability, because issues of rejection and attractiveness will be critical to the discussion. If there have been physical or health-related changes, often physical needs have been altered and communication may be more critical than ever. However, if these patterns of communication were re-established during rehabilitation, sensitive issues such as ejaculatory control perhaps may be discussed without pressure, guilt, or anger.

The man with PE completes solo exercises consisting of manual self-stimulation to help him identify the point in his sexual arousal when ejaculation is inevitable. He then experiments over time with the pause or squeeze techniques to increase or decrease his level of arousal, eventually learning to delay ejaculation for increasingly longer periods. The solo exercises, which constitute an important part of the treatment program, may have to be altered or eliminated if functional limitations dictate. The partner may also be assigned solo exercises to treat female sexual dysfunction that may coexist, or for sexual enhancement. The clinician likely will encourage a positive view of masturbation as a method of sexual self-awareness as well as a legitimate sexual choice, especially with a man with a recent disability who has little knowledge about how his body functions postdisability.

The couple may then engage in pleasuring assignments in which genital stimulation is specifically off limits. These opportunities serve to bond the couple in a mutual exploration of their needs for affection and sensual stimulation. The next step typically involves manual stimulation by the partner using some form of water-soluble lubrication. As before, the emphasis is on mutual pleasure, and the man shows his partner how to facilitate his latency by pausing or squeezing at various intervals as his enhanced awareness determines. If ejaculation occurs accidentally, it is to be enjoyed, and the couple directed to learn from all the experiences in their sexual growth process.

As the assignments continue, intercourse remains banned. Again, however, intercourse may be impossible on a more permanent basis without erectile aids for many men with disabilities. During this phase, the couple may provide orgasms for each other with manual or oral stimulation as they continue to experiment with longer latencies-to-ejaculation. When they begin to approach intercourse, the female partner agrees to provide a "quiet vagina" for her partner to experience vaginal containment. The clinician may modify positioning for this phase of the therapy to make it easier for the couple to come together without thrusting—generally in the female superior position. Active intravaginal containment follows, with the male partner giving feedback on when to move. Obviously, the consistent emphasis on maintaining a cooperative relationship is critical at this stage. Gradually, the couple resumes normal intercourse, if possible, gaining confidence and spontaneity as they increase their sexual repertoire.

When the treatment is provided for men without partners, the solo exercises are presented in the context of increasing the individual's level of comfort with his own sexuality. Because male sensual pleasure is often not encouraged early in life, his comfort level may be limited. If he has a disability, it will be critically important to explore his sensual and sexual repertoire as the first step in becoming sexually active again. The man learns ejaculatory control by way of masturbation and imagery; modifies defeating self-statements; and makes decisions about choosing appropriate partners who will work with him in integrating sexuality into the relationship. Single men with this dysfunction may be apprehensive when facing sexual contact with a new partner, especially if there have been physical changes that have affected body image and self-esteem. Zilbergeld's (1992) self-help manual for men provides support in the words of other men who have confronted problems with PE. The manual also suggest ways in which men can talk to potential sexual partners about issues of PE. Unfortunately, however, the manual deals only with men without disabilities, and such self-help manuals are not available specifically for men who are dealing with problems of disability as well as with PE.

Research (Rosen & Leiblum, 1995) has demonstrated favorable outcomes in using pharmacologic interventions in cases of severe PE or in cases that are resistant to traditional therapy. For example, after several attempts at treatment, a couple may find themselves increasingly frustrated with one another and unable to participate in the appropriate exercises together. Necessary communication, critical to successful treatment, may be difficult for the couple to achieve. At these times, medication such as fluoxetine seems to be the treatment of choice. Serotonergic antidepressants such as fluoxetine and clomipramine seem to improve ejaculatory latency by decreasing alpha-adrenergic tone or increasing serotonin levels in the blood. These drug therapies are not free of side effects, the most problematic side effect being potential decreased desire. In other cases, intracavernous injections of alprostadil are used to maintain erections after ejaculation so that couples can experience successful intercourse that is free from pressure and tension. Often, pharmacologic approaches, whether oral or injections, are integrated with cognitive–behavioral work to maximize the potential for success. An integrated medical and psychological approach can best address both the physiologic aspects and the relationship components, which both must be considered in a successful treatment program.

INHIBITED EJACULATION

Definition

Inhibited ejaculation (IE), which has also been called retarded or delayed ejaculation, or male anorgasmia (which refers to the absence of sensation that accompanies ejaculation), has been reported in the research to be rare (LoPiccolo, 1992). Clinical observation, however, has been that increasing numbers of patients with IE are being seen in urologic and sexual dysfunction clinics, especially in men with disabilities. There is little research on issues of IE for men with disabilities, and most of the work appears to have been completed in relationship to fertility issues. For the most part, clinicians have instructed patients to enhance their pleasure during sexual activity by using past sexual memories, fantasies, visual/auditory stimulation, and open communication during sexual activity. These techniques may have some ability to improve physiologic orgasm but primarily seem to contribute to what Money (1960) has referred to as a "phantom orgasm." The actual percentage of ejaculation in men with spinal cord injury is extremely low and virtually nonexistent in men with complete upper motor neuron lesions. Men with complete lower motor neuron lesions also tend not to ejaculate but occasionally perceive pleasurable sensations lower in the abdomen, pelvis, or thighs. With many other disabilities such as cerebral palsy, head injury, or various neurologic conditions, ejaculation tends to be intact physiologically, although the psychological problems can mirror the issues of the able-bodied man. The following are some of the psychological pressures that can interfere with sexual enjoyment:

- pressure to please partner
- pressure to please self
- pressure to initiate sex or relationships
- pressure to be a considerate and experienced lover
- pressure to bring partner to orgasm
- pressure to bring self to orgasm simultaneously with partner
- pressure to always be in the mood and ready for sex
- pressure to achieve and maintain erection (Silverstein, 1986)

Treatment

Few treatment manuals have referred to the problem of IE in detail, and historically the treatment approach was to apply massive stimulation, such as electroejaculation, with the notion that such stimulation would increase arousal to the point of ejaculation. This approach is certainly useful in improving fertility rates in men with disabilities (e.g., spinal cord injury and multiple sclerosis) in whom ejaculation may be impaired, but it does little to deal with the psychological issues that may accompany the dysfunction. Rather, the traditional approach of increased stimulation may inadvertently increase pressure and anxiety related to performance. For the man with a disability, there is often such a drive to ejaculate that this overriding concern can be self-defeating and add to the existing physiologic condition.

Despite the concerns regarding massive stimulation to induce ejaculation, this technique has gained widespread acceptance, especially in the United States, where it has received considerable attention in the disabled community. Its use, however, has been generally limited to cases in which improved fertility is desired. This technique involves chemical, vibratory, or electrical stimulation of the intact neurologic center below the spinal injury; the stimulation is usually done in the hospital or doctor's office. This technique tends to be most successful when the spinal segments between T-10 and T-12 have been left intact. Autonomic dysreflexia is a serious possible side effect of this procedure, so medical supervision is typically advised. During recent years, the use of chemical stimulation has been greatly reduced because of complications associated with autonomic dysreflexia (Nehra, Werner, Bastuba, Title, & Oates, 1996).

At home, many men with spinal cord injury attempt to improve ejaculation by means of vibratory stimulation of the glans penis. Success rates using this technique vary, but generally it has been reported that approximately 50% of men can expect to be successful with vibratory stimulation (Yalla, Vickers, & Sullivan, 1994). Although successful sperm retrieval with vibratory stimulation has greatly improved in recent years, there is little research on how such techniques improve sexual function and enhance ejaculation or orgasm on a regular basis. In the authors' clinical experience, many men have reported feeling extremely frustrated with their inability to ejaculate after disability and they often feel as if they are on the verge of ejaculation during peak moments of arousal. Often, they feel a sense of desperation in searching for techniques they can use successfully. In attempts to enhance their pleasure, many couples use vibrators on a regular basis while enhancing sensory levels through fantasy and stimulating thoughts and conversations. Many couples also make love during the day or leave lights on during sexual activity to improve sensory input. They also can use olfactory, taste, and auditory senses to their maximum advantage as well. Areas in which sacral sparing has occurred may also be exploited to increase stimulation, arousal, and sensual pleasure. Although limited written information aimed at enhancing sensation and ultimately ejaculation is available, little work has been done on sex therapy techniques for men with disabilities who present with IE.

Apfelbaum (1989) has suggested that IE is a disorder of both desire and arousal. He has provided case studies that demonstrate a more psychological approach in which performance anxiety is decreased and desire is enhanced. For the man with a disability, even if ejaculation is left intact, the issues of anxiety and decreased arousal may be present, as they are in the able-bodied population. At one time, it was not uncommon for sexual surrogates to be used in the treatment of this disorder; however, medical, legal, and ethical considerations have virtually eliminated surrogate therapy in the United States. Among the disabled population, surrogate therapy also played an important role in improving social skills and communication, and addressing issues of body image, but has been discontinued. In other countries, such as Israel, surrogate therapy, especially for men with disabilities, continues to be a sanctioned method of treating men with IE as well as other dysfunctions such as erectile dysfunction or desire disorders.

Among both men with and without disabilities, delayed or absent ejaculation can be the result of secondary illness, injury, or a surgical procedure, for example, prostatectomy, cancer, pelvic injury, or other neurologic conditions. IE can also be a side effect of medication, particularly antiadrenergic or neuroleptic medications that are often used in conjunction with disability. Again, in all cases of male sexual dysfunction, it is imperative that a physician such as a psychiatrist, urologist, endocrinologist, or physiatrist be a part of the overall assessment process. The best treatment method is clearly a multidisciplinary model in which the couple's total physical and emotional needs are addressed.

Psychogenic factors such as fear of pregnancy, fear of rejection by a partner, self-induced performance pressure, anxiety, anger, and relationship power struggles can also result in global anorgasmia in which masturbation, partner stimulation, or intercourse do not result in ejaculation and orgasm. The more common presentation is a delay or absence of ejaculation with intercourse, while ejaculation during masturbation is maintained. These factors may extend to all partners or be confined to a particular partner. The delay may be as much as several hours in duration or may be relatively permanent, as in the case of certain disabilities. In attempts to reduce performance anxiety for men with disabilities, it is often advised that they explore and enjoy self-stimulation as early in the recovery phase as their interest allows.

Although the stereotypic view of sexual pleasure may portray IE as a positive for both partners, the reality is that it satisfies neither the man nor his partner. Typical partner complaints include feelings of powerlessness and frustration, loss of attractiveness, rejection, and feelings of emotional disconnection. These feelings, which may be extremely intense, are typically present regardless of the partner's ability to reach orgasm or to be multiorgasmic. The patient with IE will likely not be aroused much by trying too hard to please the partner or will be distracted from arousal by her touch. On a cognitive basis, there may be self-defeating statements that are incompatible with receiving pleasure. These negative processes may lead to feelings of resentment, anger, pressure, or the sense of being used. In cases of disability, both intense emotional issues as well as negative cognitive statements can seriously impact the couple's sexual enjoyment. If couples are unable to communicate their feelings in general and about the physical changes that have occurred, they will find a positive sexual adjustment difficult to achieve. For this reason, communication, emotional intimacy, and closeness are important to maintain throughout hospitalization and rehabilitation. Many couples find it difficult to maintain communication and intimacy because they feel a need to protect each other or they may not want to share their concerns about becoming a burden to the partner. Therapy with couples can often be helpful in this regard, but is seldom used during the rehabilitation process because rehabilitation stays have become shorter as a result of managed care and other relevant reimbursement issues. Emotional and sexual adjustment tends to be a slow process that extends for many years.

Often, ejaculatory dysfunctions are further complicated by misleading signals that are difficult for the couple to interpret. Apfelbaum (1989) has described the physical manifestation of erection as "automatic" in cases of IE, that is, not accompanied by evidence of arousal. The excitement phase of the sexual response is not coordinated with feelings of desire and arousal. The presence of erection leads to the mistaken expectation on the part of each partner that the male should be aroused and perhaps ready for ejaculation. For men with disabilities who may be unable to ejaculate, partners may feel inadequate, unattractive, or undesirable. This formulation implies that treatment must emphasize learning to have enjoyable erections with the partner before proceeding to intercourse.

Instead of pressuring the man to want to ejaculate, the structure of the therapy is to encourage him to refuse any sexual behavior associated with drudgery or an exclusive focus on the partner's pleasure. He is instructed to make his complaints, frustrations, and dissatisfactions known to his partner as a method of decreasing his "response anxiety." He is also assigned a series of steps similar to the treatment protocol for female orgasm disorder. The man and his partner identify and provide stimulation that he finds increasingly arousing, with a prohibition on trying to ejaculate in favor of focusing on sensation and on managing interfering feelings or thoughts. These steps can be especially helpful as a means of enhancing pleasure for the couple dealing with disability, even though the steps may not eventually lead to ejaculation as is the goal among able-bodied couples. This change in treatment philosophy has improved outcome, but, clearly, more research on IE and its treatment is needed. It is a major issue for the man with a disability, and, except for methods aimed at improved fertility, there is a paucity of research on IE. Perhaps, some of the media attention that has been focused on the male erection will ultimately be aimed at improving ejaculation.

INHIBITED SEXUAL DESIRE

Definition

Inhibited sexual desire (ISD) is a highly prevalent dysfunction, affecting possibly 15% of adult males and accounting for up to 50% of sex cases seen in clinical settings (Beck, 1995; Rosen & Leiblum, 1989). Also known as hypoactive sexual desire disorder, ISD is characterized by persistently few or absent sexual fantasies and desire for sexual activity, and does not result from a medical condition, substance abuse, or primary psychiatric disorder. It is not uncommon for individuals with desire disorders to present themselves at a sex therapy clinic with a variety of other sexual difficulties in addition to the primary problem of low desire. Couples may also present without a desire disorder but with desire discrepancy, in which the partner's levels of desire are at variance with one another. Attempts are under way to clarify the diagnosis and the concept of normal desire and to standardize treatment. Because the psychological contributions to ISD are numerous and complex, all treatment protocols must be individualized (Exhibit 23–1). In cases of psychiatric disturbances, the treatment is generally longer and outcomes less certain. Considerable research is still needed in this area of sexual dysfunction.

Exhibit 23–1 Psychological Factors Associated with ISD

Predisposing Factors

- Substance abuse
- Sexual, physical, or emotional abuse
- Psychosis
- Personality
- Religious issues
- Disturbed family relationships
- Overly restricted upbringing

Relationship Factors

- Performance anxiety
- Poor communication
- Sexual incompatibility
- Rejection (loss of partner)
- Dysfunction in partner
- Loss of attraction
- Fears of emotional closeness

Disability Factors

- Poor self-esteem
- Body image disturbances
- Prolonged depression
- Feelings of inadequacy
- Rejection by partner
- Dependency issues
- Changes in sex roles
- Feelings of vulnerability

The sudden onset of disability or the more chronic issues of malaise, pain, fatigue, or stress can contribute to decreased libido (Gilbert, 1996). Low desire after a traumatic disability is, for the most part, of limited duration. As adjustment proceeds, sexual desire often returns slowly and steadily. The level of depression after disability may be the single greatest factor in determining the level of desire for sexual activities. If depression is more severe, or if there are substantial relationship issues that emerge after the disability (or were present before the disability), the return of sexual desire may be more protracted and may require counseling or medications for it to resolve. Depression associated with disability is a complex medical problem that requires an in-depth evaluation and treatment plan. In other instances, the precipitating factors responsible for the loss of sexual desire may be less apparent. Additional effort may be required to unravel the chain of events responsible for the diminished libido. Changes in sexual desire may also be somewhat variable over time, depending on the emotional well-being of the person with the disability and his partner.

In addition to traumatic disability, many chronic illnesses and medications can result in ISD, either temporarily or permanently (Bullard, 1988; Kaplan, 1995). Neuroendocrine disorders, cancer, heart disease, renal failure, liver disease, chronic lung disease, drug or alcohol addiction, and multiple sclerosis are among the conditions that can have a physical effect on sexual desire. Also, numerous medications may inhibit desire, including antihypertensives (e.g., propranolol or methyldopa); neuroleptics and sedatives (e.g., diazepam or phenobarbital); mood active drugs (e.g., phenelzine or alprazolam); cancer chemotherapy; glaucoma medications; and anticonvulsives (Beck, 1995). Even serotonin reuptake inhibitors, which are used to treat depression—which itself reduces desire—can result in loss of desire as well as in other sexual dysfunctions.

Evaluation of patients with ISD includes a broad assessment of psychological and relationship factors. In defining the problem, it is important to distinguish whether the lower desire has been a long-term problem or occurs only in certain situations. It is also important to know if the desire problem predated the disability. Psychological and sexual learning history may identify other psychopathology such as anxiety, affective disorders, dependency, personality disorders, gender identity disorders, posttraumatic stress disorders, and paraphilias, which can contribute to the manifestation of ISD and do not necessarily disappear when a person sustains a traumatic disability. Relationship conflict is also commonly associated with lower sexual desire and is often the focus of treatment (Beck, 1995; LoPiccolo & Friedman, 1988). Such conflict may be especially relevant after a disability, when partners find communication difficult and are unsure how to proceed with sexual intimacy. Often, there is a fear of further injury associated with sexual activity. Chronic pain may be another factor in a reduced desire for intimate contact. Furthermore, the presence of medical equipment, such as ventilators or catheters, may contribute to a sense of vulnerability and frailty.

ISD also can be the result of a specific sexual dysfunction; once symptomatic, either partner can lose interest in pursuing sexual contact. For example, men with erectile dysfunction or an ejaculatory problem may be hesitant to engage in sexual activity for fear of failure and rejection. A lower frequency of sexual contact and decreased libido are common symptoms of these disorders. Treating the primary dysfunction in such cases can usually improve or resolve the ISD. In cases of disability, the presence of neurogenic erectile dysfunction may be a significant factor in ISD. In such cases, treatment of the erection problem may improve desire. It is important for the patient to realize that, after a disability, his sexuality has not been lost and that intimacy is possible if desired. If desire does not improve within several months of treatment of the erection problem, further evaluation will be needed to explore medication, the patient's relationships, and psychological factors.

ISD needs to be distinguished from *sexual aversion*, in which sexual contact is actively avoided because of extreme negative feelings about sex. Aversion to sex after disability may be related to a number of factors, including adjustment issues to the disability, pre-injury sexual trauma, or sexual or physical abuse after onset of injury. As with all sexual problems, the clinician must consider a history of sexual abuse or trauma as a causal factor and must direct treatment at the individual or relationship sequelae (Rosen & Leiblum, 1989). The clinician also should be especially attentive to possible abuse issues after injury because it is becoming increasingly clear in clinical practice that this is a major concern.

Treatment

Because ISD is a complicated phenomenon, it should not be surprising that authorities from all therapeutic orientations have recommended treatment strategies that combine cognitive, behavioral, psychodynamic, and systems approaches. Effective treatment must recognize the influence of family of origin and early learning experiences on the development of a person's assumptions and expectations about sex and about their own sexuality. The clinician must identify and address current circumstances that serve as barriers to sexual enjoyment. For example, lifestyle factors have been implicated in the increased incidence of ISD. Dual-career couples with young children are unlikely to find much time to develop "conditions for good sex," even if they enjoy job security in these changing times. A sexual partner who also serves in the role of personal care attendant may not feel a strong desire for intimate contact. Therapy success improves if couples can alter priorities so that they can devote time to their sexual relationship. Furthermore, couples need to carefully assess their roles within the relationship, especially if disability has altered traditional roles in the home. They also must resolve relationship dissatisfaction; couples can benefit from learning the skills of conflict resolution, intimate communication, and compromise. Both the patient and partner must confront and resolve the reluctant partner's feelings of guilt, aversion, and avoidance. The partner with a strong sexual drive needs to discontinue behavior that is coercive and perceived by the patient as pressure. A significant shift in the relationship dynamics can result from a change in attitudes and expectations about sex. If intercourse is impossible because of functional limitations, the couple must discuss this matter and explore alternatives. Each partner can choose whether, and how, to be sexual, given the changes that have occurred. If this level of communication is possible, pressure disappears and many other mutually satisfying—or at least mutually agreeable—options emerge.

A method of treatment that integrates these considerations has been described by LoPiccolo and Friedman (1988). Although primarily used with an able-bodied population, the treatment can be effective with a patient with a disability or chronic illness. The treatment program, which averages 15 to 25 sessions, has four components. One component, affective awareness, is designed to identify anxiety or other unrecognized feelings about which the patient with ISD is unaware. Often, the patient tends to deny but acts out these feelings. Techniques include using feeling questions, providing encouragement, provoking feelings and giving permission to express feelings, attending to bodily cues, teaching a body awareness exercise, using gestalt techniques, offering fantasy training, and using visualization and guided imagery.

Concurrent with affective awareness, the ideal treatment facilitates insight, a second component, as well. The patient is encouraged to learn and identify what is causing his lower desire so that he can promote changes. In many cases, the patient will need to talk about the disability itself and the body image changes that have occurred. The clinician helps the patient to take responsibility for his own behavior, and the partner learns to request sexual and affectionate attention without shaming. Techniques to improve insight include asking questions about family-of-origin messages about sex; generating hypotheses about why the patient might be anxious about sex; reflecting empathetically on feelings that validate the patient's experience and invite further exploration of barriers to sexual behavior; reframing or interpreting the patient's blocked thinking in a different light; interpreting or drawing together themes in what the patient says that reveal his deepest issues; and using paradoxical interventions in which the therapist prescribes the symptom itself to use the patient's tendency to oppose the treatment—to move him in the direction of adaptive change.

The third component is cognitive restructuring. The patient identifies self-statements that mediate emotional arousal and creates a rescript. An example might be as follows: "I'm not a real man if I don't want sex whenever my partner does." The rescript might be "I don't need to live up to some unrealistic criterion to be a real man." This practice of attitude change helps the patient cope with, rather than avoid, particular sexual situations. In cases in which a disability is present, this form of cognitive therapy can be effective in addressing feelings of poor self-worth, shame, body image disturbances, inadequacy, and concerns about dependency. Self-statements may have interfered with arousal and resulted in an avoidance of sexual activity.

Behavioral interventions of many types, the fourth component, can be used to build skills and decrease resistance to change. Interventions include sensate focus exercises (which essentially comprise a systematic desensitization paradigm that reduces anxiety about sexual contact); assertiveness training; communication training; negotiation skills training; behavioral rehearsal; role playing; stress reduction; bibliotherapy; sexual education; initiation/refusal training; consultation with clergy; fantasy breaks; viewing of films and reading of books of erotica; and practice of low-level affectionate behaviors.

Pharmacologic interventions thus far have not been found for men with ISD. In men with testosterone deficiency, androgen replacement therapy resolves the disorder, but if the man's testosterone is at a normal level, androgen therapy does not improve sexual function. Many urologists are also hesitant to provide testosterone treatment for fear of increasing prostate problems. Bupropion hydrochloride and trazodone have been tried with mixed results. Yohimbine does not resolve the desire disorder per se, although it may be helpful in stimulating erection and helping to override the desire-dampening side effects of serotonin reuptake inhibitors. However, yohimbine is generally not a viable consideration in cases of neurogenic erectile difficulties.

Many men with neurogenic impotence have reported positive changes in libido following experiences with improved erection using urologic interventions. Interventions may have included penile implants, vacuum devices, or penile injection therapy with alprostadil. For many of these men, seeing, experiencing, touching, and sharing a firm erection with a partner restores a sense of masculinity and desire for sexual contact (Ducharme & Gill, 1997).

A positive psychotherapy outcome for desire disorders depends on the degree of commitment to the relationship and to resolving the marital distress. It may also involve the couple's ability to resolve issues surrounding a disability. Factors that predict negative outcome include a lack of desire for the partner at any time in the relationship, secrets, history of chronic alcohol or drug abuse, religious orthodoxy, history of depression, and significant unresolved body image concerns. Clearly, ISD is complex, and the highest levels of expertise and creativity are needed to treat it effectively. When organic issues related to disability are involved, a multidisciplinary team is required to address both the emotional and medical issues simultaneously.

PEYRONIE'S DISEASE

Definition

Peyronie's disease is a male sexual dysfunction that is less commonly observed than the erectile, ejaculatory, or desire disorders. Peyronie's disease is characterized by lesion formation in the tunica of the corpora cavernosa. During erection, this lesion results in curvature and shortening of the penis. The incidence of Peyronie's disease is about 1% (Jordan, 1994). Although the disorder is more common in older men aged 45 to 60 years, it is also seen in young men as well. In the larger urology clinics, men as young as 18 or 19 years may present with Peyronie's disease as a result of trauma. Often, they present with erectile difficulties as well as Peyronie's disease.

There is some controversy about the specific causes of Peyronie's disease and the characteristics of the men who develop the disease. Evidence seems to indicate that the inciting event of Peyronie's disease is a trauma to the penis. This trauma may be the result of vigorous sexual activity, usually with the female in the superior position, or from blunt injury to the penis as seen in sporting and motor vehicle accidents. It is generally unknown why some men develop the disease whereas other men recover after a short period. Some researchers have suggested that certain men are more prone to elastic tissue fibrosis as a result of the scarring that occurs following injury (Ami Sidi, 1988). In many cases, the disease is progressive, and not only causes pain during erection, but can render intercourse impossible because of the severe curvature of the shaft.

For the man with a disability, there is no research on whether Peyronie's disease may be more common than in the general population. To some extent, the prevalence of the condition will depend on a number of factors: presence of trauma to the pelvic region of the body, predisposition to elastic tissue problems, or presence of curvature before the onset of disability. The disease, however, is commonly seen in men with diabetes, who often have erectile problems as well (Jordan, 1994). As a result, surgery that may be used in the treatment of Peyronie's disease may not be indicated for the man with diabetes. Instead, the clinician may consider treatment by either vitamin E or penile prosthesis.

Treatment

It is important that the clinician who is working with a man or couple with whom Peyronie's disease is an issue provide reassurance, education, and assistance in managing anxiety. It is not uncommon for the disease to be misdiagnosed, because of its rarity, and for the man to feel disfigured and inadequate. Many men with Peyronie's disease question the presence of cancer because of the fibroid lesions, and have intense feelings of shame and embarrassment because of their changed penis. These men may avoid intimate relationships and discontinue sexual contact. For men with a disability, the presence of Peyronie's disease may contribute to their feelings that they are unattractive and undesirable. A patient may perceive Peyronie's disease as a further insult to his sense of self, and the disease may intensify adjustment issues surrounding the disability. The shortening of the penis, as a result of the curvature, may also contribute to feelings of emasculation.

Typically, treatment for Peyronie's disease involves a rather lengthy waiting time while observing the progression of the disease or the response to treatments such as vitamin E. During this time, the patient may find that sexual activity is difficult and that intercourse is impossible. He may also feel as if the physician is doing nothing to help his problem and question the value of treatment. Intense feelings of anger, shame, and sadness may also make compliance with medical treatment difficult.

PRIAPISM

Definition

Another male sexual dysfunction, although again not commonly seen, is *priapism,* the persistence of erection that does not result from sexual desire. Priapism is often accompanied by pain and tenderness, and the erection can persist despite orgasm and ejaculation. Over an extended period, priapism can result in erectile dysfunction on both a physiologic and psychological level. In a discussion of the causes of priapism, Lue (1992) reported that most cases are the result of either alcohol or drug abuse, sickle cell anemia, or perineal trauma. Stackl and Mee (1994) have suggested that various drugs may result in priapism: antihypertensives, drugs that act on the central nervous system, anticoagulants, and the vasoactive agents used for intracavernous injection. Other drug-induced causes of priapism include testosterone therapy, and certain parenteral nutrition therapies.

For men with disabilities, the most common cause of priapism may be a side effect of self-injections used to treat erectile problems. The most common drugs for such treatments include papaverine, phentolamine, and prostaglandin. These medications relax all components of the penile erectile tissue, culminating in a full erection. The risk of priapism after self-injection of these medications is higher in young men with better baseline erectile function and in men with neurogenic or psychogenic erectile difficulties. Severe complications from priapism may be somewhat rare, but pooling of blood and clotting in the penis are possible side effects along with pain and discomfort. Because injections of vasoactive medications are typically used in various diagnostic procedures to evaluate erectile function, prolonged erections are also common following testing. This is especially true because adjustments of dosage will usually have not occurred at the time of diagnostic testing in the urology or radiology departments.

Treatment

Because the dangers of priapism are common among men with neurogenic erections who are self-injecting, it is important that the patient and the partner be aware of the condition. An important part of self-injection training is education about priapism and the development of safeguards for prolonged erections. These safeguards may include the injection of other agents into the corpora, medical aspiration of the cavernosa, application of ice or hot packs, and clear guidelines on when to contact the physician or emergency room. Patients and their partners need to be especially cautious about drinking alcohol or using any substances that impair judgment at times when they may be injecting the man's penis.

From an emotional point of view, priapism can trigger fear regarding future erections and can decrease future interest in sexual activity. When severe, priapism can lead to depression and other affective changes that may require medication or ongoing counseling for the man and his partner. Although self-injections have contributed to great advances in sexual function, especially for the man with a disability, alertness for priapism is a necessity. Priapism is a medical emergency that must be treated as soon as possible.

CONCLUSION

Rehabilitation programs have progressed considerably from the time when sexual issues were not regarded as an important component of the rehabilitation process for people with disabilities. Today, most rehabilitation programs address sexual issues and provide a wide variety of information about the impact of disability on sexual function. Typically, information is provided to patients through books and literature, videotapes, workshops, lectures, and in individual patient–staff consultation. Despite the progress, however, little is known about male sexual dysfunctions and how they are affected by disability. Even less information is provided to patients and couples about how male sexual dysfunctions can be managed and overcome after the onset of disability. Literature and information to patients needs to provide more in-depth coverage of the various sexual dysfunctions associated with male sexuality.

As treatment programs for men have been developed, there has been a recognition that multidisciplinary approaches are the most effective. For many years, psychological and medical treatments of sexual dysfunction were seen as incompatible and competitive. The rapidly changing picture in the treatment of men with sexual dysfunctions is one in which an integrated team addresses both issues simultaneously. The team may include a psychologist, social worker, urologist, endocrinologist, and physiatrist. Moreover, once psychological intervention was considered to be important only in the differential diagnosis of organic from psychological erectile dysfunction; psychologists and mental health practitioners now make contributions in a much broader context. Supportive counseling, sex therapy, and couple's therapy are often used as an adjunct to medical treatment on the rehabilitation unit or in the urology clinic. For men who are undergoing treatment of a sexual dysfunction, the psychological issues must be addressed on an ongoing basis. In the same respect, physicians such as urologists and endocrinologists, now considered to be the experts on male sexual dysfunction, are becoming increasingly involved in rehabilitation units and with the unique sexual issues of men with disabilities. It is imperative that all members of an interdisciplinary team work in conjunction with one another to address the sexual issues of men with diabilities. Future research and clinical work should address not only the physical function of men with disabilities, but be equally concerned with the emotional and relationship aspects of the sexual experience.

REFERENCES

Ami Sidi, A. (1988). Vasoactive intracavernous pharmacotherapy. In R.J. Krane (Ed.), *The urology clinics of North America* (pp. 99–100). Philadelphia: W.B. Saunders.

Apfelbaum, B. (1989). Retarded ejaculation: A much-misunderstood syndrome. In S.R. Leiblum & R.C. Rosen (Eds.), *Principles and practice of sex therapy: An update for the 90's* (pp. 168–206). New York: Guilford Press.

Beck, J.G. (1995). Hypoactive sexual desire: An overview. *Journal of Consulting and Clinical Psychology, 63,*(6), 919–927.

Bullard, D.G. (1988). The treatment of sexual desire disorders in the medically ill and physically disabled. In S.R. Leiblum & R.C. Rosen (Eds.), *Sexual desire disorders* (pp. 348–384). New York: Guilford Press.

Ducharme, S.H., & Gill, K.M. (1995). Sexuality and disability. In L. Diamant & R. McAnulty (Eds.), *The psychology of sexual orientation, behavior and identity: A handbook* (pp. 393–409). Westport, CT: Greenwood Press.

Ducharme, S.H., & Gill, K.M. (1997). *Sexuality and spinal cord injury: Answers to your questions.* Baltimore, MD: Paul Brookes.

Feldman, H.A., Goldstein, I., & Hatzichristou, D.G. (1994). Impotence and its medical and psychological correlates: results of the Massachusetts aging study. *Journal of Urology, 54,* 151–157.

Gilbert, D.M. (1996). Sexuality issues in persons with disabilities. In R.L. Braddom (Ed.), *Physical medicine and rehabilitation* (pp. 605–629). Philadelphia: W.B. Saunders.

Jordan, G.H. (1994). Peyronie's disease and its management. In R.J. Krane, M.B. Siroky, & J.M. Fitzgerald (Eds.), *Clinical urology* (pp. 1282–1297). Philadelphia: J.B. Lippincott.

Kaplan, H.S. (1995). *The sexual desire disorders: Dysfunctional regulation of sexual motivation.* New York: Brunner/Mazel.

LoPiccolo, J.L. (1992). Postmodern sex therapy for erectile dysfunction. In R.C. Rosen & S.R. Leiblum (Eds). *Erectile disorders: Assessment and treatment* (pp. 171–197). New York: Guilford Press.

LoPiccolo, J.L., & Friedman, J.M. (1988). Broad spectrum treatment of low sexual desire: Integration of cognitive, behavioral and systemic therapy. In S.R. Leiblum & R.C. Rosen (Eds.), *Sexual desire disorders* (pp. 107–144). New York: Guilford Press.

Lue, T.F. (1992). Physiology of erection and pathophysiology of impotence. In P.C. Walsh, A.B. Retik, T.A. Stamey, & E.D. Vaughan (Eds.), *Campbell's urology* (pp. 722–725). Philadelphia: W.B. Saunders.

McCarthy, B.W. (1989). Cognitive behavioral strategies and techniques in the treatment of early ejaculation. In S.R. Leiblum & R.C. Rosen (Eds.), *Principles and practice of sex therapy: An update for the 90's* (pp. 141–167). New York: Guilford Press.

Money, J. (1960). Phantom orgasms in the dreams of paraplegic men and women. *Archives of General Psychiatry, 3,* 373–382.

Nehra, A., Werner, M., Bastuba, M., Title, C., & Oates, R. (1996). Vibratory stimulation and rectal probe electroejaculation as therapy for patients with spinal cord injury: Semen parameters and pregnancy rates. *Journal of Urology, 155,* 554–559.

Rosen, R.C., & Leiblum, S.R. (1989). Assessent and treatment of desire disorders. In S.R. Leiblum & R.C. Rosen (Eds.), *Principles and practice of sex therapy: An update for the 90's* (pp. 19–50). New York: Guilford Press.

Rosen, R.C., & Leiblum, S.R. (1995). Treatment of sexual disorders in the 1990's: An integrated approach. *Journal of Consulting and Clinical Psychology, 63*(6), 877–890.

Silverstein, J.L. (1986). *Sexual enhancement for men.* New York: Vantage Press.

Spark, R.F. (1991). *Male sexual health: A couple's guide.* Mount Vernon, NY: Consumer's Union.

Stackl, W., & Mee, S. (1994). Priapism. In R.J. Krane, M.B. Siroky, & J.M. Fitzgerald (Eds.), *Clinical urology* (pp. 1245–1258). Philadelphia: J.B. Lippincott.

Tordjman, G. (1993). A new therapeutic perspective for premature ejaculation disorder. *Cahiers de Sexologie Clinique, 19,* 5–6.

Yalla, S.V., Vickers, M.A., & Sullivan M.P. (1994). Sexual dysfunction and spinal cord injury. In A.H. Bennet (Ed.), *Impotence, diagnosis and management of erectile dysfunction in spinal cord injury* (pp. 175–185). Philadelphia: W.B. Saunders.

Zilbergeld, B. (1992). *The new male sexuality.* New York: Bantam Books.

CHAPTER 24

Management of Male Infertility

Todd A. Linsenmeyer

Ejaculatory dysfunction may occur after several types of disabilities but is most likely to occur in men with spina bifida, multiple sclerosis (MS), transverse myelitis, and traumatic spinal cord injury (SCI). With continued improvements in medical management and quality of life issues, an increasing number of men with these disabilities desire to have children. Advances and increased availability in methods for obtaining ejaculates combined with advances in assisted reproductive technologies are allowing a number of these men to have children. An understanding of the evaluation and management of ejaculatory dysfunction is important, whether a person has one of these disabilities or works with people with one of these disabilities. Such understanding will facilitate communication with the person and significant other that their hopes of having a child can often become a reality.

PHYSIOLOGY AND NEUROANATOMY OF EJACULATION

Normal ejaculation, which can occur independent of an erection, is divided into two phases: the emission phase and the ejaculatory phase. The emission phase begins during the peak of arousal. During this phase, there are secretions of a clear mucoid fluid from the bulbourethral glands. There is also peristalsis of smooth muscles of the vas deferens, seminal vesicles, and prostate, which results in secretions that travel out through the ejaculatory ducts and are deposited into the posterior urethra. These events depend on thoracolumbar sympathetic outflow from the presacral and hypogastric nerves originating at thoracic (T) level 10 through lumbar (L) level 2. Simultaneously, this sympathetic stimulation by way of the hypogastric nerves closes the bladder neck. The bladder neck has a preponderance of alpha-adrenergic receptors; therefore, sympathetic stimulation increases its tone. In this way, the bladder neck functions as a physiologic sphincter, thereby preventing the ejaculate from going in a retrograde direction. The external sphincter, which is distal to the openings of the ejaculatory ducts in the prostatic urethra, also remains closed during emission.

During the ejaculatory phase, a projectile ejaculate is produced by clonic contractions of the bulbospongiosus and ischiocavernosus muscles of the pelvic floor. These contractions result from sacral parasympathetic and somatic outflow from the pelvic nerves and pudendal nerves, respectively, originating at sacral (S) level 1 through 4. During the ejaculatory phase, the bladder neck remains closed and the external sphincter opens. Because the ejaculatory ducts are between the bladder neck and external urethral sphincter, continued closure of the bladder neck and an opening of the external urethral sphincter produces an antegrade ejaculation.

The seminal fluid is ejaculated in well-defined sequence. Before ejaculation, approximately 0.2 cc of the clear mucoid fluid from the bulbourethral glands is ejaculated. With the onset of ejaculation, the first fraction is approximately 0.5 cc of prostatic secretions combined with the spermatozoa that have been stored in the ampulla of the vas deferens. The last fraction of the ejaculate may vary between 1 and 5 cc, depending on the frequency of ejaculation originating from the seminal vesicles.

Spermatozoa pass from the testis to the head of the epididymis, which is located at the superior portion of the testis. The epididymis, a distinct structure comprising convoluted tubules, is connected to the posterior aspect of the testicle. There is controversy about the exact role of the epididymis, but it is believed to play an important part in sperm maturation and motility (Mathieu et al., 1992). Sperm pass down through the midportion of the epididymis to the tail of the epididymis, which is located at the inferior portion of the testis. From here, they pass into the vas deferens. The vas deferens is a tubular structure approximately 40 cm in length. The last 5 cm of the vas deferens, which is dilated, is called the ampulla of the vas deferens (vasal ampulla). Most of the sperm are stored in this region. During ejaculation, sperm compose approximately 10% of the total volume of the seminal fluid. Just lateral to the ampulla and behind the bladder are the seminal vesicles, which contribute approximately 70% of the total volume of the seminal fluid. The duct of the seminal vesicles joins with the vasal ampulla, which in turn empties into the ejaculatory ducts that are in the prostatic urethra. Prostatic secretions supply the additional 20% of the total volume of the seminal fluid.

CLASSIFICATIONS OF EJACULATORY DYSFUNCTION

Ejaculatory dysfunction is classified into several types: premature ejaculation, retarded (delayed) ejaculation, retrograde ejaculation, or absent ejaculation (anejaculation). Definitions for *premature ejaculation* vary from ejaculation before intromission, at the point of intromission, between 1 to 2 minutes of thrusts before ejaculation, and before female orgasm 50% of the time (McCarthy, 1980). Masters and Johnson (1970) defined premature ejaculation as rapid ejaculation and loss of erection at least 50% of the time. *Retarded ejaculation* is the significant difficulty or inability to ejaculate despite sexual excitation and an erection (Masters & Johnson, 1970). *Retrograde ejaculation* refers to the ejaculation going backward into the bladder. *Anejaculation* may be either primary (never had an ejaculation) or secondary (loss of ejaculation).

ETIOLOGIES OF EJACULATORY DYSFUNCTION

The four broad categories of etiologies of ejaculatory dysfunction are (1) functional, (2) pharmacologic, (3) anatomical, and (4) neurologic. Although the focus of this chapter is on neurologic causes of ejaculatory dysfunction, it is important to be aware of the other causes, because a person with a disability may also have a preexisting problem.

Functional Causes

Premature and retarded ejaculations generally result from functional causes. Levine (1976) reported that only rarely will a person with MS or a spinal cord tumor develop premature ejaculation as a result of the disability. In the experience of the author of this chapter, one patient complained of the onset of premature ejaculation following a traumatic incomplete upper motor neuron (UMN) lesion SCI. Retarded ejaculations are believed to be brought on by issues such as performance anxiety, guilt, or fear of pregnancy (Masters & Johnson, 1970).

Pharmacologic Causes

A wide variety of pharmacologic agents have the potential to cause ejaculatory dysfunction often because of their peripheral or central sympatholytic actions. These agents include antipsychotics (major tranquilizers); antidepressants (e.g., tricyclics, fluoxetine, and monoamine oxidase inhibitors), antihypertensives (e.g., alpha-blockers, clonidine, and ganglionic blockers); antianxiety agents (e.g., benzodiazepines); and other drugs (e.g., alcohol, baclofen, ε-aminocaproic acid, methadone, and naproxen; Brock & Lue, 1993; "Drugs That Cause Sexual Dysfunction," 1992). Those people with various disabilities may require various medications known to cause ejaculatory dysfunction. For example, a person with transverse myelitis or traumatic SCI may require baclofen to treat spasticity, or a person with quadriplegia may require an alpha-blocker to prevent autonomic dysreflexia. In general, it has been the author's experience that neurologic and anatomical changes play a much more important role than pharmacologic agents in causing ejaculatory dysfunction that occurs following the preceding disabilities. For this reason there is usually not a significant difference in ejaculatory function if agents are withheld.

Anatomical Causes

Various anatomical changes may cause ejaculatory dysfunction because they either result in an obstruction somewhere along the path of the ejaculation or change the path of least resistance so that the ejaculate goes in a retrograde manner into the bladder. Therefore, individuals with anatomical changes usually present with either retrograde ejaculation, decreased volume, or absent ejaculation.

Anatomical causes of ejaculatory dysfunction may be congenital or secondary; however, congenital causes are uncommon. Congenital causes include meatal stenosis, extrophy-epispadias posterior urethral valve complex, ectopic ejaculatory duct, urethral stricture, and obstruction of the ejaculatory duct. Patients generally present with a decreased volume or anejaculation. Secondary anatomical causes of ejaculatory dysfunction are more common than congenital causes, particularly in people with spina bifida, MS, transverse myelitis, and traumatic SCI. Men with these disabilities are more likely to have a neurogenic bladder with possible inflammation from an indwelling catheter, causing a urethral stricture, infections, or reflux of urine into the ejaculatory ducts and vas deferens, with possible scarring and obstruction of those structures. Anatomical changes that cause retrograde ejaculation may occur after bladder neck surgery (such as incision of the bladder neck); sphincterotomy; prostatectomy (open and transurethral); trauma to the bladder neck or posterior urethra; and Y-V plasty. Sphincterotomy has been a common procedure to improve voiding for men with SCI.

Neurologic Causes

Although anatomical changes can occur, neurologic changes are the major reasons for ejaculatory dysfunction following spina bifida, MS, transverse myelitis, and traumatic SCI. Any neurologic injury that affects the thoracolumbar sympathetic or sacral parasympathetic nervous system may cause ejaculatory dysfunction. For example, damage to the thoracolumbar sympathetic outflow may cause incompetence of the bladder neck, failure of the external sphincter to relax, or both, which will result in retrograde ejaculation. Damage to the parasympathetic nervous system may cause loss of the ejaculatory phase. Therefore, most individuals with neurologic causes of ejaculatory dysfunction have retrograde ejaculations or anejaculation. In people without the previously described disabilities, neurologic causes of ejaculatory dysfunction may result from surgical damage to the nerves, such as damage that may occur during retroperitoneal lymph node dissection or spinal cord surgery, or may result from medical conditions that affect the autonomic nervous system.

Most of the research has focused on ejaculatory dysfunction in people with SCI. Well-established evidence suggests that ejaculatory dysfunction that occurs following SCI is particularly significant because the majority of men who sustain SCI do so during their prime childbearing years. Recent statistics have shown that the median age of a person who sustains a spinal cord injury is 26 years and that injuries among men outnumber women 4:1 (Go, DeVivo, & Richards, 1995). Talbot (1955) evaluated erectile and ejaculatory dysfunction in 408 men with SCI using a questionnaire. In those respondents with injuries above T-12, 75% reported erections; however, only 10% reported having ejaculations. The majority of men with SCI have anejaculation, although it is possible that a number of men have retrograde ejaculations; however, those ejaculations may be undetected and unreported because they go in a retrograde direction (Horne, Paull, & Munro, 1948; Linsenmeyer & Perkash, 1991; Talbot, 1955).

In a series of 529 men with SCI, Bors and Comarr (1960) reported that only 5% of men with complete UMN lesions and 18% of those with lower motor neuron (LMN) lesions had ejaculations. Of the men with incomplete UMN lesions, 32% had ejaculations, and 70% of men with incomplete LMN lesions had ejaculations. The degree of incompleteness was not specified. Bors and Comarr suggested that patients with complete UMN lesions have less frequent ejaculations because increased sacral parasympathetic outflow inhibits emissions of spermatic fluid into the posterior urethra. This increased sacral parasympathetic outflow in those men with UMN lesions likely results from the lack of inhibition of the sacral parasympathetic center from the cerebral cortex.

Retrograde ejaculation can also occur after SCI because the external sphincter (somatic influence) fails to relax or the internal bladder neck (sympathetic influence) does not close. Although retrograde ejaculation does not pose a medical risk to the patient, urine contact with sperm has an adverse effect on sperm motility for those patients who may wish to have a child (Linsenmeyer, Wilmot, & Anderson, 1989).

There is a lack of published reports on ejaculatory dysfunction after MS, spina bifida, and nontraumatic causes of spinal cord dysfunction, such as transverse myelitis. It would be expected that some men with MS have ejaculatory dysfunction because detrusor sphincter dyssynergia during voiding has been documented (Blaivas & Barbalias, 1984). Those men with transverse myelitis and spina bifida would also be expected to have ejaculatory dysfunction similar to those patients with traumatic SCI.

In able-bodied men, a standard retroperitoneal lymph node dissection for testis cancer is a neurologic cause for ejaculatory dysfunction. This procedure involves bilateral removal of the periaortic sympathetic ganglia, which results in absence of emission or retrograde ejaculation. A more recent procedure, performed when appropriate, is a limited retroperitoneal node dissection, which may retain ejaculatory function. Other surgeries that may damage the sympathetic ganglia include various extensive retroperitoneal surgeries such as colorectal surgery, aortoiliac bypass surgery, and abdominal aneurysmectomy.

Diabetes is an example of a medical condition that can cause autonomic dysfunction and possible ejaculatory dysfunction. Approximately 30% of men with diabetes mellitus develop ejaculatory dysfunction (Greene & Kelalis, 1968). In those men, retrograde ejaculation often occurs during the emission phase because of incomplete closure of the bladder neck. Some men also have been found to have a lack of emission because of ineffective peristalsis of the vas deferens, vasal ampulla, and seminal vesicles.

EVALUATION OF EJACULATORY DYSFUNCTION

History

The clinician should obtain a thorough general medical history of past and current medical problems (Exhibit 24–1). This history should include the type of disability; length of disability; changes or progression of the disability (in patients with MS, diabetes mellitus, or a neuropathy); and completeness of injury (in patients with SCI). The clinician also should determine if there is a history of autonomic dysreflexia, which is likely to occur in those patients who are prone to dysreflexia if not premedicated before attempts to obtain an ejaculate. Current medications and past surgical procedures should also be determined, with an emphasis on those known to cause ejaculatory dysfunction, as previously discussed.

The clinician should obtain the past genitourinary (GU) history to determine if the patient had any medical problems that may potentially affect his fertility status, such as mumps orchitis, epididymitis, or sexually transmitted diseases. These problems may have had an adverse impact on the quality of semen or may have caused scar tissue within the vas deferens, epididymal, or ejaculatory ducts. The clinician should determine the patient's previous fertility status and assess ejaculatory function.

It is important for the clinician to characterize the type of ejaculatory dysfunction and character of the ejaculate. Does the patient have a premature ejaculation, delayed ejaculation, or absent ejaculation? Ask the patient about the color, consistency, and volume of the ejaculate. A person with a clear mucoid secretion may just be having bulbourethral secretions and no ejaculate. A very small volume of ejaculate or postejaculate cloudy urine may signify a retrograde ejaculate. No ejaculate may signify no ejaculation, a retrograde ejaculation, or, rarely, obstruction of the vas deferens, epididymal, or ejaculatory ducts.

Exhibit 24–1 Evaluation of Ejaculatory Dysfunction

History

- general medical history (medications, current and past problems, and surgeries)
- past genitourinary (GU) problems (mumps orchitis, epididymitis, or sexually transmitted diseases)
- previous fertility status (previous children or previous ejaculatory dysfunction)
- ejaculation (premature, delayed, or absent)
- ejaculate (color, consistency, and volume)

Physical Examination

- general physical examination
- testes (size and consistency)
- epididymis
- penis (hypospadiac meatus or meatal stenosis)
- cord structures (vas deferens present, varicocele)

Laboratory

- urine for culture and sensitivity
- postejaculation urine (retrograde ejaculation)
- semen analysis (presence of sperm)
- possible transrectal ultrasound or vasogram
- serum follicle-stimulating hormone (FSH), possible serum luteinizing hormone (LH), and serum testosterone
- possible testicular biopsy

Physical Examination

The patient should undergo a thorough physical examination (see Exhibit 24–1). In those patients with SCI, the level of injury is important because patients with injuries at or above T-6 should be premedicated before obtaining an ejaculate to prevent autonomic dysreflexia. The clinician should determine the intactness of the sacral cord by evaluating sacral sensation, the bulbocavernosus reflex, and hip flexion reflex. An intact sacral cord is particularly important when considering the use of a vibrator to obtain an ejaculate. For the GU examination, it is important for the clinician to note testicular size and check for atrophic changes. The normal testicle should be 4 to 4.5 cm in length. The clinician should examine the epididymis for any induration that may have resulted from a previous episode of epididymitis and resultant scar tissue. The clinician also should inspect the penis to determine if the patient has a hypospadiac meatus or meatal stenosis. A catheter may be needed to calibrate the meatus. There is a significant stricture in an adult male if a 9 French catheter will not pass through the stricture. Catheterization may also be needed if there is a possibility of a urethral stricture or bladder neck contracture. The clinician also needs to palpate the testicular cord to confirm that the vas deferens are present and to determine whether or not a varicocele is present. The absence of the vas deferens or the presence of a varicocele are abnormal findings.

Laboratory and Other Tests

Laboratory tests include a urine for culture and sensitivity (see Exhibit 24–1). If this test is positive, indicating urinary tract infection, treatment is warranted. Although a urinary tract infection would not cause ejaculatory dysfunction, it may affect the semen quality of patients who want to have children (Wolff et al., 1990), and it could also cause bacteremia during attempts at obtaining ejaculations. If the patient is able to experience orgasms, the clinician should obtain and examine a postcoital or postmasturbation catheterized or voided urine sample for the presence of sperm. If sperm are present, this would indicate that the patient has retrograde ejaculations. If a patient reports ejaculations with very small volumes, the clinician should examine the ejaculate to determine if it is a true ejaculate (sperm present) or if it contains secretions from the bulbourethral glands (no sperm present). The possibility of obstruction should be considered in those patients who report a very small to no semen volume.

If various modalities to obtain ejaculates are unsuccessful at obtaining sperm in the ejaculate, the clinician should consider a workup for obstruction. A transrectal ultrasound is a common method to check for ejaculatory duct obstruction. If the anatomy needs to be defined further, the clinician can perform a vasogram to evaluate for obstruction of either the ejaculatory ducts or vas deferens. Because the vasogram is an invasive procedure that carries the possibility of causing scar tissue itself, it is often done simultaneously with aspiration for sperm from the vas deferens. Absent or arrested spermatogenesis would also reflect an absence of sperm in the ejaculate. If no obstruction is found, and particularly if the testes are atrophic and if there is an elevated serum FSH, the clinician should consider testicular biopsies. In those patients with testicular atrophy or a suspected endocrine abnormality, a serum FSH should be obtained. If the serum FSH is elevated, further evaluation of the hypothalamic–pituitary–testicular axis should be performed by determining serum LH and serum testosterone.

TREATMENT OF EJACULATORY DYSFUNCTION

A person with ejaculatory dysfunction may seek medical assistance to obtain an ejaculate for a variety of reasons. Some men request help obtaining an ejaculate shortly after the onset of a disability primarily to determine whether they can have ejaculations. Other men first become interested in having an ejaculate when they enter into a serious relationship and want to know their fertility status; others become interested when they and their significant other have decided they want to have a child.

Before actually obtaining an ejaculate, the clinician must establish why the person wants to have an ejaculation. If a person wants to know his sperm count to determine his fertility status, the clinician should explain that a poor semen sample does *not* mean that it is not possible to have children. With new assisted reproductive technology techniques, success can occur with few sperm.

For those who want a child, a team approach is important, given the number of issues that must be addressed. Typical members of this team include a urologist, physiatrist, gynecologist, andrology lab worker, and, in some cases, a social worker. The urologist optimizes the person's urologic status. The physiatrist manages any medical problems. Because semen quality is often poor, a gynecologist should evaluate and treat the partner, if necessary. If the couple will be attempting intrauterine insemination (IUI), a gynecologist or reproductive endocrinologist may perform this procedure. The andrology lab is involved in washing the sperm, preparing it for insemination, or performing assisted reproductive techniques such as in vitro fertilization (IVF). The team should discuss in detail with the couple the various methods to obtain ejaculations, financial considerations, and types of assisted reproductive technologies. The couple should decide the methods they want to use and the length of time spent on each before undergoing the emotional rollercoaster involved in attempting to conceive a child. The possibility of adoption should be discussed early because there frequently is a long waiting list. If adoption is a possibility, then the couple may decide to begin the adoption process in case attempts at obtaining an ejaculate and having a child are unsuccessful.

Many strategies have been attempted to induce an ejaculate:

- use of pharmacologic agents (e.g., pseudoephedrine, ephedrine, phenylpropanolamine, or imipramine) to convert a retrograde to an antegrade ejaculation
- use of pharmacologic agents (e.g., intrathecal neostigmine or subcutaneous physostigmine) to induce an ejaculation
- vibratory stimulation
- electroejaculation
- direct aspiration of fluid from the vas deferens
- other strategies such as perineal needle stimulation or a hypogastric nerve stimulator

Intrathecal neostigmine and subcutaneos physostigmine currently are not used in the United States because of their significant side effects. In general, in patients with an intact sacral cord (UMN lesion), vibratory stimulation is usually the first technique to be attempted. If unsuccessful, electroejaculation may be attempted. If a person has a LMN injury, electroejaculation is sometimes successful. Otherwise, aspiration of sperm from the vas deferens or epididymis may be attempted.

Pharmacologic Agents That Can Induce an Ejaculate

In patients with retrograde ejaculations, who are able to ejaculate on their own, an attempt should be made to convert a retrograde ejaculate to an antegrade ejaculate. Pharmacologic agents (specifically, sympathomimetic agents) that will stimulate closure of the bladder neck are pseudoephedrine hydrochloride, 60 mg four times a day; ephedrine, 25 to 50 mg four times a day; phenylpropanolamine, 75 mg twice a day; and imipramine hydrocholoride, 25 mg twice a day or 50 mg once a day (Sigman, 1994). Patients usually try these drugs for 2 weeks. Major side effects of these agents include central nervous system stimulation, agitation, nervousness, insomnia, headache, tachycardia, and hypertension (Hoffman & Lefkowitz, 1990). Imipramine has additional potential side effects such as orthostatic hypotension and hematologic abnormalities. Urinary retention and possible autonomic dysreflexia may occur in patients with an SCI at or above T-6. The preceding drugs may be particularly useful in patients with a neuropathy (e.g., diabetes mellitus) but have not been reported to be useful in patients with an SCI (Ohl, 1994).

Gutmann and Walsh (1971) reported a 59.7% success rate in obtaining ejaculates in 70 men with suprasacral SCI lesions using intrathecal neostigmine. They reported two pregnancies, which resulted in spontaneous abortions. Side effects of intrathecal neostigmine include headaches, nausea, vomiting, and severe autonomic dysreflexia that results in death from a cerebral hemorrhage. Intrathecal neostigmine is no longer used in the United States because of the invasive method of placement and significant side effects.

Chapelle, Blanquart, Puech, and Held (1983) reported on the use of subcutaneous physostigmine followed by masturbation. Physostigmine is a lipid soluble acetylcholinesterase inhibitor and thereby acts as a parasympathomimetic agent that is able to cross the blood–brain barrier. This parasympathomimetic activity increases the sensitivity of the sacral ejaculatory reflex center (S-2 to S-4) and improves the success rate at obtaining an ejaculate when using masturbation or vibratory stimulation. To prevent severe cholinergic side effects and the possible onset of autonomic dysreflexia, the clinician must first give a peripherally acting anticholinergic agent. Subcutaneous physostigmine was found to improve the ejaculatory reflex and allowed ejaculates to occur in 8 of 20 men with complete SCI. N-buthylhyocine, 40 mg injected 30 minutes prior to the physostigmine, helps counteract the parasympathetic effects of nausea, vomiting, abdominal cramps, and diarrhea. Occasionally metoclopramide, 10 mg, and atropine, 0.25 mg, were used. All patients developed orthostatic hypotension if they did not remain in a strict decubitus position for 1 hour after the injection. Chapelle, Roby, Yakovleff, and Bussel (1988) reported obtaining an ejaculate in 55.5% ($n = 75$) of 135 men with SCI using this method. Of these men, 15 had children. More recently, Rawicki and Hill (1991) reported using subcutaneous physostigmine combined with other modalities, making it difficult to know the success of physostigmine. Nausea and vomiting occurred in two out of five men, and "marijuana-like highs" that lasted up to 1 hour occurred in two out of five men. To this author's knowledge, subcutaneous physostigmine is not being used in the United States to help augment ejaculations.

Vibratory Stimulation

Vibratory stimulation is another modality that has been used to obtain an ejaculate. Sobrero, Harlan, and Blair (1965) were the first to report the use of vibratory stimulation to obtain an ejaculate in humans. However, Brindley (1981b) was largely responsible for popularizing the use of vibratory stimulation in men with SCI. Using a powerful Ling vibrator, he reported a 77% ($n = 48$) success rate (among 62 men) at obtaining an ejaculate if the man was more than 6 months postinjury (to ensure he was out of spinal shock) and had hip flexion when scratching the soles of the feet. The vibrator produces afferent impulses that travel from the penis to the sacral cord by way of the pudendal nerve to trigger the sacral ejaculation reflex (S-2 to S-4). Impulses also stimulate the thoracolumbar emission centers, resulting in both ejaculation and emission. The hip flexion reflex test described by Brindley (1981b) tests the integrity of the L-2 to S-2 portion of the spinal cord. He reported that ejaculations were unable to be obtained in patients who did not have this reflex. Szasz and Carpenter (1989) found that failure of ejaculation could be predicted when there was an absent bulbocavernosus reflex or absent anal sphincter tone reflexes.

Until recently, electroejaculation was the major method used by fertility centers in the United States to obtain ejaculates. Slaten and Linsenmeyer (1993) found that, out of 40 centers, only 3 used vibratory stimulation; the others probably did not because of an only 30% success rate at obtaining semen using a "department store"–purchased vibrator. However, success rates are likely to dramatically improve with recent advances in vibrator technology. Sonsken, Biering-Sorensen, and Kristensen (1994) evaluated the effect of vibrator amplitude and frequency at obtaining ejaculates in men with SCI. They determined that changing the amplitude from 1 mm to 2.5 mm with a frequency of 100 Hz improved ejaculation rates from 32% to 96% in patients with an ejaculation reflex (UMN lesion). This vibrator, manufactured by Ferti Care, is commercially available (Figure 24–1). Unfortunately, despite improvements, vibratory stimulation is unsuccessful in those patients who do not have an intact sacral ejaculation reflex. However, other modalities such as electroejaculation or aspiration of the vas deferens may be used. In clinical practice, this author has used the equipment developed by the Sonsken group with similar results.

A major advantage of vibratory stimulation is that the actual stimulation procedure is noninvasive and less complicated than electroejaculation. Moreover, this method is particularly appealing for patients who do not like the idea of a rectal probe, which is required for electroejaculation. Because there is little to no discomfort, vibratory stimulation can also be used in patients with intact sensation. Recently, a model with the optimum stimulus parameters was approved by the U.S. Food and Drug Administration and is available for home use (Figure 24–2).

In their review of vibratory stimulation in men with SCI, Beckerman, Becher, and Lankhorst (1993) found that, in 357 patients treated with vibratory stimulation, side effects were reported to occur in 21 (5.9%). Side effects included autonomic dysreflexia (however, most investigators pretreated patients before vibratory stimulation); painful contractions of abdominal muscles; superficial trauma to the glans penis that resulted in bruising; bleeding; or superficial ulceration. Siosteen, Forssman, Steen, Sullivan, and Wickstrom (1990) reported that one patient no longer responded to vibratory stimulation. This author has also seen this

Figure 24–1 An example of a vibrator used to obtain an ejaculate. Courtesy of MULTICEPT ApS, Denmark.

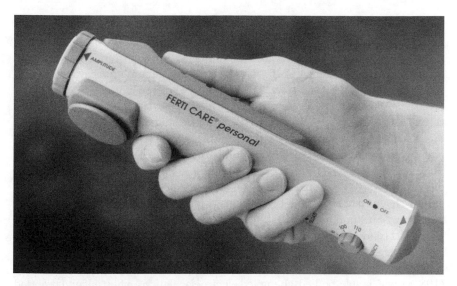

Figure 24–2 Vibrator designed for home use to obtain an ejaculate. Courtesy of MULTICEPT ApS, Denmark.

phenomenon in one patient. Of most concern is significant autonomic dysreflexia; therefore, patients with an SCI at or above T-6 must be premedicated and closely monitored during the procedure.

The new handheld home unit (Figure 24–2) has an amplitude of 2.5 mm and frequency of 100 Hz. This unit will allow couples to attempt to have children in a more private environment. If attempts are unsuccessful because of poor semen quality, assisted reproductive technologies can be attempted using semen obtained at home. The author recommends that men who develop autonomic dysreflexia (usually those with an SCI at or above T-6) should still undergo vibratory stimulation in a clinic setting under medical supervision.

Electroejaculation

Electroejaculation is one of the most common methods used to obtain an ejaculate. In 1948, Horne et al. were the first to report the use of electroejaculation in humans. They obtained an ejaculate in 8 of 15 patients with SCI and reported no complications with the procedure. Thomas, McLeish, and McDonald (1975) reported that a man with a T-12 paraplegia was able to have a child from semen obtained during electroejaculation. In 1984, Brindley reported a 62% success rate of obtaining an ejaculate in a group of 154 men with SCI who underwent electroejaculation. Of those men, 3 were able to have a child. Bennett et al. (1987) reported the first pregnancies in the United States resulting from semen obtained during electroejaculation: 4 of 10 wives became pregnant. With regard to ejaculatory dysfunction, the success rate of obtaining semen using electroejaculation has been 80% to 90% (Ohl, Bennett, McCabe, Menge, & McGuire, 1989). These researchers found that, among the 48 patients they studied, it was easiest to obtain ejaculates in men with SCI with thoracic levels of injury (90% success) compared with cervical (60% success) or lumbar (50% success) levels of injury.

Seagar and Halstead (1993) reported that, in 121 patients at risk of autonomic dysreflexia who underwent electroejaculation, medications to control blood pressures were given to 85. Of the 121 patients, 11 had transient elevations in systolic blood pressures in the range of 190 to 200 mm Hg or diastolic pressures in the range of 110 to 120 mm Hg. However, all patients exhibited normal blood pressures at the end of the procedure and there were no complications.

Patients with sensation may be unable to tolerate electroejaculation. Brindley (1981a), who is able-bodied, attempted electroejaculation on himself and reported that he was only able to tolerate one-quarter of the current necessary to obtain an ejaculate. He reported that every patient who had intact pinprick L-4, L-5, or sacral sensation was unable to tolerate electroejaculation. However, he found that electroejaculation was effective at obtaining an ejaculate in those individuals using general anesthesia and a neuromuscular blockade.

Perkash, Martin, Warner, and Speck (1990) reported their progress in developing equipment that required less current. First, they established the patient's pain threshold. Then, they used a computer program to deliver a low-intensity, repeatable current. Three patients who were unable to tolerate the full current regimen were able to tolerate the current from the new machine and produced an ejaculate in 3 to 5 minutes. Segar and Halstead (1993) reported that they induced sedation with either diazepam, meperidine, or midazolam. They also suggested inserting 30 to 50 mL of 2% lidocaine gel into the rectum just before the procedure. In their analysis of 331 men with SCI, 111 (33%) had incomplete injuries and only 27 (8%) required general anesthesia for the electroejaculation procedure.

Aspiration from the Vas Deferens

Another method for obtaining sperm is direct aspiration from the vas deferens. In 1986, Berger et al. reported successful recovery of sperm from the vas deferens. Furthermore, Bustillo and Rajfer (1986) reported a pregnancy after insemination of sperm that was obtained directly from the vas deferens. This technique is best reserved for patients who are unable to have a reflex ejaculation or emission because of a LMN lesion or absence of sperm in the ejaculate because of obstruction of the ejaculatory ducts or vas deferens. If scar tissue involves most of the vas deferens, a more complicated procedure, microscopic epididymal sperm aspiration, may be considered. This procedure, first described in 1985 by Temple-Smith, Southwick, Yates, Trounson, and deKretser, has been used for vasal agenesis but has not been reported in patients with SCI. A major concern with the procedure is the small numbers of sperm obtained and possible scar tissue from repeated aspirations. However, with new reproductive technologies that require only a few sperm and the ability to preserve sperm by freezing, aspiration techniques may play a more important role in the future.

Other Techniques

Other techniques to obtain ejaculates have been reported in the literature. However, with increased availability and excellent success rates obtaining semen using electroejaculation and vibratory stimulation equipment, those techniques have not gained popularity.

Ozkurkcugil, Cardenas, Hartsell, and Berger (1993) reported a small series on their experience using standard nerve stimulation equipment and electromyographic needles for transperineal electroejaculation. Two 6-inch needles were placed transperineally near the seminal vesicles under finger guidance. If this placement was unsuccessful, a needle was placed through the rectum over the prostate and stimulated at 5 to 10 mV at 300 to 400 mA. Seven of 12 men had sperm in the semen. Of those without sperm, 3 were reported as having ejaculatory duct obstruction. Of 5 men who had both transperineal and transrectal stimulation, 4 had sperm with both methods, but only 1 of 5 had any motile sperm with either method alone. Sperm concentrations and motilities were lower than in other reported series. The investigators reported that since performing the studies, they have obtained an electroejaculation unit. Electroejaculation was reported as more convenient for the patients, so further studies on transperineal ejaculation have not been done.

Brindley, Sauerwein, and Hendry (1989) reported on the use of a radio-linked device to stimulate the hypogastric plexus. The hypogastric plexus was surgically exposed and an electrode was wrapped around it immediately below the hypogastric plexus. Brindley et al. reported on seven patients with SCI and one with primary anorgasmia; all patients had seminal emissions. Insemination with the semen resulted in two live births (five pregnancies) in the wives of four patients. However, the researchers pointed out that this procedure is unsuitable for patients with significant pelvic pain sensitivity. Rather, they recommended that those patients first undergo a trial of electroejaculation to identify patients with significant pain or autonomic dysreflexia who should then be excluded from implantation. These researchers have recommended this procedure in patients from whom an ejaculate could not be obtained by vibratory stimulation. However, given the significant advances in electroejaculation and availability of electroejaculation equipment, electroejaculation should be performed if vibratory stimulation is unsuccessful.

Electroejaculation/Vibratory Stimulation Technique

Although there are slight differences, the electroejaculation/vibratory stimulation procedure is in general similar among institutions. The electroejaculation procedure can be divided into three phases: preejaculation (preparation) phase, ejaculation phase, and postejaculation phase. A physician and three nurses or qualified assistants are required for the procedure. The physician delivers the current and performs the ejaculation. One nurse or assistant monitors the blood pressure and administers medications, if necessary. The other nurse or assistant collects the sample. Only two nurses or assistants are needed with vibratory stimulation. However with electroejaculation, the third nurse or assistant records blood pressures, electroejaculation current, and patient data.

Preparation Phase

Before the procedure, a urine culture is obtained and treated if there are any symptoms of an infection. The night before the procedure, the patient is instructed to have a bowel program. In some centers, patients are instructed to take sodium bicarbonate, 1 g at 12 hours before the procedure and again at 2 hours before the procedure. Other researchers have found that it is the osmolarity and not the pH that affects sperm motility, so they do not have patients take sodium bicarbonate (Linsenmeyer et al., 1989). The day of the procedure, the patient is given a prophylactic antibiotic. The bladder is then prepared for the possibility of a retrograde ejaculation. Because urine has an adverse effect on sperm motility, the bladder is catheterized and drained of urine. It is important not to use a lubricant that is potentially spermicidal. The catheter is moistened with a small amount of the same solution with which the physician is going to irrigate the bladder. The bladder is irrigated with 30 cc of a physiologic solution to help to maintain sperm motility in the event of a retrograde ejaculation. Patients with injuries at or above T-6 are asked to chew and swallow 10 to 30 mg of nifedipine, depending on their history of dysreflexia, 15 minutes before the procedure. In addition, 0.5 inch of 2% nitroglycerin ointment is applied to the patient's forehead 4 to 5 minutes before the procedure. The patient is rolled onto his right side into a right lateral decubitus position. Digital rectal examination and anoscopy are performed to ensure there are no rectal lesions. The direction of the rectal vault can also be determined by this procedure.

Ejaculation Phase

With the patient laying in the right lateral decubitus position, the physician inserts a well-lubricated rectal probe into the rectal vault in the previously determined direction of the rectal vault. The rectal probe is made of polyvinyl chloride with three stainless steel electrodes arranged in parallel on the anterior surface (Figure 24–3). The electrodes are placed in the direction of the prostate and seminal vesicles. The probe also has a temperature monitor to measure the heat from the probe. This author uses Seager Model 14 Electroejaculation equipment (Figure 24–4). The equipment has an AC electrical generator controlled by a central rheostat dial. The operator turns the dial to deliver the current through the probe. One assistant continuously monitors the blood pressure and the other assistant holds a nonspermicidal cup at the tip of the penis and milks the penis to obtain an ejaculate. Ejaculation is usually heralded by a transient elevation in the blood pressure. Ejaculation usually occurs with 4 to 15 V of current. If a patient develops symptoms of dysreflexia or has a systolic blood pressure of 180, the current is stopped. If no antegrade ejaculate is obtained after 10 to 15 stimulations, the procedure is stopped.

Postejaculation Phase

The bladder is catheterized to determine if a retrograde ejaculate occurred or whether an antegrade ejaculate has been obtained. After the probe is removed, anoscopy is performed to rule out any rectal lesions. The antegrade and retro-

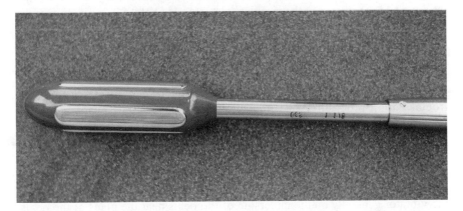

Figure 24–3 Rectal probe. Courtesy of Dalzell USA Medical Systems, The Plains, Virginia.

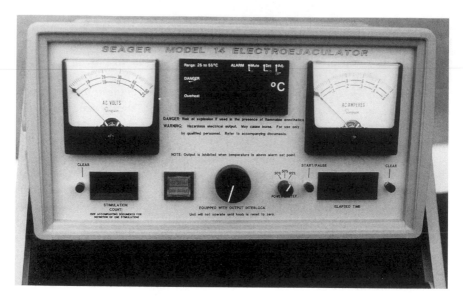

Figure 24–4 An example of the Seager Model 14 Electroejaculator with an AC electrical generator controlled by a central rheostat dial. Courtesy of Dalzell USA Medical Systems, The Plains, Virginia.

grade specimen is gently spun down and the supernatant is poured off. The collected semen is then resuspended with 20 to 30 cc of physiologic solution. The semen is then sent with the couple to the andrology laboratory, where further washing and processing of the ejaculate is performed before insemination of the semen. If the patient was given medications to prevent autonomic dysreflexia, he is assisted to sit up slowly while he is monitored for signs of hypotension. Once stable, he is discharged home and given antibiotics to take for 72 hours following the procedure.

The vibratory stimulation procedure is similar in many ways to the electroejaculation procedure. The preejaculation (preparation) phase and postejaculation phases are the same for both procedures. The one difference is that anoscopy is not performed with the vibratory stimulation procedure. In addition, this author generally places patients in a supine position rather than a right lateral decubitus position.

The ejaculation phase of the vibratory stimulation procedure involves placing the vibrator generally on the underside of the penis near the glans of the penis. The clinician holds the vibrator in place for 2 to 5 minutes. An impending ejaculation is usually signaled by abdominal and lower extremity spasms. At this point, patients with an SCI at or above T-6 may experience sudden elevations in blood pressure (autonomic dysreflexia), especially if they have not been premedicated. If there is no ejaculation after 5 minutes, the bladder is catheterized and the urine is examined for a retrograde ejaculation. If no ejaculation is obtained, the procedure may be performed again as long as there is no irritation or skin breakdown of the penis. The vibrator is placed in a slightly different position to help prevent irritation of the skin. This author has occasionally noted slight transient redness poststimulation, but has not had any patients with skin breakdown.

SEMEN QUALITY

Siosteen et al. (1990) and Beretta, Chelo, and Zanollo (1989) had patients perform vibratory stimulation on a weekly basis at home and compared first ejaculates with ejaculates at 3 to 6 months. Only the results at the end of the study were presented; however, both authors found improved semen quality at 3 to 6 months.

Now that the technology is available to obtain ejaculates, a new challenge has arisen for patients with SCI. Semen quality, particularly sperm motility, is significantly impaired in most men with SCI. The exact cause is unknown; however, in a review of the literature, Linsenmeyer and Perkash (1991) noted that possible factors were recurrent urinary tract infections, scrotal hyperthermia, prolonged sitting in a wheelchair, long-term use of medications, stasis of prostatic fluid, and sperm contact with urine (retrograde ejaculation). Other possibilities include the type of bladder management (Ohl et al., 1989), testicular denervation (Frankel & Ryan, 1981), and changes in the seminal fluid (Brackett, Lynne, Weizman, Bloch, & Abae, 1994). In a study that evaluated the effects of SCI on sperm function in an animal model, the Sprague Dawley rat, Linsenmeyer, Pogach, Ottenweller, and Huang (1994) found that sperm and testicular function undergo a profound decline during the first few weeks after SCI, with only partial recovery 4 to 6 months later. There is probably not one single cause for poor semen quality following SCI, but rather a combination of the various causes that results in poor semen quality. Further research is needed to determine which of the preceding factors, or unidentified factors or combination of factors, have the most significant impact on semen quality. Until good semen quality is able to be maintained, assisted reproductive technologies will play an important role in allowing men with SCI to have children.

ASSISTED REPRODUCTIVE TECHNOLOGIES

Despite poor semen quality, it is still possible for men with SCI to have children as a result of the significant advances and increased availability of assisted reproductive technologies. For this reason, it is important to have an infertility team, rather than a single physician, help the couple have a child. The team would typically include a urologist, rehabilitation physician, obstetrician, andrologist, nurses, and possibly a social worker. The simplest method of assisted reproductive technology is IUI into the uterus of sperm obtained from the man with SCI. Pregnancy rates per couple using IUI with sperm from a man with SCI have varied between 10% and 14% (Bennett, Seager, Vasher, & McGuire, 1988; Buch & Zorn, 1993). Bar-Chama, Ozkan, and Lipshultz (1994) found that the only distinguishing feature of ejaculation specimens that successfully resulted in a pregnancy was an average sperm motility of 33%. Unfortunately, a large number of men with SCI do not have motility of 33% or better. For this reason, IVF is playing an increasingly important role in achieving pregnancies. IVF has 30% to 40% live-birth pregnancy success rates. The IVF technique involves several steps. Ovum (eggs) are obtained from the woman by stimulating the ovaries with hormonal therapy followed by transvaginal ultrasound–guided needle aspiration of the ovum. The ovum are then incubated with sperm and the fertilized ovum are placed in the woman's uterus. For fertilization to occur, reasonable sperm motility and morphology are needed. Unfortunately, for this reason, IVF is therefore not an option for many men with SCI.

One of the newest techniques, intracytoplasmic sperm injection (ICSI), involves injection of a single sperm directly into the ovum. ICSI has pregnancy rates that are comparable with those of IVF. A significant advantage to this method is that few sperm are needed and they do not have to have any motility. Because of the lack of natural selection of sperm, there has been concern that there is a higher rate of spontaneous abortions using this method compared with other methods. Coulam et al. (1996) evaluated the outcome of pregnancies after ICSI compared with other assisted reproductive technologies. They evaluated preclinical and clinical pregnancy loss. *Preclinical pregnancy loss* was defined as one or more serum human chorionic gonadotropin concentrations greater than 5 mIU/mL beginning 11 days after embryo transfer without a gestational sac seen on ultrasound. A *clinical pregnancy loss* was defined as a spontaneous or missed abortion occurring during the first trimester after visualization of a gestational sac by transvaginal ultrasonography. They found no significant difference in preclinical pregnancy loss (28% after ICSI versus 26% after IVF) or clinical pregnancy loss (21% after ICSI versus 18% after IVF). Presently, a significant amount of research is being done to see what strategies may be useful to improve implantation rates to decrease preclinical pregnancy loss rates. It is generally believed that the rate of spontaneous and missed abortions after assisted reproductive technologies are not much higher than what normally occur. The aborted fetuses that do occur naturally are likely to have been those that would have had significant birth defects.

In summary, approximately 40% of men with SCI who have attempted to have children have done so. There is significant optimism that continued advances in IVF, ICSI, and other new assisted reproductive technologies will continue to improve pregnancy rates. For further information on assisted reproductive technologies, see Chapter 27.

FUTURE PERSPECTIVES

Advances in assisted reproductive technologies have changed the direction of research. Initially, the goal was to develop electroejaculation and medical strategies that would maintain or improve the semen quality enough so that IUI or IVF would be successful. However, with the increasing use of ICSI, further development of these strategies seems unnecessary. Presently, there is a greater challenge: to maintain or improve semen quality to such an excellent degree that no assisted reproductive technologies are necessary. Until that challenge is met, continued advances in assisted reproductive technologies will allow many men with SCI and other disorders with resultant ejaculatory dysfunction to have the opportunity to have children.

REFERENCES

Bar-Chama, N., Ozkan, S., & Lipshultz, L.I. (1994). Pregnancy in patients undergoing electroejaculation. *Journal of Urology, 151*(5) [Abstract No. 300].

Beckerman, H., Becher, M.D., & Lankhorst, G.J. (1993). The effectiveness of vibratory stimulation in anejaculatory men with spinal cord injury. *Paraplegia 31,* 689–699.

Bennett, C.J., Ayers, J.W., Randolph, F.J., Seagar, S.W., McCabe, M., Moinipanah, R., & McGuire, E.J. (1987). Electroejaculation of paraplegic males followed by pregnancies. *Fertility and Sterility, 48,* 1070–1072.

Bennett, C.J., Seager, S.W., Vasher, E.A., & McGuire, E.J. (1988). Sexual dysfunction and electroejaculation in men with spinal cord injury: Review. *Journal of Urology, 139,* 453–457.

Beretta, G., Chelo, E., & Zanollo, A. (1989). Reproductive aspects in spinal cord injured males. *Paraplegia, 27,* 113–119.

Berger, R.E., Muller, C.H, Smith, D., Forster, M., Moore, D., McIntosh, R., & Stewart, B. (1986). Operative recovery of vasal sperm from anejaculatory men: Preliminary report. *Journal of Urology, 135,* 948–950.

Blaivas, J.G., & Barbalias, G.A. (1984). Detrusor-external sphincter dyssynergia in men with multiple sclerosis: An ominous urologic condition. *Journal of Urology, 131,* 91–94.

Bors, E., & Comarr, E. (1960). Neurological disturbances of sexual function with special reference to 529 patients with spinal cord injury. *Urological Survey, 10,* 191–222.

Brackett, N.L, Lynne, C.M., Weizman, M.S., Bloch, W.E., & Abae, M. (1994). Endocrine profiles and semen quality of spinal cord injured men. *Journal of Urology, 151,* 114–119.

Brindley, G.S. (1981a). Electroejaculation, its technique, neurological implications and uses. *Journal of Neurology, Neurosurgery and Psychiatry, 44,* 9–18.

Brindley, G.S. (1981b). Reflex ejaculation under vibratory stimulation in paraplegic men. *Paraplegia, 19,* 299–302.

Brindley, G.S. (1984). The fertility of men with spinal injuries. *Paraplegia, 22,* 337–348.

Brindley, G.S., Sauerwein, D., & Hendry, W.F. (1989). Hypogastric plexus stimulators for obtaining semen from paraplegic men. *British Journal of Urology, 64,* 72–77.

Brock, G.B., & Lue, T.F. (1993). Drug induced male sexual dysfunction. *Drug Safety, 8*(6), 414–426.

Buch, J.P., & Zorn, B.H. (1993). Evaluation and treatment of infertility in spinal cord injured men through rectal probe electroejaculation. *Journal of Urology, 149,* 1350–1354.

Bustillo, M., & Rajfer, J. (1986). Pregnancy following insemination with sperm directly aspirated from vas deferens. *Fertility and Sterility, 46,* 144–146.

Chapelle, P.A., Blanquart, F., Puech, A.J., & Held, J.P. (1983). Treatment of anejaculation in the total paraplegic by subcutaneous injection of physostigmine. *Paraplegia, 21,* 30–36.

Chapelle, P.A., Roby, B.A., Yakovleff, A., & Bussel, B. (1988). Neurologic correlations of ejaculation and testicular size in men with a complete spinal cord section. *Journal of Neurology, Neurosurgery and Psychiatry, 51,* 197–202.

Coulam, C.B., Opsahl, M.S., Sherins, R.J., Thoresell, L.P., Dorfmann, A., Krysa, L., Flugger, E., & Schulman, J.D. (1996). Comparison of pregnancy loss patterns after intracytoplasmic sperm injection and other assisted reproductive technologies. *Fertility and Sterility, 65*(6), 1157–1162.

Drugs that cause sexual dysfunction: An update. (1992, August 7). *Medical Letter, 73*–78.

Frankel, A.J., & Ryan, E.L. (1981). Testicular innervation is necessary for the response of plasma testosterone levels to acute stress. *Biology of Reproduction, 24,* 491–495.

Go, B.K., DeVivo, M.J., Richards, J.S. (1995). The epidemiology of spinal cord injury. In S.L. Stover, J.A. DeLisa, & G.G. Whiteneck (Eds.), *Spinal cord injury: Clinical outcomes from the model systems* (pp. 21–55). Gaithersburg, MD: Aspen Publishers.

Greene, L.F., & Kelalis, P.P. (1968). Retrograde ejaculation of semen due to diabetic neuropathy. *Journal of Urology, 98,* 696.

Gutmann, L., & Walsh, J.J. (1971). Prostigmine assessment test of fertility in spinal man. *Paraplegia, 9,* 39–51.

Hoffman, B.B., & Lefkowitz, R.J. (1990). Catecholimines and sympathomimetic drugs. In A. Goodman, T.W. Rall, A.S. Niesm, & P. Taylor (Eds.), *The pharmacological basis of therapeutics* (8th ed., pp. 187–220). New York: Pergamon Press.

Horne, M.W., Paull, D.P., & Munro, D. (1948). Fertility studies in the human male with traumatic injuries of the spinal cord and cauda equina. *New England Journal of Medicine, 237,* 959–961.

Levine, S.B. (1976). Marital sexual dysfunction: Ejaculation disturbances. *Annals of Internal Medicine, 84,* 575–579.

Linsenmeyer, T.A., & Perkash, I. (1991). Infertility in men with spinal cord injury. *Archives of Physical Medicine and Rehabilitation, 72,* 747–754.

Linsenmeyer, T.A., Pogach, L.M., Ottenweller, J.E., & Huang, H.F.S. (1994). Spermatogenesis and the pituitary–testicular hormone axis in rats during the acute phase of spinal cord injury. *Journal of Urology, 152,* 1302–1307.

Linsenmeyer, T.A., Wilmot, C., & Anderson, R.U. (1989). The effects of the electroejaculation procedure on sperm motility. *Paraplegia, 27,* 465–469.

Masters, W.H., & Johnson, V.E. (1970). *Human sexual inadequacy*. Boston: Little, Brown.

Mathieu, C., Guerin, J.F., Cognat, M., Lejeune, H., Pinatel, M.C., & Lornage, J. (1992). Motility and fertilizing capacity of epididymal human spermatazoa in normal and pathological cases. *Fertility and Sterility, 57*(4), 871–876.

McCarthy, B.W. (1980). Cognitive-behavioral strategies and techniques on the treatment of early ejaculation. In S.R. Leiblum & R.C. Rosen (Eds.), *Principles and practice of sex therapy.* New York: Guilford Press.

Ohl, D.A. (1994). The use of electroejaculation for ejaculatory abnormalities. In D. Whitehead & H. Nagler (Eds.), *Management of impotence and infertility.* Philadelphia: J.B. Lippincott.

Ohl, D.A., Bennett, C.J., McCabe, M., Menge, A.C., & McGuire, E.J. (1989). Predictors of success in electroejaculation of spinal cord injured men. *Journal of Urology, 142,* 1483–1486.

Ozkurkcugil, C., Cardenas, D., Hartsell, C., & Berger, R.E. (1993). Electroejaculation using standard nerve stimulation equipment and Teflon coated needles. *Fertility and Sterility, 60,* 1094–1095.

Perkash, I., Martin, D.E., Warner, H., & Speck, V. (1990). Electroejaculation in spinal cord injury patients: Simplified new equipment and technique. *Journal of Urology, 143,* 305–307.

Rawicki, H.B., & Hill, S. (1991). Semen retrieval in spinal cord injured men. *Paraplegia, 29,* 443–446.

Seagar, S.W.J., & Halstead, L.S. (1993). Fertility options and success after spinal cord injury. *Urology Clinics of North America, 20*(3), 543–548.

Sigman, M. (1994). Treatment of retrograde ejaculation. In D. Whitehead & H. Nagler (Eds.), *Management of impotence and infertility.* Philadelphia: J.B. Lippincott.

Siosteen, A., Forssman, L., Steen, Y., Sullivan, L., & Wickstrom, I. (1990). Quality of semen after repeated ejaculation treatment in spinal cord injured men. *Paraplegia, 28,* 96–104.

Slaten, W., & Linsenmeyer, T.A. (1993). A survey of fertility programs for spinal cord injured men [Abstract]. *Journal of the American Paraplegia Society, 16*(2), 109.

Sobrero, A.J., Harlan, E.S., & Blair, J.B. (1965). Technique for the induction of ejaculation in humans. *Fertility and Sterility, 16,* 765–767.

Sonsken, J., Biering-Sorensen, F., & Kristensen, J.K. (1994). Ejaculation induced by penile vibratory stimulation in men with spinal cord injuries: The importance of the vibratory amplitude. *Paraplegia, 32,* 651–660.

Szasz, G., & Carpenter, C. (1989). Clinical observations in vibratory stimulation of the penis of men with spinal cord injury. *Archives of Sexual Behavior, 18*(6), 461–474.

Talbot, H.S. (1955). The sexual function in paraplegia. *Journal of Urology, 73,* 91–100.

Temple-Smith, P.D., Southwick, G.J., Yates, C.A., Trounson, A.O., & deKretser, D.M. (1985). Human pregnancy by in vitro fertilization using sperm aspirated from the epididymis. *Journal of In Vitro Fertilization and Embryo Transfer, 2*(3), 119–122.

Thomas, R.J.S., McLeish, G., & McDonald, I.A. (1975). Electroejaculation of the paraplegic male followed by pregnancy. *Medical Journal of Australia, 2,* 798–799.

Wolff, H., Politch, J.A., Martinez, A., Halmovici, F., Hill, J.A., & Anderson, D.J. (1990). Leukocytospermia associated with poor semen quality. *Fertility and Sterility, 53,* 528.

CHAPTER 25

Management of Female Sexual Dysfunction

Beverly Whipple and Karen Brash McGreer

UNDERLYING NOTIONS FOR THE MANAGEMENT OF FEMALE SEXUAL DISSATISFACTION AND DIFFICULTIES

A woman may need to make many adjustments if she is to enjoy her sexuality in the presence of a severe disability or chronic illness. She may need to redefine the meaning and purpose of sexuality in her life after a disability or with a chronic illness. She may need to decide if she will continue to grow and develop in this area of her life. She may need to consider that her best sexual experiences are not behind her, but still ahead, as she demonstrates a flexibility and maturity to accept what cannot be changed and to enjoy what she has. She will need to practice assertiveness skills to have her needs met. She will have to find that delicate balance among independence, dependence, and interdependence. She will have to accept help when necessary, without giving in to excessive dependency. She will have to overcome any tendency to view her sexuality in an "all or nothing" way. She will need a sense of humor to be able to see and appreciate the tragicomic aspects of human experience. And as she progresses toward self-actualization, she will have to appreciate her own worth in a world that may invite her to feel less worthy because of her disability or chronic illness.

Definition of Sexuality

To discuss the management of female sexual difficulties, it is important to first define sexuality and the basic underlying concepts germane to sexual response in women. In the past, sexuality was conceptualized as having one purpose: reproduction. Today, sexuality is seen as an important aspect of health and human behavior; it enhances the quality of life, fosters personal growth, and contributes to human fulfillment (Whipple & Gick, 1980). Sexuality refers to the totality of a being. This holistic view of sexuality encompasses human qualities, not just the genitals and their function. It includes all of the components—biological, psychological, emotional, social, cultural, and spiritual—that make people who they are. People have the capacity to express their sexuality in any of these arenas without necessarily involving the genitals (Whipple, 1987). An example of the psychological arena would be a person's inner self-concept: "I am a man" or "I am a woman," or "I am half a man," or "I am no longer attractive" (Whipple & Gick, 1980). Most people, for example, are aware of how even a small amount of weight gain can affect their body image. Thus, the health care professional can begin to realize the impact of a chronic illness or a disability on a person's body image.

Body Image

Nowhere is the emphasis on the "body beautiful" more apparent than in American society. Body image is an important aspect of a person's overall self-concept and self-esteem. The relationship between body satisfaction and self-satisfaction is particularly strong among females because our society places so much emphasis on attractiveness as an important indicator of female worth and value (Koch, 1995). It is no surprise, then, that an alteration in a person's appearance or even the perception of a person's body may have far-reaching social consequences (Whipple, 1987).

A person's self-concept and body image have a definite influence on how that person may interact with others. Moreover, the response of a significant other has an equally definite influence on an individual's ability to reintegrate his or her body image. The ways in which people perceive their bodies may also influence their sexual self-concept and their sexual behaviors. Those who view themselves as no longer attractive or lovable will probably shun social situations and may feel inadequate in sexual relationships. They may seek privacy and isolation from people who may be potentially shocked or disgusted by their appearance. A study by Witkin (1978) found that, for the postmastectomy patient, the fear of loss of her husband's love was greater than the fear of death.

Goals of Sexual Expression

What the health care professional and the woman or the couple view as their goal of sexual expression must also be considered. According to Timmers (1976), there are two commonly held views. The most common view is goal oriented, which is analogous to climbing a flight of stairs. The first step is touching, the next step kissing, followed by caressing, vagina–penis contact, intercourse, and then the top step of orgasm. The goal of both or one partner is orgasm. If the sexual experience does not lead to the achievement of that goal, then one or both partners do not feel satisfied with what they have experienced (Whipple, 1987).

The alternative view is pleasure oriented, which can be conceptualized as a circle, with each expression on the perimeter of the circle considered an end in itself. Whether the experience involves kissing, oral sex, or holding or other physical contact, each is an end in itself, and each is satisfying to the couple. There is no need to have this form of expression lead to anything else (Whipple, 1987). If one person in the couple is goal oriented and one is pleasure oriented, problems may occur if they do not realize their goals or do not communicate their goals to each other. In addition, if the health care professional is "genital-orgasm goal oriented," he or she may have some difficulty suggesting alternative forms of sexual expression to the woman or the couple being counseled.

Models of Sexual Response

In the past 30 years, there have been a number of contributions to our understanding of sexual response. When Masters and Johnson (1966) published their pioneering research, they reported their findings using arbitrarily chosen phases of excitement, plateau, orgasm, and resolution, which correspond to the level of sexual arousal. They described typical sexual responses for both men and women. During the excitement phase, stimulation produces physical changes resulting primarily from vasocongestion and myotonia. Vaginal lubrication begins, the upper vagina expands, the uterus is pulled upward, and the clitoris becomes engorged. The breasts enlarge slightly and the nipples erect, and muscle tension, heart rate, respiratory rate, and blood pressure increase. During the plateau phase, the outer third of the vaginal swells and the clitoris pulls back. Heart rate, respiratory rate, blood pressure, and muscle tension continue to increase. During orgasm, there is a discharge of sexual tension, with rhythmic muscular contractions of the uterus and outer vagina. Heart and respiratory rates and blood pressure reach their peak. During the resolution phase, the body returns to its unaroused state (Masters & Johnson, 1966). Masters and Johnson (1970) also were instrumental in describing the dysfunctions that occur during these phases.

Kaplan (1979) proposed a fifth phase to the sexual response cycle, the desire phase, which precedes the original four. She reported that people could be blocked from sexual pleasure and response before excitement or arousal could occur.

Zilbergeld and Ellison (1980) proposed a model of the sexual response process consisting of five phases: desire, arousal, physiological readiness, orgasm, and satisfaction. They differentiated Kaplan's (1979) desire phase into two stages, initial desire followed by arousal—the subjective experience of feeling "turned on." Physiological readiness incorporates all of the aspects of excitement identified in the previous models. They differentiate between "a peak feeling" and the physical release during orgasm. They added satisfaction as a separate phase, acknowledging that occurrence of orgasm is not the only measure of how satisfying a sexual experience is.

Reed developed a theory that overrides Kaplan's (1979) model. Although Reed has not published his theory, Stayton (1989) described Reed's theory of the Erotic Stimulus Pathway (ESP) (Figure 25-1). This model has four phases. Phase 1 is the seduction phase. This phase has two components: first, the person seduces himself or herself into being interested in another person and, second, learns how to seduce the other person into being interested in the first person. Phase 2 of ESP is the sensations phase. Reed described the senses as nature's aphrodisiacs. Touch, sight, hearing, smell, and taste contribute to sexual arousal and pleasure. Seeing and hearing one's beloved and the sight and sound of sex can be stimulating unless a person has been taught that the body is gross and the sounds of sex are frightening (Stayton, 1989). Phase 3 is called the surrender phase. For orgasm to occur a person needs to let go and give in to the experience. If a person has been taught to be overcontrolling or there are power struggles in the relationship, then the psychophysiologic response will be affected. Phase 4 of ESP is the reflection phase. How a person feels immediately after the sexual experience will act as feedback for future sexual experiences with that person or with other people. If the immediate reflection is positive, that is, warm, loving, or pleasurable, then the desire will be stimulated for the next time. If the reflection is negative, that is, the person did not like the way he or she experienced his or her response, or is negative about the partner or the situation, then the feedback will act to lower desire for the next time. Reflection appears to be the beginning of the next sexual experience. A common problem, however, in long-term relationships is that couples forget the importance of the seduction phase (phase 1) and go right for the sensations (phase 2) or orgasm phase (phase 3). Keeping seduction alive in long-term relationships is vitally important.

Physiology of Female Sexual Response

In addition to the behavioral expansions of Masters and Johnson's (1966) sexual response cycle, not all researchers or women have agreed with Masters and Johnson's monolithic pattern and their report of one reflexive pathway in sexual response. Some women have reported that they had orgasm from vaginal stimulation and some women have reported an expulsion of fluid from the urethra with orgasm, which Masters and Johnson (1966) said did not occur.

After listening to the reports of women, Perry and Whipple (1981) designed research studies that led to an identification of a sensitive area women feel through

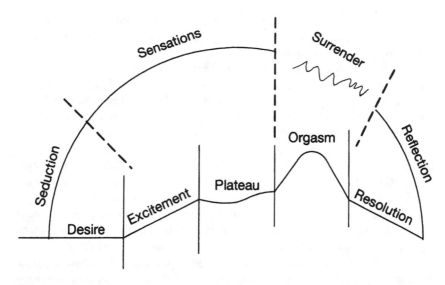

Figure 25–1 Reed's Erotic Stimulus Pathway model. *Source:* Reprinted from *American Baptist Quarterly* with permission of the American Baptist Historical Society, Valley Forge, PA 19482-0851.

the anterior wall of the vagina, which they called the Gräfenberg spot, and to their documentation of the phenomenon of female ejaculation (Addiego et al., 1981). The fluid expelled from the urethra was found to be chemically different from urine (Addiego et al, 1981; Belzer, Whipple, & Moger, 1984; Zaviacic et al., 1988). Perry and Whipple (1981) also hypothesized that there are two different nerve pathways involved in sexual response. One pathway, by way of the pudendal nerve, is the major sensory pathway from clitoral stimulation as identified by Masters and Johnson (1966). The hypogastric plexus and the pelvic nerve were identified by Perry and Whipple (1981) as the sensory pathways in sexual response in women when there is vaginal stimulation.

An additional pathway has been hypothesized based on neuroanatomical and functional studies in laboratory rats (Bianca et al., 1994; Komisaruk et al., 1996) and in women with complete spinal cord injury and without spinal cord injury (Komisaruk & Whipple, 1994, 1995; Whipple, Gerdes, & Komisaruk, 1996a). This sensory pathway, the vagus nerve, goes directly from the cervix to the brain and bypasses the spinal cord. This additional pathway may account for the report of sexual response and orgasm in women diagnosed as having complete spinal cord injury. These same researchers are currently conducting positron emission tomography (PET) scans of the brain during genital self-stimulation and orgasm to further document the pathways.

A laboratory study designed to validate the reported experience of women that they could achieve orgasm from fantasy alone, without touching their bodies, was reported by Whipple, Ogden, and Komisaruk (1992). During this study, orgasm from both self-induced imagery and genital self-stimulation was associated with significant increases in blood pressure, heart rate, pupil diameter, and pain thresholds over resting control conditions. The two orgasm conditions did not differ significantly from each other on any of the physiologic measures (Whipple et al., 1992). On the basis of these findings, it is evident that physical genital stimulation is not necessary to produce a state that is reported to be an orgasm.

Knowledge of these various models of sexual response and the variety of ways women experience sexual pleasure is important for health care professionals who are counseling women with sexual concerns. It is also important for health care professionals to be aware that there is no right or normal way to have a sexual experience. Each person is unique and responds differently depending on many variables.

Causes of Sexual Difficulties

Not all sexual interactions are pleasurable and satisfying, and almost everyone will experience some dissatisfaction or problem related to his or her sexuality (Koch, 1995). Masters and Johnson (1970) estimated that at least 50% of married people in the United States have experienced or will experience a sexual dysfunction. Not all sexual problems necessarily lead to an unhappy marriage and not all people with sexual difficulties seek treatment. In one study of 100 self-identified happily married couples (Frank, Anderson, & Rubinstein, 1978), 80% regarded themselves as sexually satisfied in their marital relationships even though 40% of the men experienced erection or ejaculation difficulties and 63% of the women had difficulties becoming aroused or reaching orgasm.

Sexual problems can affect both genders at any age, regardless of whether they prefer partners of the same or the other gender and regardless of whether there is a chronic illness, disability, or no medical problem. Most factors that impair sexual function are classified as either biologic or psychosocial in origin, however biologic and psychosocial factors interact, so there is often not a clear division of causes.

In general, any disease, injury, or surgery that affects the brain or the reflex centers in the spinal cord and the nerves that serve them can result in sexual impairment. Many of the medications used to treat various mental and physical conditions also reduce responsiveness. Several major categories may affect sexual function, according to Kaplan (1974, 1979). They are as follows:

- *Neurogenic disorders* affect the areas of the brain and spinal cord that control sexual response. Head injury, stroke, psychomotor epilepsy, spinal cord injury, and multiple sclerosis are examples of these types of disorders.
- *Vascular disorders* affect the circulatory system and appear to be more disabling for males because erection depends on blood flow. However, these disorders may be just as disabling for women in terms of sensation, lubrication, and orgasm. Disease of blood vessels, cardiac disease, leukemia, and sickle-cell disease are some of the vascular disorders that can impair sexual response.
- *Endocrine disorders* affect the hormonal balance in the body. Any problem that results in lowered levels of testosterone may affect sexual desire and response. Diabetes, hepatitis, and kidney disease are examples of endocrine disorders that can affect sexual function.
- *Debilitating diseases* refer to conditions such as advanced stages of cancer, lung disease, and degenerative disease that produce general ill health and affect sexual responsiveness. Genital disorders, such as herpes, human papilloma virus, and other infections, can impair sexual function.
- *Medications* such as tranquilizers and antidepressants can cause sexual dysfunction. Alcohol, heroin, and barbiturate abuse can have the same result. Medications that are frequently prescribed for the treatment of hypertension may cause sexual dysfunction and antihistamines may cause problems with vaginal lubrication.
- *Psychosocial factors* that can influence the development of sexual dysfunctions include communication problems, sexual misinformation, destructive relationships, as well as childhood or historical traumas.

Common Female Sexual Difficulties

In all of the following sexual disorders, organic factors, such as physical disorders or medication, must be considered as a contributory cause.

Hypoactive Sexual Desire Disorder

Previously called inhibited sexual desire, this disorder is defined as the persistent and pervasive inhibition or lack of sexual desire (American Psychiatric Association [APA], 1994). This inhibition can be selective, in that some women may experience lubrication and orgasm, but feel little pleasure; other women's desire is at such a low ebb that they have no interest in self-stimulation or in participating in sexual interaction that might lead to arousal. The suppression of sexual desire, of course, is not a dysfunction in and of itself. Problems with sexual desire are the most common complaints seen in sex therapy. Studies have indicated that 16% to 34% of the population has experienced inhibited sexual desire (Spector & Carey, 1990). In actual practice, this diagnosis will rarely be made unless the lack of desire is a source of distress to either the woman or her partner. The interest a woman has in the sexual experience will depend greatly on her purpose for having sex. There are tremendous variations in women's purposes for seeking and having sexual experiences. For some, it may be to prove themselves or their attractiveness; for others, it may be a tool for courtship and one that is no longer useful after the relationship is cemented; for others, the purposes of sex may be pleasure, or bonding, or power, or nurturing, or as an aid to relieve tension, or to sleep. The list could go on and on. The politics of sexual desire have everything to do with the experience of desire. If a woman is willing to have desire, she will find a purpose for participating.

Female Sexual Arousal Disorder

Previously called inhibited sexual excitement or lubrication inhibition, this disorder refers to recurrent and persistent failure to attain or maintain sufficient vasocongestion (vaginal lubrication; APA, 1994). Sexual arousal disorder may be either primary or secondary. A woman who has never experienced sexual arousal with any partner under any circumstance is considered to have the primary form, which is quite rare. Secondary arousal disorder is diagnosed when a woman has experienced sexual arousal in the past but is not presently responsive. Occasional unresponsiveness during sexual interaction is common. Such occasional unresponsiveness can become problematic if the woman fears that she may not be able to respond sexually in the future. This fear of failure can create anxiety about response, which can lead to actual problems in responding in the future.

Inhibited Female Orgasm

This condition involves the recurrent and persistent inhibition of orgasm as manifested by a delay in or absence of orgasm following sexual arousal and excitement, when orgasm is desired (APA, 1994). Some women are able to experience orgasm during noncoital clitoral stimulation, but are unable to experience it during coitus in the absence of manual clitoral stimulation. This represents a normal variation of female sexual response. Absolute orgasmic dysfunction is the inability to experience orgasm under any circumstances. Many therapists no longer consider a woman dysfunctional unless she fits the absolute orgasmic dysfunction category. In the general population, 5% to 10% of women have persistent or recurrent inhibited orgasm (Spector & Carey, 1990). The pejorative term "frigidity" had been used in the past to describe a lack of sexual desire, arousal, or orgasmic response in females. This term was inaccurate and gave a negative impression of women. It is no longer used.

Sexual Pain Disorder

This disorder, such as dyspareunia, involves recurrent and persistent pain in the genital area during stimulation or intercourse (APA, 1994). Repeated dyspareunia is likely to result in vaginismus in women. The pain may be experienced as repeated, intense discomfort; momentary sharp sensations of varying intensity; or intermittent twinges. Combinations of these pains may occur before, during, or after sexual intercourse. For some women, insufficient precoital stimulation may result in a lack of sexual arousal and excitement with little lubrication, leading to painful intercourse. Reportedly, 8% to 23% of women have experienced genital pain (Spector & Carey, 1990).

Vaginismus

This disorder involves the involuntary contraction of the lower one-third of the vagina. This diagnosis is made when there is a history of recurrent and involuntary spasms of the pubococcygeal muscles, which interfere with coitus. Vaginismus can be a source of dyspareunia just as recurrent dyspareunia can precede vaginismus. A reported 12% to 17% of women attending sexual dysfunction clinics have had vaginismus (Spector & Carey, 1990). No estimate of its occurrence in the general population is available.

Paucity of Research on Women

There has been a lack of interest, funding, and research focused on women's health issues, including female sexuality. According to Dr. Bernadine Healy, former National Institutes of Health (NIH) director, men were the normative standard for medical research and treatment. This, of course, meant that men's hormones set the standard for everyone. In March 1993, NIH and the Food and Drug Administration (FDA) announced new steps to help remedy the long-standing neglect of research into women's health issues. The FDA had banned drug testing in women of childbearing age in 1977 because of the concern that if a woman became pregnant during a drug trial, the drug might damage her fetus. Because of this ban, nearly half of all drug safety experiments conducted for more than a decade and a half have excluded women. Since 1977, few drugs have been tested to see whether their effect would be blocked or distorted by oral contraceptives and other drugs commonly taken by women or if there is an effect from the normal fluctuation in estrogen and progesterone in the cycling female. Also, drugs have seldom been analyzed to see if they have a different effect on women than on men. Almost all of the studies on the effects of medications on sexuality have been conducted on men, and the results have been extrapolated to women. The FDA announced that it would end its ban on participation of women in most drug safety tests (Turk, 1993). Furthermore, the FDA will require companies to carry out analysis by sex in almost all applications of new drugs.

In addition to the limited number of studies on women concerning medications, most of the studies concerning sexuality and chronic illness and disability have been conducted with men. For example, there is a paucity of literature concerning female sexual response after spinal cord injury. As Sipski (1991) has reported, perhaps the reason is that the ratio of males to females with spinal cord injury is 4:1 and that it is much easier to study sexual response in males because they have external genitalia. Whatever the reason, until the 1990s, the literature concerning female sexual function after spinal cord injury stated that women with spinal cord injury were capable of menstruating, conceiving, and giving birth (Whipple, 1990). Most of the literature was not concerned with whether women with spinal cord injury had any sexual desire or response, let alone sexual difficulties. If a woman with spinal cord injury did acknowledge that she had an orgasm, it was labeled "phantom," a label that is still used by many health care professionals.

There is a need for more research concerning female sexuality and female sexual response in women with chronic illness and disabilities. There is also a need to recognize and acknowledge the variety of sexual responses that women have and to provide information and counseling or therapy for those women who want to increase their sexual response and sexual pleasure.

SEXUAL READJUSTMENT AFTER A DISABILITY OR CHRONIC ILLNESS

A woman with a disability or a chronic illness has to make many specific adjustments to have or resume good sexual experiences. For example, she may have to work harder to have socialization experiences and skills. She may have to accept elaborate preparations before sexual experiences. She may have to give up the excessive valuing of spontaneity. She may have to cultivate a good sense of "timing" to compensate for fatigue or bodily procedures that complicate her life such as catheterizations, bowel programs, skin care, or medications. She may have to decide "it's worth it," or "I'm worth it." She may have to decide that, "despite my atrophied limbs [or poor abdominal muscle tone or being in a wheelchair], I'm still willing to have a satisfying sexual life."

"Where there's a will, there's a way." Many health care professionals have heard these words, and they are true. A beautiful book, *Incurably Romantic*, was created from photographs of the many couples who resided at what was once called "The Philadelphia Home for Incurables" (Stehle, 1985). One can gaze upon dozens of lovers with severe disabilities, having posed themselves in their wheelchairs or lying on the ground, or holding or feeding one another. What a consciousness-raising experience to see those unusual men and women. This expansion of awareness is crucial because people in general have been so thoroughly entranced to see sexuality as the right of the young, beautiful, and healthy.

The present author (K.B.M.) has estimated that 10% to 20% of adults are highly interested in sexual interactions and highly interested in intimate relationships and, for these individuals, even in the face of chronic or catastrophic disability, the prognosis for sexual recovery is good. For the estimated 10% to 20% of adults who are either totally or almost totally disinterested in sexual interactions, the disability or chronic illness may reinforce this disinterest, and even give the patient or their partner a good reason to put aside sexual activity. It is often helpful to note corresponding variabilities in sensuality, as opposed to sexuality. Some women may have high levels of interest in tender touch and affection, but little or no interest in sexual arousal or orgasm.

The concept of the lovemap, as proposed by Money (1986), and expanded by Whipple and Ogden (1989), helps to explain and predict an individual woman's sexual interests and repertoire, sexual fantasies, and hopes that get translated into action. The lovemap is the template or model that is formed in response to experiences and conditioning throughout life. A woman can explore her lovemap in the process of sex therapy as she comes to know what it is she wants and does not want sexually. As she learns to give herself the experiences and relationships she desires and to avoid any stimulation that is noxious or displeasing, she is sexually fulfilled, and the lovemap is manifested in reality.

Case Study. Before the onset of disability, L. had a satisfactory, if somewhat utilitarian, sexual lifestyle. She felt desirable to her husband, and took satisfaction in being able to satisfy him. She was diagnosed with multiple sclerosis at age 36 years. She now, 3 years later, experiences fatigue, paraparesis, and some loss of vision. After some initial depression and accommodation to decreased mobility, she began to experiment with her sexual expression. Although she had been orgasmic before her diagnosis, she now found that she needed much more physical stimulation to reach orgasm. Through sex therapy, she decided to become more assertive with her husband. She now asks for more stimulation of her breasts, specifically for him to suck, lick, or pull on and around her nipples. She finds that breast stimulation in combination with vigorous oral or manual clitoral stimulation helps her to achieve orgasm. She wishes that she could orgasm in less than 25 to 30 minutes of stimulation, but she reassures herself that her husband loves to pleasure her. He tells her that he particularly loves to hear her breathing hard and moaning with pleasure.

She says that they are closer and more sexual now than ever before. She attributes this to the feeling of vulnerability that her multiple sclerosis forced her to face. She has anxiety about the future with multiple sclerosis and fears more loss of function, but for the present, is satisfied sexually. She recently revealed that when she had to get up to empty her bladder for the second time in a lovemaking session, her husband encouraged her to just "let go" with her urine during their sexual play. She felt such appreciation for his erotic playfulness and understanding. This affirms to her that they are growing as a couple.

Stages of Sexual Readjustment

Based on a qualitative study of women with complete spinal cord injury, Whipple, Richards, Tepper, and Komisaruk (1996a) reported that three stages of sexual readjustment emerged from their data: (1) cognitive genital dissociation, (2) sexual disenfranchisement, and (3) sexual rediscovery.

Cognitive Genital Dissociation

Immediately after the onset of disability or chronic illness, there seems to be a shutting down and closing up of sexuality for many women. Often this sexual ennui is accompanied by depression and a sense of pessimism about the future. Sometimes the woman has serious doubts as to whether her partner will accept her with a disability, whether it is one that dramatically alters her appearance, such as an amputation, or one that alters her function and mobility, such as a stroke or spinal injury. She may question whether her partner will stay with her or be faithful sexually. If she is single, she may wonder whether she will ever experience the love and intimacy she desires. Sometimes a newly disabled woman stops taking any interest in her grooming or in maintaining her attractiveness. She may assume that she is hopelessly unattractive because of the disability. Body image theory has shown that people tend to allow one negative physical feature to "spread," leading to a rejection or negative feelings about the whole person. Cognitive theory has shown that people are constantly attaching meaning to human experiences. For example, if the woman's partner spends less time with her than desired, she may decide that she is being rejected or abandoned. Early developmental issues often resurface and must be reworked in the face of chronic or catastrophic disability. The woman may need to reexamine issues of trust, dependency, and autonomy.

During this early phase of sexual recovery, the health care professional can explore the previous level of sexual interest and activity. A temporary shelving of sexual interest can be normalized by letting the woman know how predictable it is. The woman and her partner can also be assessed regarding the previous value of sexuality in their relationship. Most women can be predicted to have a higher priority on other issues, such as bowel and bladder function with spinal cord injury, or survival with chronic illness, than on sexuality. However, a smaller percentage of women actually consider their sexuality a higher priority than any other area of concern. Women need to be supported in terms of their own individual priorities, not the health care professional's expectations.

Sexual Disenfranchisement

The next phase of sexual "recovery" is labeled sexual disenfranchisement (Whipple et al., 1996b). In a study of women with complete spinal cord injury, sexuality was not perceived as a high priority at first (Whipple et al., 1996b). The participants in the study reported that between 3 months and 3 years postinjury they experienced coitus. They stated that they were curious about what the experience "would be like." The experience generally resulted in sexual dissonance, a comparison between pleasure (what was) and disappointment (what is). This experience activated for most women a lengthy sexual readjustment and reevaluation of the nature of sexual pleasure.

Case Study. K. had a spastic tetraplegia after a C-6 transection of her spinal cord. Yet, as early as 3 months postinjury, she was eager to resume sexual relations with her husband. It appeared that she really needed reassurance that he still had desire for her. He was reluctant to have intercourse and, after some initial hesitancy, admitted that he was afraid of "getting caught inside" his wife. He assumed that the scissor spasms in her legs would produce a "penile captivus" if they attempted intercourse. Although he seemed reassured after some discussion, this "sexual symptom" seemed to focus the issues of how close this couple would be now and how each partner would deal with the anxiety of their new roles. He would be expected to be a caregiver to some extent, whereas previously she had been the primary nurturer in the relationship. This couple needed an extended support system to allow the husband to be "mostly" the husband, and not her major care provider. They also needed to establish boundaries that allowed them private time as a couple, without care providers in attendance. Because of her need for a hospital bed at home, they did not actually sleep together. They arranged to have sensual and often erotic "naps" on weekend afternoons in the husband's bedroom, on what had been their double bed.

Sexual Rediscovery

A period of sexual rediscovery following sexual disenfranchisement has also been described by Whipple et al. (1996b). They found that, for some women, significant life events (such as a 40th birthday), or situational events (such as a new sexual partner) were turning points. Women who were engaged in unaffirming and destructive relationships tended to move toward relationships that were affirming or constructive, sometimes 7 to 15 years postinjury.

> Affirming relationships characterized by open communication, creativity, and resourcefulness, played a key role in positive sexual self-concept. In the period of sexual rediscovery, reciprocity in relationships (partner meeting needs) was critical in the shift from negatively to positively perceived sexual readjustment. There was also a reevaluation of the meaning of sexual pleasure. Exploration resulted in self-awareness of alternative approaches to sexual arousal and, in some instances, orgasm. (Whipple et al., 1996b, p. 78)

It may be possible that the stages of sexual recovery identified in that qualitative study with women with complete spinal cord injury may also emerge from studies of women with other disabilities or chronic illness. Further research is needed in this area. However, anecdotal and case study reports from sex therapists and observations of the authors of this chapter support these stages in women with various disabilities and chronic illnesses.

TREATMENT OF FEMALE SEXUAL DISSATISFACTION AND DIFFICULTY

The following is an exploration of treatment options. Based on the PLISSIT model (Annon, 1974), the health care professional realizes that many sexual difficulties are overcome by an encouraging professional who gives the patient or couple permission to experiment in finding whatever sexual activities she or they enjoy. A knowledge of recent research concerning anatomy and physiology related to the physical disability or chronic illness that the woman experiences is helpful in giving the kind of limited information that helps the woman take the next step in her sexual recovery. Greater professional experience, knowledge gained from research found in texts, practice of the skill of talking with patients about their sexuality, and an attitude that supports the value of sexual health all empower the professional to give specific suggestions to a woman with concerns about sexual health. But when that woman has concerns beyond the scope of the health care professional, it can be useful to refer the woman to a certified sex counselor or certified sex therapist for the intensive therapy step of the PLISSIT model. Annon (1974) has pointed out that the intensive therapy step of the PLISSIT model requires obtaining a full sexual history and offering specialized advanced treatment skills.

The field of sex therapy, though, is still in its infancy, and although there are thousands of sexual health experts around the country, finding a qualified sexologist can be challenging. The first step is to contact the American Association of Sex Educators, Counselors, and Therapists (see listing under *Additional Resources* at the end of this chapter), the primary certifying association, for help in contacting a certified sexual health professional.

The postmodern practice of sex therapy borrows from several major branches within psychology, including behavioral therapy (based on prescriptive challenges); cognitive therapy (based on supporting clearer thinking); psychodynamic and object relations therapy (based on integrating early life development and experiences to resolve present difficulty); communication; and systems or family therapy. Every evaluation of a sexual problem should include a determination of whether the primary focus should be on the individual, the couple, the family, or a combination. Sex therapy is a way of helping individuals reach their sexual potential by working through their dissatisfactions to become more satisfied.

Process of Sex Therapy

The initial interview will elicit the problem as described by the woman or the couple. The words they use to label and define the problem will be useful in formulating a diagnosis and treatment plan. For example, a woman with low desire may say that she is there "to be fixed," ostensibly to reduce her partner's frustration. It will be important *not* to assume that the problem is hers alone, or even that it is unusual to be disinterested in sex. Could the health professional assume that her sexual experience is possibly not that enjoyable to her? Or that she is orgasmic in a functional sort of way? It will be helpful to determine what her idea of good sexual experience would be. It will be useful to ask about her partner's response to her lack of desire and how her partner contributes to her experience. Once the clinician understands the history of the problem, he or she should ascertain what steps the client has already taken to solve the problem or what awareness is present about significant factors influencing the problem. For example, if the woman is complaining about a lack of interest in sex, it might be useful to ask if she has noticed changes in her desire at any specific time in her menstrual cycle.

Meanwhile the clinician must also determine what phase of sexual response is affected. To use Reed's model (see Figure 25–1), is there impairment in the seduction phase? For example, how does or how doesn't the client take responsibility for her own arousal? Is the problem in some aspect of the sensations phase? For example, is the woman feeling critical of her partner's grooming, and therefore turning off, instead of asking him to shave or brush his teeth before their lovemaking proceeds? Is the problem in the surrender phase of the experience, or is there some unresolved issue or conflict that needs attention first? Or, is the problem in the reflection phase, in assessing the meaning of the experience? Is the woman aware of any positive or negative thoughts or judgments she is making about herself or her partner? One enlightened couple treated by the authors stated that they decided that "foreplay" for their next sexual experience began as soon as each experience ended—that way they were always in some phase of lovemaking. The authors of this chapter propose an additional conceptualization of Reed's ESP model: The model is circular, with the reflection phase leading to the seduction phase of the next sexual experience (Figure 25–2).

In talking with women about their sexuality, it is crucial that the clinician communicate genuine caring and respect for them. The language of the interviewer should be neither jargonistic medical terminology nor overly familiar street talk. The language used should be understood by the woman and her partner. Furthermore, the clinician needs to show sensitivity in terms of confidentiality and privacy.

Often, clients have a weak sense of their own basic worth. They are looking to have this worth validated by their partner or the health care professional. They bring their sexual concerns to therapists often because they imagine therapists have the kind of sexual experience they wish for. It is important for the therapist to avoid a "one up" stance. Usually, therapists can find a way to normalize their client's experience. For example, the therapist can disseminate information that it is normal to have sexual dissatisfaction in our culture, because more than 50% of couples have sexual problems at some point. Or, the therapist can explain that it is normal to be anxious about sex at times, especially if it is intensely erotic, which might mean being vulnerable and even experiencing pleasure anxiety.

Sex therapy is an opportunity to support the whole woman and her development. The clinician needs to examine sexual development in the context of human development. What does it mean for a woman to be working toward the fulfillment of her sexual potential? One model the present author (K.B.M.) has found most valuable is the "sexual crucible" approach developed by Schnarch (1991; 1997). It is a new paradigm for sex therapy, based on the awareness that intimacy is not common, but rare, because it requires a high level of maturation to achieve. It is based on differentiation, the ability to maintain one's self while being in close proximity to the partner. It uses sexual problems, the experience of psychotherapy, and indeed the whole relationship as a crucible, or special container, to contain the person's growth. As people grow, they may also develop the ability to tolerate intense eroticism. Eroticism is the pleasure individuals take in their sexuality or the passion and energy they invest in giving and receiving sexual pleasure. "Eroticism and passion are the missing ingredients for the vast masses of sexually functional people who never experience the full impact of their sexual potential" (Schnarch, 1991, p. 313).

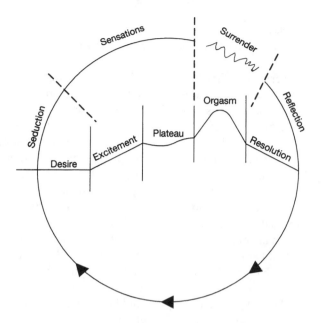

Figure 25–2 Whipple and McGreer's expansion of Reed's Erotic Stimulus Pathway model. The reflection phase leads to the seduction phase of the next sexual experience.

Schnarch (1991) has asserted that, although sex therapy has tended to divide people into only two categories, dysfunctional and functional, there is actually a third category: the blessed few, those "who have profoundly erotic intimate experiences" (p. xiv). The goal of sex therapy is to "increase the ranks of the blessed few" (p. xiv). The advantage of a focus on sexual potential, even with those people who are struggling with disability or chronic illness, is that it reduces a tendency to pathologize, and therefore supports creative progress in many clients.

Although many sex therapists are still prescribing *sensate focus exercises,* that is, structured exercises in giving and receiving touch, Schnarch (1991) has suggested that only activities chosen by patients are useful in propelling their development. He explained that when a therapist tells a person what to do, and the individual cannot do it, the therapist participates in the person's failing. For example, sensate focus exercises are often presented as if they should be pleasurable. Many clients *do not* find them so. Of course, a therapist might brainstorm with a couple or client about sensual and erotic experiences that some enjoy.

As originally conceptualized, sensate focus exercises involve initial avoidance of sexual intercourse. A couple is prohibited from engaging in any sexual activity until the therapist instructs them to do so. Over the course of treatment, they are given homework assignments to increase their range of sexual behaviors. The partners are instructed to take turns in the roles of giver and receiver as they touch and caress each other's bodies. Sensate focus activities might include massage, bathing or showering together, hand or foot holding or caressing, and eye contact exercises. Whether these activities are assigned by the therapist or are activities chosen by the clients depends on the therapist's stance.

The process of sensate focus includes awareness of thoughts, feelings, and sensations, and the meaning the person attaches to these. In the session following a particular experience, the patient may share what she had been thinking, feeling, and doing during that experience. In this way, sensate focus is useful in a diagnostic as well as a therapeutic sense. For example, a particular woman agreed that it might be enjoyable to take a shower with her husband. However, in the next session, she reported that it was a negative experience. As the therapist processed the episode, the woman admitted that she could not get her job off her mind and she did not like it that her husband had an erection the whole time. Further exploration of her thoughts and feelings helped her see how she had created intense feelings of pressure for herself. She could see that she needed to create some boundaries for herself. For example, she could decide to think about work in the time she set aside *for* work and focus herself to think about the shower experience while *there*. Processing the experience apparently gave her more freedom because the next time she took a shower with her husband, she later reported that she really participated in the moment. She chose to focus her senses more fully by noticing dozens of things related to the experience, such as water temperature and sensation, her husband's skin texture and coloring, her own nipple hardening, the nurturing experience of being dried off by her husband, and so forth. Once she realized that her husbands's erection could be ignored or played with, she had more freedom to decide what she paid attention to, and what she did not, depending on what experience she wanted to create for herself: pressure or pleasure.

Schnarch (1991) has found it most useful to work with the actual experiences patients are having as an "elicitation window" to view their development. If the couple tries an "exercise," there is no expectation of how it should feel, only that it gleans new information about each person and his or her own sexual style. Schnarch has proposed the following types of questions to understand a person's sexual style: What do you think about during sex? Who does what to whom? What is the pace? What does it mean? What is the look on your partner's face? How do you know when it is time for penetration/containment? What's off limits? What is your body telling you? These questions not only illustrate sexual style, but they challenge the patient to a higher level of individuation. Schnarch has taken a stance of inviting others to experience short-term pain (perhaps in the form of awkwardness or anxiety) for long-term gain. Schnarch's intimacy and eroticism-based model supports clients to accept the inevitable anxiety of expanding their sexual repertoire. His comprehensive text would be helpful for any health care professional who desires a greater understanding of sexual and relationship intimacy for their patients and for their own personal development.

Specific Sexual Dissatisfactions

Hypoactive Sexual Desire Disorder

Inhibited sexual desire is the most common sexual dissatisfaction women present with in sex therapy. In our culture, there is a wide range of interest and desire for sexual experience among women. The politics of desire are fascinating. There is a tendency to pathologize those people at either end of the continuum—those judged to have either too high or too low an interest in sex. Every couple can be expected to have discrepancies in their levels of desire, unless one of them is constantly adapting to the other. In courtship, this may often be the case. Compromise often brings about a tyranny of the lower common denominator, so the sex becomes boring and routine, and then one partner shuts down. There are numerous well-documented causes of a lack of sexual desire. A partial list includes religiosity or sex-negative conditioning from childhood or the family of origin, childhood sexual abuse or trauma, rape, low self-esteem, lack of intimacy skills, fear of being controlled by the partner or one's own sexual feelings, fear of pregnancy, depression, side effects of numerous medications, inability to resolve conflict with the partner, inability to work out satisfactory balance of closeness and separateness in the union, inability to integrate love and sexual desire, and unrealistic expectations about relationships. Loving and desiring when there is no guarantee of being satisfied is not easy; it takes strength and courage. As long as therapists maintain a neutral stance, patients are free to explore the meaning and value of sex for themselves. Therapists can assist patients to understand their sexual style, which alone helps many patients to overcome sexual dissatisfactions. For example, some women have a very low level of desire and have a partner whose style is either passive (in accepting continual refusals for sexual intercourse) or aggressive (in blaming or criticizing their mate's lack of interest). Such a woman might be helped by the therapist to expand her awareness of how she prefers to be seduced and then she can be encouraged to assertively communicate this to her partner. And her partner, who has a higher level of desire, may benefit from skill training in asserting his desire and need in a way that is effective with his partner. Another common difficulty in treating low sexual desire is the prevalent myth in our culture that desire is "caused" by the partner. The more accurate reality is that each person is responsible for his or her own level of desire. People are resistant to taking responsibility for their own desire. Perhaps women are especially conditioned to expect their partners to seduce and arouse them; consider fairy tales in which the kiss of the handsome prince is required to awaken the maiden. Only a mature, responsible woman is consistently able to produce her own interest and arousal by knowing what her sexual "conditions" are and seeing that they are met.

Case Study. A. (29 years old) came into sex therapy with her husband J. (34 years old). She had received a kidney transplant 4 years earlier and seems to be in great health now, although she remains on immunosuppressive drug therapy. A. and J. have been married for 9 years, and have a 2-year-old child. A. and J. both agree that they once had a happy sexual relationship. A.'s total absence of sexual desire led them into therapy at this time. J. was quite unhappy about the current level of sexual activity in the relationship. He was eager to cooperate because he really wanted to resume their previously satisfying sexual relationship. J. complained that A. had been sexually unresponsive to him since her transplant. Currently, they have sexual relations only once every 2 or 3 months. J. feels taken for granted, and both partners admit that their parents have poor marriages. A. says that she wants to be more sexually interested, but does not know how to get started. She's afraid of losing J.

In doing the sexual history on this couple, both agreed that the transplant and their pregnancy had caused fairly negative effects on their sexual relationship. In the early stages of the pregnancy, A. had been very ambivalent about being pregnant because she had hoped to progress in her career for 1 or 2 years before starting a family. J. was confused by the feeling that A. blamed him for the pregnancy. Both were willing to talk out their disappointments and clarify their expectations of one another. Each partner examined his or her own priorities and individual needs.

The therapy was successful because A. and J. had a high level of commitment and love. They began by promising to set aside more time for their relationship each week. This promise was challenging because they had allowed themselves to make their relationship a low priority timewise, so they also began a courting-type communication pattern of calling one another during the day. They gradually increased their sensual responses to one another. Because of the strains of childbearing and child rearing, and juggling dual careers, they had made sexual pleasure a low priority. They got a babysitter for a standing weekly "date" night. Recently they went on a "second honeymoon" and terminated therapy because they wanted to spend more time alone. Therapy had helped them sort out their priorities, expand intimacy, and renew their strength as a couple.

Female Sexual Arousal and Orgasmic Disorders

Female sexual arousal disorders (APA, 1994) and female orgasmic disorder (formerly referred to as inhibited female orgasm; APA, 1994) can respond well to sex therapy because sexual response is largely learned. Sex therapy tools widely used are "permission" to explore and experiment, group therapy, couples therapy, bibliotherapy and video therapy, assertiveness techniques in asking for the stimulation and experience desired, exploration of one's sexual style, improvment of body image, and expansion of the sexual repertoire to include self-stimulation alone and with the partner. Many women are helped simply through an explanation of the value of clitoral stimulation and how to incorporate it into lovemaking. Occasionally, prolonged psychodynamic psychotherapy is required for highly avoidant or anxious women. In such cases, an in-depth sexual history will usually reveal some early sexual trauma or sex-negative role modeling. The patient may need to explore and resolve any limiting decisions she made or defenses she developed. Sometimes the therapeutic relationship is a kind of reparenting experience.

Sexual Pain Disorders

Sexual pain disorders such as dyspareunia (APA, 1994) and vaginismus (APA, 1994) respond to many of the sex therapy tools described, with additional emphasis on relaxation training, with or without hypnosis, or the use of small, well-lubricated vaginal dilators, then progressing to gradually larger vaginal dilators. The woman must be fully in control of penetration and containment. To prevent a pain–tension–fear cycle from getting established, the women should always take charge of "if, when, and how" vaginal or anal penetration occurs. She should ensure there is adequate lubrication, whether natural transudate or additional water-soluble lubrication such as Astroglide or Replens, or, if the couple is not using latex for safer sex or contraception, then the use of a product such as unscented Albolene is recommended. Strong efforts may be required to reverse a well-established dyspareunia. In rare cases of a very thick, tight hymen, surgery may be indicated. If the woman has unrealistic fears of being damaged, these concerns must be raised and countered with cognitive therapy approaches. Partner involvement is crucial at the right time.

Sexual Counseling with Women with Disability or Chronic Illness

Congenital or Early-Onset Disability

When congenital or early-onset disability or chronic illness occurs, there will need to be attention for the whole family in supporting healthy sexual development. Families will need to counter tendencies toward overprotectiveness and infantilization. The therapist will need to address spasticity and contractures, whether in cerebral palsy or spinal abnormalities, which may be helped by anti-spasmodic medications. With blindness or deafness, the therapist should make a special effort to assist the patient to develop a healthy body image and perception of sexual anatomy, physiology, and function. Even teaching a young woman how to masturbate may have to be done in a specific manner, and will probably raise hackles in some sectors of our erotophobic society. The professional's and the patient's values will have to be clearly considered to be able to support healthy development. Of course, a major challenge is to support healthy socialization and social skill development, such as for dating.

Adult-Onset Disability or Chronic Illness

When adult-onset disability or chronic illness in some way interferes with sexual function, a woman may assume she can no longer be sexual in a "normal" or "proper" way. She is at risk for being desexualized and devalued by the culture at large, and then by herself to the extent that her identity is tied in to her body image or approval by others. Her previous sexual experience can be a handicap or an asset to readjustment, depending on her mindset. A sense of humor can be the most valuable asset in making flexible adjustments to physical limitations.

Patients with a disability or chronic illness may also possess one of the sexual dissatisfactions previously described and will need tailored interventions to sex therapy. Our culture tends to overvalue spontaneity and undervalue planning. For women with a disability or chronic illness, the following are some of the issues that the therapist may need to address to help the woman or couple make a satisfactory sexual adjustment (Brash, 1991):

- Timing of sexual activity in regard to energy levels or around medical procedures: It is helpful for the woman to plan sensual or sexual encounters when energy and opportunity for pleasure are optimal.
- Preparation for sexual activity (e.g., for skin care, bowel and bladder care, or contraception): These activities must be coordinated. Couples will benefit from eliminating distractions such as the telephone. Children and pets will need special care. All couples need private time without distractors.
- Transfer activities (from wheelchair to bed) and positioning with pillows or protective padding: A woman may need distant supervision or assistance from an attendant on call for these activities.
- Attention to the creation of a warm, romantic, comfortable, and private environment: The woman can create such an environment by using mood music, candles, soft lighting, and by consuming fluids and snacks to maintain energy. She may also use satin or flannel sheets, depending on whether she desires a warmer or cooler effect.
- Stimulation for arousal and lubrication: The woman may find vibrators or showerheads useful. Massage can be a wonderful way to arouse, relax, and increase awareness and flexibility. Coaching is helpful to enhance awareness

of pleasure in everyday activities such as eating, bathing, or elimination. Recommendation of selected videos or reading materials may also help some women and couples.

- Expansion of the sexual repertoire: The repertoire may include oral techniques, tantra breathing and eye contact meditation, the display of skills in self-pleasuring, and many more.
- Medication management: The woman should time her medications for pain or sedation as desired. For example, women with arthritis may be advised to take pain medication before sexual activities and women with angina may be advised to take nitroglycerin before engaging in sexual activities. Antispasmodic medication can be timed to help decrease spasms during sexual activity.
- Contraception: In addressing this issue, the woman should be aware of the risks of thromboembolic phenomena, as well as the risks of pregnancy and methods of delivery. Many women find it stimulating and helpful to have her partner insert a diaphragm or female condom, if this is the method chosen.
- Exercise: Exercise should be done to maintain range of motion and prevent deformities (e.g., hips and low back are especially important), as well as after corrective surgery (e.g., breast reconstruction after mastectomy). Changing sides in bed can be suggested (e.g., after a mastectomy if the breast usually stimulated was removed).
- Precautions: The woman should take precautions to prevent injuries, using splints or protecting her skin from pressure sores, compensating for sensory loss. She also should plan for autonomic dysreflexia if she has a spinal cord injury above T-6.

To help the woman with a disability or chronic illness and her partner to make a "sexual recovery," it is important for the therapist to appreciate the loss from her perspective, but then go on to challenge her to accept life on its own terms. The therapist may need to provide special support for the healthier partners or spouses in working through their own losses and attending to their need for rest, for time off from the caregiver role and for their own individual quality of life. The Well Spouse Foundation (see *Additional Resources*) is a national resource whose focus is to balance the needs of the "patient" and the "caregiver"; neither one to be martyred for the other. This organization holds local chapter meetings and offers a helpful newsletter. Sometimes the person with a disability or chronic illness develops an exaggerated sense of entitlement and may become demanding or unrealistic in her expectations of others, thus inviting resentment instead of tenderness. Each partner, and indeed every member of the family system, has special and universal needs for breaks from routines, adequate rest, appreciation, and so on. All need to be empowered by the health care professional to assert their own needs while respecting the needs of other members of the system.

People with disabilities and people who are at least temporarily able bodied all face a similar developmental challenge to reach their sexual potential. The concept of the temporarily able bodied refers to the premise that, if people live long enough, the odds are good that most will become disabled. Sexual counseling or therapy with a woman with a disability or chronic illness is based on the same concepts and treatment modalities used with any other woman or couple. However, it behooves the therapist to understand the meaning of the disability or chronic illness to the woman rather than impose preconceived ideas of limitations that the disability or chronic illness place on the woman or the couple.

REFERENCES

Addiego, F., Belzer, E.G., Comolli, J., Moger, W., Perry, J.D., & Whipple, B. (1981). Female ejaculation: A case study. *Journal of Sex Research, 17,* 99–100.

American Psychiatric Association. (1994). *Diagnostic and statistical manual of mental disorders* (4th ed.). Washington, DC: Author.

Annon, J.S. (1974). *The behavioral treatment of sexual problems. Vol. 1: Brief therapy.* Hawaii: Enabling Systems.

Belzer, E., Whipple, B., & Moger, W. (1984). On female ejaculation. *The Journal of Sex Research, 20,* 403–406.

Bianca, R., Sansone, G., Cueva-Rolon, R., Gomez, L.E., Ganduglia-Pirovano, M., Beyer, C., Whipple, B., & Komisaruk, B.R. (1994). Evidence that the vagus nerve mediates a response to vaginocervical stimulation after spinal cord transection in the rat. *Society for Neuroscience Abstracts, 20,* 961.

Brash, K.C. (1991). *Sexuality, sensuality, and multiple sclerosis.* Oaklyn, NJ: Multiple Sclerosis Association of America.

Frank, E., Anderson, C., & Rubinstein, D. (1978). Frequency of sexual dysfunction in normal couples. *New England Journal of Medicine, 299,* 111–115.

Kaplan, H.S. (1974). *The new sex therapy.* New York: Brunner/Mazel.

Kaplan, H.S. (1979). *Disorders of sexual desire.* New York: Simon & Schuster.

Koch, P.B. (1995). *Exploring our sexuality.* Dubuque, IA: Kendall/Hunt.

Komisaruk, B.R., Bianca, R., Sansone, G., Gomez, L.E., Cueva-Rolon, R., Beyer, C., & Whipple, B. (1996). Brain-mediated responses to vaginocervical stimulation in spinal cord-transected rats: Role of the vagus nerves. *Brain Research, 708,* 128–134.

Komisaruk, B.R., & Whipple, B. (1994). Complete spinal cord injury does not block perceptual responses to vaginal or cervical self-stimulation in women. *Society for Neuroscience Abstracts, 20,* 961.

Komisaruk, B.R., & Whipple, B. (1995). The suppression of pain by genital stimulation in females. *Annual Review of Sex Research, 6,* 151–186.

Masters, W.H., & Johnson, V.E. (1966). *Human sexual response.* Boston: Little, Brown.

Masters, W.H., & Johnson, V.E. (1970). *Human sexual inadequacy.* Boston: Little, Brown.

Money, J. (1986). *Lovemaps: Clinical concepts of sexual/erotic health and pathology.* New York: Prometheus Books.

Perry, J.D., & Whipple, B. (1981). Pelvic muscle strength of female ejaculators: Evidence in support of a new theory of orgasm. *Journal of Sex Research, 17,* 22–39.

Schnarch, D.M. (1991). *Constructing the sexual crucible: An integration of sexual and marital therapy.* New York: W.W. Norton.

Schnarch, D.M. (1997). *Passionate marriage.* New York: W.W. Norton.

Sipski, M.L. (1991). Spinal cord injury: What is the effect on sexual response? *Journal of the American Paraplegia Society, 14*(2), 40–43.

Spector, I., & Carey, M. (1990). Incidence and prevalence of the sexual dysfunctions. A critical review of the empirical literature. *Archives of Sexual Behavior, 19,* 389–408.

Stayton, W.R. (1989). A theology of sexual pleasure. *American Baptist Quarterly, 8*(2), 1–15.

Stehle, B. (1985). *Incurably romantic.* Philadelphia: Temple University Press.

Timmers, P.O. (1976). Treating goal-directed intimacy. *Social Work,* 401–402.

Turk, M. (1993). The neglected sex. *American Health,* 54–57.

Whipple, B. (1987). Sexual counseling of couples after a mastectomy or a myocardial infarction. *Nursing Forum, 23*(3), 85–91.

Whipple, B. (1990). Female sexuality. In J.F.J. Leyson (Ed.), *Sexual rehabilitation of the spinal-cord-injured patient* (pp. 19–38). Clifton, NJ: Humana Press.

Whipple, B., Gerdes, C.A., & Komisaruk, B.R. (1996a). Sexual response to self-stimulation in women with complete spinal cord injury. *Journal of Sex Research, 33*(3), 231–240.

Whipple, B., & Gick, R. (1980). A holistic view of sexuality: Education for the health professional. *Topics in Clinical Nursing, 1,* 91 98.

Whipple, B., & Ogden, G. (1989). *Safe encounters: How women can say yes to pleasure and no to unsafe sex.* New York: McGraw-Hill.

Whipple, B., Ogden, G., & Komisaruk, B.R. (1992). Relative analgesic effect of imagery compared to genital self-stimulation. *Archives of Sexual Behavior, 21,* 121–133.

Whipple, B., Richards, E., Tepper, M., & Komisaruk, B.R. (1996b). Sexual response in women with complete spinal cord injury. In D.M. Krotoski, M. Nosek, & M. Turk (Eds.), *Women with physical disabilities: Achieving and maintaining health and well-being* (pp. 69–80). Baltimore: Paul H. Brookes.

Witkin, M.H. (1978). Sex therapy and mastectomy. *Journal of Sex and Marital Therapy, 1,* 290–304.

Zaviacic, M., Dolezalova, S., Holoman, I.K., Zaviacicova, A., Mikulecky, M., & Bradzil, V. (1988). Concentrations of fructose in female ejaculate and urine: A comparative biochemical study. *Journal of Sex Research, 24,* 311–318.

Zilbergeld, B., & Ellison, C.R. (1980). Desire discrepancies and arousal problems in sex therapy. In S.R. Leiblum & L.A. Pervin (Eds.), *Principles and practice of sex therapy* (pp. 65–104). New York: Guilford Press.

ADDITIONAL RESOURCES

American Association of Sex Educators, Counselors, and Therapists (AASECT)
P.O. Box 238
Mount Vernon, IA 52314
Phone: 319-895-8407
Fax: 319-895-6203

Well Spouse Foundation
P.O. Box 801
New York, NY 10023
Phone: 800-838-0879
Fax: 212-724-5209

CHAPTER 26

Management of Female Infertility

Sandra L. Welner

INFERTILITY: SCOPE AND BACKGROUND

The World Health Organization (1987) has defined a couple as being *infertile* if they have been trying and have been unable to conceive for at least 2 years; according to the U.S. medical definition, however, a couple is infertile after only 1 year of unsuccessful attempts to achieve pregnancy (Chandra & Mosher, 1994). Infertility affects 4.9 million American couples—1 in 12—as indicated by the most recent data collected in 1988 by the National Center for Health Statistics (Mosher & Pratt, 1990). The decline in fertility among couples with advancing age has been repeatedly documented. About one-third of women who defer pregnancy until their mid- to late thirties will have an infertility problem as will at least one-half of women older than age 40 years (Jacob's Institute of Women's Health, 1995).

A 1988 National Survey of Family Growth (Mosher & Pratt, 1990) estimated that 15% of sexually active women aged 15 to 44 years (8% of all women of reproductive age) have reported *impaired fecundity*, that is, a physical inability to have children because of physical difficulty or because it is medically inadvisable to conceive. Multivariate logistic regressions have shown that older women, childless women, and married women are significantly more likely to report impaired fecundity. Likewise, women with a history of treatment for pelvic inflammatory disease or a history of diabetes, hypertension, or endometriosis are significantly more likely to report this condition (Wilcox & Mosher, 1993).

The author gratefully acknowledges the assistance of Dr. Michael Welner, Dr. Alan DeCherney, and Stephen Burns, and the inspiration and guidance of the late Mr. Nick Welner.

ETIOLOGIES OF FEMALE INFERTILITY

An evaluation of the contributing factors of infertility in couples has revealed that tubal and pelvic pathology and male problems contribute equally at approximately 35% (Speroff, Glass, & Kase, 1994). Less common difficulties in couples include ovulatory dysfunction (15%), unexplained infertility (10%), and unusual problems (10%). The most common female factors are tubal pathology (including that caused by endometriosis and pelvic adhesions) and pelvic pathology (40%) and ovulatory dysfunction (40%), specifically, oligo-ovulation and anovulation (Speroff et al., 1994). Less common etiologies include anatomic factors such as müllerian anomalies (i.e., congenital malformations of genital tract structures; Fedele et al., 1996); Asherman's syndrome (i.e., denudation of the uterine lining from infections or surgical trauma; Cisse, Andriamampandry, Diallo, Diab, & Diadhiou, 1995); fibroid uterus (Farhi et al., 1995); and a history of diethylstilbestrol exposure. The clinician will need to evaluate immunologic and hormonal factors as well, when indicated.

Another factor that contributes to infertility is cigarette smoking, which reportedly affects cervical mucus, fallopian tube motility, and oocyte viability. In addition, drug abuse, such as of marijuana and narcotics, is known to affect hypothalamic–pituitary hormone secretion (Jaffe & Jewelewicz, 1991).

IMPACT OF SPECIFIC DISABILITIES, DISEASES, AND MEDICATIONS ON FERTILITY

Women with disabilities and chronic diseases are anatomically similar to other women. The disability or chronic disease process, however, may alter physiology by affecting the hypothalamic regulation of ovulation or secretion of elevated levels of certain hormones. Chronic diseases may decrease a woman's fertility as a result of the generalized stress on her body; the stress can affect the hypothalamus as well.

Spinal Cord Injury

Approximately 30,000 women in the United States have a spinal cord injury (Ficke, 1992).

Spinal cord injury is frequently associated with alterations in menstrual patterns. Up to 60% of women with spinal cord injury demonstrate menstrual irregularities (Yarkony, 1992). The most common alteration is manifested as secondary amenorrhea, which develops in more than 50% of the women with such an injury. The duration of amenorrhea can vary, but is usually between 3 and

6 months postinjury. Secondary amenorrhea lasting up to 1 year has been reported (Yarkony, 1992). Many researchers believe stress of the injury, which affects the release of gonadotropins, alters the pituitary–hypothalamic–ovarian axis. After stabilization postinjury, fertility rates as well as rates of miscarriage are similar to those in the general population.

Galactorrhea, a result of hyperprolactinemia, has also been reported in women after spinal cord injury (Huang, Wang, Lai, Chang, & Lien, 1996). Hyperprolactinemia develops within 3 to 6 months after spinal cord injury and can persist for up to 24 months. Prolactin levels can become markedly elevated immediately postinjury, although this elevation does tend to return to normal within 1 year (Huang et al., 1996). Frequently, hyperprolactinemia is associated with menstrual disturbance. Amenorrhea resulting from a possible decrease in estrogen production likely results from a central pituitary mechanism. Osteoporosis is a potential consequence. Hence, the clinician should treat patients to restore resumption of a cyclic menstrual pattern. However, it has not been proven that hyperprolactinemia in the absence of menstrual disturbance can lead to osteoporosis (Ciccarelli et al., 1988).

Traumatic Brain Injury

More than 120,000 women suffer traumatic brain injury each year (Kraus & Sorenson, 1994). Common metabolic consequences of traumatic brain injury include short- and long-term derangements of hypothalamic function involving the adrenocorticotropic axis, thyrotropic regulation, and pituitary hypothalamic–gonadal functional disorders. The pituitary response to hypothalamic dysregulation is evidenced by increases in adrenocorticotropic hormone (ACTH), growth hormones, and prolactin, and decreases in thyroid-stimulating hormone (TSH), luteinizing hormone (LH), and follicle-stimulating hormone (FSH).

The adrenocorticotropic axis derangements can be identified soon after traumatic injury and vary in degree and duration. ACTH stimulation results in variably increased cortisol production (Carey, Clouther, & Lowery, 1971). Thyroid function may also be affected; for example, reduced thyrotropin-releasing hormone (TRH) has been found to affect TSH, resulting in reduced T_4, free T_3, and free T_4 levels. Such changes, which may persist for approximately 3 months, may be the result of changes in thyroid metabolism and binding properties or reduced biosynthesis of thyroid hormone (Madsen, Smeds, & Lennquist, 1986). Prolactin production that is normally controlled by tonic hypothalamic inhibition also may be disturbed by brain injury (de Leo, Petruk, & Crockford, 1981). The degree of prolactin elevation varies and can begin within 1 month after the traumatic event. In addition, hyperprolactinemia and galactorrhea can be managed with bromo-cryptine after the clinician has evaluated abnormalities of the pituitary gland to rule out adenoma. Hyperprolactinemia can also be induced by chest trauma or medications that are frequently administered to women to control agitation, seizures, or other problems (see *Medications* section).

The pituitary–hypothalamic–ovarian axis may also be affected by brain trauma. A small observational study found that 11 out of 84 women (13%) developed secondary amenorrhea with a duration of up to 6 months after head trauma (Cytowic, Smith, & Stump, 1986). This amenorrhea could be a result of direct suppression of gonadotropins or of abnormal levels of prolactin or thyroid hormones. In contrast, children have been reported to suffer precocious puberty after head trauma perhaps because of the premature activation of the pituitary–hypothalamic–gonadal axis (Shaul, Towbin, & Chernausek, 1985). Inhibiting factors that normally restrain pituitary gonadotropin release are believed to be affected by head trauma in these cases (Shaul et al., 1985).

Multiple Sclerosis

An estimated 350,000 to 500,000 cases of multiple sclerosis (MS) exist in the United States, with approximately 8,000 new cases reported each year, and there is a 3:1 female/male predisposition (Sibley, 1992). MS first appears most commonly in young premenopausal women. This neurologic disorder has various manifestations and may result in an unpredictable degree of disability.

Women with MS may have no impairment of fertility. However, MS may occasionally result in pituitary–hypothalamic–gonadal axis dysfunction and may induce menstrual disturbances and subsequent infertility (Grinstead, Heltberg, Hagan, & Djursing, 1989). Abnormal gonadotropin levels as well as an elevated prolactin level and ovarian androgens (testosterone) have been identified in premenopausal women with MS (Grinstead et al., 1989). Therefore, if the clinician notes secondary amenorrhea or menstrual dysfunction, he or she must evaluate and treat hyperprolactinemia or other abnormalities.

Epilepsy

Hormonal influences and neurologic conditions have been known to interact. This interaction has been specifically noted with respect to seizure disorders, which occur in 5 people per 1,000 in the general population (Banfi, Borselli, & Marinai, 1995). Estrogen reportedly lowers seizure threshold, whereas progesterone tends to stabilize it (Herzog, 1991). The neurologic conditions of those women with particularly brittle seizure control may be exacerbated by the normal fluctuation of estrogen and progesterone levels over the course of the menstrual cycle. Consequently, this interaction influences the women's choices of appropriate contraceptive methods. New preparations for oral contraception have significantly reduced amounts of estrogen, and therefore may have less impact on seizure disorders (Herzog, 1991). Menopausal hormonal replacement therapy has not been studied for its effects on those conditions.

Diabetes Mellitus

Diabetes mellitus is one of the more prevalent chronic diseases in the United States, afflicting an estimated 16 million people (Harris, 1993). This condition is strongly linked to significant disabling complications including blindness, amputations, and stroke. The association between diabetes and menstrual disturbances may result from a multiple endocrine adenopathy syndrome, which also affects thyroid function. Disorders of ovulation can occur indirectly from alterations in cortisol metabolism in mechanisms that are not well understood.

Thyroid Disease

The Thyroid Foundation of America reported that thyroid disease is one of the most common endocrinopathies, and that 80% of people affected are women (Woods, Cooper, & Ridgway, 1995). Disturbances in thyroid function are associated with alterations in metabolic rate that result in changes in body weight, hair, and other organ systems. Thyroid function is regulated through the pituitary gland, which produces TRH. Alterations in TRH secretion can affect gonadotropin-releasing hormone and prolactin release. Abnormal thyroid function also reportedly affects menstrual cyclicity (Popovich & Moore, 1993). Changes can range from amenorrhea to oligomenorrhea to menometrorrhagia. In some patients, menstrual function is unaltered.

Furthermore, thyroid abnormalities have been linked to autoimmune phenomena in some patients in whom multiple endocrine disorders are detected. These phenomena include insulin-dependent diabetes mellitus (type 1); Addison's disease; myasthenia gravis; Sjögren's syndrome; pernicious anemia; and idiopathic thrombocytopenic purpura. Hyperthyroidism and hypothyroidism can usually be treated successfully with normalization of thyroid parameters. If menstrual dysfunction has resulted from thyroid dysfunction, normal cyclicity usually resumes after treatment.

Cushing's Disease

Cushing's disease represents excess serum cortisol as a result of elevated ACTH production or excessive secretion of cortisol from the adrenal cortex. Patients with this condition may also develop hypertension, diabetes, and osteoporosis. Although Cushing's disease is relatively less common than the other aforementioned chronic diseases, menstrual disturbances are frequently found among its many manifestations.

Tuberculosis

Genital tuberculosis is apparently increasing in prevalence in the United States because of the increasing immigration from countries in which this disease is endemic. Although the prevalence of genital tuberculosis is reported to be less than 1% in the United States, that figure does not reflect the significant presence of asymptomatic infections. Moreover, the statistics have not incorporated the immigrant populations (Alvarez & McCabe, 1984). Tuberculosis, a multisystem disease primarily affecting the lungs, spreads throughout many organ systems by way of the circulation. The most common sites of extrapulmonary spread include the lymphatic system, urinary tract, and genital tract (Wolinsky, 1992). Pelvic organs of women infected with genital tuberculosis can be damaged in different ways. Genital organs and their frequency of involvement with tuberculosis infection are as follows: fallopian tubes, 90% to 100%; endometrium, 50% to 60%; ovaries, 20% to 30%; cervix, 5% to 15%; and vulva and vagina, 1% (Schaefer, 1976).

In 10% to 40% of women with genital tuberculosis, abnormal uterine bleeding may result from involvement of the ovaries or endometrial cavity. Consequences can vary from menorrhagia, menometrorrhagia, oligomenorrhea, to amenorrhea. Approximately 90% of patients infected with genital tuberculosis have very mild, subclinical presentations such as some weight loss, low-grade nocturnal fever, and fatigue (Nogales-Ortiz, Taracon, & Nogales, 1979). Up to 50% of women with genital tuberculosis are first diagnosed during an infertility workup (Nogales-Ortiz et al., 1979). Causes of infertility include tubal occlusion, endometrial infection with scarring, pelvic adhesions, or ovarian dysfunction.

Other Chronic Diseases

Women affected by chronic diseases such as malignancies, Crohn's disease, and tuberculosis, may face more than one barrier to fertility. In addition to alterations in hormonal regulation, chronic disease may affect a women's sexual desire as a result of pain, fatigue, and other related problems. A number of chronic diseases result in secondary amenorrhea. Decreased appetite and weight loss from chronic diseases also may contribute to menstrual irregularities.

Exhibit 26–1 Pharmacologic Agents Affecting Prolactin Concentrations

---

Stimulators

- Anesthetics
- Psychotropics
  - phenothiazines
  - tricyclic antidepressants
  - opiates
- Hormones
  - estrogen
  - oral steroid contraceptives
  - TRH

- Antihypertensives
  - alpha-methyldopa
  - reserpine
- Antiemetic
  - sulpiride
  - metoclopramide

Inhibitors

- L-dopa
- Dopamine

Source: Reprinted with permission from O.A. Kletzky and V. Davajan, Hyperprolactinemia, in *Infertility, Contraception, and Reproductive Endocrinology*, 3rd ed., D.R. Mishell, V. Davajan, and R.A. Lobo, eds., © 1991, Blackwell Science, Ltd.

Medications

Women with disabilities are commonly prescribed pharmaceuticals that affect ovulation either by altering thyroid function or prolactin levels or by directly suppressing ovulation (Exhibit 26–1). Steroids are often prescribed to women with rheumatologic and collagen vascular diseases. In addition, women may be treated with steroids after trauma to reduce edema in brain and spinal cord tissue. These medications can have an effect on ovulatory function by influencing T_3 to T_4 conversion. Phenytoin is commonly used by women with a history of trauma, cerebral aneurysms, or other brain tumors. Administration of this medication affects ovulation through its effects on T_4 and T_3 metabolism, serum protein binding, serum and cellular concentration of thyroid hormones, or hypothalamic and pituitary regulation of TSH (Smith & Surks, 1984). Also, aspirin may increase free T_3 levels by a poorly defined mechanism (Popovich & Moore, 1993). Nonsteroidal antiinflammatory agents are used by many women with disabilities to manage mild or moderate discomfort. It is controversial whether these agents contribute to the development of luteinized unruptured follicle syndrome. However, because of the potential effect, these agents should probably be avoided in women who are attempting conception (Akil, Amos, & Stewart, 1996).

EARLY PREGNANCY FAILURE

Incidence and Diagnostic Criteria

Recurrent pregnancy failure has been reported to occur clinically in 14% of patients and subclinically in 29%, with a combined average of 43% (Dwyer, MacLeod, Collingnon, & Sorrell, 1987). Diagnostic techniques for evaluating the viability of a pregnancy early in gestation have significantly advanced. The combination of transvaginal ultrasound evaluation and the measurement of serial titers of beta human chorionic gonadotropin (BHCG) is helpful in this respect. In patients who demonstrate BHCG levels greater than 2,000 mIU/mL, an intrauterine gestational sac will usually be visualized on transvaginal ultrasonography (Batzer, 1991). In viable pregnancies, "doubling time" of approximately 66% within 48 hours is a reassuring indicator. This trend should be followed in 1 to 2 weeks for confirmation. Conversely, BHCG titers that fall or do not rise appropriately could indicate a nonviable gestation.

The classic indicator of a confirmed viable pregnancy is the presence of fetal cardiac activity, identified at 6 weeks by transvaginal ultrasound (Molo, Kelly, Balos, Mullaney, & Radwanska, 1993). Once cardiac activity has been observed, the risk of pregnancy failure is greatly diminished (approximately 7%). Fewer than 2% of pregnancies with previously documented fetal cardiac activity may have fetal loss after 9 weeks (Molo et al., 1993). However, in patients with a history of recurrent pregnancy failure, the risk may be higher.

Genetic Causes

Genetic causes are responsible for up to 50% of pregnancy failures. Some genetic etiologies are more prevalent than others. The majority are abnormalities that occur during gonadogenesis. Autosomal trisomy is the most common abnormal karyotype, followed by monosomy, triploidy, tetraploidy, and structural abnormalities, respectively. The most common single chromosomal abnormality is monosomy 45 (Horn, Rosenkranz, & Bilek, 1990).

Different incidences of specific chromosomal anomalies have been identified in second trimester versus first trimester abortuses. These include trisomies 13, 18, and 21; monosomy X; and sex chromosomal polysomies. In the third trimester, frequency of loss as a result of chromosomal anomalies is approximately 5% compared with a frequency of loss of 0.6% in the third trimester that does not result from chromosomal factors (Simpson & Carson, 1991).

Hormonal Causes

Thyroid Disease

Thyroid disease has been implicated in infertility, in early pregnancy failure, and in problems during pregnancy. Women with poorly controlled thyroid disease are predisposed to spontaneous abortion; the fetus may also develop complications such as congenital goiter and mental retardation (Popovich & Moore, 1993).

Diabetes Mellitus

Diabetes is the most prevalent endocrinopathy and affects many women of reproductive age. Many women with diabetes may not be closely monitoring their blood sugar. When glucose control in early pregnancy has been poor, women are at increased risk for fetal loss and have an increased incidence of fetal chromosomal anomalies (The Diabetes Control and Complications Trial Research Group, 1996). Therefore, in the diabetic population, preconception counseling is essential.

Luteal Phase Defect

The luteal phase, which follows ovulation, is usually 11 to 15 days long. Luteal phase defect (LPD) in isolated cycles has been noted in up to 30% of normal fertile women (Bopp & Shoupe, 1993). Furthermore, recurrent LPDs (greater than one concurrent cycle) have been noted in 3% to 4% of women with infertility and approximately 5% of women with a history of recurrent abortion. One form of LPD occurs at the normal time in the menstrual cycle and is associated with a subnormal progesterone production. Another type is associated with a shorter normal luteal phase length (Bopp & Shoupe, 1993).

The diagnosis of LPD has two components: serum progesterone levels and endometrial biopsy. Progesterone level in the normal luteal phase should be greater than 10 ng/mL, although accurate timing of this measurement is pivotal in obtaining a valid result. The clinician should obtain more than one reading in subsequent months before confirming LPD. Progesterone levels do not always correlate with endometrial histology. The correlation of subsequent out-of-phase endometrial biopsies (greater than 3 days lag) with more than one subnormal progesterone level is more accurate than using only one of these diagnostic tests (Ilesanmi, Adeleye, & Osotimehin, 1995).

Because LPD has its origin at the phase of folliculogenesis (selection of the dominant follicle for ovulation), treatment should be addressed at this level. Agents that act on gonadotropins (LH or FSH) and stimulate folliculogenesis are preferable to supplemental progesterone. Supplemental progesterone treats the progesterone level and the endometrial histology but does not correct defective ovulation. Exclusion of contributing endocrinopathies, such as thyroid disease and prolactin abnormalities, and determination of tubal patency should precede ovulation induction.

Nonhormonal Chronic Diseases

Systemic lupus erythematosus (SLE) is an autoimmune disorder that occurs in all decades of life and has significantly greater incidence in females and in blacks (Steinberg, 1992). SLE is one of the more common autoimmune diseases in women and manifests primarily in the reproductive age group. This disorder is associated with poor pregnancy outcome with fetal losses in all trimesters. The etiology for these losses is not completely understood. Disorders of placentation possibly caused by the deposition of immune complexes in the placenta as well as thrombosis in the placenta may play a role. Preventing these effects with aspirin and prednisone is controversial; hence, this intervention must be considered on an individualized basis.

Chronic illnesses such as renal disease and poorly controlled hypertension can result in vascular changes that affect placentation. These disorders can result in decreased vascularity of the placenta, increased thrombosis in the placenta, accelerated aging, and abruptio placenta. Maternal cyanotic congenital cardiac disease may result in recurrent pregnancy losses because of impaired fetal oxygenation. Significant malnutrition such as in Crohn's disease and cancer can also be associated with pregnancy loss.

Anatomical Causes

Intrauterine adhesions (Asherman's syndrome) have been implicated in some cases of early pregnancy failure because of interference of implantation by an inhospitable, somewhat denuded intrauterine environment (Simpson & Carson, 1991). Furthermore, this syndrome has been associated with aggressive dilatation and curettage procedures or intrauterine infection (endometritis). Treatment of this condition is possible using hysteroscopic procedures with hormone supplementation. Even with these interventions, miscarriage rates may still persist in a significant number of patients.

Müllerian anomalies may also be responsible for pregnancy loss. Depending on the nature of the anomaly, the pregnancy loss may occur early, as in cases of implantation on an intrauterine septum, or somewhat later, because of anatomical compromise. Leiomyomata are yet another cause of repeated pregnancy loss, especially if the fibroid is in an intramural submucous location. The fibroid structurally inhibits implantation as well as prevents growth through spatial constraints.

In some cases, hysteroscopic resection can be attempted and has been variably successful, depending on location and size of the leiomyomata.

Infections

Various infectious agents have been linked to increased incidence of repeated pregnancy loss. Their contribution has been controversial. More common agents such as *Toxoplasma, Chlamydia trachomatis, Ureaplasma urealyticum,* and cytomegalovirus are the culprits usually sought. Uncommon agents such as variola, vaccinia, *Salmonella typhi, Vibrio fetus Malaria,* and *Brucella* also have been linked to repetitive pregnancy loss (Mishell, 1993). Special cultures and immunoassays are required to identify the offending organisms and guide appropriate treatment. Even after treatment, elimination of risk has not been predictable.

Autoimmune Disease

The fetus is a foreign entity and, without some type of immunologic suppression, the maternal antibodies would reject it. This suppression is believed to be in the form of a blocking factor, an IgG antibody, which coats the foreign fetal antigens and protects the fetus from rejection (Agrawal et al., 1995). In rare cases, women with recurrent pregnancy loss may have a defect in this protective mechanism. Treatments with paternal and maternal antibodies have not yielded consistent results.

Environmental Exposures

Maternal smoking of greater than 14 cigarettes per day (Kline et al., 1995) and maternal alcohol consumption of greater than 1 oz absolute alcohol twice per week (Parazzini et al., 1994) have been strongly linked to fetal wastage, especially in the second trimester (15 to 27 weeks). Both substances appear to act as direct fetal toxins.

In addition, although animal studies have suggested a link between ionizing radiation and early pregnancy loss, studies in humans have not yet demonstrated this link (Brent & Beckman, 1994). Ionizing radiation administered to the fetus, however, has resulted in increased incidence of congenital anomalies, a dose-dependent phenomenon.

There have been conflicting reports regarding the impact of environmental chemicals on the incidence of recurrent spontaneous abortion. Some agents implicated include anesthetic gases, arsenic, aniline, benzene, cyanide, formaldehyde, and lead. Interactions between these agents and poor pregnancy outcome requires further study (Brent & Beckman, 1994).

In summary, in evaluating a couple who has suffered recurrent pregnancy loss, intervention and diagnostic workup should follow the second episode because one episode of early pregnancy failure is seen in up to 50% of couples. If two consecutive miscarriages are documented, evaluation should begin, and efforts made to rule out treatable factors, such as hormonal, immunologic, chronic disease, and so on. If these areas are thoroughly and comprehensively evaluated and no etiology can be found, chromosomal factors should be considered. Depending on the chromosomal abnormality, recurrence risks can be determined during consultation with a skilled genetics counselor. Emotional support during this process is essential.

INHERITED DISORDERS REQUIRING GENETIC COUNSELING

The genetic influences on development are multifold. Malformations and defects are transmitted by way of a number of different genetic pathways. The most common pathways are mendelian (autosomal dominant or recessive), whereby a single gene or a pair of genes carries a specific inherited characteristic. *Multifactorial inheritance* implies involvement of both genetic and environmental factors. *Polygenic inheritance* describes traits that result from a number of genetic loci that are unaffected by the environment. The interaction between genetic predispositions and environmental exposure and the combination of genetic material of both the mother and the father is extremely complex and beyond the scope of this discussion.

The more common inherited disabilities include cleft lip or cleft palate, neural tube defects, hydrocephalus, and congenital heart disease. Although the genetic cause of cleft lip or cleft palate may vary, in the majority of babies, mendelian inheritance is implicated. Neural tube defects are attributable to multifactorial patterns of inheritance and are reported to occur in approximately 1 in 1,000 births (Lary & Edmonds, 1996). One of the more common forms is spina bifida. The mild form is spina bifida occulta; in the more disabling form, bowel and bladder dysfunction are noted as well as loss of ambulatory capability. Other forms of neural tube defects include anencephaly and meningiomyelocele. Women of reproductive age who are planning conception should take a supplement of folate (0.4 mg/day) before they attempt to conceive and while they are attempting to conceive. Folate supplementation can decrease the recurrence of neural tube defects by up to 70% (Lary & Edmonds, 1996). The pattern of hydrocephalus inheritance may be multifactorial or may result from a single-gene defect. It can sometimes be caused by environmental influences such as viral or protozoan infections. In some cases, significant deterioration of cognitive abilities can be avoided by placement of a shunt to reduce pressure on the brain tissue.

Congenital heart disease is quite common. The genetic etiologies vary from multifactorial to mendelian. Other contributing influences include rubella infection and exposure to phenytoin during pregnancy.

In summary, genetic causes of disabling conditions present a great challenge. Couples should consult with an experienced genetics counselor for advice on recurrence risks of individual conditions and other issues.

WORKUP

Women with disabilities share the identical pelvic organs as women without disabilities and are likewise subject to similar causes of infertility. Couples with disabilities have encountered negative attitudes on the part of some infertility specialists. These specialists may be consciously or subconsciously uncomfortable offering the same options and opportunities to the infertile couple with a disability as they would offer to other couples.

Furthermore, because women with certain disabilities may have ovulation problems, it is important that the infertility specialist not assume that there is only one factor causing the infertility problem. The incidence of ovulation irregularities may vary among the types of disabilities. Thus, a systematic approach to investigate every possible contributing cause is essential. The patient handout in Exhibit 26–2 may help organize and simplify the infertility evaluation. Features of the workup in the infertility handout may vary in women with different types of disabilities. For example, women with visual or fine motor coordination impairment may have difficulty reading a basal body thermometer and filling in the small squares on the chart. Partners may need to be involved. Similarly, evaluation of tubal patency and assessments of intrauterine contour by hystero-salpingogram may be difficult with some women with hip contractures, such as in women with cerebral palsy. Another evaluation option for these women would be to undergo chromotubation to assess tubal patency at the time of laparoscopy as well as a hysteroscopy to evaluate intrauterine abnormalities. Because these procedures are performed under anesthesia, the discomfort of positioning is minimized.

Physical Examination

When undergoing an infertility workup, women with disabilities need to have a physical examination to obtain cervical specimens and be evaluated for other visible or palpable pathology. The clinician needs to address special considerations, such as having an examination table that is totally accessible (low height), and preferably offering security handrails, straps, and leg boots (Welner, in press). Different segments of the infertility workup may be cumbersome and even dangerous because some procedures may trigger autonomic dysreflexia. This problem may arise in spinal cord–injured women with lesions above T-6 when the

Exhibit 26–2 Basic Infertility Workup Patient Handout

Phase 1

First Visit

1. You should have a blood count, pelvic examination including Pap smear, and cervical cultures for gonorrhea and chlamydia. Thyroid-stimulating hormone level and prolactin level may also be needed in some cases.
2. You should perform basal body temperature charting for 2 months using a basal body thermometer available at drugstores. Take your temperature in the morning before getting out of bed and mark it on chart. Do this for 2 months to reduce the chance of getting a false idea about your ovulation patterns.
3. Ask your partner to have a semen analysis. Do not have intercourse for 48 hours before collecting the semen in the provided container. This period will allow the specimen to be of optimal quality. Deliver the specimen to the lab no later than 2 hours after obtaining it.

Phase 2

After looking at the basal body temperature chart, other tests will be scheduled in their appropriate phases.

1. The hysterosalpingogram is a dye test done after the menses and before ovulation. This test is performed to find out whether the fallopian tubes are open and also is used to look at the internal shape of your uterine cavity.
2. The second test, the postcoital test, is done at midcycle (the peak of the temperature rise on the basal body temperature chart). You and your partner should have intercourse no more than 2 hours before coming to the doctor's office. The doctor will check the mucus in the cervix to see whether the sperm are alive and moving. This test can find problems of abnormal interaction between a woman's mucus in the cervix and the man's sperm. If this interaction is abnormal, the partners will need further testing.
3. Sometimes you might need a blood test around day 23 to day 24 of a 28-day menstrual cycle for progesterone level (this timing may vary depending on your cycle length and when you have your ovulation peak).
4. The next test is an endometrial biopsy on day 26 of a 28-day cycle. The doctor will take a small sample of the lining of your uterus to check whether it is thick and well developed enough to support a living embryo.
5. A laparoscopy should be performed to evaluate the presence of adhesions or endometriosis that cannot be detected with a hysterosalpingogram.

Depending on what is found during this workup, treatment will be focused on the findings determined to be abnormal. If your ovulation is unpredictable, this factor may have to be corrected before some of these tests can be performed.

clinician inserts a bulb suction cannula to aspirate cervical mucus from the endocervical canal during the postcoital test or performs a late luteal phase endometrial biopsy. Hence, the clinician must carefully monitor patients' blood pressure and keep rapid-acting antihypertensive agents nearby. In women with spinal cord injuries, preventive measures include having them empty their bladder and undergoing a bowel program before the exam. Furthermore, gentle, slow, nonforceful adjustments of leg positioning may help prevent reflex muscle spasms and discomfort. Also, the application of xylocaine gel to the perineum and cervix can help minimize the risk of autonomic hyperreflexia (Colachis, 1991), although the clinician should still watch patients for this reaction.

Treatment

Treatment of infertility factors in women with disabilities closely resembles that in women without disabilities. During the basic initial examination, the health care provider should also take a detailed history. If the workup uncovers complex problems such as sperm–mucus interactions, which would suggest antibody problems, or abnormal laparoscopic findings with apparent significant compromise of fertility potential, then the clinician should refer the patient to a fertility specialist.

The male partner's contribution to infertility cannot be underestimated. If the male partner has abnormal semen analysis, his health care provider should refer him to a urologist who specializes in fertility issues.

Ovulation disorders may be treated quite effectively. If during the initial evaluation the clinician identifies thyroid–hormone abnormalities or prolactin secretion disorders, he or she can treat to correct these factors; such treatment often will result in normalization of ovulatory function over time. If the ovulation disorder has no definable cause, treatment with ovulation induction can proceed, providing the clinician has previously documented tubal patency. The most common ovulation-inducing agent is clomiphene citrate, a medication that is also useful in the treatment of LPD. During ovulation induction, though, the ovaries can become enlarged, possibly initiating dysreflexic reactions in women with spinal cord lesions above T-6. The clinician should watch for this complication and counsel the couple to recognize warning signs and seek attention promptly.

Anatomical factors contributing to infertility include defects of the corpus uteri and damaged fallopian tubes. Endometrial causes of infertility frequently are treated successfully by hysteroscopy. Fallopian tube disorders may result from endometriosis or infections. Chlamydia infection can result in significant tubal damage, even in the absence of positive cervical cultures. Antibody titers may more accurately identify a subclinical infection. In the past, tubal disease, when documented, has been treated with microsurgical techniques. However, extensive costly tubal surgery is becoming less popular as alternative, more successful assistive reproductive technologies are being perfected. Interventions can range from straightforward techniques such as intrauterine insemination and ovulation induction to the more complicated in vitro fertilization, gamete intrafallopian transfer, or zygote intrafallopian transfer. See Chapter 27 for a more detailed discussion of assisted reproductive technologies.

Women with and without disabilities have the same anatomical contributions to infertility. Thus, during the infertility evaluation of a woman with a disability it is important that the clinician consider all contributing factors pertaining to her disability without ignoring components that require evaluation in all couples. Such a comprehensive evaluation combined with a sensitive and empathic approach will enable disabled women with fertility problems to benefit from medical knowledge and appropriate treatment.

Pregnancy Concerns

Comprehensive discussion of pregnancy and disability is beyond the scope of this chapter. However, because many women with disabilities take medications, they should be aware of the effects of those drugs. See Table 26–1 for a review of the impact of some common medications used by women with spiral cord injuries. For further information on this topic, see the references under *Suggested Readings* at the end of the chapter.

Table 26–1 Impact on Pregnancy of Medications Commonly Used by Women with Spinal Cord Injuries

Medication	Pregnancy Issues	Lactation Issues
baclofen	Teratogenesis—No data in humans; some abnormalities detected in animal models	0.1% of maternal dose in milk; considered compatible with breastfeeding by the American Academy of Pediatrics (AAP)
diazepam	Teratogenesis—Facial clefts in animals; no good evidence of anomalies in humans Neurobehavioral—Effects noted in rats but not in humans Fetal—Third trimester chronic use associated with floppy infant syndrome and diazepam withdrawal syndrome	Diazepam can accumulate in breast-fed infants as well; repeated use in nursing mothers is not recommended

continues

Table 26–1 continued

Medication	Pregnancy Issues	Lactation Issues
dantrolene	Little data exist; has been given without adverse effects in the peripartum period to prevent malignant hyperthermia	No data
oxybutynin	Teratogenesis—Anomalies seen in animals given doses toxic to the mothers	No data
pseudoephedrine	Teratogenesis—One small study found increased risk of gastroschisis Medical—The decongestant of choice in pregnancy	Not associated with adverse effects in newborns; considered compatible with breastfeeding by the AAP
phenoxybenzamine	Fetal—Animal evidence of impaired closure of the ductus arteriosus; used with apparent safety in pheochromocytoma in pregnancy	No data
prazosin	Teratogenesis—Not seen in animals; fetal and maternal toxicity at high doses in animals Fetal—Used with apparent safety for hypertension in few patients	No data
calcium channel blockers	Teratogenesis—Animal and in vitro evidence of several abnormalities Fetal—Animal evidence of acid–base disturbance Medical—Used with safety in series of women in third trimester for preterm labor	Less than 5% of maternal dose in milk; nifedipine is considered compatible with breastfeeding by the AAP
nitrofurantoin	Teratogenesis—No human or animal evidence of anomalies Medical—No reports of fetal hemolytic anemia (theoretically at risk)	Considered compatible with breastfeeding by the AAP unless the child has leukocyte G6PD deficiency
trimethoprim-sulfamethoxazole	Teratogenesis—Anomalies seen in animals; little evidence in humans Fetal—Concern over displacement of bilirubin from albumin and from impaired folate availability	Compatible with breastfeeding unless premature, jaundiced, or leukocyte G6PD deficiency
ciprofloxacin	Teratogenesis—No evidence of anomalies in animals Fetal—Arthropathy in animals; use not recommended in pregnant women	Incompatible with breastfeeding

Source: Reprinted with permission from E.R. Baker and D.D. Cardenas, Pregnancy in Spinal Cord Injured Women, *Archives of Physical Medicine and Rehabilitation*, Vol. 77, pp. 501–507, © 1996, W.B. Saunders Co.

REFERENCES

Agrawal, S., Kishore, R., Halder, A., Sharma, A., Sharma, R.K., Das, V., Shukla, B.R., & Agrawal, S.S. (1995). Outcome of pregnancy in women with recurrent spontaneous abortion following immunotherapy with allogenic lymphocytes. *Human Reproduction 10*(9), 2280–2284.

Akil, M., Amos, R.S., & Stewart, P. (1996). Infertility may sometimes be associated with NSAID consumption. *British Journal of Rheumatology, 35*(1), 76–78.

Alvarez, S., & McCabe, W.R. (1984). Extrapulmonary tuberculosis revisited: A review of experience at Boston City and other hospitals. *Medicine, 63,* 25–55.

Banfi, R., Borselli, G., & Marinai, C. (1995). Epidemiological study of epilepsy by monitoring prescriptions of antiepileptic drugs. *Pharmacy World & Science, 17*(4), 138–140.

Batzer, F.R. (1991). The use of sonography in the diagnosis and management of ectopic pregnancy. *American Journal of Gynecologic Health, 5*(3), 29–32.

Bopp, B., & Shoupe, D. (1993). Luteal phase defects. *Journal of Reproductive Medicine, 38*(5), 348–356.

Brent, R.L., & Beckman, D.A. (1994). The contribution of environmental teratogens to embryonic and fetal loss. *Clinical Obstetrics and Gynecology, 37*(3), 646–670.

Carey, L.C., Clouther, C.T., & Lowery, B.D. (1971). Growth hormone and adrenal corticol response to shock and trauma in the human. *Annals of Surgery, 174,* 451–458.

Chandra, A., & Mosher, W.D. (1994). The demography of infertility and the use of medical care for infertility. *Infertility and Reproductive Medicine Clinics of North America, 5*(2), 283–296.

Ciccarelli, E., Savino, L., Carlevatto, V., Bertagna, A., Isaia, G.C., & Camanni, F. (1988). Vertebral bone density in nonamenorrhoeic hyperprolactinaemic women. *Clinical Endocrinology, 28*(1), 1–6.

Cisse, C.T., Andriamampandry, S.D., Diallo, Y., Diab, E.H., & Diadhiou, F. (1995). The role of hysteroscopy in the diagnosis and treatment of uterine adhesions. *Revue Francaise de Gynecologie et Obstetrique, 90*(1), 17–21.

Colachis, S.C. (1991). Autonomic hyperreflexia with spinal cord injury. *Journal of the American Paraplegia Society, 15,* 171–186.

Cytowic, R.E., Smith, A., & Stump, D. (1986). Transient amenorrhea after closed head trauma. *New England Journal of Medicine, 314,* 715.

de Leo, R., Petruk, K.C., & Crockford, P. (1981). Galactorrhea after prolonged traumatic coma: A case report. *Neurosurgery, 9,* 177–178.

The Diabetes Control and Complications Trial Research Group. (1996). Pregnancy outcomes in the Diabetes Control and Complications Trial. *American Journal of Obstetrics and Gynecology, 174*(4), 1343–1353.

Dwyer, D.E., MacLeod, C., Collingnon, P.J., & Sorrell, T.C. (1987). Extrapulmonary tuberculosis—A continuing problem in Australia. *Australia New Zealand Journal of Medicine, 17,* 507–511.

Farhi, J., Ashkenazi, J., Feldberg, D., Dicker, D., Orvieto, R., & Ben Rafael, Z. (1995). Effect of uterine leiomyomata on the results of in-vitro fertilization treatment. *Human Reproduction, 10,* 2576–2578.

Fedele, L., Bianchi, S., Marchini, M., Franchi, D., Tozzi, L., & Dorta, M. (1996). Ultrastructural aspects of endometrium in infertile women with septate uterus. *Fertility and Sterility, 65,* 750–752.

Ficke, R.C. (1992). *Digest of data on persons with disabilities.* Washington, DC: National Institute of Disability and Rehabilitation Research.

Grinsted, L., Heltberg, A., Hagan, C., & Djursing, H. (1989). Serum sex hormone and gonadotropin concentrations in premenopausal women with multiple sclerosis. *Journal of Internal Medicine, 226,* 241–244.

Harris, M. (1993). Undiagnosed NIDDM: Clinical and public health issues. *Diabetes Care, 16,* 642–652.

Herzog, A.G. (1991). Reproductive endocrine considerations and hormonal therapy for women with epilepsy. *Epilepsia, 32,* S27–S33.

Horn, L.C., Rosenkranz, M., & Bilek, K. (1990). Genetic aspects of early spontaneous abortion. *Zentralbl Gynakil, 112,* 123–133.

Huang, T.S., Wang, Y.H., Lai, J.S., Chang, C.C., & Lien, I.N. (1996). The hypothalamus-pituitary-ovary and hypothalamus-pituitary-thyroid axes in spinal cord–injured women. *Metabolism, 45,* 718–722.

Ilesanmi, A.O., Adeleye, J.A., & Osotimehin, B.O. (1995). Comparison of single sperm progesterone and endometrial biopsy for confirmation of ovulation in infertile Nigerian women. *African Journal of Medical Science, 24,* 97–101.

The Jacobs Institute of Women's Health. (1995). *The women's health data book—A profile of women's health in the United States* (2nd ed). Washington, DC: Author.

Jaffe, S., & Jewelewicz, R. (1991). The basic infertility investigation. *Fertility and Sterility, 56,* 599–613.

Kline, J., Levin, B., Kinney, A., Stein, Z., Susser, M., & Warburton, D. (1995). Cigarette smoking and spontaneous abortion of known karyotype: Precise data but uncertain inferences. *American Journal of Epidemiology, 141*(5), 417–427.

Kraus, J., & Sorenson, S. (1994). Epidemiology. In J. Silver, S. Yudofsky, & R. Hales (Eds.), *Neuropsychiatry of traumatic brain injury* (pp. 3–43). Washington, DC: American Psychiatric Press.

Lary, J.M., & Edmonds, L.D. (1996). Prevalence of spina bifida at birth—United States, 1983–1990: A comparison of two surveillance systems. *MMWR CDC Surveillance Summaries, 45,* 15–26.

Madsen, M., Smeds, S., & Lennquist, S. (1986). Relationships between thyroid hormone and catecholamines in experimental trauma. *Acta Chirurgica Scandinavica, 152,* 413–419.

Mishell, D.R. (1993). Recurrent abortion. *Journal of Reproductive Medicine, 38*(4), 250–259.

Molo, M.W., Kelly, M., Balos, R., Mullaney, & Radwanska. (1993). Incidence of fetal loss in infertility patients after detection of fetal heart activity with early transvaginal ultrasound. *Journal of Reproductive Medicine, 38*(10), 804–806.

Mosher, W.D., & Pratt, W.F. (1990). *Fecundity and infertility in the United States, 1965–88. Advance data from vital and health statistics, no. 192.* Hyattsville, MD: National Center for Health Statistics.

Nogales-Ortiz, F., Taracon, I., & Nogales, F.F., Jr. (1979). The pathology of female genital tuberculosis. A 31-year study of 1436 cases. *Obstetrics and Gynecology, 53*(4), 422–428.

Parazzini, F., Tozzi, L., Chatenoud, L., Restelli, S., Luchini, L., & LaVecchia, C. (1994). Alcohol and risk of spontaneous abortion. *Human Reproduction, 9*(10), 1950–1953.

Popovich, D., & Moore, L. (1993). Pregnancy in women with thyroid disease: A delicate balance. *Journal of Perinatology and Neonatal Nursing, 7*(3), 34–36.

Schaefer, G. (1976). Female genital tuberculosis. *Clinical Obstetrics and Gynecology, 19,* 223.

Shaul, P.W., Towbin, R.B., & Chernausek, S.D. (1985). Precocious puberty following severe head trauma. *American Journal of Diseases of Children, 139,* 467–469.

Sibley, W. (1992). *Therapeutic claims in multiple sclerosis.* New York: Demos.

Simpson, J.L., & Carson, S.A. (1991). Genetic and nongenetic causes of spontaneous abortions. In J.J. Sciara (Ed.), *Gynecology and obstetrics* (pp. 1–29). Philadelphia: J.B. Lippincott.

Smith, P.J., & Surks, M.L. (1984). Multiple effects of 5,5′-Diphenylhydantoin on the thyroid hormone system. *Endocrine Review, 5*(4), 514–524.

Speroff, L., Glass, R.H., & Kase, N.G. (Eds.). (1994). Female infertility. In *Gynecologic endocrinology and infertility* (5th ed., pp. 809–851). Baltimore: Williams & Wilkins.

Steinberg, A.D. (1992). Systemic lupus erythematosus. In J.B. Wyngaarden, L.H. Smith, & J.C. Bennett (Eds.), *Cecil textbook of medicine* (19th ed., pp. 1522–1530). Philadelphia: W.B. Saunders.

Welner, S.L. (in press). Caring for the woman with a disability. In L. Wallis (Ed.), *The textbook on women's health.* Boston: Little, Brown.

Wilcox, L.S., & Mosher, W.D. (1993). Use of infertility services in the United States. *Obstetrics and Gynecology, 82,* 1.

Wolinsky, E. (1992). Tuberculosis. In J.B. Wyngaarden, L.H. Smith, & J.C. Bennett (Eds.), *Cecil textbook of medicine* (19th ed., pp. 1733–1742). Philadelphia: W.B. Saunders.

Woods, L.C., Cooper, D.S., & Ridgway, E.C. (Eds.). (1995). *Your thyroid: A home reference.* New York: Ballantine.

World Health Organization. (1987). Infections, pregnancies, and infertility: Perspectives on prevention. *Fertility and Sterility, 47,* 964–968.

Yarkony, G.M. (1992): Spinal cord injured women: Sexuality, fertility and pregnancy. In P.J. Goldstein & B.J. Stern (Eds.), *Neurologic disorders of pregnancy* (2nd rev. ed., pp. 203–222). Mt. Kisco, NY: Futura.

SUGGESTED READINGS

Allbert, L.R., & Morrison, J.C. (1992). Neurologic diseases in pregnancy. *Obstetrics and Gynecology Clinics of North America, 19*(4), 765–781.

Baker, E.R., & Cardenas, D.D. (1996). Pregnancy in spinal cord injured women. *Archives of Physical Medicine and Rehabilitation, 77*(5), 501–507.

McDonald, P.C., Gant, N.F., & Pritchard, J.A. (Eds.). (1993). *William's obstetrics* (19th ed.). East Norwalk, CT: Appleton & Lange.

Queenan, J.T. (Ed.). (1992). *Management of high risk pregnancy* (3rd ed.). Cambridge, MA: Blackwell Scientific.

Silver, R.W., & Branch, D.W. (1992). Autoimmune diseases in pregnancy. *Baillieres Clinical Obstetrics and Gynaecology, 6*(3), 565–600.

CHAPTER 27

Assisted Reproductive Technologies

José M. Colón

Since the birth of Louise Brown in 1978, the first child born after in vitro fertilization and embryo transfer (IVF-ET; Steptoe & Edwards, 1978), the field of human reproductive endocrinology and infertility has undergone a revolution that has resulted in the development of new therapies for couples who previously could not have children. *Assisted reproductive technologies (ART)* are "any techniques designed to produce pregnancy which require the involvement of third parties for success" (Toner & Hodgen, 1993, p. 219). This chapter reviews four of the most commonly used ART: (1) intrauterine insemination (IUI), (2) IVF-ET, (3) intracytoplasmic sperm injection (ICSI), and (4) gamete intrafallopian transfer (GIFT). These techniques may vary widely in terms of their indications, complexity, risks, opportunity for success, and cost. When managing infertility, no treatment will guarantee a pregnancy. The optimal treatment is the simplest one that will provide a reasonable opportunity for success with the least amount of risk, and at the lowest cost. Thus, every couple or individual making use of ART deserves a full evaluation to determine the safest and most cost-effective therapy that will result in pregnancy. Sperm, an egg or ovum, and a uterus with a functioning endometrial surface are essential to achieve pregnancy, with or without the use of ART. To better understand the rationale, indications, and management of ART, this chapter first reviews the events of the menstrual cycle and of natural, unassisted conception and implantation.

MENSTRUAL CYCLE AND UNASSISTED CONCEPTION

A woman with normal reproductive function ovulates once approximately every 28 days. The ovulatory process requires the presence of a functioning hypothalamic–pituitary axis with the pulsatile release of the gonadotropins luteinizing hormone (LH) and follicle-stimulating hormone (FSH) into the bloodstream, and a functioning ovary. LH and FSH stimulate the production and secretion of estradiol and progesterone by the ovary. Estradiol and progesterone are released into the bloodstream and feed back to the hypothalamic–pituitary axis to modulate the secretion of LH and FSH, and they induce the necessary changes in the endometrium for implantation and pregnancy to occur. During the normal, early ovulatory cycle, the hormonal interplay between the hypothalamic–pituitary axis and the ovaries results in the initial growth and maturation of a cohort of ovarian follicles (Gougeon, 1996). The follicles in the cohort are at different stages of early maturation.

By the end of the first week of the cycle, the changing sex hormone environment in the cycling woman results in the selection of a dominant follicle, the one follicle destined to ovulate. The dominant follicle continues to grow in response to hormonal stimulation, mainly LH and FSH from the pituitary gland, and the rest of the follicles from the initial cohort degenerate. The first half (2 weeks) of the cycle—the follicular phase—is characterized by the growth and maturation of the dominant follicle, which secretes increasing amounts of estradiol as well as other ovarian hormones. When the dominant follicle reaches a critical size and maturational state, the pituitary gland releases the LH surge, the final maturational stimulus and the trigger to ovulation. The ovulated egg enters the fallopian tube and travels toward the endometrial cavity. The follicle that releases the egg becomes a corpus luteum that secretes progesterone, estradiol, and other ovarian hormones during the luteal phase—the last half (2 weeks) of the cycle. This sequential pattern of hormone secretion—estrogen during the follicular phase, and estrogen plus progesterone during the luteal phase—is necessary to prepare and support the endometrium for implantation and pregnancy.

In the absence of pregnancy, the ability of the corpus luteum to secrete progesterone and other hormones is limited to approximately 14 days. At the end of the luteal phase, the corpus luteum stops secreting estrogen and progesterone and degenerates. The lack of hormonal support at the level of the endometrium results in the shedding of the lining of the uterus as a menstrual period. The decrease in the levels of estradiol and progesterone in the blood are sensed by the hypothalamic–pituitary axis, which responds with an increase in the secretion of FSH and LH. Thus, another cycle commences: The rising levels of FSH and LH induce the early growth and maturation of another cohort of immature follicles that secrete estradiol and from which the dominant follicle for that cycle will be determined. The menstrual cycle is thus characterized by ever-changing hormone levels that induce ovulation, and menstruation in the absence of pregnancy. This dynamic hormonal picture is in sharp contrast with other hormonal systems in the body, such as the pituitary–thyroid axis, which is characterized by a steady state of hormonal secretion.

If intercourse occurs at around the time of ovulation, sperm deposited in the vagina penetrate into the cervical mucus, leaving the rest of the seminal contents in the vagina. The sperm then travel into the endometrial cavity and subsequently into the fallopian tubes, where fertilization generally occurs. At present, there is no evidence that anything other than chance is involved in bringing the human sperm and egg together. A large number of spermatozoa are lost from the time of ejaculation in the vagina to the time of fertilization in the fallopian tube. A normal ejaculate contains 100 to 300 million sperm, of which a few hundred reach the vicinity of the egg (Settlage, Motoshima, & Tredway, 1973) and only one penetrates the egg in normal fertilization. Following fertilization, the fertilized egg undergoes multiple divisions and develops into an embryo as it travels toward the uterine cavity. Eventually, the embryo reaches the endometrial surface, where it implants and a pregnancy ensues. Human chorionic gonadotropin (HCG) secretion by the pregnancy rescues the corpus luteum from degeneration. The ovary continues to secrete estradiol and progesterone, which are necessary for sustaining the endometrium for the early pregnancy and preventing the shedding of the endometrium as menstruation.

STRATEGIES FOR INCREASING CONCEPTION RATES

ART can be used to overcome ovulatory dysfunction, anatomic factors, and male factor infertility. In general, the working hypothesis is that ART increases the chances of pregnancy by increasing the relative concentration of available gametes for fertilization. Thus conception rates increase if there are more eggs and sperm, or more sperm per egg available for fertilization, or both. Increased numbers of eggs can be obtained with controlled ovarian hyperstimulation protocols. Because fertilization in the natural cycle generally occurs in the fallopian tube in the presence of a few hundred sperm, increasing the relative concentration of sperm in the vicinity of the egg, in vitro or in vivo, should increase the chance of fertilization. Techniques of sperm "washing" have been developed that separate sperm from seminal plasma and concentrate the cells for ART. Either strategy, increasing the number of available eggs or increasing the relative concentration of available sperm for fertilization of the eggs, should increase conception rates. Increasing both the numbers of eggs and sperm should optimize success.

Controlled Ovarian Hyperstimulation

Controlled ovarian hyperstimulation is the manipulation of the hormones controlling ovulation to achieve the growth and maturation of multiple eggs. A number of protocols and agents are available for controlled ovarian hyperstimulation. The clinical protocols discussed in this chapter are some of the standard, most commonly used protocols in ART. Discussion is limited to the use of human menopausal gonadotropins (HMG) alone or in combination with gonadotropin-releasing hormone agonists (Gn-RH$_a$) to induce controlled ovarian hyperstimulation.

HMG is a purified preparation of LH and FSH extracted from the urine of menopausal women. The use of HMG achieves supraphysiologic levels of LH and FSH in the circulation. The normal feedback mechanism of ovarian hormones that control the levels of LH and FSH during the cycle are overridden. The high levels of LH and FSH result in the stimulation of growth and maturation of multiple follicles, including the dominant follicle as well as other follicles from the initial cohort that would have degenerated under normal conditions (Corsan & Kemmann, 1991; Ginsburg & Hardiman, 1991). Controlled ovarian hyperstimulation with HMG is generally started in the early follicular phase, around day 3 of the cycle. HMG preparations are administered as daily intramuscular injections. Response to therapy is monitored over time in two ways: (1) the size of the growing follicle is measured serially with ultrasound examinations and (2) the serum concentration of estradiol, which increases proportionally with follicular maturation, is serially determined. Once the follicles reach the appropriate size and the estradiol levels confirm adequate maturation, the patient is given an intramuscular injection of HCG, an artificial LH surge necessary for the final maturation of the eggs, and the stimulus to ovulate. Controlled ovarian hyperstimulation with HMG can be used to increase the number of ovulated eggs at the time of intercourse or at the time of IUI. The controlled ovarian hyperstimulation protocols generally used for IVF-ET, ICSI, and GIFT use a combination of agents such as Gn-RH$_a$ and HMG.

Gn-RH$_a$s are long-acting, biologically active analogues of gonadotropin-releasing hormone (Gn-RH). Gn-RH is the hormone secreted by the hypothalamus into the portal circulation that stimulates the pituitary to produce and secrete LH and FSH. There are two critical aspects of the Gn-RH stimulus in terms of pituitary production and secretion of LH and FSH: (1) hypothalamic Gn-RH is secreted in pulses and (2) the half-life of Gn-RH in the portal circulation is relatively short (Knobil, 1980). Any major disturbance of the pulsatile Gn-RH signal results in pituitary "down-regulation" and "desensitization," resulting in the shutdown of pituitary gonadotropin secretion; LH and FSH secretion stops (Vickery & Nestor, 1987). Gn-RH$_a$s are chemically altered analogues of Gn-RH that resist rapid degradation in the portal circulation. The long-acting analogues are sensed by the pituitary as a continuous Gn-RH signal rather than the normal pulsatile stimulus. The pituitary stops secreting LH and FSH. The internal gonadotropin signals that stimulate ovarian function are shut off. The use of Gn-RH$_a$ followed by the administration of HMG results in better control of controlled ovarian hyperstimulation (Meldrum, 1989; Meldrum et al., 1989). Because of pituitary gonadotrope desensitization, the supraphysiologic levels of circulating levels of LH and FSH are the result of the administration of exogenous hormones, with no influence from endogenous pituitary gonadotropins. Cycle cancellation secondary to premature luteinization or the premature release of a pituitary LH surge resulting in unpredicted ovulation is prevented (Cedars, Surey, Hamilton, Lapolt, & Meldrum, 1990). Large numbers of mature follicles are obtained with the combined use of Gn-RH$_a$ and HMG (Hughes et al., 1992; Meldrum, 1989). Gn-RH$_a$ preparations can be administered as an intranasal spray twice a day, or as a daily subcutaneous injection. In a common protocol of controlled ovarian hyperstimulation that uses Gn-RH$_a$/HMG, the Gn-RH$_a$ is started in the midluteal phase of the cycle before the cycle of HMG stimulation. Because the Gn-RH$_a$ is started after ovulation, ovarian function is little altered on the cycle in which the medication is started. However, the ovaries will not be stimulated to start a subsequent cycle. Gn-RH$_a$ administration is continued through menses and through the days of HMG administration. HMG stimulation is started anytime after the onset of menses. Gn-RH$_a$/HMG administration is continued until the follicles reach maturity in terms of size and estradiol secretion, when HCG is administered. The stimulation is monitored with serial follicle ultrasound examinations and serum estradiol determinations as described for the use of HMG alone. IUI or egg retrieval for IVF-ET, ICSI, or GIFT is performed 34 to 36 hours after the HCG injection.

Three possible complications of controlled ovarian hyperstimulation deserve mention (Schenker & Ezra, 1994): (1) ovarian hyperstimulation syndrome (OHSS), (2) an increased incidence of multiple pregnancies, and (3) a reported association of an increased incidence of ovarian cancer in patients who undergo controlled ovarian hyperstimulation. OHSS is a self-limited condition that can follow controlled ovarian hyperstimulation and is characterized by a shift of fluid from the intravascular space into the abdominal cavity (Golan et al., 1989). In mild cases, it produces ovarian enlargement, abdominal distention, and weight gain. Severe cases can present with life-threatening ascites, pleural effusion, electrolyte imbalance, and hypovolemia with hypotension and oliguria. The incidence of clinically important OHSS is in the range of 1% to 2%. Even though the pathophysiology of OHSS is not well understood, excessively high levels of estradiol secretion following HMG stimulation are likely to be involved. The full blown syndrome does not develop unless the ovulatory dose of HCG is given. Thus, it is critical to monitor the patients undergoing controlled ovarian hyperstimulation because the development of OHSS can potentially be prevented. HCG should not be administered in the presence of an excessively large number of developing follicles or a dangerously high level of serum estradiol.

Controlled ovarian hyperstimulation for ART is also associated with a high incidence of multifetal pregnancies. Multifetal pregnancies expose the mother and the fetuses to increased health risks and costs (Callahan et al., 1994; Neuman, Gharib, & Weinstein, 1994). The mother is exposed to a number of complications during pregnancy and delivery, including a higher incidence of preeclampsia, placenta previa, placental abruptio, postpartum hemorrhage, and Caesarean section. The fetuses are exposed to a higher risk of prematurity, early and late abortions, stillbirth, and perinatal morbidity and mortality. Limiting the number of embryos transferred after in vitro fertilization and limiting the number of eggs transferred for GIFT can reduce the risk of multifetal pregnancies. Today, patients with multifetal pregnancies can undergo selective reduction early in the second trimester of pregnancy to decrease the number of fetuses and to improve the chance of a favorable outcome of pregnancy (Evans et al., 1993).

A number of case reports, case-control, and cohort studies have questioned and investigated a possible association between controlled ovarian hyperstimulation and an increased risk of ovarian cancer. In a recent review and critical analysis of available data in the literature, Bristow and Karlan (1996) concluded that such an association does not necessarily indicate a causal effect between controlled ovarian hyperstimulation and ovarian cancer. Confounding factors such as infertility and nulliparity are independent risk factors for the development for ovarian cancer. The association between controlled ovarian hyperstimulation and ovarian cancer may result because infertile and, in many cases, nulliparous women compose the population that undergoes controlled ovarian hyperstimulation. The question of the oncogenic potential of controlled ovarian hyperstimulation protocols cannot be ignored. Given the available information, no change has been recommended in the manner that medications are used for controlled ovarian hyperstimulation (Riddick, 1993; Spirtas, Kaufman, & Alexander, 1993). Furthermore, the National Institute of Child and Human Development and the National Cancer Institute are funding investigations that should clarify this issue further (Bristow & Karlan, 1996).

Sperm "Washing"

Semen consists of seminal fluid with sperm, some white blood cells, and other cellular debris from the urogenital tract. The seminal fluid contains large amounts of prostaglandins, enzymes, proteinase inhibitors, and other bioactive materials that are detrimental to the fertilization process (Aümuller & Seitz, 1990; Kanwar, Yanagimachi, & Lopata, 1979). Semen is an irritant to the uterine cavity that, when placed in the womb, induces strong myometrial contractions (Hanson & Rock, 1951). To use sperm for ART, the sperm must be separated from the seminal plasma. A number of methods have been developed to "wash" sperm for ART. Basic, generally used separation techniques are the swim-up method and the density gradient centrifugation methods. A number of variants of these techniques are available. Extreme steps should be taken to ensure that samples are clearly identified throughout all laboratory procedures.

The *swim-up method,* which takes advantage of the fact that normal sperm are motile cells, consists of the layering of culture media over an aliquot of semen (Harris, Milligan, Masson, & Dennis, 1981), or over a pellet of sperm following centrifugation of the semen, after discarding the supernatant seminal fluid (Kerin et al., 1984). Sperm are allowed to swim up into the media for approximately 1 hour at 37° C. The overlay, which contains a population of highly motile sperm, is carefully aspirated without disturbing the underlying layers and is used for ART. Centrifugation, if done at all, should be kept to a minimum in terms of g force used and centrifugation time. Centrifugation has been shown to be detrimental to sperm and sperm function from the generation of reactive oxygen species that can damage the sperm membrane (Aitken & Clarkson, 1987).

Density gradient centrifugation methods use columns of colloidal suspensions of particles of specific densities through which sperm are centrifuged to separate them from the seminal fluid and its components. Liquified semen is layered at the top of the column, which is then centrifuged. The pellet at the bottom of the gradients contains a clean preparation of motile sperm that is removed and washed by resuspension and centrifugation in preparation for ART.

MOST COMMONLY USED ASSISTED REPRODUCTIVE TECHNOLOGIES

Intrauterine Insemination

IUI, in contrast to intravaginal or intracervical insemination, is the artificial placement of washed sperm in the uterine cavity at the time of ovulation. It is postulated that in a nonstimulated cycle IUI increases the chance of pregnancy by placing relatively large numbers of sperm in the endometrial cavity close to the tubal ostia, thus increasing the number of sperm entering the fallopian tubes—the site of fertilization. A cycle of controlled ovarian hyperstimulation followed by an IUI increases the number of eggs entering the fallopian tube from the peritoneal cavity, as well as the number of sperm entering the tube from the endometrial cavity. Increasing both sperm and eggs at the site of fertilization further increases the chance of success. IUI requires sperm, functioning ovaries, and a functioning reproductive tract, including the uterus and at least one functioning fallopian tube.

IUI has been used in the treatment of infertility for a variety of indications, with varying success rates. Historically, it has been difficult to compare reported results following IUI because studies have differed, among others, in the extent of the infertility workup in the couple, in the indications for insemination, in the method of sperm preparation, in the timing of the insemination, and in the number of inseminations used to achieve pregnancy (Allen et al., 1985). For a large number of reported series, poor study design or lack of adequate controls have made it difficult to arrive at meaningful conclusions. In a controlled, prospective, randomized trial, Kerin et al. (1984) demonstrated that IUI significantly increases the pregnancy rate in couples with male infertility when compared with timed intercourse. Quagliarello and Arny (1986) similarly demonstrated the effectiveness of IUI in the treatment of infertility secondary to poor cervical mucus. IUI is a relatively inexpensive treatment that will improve the chance of pregnancy in correctly chosen cases.

In 1987, Dodson, Whitesides, Hughes, Easley, and Haney first reported the use of controlled ovarian hyperstimulation with IUI for the treatment of infertility in cases in which the woman had normal pelvic anatomy. A number of studies using controlled ovarian hyperstimulation and IUI for the treatment of infertility were subsequently published with conflicting results. An examination of the literature revealed that differences in the controlled ovarian hyperstimulation protocols and in the endpoints of the hyperstimulation accounted for the conflicting results (Dodson & Haney, 1991). Studies with more aggressive protocols that induced the ovulation of multiple eggs have reported better success rates than studies that used less aggressive protocols that resulted in the ovulation of smaller numbers of eggs. Using an aggressive protocol of controlled ovarian hyperstimulation with Gn-RH$_a$/HMG and IUI, Gagliardi, Emmi, Weiss, and Schmidt (1991) reported a 26.5% pregnancy rate per IUI, a success rate that compares favorably with the results of more costly treatments such as IVF. However, the resulting multiple pregnancy rate in that study was quite high: 36%.

IUI in a nonstimulated cycle is indicated in cases of poor cervical mucus in which the sperm cannot enter the uterine cavity to reach the fallopian tubes, and in cases of mild male factor infertility to increase the number of motile sperm at the site of fertilization in the fallopian tubes. Ovulation commonly is monitored with a home urine LH kit. The insemination is scheduled relative to the identification of the LH surge. Patients treated with standard protocols of controlled ovarian hyperstimulation time the IUI of washed sperm with the HCG injection. On the day of insemination, the sperm are washed, loaded into a syringe, and placed through the vagina and cervix into the uterine cavity by means of a sterile plastic catheter. Controlled ovarian hyperstimulation is effective in cases of ovulatory dysfunction, more severe forms of male infertility, unexplained infertility, minimal to mild endometriosis, and other forms of infertility that exclude bilateral tubal disease. Success rates generally vary, depending on the aggressiveness of the controlled ovarian hyperstimulation. Therapy thus can be tailored to specific situations, using more aggressive protocols in difficult cases, such as older patients with more complex diagnoses, and less aggressive protocols in younger patients with simpler diagnoses. The goal of these therapies is to achieve pregnancy without subjecting the patients to serious complications such as severe OHSS and multiple gestations.

The main complication of IUI is infection following the insemination of sperm into the uterine cavity. The prevalence of infectious complications following IUI has been reported at 1.83 per 1,000 patients (Sacks & Simon, 1991). Preparation of the sperm samples using aseptic procedures and careful technique at the time of insemination to avoid contamination of the inseminating catheter are essential in the prevention of infections.

In Vitro Fertilization and Embryo Transfer

In vitro fertilization is extracorporeal fertilization. Eggs aspirated from the ovarian follicles and removed from the patient are placed together with sperm in the laboratory. Conception occurs in the laboratory instead of in the fallopian tube (in vivo fertilization). Following controlled ovarian hyperstimulation, multiple eggs are aspirated. Placing the eggs and a relatively large number of sperm in close proximity to each other in the laboratory increases the chance of fertilization. Transferring more than one embryo into the uterus increases the likelihood of implantation, pregnancy, and delivery of an infant. *In vitro* refers to the glass dishes and test tubes that were used in the laboratory in the early cases of extracorporeal fertilization. Today, most laboratories use sterile, disposable plastic dishes and test tubes for these procedures. IVF-ET requires sperm, functioning ovaries, and a functioning endometrial cavity. Functioning fallopian tubes are unnecessary for IVF-ET.

The history of human in vitro fertilization is relatively short (Perone, 1994). Rock and Menkin (1944) were the first to report successful in vitro fertilization using human gametes. Ova for those investigations were collected at the time of laparotomy. The fertilized eggs were not replaced into the uterus. Clinical advances such as the introduction of fiberoptics for endoscopic procedures in the 1950s allowed laparoscopic egg retrievals that obviated the need for laparotomy. The successful extraction of HMG from the urine of postmenopausal women in the 1960s led to the development of ovarian hyperstimulation protocols that increased the number of available eggs for fertilization, thus improving the chances of success. Steptoe and Edwards (1978) in Great Britain were the first to report the birth of a child, Louise Brown, following retrieval of eggs by laparoscopy, with subsequent IVF-ET. In 1981, Elizabeth Carr was the first infant born in the United States resulting from IVF-ET (Jones et al., 1982). In the 1980s, advances in ultrasound technology, such as the development of a vaginal ultrasound probe to visualize the ovaries and aspirate the follicles, further simplified the egg retrieval procedure. The majority of egg retrievals for ART today are performed by way of transvaginal, ultrasound-guided, needle aspiration of follicles. Furthermore, improvements and standardization of embryology laboratory techniques have contributed to the simplification of requirements and procedures involved in the successful establishment of a clinical in vitro fertilization program. In 1994, 6,114 babies were born in the United States following IVF-ET (Society for Assisted Reproductive Technology [SART] and The American Society for Reproductive Medicine [ASRM], 1996).

The initial indication for human in vitro fertilization was tubal disease, and IVF-ET bypasses the fallopian tubes. In vitro fertilization today is used to treat tubal as well as other causes of infertility, including male factor, immunologic, unexplained infertility, and infertility secondary to endometriosis. The procedure, which is relatively simple, is performed on an outpatient basis. Following a course of controlled ovarian hyperstimulation, the patient undergoes transvaginal ultrasound-guided egg retrieval. In general, 5 to 15 eggs are recovered at the time of retrieval. The procedure can be done under intravenous sedation or under regional anesthesia. The entire procedure—setting-up the patient, administering the sedation, and aspirating the follicles—may be completed within 1 hour. The patient goes home on the same day of the procedure. The recovered eggs are inseminated with sperm. The number of sperm used per egg is determined by the quality of the semen sample: 50,000 sperm are used if the sample is normal in terms of semen volume and sperm concentration, motility, and morphology; 500,000 sperm are used in cases of male factor infertility (Wolf, Byrd, Dandekar, & Quigley, 1984). Even though only one sperm is needed to fertilize an egg, inseminating in vitro with fewer than 50,000 to 100,000 sperm decreases the fertilization rate. Insemination with greater than 500,000 sperm increases the incidence of *polyspermy*, the penetration of an egg by more than one sperm. The sperm and egg(s) are placed together in a petri dish or in a test tube and kept in an incubator under controlled conditions where fertilization occurs.

Fertilization is a complex process by which "individual gametes from the female and male unite to create offspring whose genetic makeup is different from both parents" (Yanagimachi, 1994, p. 190). Whether in vitro or in vivo, fertilization requires that the sperm recognize, bind, attach to, and penetrate the *zona pellucida*, a protective glycoprotein coat that surrounds the egg. Once the sperm reaches the egg, the sperm membrane fuses with the egg membrane and the nuclear contents of the sperm are delivered into the egg. Following penetration by one sperm, the egg is "activated": a number of events are triggered that complete fertilization. Among these events, the zona pellucida undergoes a chemical change that excludes polyspermy, the egg completes meiosis, and the male and female genetic material combine to form the genome of the new individual. Subsequently, the fertilized egg(s) or zygote(s) cleave and develop into an embryo. In clinical in vitro fertilization these events occur in the incubator, without any outside influence, within 2 days after egg retrieval and insemination with sperm. Forty-eight to 72 hours after the retrieval, the patient returns for embryo transfer. The number of embryos transferred is critical to the success of the procedure and is determined by a number of factors such as the number and quality of the available embryos and the mother's age. Increasing the number of embryos transferred increases the chance of pregnancy as well as the chance of multiple gestations. Multiple gestations increase the rate of complications of pregnancy and delivery, as well as the rate of premature birth. Thus, the number of embryos transferred should optimize the chance of pregnancy while keeping the number of multiple gestations to a minimum. The embryos to be transferred are loaded into a catheter that is introduced into the endometrial cavity through the vagina and cervix. The embryos that are not transferred can be cryopreserved for future uterine transfer. The embryo transfer procedure takes minutes to complete and does not require any anesthesia. The patient goes home within 1 hour of the procedure. Transfer of the embryos is performed on an outpatient, same-day surgery basis.

SART of the ASRM established the United States IVF Registry to monitor the ART practiced in the United States. An annual report of ART procedures is published. The last available report from SART covered the ART procedures for 1994 (SART and ASRM, 1996). In 1994, 249 programs reported 23,254 egg retrievals for IVF-ET, which resulted in 6,114 clinical pregnancies (26.3% per retrieval) and 4,912 delivered babies (21.1% per retrieval). Of the clinical pregnancies, 19% were lost, the majority as first-trimester spontaneous abortions and 3.9% were ectopic. Of the deliveries, 63.7% were singletons, 28.3% were twins, 5.9% were triplets, and 0.6% were higher order multiple deliveries. In addition, 2.7% of the neonates delivered had a birth defect.

IVF-ET is not free of potential complications (Schenker & Ezra, 1994). Even though oocyte retrievals generally do not require general anesthesia, patients are still exposed to the possible complications associated with intravenous sedation or with the use of regional anesthesia. The complication rate of IVF-ET is small. At the time of retrieval, the aspirating needle introduced transvaginally into the pelvis can damage adjacent structures such as the bowel, bladder, uterus, and vascular structures in the pelvis. Egg retrieval as well as embryo transfer can result in pelvic infection. The risks of spontaneous abortion, ectopic pregnancy, and multifetal pregnancy are higher following assisted reproduction than following natural conception. There is no evidence, however, that IVF-ET increases the risk of congenital malformations (Schenker & Ezra, 1994).

Intracytoplasmic Sperm Injection

ICSI is the injection of a single sperm into the egg to achieve fertilization. It is a micromanipulation technique for in vitro fertilization. Some of the early steps in fertilization—sperm recognition, binding, attachment, and penetration of the zona pellucida, and the fusion of the sperm–egg membranes to deliver the chromosomal material of the sperm into the egg—are bypassed. A single sperm is aspirated into a glass micropipette and injected into the cytoplasm of the egg. It is, by definition, a form of assisted fertilization. The requirements for ICSI are similar to the requirements for IVF-ET: sperm, functioning ovaries, and a functioning endometrial cavity. Functioning fallopian tubes are unnecessary. The difference between the requirements for ICSI and the requirements for standard IFV is that, whereas traditional in vitro fertilization requires 50,000 to 500,000 sperm per egg for insemination of the eggs, ICSI can be performed with a minimal number of sperm—essentially one per egg.

The first infants delivered following ICSI were reported in 1992 (Palermo, Joris, Devroey, & Van Steirteghem, 1992). ICSI is one of a number of assisted fertilization procedures that were developed to overcome fertilization failure. Unexplained fertilization failure follows the insemination of eggs with adequate numbers of motile sperm of normal morphology. Fertilization failure is also occasionally observed following the insemination of egg(s) with sperm in relatively low numbers, with poor motility, or with abnormal morphology. It was also hypothesized that fertilization failure could occur in the presence of abnormalities of the zona pellucida, the egg membrane, or both. To improve results in cases of fertilization failure, a number of micromanipulation procedures were developed to bypass the zona pellucida and the egg membrane. With zona drilling, a portion of the zona pellucida is dissolved with acid to provide sperm easier access to the egg (Gordon et al., 1988). Partial zona dissection involves the use of a microneedle to partially open the zona pellucida, achieving the same results as zona drilling without the use of acid (Cohen et al., 1989). With subzonal sperm injection (SUZI), 5 to 10 sperm are injected through the zona pellucida into the *perivitelline space,* the space between the inner zona pellucida and the egg membrane (Ng et al., 1988). SUZI brings the sperm and egg membranes into direct apposition. Injecting a single sperm into the cytoplasm of the egg (ICSI) bypasses both the zona pellucida and the egg membrane. ICSI has been so successful in achieving fertilization and pregnancy that ICSI has replaced all forms of assisted fertilization (Palermo, Cohen, & Rosenwaks, 1996).

ICSI is generally performed in cases in which sperm recovery is too poor for IVF-ET (Yovich & Stanger, 1984). ICSI has been performed with sperm from severely oligospermic samples (Palermo et al., 1993), with sperm recovered from the epididymis (Tournaye et al., 1994), and even with sperm recovered from testicular biopsies (Schoysman et al., 1993). Because ICSI is a form of assisted fertilization in vitro, an ICSI case involves the same preparation and management of a standard in vitro fertilization cycle. The patient undergoes controlled ovarian hyperstimulation and egg retrieval. Following retrieval, the sperm are washed and placed in a solution of PVP (ICN Biochemicals, Cleveland OH). The viscous PVP (polyvinylpyrrolidone) solution slows down the sperm, facilitating the handling of the motile cells, and prevents the sperm from sticking to the injection pipette during the procedure. The micromanipulation procedure is performed under magnification using a microscope. Because motile sperm do not fertilize as well as immotile sperm, the motile sperm to be injected is immobilized by lowering the micropipette over the tail of the sperm against the bottom of the petri dish. The immobilized sperm is aspirated into the micropipette for microinjection. A metaphase II egg is held with a microsuction pipette with the extruded polar body at 12 o'clock or 6 o'clock, and a single sperm is injected into the cytoplasm. The microinjected eggs are placed in an incubator where fertilization is completed and the fertilized eggs proceed to cleave to the embryo stage. The embryos are replaced into the uterus 2 to 3 days later.

The success rate of ICSI for the treatment of couples with severe male factor infertility is comparable with the results obtained using standard IVF-ET performed in couples without male factor infertility (Daya, 1996; Palermo et al., 1996). Fertilization, implantation, and pregnancy rates are comparable between the groups, following ICSI and following standard IVF-ET. Even though the numbers are small, there is no evidence that ICSI results in an increase in the rate of congenital malformations. Because ICSI is performed as part of an in vitro fertilization cycle, the risks for patients undergoing ICSI are the same as those described for patients undergoing IVF-ET. With ICSI, however, there is an additional potential risk (6.4% to 13%) of damage to the eggs resulting from the micromanipulation procedure (Daya, 1996; Palermo et al., 1996).

Gamete Intrafallopian Transfer

GIFT is the placement of gametes—eggs and sperm—directly into the fallopian tube. Fertilization occurs in the fallopian tubes. Controlled ovarian hyperstimulation and follicular aspiration yield multiple eggs. Similar to IUI, GIFT achieves a supraphysiologic number of gametes in the fallopian tube(s), the natural site of fertilization. The chances of conception are higher than in a natural cycle. If more than one egg fertilizes, the chances of implantation and pregnancy increase. Unlike IUI, in which the ovulated egg(s) have to find their way from the peritoneal cavity into the fallopian tubes, GIFT practically ensures an extraordinary number of gametes at the site of fertilization in the tube. Generally GIFT is done by way of laparoscopy or minilaparotomy. GIFT requires sperm, functioning ovaries, and a functioning reproductive tract, including the uterus and at least one functioning fallopian tube.

The first human pregnancy following GIFT was reported by Asch, Ellsworth, Balmaceda, and Wong in 1984, 6 years following the first reported birth from IVF-ET (Steptoe & Edwards, 1978). GIFT was developed as an alternative to IVF-ET for infertile couples who had at least one functioning fallopian tube.

Even though IVF-ET could result in pregnancies, the success rate from the early procedures was relatively low, IVF-ET was expensive, the complexity of the procedure limited the availability of IVF-ET, and IVF-ET was ethically controversial (Mastroyannis, 1993; Perone, 1991). Fertilization in vivo in the fallopian tube, the site of fertilization in a natural cycle, simplified the procedure, potentially increasing the availability of GIFT compared with IVF-ET. Because fertilization occurs in its natural setting, GIFT does not require the availability of a laboratory capable of establishing the controlled conditions necessary to promote fertilization by human gametes or to maintain fertilized eggs and embryos for 48 to 72 hours until the time of transfer. Thus, it should be easier to set up a GIFT program than an IVF-ET program, hence increasing the general availability of GIFT. The need for a full embryology laboratory with IVF-ET capabilities for programs that perform GIFT, however, has been emphasized in the ASRM guidelines. The capability to perform IVF-ET is necessary for those cases in which the fallopian tubes cannot be cannulated following egg retrieval and for cases in which eggs are recovered in excess of those recommended for tubal transfer (American Fertility Society, 1990). In vivo fertilization also provided some theoretical advantages to GIFT over IVF-ET, and bypassed some of the ethical problems raised by IVF-ET. It has been suggested that fertilization in vivo is superior to fertilization in vitro because the tubal environment provides growth factors, hormones, and nutrients, some of which are undefined and cannot be artificially reproduced in the IVF-ET laboratory. Furthermore, the first stages of embryogenesis occur in a physiologic environment, and tubal transport allows the conceptus to arrive in the endometrium following a physiologic timetable, all of which may optimize the chance of survival of the embryo. The validity of these claims has yet to be established.

The indications for GIFT are the same as for IVF-ET, except that there has to be at least one functioning fallopian tube (Mastroyannis, 1993). Thus, GIFT has been used in the management of male factor infertility, unexplained infertility, and immunologic infertility, as well as for infertility secondary to endometriosis. Occasionally, a patient may require access to the fallopian tubes for GIFT because the cervix does not allow cannulation for inseminations or embryo transfer following in vitro fertilization (e.g., severe cervical stenosis following surgery for neoplasia of the cervix). The patient having GIFT undergoes controlled ovarian hyperstimulation to induce the growth and maturation of multiple follicles. Egg retrieval and cannulation of the fallopian tube(s) for GIFT have been performed in a variety of ways. The eggs can be retrieved by transvaginal ultrasound-guided follicle aspiration under intravenous sedation, at the time of laparoscopy under general anesthesia, or at the time of laparotomy under general or regional anesthesia. GIFT can be performed by way of laparoscopy or laparotomy. Hysteroscopic GIFT through the vagina, cervix, and uterus has been described but is not as effective as, and has not replaced, abdominal GIFT (Jansen &

Anderson, 1993). Just about every combination of retrieval procedures and GIFT methods has been tried and reported. Following retrieval, the eggs and a sample of washed sperm are loaded into a catheter, which is cannulated into the fallopian tube(s) by way of laparoscopy or minilaparotomy. The gametes are deposited in the tube(s) and the patient goes home the same day. There is no need for the patient to return for embryo transfer.

There are two main disadvantages to GIFT when compared with IVF-ET. First, it is evident that the second procedure needed to cannulate the fallopian tubes for GIFT, for example, a laparoscopy or a minilaparotomy, is more invasive and complex than an embryo transfer following in vitro fertilization. IVF-ET does not require a surgical procedure to access the fallopian tubes because they are bypassed. Second, in contrast to IVF-ET, when pregnancy is not achieved, it is impossible to know if fertilization occurred. Fertilization failure is in itself a cause of infertility, which can be overcome with ICSI.

The success of GIFT over the years has been consistently higher than the success of IVF-ET. In 1994, 3,692 retrievals for GIFT resulted in 1,342 clinical pregnancies (36.3% per retrieval) and 1,054 delivered babies (28.5% per retrieval). Of the clinical pregnancies, 22.5% were lost, 3.2% of the pregnancies were ectopic, and 1.8% of the neonates delivered had a birth defect. Of the deliveries, 63.6% were singletons, 29.2% were twins, 6.5% were triplets, and 0.6% were higher order multiple deliveries (SART and ASRM, 1996). It is likely that patient selection accounts to a large degree for the higher success rate achieved with GIFT when compared with IVF-ET. In general, couples who undergo IVF-ET have more severe forms of infertility than the infertility in couples who qualify for GIFT. For example, couples with higher degrees of male factor infertility, with more severe anatomic defects of the female reproductive tract, and with higher stages of endometriosis will be channeled toward IVF-ET. Couples with relatively good sperm counts and adequate fallopian tubes are channeled toward GIFT.

Prospective, controlled, randomized studies with adequate statistical power that have compared IVF-ET and GIFT in equivalent populations are unavailable. Similarly lacking are studies that have compared GIFT to controlled ovarian hyperstimulation combined with IUI. Both treatments achieve the same results: an increased number of sperm and eggs in the fallopian tubes. However, GIFT requires surgical access to the fallopian tubes under general anesthesia, whereas controlled ovarian hyperstimulation combined with IUI is simpler, safer, and less costly.

The complications encountered with GIFT are the same as those described for IVF-ET in terms of controlled ovarian hyperstimulation and egg retrieval. However, for GIFT, the patient must consider the additional risk of complications encountered from the added procedure needed to cannulate the fallopian tubes; that is, a laparoscopy under general anesthesia or a minilaparotomy under general or regional anesthesia (Schenker & Ezra, 1994).

CONCLUSION

The development of ART over the past 20 years has revolutionized the field of reproductive endocrinology and infertility. Not only are new treatments available to manage patients, but the understanding of the reproductive process has grown enormously. This understanding has opened up new areas of research that will continue to push the limits of what can be achieved at the clinical level. Progress in the field will also continue to lead to the reassessment of important social, moral, ethical, and legal questions regarding human reproduction.

Not only is basic science research needed to continue to expand our knowledge and capabilities, but appropriate clinical trials are needed to properly evaluate treatments to apply the new knowledge in a responsible way. Prospective, randomized, controlled trials are needed to compare the different available ART and to determine the efficacy of available therapies. Ideally, advances in ART should translate to generally available, realistic, cost-effective, and low-risk treatments to patients to help them achieve their reproductive goals.

REFERENCES

Aitken, R.J., & Clarkson, J.S. (1987). Cellular basis of defective sperm function and its association with the genesis of reactive oxygen species by human spermatozoa. *Journal of Reproduction and Fertility, 81,* 459–469.

Allen, N.C., Herbert, C.H., Maxson, W.S., Rogers, B.J., Diamond M.P., & Wentz, A.C. (1985). Intrauterine insemination: A critical review. *Fertility and Sterility, 44*(5), 569–580.

American Fertility Society. (1990). Revised minimum standards for in vitro fertilization, gamete intrafallopian transfer, and related procedures. *Fertility and Sterility, 53*(2), 225–226.

Asch, R.H., Ellsworth, L.R., Balmaceda, J.P., & Wong, P.C. (1984). Pregnancy after translaparoscopic gamete intrafallopian transfer. *Lancet, 2,* 1034–1035.

Aümuller, G., & Seitz, J. (1990). Protein secretion and secretory processes in male sex accessory glands. *International Review of Cytology, 121,* 127–231.

Bristow, R.E., & Karlan, B.Y. (1996). Ovulation induction, infertility, and ovarian cancer risk. *Fertility and Sterility, 66*(4), 499–507.

Callahan, T.L., Hall, J.E., Ettner, S.L., Christiansen, C.L., Greene, M.F., & Crowley, W.F. (1994). The economic impact of multiple-gestation pregnancies and the contribution of assisted-reproduction techniques to their incidence. *New England Journal of Medicine, 331*(4), 244–249.

Cedars, M.I., Surey, E., Hamilton, F., Lapolt, P., & Meldrum, D.R. (1990). Leuprolide acetate lowers circulating bioactive luteinizing hormone and testosterone concentrations during ovarian stimulation for oocyte retrieval. *Fertility and Sterility, 53*(4), 627–631.

Cohen, J., Malter, H., Wright, G., Kort, H., Massey, J., & Mitchell, D. (1989). Partial zona dissection of human oocytes when failure of zona pellucida penetration is anticipated. *Human Reproduction, 4,* 435–442.

Corsan, G.H., & Kemmann, E. (1991). The role of superovulation with menotropins in ovulatory infertility: A review. *Fertility and Sterility, 55*(3), 468–477.

Daya, S. (1996). Overview analysis of outcomes with intracytoplasmic sperm injection. *Journal de la Societe des Obstetricians et Gynecologues du Canada, 18,* 645–656.

Dodson, C.W., & Haney, A.F. (1991). Controlled ovarian hyperstimulation and intrauterine insemination for the treatment of infertility. *Fertility and Sterility, 55*(3), 457–467.

Dodson, W.C., Whitesides, D.B., Hughes, C.L., Easley, H.A., & Haney, A.F. (1987). Superovulation with intrauterine insemination in the treatment of infertility: A possible alternative to gamete intrafallopian transfer and in vitro fertilization. *Fertility and Sterility, 48*(3), 441–445.

Evans, M.I., Dommergues, M., Wapner, R.J., Lynch, L., Dumez, Y., Goldberg, J.D., Zador, I.E., Nicolaides, K.H., Johnson, M.P., Golbus, M.S., Boulot, P., & Berkowitz, R.L. (1993). Efficacy of transabdominal multifetal pregnancy reduction: Collaborative experience among the world's largest centers. *Obstetrics and Gynecology, 82*(1), 61–70.

Gagliardi, C.L., Emmi, A.M., Weiss, G., & Schmidt, C.L. (1991). Gonadotropin-releasing hormone agonist improves the efficiency of controlled ovarian hyperstimulation/intrauterine insemination. *Fertility and Sterility, 55*(5), 939–944.

Ginsburg, J., & Hardiman, P. (1991). Ovulation induction with human menopausal gonadotropins—A changing scene. *Gynecological Endocrinology, 5*(1), 57–78.

Golan, A., Ron-El, R., Herman, A., Soffer, Y., Weintraub, Z., & Caspi, E. (1989). Ovarian hyperstimulation syndrome: An update review. *Obstetrical and Gynecological Survey, 44,* 430–440.

Gordon, J.W., Grunfeld, L., Garrisi, G.J., Talanski, B.E., Richards, C., & Laufer, N. (1988). Fertilization of human oocytes by sperm from infertile males after zona pellucida drilling. *Fertility and Sterility, 50*(1), 68–73.

Gougeon, A. (1996). Regulation of ovarian follicular development in primates: Facts and hypotheses. *Endocrine Reviews, 17*(2), 121–155.

Hanson, F.M., & Rock, J. (1951). Artificial insemination with husband's sperm. *Fertility and Sterility, 2*(2), 162–174.

Harris, S.J., Milligan, M.P., Masson, G.M., & Dennis, K.J. (1981). Improved separation of motile sperm in asthenospermia and its application to artificial insemination homologous (AIH). *Fertility and Sterility, 36*(2), 219–221.

Hughes, E.G., Fedorkow, D.M., Daya, S., Sagle, M.A., Van de Koppel, P., & Collins, J.A. (1992). The routine use of gonadotropin releasing hormone agonists prior to *in vitro* fertilization and gamete intrafallopian transfer: A meta-analysis of randomized controlled trials. *Fertility and Sterility, 58*(5), 888–896.

Jansen, R.P., & Anderson, J.C. (1993). Transvaginal versus laparoscopic gamete intrafallopian transfer: A case-controlled retrospective comparison. *Fertility and Sterility, 59*(4), 836–840.

Jones, H.W., Jones, G.S., Andrews, M.C., Acosta, A., Bundren, C., Garcia, J., Sandow, B., Veek, L., Wilkens, C., Witmyer, J., Wortham, J.E., & Wright, G. (1982). The program of in vitro fertilization at Norfolk. *Fertility and Sterility, 38*(1), 14–21.

Kanwar, K.C., Yanagimachi, R., & Lopata, A. (1979). Effects of human seminal plasma on fertilizing capacity of human spermatozoa. *Fertility and Sterility, 31*(3), 321–327.

Kerin, J.F.P., Peek, J., Warnes, G.M., Kirby, C., Jeffrey, R., Matthews, C.D., & Cox, L.W. (1984). Improved conception rate after intrauterine insemination of washed spermatozoa from men with poor quality semen. *Lancet, 1,* 533–534.

Knobil, E. (1980). The neuroendocrine control of the menstrual cycle. *Recent Progress in Hormone Research, 36,* 53–88.

Mastroyannis, C. (1993). Gamete intrafallopian transfer: Ethical considerations, historical development of the procedure, and comparison with other reproductive technologies. *Fertility and Sterility, 60*(3), 389–402.

Meldrum, D. (1989). GnRH agonists as adjuncts for *in vitro* fertilization. *Obstetrical and Gynecological Survey, 44,* 314–316.

Meldrum, D.R., Wisot, A., Hamilton, F., Gutlay, A.L., Kempton, W., & Huynh, D. (1989). Routine pituitary suppression with leuprolide before ovarian stimulation for oocyte retrieval. *Fertility and Sterility, 51*(3), 455–459.

Neuman, P.J., Gharib, S.D., & Weinstein, M.C. (1994). The cost of a successful delivery with in vitro fertilization. *New England Journal of Medicine, 331*(4), 239–243.

Ng, S.C., Bongso, A., Sathananthan, A.H., Chan, C.L.K., Wong, P.C., Hagglund, L., Anandakumar, C., Wong, Y.C., & Goh, V.H.H. (1988). Pregnancy after transfer of multiple sperm under the zona. *Lancet, 2,* 790.

Palermo, G.D., Cohen, J., & Rosenwaks, Z. (1996). Intracytoplasmic sperm injection: A powerful tool to overcome fertilization failure. *Fertility and Sterility, 65*(5), 899–908.

Palermo, G., Joris, H., Derde, M.P., Camus, M., Devroey, P., & Van Steirteghem, A. (1993). Sperm characteristics and outcome of human assisted fertilization by subzonal insemination and intracytoplasmic sperm injection. *Fertility and Sterility, 59*(4), 826–835.

Palermo, G., Joris, H., Devroey, P., & Van Steirteghem, A.C. (1992). Pregnancies after intracytoplasmic injection of single spermatozoon into an oocyte. *Lancet, 340,* 17–18.

Perone, N. (1991). Gamete intrafallopian transfer: Historic perspective. *Journal of In Vitro Fertilization and Embryo Transfer, 8*(1), 1–4.

Perone, N. (1994). *In vitro* fertilization and embryo transfer: A historical perspective. *Journal of Reproductive Medicine, 39,* 695–700.

Quagliarello, J., & Arny, M. (1986). Intracervical versus intrauterine insemination: Correlation of outcome with antecedent postcoital testing. *Fertility and Sterility, 46*(5), 870–875.

Riddick, D.H. (1993, January). *AFS response to the possible association between ovulation inducing agents and ovarian cancer* [Memorandum sent by the American Fertility Society (AFS) to the AFS membership]. Birmingham, AL: American Fertility Society.

Rock, J., & Menkin, M.F. (1944). In vitro fertilization and cleavage of human ovarian eggs. *Science, 100,* 105–107.

Sacks, P.C., & Simon, J.A. (1991). Infections complications of intrauterine insemination: A case report and literature review. *International Journal of Fertility, 36*(6), 331–339.

Schenker, J.G., & Ezra, Y. (1994). Complications of assisted reproductive techniques. *Fertility and Sterility, 61*(3), 411–422.

Schoysman, R., Vanderzwalmen, P., Nijs, M., Segal, L., Segal-Bertin, G., Geerts, L., van Roosendaal, E., & Schoysman, D. (1993). Pregnancy after fertilization with human testicular spermatozoa. *Lancet, 342,* 1237.

Settlage, D.S., Motoshima, M., & Tredway, D.R. (1973). Sperm transport from the external cervical os to the fallopian tubes in women: A time and quantitation study. *Fertility and Sterility, 24*(9), 655–661.

Society for Assisted Reproductive Technology and The American Society for Reproductive Medicine. (1996). Assisted Reproductive Technology in the United States and Canada: 1994 results generated from the American Society for Reproductive Medicine/Society for Assisted Reproductive Technology Registry. *Fertility and Sterility, 66*(5), 697–705.

Spirtas, R., Kaufman, S.C., & Alexander, N.J. (1993). Fertility drugs and ovarian cancer: Red alert or red herring? *Fertility and Sterility, 59*(2), 291–293.

Steptoe, P.C., & Edwards, R.G. (1978). Birth after the re-implantation of a human embryo. *Lancet, 2,* 366.

Toner, J.P., & Hodgen, G.D. (1993). The future of assisted reproductive technologies. In R.P. Marrs (Ed.), *Assisted reproductive technologies* (pp. 218–257). Boston: Blackwell Scientific.

Tournaye, H., Devroey, P., Liu, J., Nagy, Z., Lissens, W., & Van Steirteghem, A.C. (1994). Microsurgical epididymal sperm aspiration and intracytoplasmic sperm injection: A new effective approach to infertility as a result of congenital bilateral absence of the vas deferens. *Fertility and Sterility, 61*(6), 1045–1051.

Vickery, B.H., & Nestor, J.J. (1987). Luteinizing hormone-releasing hormone analogs: Development and mechanism of action. *Seminars in Reproductive Endocrinology, 5,* 353–369.

Wolf, D.P., Byrd, W., Dandekar, P., & Quigley, M.M. (1984). Sperm concentration and the fertilization of human eggs in vitro. *Biology of Reproduction, 31*(4), 837–848.

Yanagimachi, R. (1994). Mammalian fertilization. In E. Knobil & J.D. Neill (Eds.), *The physiology of reproduction* (pp. 189–317). New York: Raven Press.

Yovich, J.L., & Stanger, J.D. (1984). The limitations of in vitro fertilization from males with severe oligospermia and abnormal sperm morphology. *Journal of In Vitro Fertilization and Embryo Transfer, 1*(3), 172–179.

CHAPTER 28

Sexual Abuse and People with Disabilities

Margaret A. Nosek and Carol Howland

My husband would get angry when I refused to have sex and he would continue to yell at me and grab me until I just gave in to shut him up. He would exert control over me by preventing me from leaving rooms, or throwing or breaking my crutches. Once he cut my clothes off me while I slept. We sought individual counseling and things are much better now because we both understand the origin of these issues. (38-year-old woman with spina bifida describing sexual abuse by husband that lasted 6 years)

Physical abuse—no physical damage, but small hits, stepping on toes purposely, hands around throat, rough assistance in transfers—lasted about 2 years. I let it continue, in large part due to access problems where we lived, and length of relationship. I spoke with close friends about it and ended it by forcing him to move out. At first I accepted it as "playful," but it hurt and I demanded that it stop. It did not stop. (42-year-old woman with muscular dystrophy describing physical abuse by live-in attendant that lasted about 2 years)

In the past two decades, sociologists and psychologists have turned more of their attention to studying the experiences of women who have been abused and assaulted. However, there has been little examination of the abuse experiences of women with disabilities or society's response to that abuse. Three important dimensions of this problem relate to the work of social services providers and clinicians. First, women with disabilities, in many cases, are unaware that they are in abusive situations. Even if they are aware of their situation, they may know little or nothing about resources available to help them resolve the violence they are experiencing. Second, people who work in rehabilitation or disability-related service settings are generally unequipped to help their clients deal with abuse and do not realize the extent to which abuse is a barrier to goal achievement for their clients. Third, workers in programs for battered women are generally unequipped to deal with their clients' disabilities and also may be operating out of facilities and programs that are inaccessible to women with various types of disabilities.

This chapter aims to increase the understanding of abuse experienced by women with disabilities. Moreover, it offers practical strategies for incorporating abuse prevention and intervention techniques into the practices of rehabilitation professionals.

DEFINITIONS OF ABUSE

In its guidelines on domestic violence, the American Medical Association (1992) defines *sexual abuse* as any form of forced sex or sexual degradation (p. 7). Examples include trying to make a woman perform sexual acts against her will; pursuing sexual activity when she is not fully conscious, or is not asked, or is afraid to say no; hurting her physically during sex or assaulting her genitals; coercing her to have sex without protection against pregnancy or sexually transmitted diseases; and criticizing her and calling her sexually degrading names. Dorothea Glass (cited in Aiello, Capkin, & Catania, 1983) has defined *sexual assault* as "an act of aggression and hostility against a whole person; not just a sexual act or a bodily violation, but an indignity, an invasion, and violation of a person that affects the victim physically, psychologically, and socially; an assault which does not necessarily end when the assailant leaves or is caught" (p. 138).

Once a label of abuse has been attached to an incident, it is necessary to determine other parameters for purposes of description and comparison. Trickett and Putnam (1993) recommended that the degree of trauma related to the severity of abuse can be indexed by the type of abuse; age at onset; frequency of abuse; closeness of the relationship to the abuser; and presence of physical violence, pain, and threats.

PREVALENCE OF VIOLENCE AGAINST WOMEN WITH DISABILITIES

Although the prevalence of abuse among women in general has been fairly well documented, only a few studies have examined the prevalence among women with disabilities (Sobsey, Wells, Lucardie, & Mansell, 1995). The Disabled Women's Network of Canada (Ridington, 1989) surveyed 245 women with disabilities and found that 40% had experienced abuse; 12% had been raped. Perpetrators of the abuse were primarily spouses, including ex-spouses (37%), and strangers (28%), followed by parents (15%), service providers (10%), and dates

(7%). Fewer than half of the women reported their experiences mostly because of fear and dependency. Of the women, 10% had used shelters or other services, 15% reported that no services were available or they were unsuccessful in their attempts to obtain services, and 55% had not tried to get services. Sobsey and Doe (1991) conducted a study of 166 cases handled by the University of Alberta Sexual Abuse and Disability Project. Of the sample, 82% were women and 70% were people with intellectual impairments; ages ranged widely, from 18 months to 57 years. In 96% of the cases, the perpetrator was known to the victim; 44% of the perpetrators were service providers. Seventy-nine percent of the individuals were victimized more than once. Treatment services were either inadequate or were not offered in 73% of the cases. The Ontario Ministry of Community and Social Services (1987) surveyed 62 women and found that more of the women with disabilities had been battered as adults compared with the women without disabilities (33% versus 22%, respectively), but fewer had been sexually assaulted as adults (23% versus 31%, respectively).

An extensive assessment of the sexuality of women with disabilities, which included a comprehensive assessment of emotional, physical, and sexual abuse, was conducted by the Center for Research on Women with Disabilities (CROWD; unpublished data) through a grant from the National Institutes of Health. The study also covered other areas that may be associated with abuse, such as sexual function, reproductive health care, dating, marriage, parenting issues, and developmental issues such as family influences and a woman's sense of self as a sexual person (Nosek et al., 1995). The design of the study consisted of qualitative interviews with 31 women with disabilities, and a national survey of 946 women, 504 of whom had physical disabilities and 442 who did not have disabilities.

Abuse issues emerged as a major theme among the 31 women interviewed in the first phase of the study. An analysis of those interviews was described by Nosek (1995). Of the 31 women, 25 reported being abused in some way. The reported abusive experiences fell into three main types: (1) sexual abuse, (2) physical abuse, and (3) emotional abuse. Of 55 separate incidents of abuse, 15 were reported as sexual abuse, 17 were physical (nonsexual) abuse, and 23 were emotional abuse. Among the 15 experiences reported, there was considerable variety in the type of sexual abuse, including fondling ($n = 3$), coerced sexual activity ($n = 3$), forced oral sex ($n = 1$), sexual assault ($n = 5$), and rape ($n = 3$). Of these experiences, six occurred in childhood, six in the teenage years, and three in adulthood. The large majority were single incidents. Of the four experiences that extended over months or years, three involved abuse by a relative. In addition, six experiences were determined to be disability related, including an inability to escape a situation because of architectural inaccessibility, lack of adaptive equipment, social stereotypes of invulnerability, increased risk in institutional settings, and impaired judgment associated with traumatic brain injury. It is obvious from these examples that women with disabilities face unique risk factors that make them susceptible to physical or sexual abuse. These risk factors included the inability to leave an abusive situation because of mobility impairments or dependency on a caregiver, as well as a perception by the perpetrator that women with disabilities can be dominated because of their physical, mental, and emotional limitations (Nosek, 1995).

The research team (Nosek et al., 1995) also identified emotional, physical, or sexual abuse in medical settings as factors that have a lifelong traumatic effect on the reproductive health maintenance practices of women with physical disabilities. For example, one participant with juvenile rheumatoid arthritis reported being sexually abused while in a hospital for surgery at age 7 years. Her disability required that she be hospitalized frequently, thereby increasing her vulnerability to the abuses that are more common in institutionalized settings.

The findings from the qualitative study (unpublished data) were used to develop items for the national survey. Two pages of the 51-page survey were devoted to abuse issues, encompassing more than 80 variables and including two open-ended questions. Analyses of the data revealed that women with disabilities appear to be at risk for emotional, physical, and sexual abuse to the same extent as women without disabilities. The prevalence of any abuse (including emotional, physical, or sexual abuse) for women with and without disabilities was 62.0% versus 62.2%, respectively. About the same proportion of women with disabilities compared to women without disabilities reported emotional abuse (51.7% versus 47.5%), physical abuse (35.5% versus 35.6%), or sexual abuse (39.9% versus 37.1%). When the categories of physical and sexual abuse were combined, 51.9% of women with disabilities and 50.6% of women without disabilities responded positively. None of these types of abuse was significantly different for women with or without disabilities.

In the survey, husbands and live-in partners were included in the same category. More husbands abused women (both with and without disabilities) emotionally (25.5% and 26.1%) and physically (17.3% and 18.5%) than other perpetrators. Mothers and fathers were the next most common perpetrators of emotional and physical abuse for both groups of women. Strangers were the most often cited perpetrators of sexual abuse for both groups (10.5% for women with disabilities; 11.6% for women without disabilities).

Women with disabilities were significantly more likely to experience emotional abuse by attendants, strangers, or health care providers than women without disabilities. There was a trend for women with disabilities to more likely experience emotional abuse by mothers, brothers, and other family members, as well. Women with disabilities were more likely to experience physical (1.6% versus 0%) or sexual (2.3% versus 0.5%) abuse by attendants. There was a trend for women with disabilities to be more likely to experience sexual abuse by health care providers.

Women who had experienced abuse that lasted longer than a single incident were examined to determine differences in the duration of abuse. Women with disabilities experienced all types of abuse (emotional, physical, or sexual) for significantly longer periods of time than women without disabilities.

Other reports have indicated that 25% of adolescent girls with mental retardation (Chamberlain, Rauh, Passer, McGrath, & Burket, 1984) have been sexually abused, as have 31% of people with congenital physical disabilities (Brown, 1988), 36% of multihandicapped children who were admitted to a psychiatric hospital (Ammerman, Van Hasselt, Hersen, McGonigle, & Lubetsky, 1989), and 50% of women who were blind at birth (Welbourne, Lipschitz, Selvin, & Green, 1983). Despite these high percentages, few abused women with disabilities receive treatment from victim services specialists (Andrews & Veronen, 1993).

INCREASED VULNERABILITY FOR ABUSE AMONG WOMEN WITH DISABILITIES

Although reliable statistics on the experience of abuse among women with disabilities are sorely lacking, there has been analysis of why they might experience a greater vulnerability. The combined cultural devaluation of women and people with disabilities is a major factor (Belsky, 1980), often further compounded by devaluation based on age (Kreigsman & Bregman, 1985). Overprotection and internalized societal expectations are other significant contributors. Womendez and Schneiderman (1991) characterized women with disabilities as having fewer opportunities to learn sexual likes and dislikes and to set pleasing boundaries. Because of frequent rejection or overprotection, they may not date, go to parties, or engage in age-appropriate sexual activity. Their first sexual experience may come much later in life. Women with disabilities often perceive celibacy or violent sexual encounters as their only choices, believing no loving person would be attracted to them. Some may believe that fate proclaims they deserve what they get, and that bad feelings (such as pain) are better than no feelings. Women with disabilities often disassociate the self from the parts of the body being assaulted. They may have experienced frequent pain inflicted by doctors and "helpers" in situations when privacy is denied, nakedness is the norm, and they are treated as if they are inhuman.

Andrews and Veronen (1993) have cited eight reasons for increased vulnerability to victimization among people with disabilities. They are (1) increased dependency on others for long-term care, (2) denial of human rights that results in perceptions of powerlessness, (3) less risk of discovery as perceived by the perpetrator, (4) difficulty some survivors have in being believed, (5) less education about appropriate and inappropriate sexuality, (6) social isolation and increased risk of manipulation, (7) physical helplessness and vulnerability in public places, and (8) "values and attitudes within the field of disability toward mainstreaming and integration without consideration for each individual's capacity for self-protection" (p. 148).

A history of abuse during childhood is a significant risk factor for domestic violence and sexual assault as an adult. The most valid and respected statistic on the prevalence of childhood sexual abuse was stated by Finkelhor (1979): 25% of female children and 9% of male children are sexually abused. Several studies have reported substantially higher rates among children with disabilities, although rates vary considerably and no attempt has been made to distinguish between physical and cognitive disabilities. Doucette (1986), for example, reported on a study of women with a variety of disabilities and found that the women were about one and one-half times as likely to have been sexually abused as children compared with nondisabled women. A survey of 62 women conducted by the Ontario Ministry of Community and Social Services (1987) found that 50% of women with disabilities reported being sexually assaulted as a child compared with 34% of women without disabilities. Sobsey and Doe (1991), citing a variety of studies, reported that the incidence of all types of abuse among children with disabilities appears to be 4.43 times the expected value. A recent congressionally mandated study conducted by the National Center on Child Abuse and Neglect (1993) documented physical and sexual abuse twice as often in children with disabilities compared with other children. Furthermore, Muccigrosso (1991) claimed that 90% to 99% of people with developmental disabilities have been sexually exploited by age 18 years—four times the rate in the nondisabled population. Mullins (1986) has claimed that 50% to 90% of people with developmental disabilities are sexually abused. Despite these widely divergent estimates, the body of evidence strongly points toward a prevalence of abuse of children with disabilities that far exceeds public awareness.

A critical risk factor for increasing the vulnerability of women to abuse is lack of economic independence. Farmer and Tiefenthaler (unpublished data) proposed that improved economic opportunity for women decreases the level of violence in abusive relationships. Women with disabilities share the problems of low wages and occupational segregation faced by women without disabilities (Schaller & DeLaGarza, 1995). However, compared with women without disabilities, and men with disabilities, economic disadvantage is greater for women with disabilities, increasing their susceptibility to entering, and remaining in, abusive relationships. Participation in the labor market is 33% for women with disabilities, dropping to 13% for full-time work, compared with 69% for men (Danek, 1992; U.S. Bureau of the Census, 1989). Their employability is also impaired by a lower educational level than women without disabilities. Even college-educated women with disabilities are less successful in obtaining employment than college-educated men with disabilities or college-educated women without disabilities (Asch & Fine, 1988). Moreover, contrary to societal expectations that women with disabilities are considered asexual and thus are exempted from sexual harassment in the workplace, sexual harassment may lead to job loss, demotion, and interrupted education for women with disabilities (Murphy, 1992, 1993). Compounding these external societal factors are internalized factors such as low self-esteem; low career self-efficacy; and affiliation concerns, that is, a woman's belief that aspiring to a particular career will jeopardize her relationships (Agonito, 1993).

VULNERABILITY OF MINORITY WOMEN TO VIOLENCE

The literature on abuse has suggested that risk factors for rape and other forms of abuse may differ with ethnic background. In general, impaired ability to recognize potential threat and to protect oneself against attack increases vulnerability to sexual assault (Giannini, Price, & Kniepple, 1987; Malamuth & Check, 1983; Myers, Templer, & Brown, 1984), factors that may be more characteristic of women with disabilities compared with women without disabilities (Nosek, 1995). African American women were found more likely than Hispanic and white women to report prior rape or incest (Scott, Lefley, & Hicks, 1993). National studies of sexual behavior have indicated that from 29% (Kinsey, Pomeroy, Martin, & Gebhard, 1953) to 39% (Wyatt, Peters, & Guthrie, 1988) of African American women have reported a history of sexual abuse as a child.

Vulnerability to abuse also tends to increase during pregnancy. When 1,243 African American and Hispanic women were asked about abuse, 7% reported physical or sexual abuse during pregnancy (Amaro, Fried, Cabral, & Zuckerman, 1990). In a primarily minority sample (72% African American or Hispanic) of pregnant teenage and adult women, 26% reported physical or sexual abuse within the past year of their first prenatal visit; 21% of teenagers and 16% of adult women reported abuse during pregnancy (Parker, McFarlane, Soeken, Torres, & Campbell, 1993). These findings confirm earlier reports that African American women historically have been more vulnerable to repeated sexual exploitation (Jackson, 1977). Battered African American women are also more likely than other women to attempt suicide; Stark and Flitcraft (1995) found that an ongoing abusive relationship was a factor in half of the suicide attempts by African American women. Hispanic women appear to be the least likely to report abuse, but this may reflect reluctance to report abuse rather than a truly reduced incidence.

PHYSICAL AND PSYCHOLOGICAL EFFECTS OF ABUSE

Violence against both nondisabled and disabled women results in homicide (Kellerman & Mercy, 1992), suicide (Browne & Finkelhor, 1986), temporary and permanent disability (Murphy, 1993), emotional problems (Ratican, 1992), medical complaints (Courtois & Watts, 1982; Cunningham, Pearce, & Pearce, 1988; Faria & Belohlavek, 1984), drug and alcohol abuse (Briere & Zaidi, 1989; Faria & Belohlavek, 1984; Finkelhor et al., 1986), and sexual dysfunction (Ratican, 1992). Ratican (1992) described the identifying symptoms of sexual abuse survivors. Survivors may present with symptoms of depression, including self-destructive and suicidal ideation (Browne & Finkelhor, 1986), chronic anxiety and tension (Briere & Runtz, 1988), anxiety attacks and phobias, and sleep and appetite disturbances. Many survivors also have more medical complaints including pelvic pain (Cunningham et al., 1988), headaches, backaches, skin disorders, and genitourinary problems (Courtois & Watts, 1982; Faria & Belohlavek, 1984). Many of these conditions are more prevalent among people with disabilities, making it more likely for physicians to attribute causation to the disability and to fail to pursue abuse as a possible cause.

Sexual abuse survivors also experience exaggerated feelings of guilt and shame, negatively affecting their self-esteem and enhancing feelings of worthlessness (Bradshaw, 1989). Such feelings often result in poor body image; consequently, women may become obese or may develop eating disorders (Courtois & Watts, 1982; Gordy, 1983; Kearney-Cooke, 1988). Self-destructive behavior, self-mutilation, drug abuse, and alcoholism occur more frequently than among nonabused women (Briere & Zaidi, 1989; Faria & Belohlavek, 1984; Finkelhor et al., 1986). A history of abuse may have serious effects on a woman's relationship and sexuality issues, engendering feelings of passivity, powerlessness, lack of trust, and isolation. Left untreated, sexual abuse may lead to sexual dysfunction, flashbacks, promiscuity, and more serious psychological sequelae, including repressed memories and dissociation (Ratican, 1992).

INTERVENTIONS IN THE ABUSE CYCLE

Successful interventions in the cycle of family violence have included asking the woman directly if her injuries were inflicted and by whom, documenting injury sites on a body map as a part of the medical record, providing educational materials that include telephone numbers of crisis hotlines and women's shelters, providing individual or group short-term therapy, and offering crisis intervention (Walker, 1984). When seeking treatment, abused women may present with symptoms related to problems other than the abuse (Courtois, 1988; Gelinas, 1983). Thus, clinicians need to directly ask women seeking treatment about any history of abuse (Briere & Zaidi, 1989).

The goal of counseling is to provide a safe environment (Cole, 1982) in which the client is in control at all times (Ratican, 1992). Counseling approaches that have been effective with survivors include transactional analysis (Courtois, 1988;

Hopping, Frady, & Plaut, 1988); gestalt techniques; guided imagery; hypnosis (Spiegel, 1989); journal keeping and letter writing; cognitive restructuring (Jehu, 1989); art, music, and dance therapy (Courtois, 1988); and group counseling (Bergart, 1986; Ratican, 1992; Westerlund, 1983). For deaf women, counseling is more effective when the counselor is sensitive to deaf culture issues and appropriate communication techniques (Merkin & Smith, 1995). Group psychotherapy using Campbell's (1986) group prototype for battered women has been implemented successfully at women's shelters (Dimmitt & Davila, 1995; Trimpey, 1989). Advocacy intervention after women leave a domestic violence shelter has also been found to help women access community resources to counteract economic dependence and lack of social support (Sullivan, Tan, Basta, Rumptz, & Davidson, 1992).

Crisis intervention involves assisting a woman to temporarily escape to a woman's shelter, escape permanently from the abuser, and have an escape plan ready in the event of imminent violence if the woman chooses to remain with the perpetrator. These options may be problematic for the woman with a disability if the shelter is inaccessible, if shelter staff are unable to meet her needs for personal assistance with activities of daily living, or if shelter staff are unable to communicate with the woman who is deaf or speech impaired. Furthermore, crisis intervention may be difficult if the woman depends primarily on the abuser for assistance with personal needs and has no family or friends with whom to stay or she is physically incapable of executing the tasks necessary to implement an escape plan, such as packing necessities and driving or arranging transportation to a shelter or friend's home. She may have to devise a safety plan with a trusted friend or relative to help her make arrangements to escape.

Four requirements are necessary to provide effective victim services to women with disabilities (Andrews & Veronen, 1993). First, service providers need to provide adequate assessment of survivors, including questions about disability-related issues. Second, survivor service providers should be trained to recognize and effectively respond to needs related to the disability, and disability service providers should be trained to recognize and respond to physical and sexual trauma. Third, barriers to services should be eliminated by providing barrier-free information and referral services; by ensuring physical accessibility to facilities; by providing 24-hour access to transportation, to interpreters, and to communication assistance; and by providing trained personnel to monitor risks and respond to victims who are receiving services through disability programs. Fourth, people with disabilities who depend on caregivers, either at home or in institutions, may need special legal protection against abuse.

A network of services, including official state agencies and statewide grassroots domestic violence coalitions, have developed across the United States in the past 20 years to meet the problems of family violence (Davis, Hagen, & Early, 1994).

There is general agreement that the existing services would not have been developed without the effective lobbying of grassroots coalitions. However, the coalitions, and the social services for which they advocate, are at risk because of diminishing resources and internal conflicts.

THEORETICAL MODELS FOR BREAKING THE ABUSE CYCLE

The woman's stage in resolving the abuse can be explained in terms of the Transtheoretical Model (Prochaska & DiClemente, 1984) and social cognitive theory (formerly called social learning theory; Bandura, 1986).The Transtheoretical Model can be applied to the initiation of self-protective as well as health-protective behavior to prevent injury and death, that is, to resolve family violence. Applying this model to the resolution of abuse by the battered woman does not in any way imply that she provokes the violent incidents and is therefore the person who needs to change; instead, it represents recognition that attempting to get the abuser to change may be futile, so the woman needs to initiate behavior to protect herself from further abuse. The Transtheoretical Model views behavior change as a process consisting of five stages: (1) precontemplation, (2) contemplation, (3) preparation, (4) action, and (5) maintenance. A battered woman is in the precontemplation stage if she does not believe she is being abused despite physical evidence to the contrary, she minimizes the extent of the abuse, she makes excuses about the abuser's behavior and believes he will not hurt her again despite repeated past incidents of abuse, or she believes she should continue to endure the abuse. Contemplators are actively considering options for resolving the abuse, for example, by examining the pros and cons of leaving the abusive situation. Preparation indicates a readiness to end the abusive situation in the near future and being on the verge of taking action. The person in this stage may have already made attempts to leave and failed. She has entered the action stage by telling another person about the abuse who could potentially assist her to prevent further abuse, calling a women's shelter, or physically leaving the abuser. She is in the maintenance stage if she has left the abuser and not entered into another abusive relationship.

Within the three-phase cycle of violence described by Walker (1979), the woman is most receptive to interventions in a brief period called Open Window Phase (Curnow, 1993, 1995). The Open Window Phase occurs between the acute battering phase and the honeymoon (calm) phase, before the next tension-building phase begins a new cycle of violence. Battered women will probably be the most receptive to progressing to the next stage of change (e.g., precontemplation to contemplation or preparation to action) during the Open Window Phase.

Progress along the continuum of behavioral change is not linear, but tends to be characterized by frequent relapses to the point of contemplation or precontemplation in a cyclic manner. Intervention and treatment are the most effective when they are compatible with a client's current stage of change. The clinician can plan the most effective intervention through the use of a 32-item questionnaire that was developed to identify a client's current stage of change (McConnaughy, Prochaska, & Velicer, 1983).

Considerable *self-efficacy* (DiClemente, Prochaska, & Gilbertini, 1985), that is, confidence in one's ability to perform a particular behavior, is needed both to leave the abusive situation and to remain free of abusive relationships. Self-efficacy is a major construct of social cognitive theory (Bandura, 1986). The interaction of behavior, personal factors, and environmental influences—all emphasizing self-efficacy—in tolerating abuse needs to be explored based on social cognitive theory. Social cognitive theory has been used to predict family violence in terms of modeling, the role of stress, the use of alcohol, the presence of relationship dissatisfaction, and aggression as a personality style (O'Leary, 1988). However, studies that have applied this theory to influence a battered woman's decision to leave or otherwise resolve an abusive relationship are scarce. Bandura (1986) has suggested that self-referent thought is an important mediator between knowledge and action and that perception of self-efficacy influences motivation and behavior. Efficacy evaluations have had strongest relationships with the maintenance stage of change and relapse problems (Donovan & Marlatt, 1988; Marlatt & Gordon, 1985). Women with low self-efficacy may be more likely to return to an abusive relationship or enter into another abusive relationship.

ABUSE INTERVENTION GUIDELINES FOR REHABILITATION SERVICE PROVIDERS

The first and most important step for rehabilitation service providers is to abandon the belief that no one would ever abuse a woman with a disability and that abuse does not affect the services they provide. Statistics have shown that women with disabilities are just as likely to experience abuse as other women, and they face extraordinary obstacles to resolving abusive relationships. Abusive spouses or caregivers may seriously interfere with a woman's participation and progress in rehabilitation programs. It is important for people in rehabilitation or other types of service settings who work with women with disabilities to understand the symptoms and consequences of abuse. There are effective strategies they can use to assist their clients in dealing with abusive situations (Salber & Taliaferro, 1995).

A woman may not tell her therapist or counselor about abuse for many reasons (Salber & Taliaferro, 1995):

- She may fear retribution if the perpetrator learns the violence has been disclosed.
- She may feel shame and humiliation that the abuse is happening to her.

- She may think she deserved the abuse. She may think that, because of her disability, she cannot hope for better treatment.
- She may feel protective of her partner. She may have been told that no one else would have her or take care of her because of her disability.
- She may not fully comprehend her situation. She may not recognize that what she is experiencing is abuse, especially if she has been exposed to it most of her life.
- She may think that problems with abuse are inappropriate to bring up with her counselor, and that he or she may not be knowledgeable or does not care about abuse.
- She may think her counselor is too busy to spend time talking about this problem.
- She may think her counselor could not help her with this problem.

Correspondingly, counselors may feel uncomfortable bringing up questions of abuse with their clients. Some reasons are listed below (Salber & Taliaferro, 1995):

- They believe that abuse does not occur in the population of women with disabilities.
- The client is not articulate or may have cognitive impairments that make it difficult to get the history.
- They think the woman provoked or deserved the abuse.
- They believe what happens in the home, in terms of domestic violence, is a private matter and therefore should not be discussed.
- They think she can just leave if she wants to.
- They know the perpetrator and believe he or she is incapable of abuse.
- They do not know what to do if they uncover the abuse or they believe it is the job of other professionals, such as social workers.
- They know what to do, but believe it will not help—"she just goes back to him anyway."

Furthermore, it is useful for all types of service providers to be aware of the constellation of symptoms that are often presented by victims of abuse in medical settings (Salber & Taliaferro, 1995). These include:

- A description of an incident that is inconsistent with the kind of injury, such as "I bumped into something," when bruises are on the inside of the arm.
- A time delay between the occurrence of an injury and the receipt of medical attention.
- An "accident"-prone history.
- Suicide attempts or depression.

- Repetitive psychosomatic complaints or recurring physical complaints with no physical signs of organic disease, including headaches, chest pains, heart palpitations, choking sensations, numbness and tingling, nervousness, dyspareunia, or pelvic pain.
- Emotional complaints, including anxiety, panic attacks, sleep disorders, nervousness, depression, difficulty coping with parenting, or nonspecific complaints of marital problems.
- Signs and symptoms of alcoholism and drug abuse.
- Injury during pregnancy, or "spontaneous" abortions, premature labor, low-birth-weight babies, and fetal injuries.
- Other pregnancy-related problems, such as substance abuse, poor nutrition, depression, and late or sporadic access to prenatal care.
- Signs and symptoms of posttraumatic stress disorder: increased arousal, sleep difficulties, irritability, difficulty concentrating, and hypervigilance.
- Injuries resulting from abuse that may have a "central pattern," that is, injuries to the face, neck, throat, chest, breasts, abdomen, and genitals.
- Multiple injuries in various stages of healing, which suggests physical violence occurring over time.

If a service provider suspects that a client is experiencing abuse, he or she can take six important steps to assist her:

1. Talk with her directly and privately about the suspected abuse. Validate her experience and approach it as a problem that can be solved.
2. Assess the degree of danger she is experiencing. If she is in imminent danger, she should be immediately referred to the police or a battered women's shelter. Some states have mandatory reporting requirements to adult protective services for people who are elderly or disabled and are living in an institutional setting. Other states require only that information about community resources be given.
3. Help her develop a safety plan that addresses emergency shelter, transportation, supplies, medication, cash, keys, and so forth.
4. Document the incident in her record, including your suspicions of abuse.
5. Plan for follow-up on referrals.
6. Give her information on resources that could help her, including
   - local battered women's program (listings are available from the National Coalition Against Domestic Violence in Denver, CO, 303-839-1852)
   - state departments of human resources, adult protective services
   - advocates for victims of domestic abuse
   - a lawyer referral service
   - the local police department, family violence division

CONCLUSION

Women with disabilities face the same vulnerabilities to abuse that all women face, plus additional vulnerabilities specifically related to their disability. It is notable that women with disabilities tend to experience abuse for longer periods of time, reflecting the reduced number of escape options open to them because of more severe economic dependence, the need for assistance with personal care, environmental barriers, and social isolation. It is difficult to separate the effect of disability from the effects of poverty, low self-esteem, and family background in identifying the precursors to violence against this population. More information is needed on how women with disabilities escape or resolve abusive situations. Steps must be taken to train girls and women with disabilities to understand inappropriate touch, including in medical settings, and to learn how to recognize and avoid or resolve abusive situations in the family and in the community. An important element in this training is informing women that they do not need to tolerate abuse and linking them to community resources that could help them expand their options for removing violence from their lives.

REFERENCES

Agonito, R. (1993). *No more "nice girl": Power, sexuality, and success in the workplace.* Holbrook, MA: Bob Adams.

Aiello, D., Capkin, L., & Catania, H. (1983). Strategies and techniques for serving the disabled assault victim: A pilot training program for providers and consumers. *Sexuality and Disability, 6(3–4),* 135–144.

Amaro, H., Fried, L., Cabral, H., & Zuckerman, B. (1990). Violence during pregnancy and substance use. *American Journal of Public Health, 80,* 575–579.

American Medical Association. (1992). *Diagnostic and treatment guidelines on domestic violence.* Chicago: Author.

Ammerman, R.T., Van Hasselt, V.B., Hersen, M., McGonigle, J.J., & Lubetsky, M.J. (1989). Abuse and neglect in psychiatrically hospitalized multihandicapped children. *Child Abuse & Neglect, 13,* 335–343.

Andrews, A.B., & Veronen, L.J. (1993). Sexual assault and people with disabilities [Special issue: Sexuality and disabilities: A guide for human service practitioners]. *Journal of Social Work and Human Sexuality, 8(2),* 137–159.

Asch, A., & Fine, M. (1988). Introduction: Beyond pedestals. In M. Fine & A. Asch (Eds.), *Women with disabilities: Essays in psychology, culture, and politics* (pp. 1–37). Philadelphia: Temple University Press.

Bandura, A. (1986). *Social foundations of thought and action: A social cognitive theory.* Englewood Cliffs, NJ: Prentice Hall.

Belsky, J. (1980). Child maltreatment: An ecological integration. *American Psychologist, 35(4),* 320–335.

Bergart, A.M. (1986). Isolation to intimacy: Incest survivors in group therapy. *Social Casework, 67,* 266–275.

Bradshaw, J. (Speaker). (1989). *Healing the shame that binds you* (Cassette Recording No. 1-55874-043-0). Deerfield Beach, FL: Health Communications.

Briere, J., & Runtz, M. (1988). Symptomatology associated with childhood sexual victimization in a nonclinical adult sample. *Child Abuse & Neglect, 12,* 51–59.

Briere, J., & Zaidi, L.Y. (1989). Sexual abuse histories and sequelae in female psychiatric emergency room patients. *American Journal of Psychiatry, 146,* 1602–1606.

Brown, D.E. (1988). Factors affecting psychosexual development of adults with congenital physical disabilities. *Physical and Occupational Therapy in Pediatrics, 8*(2–3), 43–58.

Browne, A., & Finkelhor, D. (1986). Impact of child sexual abuse: A review of the research. *Psychological Bulletin, 99,* 66–77.

Campbell, J. (1986). A survivor group for battered women. *Advances in Nursing Science, 8*(2), 13–20.

Chamberlain, A., Rauh, J., Passer, A., McGrath, M., & Burket, R. (1984). Issues in fertility control for mentally retarded female adolescents: I. Sexual activity, sexual abuse, and contraception. *Pediatrics, 73,* 445–450.

Cole, E. (1982). Sibling incest: The myth of benign sibling incest. *Women and Therapy, 1*(3), 79–89.

Courtois, C.A. (1988). *Healing the incest wound: Adult survivors in therapy.* New York: W.W. Norton.

Courtois, C.A., & Watts, D.C. (1982). Counseling adult women who experienced incest in childhood or adolescence. *The Personnel and Guidance Journal, 60,* 275–279.

Cunningham, J., Pearce, T., & Pearce, P. (1988). Childhood sexual abuse and medical complaints in adult women. *Journal of Interpersonal Violence, 3,* 131–144.

Curnow, S.A.M. (1993). *The open window phase of help seeking and reality behaviors by battered women.* Spokane, WA· Whitworth College, Intercollegiate Center for Nursing Education.

Curnow, S.A.M. (1995). Battered women in the critical care setting: Strategies for critical care nurses. *Dimensions of Critical Care Nursing, 14*(3), 160–167.

Danek, M.M. (1992). The status of women with disabilities revisited. *Journal of Applied Rehabilitation Counseling, 23*(4), 7–13.

Davis, L.V., Hagen, J.L., & Early, T.J. (1994). Social services for battered women: Are they adequate, accessible, and appropriate? *Social Work, 39*(6), 695–704.

DiClemente, C.C., Prochaska, J.O., & Gilbertini, M. (1985). Self-efficacy and the stages of self-change of smoking. *Cognitive Therapy and Research, 9,* 181–200.

Dimmitt, J., & Davila, Y.R. (1995). Group psychotherapy for abused women: A survivor-group prototype. *Applied Nursing Research, 8*(1), 3–7.

Donovan, D.M., & Marlatt, G.A. (Eds.). (1988). *Assessment of addictive behaviors.* New York: Guilford Press.

Doucette, J. (1986). *Violent acts against disabled women.* Toronto: DisAbled Women's Network.

Faria, G., & Belohlavek, N. (1984). Treating female adult survivors of childhood incest. *Social Casework, 65,* 465–471.

Finkelhor, D. (1979). *Sexually victimized children.* New York: Free Press.

Finkelhor, D., Araji, S., Baron, L., Browne, A., Peters, S.D., & Wyatt, G.E. (1986). *Sourcebook on child sexual abuse.* Newbury Park, CA: Sage.

Gelinas, D.J. (1983). The persisting negative effects of incest. *Psychiatry, 46,* 312–332.

Giannini, A.J., Price, W.A., & Kniepple, J.L. (1987). Decreased interpretation of nonverbal cues in rape victims. *International Journal of Psychiatry in Medicine, 16,* 389–393.

Gordy, P.L. (1983). Group work that supports adult victims of childhood incest. *Social Casework, 64,* 300–307.

Hopping, M.W., Frady, B.J., & Plaut, M.W. (1988). Wounded kid therapy. *Transactional Analysis Journal, 18*(3), 199–206.

Jackson, J.J. (1977). Black women in a racist society. In C.V. Willie, B.M. Kramer, & B.S. Brown (Eds.), *Racism and mental health* (pp. 185–268). Pittsburgh: University of Pittsburgh Press.

Jehu, D. (1989). Mood disturbances among women clients sexually abused in childhood. *Journal of Interpersonal Violence, 4,* 164–184.

Kearney-Cooke, A. (1988). Group treatment of sexual abuse among women with eating disorders. *Women and Therapy, 7*(1), 5–21.

Kellerman, A., & Mercy, J. (1992). Men, women, and murder: Gender-specific differences in rates of fatal violence and victimization. *Journal of Trauma, 33*(1), 1–5.

Kinsey, A.C., Pomeroy, W.B., Martin, C.E., & Gebhard, D.H. (1953). *Sexual behavior in the human female.* Philadelphia: W.B. Saunders.

Kreigsman, K.H., & Bregman, S. (1985). Women with disabilities at midlife [Special issue: Transition and disability over the life span]. *Rehabilitation Counseling Bulletin, 29*(2), 112–122.

Malamuth, N.M., & Check, J. (1983). Sexual arousal to rape depictions: Individual differences. *Journal of Abnormal Psychology, 92,* 55–67.

Marlatt, G.A., & Gordon, J.R. (Eds.). (1985). *Relapse prevention: Maintenance strategies in the treatment of addictive behaviors.* New York: Guilford Press.

McConnaughy, E.A., Prochaska, J.O., & Velicer, W.F. (1983). Stages of change in psychotherapy: Measurement and sample profiles. *Psychotherapy, 20*(3), 368–375.

Merkin, L., & Smith, M.J. (1995). A community based model providing services for deaf and deaf–blind victims of sexual assault and domestic violence. *Sexuality and Disability, 13*(2), 97–106.

Muccigrosso, L. (1991). Sexual abuse prevention strategies and programs for persons with developmental disabilities. *Sexuality and Disability, 9*(3), 261–272.

Mullins, J.B. (1986). The relationship between child abuse and handicapping conditions. *Journal of School Health, 56*(4), 134–136.

Murphy, P.A. (1992). Taking an abuse history in the initial evaluation. *NARPPS, 7*(5), 187–190.

Murphy, P.A. (1993). *Making the connections: Women, work, and abuse.* Orlando, FL: Paul M. Deutsch Press.

Myers, M.B., Templer, D.I., & Brown, R. (1984). Coping ability of women who become victims of rape. *Journal of Consulting and Clinical Psychology, 52,* 73–78.

National Center on Child Abuse and Neglect. (1993, October 7). National Center on Child Abuse and Neglect: Study mandated by Congress. *The New York Times,* p. A21.

Nosek, M.A. (1995). Sexual abuse of women with physical disabilities. *Physical Medicine and Rehabilitation: State of the Art Reviews, 9*(2), 487–502.

Nosek, M.A., Young, M.E., Rintala, D.H., Howland, C.A., Foley, C.C., & Bennett, J.L. (1995). Barriers to reproductive health maintenance among women with physical disabilities. *Journal of Women's Health, 4*(5), 505–518.

O'Leary, K.D. (1988). Physical aggression between spouses. In V.B. Van Hasselt, R.L. Morrison, A.S. Bellack, & M. Hersen (Eds.), *Handbook of family violence* (pp. 31–55). New York: Plenum Press.

Ontario Ministry of Community and Social Services. (1987, April 1). Disabled women more likely to be battered, survey suggests. *The Toronto Star,* p. F9.

Parker, B., McFarlane, J., Soeken, K., Torres, S., & Campbell, D. (1993). Physical and emotional abuse in pregnancy: A comparison of adult and teenage women. *Nursing Research, 42*(3), 173–178.

Prochaska, J.O., & DiClemente, C.C. (1984). *The transtheoretical approach: Crossing traditional boundaries of therapy.* Homewood, IL: Irwin.

Ratican, K.L. (1992). Sexual abuse survivors: Identifying symptoms and special treatment considerations. *Journal of Counseling and Development, 71*(1), 33–38.

Ridington, J. (1989). *Beating the "odds": Violence and women with disabilities* (Position Paper No. 2). Toronto, Canada: DisAbled Women's Network.

Salber, P.R., & Taliaferro, E. (1995). *The physician's guide to domestic violence: How to ask the right questions and recognize abuse—Another way to save a life.* Volcano, CA: Volcano Press.

Schaller, J., & DeLaGarza, D. (1995). Issues of gender in vocational testing and counseling. *Journal of Job Placement, 11*(1), 6–14.

Scott, C.S., Lefley, H.P., & Hicks, D. (1993). Potential risk factors for rape in three ethnic groups. *Community Mental Health Journal, 29*(2), 133–141.

Sobsey, D., & Doe, T. (1991). Patterns of sexual abuse and assault. *Sexuality and Disability, 9*(3), 243–260.

Sobsey, D., Wells, D., Lucardie, R., & Mansell, S. (Eds.). (1995). *Violence and disability: An annotated bibliography.* Baltimore, MD: Paul H. Brookes.

Spiegel, D. (1989). Hypnosis in the treatment of victims of sexual abuse. *Psychiatric Clinics of North America, 12,* 295–305.

Stark, E., & Flitcraft, A. (1995). Killing the beast within: Woman battering and female suicidality. *International Journal of Health Services, 25*(1), 43–64.

Sullivan, C.M., Tan, C., Basta, J., Rumptz, M., & Davidson, W.S. II. (1992). An advocacy intervention program for women with abusive partners: Initial evaluation. *American Journal of Community Psychology, 20*(3), 309–332.

Trickett, P.K., & Putnam, F.W. (1993). Impact of child sexual abuse on females: Toward a developmental psychobiological integration. *Psychological Science, 4*(2), 81–87.

Trimpey, M.L. (1989). Self-esteem and anxiety: Key issues in abused women's support group. *Issues in Mental Health Nursing, 10,* 297–308.

U.S. Bureau of the Census. (1989). *Labor force status and other characteristics of persons with a work disability: 1981 to 1988* (Current Population Reports Series P-23, No. 160). Washington, DC: U.S. Government Printing Office.

Walker, L.E. (1979). *The battered woman.* New York: Harper & Row.

Walker, L. (1984). *The battered woman syndrome.* New York: Springer.

Welbourne, A., Lipschitz, S., Selvin, H., & Green, R. (1983). A comparison of the sexual learning experiences of visually impaired and sighted women. *Journal of Visual Impairment and Blindness, 77,* 256–259.

Westerlund, E. (1983). Counseling women with histories of incest. *Women and Therapy, 2*(4), 17–31.

Womendez, C., & Schneiderman, K. (1991). Escaping from abuse: Unique issues for women with disabilities. *Sexuality and Disability, 9*(3), 273–280.

Wyatt, G.E., Peters, S.D., & Guthrie, D. (1988). Kinsey revisited, Part II: Comparisons of the sexual socialization and sexual behavior of black women over 33 years. *Archives of Sexual Behavior, 17*(4), 289–332.

CHAPTER 29

Issues for the Partner of the Person with a Disability

Elizabeth A. McNeff

Change and loss associated with disability or illness demands major adjustments from both partners and their families in personal relationships. A partner's disability or illness can powerfully affect couples' relationship rules and sacred boundaries in complex ways (Rolland, 1994). Whether the disability or illness occurs suddenly or over time, resulting changes in physiologic function can be permanent and can require substantial psychological adjustment for both partners.

Some of the effects of disability or illness may be positive, such as family members' drawing closer together, renewed opportunities for personal growth and development, and reevaluation of interpersonal values (Crewe, 1993). Unfortunately, negative effects may outweigh the positive and can include a perceived sense of loss, financial upheaval, unwanted responsibilities, resentment over imposed changes, and loss of confidence and control in one's life (Crewe, 1993). Individuals in a relationship may experience frustration over lost goals and internalized anger, which can create guilt, depression, injured self-esteem, and anxiety. Disability and illness may pose new and somewhat frightening threats to a personal world that seems too delicate to endure yet another loss (Hayes, Potter, & Hardin, 1995). Partners are challenged to develop strategies to cope with the stresses and uncertainties of planning and achieving normative life cycle goals and to maintain a balanced, healthy, and mutual relationship (Rolland, 1994).

It is important for both parties in a relationship to understand the dynamics and aspects of loss associated with disability and how individuals experience loss differently. The manner in which individuals conceptualize these losses can complicate a relationship. Individual differences in cognitive development, coping skills, personal resources, social support systems, and access to health care all contribute to the recovery process (Hayes et al., 1995).

A multitude of emotions are associated with loss. The order of occurrence and intensity of each of the emotions varies from individual to individual (Hayes et al., 1995). What is important to remember, however, is that how a person responds to loss is at least as much a function of the individual as it is of the nature of loss itself. Responses to disability and illness of the individual with the disability are both physical (e.g., mobility, body temperature regulation, cognitive, and sexual function) and psychological (e.g., body image, self-efficacy, vocation and finance). Factoring in time since onset of disability, responses of the individual with the disability and the partner may include pain, anger, denial, panic, guilt, bargaining, depression, and worry. Dealing with the issues surrounding disability and illness can be a lengthy process for individuals in an intimate personal or marital relationship as well as for family and friends. This chapter identifies and discusses key variables that may moderate the impact of a disability on partner relationships; reviews research on disability, sexuality, and partner relationships; and identifies treatment issues, concerns, and recommendations for rehabilitation or counseling services.

KEY VARIABLES THAT MAY AFFECT INTIMACY

Crewe (1993) identified the role of the person with a disability and the characteristics of the person's relationship, disability, and environmental support as relevant variables that may influence the effect of disability on intimate personal relationships and marriage. In terms of role, is the individual with a disability a spouse, sibling, boyfriend, girlfriend, or other significant family member? Partners with disabilities encounter different obstacles in interpersonal relationships than a child or sibling may face with a parent or guardian. Partners should consider the gender and role of the person with the disability within the definition of the relationship to determine the effect of the disability on the relationship. Role reversals often occur in relationships in which disability is a factor.

The characteristics of the relationship are also important to consider. How long have the individuals been involved? What is the level of commitment? In what stage of life are the partners? What was the sequence of disability and partnership? Did the disability come before the relationship? Did the relationship come before the disability? Another factor to consider is whether the relationship is between individuals with disabilities. Likewise, the characteristics of the disability must be assessed. In what phase of "disability" is the disability? Is it progressive or stable? If progressive, in what phase? What are the psychological and physiologic functions of the disability? What are the real, and perceived, limitations of the disability? In addition, partners should also examine the characteristics of environmental support. What are the internal and external environmental support systems? Who is providing assistance to meet the demands of additional needs acquired through the disability and illness? The partner? Siblings? Parents? How are those responsibilities distributed? Is respite or relief care conveniently obtainable? Are there adequate financial resources available? What options are at hand?

According to Rolland (1994), when disability or illness strikes a couple's relationship, a number of significant structural and emotional variables are likely to occur that can affect an intimate partnership. Dealing with these variables can help promote couples' resilience in the face of loss and can enhance opportunities for increased intimacy between partners (Rolland, 1994).

Whose problem is it? This is the first variable that a couple must address. If the disability or illness is the exclusive domain of the "patient," it will skew a couple's relationship. Even though the immediate loss may be more acute for the disabled individual, the nondisabled spouse experiences many of the same dilemmas as the disabled or ill partner. Therefore, dealing with and accepting the loss should not be the sole responsibility of the disabled partner. Optimal functioning relies on the willingness of both partners to challenge stereotypical assumptions of the "patient as the diseased" model. If partners view the disability as a conjoined issue, they are more likely to feel empowered by their circumstances.

Couples should also consider the need to establish healthy boundaries. Identification with the disability or illness as a key aspect of the relationship is a major risk for couples. If this process (identification) invades the relationship, possibilities for growth become limited and the idea of living a normalized life is externalized "outside" the relationship with "illness" inside it. This focus creates distancing, or a "split," between partners. To counteract this split, couples should delineate time for self-care whenever possible. They should establish boundaries that serve to remind that the partner is not the disability and the relationship is about more than the illness. Boundaries can promote a belief in the possibility for greater control over the psychosocial processes generated by disability in the partners' lives.

Couples need to also address the balance in the relationship between partner and caregiver roles. Couples' expectations for a shared, balanced role within the relationship may become impossible with a disability. Both partners need to be aware that sustaining intimacy predominantly depends on creating viable caregiving boundaries. Couples need to specify which aspects of caregiving are to be done by the partner or the disabled individual, and which need professional assistance. It is imperative that couples understand and negotiate caregiver–patient roles that are realistic to the conditions of the disability. This delineation of duties will help couples establish clear, healthy boundaries that can foster and enhance the relationship. Sharing concerns about caregiving roles may be painful, especially for the nondisabled partner; however, defining limits is a critical issue for partners when disability is a component of the relationship.

A key component of healthy relationships is a balance between time together and time spent apart. For couples facing disability and chronic illness, a manageable balance is extremely challenging. The disabled partner may foster a pull for increased closeness, whereas the nondisabled partner may require more time and space apart. As a result, the disabled partner may feel engulfed and controlled by the illness and the nondisabled partner may experience feelings of guilt. Setting realistic limits requires each partner to consider the other's predicament while affirming the basic entitlement of two committed, equal individuals to make caring, personal decisions.

Each partner should consider the degree of psychosocial recovery a person has undergone. If the pace of adapting to the disability or illness is different for each partner, misunderstanding and conflict may result. If there is an extended period of cognitive impairment, the "affected" partner may have difficulty understanding a partner's needs because of problems with recollection and perception of time. Couples can help the healing process by sharing their perceptions and feelings about what has occurred.

Conditions involving permanent cognitive impairment are among the most challenging for couples to face. Most healthy relationships involve a balance of cognitive abilities. Loss of the intellectual and emotional aspects of intimacy can be devastating for couples. For many, the old, comfortable relationship dies, and they must attempt to construct a new relationship. The possibilities for intimacy may become quite different or limited. Because of the fundamental change in the capacity for intimacy, the nondisabled partner may lose interest in his or her mate. It may be useful for couples to highlight the unaffected areas of the relationship and emphasize the development of new, shared interests.

The role of gender is a critical dimension in understanding couples' issues when a disability is present. Men may experience more difficulty than women in adapting to a disabled, or dependent, partner because gendered social expectations have not prepared them to deal effectively with loss. As a result of gender socialization, men and women may be more adept at different aspects of coping. Disability or illness can provide couples with an opportunity to reexamine habitual role constraints. Early intervention to help couples identify and renegotiate, if necessary, their gender-defined roles in a more healthy and balanced way can help avert a crisis.

Couples should have access to comprehensive information explaining how a disability or illness can be expected to affect their sexuality. Certain conditions are associated with diminished sexual desire and may interfere with sexual function. Promoting sensitive and open communication between partners about the meaning of their loss or change should be a priority for intervention. Couples who are unaccustomed to communicating about their sexual lives can learn to express and effectively communicate limitations, preferences, and emotions that will promote a healthier relationship. Partners may need to redefine intimacy and nurturance in broader, other than sexual, terms. This strategy may help them adapt more successfully to losses in the sexual component of their relationship by valuing a mutually caring and compassionate relationship in other inclusive dimensions.

Significant differences between partners' beliefs and values can precipitate a relationship crisis when individuals are faced with disability or illness. Within this context, however, couples have the opportunity to examine and alter constraining beliefs in new, healthy directions. Partners can identify their fundamental beliefs about how to manage diversity and adjust their lives accordingly, engendering renewed confidence in themselves and the relationship.

Life cycle skews can occur during any transition period of the couple's and individual's life cycle when they must experience the normative developmental tasks of the next phase in the context of illness or disability. Stark differences in each partner's capacity to carry out life goals may be brought to light at those times. Each partner may reevaluate personal and relationship goals. With more serious debilitating illnesses, long-standing, unmet relationship needs may interact with an awareness of one's mortality.

EFFECT OF DISABILITY AND ILLNESS ON INTIMATE AND MARITAL RELATIONSHIPS

Sexuality, sexual relationships, intimacy, marriage, and partnering issues are important concerns among individuals living with a disability and their loved ones. Unfortunately, these concerns are surprisingly neglected in the literature (Rolland, 1994). The majority of research has been devoted to the physiologic aspects of sexual function or dysfunction in a variety of disabling conditions (Yoshida, 1994). Most of the research on psychosocial issues of people with a disability has focused on marital status before and after the onset of disability (Yoshida, 1994). Interestingly, the literature contains conflicting reports about the correlation between disability and rates of marriage and divorce (Crewe, 1993; Crewe, Athelstan, & Krumberger, 1979).

Investigators have often disagreed about the effects of severity of disability on marital and partnership status (Brown & Giesy, 1986). Studies of people with disabilities and illness, other than people with a spinal cord injury (SCI), have generally failed to demonstrate a clear relation between severity of condition and marital satisfaction or family functioning (Brown & Giesy, 1986). It has been argued by Klein, Dean, and Bogdanoff (1968) and Zahn (1973) that, because of their lesser role for ambiguity, severely disabled people enjoy greater marital satisfaction and better family relations than moderately disabled people. With specific reference to people with SCI, Comarr (1963) as well as Brown and Giesy (1986) claimed there was no relation between divorce rates and severity of disability (paraplegia versus quadriplegia) for people married before the injury occurred. El Ghatit and Hanson (1976) claimed that severity of disability had no effect on whether single males contracted a first marriage after injury, but was related to whether they subsequently divorced; the more severely disabled individuals manifested the higher divorce rate.

The issue of disability and pre-injury marriages or partnerships also has been studied. DeVivo and Fine (1985) followed 276 patients who sustained SCIs between 1973 and 1980 and compared their rates of marriage and divorce with the general U.S. population. The researchers found that their sample had experienced substantially fewer marriages and significantly more divorces than would be expected, according to base rates for age in the United States. They discovered groups with early-onset disabilities are more likely to experience a lower incidence of marriage, and a substantial proportion of those individuals remain single throughout their lives. According to Crewe (1993), the reasons are speculative, and may include reduced social opportunities, financial disadvantage, attitudinal barriers, and physical restrictions. DeVivo and Fine's (1985) findings must be carefully interpreted because the study covered only 3 years and no demographic variables were reliably related to marrying. The authors, however, did identify several significant correlates of divorce: Divorcing patients were significantly more likely to be young African American women who had been previously divorced and had no children.

DeVivo, Hawkins, Richards, and Go (1995) conducted a study to compare the divorce rates of people who got married after SCI with rates of the non-SCI population of comparable age and gender to identify factors associated with increased likelihood of divorce. The study involved 622 people enrolled in the National Spinal Cord Injury Statistical Center data set since 1973. The people were followed from 1 to 15 years after their marriage. The status of each marriage was determined at the time of the most recent follow-up interview. Based on the specific annual divorce rates for the U.S. population, 74 divorces were expected; 120 divorces occurred. The study revealed men and remarried people had divorce rates higher than women and people married for the first time. Overall, the impact of SCI appeared to be almost as great on postinjury marriages as it was on preexisting marriages. The authors, warned, however, that the study yielded descriptive rather than causal information. Hence, researchers must identify other factors before developing a clinically useful model to predict people at high risk for divorce.

A research project conducted by Brown and Giesy (1986) studied the proposition that people are selected into and out of marriage on the basis of their health or disability status. The researchers provided a test of the proposition by comparing the marital status of people with SCI with the marital status of the general public. It was anticipated that people with SCI would marry or remarry significantly less often than other people, and separate or divorce significantly less often. The selected factors were sex; severity of disability (indicated by the need for assistance, perceived health, and extent of paralysis); socioeconomic status (indicated by adequacy of income and welfare status); current age; and age at onset of disability. In a secondary analysis of existing survey data, 251 Oregon residents with SCI (182 males and 69 females) found the marital selection proposition was supported in that the marital status of the sample differed markedly from that of the general population, the disability exerted a greater effect on the marital status of females than males, and all of the selected variables were significantly associated with the marital status of one or both genders.

Research has indicated that marital status is the most powerful predictor of independent living outcome variables for SCI. Urey, Viar, and Henggler (1987) examined predictors of positive marital adjustment among people with SCI. They studied 20 couples in which one spouse sustained an SCI. Results indicated that, for both husbands and wives, the numbers of recreational and social activities in which they engaged with others was the strongest predictor of positive marital adjustment.

Another component of the study conducted by Urey et al. (1987) examined marital characteristics of couples who were coping successfully with SCI versus those who were not, as well as the relationship of positive marital adjustment in couples with SCI compared with positive adjustment among able-bodied couples. The data revealed significant interaction effects with post hoc comparisons that indicated that spouses with SCI in distressed marriages engaged in significantly fewer activities alone and with their spouse and requested the greatest degree of change in the marital relationship compared with other groups. Distressed couples expressed more dissatisfaction in sexual relations and more negative communication during conflict resolution tasks.

Although there has been much discussion concerning the effects of disability and illness on existing marriages, less attention has been given to the subject of marriages contracted after the onset of disability. El Ghatit and Hanson (1976) studied the outcome of marriages contracted after males sustained SCI. They found that divorce rates after SCI were no higher than in the general population and were actually quite close to the U.S. rates as a whole. Despite severe loss of genital function and decreased sensory and mobility function, the majority of the sample claimed their sexuality was still an important part of their lives and their sexual desire was unaltered after injury. However, the numbers of complete and incomplete paraplegics, the relative youth of the subjects, and the short time elapsed since injury were factors that would potentially limit the generalizability of the data. In contrast to males, research (Crewe et al., 1979; Crewe & Krause, 1988) has suggested that married women who become disabled are especially vulnerable to divorce. Although the numbers of women who participated in the study (Crewe et al., 1979) were small, six out of seven women who had been married at the time of SCI were divorced within the first few years afterward.

According to Crewe and Krause (1988), the distinction between unions that occur after the onset of disability (referred to as postinjury marriages/partnerships) and those that precede and survive the injury (pre-injury marriage/partnerships) merits attention. Most studies of the marriages of individuals with SCI have focused on survival versus divorce (Crewe et al., 1979). Little information has been available about matters such a communication patterns, social life, satisfaction, and quality of life.

A 1979 study by Crewe and colleagues compared pre-injury and postinjury marriages of 55 people with SCI and their partners. Comparisons were made in terms of sexual function, satisfaction with various aspects of life, physical dependency, social life, medical condition, and employment. The data revealed several differences between the relationships. The disabled individuals in pre-injury marriages were judged to have less motivation for independence; a larger proportion of them received daily personal care assistance from their partner. Individuals in postinjury marriages were more likely to be employed and were judged to be better adjusted psychologically. It was revealed that subjects and their partners who coupled after onset of disability were happier than the subjects who experienced pre-injury marriages. Age, state of health, the impact of disability on the relationship, and the personal assets of disabled individuals who attract new partners are possible explanations for the findings.

In another study by Crewe and Krause (1988), couples who married after the onset of disability reported greater satisfaction with their sex lives, living arrangements, social lives, health, emotional adjustment, and control over their lives. They also indicated that they were more likely to be working, loneliness was less of a problem, and they were frequently socially active outside of their homes. Several factors might explain the advantages of the postinjury marriages. Disability was a factor in the relationship from the beginning of postinjury marriages. Pre-injury marriages were likely to undergo stress as a result of the injury; the disability frequently caused resentment or resignation. Partners had to undergo a reversal of roles or had to learn new ways of communicating feelings, wants, and needs.

There are additional possibilities that might explain the success of postinjury partnerships that cannot be tested with the data collected. The spouses in postinjury marriages may exhibit unusual qualities that contribute to the success of these unions. They may have the maturity and independence to look beyond and ignore society's stereotypes and pursue intimate involvement with someone who is stigmatized with a disability. They may also possess better than average communications skills that would help them overcome initial barriers to nonverbal communication and spontaneous action imposed by disability. The sexual relationship is less likely to be spontaneous because the partners are more likely to discuss sexual activity in advance. Being honest, open, and explicit about needs and feelings may be a contributing factor to healthier communication during a marriage or partnership.

Because Crewe et al. (1979) have shown that people married after injuries have better marital adjustment than those married before injuries, a study conducted by Simmons and Ball (1984) predicted that comparable differences also would be reflected in personality data. The researchers studied marital adjustment and self-actualization in couples married before and after SCI. Their research revealed that both husbands and wives who married after the injuries occurred were significantly more inner directed and experienced better marital adjustment than those married before the onset of injury or disability. Wives in the married pre-injury group had better marital adjustment if they were more inner directed, whereas wives in the postinjury group were better adjusted if they were more present centered and capable of intimate contact.

Crewe (1993) identified factors that could contribute to difficult relationship adjustments in pre-SCI marriages. The first is the tendency of the rehabilitation system to identify the individual with a disability as the patient and the spouse as the caregiver and, therefore, as a part of the "patient's" support system. Government systems that provide financial assistance for personal care also may not pay spouses who assist in that care. Nondisabled spouses may be put in the position of maintaining a household, holding an outside job, and providing personal care for their partner with a disability. Furthermore, conflicts may arise between maintaining a sexual relationship with the disabled partner while also providing intimate personal care. Functional limitations may lead to an omission of activities or changes in the way they are conducted. These factors can have a negative impact on maintaining a healthy intimate relationship. The relationship can become stressed and anxiety ridden, and may lose equilibrium. When there is no longer a satisfactory exchange of instrumental affective positive behaviors, and communication patterns break down, marital happiness is prone to decline (Urey & Henggler, 1987).

Crewe (1993) described in detail the 1973 Minnesota Spinal Cord Injury Study; the study included marriage as a primary topic of interest. The sample consisted of 256 subjects who provided information about themselves using the Life Satisfaction Questionnaire (LSQ). The LSQ contains information about the date and type of SCI; need for assistance with activities of daily living; dating and social activities; marital and family status; work activities; educational level and school involvement; sitting tolerance and need for medical services; rating scales of satisfaction for various aspects of life; and a 10-point rating scale ranging from 1 (poor adjustment) to 10 (easy adjustment) of the individual's present personal adjustment to SCI and that projected for the future. The study collected data to investigate if there were measurable differences between married and single subjects on measures of demographic characteristics, life satisfaction, social and work activities, and reported problems; if there were significant differences that could be observed in the marriages that survived SCI and in those that occurred after injury; and if it was possible to predict, among people who were single at the time of SCI, who would later marry and who would remain single. The study found that the surviving marriages demonstrated strength and commitment, but they also included noticeable areas of loss and regret. Spouses in pre-injury marriages were much more likely to be providing personal care than spouses in postinjury marriages, even when the level of injury was constant. Disabled individuals in pre-injury marriages appeared to be much less likely to be working compared with individuals in postinjury marriages.

In 1985, data were collected for a follow-up study (Crew & Krause, 1990) of 33 individuals from sample one and 89 individuals from sample two. Significant differences between the two groups were found on many of the emotional and behavioral measures. Individuals in postinjury marriages were generally more active socially, had higher levels of educational attainment, and were more likely to be working. Overall, individuals in postinjury marriages were more satisfied with their living arrangements and sex lives, social lives, general health, emotional adjustment, and sense of control in their lives. Despite the wide discrepancy in employment rates between the two groups, they did not differ in terms of satisfaction with employment or financial means or in terms of their family relationships, recreational opportunities, or general life opportunities.

Ratings of personal adjustment and life satisfaction were fairly high among both groups (Crew & Krause, 1990). Ratings were significantly higher for younger people with no statistically significant difference being attributed to the timing of the marriage. Out of 13 problem areas, only loneliness was significantly less troublesome for individuals in postinjury marriages than for those in pre-injury marriages. Work status stood out as a potent predictor for the possibility that individuals would attract a spouse following disability. Other factors that frequently characterized the group that married were the following: they frequently went out socially; they rated their overall adjustment as higher; and they scored higher on the life satisfaction items involving social life, sex life, and general health. The studies suggest that marriage serves to enhance life satisfaction and productivity.

DISABILITY AND MEETING SIGNIFICANT OTHERS

The topic of sexuality and intimate relationships is an important concern among people living with a disability or illness. Research has focused on a multitude of issues surrounding marital status pre-injury and postinjury but has ignored the difficulties of meeting others with the intent of developing intimate marriages or partnerships. Moreover, the vast majority of research in this area has been conducted and published by people without a disability (Yoshida, 1994). To obtain a greater understanding of issues surrounding sexual relationships and intimate partnerships, it is imperative that researchers articulate the experiences and concerns shared by people living with disabilities (Yoshida, 1994).

A recent study by Yoshida (1994) studied the experiences of 28 men with SCI, specifically paraplegia, regarding meeting significant others and making decisions about long-term relationships. The study identified five major factors to consider when discussing potential intimate partner relationships and determining if the potential partner could cope with disabled life. These factors are acceptance of the individual, awareness and assistance with accessibility, altered divisions of labor, comfort with sexuality, and long-term plans. In addition to using these five key variables to assess potential relationships, the single most important question participants considered when assessing a potential relationship was, "Can the person deal with the life of someone in a chair?" It is especially important that the partner understand from the beginning the nature and scope of the disabled partner's physical differences. It is easier to accept a disability when the disabled partner outlines all the facts openly and honestly. If the relationship involves a disabled and nondisabled partner, a number of challenges must be overcome. If the disability is permanent, the nondisabled partner must accept that fact. If the disability is progressive, the partner must be prepared for that reality also. The role of open and honest communication cannot be underestimated at any point during a relationship.

In addition, both partners must acknowledge that the need for sexual expression is not lost as a result of disability or illness. Every person is a sexual being and every person has a right to sexual expression. Therefore, it is up to each partner to discover the type of sexual expression with which he or she is comfortable and the best way to achieve that expression.

GAY MALE AND LESBIAN PARTNERSHIP ISSUES

In addition to issues related to social stigma, gay male and lesbian couples may face some of the same issues as opposite-sex couples (Rolland, 1994). Sudden disability or chronic illness spotlights attention for health care needs and may frequently force a hidden or private relationship into public for the first time during a moment of great vulnerability (Rolland, 1994). It can be particularly disconcerting for gay male and lesbian couples to deal with disapproving health professionals who may associate homosexual activity with a deviant lifestyle (Landau-Stanton, 1993; Walker, 1991). Health care professionals may experience discomfort and be forced to confront personal prejudices when first encountering gay male and lesbian couples during the course of treatment. This experience may be a health care worker's first experience with an intimacy feared by many people in society (Rolland, 1994). It is important, however, that lesbians and gay males with disabilities discuss their sexuality with their primary care providers. However, they have much to lose by being open with homophobic or heterosexist providers who may subscribe to prevailing negative attitudes and stereotypes about individuals with a disability who are gay males or lesbians (O'Toole & Bregante, 1992).

Chronic illness or disability can bring a couple's personal life and family of origin face to face for the first time (Rolland, 1994). Unfortunately, this is not always a positive experience. Most states do not legally recognize gay marriages or relationships. If the couple is co-parenting children, they may encounter a maze of legal problems when a medical crisis arises. Families of origin may attempt to exclude gay male or lesbian partners from visitation, medical caregiving, or memorial services (O'Toole & Bregante, 1992; Rolland, 1994). The experience of Kowalski and Thompson is a case in point (O'Toole & Bregante, 1992): Committed lesbian partners for four years, the women owned a home and considered each other lifelong partners. At this point, neither was disabled; they were not identified as lesbians by their families, nor did they have any legal paperwork to identify them as partners. One of them was struck by a drunk driver, requiring extensive hospitalization. She was permanently and severely disabled. The uninjured partner was denied any role in her partner's recovery since the partner's birth family presumed themselves to be her only family (Thompson & Andrzejewksi, 1988).

In treating lesbians and gay males, health care providers need to address homosexuality by examining the complexity of human behavior, affective preference, and gender identity from a more positive stance (O'Toole & Bregante, 1992). They must overcome attitudinal barriers to interaction through understanding and acceptance. Many gay men and lesbians experience limited access to services, information, and support (O'Toole & Bregante). In addition, according to Laird (1993), clinicians should address issues relating to disenfranchisement and exclusion from family leave policies and survivor benefits for the well partner, as well as the lack of legal rights for visitation and sustained contact with the children of a partner who dies.

Anstett, Kiernan, and Brown (1987) have recommended that allied health care workers dealing with gay male or lesbian health-related concerns ask open and direct questions, keep a good sexual and social history, and assist the individual in identifying peer support systems. Furthermore, providers should be open with answers; remember that sexual practices influence health; and remember that consumers want good care, not interference. Professionals should be aware that there are different types of family configurations that include significant others and support systems. Also, confidentiality is an important issue because there are significant insurance and employment concerns.

SEXUAL ADJUSTMENT, ACTIVITY, AND SATISFACTION

The occurrence of a disabling condition can exert a pervasive, long-term influence on many spheres of an individual's life, and sexuality is no exception (Kreuter, Sullivan, & Siosteen, 1994b). All aspects of sexuality are potentially affected—physiologic, psychological, behavioral, and social (Kreuter et al., 1994b). In addition to the physical limitations caused by disability, the possible loss of genital sensation or erectile function and difficulties with bowel and bladder control can interfere with sexual function, body image, self-concept, and psychological adjustment (Kreuter et al., 1994b).

According to Kreuter et al. (1994b), the premise in an existing intimate relationship may be totally altered by disability because the injury was something neither partner had bargained for. The nondisabled partner, as well as the disabled person, may experience difficulties adjusting to the changes imposed by disability. The literature (Crewe et al., 1979; Crewe & Krause, 1988; David, Gur, & Rozin, 1977; Kreuter, Sullivan, & Siosteen, 1994a) has suggested that, if the disability is present at the beginning of the relationship, the opportunity for a successful partnership is enhanced. It has been assumed that the consequences of disability and illness also affect the sexuality and intimacy of the noninjured partner; however, relatively little research has concentrated on the noninjured partner's marital and sexual lives (Kreuter et al., 1994a; Siosteen, Lundqvist, Blomstrand, Sullivan, & Sullivan, 1990).

Kreuter et al. (1994a) compared the emotional and sexual aspects of relationships before and after SCI, from the partner's point of view. In addition, the researchers investigated the subjects' personality characteristics. Of the partners, 88% in pre-injury and 86% in postinjury relationships considered their overall relationship to be satisfactory. Several sexual aspects of the relationships were revealed that favored postinjury marriages and partnerships. Perceived deterioration of sex life as a result of the injury was higher among pre-injury partners and the frequency of sexual activity and variety of sexual expression used was lower in the pre-injury relationships. However, there was no significant difference reported between the two groups in satisfaction with current sex life.

The results suggest that clinicians emphasize sexual counseling designed to enhance communication that will encourage sensualism and experimentation with a wide variety of options. Practitioners should include partners and spouses early in the counseling process, and pay particular attention to older couples who experience disability or chronic illness. Counseling and comprehensive human sexuality information may help these couples overcome taboos, inhibitions, and stereotypes so they may develop greater acceptance of a variety of sexual activities. Because sexual needs, desires, and concerns may change over time, practitioners should repeat the sessions offered and have reference or referral information readily available.

Kreuter et al. (1994b) also investigated partners' overall experiences in relation to sexual interest, behavior, and satisfaction. A measure of satisfaction within relationships also was included. Of the partners studied, 61% appreciated the quality of their sexual relationship and most partners (84%) considered their relationship to be satisfying overall. About 50% of the couples engaged in sexual activity, with or without intercourse, once a week or more. Of the partners, 55% reported being content with the frequency of their sexual interaction, whereas slightly more than 30% would have liked more frequent activity. Of the partners, 45% considered their sex life to be as good as or even better than their previous sex life. Qualities that were identified as contributing to an active, fulfilling, and satisfactory sexual relationship were high general satisfaction with life, a varied repertoire of rewarding sexual expressions, including intercourse and concern about the able-bodied partner's sexual pleasure. From the partner's perspective, feelings of emotional closeness, mutual concern, and a willingness to engage in a variety of sexual activities appeared to be more important for sexual fulfillment than the physiologic aspects of sexuality.

PSYCHOSOCIAL CONCEPTS OF DISABILITY AND PARTNER ADJUSTMENT

The profound psychosocial impact of disability on individuals and their loved ones has been reported (Marinelli & Dll Orto, 1977; Moos, 1984; Siosteen et al., 1990; Trieschmann, 1980; Wright, 1983). Disability affects the entire family, and the performance of a person living with a disability is a function of the individual's needs and demands of his or her environment (Feigin, 1994). An examination of the social context in which disability occurs reveals a broader concept of the effects of disability as it relates to the individual's social function.

There is an increased need to understand how couples adjust to disability or illness. Individuals who continue in their marriage after having experienced the disability of a partner have a higher degree of reciprocity in their relational adjustment to the disability, although they may differ in their adjustment experience (Feigin, 1994; Rolland, 1994). Family members are expected to sustain and help the individual with disability or illness even though they, too, have been affected. They provide the closest physical and emotional environment and play a key role in helping the family member adjust to the disabling situation (Feigin, 1994; Rolland, 1994). The literature on rehabilitation has linked social support systems with physical and emotional well-being (Cobb, 1976; Rintala, Young, Hart, Clearman, & Fuhrer, 1992). Socioemotional support from family members as part of the personal caregiving role is positively associated with coping systems of the individual with disability (Feigin, 1994; Umberson, 1987).

There are limited broad-based, generalizable research data in studies of illness and disability regarding the functions of the family in general and spouses or partners in particular (Feigin, 1994). As a result, little information exists about how adjustment is actually achieved in intimate couple relationships. Although there has been increasing theoretical interest in disability adjustment with regard to family context, limited empirical data have dealt with the subject of spouse or partner adjustment and function. Few studies have investigated both partners; most of the studies have been patient centered and have disregarded the possible effects on the nondisabled partner (Feigin, 1994; Kelly & Lambert, 1992; Kessler & McRae, 1984).

Kelly and Lambert (1992) conducted an extensive review of the research (from 1980 to 1990) on family support in rehabilitation. They located and reviewed more than 13,000 publications on this topic. Even though the topic was addressed widely, fewer than 40 of the publications were data-based studies. Of those studies, only four examined personal and family adjustment to disability and emphasized the interdependent nature of this adjustment by demonstrating that family support has a direct influence on the behavior of people with disabilities. However, not one of the four studies examined partner issues by studying both partners, and only one investigated spousal adaptation in wives of husbands with a disability.

Feigin (1994) conducted a study that examined the adjustment of both spouses to a postmarital disability of one partner. The research investigated the personal, marital, and social aspects of the couple's relationship in an attempt to understand the multidimensional patterns of adjustment as related to disability status. The study also dealt with gender differences in relation to the differential status of disability. The results revealed a positive correlation between the adjustment of both spouses to the disability situation and indicated significant differences between the adjustment of the disabled individual and that of the nondisabled spouse. The most interesting finding was that the nondisabled spouse reported a higher level of vulnerability in the marital relationship, in the sense of having a stronger fear of separation and a higher sense of dependency. Regarding gender, the results of the study indicated that females were more anxious than males, whereas males engaged in more work and study activities.

Disability clearly is not an individual matter; the adjustment process becomes a mutual experience for partners. Adjustment to disability should be understood and treated by viewing it in a social context, recognizing changes in relationship roles and their effect on interactional processes. Furthermore, interventions should be directed toward helping couples achieve a positive balance of roles and functions that meets the needs of both partners. Such couples intervention is probably more effective in the long run than help offered only to disabled people. Unfortunately, the present approach used by the majority of social and psychological services is still mostly client centered and needs to be reviewed to include the partners of people with an illness or disability.

Overall, there are a number of conflicting opinions regarding the effects of disability on marriage and partnerships. According to Brown and Giesy (1986), previous research has not clearly indicated whether the marital status of people with disability or illness differs significantly from the general population, nor has it explicated the effects of other factors on their marital status. The research has suggested, however, that people of lower socioeconomic status, younger individuals, and people who were younger at the onset of the disability or illness were less likely to be married than their counterparts (Brown & Giesy, 1986; Crewe, 1993). Further research may provide additional insight, perhaps by indicating that disabled or chronically ill people attribute their marital or partnership problems (if partnered) and their difficulties in meeting and courting partners (if single) to their physical condition.

Other factors are clearly involved in the formation, maintenance, or disruption of marriage and intimate partnerships. Duration of partnership, pre-injury versus postinjury relationships, timing of the union, number and ages of dependent children, personality factors, emotional status, and extent of individuals' social participation are contributing factors to the success or failure of a relationship. From future investigations of these and other factors, a theory may gradually develop that will elaborate the mechanisms by which disability or chronic ill health affect marital and partnership status, thereby explicating the circumstances under which the effects of disability or chronic ill health are accentuated, muted, or neutralized (Brown & Giesy, 1986).

Considering the evidence documenting the positive role that family, and the spouse in particular, can have on rehabilitation and adjustment to disability and illness, it is surprising how little research has examined the spouses' perception of the marriage or their perception of the social behavior of the partner with a disability (Stambrook et al., 1991). Psychosocial and spousal issues should not be overlooked. How an individual with a disability adjusts and the social behavior he or she exhibits may adversely affect the marital relationship, thereby jeopardizing support the individual needs for successfully adjusting to the injury.

In addition, sexual expression of individuals with a disability or illness may be affected not only by their particular physical condition but also by the attitudes of society and of their partners toward the disability (Kreuter et al., 1994b; Stambrook et al., 1991). The impact of disability on a person's sexuality will be closely related to their view of themselves; body image, self-efficacy, and self-esteem will all be influenced by his or her confidence in interpersonal relationships (Kreuter et al., 1994b; Teal & Athelson, 1975). Sexuality should be viewed as an interactive, dynamic learning process comprising psychological, social, and behavioral components. According to Kreuter et al. (1994b), sexual interaction is a joint responsibility. Recognizing this, the clinician may most adequately assess the impact of disability by asking both partners about their experiences and perceptions during the sexual aspects of their relationship. A more complete knowledge of sexual adjustment following disability or illness, which includes the perspective of the partner of the individual with the disability or illness, would improve the caliber of sexual counseling currently available to clients and their partners (Kreuter et al., 1994a).

CRITICAL ASPECTS OF COUPLE RELATIONSHIPS

The issues and challenges of couples dealing with disability or illness as it affects their intimate personal partnerships have been well delineated, especially by Rolland (1994). Of great importance is what the treatment community, especially counselors, educators, mental health therapists, physicians, nurses, and other health care providers, does in applying their expertise and knowledge to alleviate problems for couples.

Practitioners need to recognize that couples affected by disability share many issues and concerns, yet do not necessarily share them all. For example, there are distinct differences between marriages and partnerships established pre-disability and those established postdisability (Crewe & Krause, 1988; Crewe et al., 1979). Furthermore, homosexual couples face stresses in addition to those faced by heterosexual couples (O'Toole & Bregante, 1992).

Another issue important to treatment is the provider's recognition that each relationship is created by a particular, individual couple and that many factors contribute to the characteristics of that relationship (Crewe, 1993). Each couple will bring to counseling their unique ways of adjusting to the disability as it affects them. Respect for those unique coping mechanisms must be part of the therapeutic relationship, yet, the therapist may simultaneously be called on to confront and change aspects of the adjustment that are not working or are dysfunctional.

TREATMENT MODELS, INTERVENTIONS, AND
RECOMMENDATIONS

It is important to consider that whether or not individuals are in intimate relationships, they are still emotional, social, and sexual beings who need information and possibly counseling related to self, sexuality, and partnerships. Early and ongoing treatment related to the impact of illness or disability on self and relationships is an issue for the person affected from the onset of illness or disability; yet, all too often, practitioners overlook this critical juncture of treatment. It is important to have educational and therapeutic counseling available from the time the disability or illness first occurs or is diagnosed, and over time as well. Windows of opportunity vary with each individual and couple. Counseling or information should be available to physically disabled people and their partners whenever they are ready to use it (Anderson & Cole, 1975).

Qualifications of Treatment Providers

For couples counseling, a high level of skill is required to effectively intervene as a therapist. It is advisable that treatment providers working in this area possess the training and skills needed to work with any couple, whether or not disability or illness is a factor. The professional should attempt to gain additional expertise in the areas of loss, grief, disability, and sexuality. With specific disabilities or illnesses, it is crucial that the treatment provider understand the ways that disability or illness impacts not only the person with the disability, but the person's family and significant others. It is important that the treatment provider know his or her limits and not exceed them. Clients have the right to the best possible care, and should receive nothing less as they grapple with the stresses of disability or illness on self, their relationships, and family life.

Treatment Models

Communication is a key ingredient in all relationships and needs to be the focus of any treatment program or service. Effective communication between partners in an intimate relationship is crucial to satisfaction in that relationship. A disability or long-term health problem requires sensitive, open, and direct discussion about a range of issues for couples to live well with chronic conditions (Rolland, 1994). Kaplan (1979) has identified four main counseling techniques used by counselors of individuals with disability or illness: group counseling, positive self-concept and body image training, information dissemination, and incorporation. Extending these techniques to include partners may assist in recovery or adjustment. A brief discussion of each technique as it applies follows (Kaplan, 1979).

Group Counseling

The focus is on in-group support and empathy with the clients. Advocates for group counseling believe clients gain a great deal from each other in terms of the exchange of ideas and information about sexuality, as well as the emotional support people in similar circumstances can give to one another. Another advantage is the dissemination of knowledge to a large group within a relatively short time.

Positive Self-Concept and Body Image Training

Proponents of the approach to sexuality counseling believe an improved self-concept is vital to sexual adjustment and, conversely, that adequate sexual adjustment improves self-concept. Counselors using this approach concentrate on the positive aspects of self-concept and body image they feel are inherent in all humans.

Information Dissemination

This technique focuses on what a disabled client can and cannot do sexually. This is a matter-of-fact discussion, and various sexual techniques are outlined. The emphasis is on what the person can do, rather than on what he or she is prevented from doing.

Incorporation

Incorporation of sexual function into the client's total lifestyle combines self-concept, information dissemination, and supportive counseling techniques. The goal is to help the client regain his or her sense of sexual self within the context of a total lifestyle. Sexuality is discussed within the context of other subjects concerning the client's function. Bowel and bladder training, grooming habits, sexual function, dating, and other interpersonal activities may be discussed along with their interrelationships in a total lifestyle "package."

CONCLUSION

Whatever the larger treatment configuration (e.g., initial medical facility, rehabilitation setting, transitional care, or outpatient treatment), counseling and education for couples affected by disabilities needs to be an integral aspect of that treatment. Treatment should provide a structured time and process for couples to address the disability as "our" problem and deal with the resulting issues (Rolland, 1994). Within that framework, treatment should include marital or couples therapy, including sexual therapy if indicated. Educational counseling, especially in relation to the impact of the disability, is important as well. Key to successful treatment is a holistic approach that looks at and values each individual as a whole person, helps people to successfully redefine and balance their lives as they deal with a disability, and recognizes the importance of giving couples the opportunity to work through and resolve the critical aspects of intimate couple relationships.

REFERENCES

Anderson, T., & Cole, T. (1975). Sexual counseling of the physically disabled. *Postgraduate Medicine, 58*(1), 117–123.

Anstett, R., Kiernan, M., & Brown, R. (1987). The gay–lesbian patient and the family physician. *Journal of Family Practice, 25*(4), 339–344.

Brown, J., & Giesy, B. (1986). Marital status of persons with spinal cord injury. *Social Science and Medicine, 23*(3), 313–322.

Cobb, S. (1976). Social support as a moderator of life stress. *Psychosomatic Medicine, 38,* 300–314.

Comarr, A.E. (1963). Marriage and divorce among patients with spinal cord injury, II-V. *Journal of the Indian Medical Profession, 9,* 4162–4168, 4181–4186, 4378–4384, 4424–4430.

Crewe, N. (1993). Spousal relationships and disability. In F.P. Haseltine, S.S. Cole, & D.B. Gray (Eds.), *Reproductive issues for persons with physical disabilites.* Baltimore: Paul H. Brookes.

Crewe, N., Athelstan, G., & Krumberger, J. (1979). Spinal cord injury: A comparison of preinjury and postinjury marriages. *Archives of Physical Medicine and Rehabilitation, 60,* 252–256.

Crewe, N., & Krause, J. (1988). Marital relationships and spinal cord injury. *Archives of Physical Medicine and Rehabilitation, 69,* 435–438.

Crewe, N., & Krause, J. (1990). An eleven-year follow-up of adjustment to spinal cord injury. *Rehabilitation Psychology, 35,* 205–210.

David, D., Gur, M., & Rozin, R. (1977). Survival in marriage in the paraplegic couple: Psychological study. *Paraplegia, 15,* 198–201.

DeVivo, M., & Fine, P. (1985). Spinal cord injury: Its short-term impact on marital status. *Archives of Physical Medicine and Rehabilitation, 66,* 501–504.

DeVivo, M., Hawkins, L., Richards, J., & Go, B. (1995). Outcomes of post-spinal cord injury marriages. *Archives of Physical Medicine and Rehabilitation, 76,* 130–138.

El Ghatit, A.A., & Hanson, R.W. (1976). Marriage and divorce after spinal cord injury. *Archives of Physical Medicine and Rehabilitation, 57,* 470–472.

Feigin, R. (1994). Spousal adjustment to a postmarital disability in one partner. *Family Systems Medicine, 12*(3), 235–247.

Hayes, R., Potter, C., & Hardin, C. (1995). Counseling the client on wheels: A primer for mental health counselors new to spinal cord injury. *Journal of Mental Health Counseling,* 18–30.

Kaplan, S. (1979). Sexual counseling for persons with spinal cord injuries: A literature review. *Journal of Applied Rehabilitation Counseling, 10*(4), 200–204.

Kelly, S.D.M., & Lambert, S.S. (1992). Family support in rehabilitation: A review of research, 1980–1990. *Rehabilitation Counseling Bulletin, 36,* 98–119.

Kessler, R.C., & McRae, J.A. (1984). A note on the relationships of sex and marital status to psychological distress. *Research in Community and Mental Health, 4,* 109–130.

Klein, R.F., Dean, A., & Bogdanoff, M.D. (1968). The impact of illness upon the spouse. *Journal of Chronic Diseases, 20,* 241–248.

Kreuter, M., Sullivan, M., & Siosteen, A. (1994a). Sexual adjustment after spinal cord injury— Comparison of partner experiences in pre- and postinjury relationships. *Paraplegia, 32,* 759–770.

Kreuter, M., Sullivan, M., & Siosteen, A. (1994b). Sexual adjustment after spinal cord injury (SCI) focusing on partner experiences. *Paraplegia, 32,* 225–235.

Laird, J. (1993). Lesbian and gay families. In F. Walsh (Ed.), *Normal family practices* (2nd ed.). New York: W.W. Norton.

Landau-Stanton, J. (1993). *AIDS, health and mental health: A primary sourcebook.* New York: Brunner/Mazel.

Marinelli, R.P., & Dll Orto, A.E. (1977). *The psychological and social impact of physical disability.* New York: Springer.

Moos, R.H. (1984). *Coping with physical illness. Vol. 1: New perspectives.* New York: Plenum Press.

O'Toole, C., & Bregante, J. (1992). Lesbians with disabilities. *Sexuality and Disability, 10*(3), 163–172.

Rintala, D.H., Young, M.E., Hart, K.A., Clearman, R., & Fuhrer, M.J. (1992). Social support and the well-being of persons with spinal cord injury living in the community. *Rehabilitation Psychology, 37*(3), 155–163.

Rolland, J. (1994). In sickness and in health: The impact of illness on couples' relationships. *Journal of Marital and Family Therapy, 4*(20), 327–347.

Simmons, S., & Ball, S. (1984). Marital adjustment and self-actualization in couples married before and after spinal cord injury. *Journal of Marriage and the Family, 46,* 943–945.

Siosteen, B.A., Lundqvist, M.D., Blomstrand, M.D., Sullivan, L., & Sullivan, M. (1990). Sexual ability, activity, attitudes and satisfaction as part of adjustment in spinal cord-injured subjects. *Paraplegia, 28,* 285–295.

Stambrook, M., Psych, C., MacBeath, S., Moore, A.D., Peters, L.C., Zubek, I.C., & Friesen, I.C. (1991). Social role functioning following spinal cord injury. *Paraplegia, 29,* 318–323.

Teal, J. & Athelson, G. (1975). Sexuality and spinal cord injury: Some psychosocial considerations. *Archives of Physical Medicine and Rehabilitation, 56,* 264–268.

Thompson, K., & Andrzejewski, J. (1988). *Why can't Sharon Kowalski come home?* San Francisco, CA: San Francisco Spinsters/Aunt Lute.

Trieschmann, R.B. (1980). *Spinal cord injuries: Psychological, social and vocational adjustment.* New York: Pergamon Press.

Umberson, D. (1987). Family status and health behaviors: Social control as a dimension of social integration. *Journal of Health and Social Behavior, 28,* 306–320.

Urey, J., & Henggler, S. (1987). Marital adjustment following spinal cord injury. *Archives of Physical Medicine and Rehabilitation, 68,* 69–74.

Urey, J., Viar, V., & Henggler, S. (1987). Prediction of marital adjustment among spinal cord injured persons. *Rehabilitation Nursing, 12*(1), 26–30.

Walker, G. (1991). In the midst of winter: Systematic therapy with families, couples and individuals with AIDS infection. New York: W.W. Norton.

Wright, B. (1983). *Physical disability: A psychological approach* (2nd ed.). New York: Harper & Row.

Yoshida, K. (1994). Intimate and marital relationships: An insider perspective. *Sexuality and Disability, 12*(3), 179–189.

Zahn, M.A. (1973). Incapacity, impotence and invisible impairment: Their effects upon interpersonal relations. *Journal of Health and Social Behavior, 14,* 115–123.

Index

Page numbers in *italics* denote
exhibits and figures; those followed by "t" denote tables.

617